The

AUTHENTIC LIBRETTOS

of the

ITALIAN OPERAS

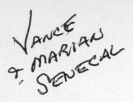

The
AUTHENTIC
LIBRETTOS
of the
ITALIAN OPERAS

AÏDA   BARBER OF SEVILLE

CAVALLERIA RUSTICANA   DON GIOVANNI

LA FORZA DEL DESTINO   LA GIOCONDA

LUCIA DI LAMMERMOOR   I PAGLIACCI

RIGOLETTO   LA TRAVIATA

IL TROVATORE

*Complete with English and Italian Parallel Texts
and Music of the Principal Airs*

CROWN PUBLISHERS
NEW YORK

PRINTED IN THE UNITED STATES OF AMERICA

CONTENTS

CONTENTS

FOREWORD

The music is not everything in opera. Its full enjoyment can be achieved only with the knowledge of the words that are being sung—usually in a foreign language. In this series, the librettos are presented in the original language with an English line by line translation. Thus, it is possible to follow the song and to understand the meaning of the foreign words.

The natural grouping of Italian operas suggested itself as a logical volume in this Libretto series which was inaugurated with "The Authentic Librettos of the Wagner Operas."

It was in Italy that opera received its most enduring impetus. The Italian composers' "Musica Parlante" (Speaking Music) spread throughout the continent and made Italian opera supreme. And today undoubtedly more opera performances are given in Italian than in any other language.

But there is no one Italian composer who stands out as Wagner does among the Germans. Verdi, of course, is most important. He was prolific and his "Aïda" has the distinction of being first in number of performances by the Metropolitan. But only a few of his operas have retained their popularity.

The selection of the operas to be included in this volume was determined largely by importance and popularity as indicated by the number of performances at the Metropolitan Opera House in the past 56 years. The Puccini operas had to be omitted because of insurmountable copyright difficulties. Mozart's "Don Giovanni" may seem out of place among Italian operas. But since the libretto, by Lorenzo da Ponte, is in Italian and it is sung invariably in that language, it is included in this volume.

The record of performances of these operas at the Metropolitan Opera House, 1883-1938: Aïda, 284; I Pagliacci, 214; Cavalleria Rusticana, 187; La Traviata, 157; Rigoletto, 155; Il Trovatore, 127; Lucia di Lammermoor, 106; Barber of Seville, 96; La Gioconda, 94; Don Giovanni, 54; La Forza del Destino, 37.

RIGOLETTO

by

GIUSEPPE VERDI

THE STORY OF "RIGOLETTO"

RIGOLETTO, a hunchback buffoon, or jester to the libertine Duke of Mantua, and willing pander to his licentious habits, has by his ribald and unfeeling jests, together with his villanous connivance at the Duke's open disdain for all considerations of honor, rendered himself highly objectionable to the courtiers, particularly the Counts of Ceprano and Monterone, whose wife and daughter respectively have become victims to the unbridled passions of the Duke. Monterone, in indignation at the dishonor to which he is subjected, seeks the Duke's presence and boldly denounces his conduct, and that of his vile abettor, Rigoletto, who is inwardly terror-stricken by his vehement maledictions.

Rigoletto has a young and beautiful daughter, whom he conceals from public observation with the most jealous care; so strictly has she been guarded that she has not been allowed to leave her home, except to attend her religious observances at church. She, however, has not escaped the notice of the Duke, who has repeatedly observed her at her devotions, and contrived to track her to her humble habitation, where, by bribing her servant, he gains access to her. Representing himself to be a poor student deeply impressed with her attractions, he succeeds in inspiring her with reciprocal sentiments, never dreaming that it is the daughter of his buffoon he is thus beguiling.

The fact of the existence of a young and lovely woman in the dwelling of Rigoletto becoming known to the courtiers, they form a plot to abduct her therefrom by force and deliver her to the Duke. At a late hour in the evening they assemble (masked) in the neighborhood of Rigoletto's dwelling, and, under pretence that they are going to carry off the wife of Ceprano, whose house adjoins Rigoletto's, they induce him to assist. He is accordingly masked and bandaged, and is made to hold the ladder by which some of the party ascend to the window of his house, which they enter, and tear away the bewildered Gilda, whose mouth they cover, to prevent her giving any alarm, and carry her off triumphantly to the Ducal Palace.

The outwitted jester, finding himself deserted, immediately suspects that all is not right, and tearing off the bandage, perceives the scarf of his daughter, which has been dropped in the flight; he is instantly struck with the conviction that he has been robbed of his beloved Gilda, his only treasure, and that the curse of Count Monterone has already begun to work.

The courtiers relate to the Duke as a good joke how they have carried off the jester's *mistress*, but he knows full well from their description that it is Gilda they have abducted, and the unfortunate girl soon becomes a prey to his insatiate passions.

Rigoletto hastens to the palace, and demands his daughter from the courtiers, who treat him with contempt and derision, baffling all his endeavors to obtain access to the Duke. He is presently joined by his daughter, who has at length freed herself from the vicious attentions of the Duke, and after mutual condolence they quit the place, cursing the scene of their disgrace. Resolving to be revenged on the author of his daughter's and his own misery, Rigoletto hires a bravo named Sparafucile, for a stipulated sum, to assassinate the Duke, who is enticed by the blandishments of Maddelene, the sister of Sparafucile, to the bravo's house, a ruinous and lonely inn.

Gilda has been desired by her father to put on male attire and fly to Verona, but previous to starting, in order to extinguish the lingering affection which she still entertains for her unprincipled seducer, she is made an eye-witness, through crevices in the wall of the inn, of his inconstancy and perfidy. She overhears the sister of the bravo earnestly endeavoring to dissuade him from murdering the handsome guest; but he resolutely persists in his determination to fulfil his contract, unless some person should chance to come to the inn before midnight whom he might kill instead, and pass the body in a sack to Rigoletto as that of the murdered Duke. Upon hearing this Gilda at once resolves to save the life of the undeserving object of her affections by sacrificing her own. She knocks at the door of the inn, is admitted, and instantly stabbed by the cold-blooded assassin. Shortly after, Rigoletto appears, pays the bravo, and receives from him the sack containing (as he supposes) the body of the Duke; he proceeds to throw it into the river which runs at the back of the inn, but before he has time to accomplish it, he is astounded by the voice of the living Duke, which he hears at a short distance; he instantly suspects foul play, tears open the sack, and is horrified to find, instead of the dead body of the hated Duke, the dying form of his beloved daughter, who almost immediately expires. Overwhelmed with terror and anguish at the fulfilment of the dreaded malediction, he falls senseless on the body of his unfortunate daughter.

RIGOLETTO

ACT I.

SCENE I—Magnificent salon in the Ducal Palace, with opening in the back scene, through which other salons are seen, the whole brilliantly lighted for a Fête, which is at its height. Nobles and ladies in magnificent costumes moving in all directions. Pages passing to and fro. Music heard in the distance, and occasional bursts of merriment.

(Enter the DUKE and BORSA, from the back.)

Duke.

Beautiful as youthful is my unknown charmer,
And to the end I will pursue the adventure.

Borsa.

The maiden, you mean, whom you see at the church?

Duke.

For three months past, on every Sunday.

Borsa.

Know you where she lives?

Duke.

In a remote part of the city,
Where a mysterious man visits her nightly.

Borsa.

And do you not know who he is?
Is he her lover?

Duke.

I do not know.

(A group of ladies and gentlemen cross the stage.)

Borsa.

What beauty!—Do you not admire it?

Duke.

Ceprano's wife surpasses the handsomest of them.

Borsa.

Mind the Count does not hear you, Duke.

(Softly.)

Duke.

What care I for him?

Borsa.

It may get talked about.

ATTO I.

SCENA I—Sala magnifica nel Palazzo Ducale, con porte nel fondo, che mettono ad altre sale, pure splendidamente illuminate; folla di cavalieri e dame in gran costume nel fondo delle sale; paggi che vanno e vengono. La festa è nel suo pieno. Musica interna da lontano e serosci di risa di tratto in tratto.

(Il DUCA e BORSA, che vengono da una porta del fondo.)

Duca.

Della mia bella incognita borghese,
Toccare il fin dell' avventura io voglio.

Borsa.

Di quella giovinche vedete al tempio?

Duca.

Da tre lune ogni festa.

Borsa.

La sua dimora?

Duca.

In un remoto calle;
Misterioso un uom v'entra ogni notte.

Borsa.

E sa colei chi sia
L'amante suo?

Duca.

Lo ignora.

(Un gruppo di dame e cavalieri attraversan la sala.)

Borsa.

Quante beltà!—Mirate.

Duca.

Le vince tutte di Cepran la sposa.

Borsa.

Non v'oda il Conte, o Duca—

(Piano.)

Duca.

A me che importa?

Borsa.

Dirlo ad altra ei potria—

Duke.
That would not much affect me.

Duca.
Nè sventura per me certo saria.

QUESTA O QUELLA——'MID THE FAIR THRONG Air (Duke)

Ques-ta o quel - la___ per me pa - ri so-no A quan-t'al - tre d'in-
'Mid the fair throng that spar-kles a - round me, Not one___ o'er my

tor - no,___ d'in-tor-no mi ve - do, Del mio co - re___
heart— no!___ not one o'er my heart holds sway; Though a sweet smile___

___ l'im-pe - ro non ce - do___ Meg-lio_ad u - na___
___ one mo-ment may charm me,___ A glance from some bright eye___

___ che_ad al - tra bel - tà. La co - sto-ro_av-ve - nen-za_e qual
___ its spell drives a - way. All a - like may at - tract, each in

do - no Di che_il fa - to ne_in - fio - ra la
turn___ may please; Now with one I may tri - fle and

vi - ta;___ S'og-gi ques-ta___ mi tor-na gra - di - ta, For-se_un'
play,___ Then an - oth - er___ may sport with and tease— Yet all my

al - tra, for - se_un' al - tra___ do-man lo sa - rà, un' al-
heart to en - slave their wiles dis-play,___ my heart to en - slave their wiles___

- tra, for-se_un' al - tra___ do-man lo sa - rà.
dis-play, their wiles dis - play,___ their wiles___ dis - play.

As a dove flies, alarmed, to seek shelter,
  Pursued by some vulture, to bear it aloft
  in flight,
Thus do I fly from constancy's fetter:
  E'en women's spells I shun—all their ef-
  forts I slight.
A husband that's jealous I scorn and de-
  spise,
  And I laugh at and heed not a lover's
  sighs;
If a fair one take my heart by surprise,
  I heed not scornful tongues or prying
  eyes.

(Enter COUNT CEPRANO, watching his wife, who is seen advancing from the distance, attended by a cavalier. Lords and ladies promenading at back.)

Duke
(meeting the COUNTESS, and addressing her with gallantry).

Are you already going, cruel one?

Countess.

I must obey my husband:
Ceprano desires me to leave.

Duke.

The light of your face
Sheds upon the court more lustre than the
  sun;
For your smile all alike must sigh;
For you love's flame doth all around con-
  sume;
Enslaved, enchanted, for you my heart is
  breaking.
        (Kissing her hand with warmth.)

Countess.

Be more circumspect.

Duke.

No! (Giving her his arm, and leading her off.)
(Enter RIGOLETTO, meeting the COUNT CEPRANO and nobles.)

Rigoletto.

What troubles your thoughts,
Signor Ceprano?

(COUNT shows impatience, and goes off after the DUKE.)

Rigoletto   (to the Cavaliers).
He is out of temper, I see.

Chorus.

What sport!

Rigoletto.

Indeed!

La costanza tiranna del core
  Detestiamo qual morbo crudele,
  Sol chi vuole si serbi fedele;
  Non v' ha amor, se non v' è libertà.
De' mariti il geloso furore,
  Degli amanti le smanie derido,
  Anco d'Argo i cent' occhi disfide
  Se mi punge una qualche beltà.

(Entra il CONTE DI CEPRANO, che segue da lungi la sua sposa, seguita da altre cavaliere. Dame e signori entrano du varie parti.)

Duca
(alla SIGNORA DE CEPRANO, movendo ad incontrarla con
        molta galanterie).

Partite? Crudele!

Conte.

Seguire lo sposo.
M' è forza a Ceprano.

Duca.

Ma dee luminoso
In Corte tal astro qual sole brillar.
Per voi qui ciascuno dovrà palpitar.
Per voi già possente la fiamma d'amore
Inebria, conquide, distrugge il mio core.
        (Con enfasi baciandole la mano.)

Conte.

Calmatevi—

Duca.

No! (Ce da il braccio, ed esce con lei.)
Entra e RIGOLETTO, che s'incontra nel SIGNOR DI CEPRANO,
poi cortigiani.)

Rigoletto.

In testa che avete,
Signor di Ceprano?

(CEPRANO fa un gesto d'impazienza, e segue il DUCA.)

Rigoletto   (ai Cortigiani).
Ei sbuffa, vedete?

Coro.

Che festa!

Rigoletto.

Oh sì—

Borsa.

The Duke is having his diversion.

Rigoletto.

Is it not always so? What is there new in
it?

Gambling and drinking, feasting and dancing,

Fighting and banqueting, all come to him
alike.

Now 'gainst the Countess siege he is laying,

Her husband's jealousy wholly deriding.

(Exit.)

(Enter MARULLO.)

Marullo

(eagerly).

Oh, such news! such news I have!

Chorus.

What has happened? Tell us!

Marullo.

You will be quite surprised.

Chorus.

Narrate it! narrate it!

Marullo.

Ah! ah! Rigoletto—

Chorus.

What of him?

Marullo.

A strange adventure.

Chorus.

Has he lost his hump? Is he no longer
deformed?

Marullo.

Stranger much than that! The idiot has
taken—

Chorus.

Taken what?

Marullo.

An inamorata!

Chorus.

An inamorata!—Incredible.

Marullo.

Into a Cupid the hunchback is transformed.

Chorus.

Oh, what a Cupid!—What a comical
Cupid!

(Enter the DUKE, followed by RIGOLETTO, and CEPRANO in
the background.)

Borsa.

Il Duca qui pur si diverte.

Rigoletto.

Così non è sempre? che nuove scoperte!

Il giuoco ed il vino, le feste, la danza,

Battaglie, conviti, ben tutto gli sta.

Or della Contessa l'assedio egli avanza,

E intanto il marito fremendo ne va.

(Esce.)

(Entra MARULLO.)

Marullo

(premuroso).

Gran nuova! gran nuova!

Coro.

Che avvenne? parlate!

Marullo.

Stupir ne dovrete—

Coro.

Narrate, narrate—

Marullo.

Ah! ah!—Rigoletto—

Coro.

Ebben?

Marullo.

Caso enorme!—

Coro.

Perduto ha la gobba? non è più difforme!

Marullo.

Più strana è la cosa!—Il pazzo possiede—

Coro.

Infine?

Marullo.

Un' amante!

Coro.

Amante! Chi il crede?

Marullo.

Il gobbo in Cupido or s' è trasformato!—

Coro.

Quel mostro Cupido!—Cupido beato!—

(Entra il DUCA, seguito da RIGOLETTO, indi CEPRANO.)

Duke (to RIGOLETTO).

What a troublesome fellow is that Ceprano!
But his wife—to my mind she's an angel!

Rigoletto.

Then carry her off.

Duke.

That is easily said—but how to do it?

Rigoletto.

Do it to-night.

Duke.

You do not consider the Count.

Rigoletto.

Can you not put him in prison?

Duke.

Ah! no.

Rigoletto.

Then why not banish him?

Duke.

Buffoon, I dare not.

Rigoletto.

His head, then.
(Making signs of cutting it off.)

Ceprano (coming forward).

(Black-hearted villain!)

Duke.

Is this the head you speak of?
(Placing his hand on the shoulder of the COUNT.)

Rigoletto (laughing).

Of what value is such a head as that?

Ceprano.

Miscreant!
(Furiously, and drawing his sword.)

Duke.

Forbear. (To CEPRANO.)

Rigoletto.

He only makes me laugh.

Chorus.

He is frantic with rage.
(Among themselves.)

Duke.

Buffoon, come hither.
(To RIGOLETTO.)
You always carry your jokes too far;—
The anger you provoke may one day on
    your head alight.

Rigoletto.

Who can hurt me?—I have no fear.

Duca (a RIGOLETTO).

Ah, quanto Ceprano, importuno niun v' è.
La cara sua posa è un angiol per me!

Rigoletto.

Rapitela.

Duca.

E detto; ma il farlo?

Rigoletto.

Stassera.

Duca.

Nè pensi tu al Conte?

Rigoletto.

Non c' è la prigione?

Duca.

Ah, no.

Rigoletto.

Ebben—s'esilia.

Duca.

Nemmeno, buffone.

Rigoletto.

Adunque la testa—
(Indicando di farla tagliare.)

Ceprano.

(Oh, l'anima nera!)

Duca.

Che di' questa testa?—
(Battendo colla mano una spalla al Conte.)

Rigoletto.

Che far di tal testa?—A cosa ella vale?

Ceprano.

Marrano.
(Infuriato, battendo la spada.)

Duca.

Fermate— (A CEPRANO.)

Rigoletto.

Da rider mi fa.

Coro.

In furia è montato!
(Tra loro.)

Duca.

Buffone, vien quà.
(A RIGOLETTO.)
Ah! sempre tu spingi lo scherzo all' estremo.
Quell' ira che sfida colpir ti potrà.

Rigoletto.

Che coglier mi puote? Di loro non temo;

The Duke's protégé no one dares to injure!

Ceprano (aside to Courtiers).

Vengeance on the buffoon!

Chorus.

And who amongst us
Has not some wrong to be avenged!

Ceprano.

And they shall be avenged!

Chorus.

But how?

Ceprano.

To-morrow, let all who have the courage,
By my side, and armed, appear.

Chorus.

Be it so.

Ceprano.

At night.

Chorus.

Agreed.

(Groups of Dancers appear.)

All here is joyful—all here is festive;
To pleasure all here invites;
Oh, look around, and in all faces see
The reign of voluptuous delights.

Count Monterone (from without).

I will speak to him.

(Enter COUNT MONTERONE.)

Duke.

No.

Monterone.

But I will.

Chorus.

Monterone!

Monterone (looking scornfully at the DUKE).

Yes, Monterone—against crimes like thine
There is yet one to raise a voice.

Rigoletto (to the DUKE, mimicking the voice of MONTERONE).

I will speak to him.

(With mock gravity.)

Against us you have conspired, signor,
And we, in our clemency, have pardoned
you.
'Tis madness in all seasons to come here,
Wailing about the honor of your daughter.

Del Duca un protetto nessun toccherà.

Ceprano (ai Cortigiani, a parte).

Vendetta del pazzo—

Coro.

Contr' esso un rancore
Pei tristi suoi modi, di noi chi non ha?

Ceprano.

Vendetta.

Coro.

Ma come?

Ceprano.

Domani, chi ha core,
Sia in armi da me.

Tutti.

Sì.

Ceprano.

A notte.

Tutti.

Sarà.

(La folla de' danzatori invade la sala.)

Tutto è gioja, tutto è festa,
Tutto invitaci a goder!
Oh, guardate, non par questa,
Or la reggia del piacer!

Conte di Monterone (dall intorno).

Ch' io gli parli.

(Entra il CONTE DI MONTERONE.)

Duca.

No.

Monterone.

Il voglio.

Tutti.

Monterone!

Monterone (fissando il DUCA con nobile orgoglio).

Sì Monteron—la voce mia qual tuono
Vi scuoterà dovunque—

Rigoletto (al DUCA, contraffacondo la voce di MONTERONE).

Ch' io gli parli.

(Si avanza con ridicola gravita.)

Voi congiuraste contro noi, signore,
E noi, clementi in vero, perdonammo—
Qual vi piglia or delirio—a tutte l'or
Di vostra figlia reclamar l'onore?

Monterone (looking scornfully at RIGOLETTO).

Despicable buffoon!—
(To DUKE.)
Ah! thus will I
Thy vile orgies ever disturb.   In all places
Shall my weeping voice attend you,
While unavenged shall remain
The gross insult on my family inflicted.
And if to the hangman you consign me,
As a spirit will I again visit thee,
Till the vengeance of God and man o'er-
whelm thee.

Duke.

No more of this—arrest him.

Rigoletto.

He is mad!

Chorus.

What ravings!

Monterone.

Oh! on both of ye be my malediction!
(To the DUKE and RIGOLETTO.)
Vile is he who hounds the dying lion,
But viler thou, O Duke, and thy serpent
there,
Who the anguish of a parent can deride!
A parent's curse be on ye both!

Rigoletto.

(What do I hear? Oh, horror!)
(Greatly agitated.)

All   (except RIGOLETTO).

Audaciously thou hast this fête disturbed,
By an infernal spirit hither led.
Vain are thy words—deaf to them our ears.
Go, tremble, old man, at the sovereign anger
Thou hast provoked. No hope for thee re-
mains;
Fatal will this day prove to thee.

MONTERONE is marched off between halberdiers—the others
follow the DUKE.)

SCENE II—The extremity of a street that has no thor-
oughfare. On the left a house of retired appearance, within
a court-yard, from which there is a doorway into the
street. In the court-yard are seen a tall tree and a marble
seat. At the top of the wall, a terrace, supported by arches,
and reached by a flight of steps in front. On the right of
the passage is the highest wall of the garden, and the gable
end of the palace of CEPRANO. It is night.

(Enter RIGOLETTO, enveloped in a cloak, followed by SPAR-
AFUCILE, who has a long sword under his cloak.)

Rigoletto.

(How fearfully that man cursed me!)

Monterone (guardando RIGOLETTO con ira sprezzante).

Novello insulto!—
(Al DUCA.)
Ah, sì a turbare
Sarò vestr' orgie—verrò a gridare,
Fino a che vegga restarsi inulto
Di mia famiglia l'atroce insulto;
E se al carnefice pur mi darete
Spettro terribile mi rivedrete,
Portante in mano il teschio mio,
Vendetta chiedere al mondo e a Dio.

Duca.

Non più, arrestatelo.

Rigoletto.

E matto!

Coro.

Quai detti!

Monterone.

Oh, siate entrambi voi maledetti.
(Al DUCA e RIGOLETTO.)
Slanciare il cane al leon morente
E vile, o Duca—e tu serpente,
(A RIGOLETTO.)
Tu che d'un padre ridi al dolore,
Sii maledetto!

Rigoletto.

(Che sento? orrore!)
(Colpito.)

Tutti   (meno RIGOLETTO).

Oh, tu che la festa audace hai turbito,
Da un genio d'inferno qui fosti guidato;
E vano ogni detto, di quà t'allontana—
Va, trema, o vegliardo, dell' ira sovrana—
Tu l' hai provocata, più speme non v' è.
Un' ora fatale fu questa per te.

(MONTERONE parte fra due alabardieri; tutti gli altri
seguirono il DUCA in altra stanza.)

SCENA II—L'estremità più deserta d'una Via Cieca. A
sinistra, una casa di discreta apparenza, con una piccola
corte circondata da muro. Nella corte un grosso ed alto
albero ed un sedile di marmo; nel muro una porta che mette
ella strada; sopra il muro un terrazzo practicabile, sostenuto
da arcate. La porta del primo piano dà su detto terrazzo,
a cui si ascende per una scala di fronte. A destra, della
via è il muro altissimo del giardino, e un fianco del Palazzo
di CEPRANO. E notte.

(RIGOLETTO chiuso nel suo mantello. SPARAFUCILE lo
segue, portando sotto il mantello una lunga spada.)

Rigoletto.

(Quel vecchio maledivami!)

Sparafucile.

    Signor—

Rigoletto.

    Go: I have no need of you.

Sparafucile.

    Be that as it may, you have before you
    A man who knows how to use a sword.

Rigoletto.

    A robber?

Sparafucile.

    No— a man who, for a trifle,
    Will from a rival free you;—
    And have you not one?

Rigoletto.

    Who is he?

Sparafucile.

    Have you not a mistress here?

Rigoletto.

    (What do I hear?) What would it cost me
    To rid me of a signor?

Sparafucile.

    More than for a lesser man.

Rigoletto.

    When must it be paid?

Sparafucile.

    One-half beforehand,
    The other when the deed is done.

Rigoletto.

    (O demon!) And how can you
    Be sure of success?

Sparafucile.

    In the street sometimes they fall.
    At other times in my own house;—
    I waylay my man at night—
    A single blow, and he is dead.

Rigoletto.

    And how in your own house?

Sparafucile.

    All the easier—
    I have a sister there who helps.
    She dances in the streets—she is handsome—
    Those I want she decoys—and then—

Rigoletto.

    I comprehend

Sparafucile.

    Signor?

Rigoletto.

    Va non ho niente.

Sparafucile.

    Nè il chiesi—a voi presente
    Un uom di spada sta.

Rigoletto.

    Un ladro?

Sparafucile.

    Un uom che libera
    Per poco da un rivale,
    E voi ne avete—

Rigoletto.

    Quale?

Sparafucile.

    La vostra donna è là.

Rigoletto.

    (Che sento?) E quanto spendero
    Per un signor dovrei?

Sparafucile.

    Prezzo maggior vorrei—

Rigoletto.

    Com' usasi pagar?

Sparafucile.

    Una metà s'anticipa,
    Il resto si da poi—

Rigoletto.

    (Dimonio!) E come puoi
    Tanto securo oprar?

Sparafucile.

    Soglio in cittade uccidere,
    Oppure nel mio tetto.
    L'uomo di sera aspetto—
    Une stoccata, e muor.

Rigoletto.

    E come in casa?

Sparafucile.

    E facile—
    M'ainta mia sorella—
    Per lè vie danza—è bella—
    Chi voglio attira—e allor—

Rigoletto.

    Comprendo—

Sparafucile.

There is nothing to fear;

My trusty weapon never betrays me.

(Showing his sword.)

Can I serve you?

Rigoletto.

No; not at present.

Sparafucile.

The worse for you.

Rigoletto.

Your name?

Sparafucile.

Sparafucile is my name.

Rigoletto.

A foreigner?

Sparafucile.

From Burgundy.

(About to go.)

Rigoletto.

Where are you to be found?

Sparafucile.

Hereabouts, every night.

Rigoletto.

Go. (Exit SPARAFUCILE.)

How like are we!—the tongue my weapon,
    the dagger his!

To make others laugh is my vocation—his
    to make them weep!

How that old man cursed me!

O man!—O human nature!

What scoundrels dost thou make of us!

O rage! To be deformed—the buffoon to
    have no play!

Whether one will or not, to be obliged to
    laugh!

Tears, the common solace of humanity,

Are to me prohibited!

Youthful, joyous, high-born, handsome,

An imperious master gives the word—

"Amuse me, buffoon,"—and I must obey.

Perdition! How do I not despise ye all,

Ye sycophants—ye hollow courtiers!

If I am deformed, 'tis ye have made me so;

But a changed man will I now become.

Sparafucile.

Senza strepito—

E questo il mio stromento.

(Mostra la spada.)

Vi serve?

Rigoletto.

No—al momento—

Sparafucile.

Peggio per voi—

Rigoletto.

Chi sa?

Sparafucile.

Sparafucile mi nomino—

Rigoletto.

Straniero?—

Sparafucile.

Borgognone—

(Per andarsene.)

Rigoletto.

E dove all' occasione?—

Sparafucile.

Quì sempre a sera.

Rigoletto.

Va. (SPARAFUCILE parte.)

Pari siamo!—Io la lingua, egli ha il pug-
    nale;

L'uomo son io che ride, ei quel che spegne!

Quel vecchio maledivami!

O uomini!—o natura!

Vil scellerato mi faceste voi!

Oh rabbia!—esser difforme!—esser buffone!

Non dover, non poter altro che ridere!

Il retaggio d'ogni uom m' è tolto—il pianto!

Questo padrone mio,

Giovin, giocondo, sì possente, bello

Sonnecchiando mi dice;

Fa ch'io rida, buffone.

Forzarmi deggio, e farlo! Oh, dannazione!

Odio a voi, cortigiani schernitori!

Quanta in mordervi ho gioia!

Se iniquo so, per cangion vostra e solo—

Ma il altr' uom quì mi cangio!

Quel vecchio malediami! Tal pensiero

Perchè conturba ognor la mente mia?

That old man cursed me! Why does that curse
Thus ever haunt my harassed mind?
What have I to fear? Ah, no, this is mere folly!
(Opens a door with a key, and enters the yard.)

(Enter GILDA, coming from the house, and throwing herself into her father's arms.)

Rigoletto.

My daughter!

Gilda.

My dear father!

Rigoletto.

Only when near to thee
Does my oppressed heart know joy.

Gilda.

Oh, what affection!

Rigoletto.

My only life art thou!
What other earthly happiness have I?
(Sighing.)

Gilda.

Why do you sigh? What ails you?
Open your mind to your poor daughter.
If any secret you have, to her confide it;
And do about her family inform her.

Rigoletto.

Thou hast not any.

Gilda.

What is your real name?

Rigoletto.

What matters it to thee?

Gilda.

If you are not willing
Of your family to speak—

Rigoletto.

Do you ever go out?
(Interrupting her.)

Gilda.

Only when I go to church.

Rigoletto.

In that thou dost right.

Gilda.

If of yourself you will not speak,
At least tell me something of my mother.

Mi coglierà sventura? Ah no, è follia.
(Apre con chiave, ad entra nel cortile.)

(Entra GILDA, ch'esce dalla casa e segetta nelle sue braccia.

Rigoletto.

Figlia!

Gilda.

Mio padre!

Rigoletto.

A te dapresso
Trova sol gioia il core oppresso.

Gilda.

Oh, quanto amore!

Rigoletto.

Mia vita sei!
Senza te in terra qual bene avrei?
(Sospira.)

Gilda.

Voi sospirate!—che v'ange tanto?
Lo dite a questa povera figlia—
Se v' ha mistero—per lei sia franto—
Ch'ella conosca la sua famiglia.

Rigoletto.

Tu non ne hai—

Gilda.

Qual nome avete?

Rigoletto.

A te che importa?

Gilda.

Se non volete
Di voi parlarmi—

Rigoletto.

Non uscir mai.
(Interrompendola.)

Gilda.

Non vo che al tempio.

Rigoletto.

Or ben tu fai.

Gilda.

Se non di voi, almen chi sia.
Fate ch'io sappia la madre mia.

DEH NON PARLARE —— *SPEAK NOT OF ONE* Air (Rigoletto)

Deh non par-la-re al mi - se-ro   Del suo per-du - to be - - ne;
Speak not of one, whose loss to thee,   All earth can boast could ne'er— re-store;

El - la sen-tia, quell' an - ge-lo, Pie - tà— del - le— mie
Her an-gel form me - thinks I see, Who loved me, though de - form'd and

pe - ne;   So - lo, dif-for-me, po-ve-ro,   Per com-pas-sion mi a-
poor.—   Pi - ty, O Gil-da; spare me!   Ask it, my child, no

mò. Ah! mo-ri - a,   mo - ri - a, le zol - le co-pra-no Lie-vi quel ca-po a-
more. Ah! she died;—   may earth   rest light-ly on— her; To me she's lost for-

ma-to;   So-la or tu re - sti, So-la or tu res-ti al mi - se - ro;—
ev - er.   Thou art my on - ly hope, Thou art my on - ly hope, my child!

Di - o, sii rin - gra - zia - to, si rin - gra - zia - to.
Fa - ther of all!— oh! bless her with Thy mer - cy mild!

Gilda.

Alas! what anguish! such bitter grief
What language can express!
Father, dear father, calm yourself,
Or my heart will surely break.
To me your name pray tell;
The grief that saddens you impart.

Rigoletto.

'Twere useless myself to discover;
Suffice it that thy father I am.
Some in the world there are who fear me,
In others, perhaps, envy I excite;
But one there is who has cursed me!

Gilda.

Quanto dolor! che spremere
Sì amaro pianto può?
Padre, non più, calmatevi—
Mi lacera tal vista—
Il nome vostro ditemi,
Il duol che sì v'attrista—

Rigoletto.

A che nomarmi? è inutile!
Padre ti sono, e basti—
Me forse al mondo temono,
D' alcuno ho forse gli asti:
Altri mi maledicono—

Gilda.
>Country, family, friends,
>Possess you none of them?

Rigoletto.
>Country, family, friends, say'st thou?
>Thou art my country, family, and friends!
>The whole universe thou art to me!
>>(Passionately.)

Gilda.
>Ah! if happier I could render you,
>What joy to my heart it would bring!
>Three months full it is since hither I came,
>And nothing yet have I of the city seen.
>With your permission I should like to see it.

Rigoletto.
>Never! never!   Hast thou ever left the
>house?

Gilda.
>No.

Rigoletto.
>That's well.

Gilda.
>(What have I said?)

Rigoletto.
>I'll take care thou shalt not!
>(She might be followed—stolen from me!
>To dishonor the daughter of a buffoon
>Would here be laughed at.   Horror!)   Ho,
>there!
>>(Turning towards the house.)

>>(Enter GIOVANNA, from the house.)

Giovanna.
>Signor?

Rigoletto.
>Has any one seen me come hither?
>Mind—speak the truth.

Giovanna.
>Oh, no—no one.

Rigoletto.
>That is well.   The gate that to the bastion
>leads—
>Is that always closed?

Giovanna.
>It is, and shall be.

Gilda.
>Patria, parenti, amici,
>Voi dunque non avete?

Rigoletto.
>Patria! parenti! dici?
>Culto, famiglia, patria,
>Il mio universo è in te!
>>(Con effusione.)

Gilda.
>Ah! se può lieto rendervi,
>Gioia è la vita a me!
>Già da tre lune son quì venuta,
>Nè la cittade ho ancor veduta;
>Se il concedete, farlo or potrei—

Rigoletto.
>Mai! mai! uscita, dimmi, unqua sei?

Gilda.
>No.

Rigoletto.
>Guai!

Gilda.
>(Che dissi?)

Rigoletto.
>Ben te ne guarda!
>Potrian seguirla, rapirla ancora!
>Qui d'un buffone si disonora
>La figlia, e ridesi—Orror! Olà?
>>(Verso la casa.)

>>(Entra GIOVANNA, dalla casa.)

Giovanna.
>Signor?

Rigoletto.
>Venendo, mi vide alcuno?
>Bada, di' il vero—

Giovanna.
>Ah, no, nessuno.

Rigoletto.
>Sta ben—la porta che dà al bastione
>E sempre chiusa?

Giovanna.
>Lo fu e sarà

VEGLIA O DONNA —— *SAFELY GUARD THIS TENDER BLOSSOM* Duet (Rigoletto and Gilda)

RIGOLETTO

(The DUKE, in disguise, is seen to arrive in the street.)

Rigoletto.

There is some one outside.

(RIGOLETTO comes through the garden-gate, and looks about the street; while doing so, the DUKE stealthily glides in, and hides himself behind a tree, throwing a purse to GIOVANNA.)

Gilda.

Oh, Heavens!
He is always suspicious.

Rigoletto   (returning to GILDA.)

Does any one ever follow you to church?

Gilda.

No.

Duke.

(Rigoletto.)

Rigoletto.

Should any one knock,
On no account admit him.

Giovanna.

Not even the Duke?

Rigoletto.

Above all others keep him out. Daughter, adieu!

Duke.

(His daughter!)

Gilda.

Adieu, dear father.

(They embrace, and RIGOLETTO departs, closing the door after him.)

Gilda   (in the yard).

Giovanna, I am struck with remorse.

Giovanna.

What about, pray?

Gilda.

I did not tell him of the youth who follows me to church.

Giovanna.

Why should you tell him? Do you hate the youth,
And would you thus dismiss him?

Gilda.

No, no! his looks are pleasing to me.

Giovanna.

And he has the appearance of a wealthy signor.

Gilda.

Neither signor nor wealth do I wish to have;

(Entra il DUCA, in costume borghese, della strada.)

Rigoletto.

Alcuno è fuori—

(Apre la porta della corte e, mentre esce a guardar sulla strada, il DUCA guizza furtivo nella corte, e si nasconde dietro l'albero; gettando a GIOVANNA una borsa la fa tacere.)

Gilda.

Cielo!
Sempre novel sospetto—

Rigoletto   (a GILDA, tornando).

Vi seguiva alla chiesa mai nessuno?

Gilda.

Mai.

Duca.

(Rigoletto.)

Rigoletto.

Se talor quì picchiano
Guardatevi d'aprire—

Giovanna.

Nemmeno al Duca?

Rigoletto.

Meno che a tutti a lui. Mia figlia, addio.

Duca.

(Sua figlia!)

Gilda.

Addio, mio padre.

(S'abbracciano, e RIGOLETTO parte, chiudendosi dietro la porta.)

Gilda   (nella corte).

Giovanna, ho dei rimorsi—

Giovanna.

E perchè mai?

Gilda.

Tacqui che un giovin ne sequiva al tempio.

Giovanna.

Perchè ciò dirgli?—l'odiate dunque
Cotesto giovin, voi?

Gilda.

No, no, chè troppo è bello, e spira amore—

Giovanna.

E magnanimo sembra e gran signore.

Gilda.

Signor nè principe—io lo vorrei:

The poorer he prove, the more shall I love
    him.
Sleeping or waking, my thoughts are all of
    him,
And my heart longs to tell him I lo—

Duke
(suddenly coming forward, motioning GIOVANNA to retire,
    and kneeling at the feet of GILDA).
    I love thee!
    The words repeat! Such delicious accents
    Open to me a heaven of enjoyment.

Gilda.
    Giovanna? Alas, no one answers me!
    There's no one here! Oh, heavens, I'm
        alone!

Duke.
    No! I am here; and to thee I respond—
    Against all the world I will protect thee!

Gilda.
    Why thus address yourself to me?

Duke.
    Whate'er your state, to me it matters not—
    I love thee!

Gilda.
    Oh, go away.

Duke.
    Go away! No, not yet!
    If love's fire within us both be lighted,
    Inseparable we should henceforth be;
    O maiden bright, thy lot with mine unite!

Sento che povero—più l'amerei.
Sognando o vigile—sempre lo chiamo,
E l'alma in estasi—gli dice t'a—

Duca
(esce improvviso, fa cenno a GIOVANNA d'andarsene, e in.
    ginocchiandosi a' pied di GILDA termina la frase).
    T'amo!
    T'amo, ripetilo—si caro accento,
    Un puro schiudimi—ciel di contento!

Gilda.
    Giovanna? Ahi, misera! non v' è più alcuna
    Che qui rispondami! Oh Dio! nessuno!

Duca.
    Son io coll' anima—che ti rispondo—
    Ah, que che s'amano—son tutto un mondo!

Gilda.
    Chi mai, chi giungere—vi fece a me?

Duca.
    S'angelo o demone—che importa a te?
    Io t'amo—

Gilda.
    Uscitene.

Duca.
    Uscire! adesso!
    Ora che accendene—un fuoco istesso!
    Ah, inseparabile—d'amore, il dio
    Stringeva, o vergine—tuo fato al mio!

E IL SOL DELL' ANIMA — *LOVE IS THE SUN* Air (Duke)

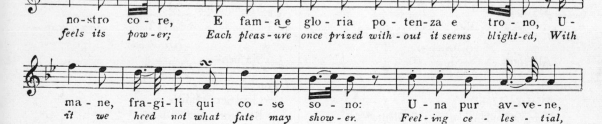

so - la, di - vi - na,   Ea - mor chea gl'an - ge - li, a -
no   joy ter - res - trial Can e'er to   me such sweet__

gl'an - ge - li più ne av - vi - ci - na! ___   A - dun - quea - mia - mo - ci,
rap - ture im - part. Ah! ___   May no blight ev - er this

don - na ce - le - ste, D'in - vi - di a gl'uo - mi - ni   sa - rò per
heart from thee sev - er; Rest in my bos - om, ne'er to de -

te,   D'in - vi - dia a - gl'un - mi - ni sa - rò per   te.
part,   Rest in__ my__ bos - om, and - ne'er de - part.

Gilda.

(Ah! how these words my ears delight!
His tones, how tender—and how pure his
love!)

Duke.

That you love me—oh, the words repeat—

Gilda.

You have heard.

Duke.

O joy unlooked for!

Gilda.

Your name, now, I pray you tell me;
For I never yet have heard it.

(Enter CEPRANO and BORSA, from the street.)

Ceprano   (to BORSA).

This is the place.

Duke   (to GILDA).

My name is—
                 (Considering.)

Borsa   (to CEPRANO).

All right.
                 (They depart.)

Duke.

Walter Maldè.
I am a student—a poor student.

Gilda.

(Ah de' miei vergini—sogni son queste—
Le voci tenere—si care a me!)

Duca.

Che m'ami—deh! ripetimi—

Gilda.

L'udiste.

Duca.

Oh, me felice!

Gilda.

Il nome vostro ditemi;
Saperlo non mi lice?

(Entra CEPRANO e BORSA sulla via.)

Ceprano   (a BORSA).

Il loco è quì—

Duca   (a GILDA).

Mi nomino—
                 (Pensando.)

Borsa   (a CEPRANO).

Sta ben—
                 (E partono.)

Duca.

Gaultier Maldé.
Studento sono, povero.

Giovanna. (In alarm.)	*Giovanna.* (Spaventata.)
I hear footsteps outside.	Rumor di passi è furore.
Gilda.	*Gilda.*
Perhaps it is my father.	Forse mio padre.
Duke.	*Duca.*
Ah! could I the traitor catch	Ah! cogliere
Who thus presumes to interrupt	Potessi il traditore
The joy I have in being with thee!	Che sì mi sturba!
Gilda (to GIOVANNA).	*Gilda* (a GIOVANNA).
(Quickly away!	(Adducilo
To the bastion conduct him—go!)	Di quà al bastione, ite!)
Duke.	*Duca.*
First say that you love me?	Di m'amerai tu?
Gilda.	*Gilda.*
And you?	E voi?
Duke.	*Duca.*
With my whole heart I swear it.	L'intera vita, poi.
Gilda.	*Gilda.*
No more, no more, at once depart.	Non più, non più, partite.
Both.	*A 2.*
Farewell, my hope, my soul, farewell;	Addio, speranza ed anima
For thee alone henceforth I'll live;	Sol tu sari per me.
Farewell! Immutable as Fate	Addio, vivrà immutabile
Shall be my love and truth to thee.	L'affretto mio per te.
(Exit the DUKE, escorted by GIOVANNA, GILDA following his steps with her eyes.)	(Parte il DUCA scortato da GIOVANNA, GILDA resta fissando è partito.)
Gilda (alone).	*Gilda* (sola).
Walter Maldè! What a romantic name!	Gualtier Maldé! nome di lui si amato.
Already is it on my heart engraven!	Scolpiciti nel core innamorato!

CARO NOME CHE IL MIO COR — *DEAR NAME WITHIN THIS BREAST* Air (Gilda)

ra, E fin l'ul - ti - mo so - spir, Ca - ro no - me, tuo_ sa -
heart; 'Twill beat for thee a - lone; Till death 'twill ne'er de -

rà.   Col pen - sier il mio de - sir A te sem - pre vo - le - rà._
part!   'Twill_ beat for thee a - lone; Ah! till death 'twill ne'er de - part!_

E fin l'ul - ti - mo_ mi - o_ so -
'Twill beat, 'twill beat for thee a -

spir, Ca - ro no - - - me, tuo sa - rà.
lone, Ah!_ till death _ 'twill ne'er de - part.

(She ascends the terrace, with a lantern in her hand.)	(San al terrazzo con una lanterna, che tono entra in casa.)
(Enter MARULLO, CEPRANO, and BORSA, accompanied by courtiers, in masks, and armed.)	(Entrano MARULLO, CEPRANO, e BORSA, cortigiani, armati e mascherati, dalla via.)
Borsa.	*Borsa.*
Look there!	E là.
(Pointing towards GILDA.)	(Indicanda GILDA.)
Ceprano.	*Ceprano.*
Ah! there she is—	Miratela—
Chorus.	*Coro.*
Oh! how beautiful she is!	Oh! quanto è bella!
Marullo.	*Marullo.*
A fairy or an angel!	Par fata od angiol!
Chorus.	*Coro.*
Can that the mistress be	L'amante è quella
Of Rigoletto?	Di Rigoletto?
(They all laugh.)	
(Enter RIGOLETTO, absorbed in thought.)	(Entra RIGOLETTO, concentrato.)
Rigoletto.	*Rigoletto.*
(Laughing! what can it mean?)	(Riedo! perche?)
Borsa.	*Borsa.*
Silence, to our work; we've no time for laughing.	Silenzio, all' opra, badate a me.
Rigoletto.	*Rigoletto.*
(Ah, how fiercely that old man cursed me!)	(Ah da quel vecchio fui maledetto!)
Who is there?	Chi è là?

Borsa *(to his companions).*

Be silent, 'tis Rigoletto.

Ceprano.

A double capture! We can also slay him.

Borsa.

No; to-morrow it will make more sport.

Marullo.

But now everything is ready.

Rigoletto.

(Who is speaking there?)

Marullo.

Is't you, Rigoletto—say.

Rigoletto *(considerably agitated).*

Who goes there?

Marullo.

You will not betray us—I am—

Rigoletto.

Who?

Marullo.

Marullo.

Rigoletto.

In the dead of night for good you are not
here.

Marullo.

'Tis a ridiculous frolic brings us here;
Ceprano's wife we mean to carry off.

Rigoletto.

(Once more do I breathe.) But how do you
enter?

Marullo *(to CEPRANO).*

Hand here the keys!

(To RIGOLETTO.)

Doubt us not;

We are not to be foiled in a stratagem.

(Handing him the keys taken from CEPRANO.)

Here are the keys.

Rigoletto *(feeling the keys).*

I feel that this is his crest.

(Ah! then all my terrors have been need-
less!)

(He breathes more freely.)

Yonder is his palace—I will go with you.

Marullo.

We are all disguised.

Borsa *(ai compagni).*

Tacete, c' è Rigoletto.

Ceprano.

Vittoria doppia! L'uccideremo.

Borsa.

No: chè domani più rideremo.

Marullo.

Or tutto aggiusto.

Rigoletto.

(Chi parla quà?)

Marullo.

Ehi, Rigoletto?—di

Rigoletto *(con voce terribile).*

Chi va là?

Marullo.

Eh, non mangiarci—son—

Rigoletto.

Chi?

Marullo.

Marullo.

Rigoletto.

In tanto bugo lo squardo è nullo.

Marullo.

Quì ne condusse ridevol cosa;
Tòrre a Ceprano vogliam la sposa.

Rigoletto.

(Ohimè, respiro.) Ma come entrare?

Marullo *(a CEPRANO).*

La vostra chiave?

(A RIGOLETTO.)

Non dubitare;

Non de mancarci lo stratagemma.

(Gli dà chiave avuta da CEPRANO.)

Ecco le chiavi.

Rigoletto *(palpandole).*

Sento il suo stemma.

(Ah, terror vano fu dunque il mio!)

(Respirando.)

N' è là palazzo—con vio son io.

Marullo.

Siam mascherati.

Rigoletto.

Then so will I be;

Give me here a mask.

Marullo.

Well, here is one.

You shall hold the ladder.

(Puts a mask on the face of RIGOLETTO, fastens it by a handkerchief across his eyes, and places him at a ladder, against the terrace wall, to keep it steady.)

Rigoletto.

How very dark it has become!

Marullo.

The bandage renders him both blind and deaf.

(To his companions.)

All.

Silence! silence! while vengeance we seek;

In his own trap now let him be caught;

The jester who constantly makes us his sport,

Shall now, in his turn, our laughter provoke.

Hush! be quiet! his mistress we'll seize,

And, to-morrow, at court have our laugh.

(Some ascend to the terrace, force a window, by which they enter, and descend to the door, which they open to others, who enter and drag out GILDA. She has her mouth gagged with a handkerchief. While being dragged across the stage, a scarf falls from her.)

Gilda.

Help! help! Father, dear, help!

Chorus.

Victory!

Gilda.

Help! help!

(At a distance.)

Rigoletto.

Is it not yet done? What a capital joke!

(Putting his hands to his face.)

Why, my eyes are bandaged!

(He snatches off the bandage and mask, and, by the light of the lantern, recognizes the scarf, and sees the door open; he rushes in, and drags out GIOVANNA, greatly frightened; he fixes his eyes upon her in stupefaction, tears his hair in agony, and, after many ineffectual efforts to speak, exclaims:)

Ah! this is the Malediction!

(Swoons.)

END OF ACT I.

Rigoletto.

Ch' io pur mi mascheri;

A me una larva?

Marullo.

Sì pronta è già.

Terrai la scala.

(Gli mette una maschera, e nello stesso tempo lo benda con un fazzoletto, e lo pone a reggere una scala, che avranna appostata al terrazzo.)

Rigoletto.

Fitta è la tenebra!

Marullo.

La benda cieco e sordo il fa.

(A compagni.)

Tutti.

Zitti, zitti, moviamo a vendetta,

Ne sia còlto, or che meno l'aspetta.

Derisorë sì audace constante

A sua volta schernito sarà!

Cheti, cheti, rubiamgli l'amante,

E la Corte doman riderà.

(Alcuni salgono al terrazzo, rompon la porta del primo piano, scendono, aprono ad altri ch'entrano dalla strada, e riescono, trascinando GILDA, la quale avrà la bocca chiusa da un fazzoletto. Nel traversare la scena ella perde una sciarpa.)

Gilda.

Soccorso, padre mio—

Coro.

Vittoria!

Gilda.

Aita!

(Più lontano.)

Rigoletto.

Non han finito ancor! qual derisione!

(Si tocca gli occhi.)

Sono bendato!

(Si strappa impetuosamente la benda e la maschera, ed al chiarore d'una lanterna scordata riconosce la sciarpa: vede la porta aperta, entra, ne trae GIOVANNA spaventata; la fissa con istapore, si strappa i capelli senza poter gridare; finalmente, dopo molti sforzi, esclama:)

Ah!—la Maledizione!

FINE DELL' ATTO PRIMO.

ACT II.

SCENE I—Salon in the Duke's Palace. Large folding-doors in back-scene, and smaller ones on each side, above which hang portraits of the Duke and the Duchess. A table covered with velvet, handsome chairs, and other appropriate furniture.

(Enter the Duke, by centre doorway, much agitated.)

Duke.

She has been stolen from me!

But how, and by whom? Oh, heavens!

Thus to lose her at the very moment

When my passion most demanded her!

The door was wide open—the house deserted!

Whither can the dear angel have flown!

She who first within this wandering heart

The joys of a true love hath awakened—

She so pure that, by her modest bearing,

To truthfulness I feel me now inclined.

She has been stolen from me! But, to do it,

Who has dared! On him shall vengeance alight!

Grief for my beloved one vengeance demands!

ATTO II.

SCENA I—Salotto nel Palazzo Ducale. Vi sono due porte laterali, una maggiore nel fondó che si chiude. A' suoi lati pendono i ritratti, in tutta figura, a sinistra, del Duca, a destra della sua sposa. V' ha un seggiolone presso una tavola coperta di velluto, ed altri mobili.

(Entra il Duca, dal mezzo, agitato.)

Duca.

Ella mia fu rapita!

E quando, o ciel?—ne' brevi istanti, prima

Che un mio presagio interno

Sull' orma corsa ancora mi spingesse!

Schiuso era l'uscio! la magion deserta!

E dove ora sarà quell' angiol caro!

Colei che potè prima in questo core

Destar la fiamma di costanti affetti?

Colei sì pura, al cui modesto accento

Quasi tratto a virtù talor mi credo!

Ella mi fu rapita!

E chi l'ardiva?—ma ne avro vendetta:

Lo chiede il pianto della mia diletta.

PARMI VEDER LE LAGRIME — *DEAR MAID, EACH TEAR*   Air (Duke)

Par - mi ve - der le la - gri - me   Scor - ren - ti da___ quel ci - glio,
Dear maid, each tear of thine that falls,   Each sad sigh that bos - om heav - ing,

Quand - do fra il dub - bio e l'an - sia Del   su - bi - to pe -
Pin - ing with - in some dark walls, Fills me___ with pain and

reg - lio, Dell' a - mor no - stro me - mo - re, Dell' a - mor no - stre
griev - ing. Ah! vain - ly didst thou cry to me, Ah!_ vain - ly didst thou.

me - mo - re, Il suo Gual - tier chia - mò.   Ned ei pe - tea soc -
cry___ to me, "Help me, dear Wal - ter, help!"   I then, a - las! was

cor - rer - ti,   Ca - ra fan - ciul - la a - ma - ta;
far   a - way,   No   aid   could I___ af - ford thee;

Ei che vor-ria coll' a - ni - ma___   Far - ti quag-giù be -
Yet, could my life thy woes re - pay,___   Glad - ly ex-changed it

a - ta; Ei che le sfe-re a gl'an - ge - li, Ei__ che le sfe-re a
should be. Not e'en the an-gels' blest a - bode Could peace to me re -

gl'an - ge - li Per te non in - vi - diò,   Ei che le
store,___   to me re - store, from thee a - part;   Could peace to

sfe - re; Le sfe-re a gl'an - ge - li Per te, per te___   Le sfe - re a
me re-store: Not e'en the an - gels' blest a - bode___ Could peace to

gl'an - ge - li Per te ___   non in - vi - diò,   non in - vi - diò.
me re-store, Could peace ___   to me re - store,   from thee a - part.

(Enter MARULLO, CEPRANO, BORSA, and other courtiers.)	(Entrano MARULLO, CEPRANO, BORSA, ed altri cortigiani.)
All.	*Tutti.*
Oh, Duke! oh, Duke!	Duca, Duca!
Duke.	*Duca.*
What news?	Ebben?
All.	*Tutti.*
From Rigoletto	L'amante
We have carried off his mistress.	Fu rapita a Rigoletto.
Duke.	*Duca.*
Capital! Where is she?	Bella! e d'onde?
All.	*Tutti.*
In your palace.	Dal suo tetto.
Duke.	*Duca.*
Ah, ah! tell me how 'twas done?	Ah, ah; dite, come fu?

SCORRENDO UNITI — *AS WE WITH GLEE* (Chorus)

Scor-ren - dou - ni - ti re - mo - ta
As we with glee on mis - chief bent last

vi - a Bre - v'o - ra do - po ca - du - to il
night roved, When hush'd in peace - ful sleep the world seem'd

dì, Co - me pre - vi - sto ben s'e - ra in pri - a, Ra - ra bel -
bu - ried, The one we sought we met, a - lone, mis - trust - ing, Be - side the

tà ci si sco - pri, ci si sco - prì. E - ra l'a -
house in which we guess'd the bird was caged. The charm - ing

man - te di Ri - go - let - to Che, vis - ta ap -
fair was Ri - go - let - to's mis - tress; But she af -

pe - na, si di - le - guò. Già di ra - pir - la s'a - vea il pro -
fright - ed to her home then ran; The jest - er then ap - pear'd, with whom we

get - to, Quan - do il buf - fon ver noi spun - tò, ver noi spun -
sport - ed: "Give us thy aid, Ce - pra - no's wife to steal a -

tò; Che di Ce - pra - no noi la Con - tes - sa Ra - pir vo -
way!" The trap he fell in; oh, sport worth tell - ing! A ban - dage

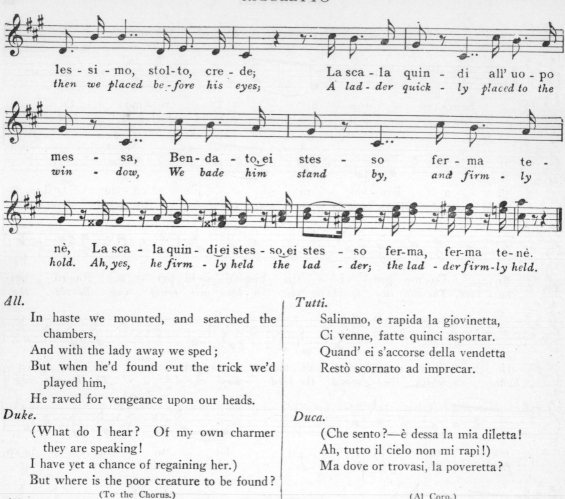

les - si - mo, stol - to, cre - de; La sca - la quin - di all' uo - po
then we placed be - fore his eyes; *A lad - der quick - ly placed to the*

mes - sa, Ben - da - to ei stes - so fer - ma te -
win - dow, We bade him stand by, and firm - ly

nè, La sca - la quin - di ei stes - so ei stes - so fer - ma, fer - ma te - nè.
hold. Ah, yes, he firm - ly held the lad - der; the lad - der firm - ly held.

All.	**Tutti.**
In haste we mounted, and searched the chambers,	Salimmo, e rapida la giovinetta,
And with the lady away we sped;	Ci venne, fatte quinci asportar.
But when he'd found out the trick we'd played him,	Quand' ei s'accorse della vendetta
He raved for vengeance upon our heads.	Restò scornato ad imprecar.
Duke.	**Duca.**
(What do I hear? Of my own charmer they are speaking!	(Che sento?—è dessa la mia diletta!
I have yet a chance of regaining her.)	Ah, tutto il cielo non mi rapì!)
But where is the poor creature to be found?	Ma dove or trovasi, la poveretta?
(To the Chorus.)	(Al Coro.)
All.	**Tutti.**
All proper care we have taken of her.	Fu da noi stessi addotta or qui.

POSSENTE AMOR — *TO HER I LOVE*   Air (Duke)

Pos - sen - te a - mor mi chia - ma, Vo - lar io deg - gio a
To her I love with rap - ture, I must with speed flee a -

le - i; Il ser - to mio da - rei Per con - so - lar quel
way; All thought of her base cap - ture I'll gen - tly soothe a -

cor.   Il ser - to mio da - rei _____ Per con - so - lar_ quel_
way;   All thought of her base cap - ture I'll gen - tly soothe a -

cor.   Ah! sap - pi al - fin chi l'a - ma Co - no - sca al - fin chi
way.   From her my name and sta - tion I can - not now con -

so - no, Ap - pren - do ch'an - co in tro - no Ha deg - li schia - vi A-
ceal, ____ Yet, free from ob - ser - va - tion, I may my love re -

mor;   Ap - - pren - do ch'an - co in tro - no, ch'an - co in
veal;   I _____ may_ my_ love re - veal_ I ___ may my

tro - no Ha deg - li schia - vi, Ha_ deg - li schia - vi A - mor.
love, yes, my love to her_ re - veal, My_ love to her may re - veal.

(What new thought now has seized him—	(O qual pensiero l'agita
A sudden change has just come o'er him.)	Come congiò d' umor!)
Marullo.	*Marullo.*
Unlucky Rigoletto!—	Povero Rigoletto!—
Chorus.	*Coro.*
Here he comes—be silent, all.	Ei vien—silenzio.
(Enter RIGOLETTO.)	(Entra RIGOLETTO.)
All.	*Tutti.*
Good morning to you, Rigoletto.	Buon giorno, Rigoletto—
Rigoletto.	*Rigoletto.*
(They are all of them in the plot.)	(Han tutti fatto il colpo!)
Ceprano.	*Ceprano.*
What news do you bring,	Ch' hai di nuovo,
Buffoon?	Buffon?
Rigoletto.	*Rigoletto.*
More than ever	Che dell' usato
Are you wearisome to me.	Più noioso voi siete.
All.	*Tutti.*
Ah! ah! ah!	Ah! ah! ah!

Rigoletto.

(Whither can they have carried her?)
(Looking about anxiously.)

All.

(See how uneasy he appears!)

Rigoletto (sardonically).

Happy I am
To see that no hurt you have taken
From the cold air of last night.

Marullo.

Last night, said you?

Rigoletto.

Yes—Ah! 'twas a capital trick.

Marullo.

I was asleep, all night.

Rigoletto.

Oh! you were asleep! then I have been
    dreaming!

(He is about to go, when, seeing a handkerchief on the table, he anxiously examines the cipher on it.)

All.

(See how everything he scrutinizes!)

Rigoletto.

(It is not hers.)
(Throwing it down.)

Is the Duke still sleeping?

All.

Yes, he is still sleeping!
(Enter a Page of the DUCHESS.)

Page.

The Duchess desires to speak to her lord.

Ceprano.

He sleeps.

Page.

Was he not here but lately?

Borsa.

He has gone hunting.

Page.

Without his suite! without arms!

All.

Canst thou not understand,
That for a short time he cannot be seen?

Rigoletto

(who has been anxiously listening, suddenly rushes amongst them, and exclaims:)

Ah! she is here, then   She is with the Duke!

All.

Who?

Rigoletto.

(Dove l'avran nascosta?)
(Spiando inquieto dovunque.)

Tutti.

(Guardate com' è inquieto!)

Rigoletto.

Son felice
Che nulla a voi nuocesse
L'aria di questa notte.

Marullo.

Questa notte!

Rigoletto.

Sì—Ah! fu il bel colpo!

Marullo.

S' ho dormito sempre!

Rigoletto.

Ah! voi dormiste! avrò dunque sognato!

(S'allontana, e vendendo un fazzoletto sopra una tavola ne osserva inquieto la cifra.)

Tutti.

(Ve' come tutto osserva!)

Rigoletto.

(Non è il suo.)
(Gettandolo.)

Dorme il Duca tuttor?

Tutti.

Si, dorme ancora.
(Entra un Paggio della DUCHESSA.)

Paggio.

Al suo sposo parlar vuol la Duchessa

Ceprano.

Dorme.

Paggio.

Quì or or con voi non era?

Borsa.

E a caccia.

Paggio.

Senza paggi! senz' armi!

Tutti.

E non capisci
Che vedere per ora non può alcuno?

Rigoletto

(che a parte e stato attentissimo al dialogo, balzande im provviso tra loro prorompe).

Ah, ell' è quì dunque! Ell' è col Duca!

Tutti.

Chi?

Rigoletto.

The maiden whom last night
From my house you forced away.

All.

You must be mad.

Rigoletto.

But I will have her back—she must be here.

All.

If your mistress you have lost, elsewhere
Seek for her.

Rigoletto.

I will have back my daughter!

All.

His daughter, says he?

Rigoletto.

Yes, she is my daughter; you will not now
O'er such a victory exult.
She is here, I will have her, give her back
to me!

(He rushes towards the door in the centre, but the courtiers bar his progress.)

Minions, sycophants, panders, thieves,
At what price have you my daughter sold?
Your sordid souls no crime intimidates,
But priceless is a daughter to her father.
Restore her, or, though unarmed I am,
Fearfully shall this hand assail ye;
Naught on earth can a father dismay,
When the honor of his child he doth defend!
Assassins, open that door, and let me pass.

(He again attempts to pass the door, but is restrained by the courtiers; he struggles with them for a while and then sinks exhausted to the ground.)

Ah! come ye thus all against me!

(Weeping.)

Well, see; I weep! Marullo—Signor,
In heart and mien thou seemest gentle,—
Tell me where they have my daughter hidden!
Is she here? Tell me truly! Silent! Why?
O, my lords, I pray you to have pity on me—
To an old man give back his daughter!
To restore her will you nothing cost,
While to me my child is all the world.

(Enter GILDA, through the doorway on the left. She rushes into the arms of her father.)

Gilda.

O, my father!

Rigoletto.

Le giovin che stanotte
A mio tetto rapisti—

Tutti.

Tu deliri!

Rigoletto.

Ma la saprò riprender—Ella è quì.

Tutti.

Se l'amante perdesti, la ricerca
Altrove.

Rigoletto.

Io vo' mia figlia!

Tutti.

La sua figlia!

Rigoletto.

Sì, la mia figlia—D'unta tal vittoria—
Che? adesso non ridete?
Ella è là, la vogl' io, la renderete.

(Corre verso la porta di mezzo, ma i cortigiani gli attraversano il passaggio.)

Cortigiani, vil razza dannata,
Per qual prezzo vendeste il mio bene?
A voi nulla per l'oro sconviene,
Ma mia figlia è impagabil tesor.
La rendete—o se pur disarmata
Questa man per voi fora cruenta;
Nulla in terra più l'uomo paventa,
Se dei figli difende l'onor.
Quella porta, assassina, m'aprite:

(Si getta ancor sulla porta che gli è nuovamente contesa dai gentiluomini; lotta alquanto, poi torna spossato sul davanti del teatro.)

Ah! voi tutti a me contro venite!

(Piange.)

Ebben piango—Marullo—signore,
Tu ch' hai l'alma gentil come il core,
Dimmi or tu, dove l'hanno nascosta?
E là? E vero? tu taci? perchè?
Miei signori—Perdono, pietate;
Al vegliardo la figlia ridate;
Ridornarla a voi nulla ora costa,
Tutto il mondo è tal figlia per me.

(Entra GILDA, ch'esce dalla stranza a sinistra, e si getta nelle paterne braccia.)

Gilda.

Mio padre!

Rigoletto.

O God! my own Gilda!
Signors, in her you behold
My whole family.   Have no further fear,
My angel child!   It was a joke—was it not
so?   (To the courtiers.)
I wept, but now I laugh.   Yet thou—why
weepest thou?

Gilda.

For shame, father!   I have been maltreated!

Rigoletto.

Heaven! what say'st thou?

Gilda

What I have to say no one else must hear.

Rigoletto

(turning towards the courtiers, imperatively).
Away, away! all of ye!
And if your Duke should hither dare approach,
Tell him not to enter—for I am here.
(Falling into a chair.)

All.

(With children and madmen
It is sometimes well to simulate;
Therefore will we depart; but what he does
We will not fail unseen to watch.)
(Exeunt through doorway in front, closing it after them.

Rigoletto.

Now speak—we are alone.

Gilda.

(Heaven, now grant me courage!)
Whene'er to church I went,
There my prayers to say,
A youth of handsome mien
Before me always stood.
Although our lips were silent,
Our hearts discoursed through our eyes.
Stealthily, in night's darkness,
While alone, he came to me:
"A student poor am I,"
Plaintively he said to me;
And with ardent sighings
His love for me protested.
Then he left me; and my heart
To hope's bright visions opened,
When men ferocious and unlook'd-for
Tore me from our home away.

Rigoletto.

Dio! mia Gilda!
Signori, in essa è tutta
La mia famiglia.   Non temer più nulla,
Angelo mio—fu scherzo non è vero?
(Ai cortigiani.)
Io che pur piansi or rido—E tu a che piangi

Gilda.

Ah! l'onta, padre mio!

Rigoletto.

Cielo! che dici?

Gilda.

Arrossir voglio innanzi a voi soltanto.

Rigoletto

(trivolto ai cortigiani, con imperioso modo.)
Ite di quà, voi tutti—
Se il Duca vostro d'appressarsi osasse,
Che non entri gli dite, e ch' io ci sono
(Si abbandona sul seggiolone.)

Tutti.

(Co' fanciulli e coi dementi
Spesso giova il simular.
Partiam pur, ma quel ch' ei tenti
Non lasciamo d'osservar.)
(Escon dal mezzo e chindon la porta.

Rigoletto.

Parla—siam soli.

Gilda.

(Ciel, dammi corraggio!)
Tutte le feste al tempio
Mentre pregava Iddio,
Bello e fatale un giovane
S'offerse àl guardo mio—
Se i labbri nostri tacquero,
Dagli occhi il cor parlò.
Furtivo fra le tenebre
Sol iera a me giungeva;
Sono studente, povero,
Commosso mi diceva,
E con ardente palpito
Amor mi protestò.
Parti—il mio core aprivasi
A speme più gradita,
Quando improvvisi apparvere
Color che m' han rapita.

And hither forcibly brought me,
To my ruin and dismay.

Rigoletto.

Stop—say no more, my angel—
(I know all! Avenging Heaven,
Upon my head falls the infamy
I have of thee invoked!) O God!
That she might be exalted,
How miserably have I fallen!
Ah! often near the altar
The scaffold should be reared;
But now all is out of order,
And e'en the altar desecrated.
Weep, my child, and let thy tears
Within thy father's bosom fall.

Gilda.

Father, like an angel you speak to me
These words of consolation.

Rigoletto.

What must be done I will quickly dispose
of,
And then for ever will we quit this fatal
place.

Gilda.

Yes!

Rigoletto.

How changed in one short day may be our
destiny!

(Enter a Herald and the COUNT MONTERONE, who is
marched across the back of the stage, between guards.)

Herald.

Make way; he is ordered to the prison of
Castiglion.

(To the guards.)

Monterone.

Since in vain thou hast by me been cursed,

(Stopping before the portrait.)

The wrath of neither heaven nor earth can
reach thee,
And happy wilt thou yet live, O Duke!

(Exit, between the guards.)

Rigoletto.

No, old man, not so—thou shalt be avenged!
Yes, vengeance, dire vengeance, awaits thee!
The one hope of my soul is thee to punish!
And the hour of retribution is nigh
That to thee shall prove fatal.

E a forza quì m'addussero
Nell' ansia più crudel.

Rigoletto.

Non dir; non più, mio angelo.
(T'intendo, avverso ciel!
Solo per me l'infamia
A te chiedeva, o Dio!
Ch' ella potesse ascendere
Quanto caduto er' io;
Ah! presso del patibolo
Bisogna ben l'altare!
Ma tutto ora scompare;
L'altar si roversciò!)
Piangi, fanciulla, e scorrere
Fa il pianto sul mio cor.

Gilda.

Padre, in voi parla un angelo
Per me consolator.

Rigoletto.

Compiuto pur quanto a fare mi resta,
Lasciare potremo quest' aura funesta.

Gilda.

Sì.

Rigoletto.

(E tutto un sol giorno cangiare potè!)

(Entra un Usciere ed il CONTE DI MONTERONE, che dalla
destra attraversa il fondo della sala fra gli alabardieri.)

Usciere.

Schiudete—ire al carcere Castiglion dee.

(Alle guardie.)

Monterone.

Poichè fosti invano da me maledetto,

(Fermandosi verso il ritratto.)

Nè un fulmine o un ferro colpiva il tuo
petto,
Felice per anco, o Duca, vivrai—

(Esce fra le guardie dal mezzo.)

Rigoletto.

No, vecchio, t'inganni—un vindice avrai.
Sì, vendetta, tremenda vendetta
Di quest' anima è solo desio—
Di punirti giè—l'ora s'affretta,
Che fatale per te tuonerà.

Like thunder from the heavens hurled,
Shall fall the blow of the despised buffoon.

Gilda.

O father dear, what joy ferocious
I see your flashing eyes light up!
Ah! pardon him, as we ourselves
The pardon of heaven hope to gain.
(I dare not say how much I love him,
And pity him who none for me hath
    shown!)

(Exeunt, through centre door.)

END OF THE SECOND ACT.

———

ACT III.

SCENE I—A desolate place on the banks of the Mincio. On the right, with its front to the audience, a house, two stories high, in a very dilapidated state, which is nevertheless used as an inn. The doors and walls are so full of crevices, that whatever is going on within can be seen from without. In front, the road and the river. In the distance, the city of Mantua. It is night.

(GILDA and RIGOLETTO discovered, in apparent altercation, SPARAFUCILE seen in the house, cleaning his belt, unconscious of what is going on outside.)

Rigoletto.

Yet you love him?

Gilda.

I cannot help it.

Rigoletto.

Surely
This madness ere now you should have con-
    quered.

Gilda.

Yet I love him!

Rigoletto.

How weak is the heart of woman!
Her vile seducer she'd forgive—
But avenged thou shalt be, my Gilda.

Gilda.

Have pity on him, dear father!

Rigoletto.

If of his treachery I convince you,
Will you then from your heart discard him?

Gilda.

I do not know;—but he to me is true.

Rigoletto.

He!

Come fulmin scagliato da Dio
Il buffone colpirti saprà.

Gilda.

O, mio padre, qual gioja feroce,
Balenarvi negli occhi vegg' io!
Perdonate—a noi pure una voce
Di perdono dal cielo verrà.
(Mi tradiva, pur l'amo, gran Dio,
Per l'ingrato ti chiedo pietà!)

(Escon dal mezzo.)

FINE DELL' ATTO SECONDO.

———

ATTO III.

SCENA I—Deserta sponda del Mincio. A sinistra è una casa in due piani, mezzo diroccata, la cui fronte, volta allo spettatore, lascia vedere per una grande arcata l'interno d'una rustica osteria; il muro poi n' è si pien di fessure, che dal di fuori si può facilmente scorgere quanto avviene nell' interno. Al di là del fiume è Mantova. E notte.

(GILDA e RIGOLETTO inquieto, sono sulla strada. SPARAFUCILE nell' interno dell' osteria, seduto presso una tavola sta ripulendo il suo cinturone, senza nulla intenders di quanto accade al di fuori.)

Rigoletto.

E l'ami?

Gilda.

Sempre.

Rigoletto.

Pure
Tempo a guarirne t' ho lasciato.

Gilda.

Io l'amo.

Rigoletto.

Povero cor di donna! Ah, il vile infame!
Ma avrai vendetta, o Gilda—

Gilda.

Pietà, mio padre—

Rigoletto.

E se tu certa fossi
Ch' ei ti tradisse, l'ameresti ancora?

Gilda.

Nol so, ma pur m'adora.

Rigoletto.

Egli!

Gilda.

Yes.

Rigoletto.

Well, then, this way come, and see.

(He conducts her to one of the crevices in the wall, and motions her to look through.)

Gilda.

A man, surely,

I see!

Rigoletto.

Wait a little longer.

(Enter the DUKE, dressed as a private soldier, through a door on the left, opening into the ground-floor room.)

Gilda.

Ah, my father!

(Surprised.)

Duke.

Two things I want, and quickly.

(To SPARAFUCILE.)

Sparafucile.

What are they?

Duke.

A room and some wine.

Rigoletto.

(His usual custom, no doubt.)

Sparafucile.

(Oh! the fine gentleman!)

(Goes off into an adjoining room.)

Gilda.

Sì.

Rigoletto.

Ebbene, osserva dunque.

(La conduce presso una delle fezzure del muro, ed ella vi guarda.)

Gilda.

Un uomo

Vedo.

Rigoletto.

Per poco attendi.

(Entra il DUCA, in assisa di semplice officiale di cavalleria, nella sala terrena per un aporta a sinistra.)

Gilda.

Ah, padre mio!

(Trasalendo.)

Duca.

Due cose, e tosto—

(A SPARAFUCILE.)

Sparafucile.

Quali?

Duca.

Una stanza e del vino—

Rigoletto.

(Son questi i suoi costumi!)

Sparafucile.

(Oh, il bel zerbino!)

(Parte nella vicina stanza.)

LA DONNA E MOBILE — *HOW FICKLE WOMEN ARE*   Air (Duke)

gne - ro La__ don-na è - mo - bil Qual piu-ma al ven - to,
o - cean. Yet__ there's no feel - ing Love's pleas-ure steal - ing,

Mu - ta d'ac - cen - to__ e__ di pen - sier,
Like that of seal - ing Their lips__ with a kiss, Their

e__ di pen - sier! e, _____ e__ di pen - sier!
lips__ with a kiss! Their _____ lips with a__ kiss!

(Re-enter SPARAFUCILE, with a bottle of wine and two glasses, which he places on the table, and then twice strikes the ceiling with the hilt of his sword. At this signal, MAD-DELENE, a smiling lass, in Gipsy costume, descends by a ladder. The DUKE approaches to embrace her, but she repulses him. Meanwhile SPARAFUCILE goes out into the road, and says to RIGOLETTO:)	(Rientra SPARAFUCILE, con una bottiglia di vino e due bic-chieri, che depone sulla tavola, quindi batte col pomo della sua lunga spada due colpi al soffito. A quel segnale, una ridente GIOVANE, in costume di Zingara, scenda a salti la scala. Il DUCA corre per abbracciarla, ma ella gli sfugge. Frattanto SPARAFUCILE, uscito sulla via, dice a parte a RIGOLETTO:)
Your man is there! Is he to live or die?	E là il vostr' uomo—viver dee o morire?
Rigoletto.	*Rigoletto.*
Wait awhile; and then my pleasure you shall learn.	Più tardi tornero l'opra a compire.
(SPARAFUCILE goes off between the house and the river, GILDA and RIGOLETTO remaining in the road.)	(SPARAFUCILE si allontana dietro la casa lungo il fiume. GILDA e RIGOLETTO sulla via.)
Duke.	*Duca.*
One day, if I remember rightly,	Un dì, se ben rammentomi,
O beauty bright, I thee encountered,	O, bella, t'incontrai,
And ever since I've sought thee out,	Mi piacque di te chiedere,
Till here at last I've found thee;	E intesi che quì stai.
Ah! now believe me, while I swear,	Or sappi, che d'allora
That henceforth this heart will thee adore.	Sol te quest' alma adora.
Maddelene.	*Maddalena.*
Ah, ah! and since then twenty others	Ah, ah!—e vent' altre appresso
Are by you quite as much remembered,	Le scorda forse adesso?
(To give the gentleman his due, though,	(Ha un' aria il signorino
He has a cavalier-like bearing.)	Da vero libertino.)
Duke.	*Duca.*
Yes; a bad one I am!	Sì; un mostro son!
(Attempts to kiss her.)	(Per abbracciarla.)
Maddelene.	*Maddalena.*
Leave me alone,	Lasciatemi,
Stupid, do.	Stordito.
Luke.	*Duca.*
Eh! what a fuss!	Ih! che fracasso!

Maddelene.
Be quiet, will you?

Duke.
If you'll be gentle,
And not make so much resistance.
When the joys of love await us,
Virtue need not be so prudish.
(Taking her hand.)
How beautiful and white your hand is.

Maddelene.
You're pleased to joke me, signor.

Duke.
No, no.

Maddelene.
I know I'm ugly.

Duke.
Embrace me.

Maddelene.
Thou'rt drunk!

Duke.
With love of thee I may be.
(Laughing.)

Maddelene.
Signor, these words unmeaning
Why to me address?

Duke.
No, no—I will marry you.

Maddelene.
Your word of honor, then, give me.

Duke.
Most lovely of your sex art thou!
(Ironically.)

Rigoletto.
Well! have you now heard enough?
(To GILDA, who has seen and heard all that has passed.)

Gilda.
Oh! the wicked traitor!

Duke.
Ah! of Venus the fairest daughter,
The slave of your charms here behold;
One word from thy beautiful lips
My suffering alone can assuage;
Come, and my fond heart relieve
Of its anxious palpitations.

Maddelene.
Ah, ah! with all my heart I laugh
At stories which so little cost;

Maddalena.
Stia saggio.

Duca.
E tu sii docile,
Non farmi tanto chiasso.
Ogni saggezza chiudesi
Nel guadio e nell' amore.
(Le prende la mano.)
La bella mano candida!

Maddalena.
Scherzate voi, signore.

Duca.
No, no.

Maddalena.
Son brutta.

Duca.
Abbracciami.

Maddalena.
Ebro.

Duca.
D'amore ardente.
(Ridendo.)

Maddalena.
Signor, l'indifferente,
Vi piace canzonar?

Duca.
No, no—ti vo' sposar.

Maddalena.
Ne voglio la parola.

Duca.
Amabile figliuola!
(Ironico.)

Rigoletto.
Ebben?—ti basta ancor?
(A GILDA, che avrà tutto osservato ed inteso.)

Gilda.
Iniquo traditor!

Duca.
Bella figlia dell' amore,
Schiavo son de' vezzi tuoi;
Con un detto sol tu puoi
Le mie pene consolar.
Vieni, e senti del mio core
Il frequente palpitar.

Maddalena.
Ah! ah! rido bèn di core,
Chè tai baie costan poco;

Your jokes I prize, you may believe me,
At just as much as they are worth.
Accustomed am I, my gallant signor,
To badinage as good as this.

Gilda.

Ah! thus to me of love he spoke,
Thus the wretch hath me betrayed;
Unhappy me!—forlorn, deserted,
With anguish how my heart doth ache!
Oh! what a weak credulity
In such a libertine to trust!

Rigoletto.

Be silent;—now to grieve is useless;
That he deceived thee thus thou see'st;
Be silent, and on me depend
Vengeance eternal to insure;
Prompt as dreadful shall it be—
Like thunder on his head 'twill fall!
Hear me;—at once to the house return,
What gold you may require there obtain;
A horse provide, and the apparel of a youth;
Then to Verona hasten,
Where to-morrow I will join thee.

Gilda.

Come now with me.

Rigoletto.

Impossible.

Gilda.

I tremble.

Rigoletto.

Go.

(Exit GILDA.)

(RIGOLETTO goes behind the house, and returns in conversation with SPARAFUCILE. During the scene between them the DUKE and MADDELINE remain seated in the inn, talking, laughing, and drinking.)

Rigoletto.

Twenty crown-pieces, say you?—Here are
   ten;
When the deed is done, ten more you shall
   have.
Is he still here?

Sparafucile.

Yes.

Rigoletto.

At the hour of midnight.
I shall return.

Quanto valga il vostro giuoco,
Mel credete, so apprezzar.
Sono avvezza, bel signore,
Ad un simile schervar.

Gilda.

Ah! così parlar d'amore
A me pur l'infame ho udito!
Infelice cor tradito,
Per angoscia non scoppiar.
Perchè o credulo mio core,
Un tal uom dovevi amar!

Rigoletto.

Taci, il piangere non vale;
                (A GILDA.)
Ch' ei mentiva or sei secura—
Taci, e mia sarà la cura
La vendetta, d'affrettar.
Pronta fia, sarà fatale;
Io saprollo fulminar.
M'odi, ritorna a casa—
Oro prendi, un aestriero,
Una veste viril che t'apprestai,
E per Verona parti—
Sarrovvi io pur domani—

Gilda.

Or venite.

Rigoletto.

Impossibil.

Gilda.

Tremo.

Rigoletto.

Va.

(GILDA parte.)

(RIGOLETTO va dietro la casa, e ritorna parlando con SPARAFUCILE e contandogli della monete. Durante questa scena e la sequente il DUCA e MADDALENA stanno fra loro parlando, ridendo, bevendo.)

Rigoletto.

Venti scudi hai tu detto?   Eccone dieci;
E dopo l'opera il resto.
Ei quì rimane?

Sparafucile.

Sì.

Rigoletto.

Alla mezzanotte
Ritornerò.

Sparafucile.

You need not hurry.

Alone into the river I can cast him.

Rigoletto.

No, no,—I wish to throw him in myself.

Sparafucile.

Well, so let it be.   But what is his name?

Rigoletto.

Perhaps of both you'd like to know the names?

His name is *Crime,* and mine is *Punishment.*

(Exit—the darkness increases, distant thunder heard.)

Sparafucile.

A storm in the distance is arising;

Darker the night is becoming.

Duke.

Maddelene!

(Attempting to take hold of her.)

Maddelene.

Desist—my brother comes.

(Repelling him.)

Duke.

Well, what matters his coming?

(Thunder.)

Maddelene.

It thunders.

(Enter SPARAFUCILE.)

Sparafucile.

And rain is coming.

Duke.

So much the better;

I will lodge here—in the stable you may sleep—

Or in the regions below—or where you please.

Sparafucile.

Thank you.

Maddelene.   (Aside to the DUKE.)

(Ah, no—depart.)

Duke   (to MADDELENE).

In such weather as this?

Sparafucile   (to MADDELENE).

Twenty crowns of gold, remember.

Signor,

To offer you my room I shall be happy:

At once I'll show you to it, if you please.

(He takes a light, and goes toward the staircase.)

Sparafucile.

Non cale,

A gettarlo nel fiume basto io solo.

Rigoletto.

No, no,—il vo' far io stesso.

Sparafucile.

Sia—il suo nome?

Rigoletto.

Vuoi saper anco il mio?

Egli è *Delitto, Punizion* son io.

(Parte—Il cielo ci oscura e tuona.)

Sparafucile.

La tempesta è vicinia.

Più scura fia la notte.

Duca.

Maddalena!

(Per prenderla.)

Maddalena.

Aspettate—mio fratello viene.

(Sfuggendogli.)

Duca.

Che importa?

(S' ode il tuona.)

Maddalena.

Tuona.

(Entra SPARAFUCILE.)

Sparafucile.

E pioverà tra poco.

Duca.

Tanto meglio.

Io qui mi tratterrò—tu dormirai

In scuderia—all' inferno—ove vorrai

Sparafucile.

Grazie.

Maddalena.   (Piano al DUCA.)

(Ah, no—partite.)

Duca   (a MADDALENA).

(Con tal tempo?)

Sparafucile   (piano a MADDALENA).

Son venti scudi d'ore.

Ben felice.   (Al DUCA.)

D' offrivi la mia stanza—se a voi piace

Tosto a vederla andiamo.

(Prende una lume, e s' avvia per la scaia.)

Duke.

With all my heart—be uick, let me see it.
(Whispers to MADDELENE, and follows SPARAFUCILE.)

Maddelene.

(Poor young man! so much, too, the gentleman!

O God!—what a fearful night is coming!)
(Thunder.)

Duke

(observing that the window has no shutters).

If here you sleep, plenty of air you get.

Well, good night!

Sparafucile.

May God protect you, signor.

Duke.

Quickly I shall be asleep, so weary am I.
(He lays down his hat and sword, throws himself on the
bed, and in a short time falls asleep. MADDELENE, below,
stands by the table. SPARAFUCILE finishes the contents of
the bottle left by the DUKE. Both remain silent for awhile,
and apparently in deep thought.)

Maddelene.

What pleasing manners the young man has!

Sparafucile.

Oh, truly; but twenty crowns I'm to have.

Maddelene.

Only twenty! too little! much more he's
worth!

Sparafucile.

Go—and, if he sleeps, his sword bring
hither.

Maddelene

(ascending, and contemplating him while sleeping).

It is a sin to kill so nice a youth!
(She takes up the DUKE's sword, and begins to descend.)
(Enter GILDA, approaching by the passage, in the attire
of a youth, with whip and spurs; she advances slowly
towards the house; SPARAFUCILE continues drinking. It
lightens and thunders.)

Gilda.

Ah! my reason seems quite to desert me!

Love overcomes me! O father, pardon!
(Thunder.)

What a night of horrors! How will it end?

Maddelene.

Brother!
(Having descended, she deposits the DUKE's sword on the
table.)

Gilda.

Who speaks?
(Looking through the crevices.)

Duca.

Ebben sono con te—presto, vediamo.
(Dice una parola all' orecchio di MADDALENA e segue
SPARAFUCILE.)

Maddalena.

(Povero giovin!—grazioso tanto!

Dio!—qual mai notte è questa!)
(Tuona.)

Duca

(vedendone il balcone senza imposte).

Si dorme all' aria aperta? bene, bene—

Buona notte.

Sparafucile.

Signor, vi guardi Iddio.

Duca.

Breve sonno dormiam—stanco son io.
(Depone il capello, la spada, e si stende, sul letto, dove
in breve addormentasi. MADDALENA frattanto siede presso
la tavola. SPARAFUCILE beve dalla bottiglia lasciata dal
DUCA—Rimangono ambidue taciturni per qualche istante,
e preoccupati da gravi pensieri.)

Maddalena.

E amabile invero cotal giovinotto.

Sparafucile.

Oh sì—venti scudi ne dà di prodotto.

Maddalena.

Sol venti!—son pochi—valeva di più.

Sparafucile.

La spada, s' ei dorme, va, portami giù.

Maddalena

(sale, e contemplando il dormente).

Peccato! è pur bello!
(Prende la spada del DUCA, e scende.)
(Entra GILDA, che comparisce nel fondo della via in costume virile, con stivali e speroni, e lentamente si avanza
verso l' osteria, mentre SPARAFUCILE continua a beve. Spess
lampi e tuoni.)

Gilda.

Ah, più non ragiono!

Amor mi trascina!—mio padre, perdono!
(Tuona.)

Qual notte d' orrore! Gran Dio, che ac-
cadrà.

Maddalena.

Fratello!
(Sara discesa, ed avrà posata la spada del DUCA sulla tavola.)

Gilda.

Chi parla?
(Osserva pella fessura.)

Sparafucile.
  To the devil be gone!
  (Seeking something in a cupboard.)
Maddelene.
  Handsome as an Apollo is this youth—
  I love him—he loves me—so slay him not.

Gilda.
  Oh, heavens! *(Listening.)*
Sparafucile.
  Mend the holes in that sack.
Maddelene.
  Why?
Sparafucile.
  Thy beautiful Apollo I must kill,
  And into the river cast.
Gilda.
  O hellhound!
Maddelene.
  The promised money you may yet obtain
  And spare his life.
Sparafucile.
  I think that difficult.
Maddelene.
  Listen, and hear how easy my project.
  Ten crowns already from the hunchback
  Thou hast received. In a little time
  Hither with the other ten he will come;
  Kill him, and then the twenty thou wilt
    have.
Sparafucile.
  Kill the hunchback! What dost thou sug-
    gest?
  For a thief, or a swindler, do you take me?
  Did I ever a client betray? No!
  The man who pays me faithful ever finds
    me!
Gilda.
  What do I hear? My father!
Maddelene.
  Ah, mercy on him!
Sparafucile.
  He must die!
Maddelene.
  I'll give him a hint to fly.
  (About to go.)

Sparafucile.
  Al diavol ten va.
  (Frugando in un credenzone.)
Maddalena.
  Somiglia un Apollo quel giovine—io l'amo—
  Ei m'ama—riposi—nè più l'uccidiamo.

Gilda.
  Oh, cielo! *(Ascoltando.)*
Sparafucile.
  Rattoppa puel sacco
Maddalena.
  Perche?
Sparafucile.
  Entr' esso il tuo Apollo, sgozzato da me,
  Gettar dovro al fiume.
Gilda.
  L'inferno qui vedo!
Maddalena.
  Eppure il danaro salvarti scommetto,
  Serbandolo in vita.
Sparafucile.
  Difficile il credo.
Maddalena.
  M'ascolta—anzi facil ti svelo un progetto.
  De' scudi, già dieci dal gobbo ne avesti;
  Venire cogli altri più tardi il vedrai—
  Uccidilo, e venti allora ne avrai,
  Così tutto il prezzo goder si potrà.

Sparafucile.
  Uccider quel gobbo!—che diavol dicesti!
  Un ladro son forse? Son forse un bandito!
  Qual altro cliente da me fu tradito?
  Mi paga quest' uomo—fedele m' avrà.

Gilda.
  Che sento! mio padre!
Maddalena.
  Ah, grazia per esso.
Sparafucile.
  E d'uopo ch' ei muoia—
Maddalena.
  Fuggire il fo adesso.
  (Va per salire.)

Gilda.

O kind-hearted woman!

Sparafucile.

The reward we shall lose.

Maddelene.

That's true.

Sparafucile.

Let me do it.

Maddelene.

He must be saved.

Sparafucile.

Should any other before midnight arrive,

Him I will slay instead of him now here.

Maddelene.

The night is dark, through the sky the
thunder roars,

No one at such a time this place will pass.

Gilda.

Oh, what a temptation—for th' ingrate to
die!

And for thee, father! O heaven, guide me!

(The clock strikes the half-hour.)

Sparafucile.

There is still half an hour.

Maddelene.

Brother, wait.

(Weeping.)

Gilda.

What! that woman weep, and I not help
him!

Ah! although to my love truthless he be,

My life for his shall be the sacrifice!

(Knocks at the door.)

Maddelene.

Who knocks?

Sparafucile.

'Tis the wind.

Maddelene.

Some one knocks, I'm sure.

Sparafucile.

It is strange.

Maddelene.

Who's there?

Gilda.

Have pity on a stranger;

A lodging grant him for this bitter night.

Gilda.

Oh, buona figliuola!

Sparafucile.

Gli scudi perdiamo.

Maddalena.

E ver!

Sparafucile.

Lascia fare—

Maddalena.

Salvarlo dobbiamo.

Sparafucile.

Se pria ch' abbia il mezzo la notte toccat

Alcuno qui giunga, per esso morrà.

Maddalena.

E buia la notte, il ciel troppo irato,

Nessuno a quest' ora di qui passerà.

Gilda.

Oh, qual tantazione! morir per l'ingrato

Morire! e mio padre! Oh, cielo pietà!

(Battono le undici e mezzo.)

Sparafucile.

Ancor c' è mezz' ora.

Maddalena.

Attendi, fratello.

(Piangendo.)

Gilda.

Che! piange tal donna! Nè a lui darò ait

Ah, s' egli al mio amore divenne rubell

Io vo' per la sua gettar la mia vita.

(Picchia alla porta.)

Maddalena.

Si picchia?

Sparafucile.

Fu il vento—

Maddalena.

Si picchia, ti dico

Sparafucile.

E strano!

Maddalena.

Chi è?

Gilda.

Pietà d'un mendico;

Asil per la notte a lui concedete.

Maddelene.

A long night 'twill be for him!

Sparafucile.

Wait awhile.

(He searches the cupboard for something.)

Gilda.

Ah! so near to death, and yet so young!

Oh! for these wretches God's pardon I ask;

Forgive, O father, thine unhappy child!

And happy live the man I die to save!

Maddelene.

Now hasten, quick, the fatal deed enact;

To save one life another I yield up.

Sparafucile.

Well, I am ready the issue to abide,

I care not so that the reward I get.

(He goes behind the doorway with a dagger. MADDELENE opens the door, and then runs forward, to close that in front. GILDA enters and SPARAFUCILE closes the door. All the rest is buried in silence and darkness.)

(Enter RIGOLETTO, enveloped in a cloak; he advances from the road to the front of the scene. The violence of the storm has abated, the lightning and thunder still continuing occasionally.)

Rigoletto.

At last the hour of my revenge is nigh;

Full thirty days and nights for this I've waited,

My soul with tears of blood consuming,

Under the guise of a buffoon. That door

(Examining the house.)

Is shut! 'Tis not yet the hour—I must wait.

What a night of foul mystery is this!

The heavens in a tempest,

On the earth a homicide!

Oh, how truly great do I now feel!

'Tis midnight!

(The clock strikes twelve.)

(Enter SPARAFUCILE, from the house.)

Sparafucile.

Who is there?

Rigoletto.

It is I.

(About to enter.)

Sparafucile.

Wait where you are.

(Re-enters the house, and returns, dragging a sack.)

Your man is here disposed of.

Rigoletto.

O joy—a light!

Maddalena.

Fia lunga tal notte!

Sparafucile.

Alquanto attendete.

(Va a cercare nel credenzone.)

Gilda.

Ah, presso alla morte, sì giovane, sono!

Oh cielo, pegli empi ti chiedo perdono.

Perdona tu, o padre, a questa infelice!

Sia l' uomo felice—ch' or vado a salvar.

Maddalena.

Su, spicciati, presto, fa l'opra compita;

Anelo una vita—con altra salvar.

Sparafucile.

Ebbene—son pronto, quell' uscio dischiudi;

Piucch' altro li scudi—mi preme salvar.

(Va a postarsi con un pugnale dietro la porta. MADDALENA apre, poi corre a chiudere la grande arcata di fronte. Mentre entra GILDA, dietro a cui SPARAFUCILE chiude la porta, e tutto resta sepolto nel silenzio e nel buoi.)

(Entra RIGOLETTO, solo, si avanza dal fondo della scena chiuso nel suo mantello. La violenza del temporale è diminuita, nè più si vede e sente che qualche lampo e tuono.)

Rigoletto.

Della vendetta olfin giunge l'istante!

Da trenta di l'aspetto

Di vivo sangue a lagrime piangendo

Sotto la larva del buffon—Quest' uscio!

(Esaminando la casa.)

E chiuso! Ah, non è tempo ancor! S'attenda.

Qual notte di mistero!

Una tempesto in cielo!

In terra un omicidio!

Oh, come invero qui grande mi sento!

Mezza notte!

(Suona mezza notte.)

(Entra SPARAFUCILE, dalla casa.)

Sparafucile.

Chi è là?

Rigoletto.

Son io.

(Per entrare.)

Sparafucile.

Sostate.

(Rientra, e torna, trascinando un sacco.)

E qui spento il vostr' uomo—

Rigoletto.

Oh, gioja! un lume!

Sparafucile.

A light? No—first the money.
(RIGOLETTO hands him a purse.)

Sparafucile.

Let us into the river cast him.

Rigoletto.

No! alone I'll do it.

Sparafucile.

As you please; but this place is not the best;

Higher up, the stream is deeper. Be quick,

That no one may observe you. Good night.
(He re-enters the house.)

Rigoletto.

Here he is!—dead. I should like to see him!

But what matters? 'Tis done! Here are his spurs.

Now will the world again look well with me!

Here is the buffoon, and here his master!

At my feet he lies. It is he! It is he!

Now hath my grief its just revenge attained!

In the sea shall be his sepulchre,

This sack his winding-sheet!
(He tries to drag the sack towards the river, when he is surprised at hearing the voice of the DUKE, who passes along the background.)

What voice is that! Or is it an illusion?

No! no! it is he! it is he himself!
(Greatly alarmed.)

The Malediction! Oh, there! demon of hell!
(Nearing the house with the sack.)

But who, instead of him, can be in the sack!
(Tearing open the sack.)

I tremble. It is a human body!
(Lightning.)

My daughter! O God, my daughter!

Ah, no! it is impossible;

Towards Verona she journeyeth;

A dreadful vision this must be.
(Kneeling down.)

O my Gilda! Tell me who this has done?

The assassin to me reveal! Ho! who's here?
(Knocking violently at the door.)

No one! Oh, my daughter!

Sparafucile.

Un lume? No, il danaro.
(RIGOLETTO gli dà una borsa.)

Sparafucile.

Lesti all' onda il gettiam—

Rigoletto.

No—basto io solo.

Sparafucile.

Come pi piace—Qui men atto è il sito—

Più avanti è più profondo il gorgo—Presto

Che alcun non vi sorprenda—Buono notte.
(Rientra in casa.)

Rigoletto.

Egli è là! morto! O sì—vorrei vederlo!

Ma che importa! è ben desso! Ecco i suo sproni!

Ora mi guardo, o mondo—

Quest' è un buffone, ed un potente è questo!

Ei sta sotto a' miei piedi. E desso! E desso!

E giunta alfin la tua vendetta, o duolo!

Sia l'onda a lui sepolcro,

Un sacco il suo lenzuolo!
(Fa per trascinare il sacco verso la sponda, quando è sorpreso dalla lontana voce del DUCA, che nel fondo attraversa la scena.)

Qual voce! illusion notturna è questa!

No! no! egli è desso! è desso!

Maledizione! Olà—dimon bandito?
(Trasalendo verso la casa.)

Chi è mai, chi è qui in sua voce;
(Taglio il sacco.)

Io tremo—E umano corpo!
(Lampeggia.)

Mia figlia! Dio! mia figlia!

Ah no—è impossibil! per Verona è in via!

Fu visïon! E dessa!
(Inginocchiandosi.)

Oh, mia Gilda! fanciulla a me rispondi!

L' assassino mi svela—Olà? Nessuno!
(Picchia disperatamente alla casa.)

Nessun! mia figlia—

Gilda.

Who calls on me?

Rigoletto.

She speaks! she moves! she lives! Oh,
  heaven!

Ah! my only worldly solace,

Look on me; dost thou not know me?

Gilda.

Father!

Rigoletto.

Unveil this mystery! Art thou wounded?

Gilda.

The sword pierced me here.

(Points to her breast.)

Rigoletto.

Who was it stabbed you?

Gilda.

I have deceived you! I am guilty!

Too much I loved him—now I die for him.

Rigoletto.

(O awful fate, by my hand hath she fallen,

Of my righteous vengeance the sole victim.)

Angel dear, look on me, to me listen;

Speak, oh, speak to me, my darling daughter!

Gilda.

More I cannot say; pardon me and him!

O my father, bless your dying daughter.

Gilda.

Chi mi chiama?

Rigoletto.

Ella parla! si move! è viva! oh Dio!

Ah! mio ben solo in terra;

Mi guarda—mi conosci—

Gilda.

Ah, padre mio—

Rigoletto.

Qual mistero! che fu! sei tu ferita?

Gilda.

L'acciar qui mi piagò—

(Indicando il core.)

Rigoletto.

Chi t' ha colpita?

Gilda.

V' ho ingannata—colpevole fui;

L'amai troppo—ora muoio per lui!

Rigoletto.

(Dio tremendo! ella stesso fu côlta

Dallo stral di mia giusta vendetta!)

Angiol caro; mi guarda, m'ascolta.

Parla; parlami, figlia diletta!

Gilda.

Ah! ch'io tacchia! a me—a lui perdonate;

Benedite alla figlia, o mio padre.

LASSU IN CIELO — *IN HEAV'N ABOVE* Duet (Rigoletto and Gilda)

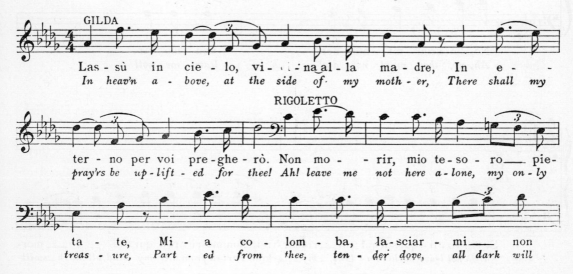

GILDA

Las - sù in cie - lo, vi - ci - na al - la
In heav'n a - bove at the side of my

dêi, no' la - sciar - mi non dêi
be. all dark. all dark will be!

RIG.

ma - dre In e - ter - no per voi pre - ghe -
moth - - er, There shall my pray'rs be up - lift - ed for

Oh mia fi - glia!
Oh, stay, dear child!

rò, Pre - ghe - rò, Per voi pre - ghe -
thee! There I will pray, I will pray for

No, la - sciar - mi non dêi non mo - rir
Ah, no, thou must not die! leave me not!

rò
thee.

Se t'in - vo - li - qui sol qui sol - ri - mar - rei, Non mo - ri - reo qui te - co — mor -
Ah! do not leave me here a - lone, — my — child. Part-ed from thee, my child, all dark — will

Non più   A lui   per-do-na-te,   mio pa-dre,   Ad-
And when I'm gone,   give him par-don,   my fa-ther!   Then

ró!   O mia fi-glia!   o mia Gil-da!   no, la-sciar-mi non
be!   Oh! stay, my child!   Oh! my Gil-da!   Leave me not here a-

di   -   o!   las-sù in ciel,   las-sù in
fare   -   well!   In heav'n a-bove,   In heav'n a-

dêi,   non mo-rir,
lone!   do not die!

ciel   Pre   -   ghe-rò,   per voi, pre-ghe-
bove,   There shall my pray'rs   be raised   for

No, la-sciar-mi non dêi,   non mo-rir,
Leave me' not here a-lone!   do not die!

RIG.
Gil-da! mia Gil-da! È mor-ta!   Ah! la ma-le-di-zio-ne!
Gil-da! my Gil-da! All's dark, now!   Ah! yes, his curse is on   me!

(Falling and tearing his hair over the corpse of his | (Strappendosi e capelli, cade sul cadavere della figlia.)
daughter.)

END OF THE OPERA.

IL TROVATORE
(The Troubadour)

by

GIUSEPPE VERDI

THE STORY OF "IL TROVATORE"

THE old Count di Luna, now deceased, had two sons, not much apart in age. One night, while they were both yet in their infancy and under the care of a nurse, an old gipsy-woman — a tribe which, at that dark age, was universally believed to be closely allied to evil spirits, and possessing great magic powers — was discovered by the servants near the cradle of the youngest of the two children, to whose chamber she had stealthily gained access, while the nurse was asleep. The gipsy was quickly and violently expelled from the castle, but from that day the child's health began to fail. No remedies proving of avail, the old gipsy was suspected of having bewitched the child. Search was instituted, the woman taken prisoner, and, agreeably to the barbarous modes of punishment of the times, burned alive. A daughter of the gipsy, with her child in her arms, witnessed the execution. To her the unhappy victim of superstition bequeathed the task of vengeance. During the night following the young gipsy managed to steal the youngest child of the Count from the castle. She hurried with it to the stake, where the flames were still raging over the remains of her ill-fated mother. Arrived there, and almost out of her senses by the vivid recollection of the horrible scene she had just witnessed, she, by a fatal mistake, hurled her own child into the flames instead of the young Count. She discovered her error too late. But still she was not to be baffled in her dark designs. She fled, taking the child with her, joined her tribe, and brought him up — Manrico, the Troubadour — as her own son, trusting the secret

of his parentage to no one, and waiting for a favorable moment to make him the tool of her vengeance against his own kindred.

In the meanwhile the old Count died, leaving the oldest son sole heir of his title and possessions, but doubting, up to his last moment, the death of his last born, although a heap of infant's bones, found among the ashes around the stake, seemed to be proof conclusive.

After this preliminary knowledge we now come to the actual business of the piece.

Manrico, grown up a valiant and daring knight, well skilled in arms, and of high mind and bearing, entered the contest at a tourney disguised, won all the honors, and was crowned victor by the hands of the Duchess Leonora, lady attendant on the Queen. From this moment dated a passionate love, shared by both. The Troubadour made his feelings known by nightly serenades performed below the window of the Duchess.

Unhappily, the Count di Luna (brother to Manrico, although this was unknown to both of them) was also smitten with a deep passion for the Duchess. One night, while the Count was lingering in the gardens attached to the Royal palaces, he suddenly heard the voice of the Troubadour in a thicket close by. Presently a door in the palace buildings opened, the Duchess stole out, and mistaking the Count for his sweet-voiced rival, she hastened towards him. Manrico stepping out from the foliage, she saw her mistake and sought his protection. Hard words passed between the two rivals. The Troubadour unmasked himself, revealing to his antagonist the features of one whose life had been forfeited to the laws by some act of violence against the existing government. The two knights retired with drawn swords to a more secluded spot, leaving the Duchess insensible on the ground.

The duel — this we learn from a conversation between Azucena and her supposed son, at the beginning of the second act — quickly terminated in favor of the Troubadour. The latter had already lifted his sword, to pierce the heart of his adversary, when he felt the influence of some secret power suspending the intended motion. A voice from heaven seemed to say to him, "Spare thy foe." Manrico, obeying reluctantly, retired. Joining the army, opposing his country's forces, he was left for dead on the battle-field of Pelilla. His mother sought him out by night, intending to give him fit burial. She discovered that life was not yet extinct, and had him removed to one of the mountain resorts of her tribe, and there restored him to health. Thus we find him at the beginning of Act Second, yet feeble and suffering.

His Prince, having heard of Manrico's being still alive, despatched a messenger to his retreat, bidding him to repair to the fortress of Castellar and to defend it against the forces of the Count di Luna. At the same time he communicated to him that the Duchess Leonora, believing in the current reports of his death, was about to take the veil that very evening, at a convent in the neighborhood of Castellar. Upon receipt of this message Manrico at once departed, and arrived at the convent just in time to rescue Leonora, who was about to be carried off forcibly by the Count di Luna and his followers. The Troubadour conducted the Duchess to Castellar, which place was immediately enclosed and besieged by the Count di Luna's troops.

Azucena, following Manrico (to whom she had become unconsciously attached) to Castellar, had ventured too far in the lines of the enemy, was taken prisoner and led before the Count,

charged with being a spy. Here it happened that an old servant of the house of Luna, Ferrando, recognized her features. The gipsy, frightened and confounded by this unexpected discovery, called for her son Manrico to protect her. This only added to the Count's wrath, who gave orders to have her burned immediately in face of the castle.

The Troubadour, in the meanwhile, was making preparations to celebrate his union with Leonora on the morrow, when he was informed by the sentinels that a gipsy woman was about to be burned alive in front of the enemy's camp. Quickly recognizing the form of his mother, he gathered a squad of his troops around him and sallied out to rescue his ill-fated mother. But fortune was against him; his forces were repulsed and himself taken.

The Count di Luna, after storming the fortress of Castellar on the day following — but without finding a trace of Leonora — took his prisoners to the capital of the province. Here, on the eve before the day fixed for the execution of son and mother, Leonora suddenly appeared before the Count, offering him her hand in exchange for the life of Manrico. The Count consents, and Leonora is admitted into the dungeon, to restore Manrico to liberty. Before she enters, however, she takes poison, which she carried concealed in a ring on her finger. Manrico refuses to accept of his liberty, accusing the Duchess of basely betraying his affections. During this delay the poison begins to take its effect. Manrico discovers the extent of her sacrifice too late. The Count enters, understands at a glance what has happened, and orders Manrico to be beheaded immediately. While his order is being obeyed, he rouses the gipsy from the stupor in which she has been lying, motionless, in a corner of the dungeon. He drags her to the window, showing her the execution of her supposed son. Then the gipsy triumphantly divulges her secret. "Manrico is thy brother!" exclaims she to the horror-stricken Count, and with a "Mother! thou art avenged," she falls lifeless

IL TROVATORE

(THE TROUBADOUR)

ACT I.

THE DUEL.

SCENE I—Vestibule in the palace of Aliaferia, with side door conducting to the apartments of COUNT DI LUNA. FERRANDO and servants of the COUNT reclining near the door. Armed men are seen walking in the background.

Ferrando
(to the servants, who are falling asleep).

Arouse ye! arouse ye! The Count's approach
Must find us watchful:
Ye know 'tis his wont
Under the casement of his beloved one
To pass whole nights unsleeping.

Servants.

'Tis the venom of jealous doubt
That has entered his bosom.

Ferrando.

This minstrel knight, who in the garden
Sings with his lute at midnight,
Seems a rival not idly dreaded.

Servants.

Pray dispel from our eyelids
The sleep that on us falls,
By now relating the truthful tale
Of Garzia, late brother to Count Luna.

Ferrando.

Be it so;
Come close around me here.
(The servants cluster around him.)

Soldiers.

We're ready.

Servants.

We hear thee.
(All surround FERRANDO.)

Ferrando.

With two sons, heirs of fortune and affection,

ATTO I.

IL DUELLO.

SCENA I—Atrio nel palazzo dell' Aliaferia; porta da un lato, che mette agli appartamenti del CONTE DI LUNA. FERRANDO, e molti famigliari del CONTE, che giacciono presso la porta, alcuni uomini d'arme che passeggiano in fondo.

Ferrando
(parla ai famigliari).

All' erta, all' erta! Il Conte
N' è d'uopo attender vigilando; ed egli
Talor, presso i veroni
Della sua cara, intere
Passa le notti.

Famigliari.

Gelosia le fiere
Serpi gli avventa in petto!

Ferrando.

Nel Trovator, che dai giardini muove
Notturno il canto, d'un rivale a dritto
Ei teme.

Famigliari.

Dalle gravi
Palpêbre il sonno a discacciar, la vera
Storia ci narra di Garzia, germano
Al nostro Conte.

Ferrando.

La dirò: venite
Intorno a me.
(Famigliari eseguiscono accostandosi pur essi.)

Arme.

Noi pure—

Famigliari.

Udite, udite.
(Tutti accerchiano FERRANDO.)

Ferrando.

Di due figli vivea, padre beato,
Il buon Conte di Luna

Lived the Count in enjoyment;
Watching the younger for his safe protection
The good nurse found employment.
One morning, as the dawn's first rays were shining,
From her pillow she rose,—
Who was found, think ye, near the child reclining?

Fida nutrice del secondo nato
  Dormia presso la cuna
Sul romper dell' aurora un bel mattino
  Ella dischiude i rai,
E chi trova d'accanto a quel bambino?

Chorus.
Who? Pray tell us! speak, disclose!

Coro.
Chi?—Favèlla—chi mai?

ABBIETTA ZINGARA — *SAT THERE A GIPSY HAG*   Ballad (Ferrando)

Allegretto

Ab-biet-ta Zin-ga-ra fo-sca ve-gliarda! Cin-ge-vai sim-bo-li
Sat there a gip-sy-hag, witch-like ap-pearing; Of her dark mys-te-ries

di-ma-li-ar-da; e sul fan-ciul-lo con vi-so ar-ci-gno,
strange sym-bols wear-ing. O'er the babe sleep-ing with fierce looks bend-ing,

l'oc-chio af-fig-ge-a tor-vo, san-gui-gno! D'or-ror com-
Gazed she up on him, black deeds in-tend-ing! Hor-ror pro-

pre-sa com-pre-sa è la nu-tri-ce a-cu-to un gri-do
found seized the nurse at that dark vi-sion; Sharp cries of ter-ror

un gri-do all'au-ra scio-glie, ed ec-co, in me-no che lab-bro il
soon rent the air a-bove her, And swift-ly as thought flies, with speed-y de-

di-ce, i ser-vi, i ser-vi ac-cor-ro-no, i servi ac-cor-ro-no in quel-la so-glie;
ci-sion, The serv-ants, the serv-ants all a-larm'd, the servants round a-bout the threshold hov-er;

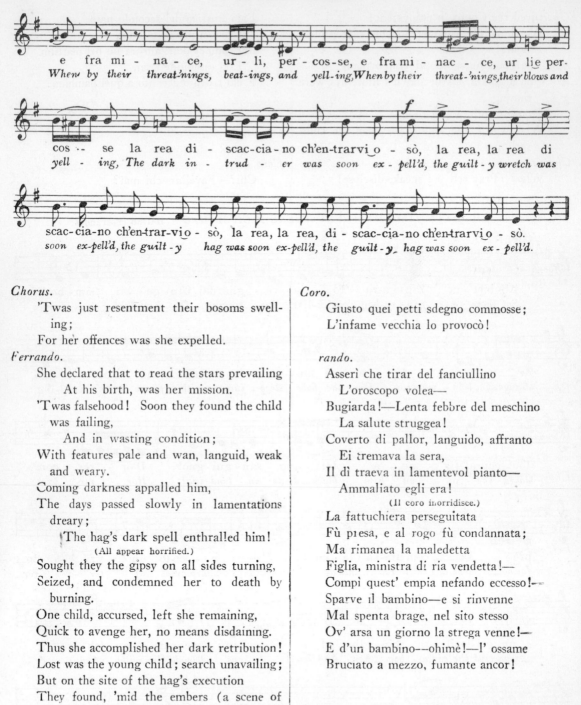

e fra mi - na - ce, ur - li, per - cos-se, e fra mi - nac - ce, ur lie per-
When by their threat-'nings, beat-ings, and yell-ing,When by their threat-'nings,their blows and

cos .. - se la rea di - scac-cia - no ch'en-trar vi_o - sò, la rea, la rea di
yell - ing, The dark in - trud - er was soon ex - pell'd, the guilt - y wretch was

scac-cia-no ch'en-trar-vi_o - sò, la rea, la rea, di - scac-cia-no ch'en-trarvi_o - sò.
soon ex-pell'd, the guilt - y hag was soon ex-pell'd, the guilt-y_ hag was soon ex - pell'd.

Chorus.

'Twas just resentment their bosoms swell-
ing;
For her offences was she expelled.

Ferrando.

She declared that to read the stars prevailing
At his birth, was her mission.
'Twas falsehood! Soon they found the child
was failing,
And in wasting condition;
With features pale and wan, languid, weak
and weary.
Coming darkness appalled him,
The days passed slowly in lamentations
dreary;
The hag's dark spell enthralled him!
(All appear horrified.)
Sought they the gipsy on all sides turning,
Seized, and condemned her to death by
burning.
One child, accursed, left she remaining,
Quick to avenge her, no means disdaining.
Thus she accomplished her dark retribution!
Lost was the young child; search unavailing;
But on the site of the hag's execution
They found, 'mid the embers (a scene of
horror
Their eyes assailing), of a young infant,
Alas! the bones half consumed and burning.

Coro.

Giusto quei petti sdegno commosse;
L'infame vecchia lo provocò!

rando.

Asserì che tirar del fanciullino
L'oroscopo volea—
Bugiarda!—Lenta febbre del meschino
La salute struggea!
Coverto di pallor, languido, affranto
Ei tremava la sera,
Il dì traeva in lamentevol pianto—
Ammaliato egli era!
(Il coro inorridisce.)
La fattuchiera perseguitata
Fù presa, e al rogo fù condannata;
Ma rimanea la maledetta
Figlia, ministra di ria vendetta!—
Compì quest' empia nefando eccesso!—
Sparve il bambino—e si rinvenne
Mal spenta brage, nel sito stesso
Ov' arsa un giorno la strega venne!—
E d'un bambino—ohimè!—l' ossame
Bruciato a mezzo, fumante ancor!

Chorus.	*Coro.*
Ah! fiend inhuman! such deeds revolting	Oh, scellerata!—oh, donna infame!
My soul with horror and hatred fill!	Del par m'investe odio ed orror.
Some of Chorus.	*Alcuni.*
The father?	E il padre?
Ferrando.	*Ferrando.*
Few his days, and filled with sorrow;	Brevi e tristi giorni visse;
Yet a secret presentiment at heart made him still hopeful;	Pure ignoto del cor presentimento Gli diceva, che spento
It told him his son was living;	Non era il figlio; ed a morir vicino
And on his dying bed he claimed of the Count, our master,	Bramò che il signor nostro a lui giurasse
His solemn promise, a careful search to instigate.	Di non cessar le indagini—ah!—fur vane!
Ah! how vainly!	
Chorus of Soldiers.	*Arme.*
But what of her?	E di colei non s'ebbe
No tidings as yet you've heard?	Contezza mai?
Ferrando.	*Ferrando.*
No word hath reached us! Oh, heaven grant	Nulla contezza—Oh! dato
That haply we may meet one day!	Mi fosse rintracciarla
	Un dì!
Chorus of Servants	*Famigliari.*
And were it so, would'st thou know her?	Ma ravvisarla potresti?
Ferrando.	*Ferrando.*
Yes, by counting the years	Calcolando
That have vanished, I should know her.	Gli anni trascorsi—lo potrei.
Chorus of Soldiers.	*Arme.*
Be that	Sarebbe
The moment, down near her mother	Tempo presso la madre
In perdition to send her!	All' inferno spedirla.
Ferrando.	*Ferrando.*
To perdition? 'Tis believed, that on this earth	All' inferno?—E credenza, che dimori
She's doomed to wander—she, the soul-accursed, the witch infernal.	Ancor nel mondo l'anima perduta Dell' empia strega, e quando il cielo è nero
And when the skies are darkened,	In varie forme altrui si mostri.
In forms oft-changing have some beheld her.	
Chorus.	*Coro.*
'Tis true!	E vero!
Some of Chorus.	*Alcuni.*
They say some have seen her o'er housetops careering!	Sull' orlo dei tetti alcun l' ha veduta!

Others.	*Altri.*
Transformed to a bird, or a vampire appearing!	In upupa o strige talora si muta!
Still Others.	*Altri.*
Sometimes like a raven, or owl, shrilly crying,	In corvo tal' altra; più spesso in civetta,
From daylight and thunder she's seen madly flying!	Sull' alba fuggente al par di saetta!
Ferrando.	*Ferrando.*
The Count's faithful servant, the old witch assaulting,	Mori di paura un servo del conte,
Soon died in an access of terror revolting!	Che avea della zingara percossa la fronte!
(All manifest great terror.)	(Tutti si pingono, di superstizzoso terrore.)
She came to his chamber, an owl's form assuming,	Apparve a costui d' un gufo in sembianza,
The silence disturbing, the darkness illuming;	Nell' alta quiete di tacita stanza!—
She gazed on him fiercely with eyes brightly flaming;	Con occhi lucenti guardava—guardava,
With loud cries of anguish the still air was rent!	Il cielo attristando con urlo feral!
That moment the bell struck, midnight proclaiming.	Allor mezzanotte appunto suonava—
(A bell suddenly strikes the hour of midnight.)	(Suona mezzanotte.)
Chorus.	*Tutti.*
Ah! maledictions fall on the witch of infernal descent!	Ah! sia maledetta la strega infernal!
	(Con subito soprasalto.)
(The servants hasten towards the door. The soldiers retire in the background.)	(Odonzi alcuni tocchi di tamburo. Gli uomini d'armi accorrono in fondo; i famigliari traggonsi verso la porta.)

SCENE II—Gardens of the Palace; on one side a flight of marble steps, leading to the apartments. Thick clouds conceal the moon.

SCENA II—Giardini del palazzo; sulla destra narmora scalinata che mette negli appartamenti. La notte è inoltrata ed dense nubi cuoprono la luna.

(Enter LEONORA and INEZ.)	(Entra LEONORA ed INEZ.)
Inez.	*Ines.*
What still detains thee? late 'tis growing;	Che più t'arresti?—l'ora è tarda; vieni,
Come then; already her Highness has called thee;	Di te la regal donna
Did'st hear her?	Chiese, l'udisti.
Leonora.	*Leonora.*
Another night goes by,	Un' altra notte ancora
Yet him I behold not!	Senza vederlo!
Inez.	*Ines.*
Peril tends the flame	Perigliosa fiamma
That thou dost nourish.	Tu nutri!—Oh, come, dove
Oh, tell me, prithee, how the spark	La primieri favilla
First was kindled in thy bosom?	In te s'apprese?

Leonora.

At the Tournay. He entered;
Dark were his vestments and his crest;
His shield and banner no devices bearing;
An unknown Knight he came,
And in the lists bore away all the honors;
   mine was the hand
That crowned his brow as victor. Soon, a
   civil war outbreaking,
He disappeared. Ah! like a golden vision
Fled his dear image! One other moment,
Long after this,—but then—

Inez.

What chanced then?

Leonora.

Now hear!

Leonora.

Ne' tornei. V'apparvo
Bruno le vesti ed il cimier, lo scudo
Bruno e di stemma ignudo,
Sconosciuto guerrier, che dell' agone
Gli onori ottente—Al vincitor sul crine
Il serto io posi—Civil guerra intanto
Arse—nol vidi piú!—come d'aurato
Sogno fuggente imago!—ed era volta
Lunga stagion—ma poi—

Ines.

Che avvenne?

Leonora.

Ascolta!

TACEA LA NOTTE PLACIDA — *THE NIGHT, CALMLY AND PEACEFULLY*   **Air (Leonora)**

Ta - cea la not-te plac - ci - da, E bel-lain ciel se - re - no; La
The night, calm-ly and peace-ful - ly, In beau-ty seem'd re - pos - ing; The

lu - nail vi-so ar-gen-te - o Mos - tra-va lie-to a pie - no! Quan-do suo-nar per
moon float-ed in sil - ver light, Her fair-est beams dis - clos-ing; When thro' the air re-

l'a - e - re, In-fi-no al-lor si mu - to, Dol ci s'u - di - ro e fle - bi -
sound-ing clear, Till then in si - lence wreath-ing, Gen-tly and sad-ly on___ mine

li, Gli ac-cor - di d'un li u - to, E ver-si me - lan-
ear A lute's sweet chords were breath - ing, And words that pen - sive

co - ni-ci, E ver-si me-lan-co-ni-ci, Un tro-va-tor can - tò.
im-port bear, And words that pen - sive im-port bear, A wan-d'ring min-strel sang.

Words, like the prayers, a humble heart
Outpours to heaven when lonely,
In which one well-known name was oft
Repeated; 'twas mine, mine only!
Reaching in haste the balcony,
I saw him standing before me!
Joy, such as only angels know,
With glowing thrill came o'er me!
To heart, and eyes, with rapture filled,
The earth like heaven appeared.

Inez.
What thou relatest sadly disturbs me,
Filling my bosom with terror.

Leonora.
'Tis idle!

Inez.
Doubtings and dark forebodings arise within
  me,
Concerning this Knight's strange move-
  ments!
Try to forget him!

Leonora.
What saidst thou! No more, then!

Inez.
Heed friendly counsel; heed it,
I pray; heed it!

Leonora.
To forget him! Ah, thou art speaking
  words
Which the soul can ne'er comprehend.

Versi di prece, ed umile,
Qual d'uom che prega Iddio;
In quella ripeteasi
Un nome—il nome mio!
Corsi al veron sollecita—
Egli era, egli era desso!—
Gioja provai che agli angeli
Solo è provar concesso!—
Al core, al guardo estatico
La terra un ciel sembrò!

Ines.
Quanto narrasti di turbamento
M' ha piena l'anima!—Io tremo—

Leonora.
Invano!

Ines.
Dubbio, ma tristo presentimento
In me risveglia quest' uomo arcano!
Tenta obliarlo—

Leonora.
Che dici!—Oh, basti!

Ines.
Cedi al consiglio dell' amistà—
Cedi—

Leonora.
Obliarlo!—Ah! tu parlasti
Detto, che intendere l'alma non sà.

DI TALE AMOR — *OF LOVE LIKE THIS, HOW VAINLY* . Air (Leonora)

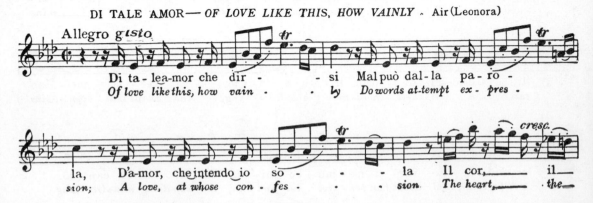

Di ta - lea-mor che dir - - si Mal può dal-la pa - ro-
Of love like this, how vain - - ly Do words at-tempt ex - pres -

la, D'a-mor, che intendo io so - - la Il cor, il
sion; A love, at whose con - fes - - sion The heart, the

cor,____ il_ cor sì - ne-bri - ò. Il mio des - ti - no com - pir - ed
heart,____ the_ heart with rap-ture glows. My fate would not com - plet - ed

si, non puo che a lui d'ap - pres - so, S'io non vi - vrò per es -
be, If he were not be - side__ me; Were life with him de - nied____

so, Per es - so, per es - so, per es-so,_ mo - ri - rò! S'i-o non vi-vrò per
me, Then wel - come, then wel - come, then wel-come death's re - pose. Yes, were life with him de-

es - so, per es-so io mo - ri - rò, Ah! sì per es - so,_ mo - ri
nied_ me, I'd wel - come death's re - pose, ah! yes, for him, in_ death re -

rò! per_ es - so mo-ri - rò, mo - - - - ri - rò!
pose, in_ death would I re - pose, I'd _____ re-pose.

Inez   (aside).
 	
No cause for sad repentance
May coming time disclose!
     (They ascend to the apartments.)
     (Enter the COUNT.)
 	
Count.
 	
Night reigns in silence! Her Highness, no doubt,
Is now immersed in peaceful slumber;
Not yet sleeps her companion—Oh! Leonora,
Thou art still wakeful; the tremulous light
Now shining from thy casement tells me
Of thy nocturnal vigils—
Ah! how this amorous passion
Thrills each nerve within me!—I must now behold thee,
And thou shalt hear me! Loved one! To us belongs
This blissful moment—
(Blinded by passion, he approaches the steps, but suddenly pauses, on hearing the sound of a lute.)
 	
The Troubadour! I tremble!
	Ines (da se).
	
	Non debba mai pentirsi
	Chi tanto un giorno amò!
	     (Ascendono agli appartamenti.)
	     (Entra il CONTE.)
	
	Conte.
	
	Tace la notte! Immersa
	Nel sonno è, certo, la regal signora;
	Ma veglia la sua dama—Oh! Leonora,
	Tu desta sei; mel dice
	Da quel verone tremolante un raggio
	Della notturna lampa—
	Ah!—l'amorosa vampa
	M'arde ogni fibra!—Ch'io ti vegga è d'uopo,
	Che tu m'intenda—Vengo—A noi supremo
	E tal momento—
	(Cieco d'amore avviasi alla gradinata; odonsi gli accordi d'un liuto; egli si arresta.)
	
	Il Trovator!—Io fremo.

DESERTO SULLA TERRA— *LONELY ON EARTH ABIDING*   Romanza (Manrico)

De - ser - to sul - la ter - - ra, col__rio de -
Lone - ly on earth__ a - bid - - ing, War - ring 'gainst

sti - no in guer - - ra, è so - la spe-me un cor, è so - la spe-me un
fate's cru - el chid - - ing, Hope doth one heart im - plore, Hope doth one heart im -

cor, è so - la spe-me un cor,___ · un cor al Tro - va - tor!
plore, Hope doth one heart im - plore,___ To love the Trou - ba - dour!

Count.	Conte.
Oh, accents! I shudder!	Oh, detti! Io fremo!
Manrico.	Manrico.
But that fond treasure gaining,	Ma s'ei quel cor possiede,
Its faith and love obtaining,	Bello di casta fede,
High o'er all kings would soar,	E d'ogni re maggior
The happy Troubadour!	Il Trovator!
Count.	Conte.
Oh, accents! Oh, jealous anger!	Oh detti, oh gelosia!—
'Tis no error—she approaches!	Non m'inganno--Ella scende;
(Wraps himself in his mantle.)	(Si avvolge nel suo mantello.)
(Enter LEONORA.)	(Entra LEONORA.)
Leonora	Leonora
(hastening towards the COUNT).	(correndo verso il CONTE).
Oh, my beloved!	Anima mia!
Count.	Conte.
What now?	(Che far!)
Leonora.	Leonora.
More late than usual	Più dell' usato
Is thy coming; each moment have I counted	E tarda l'ora; io ne contai gl'istanti
With heart and pulses beating!—At length	Coi palpiti del core!—Alfin ti guida
'Tis love filled with pity that brings thee	Pietoso amor tra queste braccia—
to these loving arms.	
Voice of the Troubadour.	Le Voce del Trovatore.
Deceiver!	Infida.
(The moon emerging from the clouds reveals the figure of a masked cavalier.)	(La luna mostrasi dai nugoli, e lascia scorgere una persona di cui la visiera nasconde il volto.)
(Enter MANRICO.)	(Entra MANRICO.)
Leonora	Leonora.
(recognizing each and falling at the feet of MANRICO).	(Riconoscendo entrandi, e gettandosi ai piedi di MANRICO.)
That voice!—Ah, darkness and unrest	Qual voce!—Ah, dalle tenebre

My eager steps misguided!
'Twas thee, I thought, my words addressed!
In thee, not him, confided.
To thee my soul expandeth!
No other bliss demandeth!
I love thee, ah, believe me,
With lasting, boundless love!

Count.

And dar'st thou?

Manrico

(raising LEONORA).

Enough, forgive me!

Count.

With rage my heart doth move!
If thou'rt not base, reveal thyself!

Leonora.

Alas!

Count.

Thy name declaring—

Leonora.

Oh, speak, I pray!

(Aside to MANRICO).

Manrico.

Behold me, then,
Manrico!

Count.

Thou?—wherefore?
Rash traitor! bold and daring!
Urgel's accomplice, the laws have condemned
    thee.
And dar'st thou thus return
Within these royal portals?

Manrico.

What stays thee? Go call the guards, to
    aid thee;
Seize me, thy rival,
And to the headsman's gleaming axe
Consign me.

Count.

Thy fatal hour.
Perchance, already is at hand!
Oh, insensate! Come then—

Leonora.

Stay thee!

Tratta in errore io fui!
A te credei rivolgere
L'accento, e non a lui—
A te, che l'alma mia
Sol chiede, sol desia—
Io t'amo, il giuro, io t'amo
D' immenso eterno amor!

Conte.

Ed osi?—

Manrico

(sollevandola).

(Ah, più non bramo!)

Conte.

Avvampo di furor!
Se un vil non sei, discovriti.

Leonora.

(Ohimè!)

Conte.

Palesa il nome—

Leonora.

Deh, per pietà!—

(Sommessamente a MANRICO.)

Manrico.

Ravvisami,
Manrico io son.

Conte.

Tu!—Come!
Insano, temerario!
D'Urgel seguace, a morte
Proscritto, ardisci volgerti
A queste regie porte?—

Manrico.

Che tardi?—or via le guardie
Appella, ed il rivale
Al ferro del carnefice
Consegna.

Conte.

Il tuo fatale
Istante assai più prossimo
E, dissennato!—Vieni—

Leonora.

Conte!—

Count.

To my rage thou'rt victim doomed,
And fate wils I must slay thee.

Leonora.

One moment stay thee!

Count.

Follow me.

Manrico.

Lead on!

Leonora.

(What must I do?—
A single cry from me
May cause his ruin!)   Hear me.

Count.

No!
Fires of jealous, despised affection
In my heart are fiercely raging!
Wretch! thy blood for this foul defection
Soon shall flow, its pains assuaging!
(To LEONORA.)
Thou hast dared me, thy passion revealing!
He thou lovest in death shall lie,
Thy fond words his fate now sealing,
By this hand he's doomed to die!

Leonora.

One short moment thy fury restraining,
Let thine anger give way to reason;
I, alone, thy base passion disdaining,
Roused thy hateful charge of treason!
Let thy vengeance on me then descending,
Who have scorned thee, and still can defy,—
Strike thy dagger in this heart offending,
From thy love that dared to fly.

Manrico.

Vainly anger his proud heart is moving,
He shall soon fall by death inglorious;
Haply he who inspires thee with loving
Is by thy love made ever victorious.
(To the COUNT.)
Thy dark fate is already decided,
Doomed to perish, thy last hour is nigh!
Heart and life to my hand are confided,
Heaven condemns thee, and thou shalt die!

(The two rivals retire with drawn swords. LEONORA falls senseless.)

END OF FIRST ACT.

Conte.

Al mio sdegno vittima
E forza ch' io ti sveni—

Leonora.

Oh ciel!—t'arresta—

Conte.

Seguimi—

Manrico.

Andiam—

Leonora.

Che mai farò?—
Un sol mio grido perdere
Lo puote!)—M'odi—

Conte.

No.
Di geloso amor sprezzato
Arde in me tremendo foco!
Il tuo sangue, o sciagurato,
Ad estinguerlo fia poco!
(A LEONORA.)
Dirgli, o folle—io t'amo—ardisti—
Ei più vivere non può—
Un accento proferisti,
Che a morir lo condannò!

Leonora.

Un istante almen dia loco
Il tuo sdegno alla ragione—
Io, sol io di tanto foco
Son, pur troppo, la cagione!
Piombi, ah! piombi il tuo furore
Sulla rea che t'oltraggiò—
Vibra il ferro in questo core,
Che te amar non vuol, non può.

Manrico.

Del superbo vana è l'ira;
Ei cadrà da me trafitto.
Il mortal che amor t'inspira,
Dall' amor fu reso invitto.
La tua sorte è già compita—
(Al CONTE.)
L'ora omai per te suonò!
Il tuo core e la tua vita
Il destino a me serbò!

(I due rivali si allontanano con le spade sguainate; LEONORA cade priva di sentimento.)

FINE DELL' ATTO PRIMO.

ACT II.
THE GIPSY.

SCENE I—A ruined house at the foot of a mountain in Biscay; the interior is partly exposed to view; within, a great fire is lighted. Day begins to dawn.

(AZUCENA is seated near the fire. MANRICO, enveloped in his mantle, is lying upon a mattress; his helmet is at his feet; in his hand he holds a sword, which he regards fixedly. A band of gipsies are sitting in scattered groups around them.)

Gipsies.

See, how the shadows of night are flying!

Morn breaketh, heaven's glorious arch unveiling;

Like a young widow, who, weary of sighing,

Lays by her garments of sorrow and wailing.

Rouse up to labor! Take each his hammer!

Who makes the gipsy's a life with pleasure laden?

The gipsy maiden.

(They take up the implements of labor, and strike with their hammers upon anvils, in regular measure.)

Men

(resting awhile from their labor, they address the women).

Fill me a bumper; both arm and hand

New strength and courage draw from flowing beakers.

(The women pour out wine for them in rustic cups.)

All.

See how the sunlight, radiantly glowing,

Borrows new beams from our wine-cups o'erflowing!

Resume our labor! Take each his hammer!

Who makes the gipsy's a life with pleasure laden?

The gipsy maiden!

Azucena

(as she begins to sing, the gipsies gather about her).

ATTO II.
LA GITANA.

SCENA I—Un diruto abituro sulle falde d'un Monte della Biscaglia—nel fondo, quasi tutto aperto, arde un gran fuoco. I primi albori.

(AZUCENA siede presso il fuoco—MANRICO, le sta disteso accanio sopra una coltrice, ed avviluppato nel suo mantello; ha l'elmo ai piedi, e fra le mani la spada, su cui figge immobilmente lo sguardo—Una banda di Zingari è sparso all'intorno.)

Zingari.

Vedi! le fosche notturne spoglie

De' cieli sveste l'immensa volta;

Sembra una vedova che alfin si toglie

I bruni panni ond' era involta.

All' opra, all' opra. Dagli, martella.

Chi del gitano i giorni abbella?

La zingarella.

(Danno di piglio ai loro ferri di mestiere—al misurato tempestar dei martelli cadenti sulle incudini, ou uomini, ou donne, e tutti in un tempo in fine intuonano la cantilena seguente.)

Uomini

(alle donne, sostando un poco dal lavoro).

Versami un tratto: lena e coraggio

Il corpo e l'anima traggon dal bere.

(Le donne mescono ad essi in rozze coppe.)

Tutti.

Oh, guarda, guarda! del sole un raggio

Brilla più vivido nel ⎰tuo⎱ bicchiere—
⎱mio⎰

All' opra, all' opra—Dagli, martella—

Quale a ⎰voi⎱ splende propizia stella?—
⎱noi⎰

La zingarella.

Azucena

(canta: gli zingari le si fanno allato).

STRIDE LA VAMPA — *UPWARD THE FLAMES ROLL*   Air (Azucena)

Stri - de la vam- -pa! La___ fol-la in-do - mi-ta Cor -

Up - ward the flames___ roll; crowds___ press-ing fierce - ly on, Rush

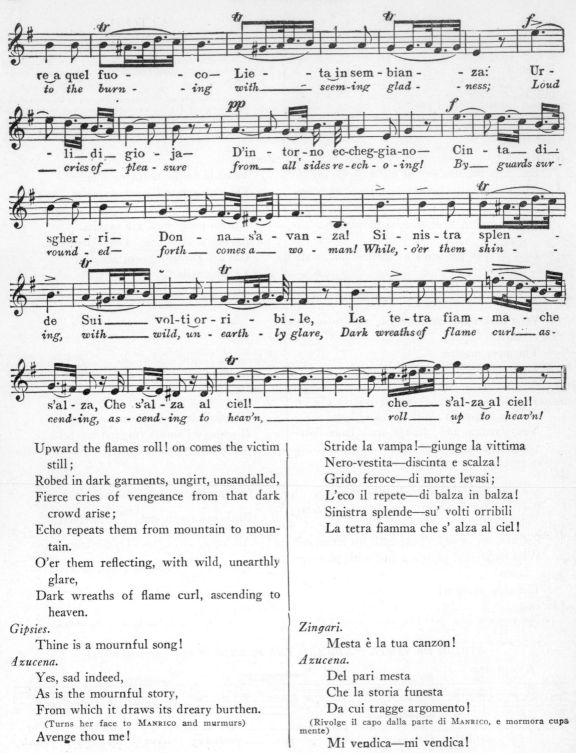

re a quel fuo - - co— Lie - - ta in sem - bian - - za: Ur-
to the burn - - ing with seem-ing glad - - ness; Lòud

-li - di gio - ja— D'in - tor-no ec-cheg-gia-no— Cin - ta di_
cries of plea - sure from all' sides re-ech - o - ing! By guards sur -

sgher - ri— Don - na s'a - van - za! Si - nis - tra splen -
round - ed forth comes a wo - man! While, - o'er them shin -

de Sui vol-ti or - ri - bi - le, La te - tra fiam - ma - che
ing, with wild, un - earth - ly glare, Dark wreaths of flame curl as-

s'al - za, Che s'al - za al ciel! che s'al-za al ciel!
cend-ing, as - cend-ing to heav'n, roll up to heav'n!

Upward the flames roll! on comes the victim still;	Stride la vampa!—giunge la vittima
Robed in dark garments, ungirt, unsandalled,	Nero-vestita—discinta e scalza!
Fierce cries of vengeance from that dark crowd arise;	Grido feroce—di morte levasi;
Echo repeats them from mountain to mountain.	L'eco il repete—di balza in balza!
O'er them reflecting, with wild, unearthly glare,	Sinistra splende—su' volti orribili
Dark wreaths of flame curl, ascending to heaven.	La tetra fiamma che s' alza al ciel!

Gipsies.

Thine is a mournful song!

Azucena.

Yes, sad indeed,

As is the mournful story,

From which it draws its dreary burthen.

(Turns her face to MANRICO and murmurs)

Avenge thou me!

Zingari.

Mesta è la tua canzon!

Azucena.

Del pari mesta

Che la storia funesta

Da cui tragge argomento!

(Rivolge il capo dalla parte di MANRICO, e mormora cupamente)

Mi vendica—mi vendica!

Manrico.

(Again those mysterious words!)

Elderly Gipsy.

Companions, day advances;
'Tis time to seek for food; let us descend
To the towns that lie beneath us.

Manrico.

Come on, then!
(Putting away their tools.)

Women.

Come on, then!
Commence descending promiscuously; their song is heard
growing fainter in the distance.)

Gipsies.

Who makes the gipsy's a life with pleasure
   laden?
The gipsy maiden!

Manrico
(rising).

All have left us; ah, now relate
That dark mournful story!

Azucena.

Thou dost not know it as yet?
Thou wert but still young, when,
Spurred on by ambition, far away
Thou didst wander!—My mother's final
   doom
This tale relateth. She was charged
With fearful crimes by a haughty noble,
Whose failing infant she was accused of
   charming!
Doomed to the stake, she perished
Where this fire is burning!

Manrico.

Ah, fate unhappy!
(Drawing back with horror from the fire).

Azucena.

In fetters, they led her onward to meet her
   dark fate impending;
With babe in hand, I followed sadly, with
   tears descending.
In vain tried I to approach her, through
   crowds that round her were pressing;
In vain did she attempt to stay, to leave
   with me her blessing.
Goaded by spears and lances, with oaths and
   jeers assaulted,

Manrico.

(L'arcana parola ognor!)

Vecchio Zingara.

Compagni, avanza il giorno;
A procacciarci un pan, sù, sù!—scendiamo
Per le propinque ville.

Uomini.

Andiamo.
(Ripongona sollecitamente nei sacchi i loro arnesi.)

Donne.

Andiamo.
(Tutti scendono alla rinfusa giù per la china; tratto tratto
e sempre a maggior distanza, odesi il loro canto.)

Zingari.

Chi del gitano i giorni abbella?
La zingarella!

Manrico
(sorgendo).

Soli or siamo; deh narra
Quella storia funesta.

Azucena.

E tu la ignori,
Tu pur!—Ma giovinetto i passi tuoi
D'ambizïon lo sprone
Lungi traca!—Dell' ava il fine acerbo
E quella storia—La incolpò superbo
Conte di malefizio, onde apparia
Côlto un bambin suo figlio—Essa bruciata
Fù dov' arde or quel foco!

Manrico.

Ahi! sciagurata!
(Rifuggendo con raccapriccio dalla fiamma.)

Azucena.

Condotta ell' era in ceppi al suo destin
   tremendo
Col figlio—teco in braccio io la seguia pian-
   gendo:
Infino ad essa un varco tentai, ma invano,
   aprirmi—
Invan tentò la misera fermarsi, e benedirmi!
Che, fra bestemmie oscene, pungendola coi
   ferri
Al rogo la cacciavano gli scellerati sgherri!

The guards pursued her ruthlessly, 'till at the stake they halted.

At length, with broken accents, "Avenge thou me," she cried!

Those dying words will ever within my heart abide.

Manrico.

Didst thou avenge her?

Azucena.

The Count's young child, ere the day was ended,

I stole and brought him hither; the flames still to heaven ascended!

Manrico.

The flames?—Oh, heav'n—thou couldst not—

Azucena.

Sadly the child began weeping;

Rent was my heart with his sorrow, o'er me pity was creeping,

When quickly, my mind disordered, saw what like dreams came o'er me.

Deadly shapes and phantoms brought the dark scene before me;

The guardsmen, this place of torture, the mother pale, confounded,

Barefoot, ungirdled, the outcry of anguish,

That cry within me resounded: "Avenge thou me!"

All heedless, my hand extended held fast the victim pale;

The flames rolled expectant; in I hurled him!

Calmed was the fatal madness, fled was the horrid vision;

The fire still glowed in silence, gorged with its foul commission!

Gazing around in sadness, I saw the infant cherished

Of that vile Count approaching!

Manrico.

Ah, what say'st thou?

Azucena.

My child had perished,

My child through me had perished!

Allor, con tronce accento, mi vendica! es-clamò—

Quel detto un eco eterno in questo cor lasciò.

Manrico.

La vendicasti?

Azucena.

Il figlio giunsi a rapir del Conte;

Lo trascinai quì meco—le fiamme ardean già pronte.

Manrico.

Le fiamme?—oh ciel!—tu forse?—

Azucena.

Ei distruggeasi in pianto—

Io mi sentiva il cor dilaniato, infranto!—

Quand'ecco agli egri spirti, come in un sogno, apparva.

La vision ferale di spaventose larve!—

Gli sgnerri ed il supplizio!—la madre smorta in volto—

Scalza, discinta!—il grido, il noto grido ascolto—

Mi vendica!—La mano convulsa tendo stringo

La vittima—nel foco la traggo, la sospingo!—

Cessa il fatal delirio—

L'orrida scena fugge—

La fiamma sol divampa,

E la sua preda strugge!

Pur volgo intorno il guardo,

E innanzi a me vegg' io

Dell' empio Conte il figlio!—

Manrico.

Ah! come?

Azucena.

Il figlio mio,

Mio figlio avea bruciato!

Manrico.

Horrid crime!

Azucena.

Once more my thin locks with horror rise
   up, unsoothed by time!

(Azucena falls fainting on her seat; Manrico is struck
dumb with surprise and horror.)

Manrico.

I'm not thy son, then? tell me, who am I,
   I pray thee?

Azucena

(hastily, as if to repair an involuntary admission).

Mine art thou ever.

Manrico.

Thy words denied it.

Azucena.

It may be; what wouldst thou?

When wandering thoughts such terrible
   scenes encounter!

The mind, disordered, heeds not all the follies

Unguarded lips may utter. Mother tender
   and true.

Hast thou not found me ever?

Manrico.

Can I disown it?

Azucena.

To me thy life's protection

Thou owest. At midnight, on the field of
   battle

At Petilla, where reports declared thou hadst
   fallen,

Did I not come to give thee fit burial?

In thy breast, my cares revived the vital
   spark,

But there the affection fond, maternal,
   stayed not.

How many hours did I tend thee, healing
   thy wounds

So ghastly and numerous?

Manrico   (with noble pride).

Wounds obtained on that dark morning;

My breast alone received them! 'Mid all
   the thousands that disbanded,

I alone faced the foe, still firm, unyielding.

The vile de Luna then

Manrico.

Che dici quale orror!

Azucena.

Sul capo mio le chiome sento drizzarsi ancor!

(Azucena ricade trambasciata sul proprio seggio: Manrico ammutisce, colpito d'orrore e di sorpresa—Momenti di
silenzio.)

Manrico.

Non son tuo figlio?—E chi son io, chi dunque?

Azucena

(con sollecitudine di chi cerca emendare involontario fallo).

Tu sei mio figlio!

Manrico.

Eppur dicesti—

Azucena.

Ah!—forse—

Che vuoi!—Quando al pensier s'affaccia il
   truce

Caso, lo spirto intenebrato pone

Stolto parole sul mio labbro—Madre,

Tenera madre non m'avesti ognora?

Manrico.

Potrei negarlo?—

Azucena.

A me, se vivi ancora,

Nol dêi? Notturna, nei pugnati campi

Di Petilla, ove spento

Fama ti disse, a darti

Sepoltura non mossi? La fuggente

Aura vital non iscovri, nel seno

Non l'arrestò materno affetto?—E quanta

Cure non spesi a risanar le tante ferite!

Manrico   (con nobile orgoglio).

Che portai quel dì fatale—

Ma tutte qui, nel petto?—Io sol, fra mille

Già sbandati, al nemico

Volgendo ancor la faccia!—Il rio de Luna,

Sù me piombò col suo drappello; io caddi,

Charged me with his troops o'erwhelming;
I faltered and fell,
Yet brave and unconquered!

Azucena.
Such were the thanks
Which the villain did repay thee,
For sparing his base life in that combat at
night!
What then did blind thee?
Was it a strange compassion?

Manrico.
Oh, mother! I cannot tell thee! I know
not!

Però da forte io caddi!

Azucena.
Ecco mercede
Ai giorni, che l'infame
Nel singolar certame
Ebbe salvi da te?—qual t'acciecava
Strana pietà per esso?

Manrico.
Oh madre!—non saprei dirlo a me stesso!

MAL REGGENDO — *ILL SUSTAINING* Air (Manrico)

Azucena.

But within that soul ungrateful
Not one word from heaven hath resounded!
Oh! if with that villain hateful
Thou in fight shouldst be confounded,
Haste to accomplish (Heaven doth will it)
What I command thee, hear and fulfil it!
To the handle send this weapon
Through the monster's cruel heart.

(The prolonged note of a horn is heard.)

Manrico.

Ruiz sends hither th' accustomed courier,
Haply—

(Sounds his horn in reply.)

Azucena.

Avenge thou me!

(Remains in thought and seemingly unconscious of what is passing.)

(Enter a Messenger.)

Manrico

(to the Messenger).

Approach this way. Proceed
And tell me what news thou bringest.

Messenger.

The scroll I bring here will tell thee all.

(Presenting a letter.)

Manrico

(reads).

"Within our power is Castellor;
By the order of our prince thou must watch o'er
And defend it. Wherever this may reach thee,
Come in haste. Kept in error still by thy reported death,
This very evening Leonora will assume the nun's dark veil within the neighboring convent."

Just heaven, forbid it!

(With exclamations of sorrow.)

Azucena

(starting).

What dost thou?

Manrico

(to the Messenger).

Hence quickly down to the valley
Without delay, a steed provide me.

Messenger.

Be it so.

Azucena.

Ma nell' alma dell' ingrato
Non parlò del cielo il detto!
Oh! se ancor ti spinge il fato
A pugnar col maledetto,
Compi, o figlio, qual d'un Dio,
Compi allora il cenno mio:
Sino all' elsa questa lama
Vibra, immergi all' empio in cor.

(Odesi un prolungato suono di corno.)

Manrico.

L'usato messo Ruiz invia!—
Forse—

(Dà fiato anch' esso al corno che tiene ad armacello.)

Azucena.

Mi vendica!

(Resta concentrata, quasi inconsapevole di ciò che succede.)

(Entra il Messo.)

Manrico

(al Messo).

Inoltra il piè.
Guerresco evento, dimmi, seguia?

Messo.

Risponda il foglio che reco a te.

(Porgendo il foglio, che MANRICO legge.)

Manrico.

"In nostra possa è Castellor: ne dêi,
Tu, per cenno del prence,
Vigilar le difese. Ove ti è dato,
Affrettati a venir. Giunta la sera
Tratta in inganno di tua morte al grido,
Nel vicin claustro della croce il velo
Cingerà Leonora." Oh, giusto cielo!

(Con dolorosa esclamazione.)

Azucena

(scuotendosi).

(Che fia!)

Manrico

(al Messo).

Veloce scendi la balza,
E d'un cavallo a me provvedi—

Messo.

Corro—

Azucena   (interposing).

Manrico!

Manrico.

The time flies swiftly.   Haste thee, and
   yonder
My coming awaits thee.
            (The MESSENGER departs hastily.)

Azucena.

What hopest thou? what wouldst thou?

Manrico.

(Lose her thus! Oh, torment!
Thus lose that angel!)

Azucena.

(His brain is turned!)

Manrico.

Farewell now.
   (Replacing his helmet upon his head, and wrapping his
cloak around him.)

Azucena.

No! stay thee! hear me!

Manrico.

Release me!
But a moment lost may wither
All the hopes that now sustain me;
Earth and heaven, combined together,
Would be powerless to restrain me!

Azucena.

Insensate!

Manrico.

Ah, release me, O mother, I pray thee!
Woe betide if here I stay me!
Thou wilt see thy son, extended
At thy feet, with grief expire.

Azucena.

No, I'll ne'er permit thy going.
In thy veins my blood is flowing;
Every crimson drop thou losest
From thy mother's heart doth flow.
   (MANRICO departs, AZUCENA striving in vain to detain
him.)

SCENE II—Cloister of a Convent in the vicinity of
Castellor. Night.
   (The COUNT, FERRANDO and followers advance cautiously,
enveloped in their cloaks.)

Count.

All is deserted; through the air comes yet
No sound of th' accustomed chanting.
I come in time then.

Azucena   (frapponendosi).

Manrico!—

Manrico.

Il tempo incalza—
Vola; m'aspetta dell cole a' piedi.
            (Il Messo parte, affrettatamente.)

Azucena.

E speri, e vuoi?

Manrico.

(Perderla?—Oh, ambascia!—
Perder quell' angelo?—)

Azucena.

(E fuor di sè!)

Manrico.

Addio—
   (Postosi l'elmo sul capo, ed afferrando il mantello.)

Azucena.

No—forma—odi—

Manrico.

Mi lascia—
Un momento può involarmi
Il mio ben, la mia speranza!
No, che basti ad arrestarmi
Terra e ciel non ha possanza.

Azucena.

Demente!

Manrico.

Ah! mi sgombra, o madre, i passi—
Guai per te, s'io qui restassi:
Tu vedresti a' piedi tuoi
Spento il figlio di dolor!

Azucena.

No soffrirlo non poss' io.
Il tuo sangue è sangue mio!
Ogni stilla che ne versi
Tu la spremi dal mio cor!
   (Si allontana, indarno trattenuto da AZUCENA.)

SCENA II—Chiostro d'un cenobio, in vicinanza di Castel
lor. E notte.
   (Il CONTE, FERRANDO, ed alcuni sequaci, ed avviluppati nei
loro mantelli, inoltrandesi cautamente.)

Conte.

Tutto è deserto; nè per l'aura ancora
Suona l'usato carme—
In tempo io giungo!

Ferrando.

    A daring labor here, my lord,
    Awaits thee.

Count.

    'Tis daring; and such alone as burning passion
    And wounded pride from me should demand.
    My rival dead—each hindrance opposed to my wishes
    Seemed fallen and vanquished;
    Till lately she discovered one still more potent,
    The altar. Ah, no! For none else is Leonora!
    She is mine, mine only!

Ferrando.

    Ardita opra, o signore,
    Imprendi.

Conte.

    Ardita, e quel furente amore
    Ed irritato orgoglio
    Chissero a me. Spento il rival, caduto
    Ogni ostacol sembrava a' miei desiri;
    Novello e più possente ella ne appresta—
    L'altare!—Ah no, non fia
    D'altri Leonora!—Leonora è mia!

IL BALEN DEL SUO — *OF HER SMILE THE RADIANT*   Air (Count)

d'ar-do le fa-vel-li in mio fa-vo-re, sper-da il so-le d'un suo
burn-ing, More than words shall win me fa-vor, Her bright glan-ces on me

sguar-do la tem-pe-sta del mio cor. Ah! l'a-mor, l'a-mor on-
turn-ing calm the tem-pest in my heart. Ah! this love with-in me

d'ar-do le fa-vel-li in mio fa-vore, sper-da il so-le d'un suo sguar-do la tem-pe-sta,
burn-ing More than words shall win me fa-vor, Her bright glan-ces on me turn-ing, Calm the tem-pest,

Ah!_____ si la tem-pes-ta del mio cor.
Ah!_____ calm the tem-pest in my heart.

(A sound of bells is heard.)	(Odesi il rintocco de' sacri bronzi.)
What soundeth? Oh, heaven!	Qual suono!—oh, ciel!—
Ferrando.	*Ferrando.*
The bell	La squilla
That proclaims the rite's commencing.	Vicino il rito annunzia!—
Count.	*Conte.*
Ere at the altar she kneels	Ah! pria che giunga.
I must seize her.	All' altar, si rapisca!
Ferrando.	*Ferrando.*
Ah! heed thee!	Oh, bada!
Count.	*Conte.*
Silence!	Taci!
Didst hear not? Depart then! 'Mid the	Non odo—andate—Di quei faggi all' ombra
trees' dark shadows	Celatevi—Ah! fra poco.
Conceal yourselves.	(FERRANDO e gli altri seguaci si allontanano.)
(FERRANDO and followers retire.)	Mia diverrà!—Tutto m' investe un foco!
Ah! how quickly mine she will be!	
Fires in my heart are burning!	
(Watching anxiously in the direction from which LEONORA is expected.)	(Ansioso, guardingo osserva dalla porte onde deve giunger LEONORA.)
Ferrando and Followers.	*Ferrando e Seguaci.*
How bold! Let's go—conceal ourselves	Ardire!—Andiam—celiamoci
Amid the shades in haste.	Tra l'ombre—nel mister!—
How bold! Come on—and silence keep,	Ardire!—Andiam—silenzio!—
The prize he soon will hold.	Si comia il suo voler!

PER ME ORA FATALE — OH, FATAL HOUR Air (Count)

Alla marcia

Per me o - ra fa - ta - le, i tuoi mo - men - ti af - fret - ta, af - fret - ta. La
Oh, fa - tal hour im - pend - ing, Thy mo - ments urge with speed e - lat - ing, The

gio - ja che m'a - spet - ta, gio - ja mor - tal non è,___ gio - ja mor-
joy my heart's a - wait - ing Is not of mor - tal birth,___ of mor - tal

tal, no, no, no, non è. In va - no un Dio, ri - va - - le S'op-
birth, no, it can - not be. In vain doth Heav'n, con - tend - - ing With

po - ne all' a - mor mi - o,___ non può nem - men un Di - o, don - na, ra-
ri - val claims, op - pose me,___ If once these arms en - close thee, No pow'r in

pir - ti a me,___ non può, ra - pir - ti a me.
heav'n or earth,___ no pow'r shall tear thee from me.

Chorus of Nuns (within).	Coro de Religioso (interno).
Error thy soul encumbers,	Ah! se l' error t'ingombra,
Daughter of Eve, but know thee,	O figlia d'Eva, i rai,
Death's swift approach will show thee	Presso a morir, vedrai
Life's but a fleeting dream.	Che un' ombra, un sogno tù,
Phantoms in restless slumbers	Anzi del sogno un' ombra
All earthly hopes will seem!	La speme di quaggiù!
Come, let this veil concealing,	Vieni, e t'asconda il veio
Hide thee from human vision,	Ad ogni sguardo umano,
Nor worldly thought, nor feeling	Aura, o pensier mondano
Can here admitted be.	Qui vivo più non è.
To heaven, for grace appealing,	Al ciel ti volgi, e il cielo
Opening it waits for thee.	Si schiuderà per te.
(Enter LEONORA with INEZ and female followers.)	(Entra LEONORA con INES, e seguiti.)
Leonora.	*Leonora.*
Why art thou weeping?	Perchè piangete?

Inez.

Ah! truly
Thou wilt leave us forever!

Leonora.

Oh, dear companions,
No fond smile, no hope to cheer me,
No flower remaining on earth for me!
Now must I turn unto Him, the whole
    support
Of those in affliction, and after days of
    prayer and penitence,
I may haply rejoin my lost beloved one
With the blest in heaven. Restrain thy
    weeping;
To the altar now lead me.
(About to proceed.)
(Enter the COUNT, suddenly.)

Count.

No, withhold!

Ladies.

The Count here!

Leonora.

Gracious heaven!

Count.

For thee no altar now waits
But one hymenial.

Ladies.

Such daring boldness!

Leonora.

Why comest thou here, insensate?

Count.

To make thee mine now!
(On saying so, he approaches, and seizes LEONORA—but MANRICO appears, like a phantom, and places himself between them—general consternation.)

Leonora.

And can I still my eyes believe
That see thee here before me!
Or is it but a dream of bliss,
A charm that hovers o'er me!
Unused to such excessive joy
My heart with doubts contended!
Art thou from heaven descended,
Or am I there with thee?

Count.

Do souls departed thus return
From death's domains eternal?

Ines.

Ah!—dunque
Tu per sempre ne lasci!

Leonora.

O dolci amici
Un riso, una speranza, un fior la terra
Non ha per me! Degg' io
Volgermi a quei che degli afflitti è solo
Conforto, e dopo i penitenti giorni,
Puó fra gli eletti al mio perduto bene
Ricongiùngermi un di. Tergete i rai,
E guidatemi all' ara.
(Incamminandosi.)

Conte.

No, giammai!—

Donne.

Il conte!

Leonora.

Giusto ciel!

Conte.

Per te non havvi
Che l' ara d' imeneo—

Donne.

Cotanto ardia!—

Leonora.

Insano! e qui venisti?

Conte.

A farti mia.
(E si dicendo, scagliasci verso de LEONORA onde impadronirsi di lei; ma fra esso e la preda trovasi, qual fantasma surle di sotterra, MANRICO. Un grido universal irrompe.)

Leonora.

E deggio?—e posso crederlo?—
Ti veggo a me d'accanto!
E questo un sogno, un' estasi,
Un sovrumano incanto!
Non regge a tanto giubilo
Rapito il cor, sorpreso!—
Sei tu dal ciel disceso,
O in ciel son io con te?

Conte.

Dunque gli estinti lasciano
Di morte il regno eterno!

Thus to condemn me, doth hell indeed
Renounce its prey infernal!
But if as yet thy fatal thread
Of time remains unmeasured,
If life by thee is treasured,
Then fly from her and me.

Manrico.

Heaven's blest abode, nor regions infernal
Have yet possessed me.
True, base assassins mortal blows may deal,
Thy deeds impressed me.
O'erwhelming power that naught can stay
Have ocean's waves unbounded!
He, who thy guilt confounded!
His arm has aided me.

Ladies.

In heaven thy faith reposing,
(To LEONORA.)
Thence comes this aid to thee.

Ferrando and Followers.

'Tis fate thou'rt now opposing,
From harm it holds him free.
(Enter RUIZ and Soldiers.)

Ruiz and Followers.

Long live Urgal!

Manrico.

My brave-hearted soldiers!

Ruiz.

Come then.

Manrico
(To LEONORA).
Lady, I wait thee.

Count.

Wouldst thou rob me of her?
(Opposing him.)

Leonora.

Oh!

Manrico
(to the COUNT).
Withhold there!

Count.

Wouldst thou deprive me of her?
No!
(Drawing his sword.)

Ruiz and Soldiers.

He raveth!
(Surrounding the COUNT.)

A danno mio rinunzia
Le prede sue l' inferno!—
Ma se non mai si fransero
De' giorni tuoi gli stami,
Se vivi e viver brami,
Fuggi da lei, da me.

Manrico.

Nè m' ebbe il ciel, nè l' orrido
Varco infernal sentiero—
Infami sgherri vibrano
Colpi mortali, è vero!
Potenza irresistibile
Hanno de fiumi l' onde!—
Ma gli empj un Dio confonde!—
Quel Dio soccorse a me!

Donne.

Il cielo in cui fidasti,
(A LEONORA.)
Pietade avea di te.

Ferrando e Seguaci.

Tu col destin contrasti;
(Al CONTE.)
Suo difensore egli è.
(Entra RUIZ, seguito da lunga tratta d' armati.)

Ruiz.

Urgel viva!

Manrico.

Miei prodi guerrieri!—

Ruiz.

Vieni.

Manrico
(A LEONORA.)
Donna, mi segui.

Conte.

E tu speri?
(Opponendosi.)

Leonora.

Oh!

Manrico
(Al CONTE.)
T'arretra.

Conte.

Involarmi costei!
No!
(Sguainando la spada.)

Ruiz e Armati.

Vaneggi!
(Accerchiando il CONTE.)

Ferrando and Followers.

What wouldst thou, my lord?

(The COUNT is disarmed by the soldiers of RUIZ.)

Count.

All my reason in fury is lost!

(with gestures and accents of fury.)

Leonora.

(He affrights me!)

Count.

Furies dwell in my heart!

Ruiz and Soldiers.

Come then, a future of smiles waits for thee.

(TO MANRICO.)

Ferrando and Followers.

Yield thee, since yielding no baseness implies.

(Exit MANRICO, leading LEONORA—the COUNT is driven back, the ladies retreat to the Convent, as the curtain falls.)

END OF THE SECOND ACT.

ACT III.

THE GIPSY'S SON.

SCENE I—A camp. On the right, the tent of the COUNT DI LUNA, on which is displayed a banner, indicative of his supremacy. The fortress of Castellor seen in the distance. The scene full of Soldiers, some playing, some polishing their accoutrements, some walking in apparent conversation, while others are on duty as Sentinels.

(Enter FERRANDO, from the tent of the COUNT.)

Some of the Soldiers.

Now with dice, may fortune speed us;
Other games will shortly need us!
From our swords this blood we burnish,
Coming deeds fresh stains will furnish.

(Sounds of warlike instruments are heard; all start and turn towards the sounds.)

Some Soldiers.

Lo! they come for succor praying!

(A strong band of soldiers crosses the camp.)

Other Soldiers.

Still, they make a brave display!

All.

Let us, without more delaying
Castellor attack to-day.

Ferrando.

Yes, brave companions; at dawn, to-morrow,

Ferrando e Seguaci.

Che tenti, signor!

(Il CONTE è disarmato oa quei di RUIZ.)

Conte.

Di ragione ogni lumi perdei!

(Con gesti ed accenti di maniaco furore.)

Leonora.

(M'atterrisce.)

Conte.

Ho lo furie nel cor!

Ruiz e Armati.

Vieni; è lieta la sorte per te.

(A MANRICO.)

Ferrando e Seguaci.

Cedi; or ceder viltade non è!

(MANRICO tragge seco LEONORA—il CONTE è respinto, le donne rifuggono al cenobio—scende subito la tela.)

FINE DELL' ATTO SECONDO.

ATTO III.

IL FIGLIO DELLA ZINGARA.

SCENA I—Accampamento—A destra, il padiglione del CONTE DI LUNA, su cui sventola la bandiera in segno di supremo comando—da lungi Torreggia Castellor.—Scolte di uomini d'arme da per tutto; altri giocano, altri forbiscono le armi, altri passeggiano.

(Entra FERRANDO, dal padiglione del CONTE.)

Alcuni Uomini d'Arme.

Or co' dadi, ma fra poco
Giocherem ben altro gioco!
Questo acciar, dal sangue or terso,
Fia di sangue in breve asperso!

(Odonsi strumenti guerrieri; tutti si volgono là dove si avanza il suono.)

Alcuni.

Il soccorso dimandato!

(Un grosso drappello di balestrieri, in completa armatura, traversa il campo.)

Altri.

Han l'aspetto del valor!

Tutti.

Più l'assalto ritardato
Or non fia di Castellor.

Ferrando.

Sì prodi amici; al dì novello, è mente

Our leader has now resolved
On storming the fortress on all sides.
Within its walls a booty immense
We're sure to find; 'tis more than hopeful;
If conquered 'tis ours then.

Some of the Soldiers.

Pleasure there invites us.

Ferrando and Chorus.

Now let the trumpet in war tones resound-
ing,
Call to arms; with courage bold, we'll march
undaunted.
Haply, to-morrow, our proud foes confound-
ing,
On those walls shall our banners be planted.
Ne'er more brilliant were prospects victor-
ious
Than the hopes which our hearts now elate.
Thence, we'll gather renown, bright and
glorious;
Pleasure, honor and profit there await us,
Honor and booty for us there await.

(Enter the Count, from the tent; turns with lowering
gaze towards Castellor.)

Count.

Within my rival's arms! How this reflec-
tion,
Like a taunting demon, follows me
Wherever I wander. Within my rival's
arms! To-morrow
Ere the day dawns, I'll hasten to sunder
them forever!
Oh! Leonora!

(A tumult is heard.)
(Enter Ferrando.)

Count.

What now?

Ferrando.

Around the camp
Was seen a gipsy-woman, loitering:
Surprised by the sentinels on duty
To escape she attempted. With reason
They suspected her of spying out our move-
ments,
And pursued.

Count.

Was she taken?

Del capitan la rôcca
Investir da ogni parte.
Colà pingue bottino
Certezza è rinvenir, più che speranza.
Si vinca, è nostro.

Uomini d'Arme.

Tu c'inviti a danza!

Ferrando con Coro.

Squilli, eccheggi la tromba guerriera
Chiami all' armi, alla pugna, all' assalto;
Fia domani la nostra bandiera
Di quei merli piantata sull' alto.
No, giammai non sorrise vittoria
Di più liete speranze finor!
Ivi l'util ci aspetta e la gloria;
Ivi opimi la preda e l'onore!
Ivi opimi la preda e l'onor!

(Entra il Conte, uscito dalla tenda, volge uno sguardo
bicco a Castellor.)

Conte.

In braccio al mio rival!—Questo pensiero
Come persecutor demone ovunque
M'insegue! In braccio al mio rival!—Ma
corro
Surta appena l'aurora,
Io corro a separavi—Oh, Leonora!

(Odesi tumulti.)

(Entra Ferrando.)

Conte.

Che fu?

Ferrando.

D'appresso il campo
S'aggirava una zingara; sorpresa
Da' nostri esploratori,
Si volse in fuga; essi, a ragion temendo
Una spia nella trista,
L'inseguir—

Conte.

Fu raggiunta?

Ferrando.

They seized her.

Count.

Hast seen her yet?

Ferrando.

No; the conductor
Of the escort hath so
Informed me.

Count.

Here she comes.

(AZUCENA, with her hands bound together, is dragged
in by the Sentinels.)

Soldiers.

Come on, thou sorceress, come forward!

Azucena.

Oh, help me! Pray release me! Ah, maddened wretches,
Of what accuse me?

Count.

Come hither.

(AZUCENA is led before the COUNT.)

To me reply now, and tremble if thou liest.

Azucena.

Ask, then.

Count.

Whither bound?

Azucena.

I know not.

Count.

How?

Azucena.

'Tis a custom of the gipsies
Without purpose to wander
Wherever fancy leads them,
Their only shelter heaven,
The wide world their country.

Count.

Whence comest thou?

Azucena.

From Biscalia, where, till of late,
Was my sole abode, amid its wild, barren
mountains.

Count.

(From Biscalia!)

Ferrando.

E presa.

Conte.

Vista l' hai tu?

Ferrando.

No; della scorta
Il condottier m'apprese
L'evento.

(Tumulto più vicino.)

Conte.

Eccola.

(Entra AZUCENA, con le mani avvinte, è trascinata dagli Es
ploratori—un codazzo d'altri soldati.)

Esploratori.

Innanzi, o strega, innanzi.

Azucena.

Aìta!—Mi lasciate—Oh! furibondi,
Che mal fec' io?

Conte.

S'appressi.

(AZUCENA è tratta innanzi il CONTE.)

A me rispondi.
E trema dal mentir!

Azucena.

Chiedi.

Conte.

Ove vai?

Azucena.

Nol so.

Conte.

Che?

Azucena.

D'una zingara è costume
Muover senza disegno
Il passo vagabondo,
Ed è suo tetto il ciel, sua patria il mondo.

Conte.

E vieni?

Azucena.

Da Biscaglia, ove finora
La sterili montagne ebbi ricetto.

Conte.

(Da Biscaglia!)

Ferrando.

(What heard I? oh, dark suspicion.)

Ferrando.

(Che intesi!—Oh, qual sospetto!)

GIORNI POVERI — *I WAS POOR, YET UNCOMPLAINING* (Azucena)

Gior- ni po- ve- ri vi- ve- a, pur con- ten- ta del mio
I was poor, yet un-com- plain-ing, Lived con- tent- ed, grate-ful

sta- to; so- la spe-me un fi- glio a- ve- a, Mi la- sciò! m'ob-
heart- ed With one son, sole hope re- main- ing, But, a- las! from

bli- a l'in- gra- to. Io de- ser- ta, va-do er- ran- do di quel
me he hath part- ed. Now I wan- der sad and lone- ly Through the

fi- glio ri- cer- can- do, di quel fi- glio che al mio co-
world, seek- ing him on- ly; All my heart's trou- bled e- mo-

re pe-ne or- ri- bi- li- co- stò!— Qual per es- so pro-vo a- mo- re,
tion For his loss, no words can show!— Ah! for him my warm de- vo- tion,

qual per es- so pro-vo a-mo- re ma-dre in ter- ra non- pro- vò.
Ah! for him, my warm de- vo- tion, No earth-ly moth-er else— can know.

Ferrando.

Ah! those features!

Count.

Say, long time
Didst thou abide among those mountains?

Azucena.

Long time, yes.

Ferrando.

(Il suo volto.)

Conte.

Di' traesti
Lunga etade fra quei monti?

Azucena.

Lunga, sì.

Count.
Dost thou remember
A child, son of a noble,
Who was stolen from his castle
Many years since and carried thither?

Azucena.
And thou, tell me—art?

Count.
A brother
Of the lost one.

Azucena.
Ah!

Ferrando.
Yes!
(Noting the ill-concealed terror of AZUCENA.)

Count.
Hast heard what there befell him?

Azucena.
I?—No!—Oh! grant
That I may now my search continue.

Ferrando.
Stay, impostor!

Azucena.
(Alas!)

Ferrando.
Thou seest here
The guilty wretch who that dark crime
Committed!

Count.
Continue!

Ferrando.
Behold her.

Azucena.
Silence!
(Softly to FERRANDO.)

Ferrando.
'Tis she, who stole the child, and burned
him!

Count.
Ah! guilty one!

Chorus.
'Tis the same one!

Azucena.
He speaks falsehood.

Conte.
Rammenteresti
Un fanciul, prole di conti,
Involato al suo castello,
Son tre lustri, e tratto quivi?

Azucena.
E tu, parla—sei?

Conte.
Fratello
Del rapito.

Azucena.
(Ah!)

Ferrando.
(Sì!)
(Notando il mal nascoto terrore di AZUCENA.)

Conte.
Ne udivi
Mai novella?

Azucena.
Io?—No!—Concedi
Che del figlio l'orme io scopra.

Ferrando.
Resta, iniqua—

Azucena.
(Ohimè!)

Ferrando.
Tu vedi
Chi l'infame, orribil opra
Commettea!

Conte.
Finisci.

Ferrando.
E dessa!

Azucena.
(Taci.)
(Piano a FERRANDO.)

Ferrando.
E dessa, che il bambino arse!

Conte.
Ah, perfida!

Coro.
Ella stessa!

Azucena.
Ei mentisce

Count.
Thou canst not fly
Thy fate impending.

Azucena.
Ah!

Count.
Those bonds
Draw still more closely.
(The soldiers obey.)

Azucena.
Oh! heaven! Oh! heaven!

Chorus.
Vent thy rage!

Azucena.
And comest thou not,
My son, Manrico, to release me?
Thy unhappy mother now
To aid and succor?

Count.
Thou the mother of Manrico?

Ferrando.
Tremble!

Count.
Oh! fate! thus in my power!

Azucena.
Ah! loose awhile, ye monsters vile,
These bonds that now confine me.
Such fierce and cruel torments
To lingering death consign me!
Descendant of a wicked sire,
Than he more guilty, tremble!
For God protects the weak,
And he will punish thee!

Count.
Thy son, oh, wretched Zingara,
Is he that base betrayer?
And can I, thee condemning,
Strike, too, the traitor's heart?
The joy my soul o'erflowing,
Words lack the power of showing!
To my arm, for vengeance, a brother's ashes
    call!
Avenged in full shall they be!

Ferrando and Chorus.
Base wretch, the fatal pile prepared,

Conte.
Al tuo destino.
Or non fuggì.

Azucena.
Deh!

Conte.
Quei nodi
Più stringete
(I soldati esequiscono.)

Azucena.
Oh, Dio! Oh, Dio!

Coro.
Uria pure.

Azucena.
E tu non m'odi,
Oh, Manrico,—oh, figlio mio?
Non soccorri all' infelice
Madre tua!

Conte.
Di Manrico genitrice!

Ferrando.
Trema!

Conte.
Oh, sorte! in mio poter!

Azucena.
Deh, ralentate, o barbari,
Le acerbe mie ritorte—
Questo crudel supplizio
E prolungata morte!
D' iniquo genitore
Empio figliuol peggiore,
Trema—V' è Dio pe' miseri,
E Dio ti punirà!

Conte.
Tua prole, o turpe zingara,
Colui, quel seduttore!
Portò col tuo supplizio
Ferirlo in mezzo al core!
Gioja m'inonda il petto,
Ciu non esprimo il detto!
Meco il fraterno cenore
Piena vendetta avra!

Ferrando e Coro.
Infame, pira sorgere;

Ah! yes, thou soon shalt see
Bright flames the heavens illuming!
Not this alone awaits thee,
These earthly fires consuming!
Condemned to flames infernal
There shall thy wicked spirit dwell!

(AZUCENA is dragged away by the soldiers, by command
of the COUNT.   He enters the tent, followed by FERRANDO.)

SCENE II—Hall adjoining the Chapel of Castellor; a
balcony in the background.

(MANRICO, LEONORA, RUIZ.)

Leonora.

Ah! what clamor of arms
Is that which reached me?

Manrico.

Great is the danger;
Vain are all my attempts to hide it!
At early dawn to-morrow
The foe will assail us.

Leonora.

Alas! what sayst thou?

Manrico.

Be assured that our swords will be victori-
ous!
We can equal them
In arms, boldness, and courage.
Depart.
(To RUIZ.)
The preparations for the strife
In my absence, thou wilt accomplish.
Let nought be wanting.
(Exit RUIZ.)

Leonora.

What a sombre splendor
Is o'er our bridal shining!

Manrico.

All this mournful foreboding
Pray banish, dearest!

Leonora.

And can I?

Manrico.

'Tis love, sublime emotion, at such a mo-
ment
Bids thy heart still be hopeful.
Ah! love; how blest our life will be

Empia, vedrai tra poco—
Nè solo tuo supplizio
Sarà l'orrendo foco!
Le vampe dell' inferno
A te fian rogo eterno;
Ivi penare ed ardere
L'anima tua dovrà!

(Al cenno del CONTE, i soldati traggono seco loco AZUCENA.
Egli entra nella sua tenda, seguito da FERRANDO.)

SCENA II—Sala adjacente alla Cappella in Castellor, con
verone in fondo.

(MANRICO, LEONORA, e RUIZ.)

Leonora.

Quale d'armi fragore
Foc' anzi intesi?

Manrico.

Alto è il periglio!—Vano
Dissimularlo fora!
Alla novella aurora
Assaliti saremo!

Leonora.

Ahimè!—che dici!

Manrico.

Ma de' nostri nemici
Avrem vittoria.—Pari
Abbiamo al loro ardir, brando e coraggio
Tu va.
(a RUIZ).
Le belliche opre,
Nell' assenza mia breve, a te commetto.
Che nulla manchi!
(RUIZ parte.)

Leonora.

Di qual tetra luce
Il nostro imen risplende!

Manrico.

Il presagio funesto,
Deh, sperdi, o cara!

Leonora.

E il posso?

Manrico.

Amor—sublime amore,
In tal istante ti favella al core.
Ah! sì, ben mio, coll' essere
Io tuo, tu mia consorte,

Our fond desires attaining,
My soul shall win fresh ardor,
My arm new courage gaining.
But, if, upon the fatal page
Of destiny impending,
I'm doomed among the slain to fall,
'Gainst hostile arms contending,
In life's last hour, with fainting breath,
My thoughts will turn to thee.
Preceding thee to heaven, will death
Alone appear to me.

(Tones of organ heard from the neighboring chapel.)

Leonora.

The mystic tide of harmony
Within our hearts doth flow!
The church unfolds the raptures
From holy love that grow!

(While they are about to enter the chapel, RUIZ enters hurriedly.)

Ruiz.

Manrico!

Manrico.

How?

Ruiz.

The Zingara,
Yonder, in chains, behold her!

Manrico.

Oh, heaven!

Ruiz.

Led on by cruel men,
They near the stake already.

Manrico.

Oh, heavens! my limbs are failing me;
Shadows my eyes are veiling!

(Approaching the balcony.)

Leonora.

Thou tremblest!

Manrico.

With reason. Know the cause:
I am—

Leonora.

Thou'rt what?

Manrico.

Her offspring.
Ah! monsters! this dark revolting scene
Almost of my breath deprives me!

Avrò più l' alma intrepida,
Il braccio avrò più forte.
Ma pur, se nella pagina
De' miei destini è scritto,
Ch' io resti fra le vittime,
Dal ferro ostil trafitto,
Fra quegli estremi aneliti,
A te il pensier verrà, verrà,
E solo in ciel precederti
La morte a me parrà!

(Odesi il suono dell' organo dalla vicina cappella.)

Leonora.

L'onda de suoni mistici
Pura discende al cor!
Vieni; ci schiude il tempio
Gioje di casto amor!

(Mentre s' avviano giubilanti al tempio, RUIZ soppraggiunge frettoloso.)

Ruiz.

Manrico!

Manrico.

Che?

Ruiz.

La zingara,
Vieni, tra ceppi mira!

Manrico.

Oh, Dio!

Ruiz.

Per man de' barbari
Accesa è girà la pira.

Manrico.

Oh, ciel! mie membra oscillano—
Nube me copre il ciglio!

(Accostandosi al verone.)

Leonora.

Tu fremi.

Manrico.

E il deggio! Sappilo,
Io son—

Leonora.

Che mai?

Manrico.

Suo figlio!
Ah, vili! Il rio spettacolo
Quasi il respir m'invola!

Collect our forces without the least delay.
Ruiz—go—speed thee, quickly!
(Ruiz departs hastily.)

Raduna i nostri—affrettati.
Ruiz—va—torna—vola!
(Ruiz parte.)

DI QUELLA PIRA — *OF THAT DARK SCAFFOLD*   Air. (Manrico)

Di quel-la pi-ra l'or-ren-do fo-co   Tu-te le fi-bre
Of that dark scaf-fold, those flames as-cend-ing   Thrill thro' each fi-bre

m'ar-se av-vam-po!   Em-pi, spe-gne-te-la, o ch'io fra po-co   Col san-gue
with mad-d'ning glow!   Quench them, ye mon-sters vile or, still of-fend-ing,   To stay their

vos-tro la spe-gne-rò.   E-ra già fi-glio pri-ma d'a-
fu-ry, your blood shall flow!   I was her off-spring, ere love I

mar-ti, Non puo fre-nar-mi il tuo mar-tir!__ Ma-dre in-fe-
gave__ thee, In vain to hold__ me, thy griefs would try.__ Moth-er un-

li-ce, cor-ro a sal-var-ti, O te-co al-me-no cor-ro a mo-rir!
hap-py! I fly to save thee, Or, all else fail-ing, with thee to die.

Leonora.

Such heavy sorrows my heart o'erpowering.
Oh! better far would it be to die!
(Re-enter Ruiz, with Soldiers.)

Ruiz.

Arouse ye to arms now!
The foe we will defy!

(Manrico rushes out, followed by Ruiz and Soldiers. From within a noise of arms and warlike instruments is heard.)

END OF THE THIRD ACT.

Leonora.

Non reggo a colpi tanto funesti.
Oh, quanto meglio saria morir!
(Entra Ruiz, torna armati.)

Ruiz.

All' armi, all' armi! eccone presti
A pugnar teco, teco a morir.

(Manrico parte frettoloso seguìto da Ruiz, e dagli armati, mentre odesi dall' interno fragor d'armi e di bellici strumenti.)

FINE DELL' ATTO TERZO.

ACT IV.

THE PUNISHMENT.

SCENE I—A wing of the palace of Aliaferia; in the angle, a tower with window secured by iron bars. Night; dark and clouded.

(Enter LEONORA and RUIZ, enveloped in cloaks.)

Ruiz (in an undertone).

Here stay we;
Yonder's the tower where are confined the prisoners for state offences;
Hither they brought him whom we are seeking.

Leonora.

Go thou:
Leave me here; be not anxious for my safety;
Perchance I yet may save him.
(RUIZ retires.)
Afraid for me? Secure
And ready are my defences!
(She gazes upon a jewel which she wears on her right hand.)
In this dark hour of midnight
I hover round thee near approaching.
Unknown to thee, love! Ye moaning breezes around me playing.
In pity aid me, my sighs to him conveying!

ATTO IV.

IL SUPPLIZIO.

SCENA I—Un' ala del palazzo dell' Aliaferia—all' angolo una torre, con finestre assicurate da spranghe dì ferro. Notte oscurissima.

(Si avanzano due personne ammentellate; sono RUIZ e LEONORA.)

Ruiz (sommessamente).

Siam giunti:
Ecco la torre, ove di stato
Gemono i prigionieri.—Ah! l'infelice
Ivi fu tratto!

Leonora.

Vanne.
Lasciami, nè timor di me te prenda—
Salvarlo io potrò, forse.
(RUIZ si allontana.)
Timor di me?—Sicura,
Presta è la mia difesa!
(I suoi occhi figgonsi ad una gemma che le fregia la man destra.)
In questa oscura
Notte ravvolta, presso a te son io,
E tu nol sai! Gemente
Aura, che intorno spiri,
Deh, pietosa gli arreca i miei sospiri.

D'AMOR SULL' ALI ROSEE — *ON ROSY WINGS OF LOVE*   Air. (Leonora)

de-sta_al-le me - mo - rie, Ai so-gni, ai so-gni dell' a - - mor,—
call to his fond re - mem - brance Sweet vi-sions, sweet vi-sions of our— love;—

Ma, deh! non dir-gli im-prov-vi-do le pe - ne, le pe-ne, le pe-ne del mio cor.
But, let no ac-cent re-veal to him The sor - rows, the sor-rows, the griefs my heart doth prove.

Deh! non dir - gli im-prov-vi-do le pe - - ne del mio cor, le pe -
Let no ac - cent re-veal to him the tri - - als I now prove, the sor -

ne, le pe - - - - - - - - ne del cor.
rows, the sor - - - - - - - - rows I prove.

Chorus (The passing bell.) (within).	**Voci** (Suona la campana dei morti.) (interne).
Have compassion upon a soul departing	Miserere d'un' alma già vicina
For that abode, from whence there's no re-turning;	Alla partenza che non ha ritorno;
Thy forgiveness, oh! power divine, imparting,	Miserere di lei, bontà divina,
Let him not be a prey to endless burning.	Preda non sia dell' infernal soggiorno.
Leonora.	**Leonora.**
That solemn petition, so sadly ascending,	Quel suon, quelle preci solemni, funeste,
With terror and mystery the air seems to fill!	Empiron quest' aere di cupo terrore!
'Gainst fatal foreboding my heart is con-tending,	Contende l'ambascia, che tutta m'investe
My breath is suspended, my pulses are still.	Al labbro il respiro. i palpiti al core!

AH, CHE LA MORTE — *AH, HOW DEATH*   Air (Manrico)

Ah!— che la mor-te o-gno - ra   È — tar-da nel ve-nir A chi de-
Ah!— how death still de - lay - eth,   Lin - gers, or seems to fly From him, who

si - a, a chi de - si - a mo-rir! Ad-dì - o, ad - dio, Leo-no-ra ad-di - o!

long-eth, from him who long-eth to die! Fare-well,— love, fare-well, Leo - no - ra, fare - well!

Leonora.

Oh, heaven! faintness o'erpowers me!

Chorus
(within).

Have compassion upon a soul departing

For that abode, from whence there's no returning;

Thy forgiveness, oh! power divine, impart-
ing,

Let him not fall a prey to endless burning.

Leonora.

O'er yonder dark tower, ah, death waits the
morrow

With wings pale and shadowy his watch
seems to hold.

Ah! ne'er will they open those portals of sorrow

'Till after the victim is lifeless and cold.

Manrico
(in the tower).

Now with my life fulfilling

Love's fervent vows to thee!

Do not forget; let me remembered be.

Farewell, my love, farewell, Leonora!

Leonora.

And can I ever forget thee!

Thou shalt see that more enduring

Love, than mine, ne'er had existence,

Triumph over fate securing,

Death shall yield to its resistance.

At the price of mine, now blighted,

Thy dear life will I defend,

Or again with thee united,

To the tomb will I descend!

(Enter the COUNT and his followers. LEONORA stands
aside.)

Count.

You hear me? Give the son to the axe

At daybreak; lead to the stake the mother.

(The followers enter the tower.)

Perhaps, thus acting, I abuse the power

Leonora.

Oh, ciel!—sento mancarmi!

Voci
(internè).

Miserere d'un' alma già vicina

Alla partenza che non ha ritorno!

Miserere di lei, bontà divina,

Preda non sia dell' infernal soggiorno!

Leonora.

Sull' orrida torre, ah! par che la morte

Con ali di tenebre librando si và!

Ahi! forse dischiuse gli fian queste port

Sol quando cadavere già freddo ei sarà!

(Rimane assorta, dopo qualche momento scuotesi, ed _ in
procinto di partire, allorchè vienne dalla torre un gemito
e quindi un mestò suono; elle si ferma.)

Manrico.
(Dalla torre.)

Sconto col sangue mio

L'amor che posi in te!

Non ti scordar di me!

Leonora, Addio!

Leonora.

Di te, di te scordar me!

(S'apre una porta.)

Tu vedrai che amore in terra

Mai del mio non fù più forte:

Vinse il fato in aspra guerra,

Vincerà la stessa morte.

O col prezzo di mia vita

La tua vita salverò,

O con te per sempre unita

Nella tomba scenderò.

(Entra il CONTE, ed alcuni seguaci. LEONORA si pene in
disparte.)

Conte.

Udiste? Come albeggi,

La scure al figlio, ed alla madre il rogo.

(Entrano i seguaci per un piccolo uscio nella torre.)

Abuso io forse quel poter che pieno

The prince to me confided.

To such excesses that woman's love constrains me!

But where to find her? Since Castellor is ours

Of her no tidings have reached me;

All my researches on every side are fruitless!

Ah! cruel love, where art thou?

Leonora   (advancing).

Standing before thee!

Count.

Those accents! Lady! thus near me?

Leonora.

Thou see'st me.

Count.

What brought thee hither?

Leonora.

Already his last hour approaches

And thou dost ask me?

Count.

Thou still wouldst dare me?

Leonora.

Ah, yes! for him

I would ask of thee compassion.

Count.

How? art thou raving?

Mercy to him, my rival, show?

Leonora.

May heaven with mercy inspire thee!

Count.

My whole desire is for vengeance. Go!

(LEONORA throws herself despairingly at his feet.)

In me trasmise li prence! A tal mi tragg:

Donna per me funesta!—Ov' ella è mai?

Ripresso Castellor, di lei contezza

Non ebbi, e furo indarno

Tante ricerche e tante!

Oh!—dove sei crudele?

Leonora   (avanzandosi).

A te dinante.

Conte.

Qual voce!—Come!—tu, donna?

Leonora.

Il vedi.

Conte.

A che venisti?

Leonora.

Egli è gia presso

All' ora estrema, e tu lo chiedi?

Conte.

Osar potresti?

Leonora.

Ah, si, per esso

Pietà domando—

Conte.

Che! tu deliri!

Io del rivale sentir pietà?

Leonora.

Clemente il Nume a te l'inspiri—

Conte.

E sol vendetta mio nume. Va!

(LEONORA si getta disperata ai suoi piedi.)

MIRA DI ACERBE — *WITNESS THE TEARS OF AGONY*   Air (Leonora)

Mi - ra, dia-cer - be la-gri-me Spar - gqal tuo pie-deun ri - o.
Wit-ness the tears of ag - o - ny Here, at thy feet, now rain-ing

Non bas-tail pian-to? sve - na-mi, Ti be - vi il san-gue mi - o!
If these suf-fice not, tor-ture me, My life's crim-son cur-rent drain-ing!

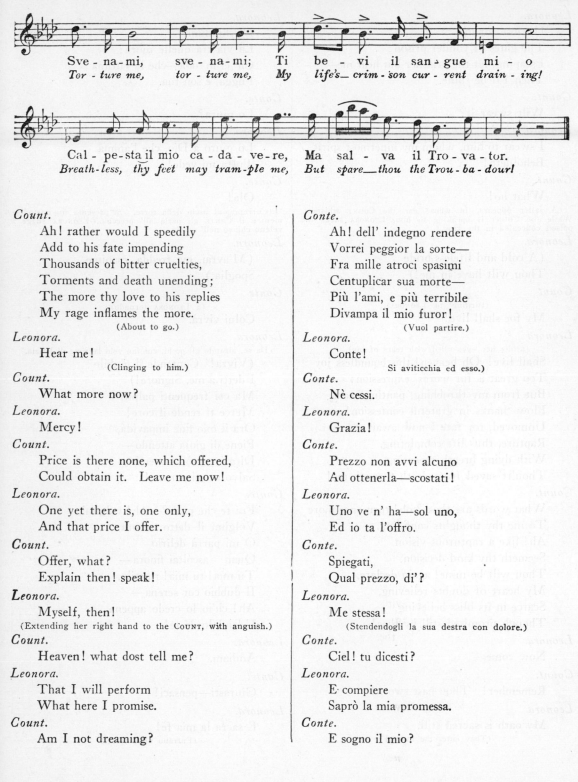

Sve - na - mi, sve - na - mi; Ti be - vi il san - gue mi - o
Tor - ture me, tor - ture me, My life's__ crim - son cur - rent drain - ing!

Cal - pe - sta il mio ca - da - ve - re, Ma sal - va il Tro - va - tor.
Breath - less, thy feet may tram - ple me, But spare__ thou the Trou - ba - dour!

Count.
Ah! rather would I speedily
Add to his fate impending
Thousands of bitter cruelties,
Torments and death unending;
The more thy love to his replies
My rage inflames the more.
(About to go.)

Leonora.
Hear me!
(Clinging to him.)

Count.
What more now?

Leonora.
Mercy!

Count.
Price is there none, which offered,
Could obtain it. Leave me now!

Leonora.
One yet there is, one only,
And that price I offer.

Count.
Offer, what?
Explain then! speak!

Leonora.
Myself, then!
(Extending her right hand to the COUNT, with anguish.)

Count.
Heaven! what dost tell me?

Leonora.
That I will perform
What here I promise.

Count.
Am I not dreaming?

Conte.
Ah! dell' indegno rendere
Vorrei peggior la sorte—
Fra mille atroci spasimi
Centuplicar sua morte—
Più l'ami, e più terribile
Divampa il mio furor!
(Vuol partire.)

Leonora.
Conte!
(Si aviticchia ed esso.)

Conte.
Nè cessi.

Leonora.
Grazia!

Conte.
Prezzo non avvi alcuno
Ad ottenerla—scostati!

Leonora.
Uno ve n' ha—sol uno,
Ed io ta l'offro.

Conte.
Spiegati,
Qual prezzo, di'?

Leonora.
Me stessa!
(Stendendogli la sua destra con dolore.)

Conte.
Ciel! tu dicesti?

Leonora.
E compiere
Saprò la mia promessa.

Conte.
E sogno il mio?

Leonora.

Unclose for me
The gates of yonder prison;
Escaping, let the prisoner but hear me—
Then I'll be thine.

Count.

Wilt swear it?

Leonora.

I swear to him, whom my innermost spirit
Beholdeth!

Count.

What ho!

(A jailer appears, in whose ear the COUNT whispers. While the COUNT is speaking to him, LEONORA sucks the poison concealed in the ring.)

Leonora.

(A cold and lifeless bride
Thou wilt have in me!)

Count
(turning to LEONORA).

My foe shall live!

Leonora
(aside, her eyes filled with tears of joy).

Shall live! Oh heaven! this boundless joy
Too great is for words' expression;
But from my throbbing, panting heart
Flow thanks in grateful confession!
Unmoved, my fate I now await;
Rapture, thus life completing,
With dying breath repeating
Thou'rt saved from death through me!

Count.

What words are those? oh! turn once more
To me thy thoughts confiding.
Ah! like a rapturous vision
Seemeth thy kind decision.
Thou wilt be mine! again declare,
My heart of doubts relieving,
Scarce in its bliss believing,
Though promised still by thee!

Leonora.

Now come—

Count.

Remember! Thou hast sworn!

Leonora.

My oath is sacred still.

(They enter the tower.)

Leonora.

Dischiudimi
La via tra quelle mura;
Ch' ei m' oda—che la vittima
Fugga, e son tua.

Conte.

Lo giura?

Leonora.

Lo giuro a Dio, che l'anima
Tutta mi vede!

Conte.

Ola!

(Correndo al uscio della torre. Si presenta un custode—mentre il CONTE gli parla all' orecchio, LEONORA sugge il veleno chiuso nell' anello.

Leonora.

(M'avrai, ma fredda, esanime
Spoglia.)

Conte
(a LEONORA tornado).

Colui vivrà.

Leonora
(Da sè, alzando gli occhi, cui fan velo lagrime di letizia.)

(Vivra! Contende il giubilo
I detti a me, Signore!)
Ma coi frequenti palpiti
Mercè ti rende il core!
Ora il mio fine impavida,
Piene di gioja attendo—
Dirgli potrò, morendo;
Salvo tu sei per me!

Conte.

Fra te che parli?—Ah! volgimi.
Volgimi il detto ancora,
O mi parrà delirio
Quan ascoltai finora—
Tu mia! tu mia! ripetilo,
Il dubbio cor serena—
Ah! ch'io lo credo appena
Udendolo da te!

Leonora.

Andiam.

Conte.

Giurasti—pensaci!

Leonora.

E sacra la mia fè!

(Entrano nella torre.)

SCENE II—A gloomy dungeon.

(AZUCENA lying upon an old mattress, MANRICO seated near her.)

Manrico.

Mother, thou sleepest not?

Azucena.

I have sought for slumber,
But, ah! it flies from my weary eyelids!—
I'll pray.

Manrico.

'Tis the air, cold and damp,
Perchance, with chills disturbs thee?

Azucena.

No; but from this tomb
Of the living would I escape forever,
Where confinement o'erpowers and suffo-
cates me.

Manrico.

Escape!   (Wringing his hands.)

Azucena.

Do not distress thee;
                    (Rising.)
These cruel tyrants cannot long oppress me.

Manrico.

Ah, wherefore?

Azucena.

Look ye! and behold already upon my brow
The finger of death has left its impress!

Manrico.

Ah!

Azucena.

They will find here
But a lifeless form, silent, cold and dead!
Merely a skeleton!

Manrico.

Cease ye!

Azucena.

Dost hear not?—coming footsteps—
Ah! the jailors approach, who to the stake
will drag me!
Defend, and save thy mother!

Manrico.

There's no one,
Resume thy courage. There's no one here
approaching.

SCENA II—Orrido carcere.

(AZUCENA giacente sopra una specie di rozza coltre, MANRICO seduto a lei d'appresso.)

Manrico.

Madre, non dormi!

Azucena.

L'invocai più volte,
Ma fugge il sonno a queste luci, prego.

Manrico.

L'aura fredda è molesta
Alle tue membre forse?

Azucena.

No; da questa
Tomba di vivi sol fuggir vorrei,
Perchè sento il respiro soffocarmi!

Manrico.

Fuggir!   (Torcendosi le mani.)

Azucena.

Non attristarti;
                    (Sorgendo.)
Far di me strazio non potranno i crudi!

Manrico.

Ah! come?

Azucena.

Vedi? le sue forsche, impronte
M' ha già stampate in fronte
Il dito della morte!

Manrico.

Ahi!

Azucena.

Troveranno
Un cadavere muto, gelido!—anzi
Uno scheletro!

Manrico.

Cessa!

Azucena.

Non odi?—gente appressa!
I carnefici son—vogliono al rogo
Trarmi!—Difendi la tua madre!

Manrico.

Alcuno.
Ti rassicura, quì non volge.

Azucena.

    The scaffold!

    That word of terror!

Manrico.

    Oh! mother! oh! mother!

Azucena.

    One morning

    Fierce crowds assembled, seized my mother and led her

    To torture! Mark how the abhorrent flames curl!

    Round her they madly cling! her hair consuming

    Now streams upward to heaven!

    Observe the glaring eyeballs

    From their orbits protruding! Ah! who has brought me

    To behold this dread vision?

    (Falls convulsed in the arms of MANRICO.*)*

Manrico.

    If filial love and words of affection

    Have power to move thy feelings maternal,

    Strive to banish these terrors,

    And seek in slumbers forgetful, both rest and composure.

    (Conducts her to the mattress.)

Azucena.

    Il rogo!

    Parola orrenda!

Manrico.

    Oh, madre!—oh, madre!

Azucena.

    Turba feroce l'ava tua condusse

    Al rogo—mira la terribil vampa!

    Ella n' è tocca già!—già l'arso crine

    Al ciel manda faville!—

    Osserva le pupille

    Fuor dell' orbita lor!—Ahi!—chi mi toglie

    A spettacol sì stroce!

    (Cadendo tutta convulsa tra le braccia di MANRICO.*)*

Manrico.

    Se m'ami ancor, se voce

    Di figlio ha possa di una madre in core,

    Ai terrori dell' alma

    Obli cerca nel sonno, e posa e calma.

    (La conduce presso la coltre.)

SI, LA STANCHEZZA – *YES, HEAVY WOES* Duet. (Manrico and Azucena)

Sì; la stan-chez-za m'op-pri-me o figlio, Al-la qui-e-te io
Yes; heav-y woes, and fa-tigue op-press me, Clos-ing my eyes, I to

chiu-do il ci-glio. Ma, se del ro-go ar-der si ve-da L'or-ri-da
sleep ad-dress me. But, should that dark pile rise up be-fore thee, With flames as-

fiam-ma, de-sta-mi al-ler. Ri-po-sa, o ma-dre; Id-di-o con-ce-da
cend-ing, wake me a-gain. Re-pose, O mo-ther: may Heav'n watching o'er thee

Men tri-sti im-ma-gi-ni al tuo cor.   Ai no-stri mon-ti
Send thee bright vi-sions, sooth-ing thy pain   *Back to our moun-tains,*

ri-tor-ne-re-mo, L'an-ti-ca pa-ce i vi go-dre-mo! Tu can-te-
our steps re-tra-cing, There, peace and qui-et once more em-bra-cing, Songs thou wilt

ra-i,   sul tuo li-u-to,   In son-no pla-ci-do io dor-mi-rò.
sing me   with lute at tend-ing, Sweet dreams shall vis-it our sleep as of yore.

MAN.

Ri-po-sa o ma-dre; io pro-no e mu-to La mente al cie-lo_ ri-vol-ge-
Re-pose, O moth-er;— si-lent-ly bend-ing O'er thee, my spir-it_heav'n-ward shall

AZU.

Tu can-te-ra-i sul tu-o li-u-to   In son-no
Loved songs thou'lt sing me thy soft lute aid lend-ing. Sweet dreams shall

MAN.

rò.   La men-te al
soar.   *My soul, with de-*

pla-ci-do io dor-mi-rò, tu can-te-ra-i, sul tu-o li-
vis-it our sleep as of yore. Loved songs thou'lt sing me, thy soft lute aid

cie-lo_ ri-vol-ge-rò,
vo-tion heav'n-ward shall soar.

u - to, In son - no pla - ci - do io dor - mi - rò, Io
lend - ing, Sweet dreams shall vis - it our sleep as of yore, Sweet

La men - te al cie - lo___ ri - vol - ge - rò.
My soul, with de - vo - tion,___ heav'n-ward shall soar.

dor - mi - rò, Io dor - mi - rò, Io dor - mi - rò,
dreams of yore, Sweet dreams of yore, Sweet dreams of yore,

Ri - po - sa, o ma - dre, ri - po - sa, o
Re - pose thee, O moth - er, re - pose thee, O

Io dor - mi - rò, Io dor - mi - ro, Io dor - mi - ro.___
Sweet dreams of yore, Sweet dreams of yore, Sweet dreams of yore.___

ma - dre la men - te al ciel ri - vol - ge - rò.___
moth - er, my wear - y soul heav'n-ward shall soar.___

(Azucena yields herself to sleep; Manrico remains kneeling beside her.)

SCENE III—The door opens; enter Leonora.

Manrico.

How! In this darkness do I deceive me?

Leonora.

'Tis I, Manrico!

Manrico.

Oh! my Lenora!

Oh, heaven, dost grant me in thy compassion

Rapture so boundless ere to death they lead
me?

(Azucena si addormenta; Manrico resta genuflesso accante
a lei.)

SCENA III—Si apre la porta, entra Leonora.

Manrico.

Che!—non m'inganno! quel fioco lume!

Leonora.

Son io, Manrico—

Manrico.

Oh, mia Leonora!

Ah, mi concedi, pietoso Nume,

Gioja si grande, anzi ch'io morra?

Leonora.

Thou shalt not die, love! I come to save thee.

Manrico.

Truly! to save me? What meanest thou?

Leonora.

Farewell, love!
Let nought delay thee, depart now, quickly!

Manrico.

Thou comest not with me?

Leonora.

I must remain here!

Manrico.

Remain!

Leonora.

Ah, fly thee!

Manrico.

No.

Leonora.

Woe awaits thee!
(Endeavoring to force him towards the door.)

Manrico.

No!

Leonora.

Life's before thee!

Manrico.

Ah! no, I scorn it!
But, lady, bend thy gaze upon me!
Whence comes this power? what price has bought it?
Thou wilt not speak? oh, dark suspicion!
'Twas from my rival thou purchased thy mission!
Ah! thou hast sold him thy heart's affection!
Bartered a love, once devoted to me!

Leonora.

Oh, how thine anger doth blind thy vision!
Oh, how unjust is thy cruel suspicion!
Obey. and fly thee, not heaven's protection,
If thou dost linger, can succor thee!

Azucena
(sleeping).

Back to our mountains, our steps retracing.
There peace and quiet once more embracing.

Leonora.

Tu non morrai—vengo a salvarti.

Manrico.

Come!—a salvarmi?—Fia vero!

Leonora.

Addio!
Troncá ogni indulgio!—t'affretta!—parti!
(Accennandogli la porta.)

Manrico.

E tu non vieni?

Leonora.

Restar degg' io!

Manrico.

Restar!

Leonora.

Deh! fuggi!

Manrico.

No.

Leonora.

Guai se tardi!
(Cercando di trarlo verso l'uscio.)

Manrico.

No!

Leonora.

La tua vita!

Manrico.

Io la dispresso—
Pur—figgi, o donna, in me gli sguardi!—
Da chi l'avesti?—ed a qual prezzo?—
Parlar non vuoi?—Balen tremendo!—
Dal mio rivale!—intendo—intendo!—
Ha quest' infame l'amor venduto—
Venduto un core che mio giurò!

Leonora.

Ahi, come l'ira ti rende cieco!—
Ahi, quanto ingiusto, crudel sei meco!—
T' arrendi—fuggi, o sei perduto!—
O, il ciel nemmen salvar ti può!

Azucena
(Dormendo.)

Ai nostri monti ritorneremo—
L'antica pace—ivi godremo!

Songs thou wilt sing me with lute attending,
Sweet dreams shall visit our sleep as of yore.

Manrico.

Begone now!

Leonora
(casting herself down at the feet of MANRICO).

Oh! repulse me not!
See'st thou? I languish,
Oppressed and fainting.

Manrico.

Go! I hate thee now;
May curses blight thee!

Leonora.

Ah! cease reviling;
Curse me no more, but raise thy thoughts
To heaven in prayers for me
At this dark moment!

Manrico.

A chill through my bosom is swiftly coursing.

Leonora.

Manrico!
                    (Falls on her face.)
Manrico
                    (hastening to lift her up).

Lady! what mean you?
Tell me!

Leonora.

Death's cold hand is on me!

Manrico.

What, dying?

Leonora.

Ah! far more rapidly
The poison sped its mission
Than I intended!

Manrico.

Oh! mortal blow!

Leonora.

Feel now, my hand is freezing—
But here, within me, dread fires are burning!
                    (Placing her hand on her breast.)
Manrico.

Oh, heaven, what didst thou?

Leonora.

Sooner than live, another's bride,
Near thee, I preferred to die!

Tu canterai—sul tuo lïuto—
In sonno placido—io dormirò—

Manrico.

Ti scosta.

Leonora
                    (è caduta ai piedi di MANRICO).

Non respingermi—
Vedi?—Languente, oppressa,
Io manco—

Manrico.

Va—ti abbomino—
Ti maledico—

Leonora.

Ah, cessa!—
Non d'imprecar, di volgere
Per me la prece a Dio
E questa l'ora!

Manrico.

Un brivido corse nel petto mio!

Leonora.

Manrico!—
                    (Cade boccone.)
Manrico
                    (accorrendo a sollevarla).

Donna, svelami—
Narra—

Leonora.

Ho la morte in seno.

Manrico.

La morte!—

Leonora.

Ah, fu più rapida
La forza del veleno
Ch'io non pensava!—

Manrico.

Oh, fulmine!

Leonora.

Senti!—la mano è gelo—
Ma quì foco orribile
Arde—
                    (Toccandosi il vetto.)
Manrico.

Che festi—oh, cielo!

Leonora.

Prima che d'altri vivere,—
Io volli tua morir!—

Manrico.

    Insensate! and I this angel's love
    With curses dared repay!

Leonora.

    I strive no longer!

Manrico.

    Ah! hapless one!
        (The COUNT enters, but stops on the threshold.)

Leonora.

    Behold the moment! I'm dying, Manrico!
    Now, heavenly Father, pardon me, I implore
      Thee!

Count.

    (Ah! she deceived me purposely,
    That for him she might die!)
    The block awaits him!
        (To the soldiers, pointing out MANRICO.)

Manrico.

    Mother! farewell forever!
        (Goes out with the soldiers.)

Azucena
        (awakening).

    Manrico! my son, where art thou?

Count.

    To death delivered!

Azucena.

    Ah, stay thee! hear me—
        (The COUNT drags AZUCENA to the window.)

Count.

    Look ye!

Azucena.

    Heaven!

Count.

    'Tis over!

Azucena.

    The victim was thy brother!

Count.

    He! horrid fate!

Azucena.

    Thou art avenged, O mother!
        (Falls near the window.)

Count
        (with horror).

    And I still live!

Manrico.

    Insano!—Ed io quest' angelo
    Osava malodir!

Leonora.

    Più non— resisto!—

Manrico.

    Ahi, misera!—
        (Entra il CONTE, arrestandosi sulla seglia.)

Leonora.

    Ecco l'instante—io moro—
    Manrico!—Or la tua grazia,
    Padre del cielo, imploro!

Conte.

    (Ah! volle me deludere
    E per costui morir!)
    Sia tratto al ceppo!
        (Indicando agli armati MANRICO.)

Manrico.

    Madre!—Oh, madre, addio!
        (Parte, tra gli armati.)

Azucena
        (Destandosi.)

    Manrico!—Ov' è mio figlio?

Conte.

    A morte ei corre!—

Azucena.

    Ah ferma!—m'odi—
        (Franscinando AZUCENA presso la finestra.)

Conte

    Vedi!

Azucena.

    Cielo!

Conte.

    E spento!

Azucena.

    Egli era tuo fratello!—

Conte.

    Ei!—quale orror!

Azucena.

    Sei vendicata, O madre!
        (Cade a piè della finestra.)

Conte.

    E vivo ancor!
        (Inorridito.)

END OF THE OPERA.

LA TRAVIATA

by

GIUSEPPE VERDI

LIBRETTO ADAPTED FROM "LA DAME AUX CAMELIAS"
BY ALEXANDRE DUMAS FILS

THE STORY OF "LA TRAVIATA"

THE first act commences with a gay party in the house of Violetta (the heroine), a young and beautiful creature, thrown by circumstances, and the loss of her parents in childhood, into a course of voluptuous living. She is surrounded by a circle of gay and thoughtless beings like herself, who devote their lives to pleasure. Amongst the throng who crowd to her shrine is Alfred Germont, a young man, who becomes seriously enamored with Violetta. Touched by the sincerity of his passion, she yields to its influence, a new and pure love springs up in her heart, and for the first time she becomes conscious of the misery of her position, and the hollowness of the pleasures in which she has basked. In the second act, we discover her living in seclusion with her lover, in a country-house near Paris, three months after the events narrated in the preceding act. Alfred accidentally discovers that Violetta has been secretly selling her houses and property in Paris, in order to maintain this establishment; and, revolting at the idea of being a dependent on her bounty, he leaves hurriedly for Paris, to redeem his honor from this disgrace. During his absence, his father, who has discovered his retreat, arrives, and, representing to Violetta that his son's connection with her is not only lowering him in the opinion of the world, but will be ruinous to his family, inasmuch as his sister was betrothed to a wealthy noble, who had, however, declared his intention of renouncing her, unless Alfred would give up Violetta, the generous girl resolves to sacrifice her affections and happiness for her lover's sake, and returns alone to Paris, whither Alfred, overwhelmed with despair when he discovers her flight, follows her. We are then transported to a saloon in the hotel of Flora, one of Violetta's former friends, during a festival given by the fair mistress of the mansion. There Alfred again meets Violetta, now under the protection of the Baron Dauphol, and being unaware of the generous motive which made her desert him, he overwhelms her with reproaches, and flings a purse containing money at her feet, in the presence of the company. Degraded and heartbroken, the unfortunate Violetta returns home to die; and in the last act we find the sad romance of her life drawing to its close. Alfred, too late, learns the truth, and discovers the sacrifice she has made to secure his happiness. Penetrated with grief and shame, he hastens, with his father, to comfort and console her, and to offer her his hand and name in reparation of the wrong he has done her, — but too late. The fragile flower, broken on its stem, can never more raise its beauteous head. One gleam of happiness, the purest and brightest that she has known, arising from her lover's assurance of his truth, and his desire to restore her reputation, gilds the closing moments of her life, and in a transport of joy her soul suddenly quits its fragile tenement of clay.

LA TRAVIATA

ACT I.

SCENE I—A salon in the house of VIOLETTA; in the back scene is a door, which opens into another salon; there are also side doors; on the left is a fireplace, over which is a mirror. In the centre of the apartment is a dining-table, elegantly laid.

(VIOLETTA, seated on a couch, is conversing with the DOCTOR and some friends, whilst others are receiving the guests who arrive, among whom are the BARON, and FLORA on the arm of the MARQUIS.)

Chorus 1.

Past already's the hour of appointment—
You are tardy.

Chorus 2.

We played deep at Flora's,
And while playing the hours flew away.

Violetta.

Flora, and kind friends, the night is before
us.
Other pleasures we here will display.
(Goes to meet them.)
'Mid the wine-cups the hours pass more
gaily.

Flora.
Marquis. } Can you there find enjoyment?

Violetta.

I strive to;
Yes, to pleasure I yield, and endeavor
With such remedies illness to stay.

All.

Yes! enjoyment will lengthen our days.

SCENE II—The same. GASTON and ALFRED enter. Servants are busy about the table.

Gaston.

In Alfred Germont, fairest lady,
Another behold, who esteems you;
There are few friends like him; he's a treasure.

Violetta.

Thanks, dear Viscount, for so great a pleasure.
(She gives her hand to ALFRED, who kisses it.)

ATTO I.

SCENA I—Salotto in casa di VIOLETTA; nel fondo è la porta che mette ad altra sala; ve ne sono altre due laterali; a sinistra un caminetto con sopra uno specchio. Nel mezzo è una tavola riccamente imbandita.

(VIOLETTA seduta sur un divano sta discorrendo col DOTTORE, e con alcuni amici, mentre altri vanno ad incontrare quelli che sopraggiungono, tra' quali sono il BARONE e FLORA al braccio del MARCHESE.)

Coro 1.

Dell' invito trascorsa è già l' ora—
Voi tardaste.

Coro 2.

Giocammo da Flora,
E giocando quell' ore volâr.

Violetta.

Flora, amici, la notte che resta
D'altre gioie quì fate brilla—
(Andando ore incontre.)
Fra le tazze è più viva la festa.

Flora.
Marchese. } E goder voi potrete?

Violetta.

Lo voglio;
Alla danza m'affido, ed io soglio
Con tal farmaco i mali sopir

Tutti.

Sì, la vita s'addoppia al gioir.

SCENA II—Detti, il Visconte GASTONE DI LETORIERES, ALFREDO GERMONT; servi affaccendati interno all mensa.

Gastone.

In Alfredo Germont, o signora,
Ecco un altro che molto vi onora:
Pochi amici a lui simili sono.

Violetta.

Mio Visconte, mercè di tal dono.
(Dà la mano ad ALFREDO, che gliela bacia.)

Marquis.

Dear Alfred!

Alfred.

Kind Marquis!

(They shake hands.)

Gaston

(to ALFRED).

I told you

That combined here are friendship and pleasure.

(During this dialogue the servants have placed the viands upon the table.)

Violetta.

All is ready?

(A servant bows assent.)

My dear friends, be seated;

'Tis at the banquet that each heart unfolds.

Chorus.

Thou hast wisely the maxim repeated,

Cure for trouble the wine-cup still holds.

(They seat themselves, VIOLETTA between ALFRED and GASTON, and opposite to them FLORA, the MARQUIS, and the BARON; the rest take their seats promiscuously; there is a momentary silence, during which the dishes are passed round, and VIOLETTA and GASTON converse in an undertone.)

Gaston

(to VIOLETTA).

Thou'rt the sole thought of Alfred.

Violetta.

Art jesting?

Gaston.

Thou wert ill, and each day in distress

He came to ask thy condition.

Violetta.

Be silent;

No, I am naught to him.

Gaston.

I deceive not.

Violetta

(to ALFRED).

Is it true then? Can it be? Ah, I know not.

Alfred

(sighing).

Yes, it is true.

Violetta

(to ALFRED).

Grateful thanks, then, I give you.

(To the BARON.)

You, dear Baron, were not so enamored.

Baron.

But 'tis only a year I have known you.

Marchese.

Caro Alfredo!

Alfredo.

Marchese!

(Si stringono la mano.)

Gastone

(ad ALFREDO).

T' ho detto

L' amistà quì s' intreccia al diletto.

(I servi frattanto avranno imbandite le vivande.)

Violetta.

Pronto è il tutto?

(Un servo accenna che sì.)

Miei cari, sedete;

E al convito che s' apre ogni cor.

Tutti.

Ben diceste—le cure segrete

Fuga sempre l'amico licor.

(Siedono in modo che VIOLETTA resti tra ALFREDO e GASTONE; di fronte vi sarà FLORA, il MARCHESE ed il BARONE; gli altri siedono a piacere. Vi ha un momento di silenzio; frattanto passano i piatti, e VIOLETTA e GASTONE parlano sotto voce tra loro.)

Gastone.

Sempre Alfredo a voi pensa.

Violetta.

Scherzate?

Gastone.

Egra foste, e ogni dì con affanno

Quì volò, di voi chiese.

Violetta.

Cessate.

Nulla son io per lui.

Gastone.

Non v' inganno.

Violetta

(ad ALFREDO).

Vero è dunque?—Onde ciò? Nol comprendo.

Alfredo

(sospirande).

Sì, egli è ver.

Violetta.

Le mie grazie vi rendo.

(Al BARONE.)

Voi, barone, non feste altrettanto.

Barone.

Vi conosco da un anno soltanto.

Violetta.

And Alfred a few minutes only.

Flora

(softly to the BARON).

'Twould be better if you had not spoken.

Baron

(softly to FLORA).

For this youth I've no liking.

Flora.

But why?

As for me, now, he pleases me well.

Gaston

(to ALFRED).

Thou art silent; hast nothing to offer?

Marquis.

Madame alone has the power to arouse him.

Violetta

(fills the glass of ALFRED).

I will fill, then, like Hebe!

Alfred.

And, like her,

I proclaim thee immortal.

All.

We pledge thee!

Gaston

(to the BARON).

Can you not, in this moment of pleasure,

Give a toast, or a gay tuneful measure?

(The BARON declines.)

(To ALFRED.)

Then wilt thou—

All.

Yes, yes, a drinking song.

Alfred.

I've no inspiration.

Gaston.

Art thou not then a singer?

Alfred

(to VIOLETTA).

Will it please you?

Violetta.

Yes.

Alfred

(rising).

Yes? Then I yield.

Marquis.

Pay attention!

Violetta.

Ed ei solo da qualche minuto.

Flora

(piano al BARONE).

Meglio fora, se aveste taciuto.

Barone

(piano a FLORA).

M'è increscioso quel giovin.

Flora.

Perchè?

A me invece simpatico egli è.

Gastone

(ad ALFREDO).

E tu dunque non apri più bocca?

Marchese

(a VIOLETTA).

E a madama che scuoterlo tocca.

Violetta

(mesce ad ALFREDO).

Saro l'Ebe che versa.

Alfredo.

E ch' io bramo

Immortal come quella.

(Con galanteria.)

Tutti.

Beviamo.

Gastone.

O Barone, nè un verso, nè un viva

Troverete in quest' ora giuliva?

(BARONE accenna di nò.)

(Ad ALFREDO.)

Dunque a te.

Tutti.

Sì, sì, un brindisi.

Alfredo.

L'estro non m'arride.

Gastone.

E non se' tu maestro?

Alfredo

(a VIOLETTA).

Vi fia grato?

Violetta.

Sì.

Alfredo

(si alza).

Sì?—L'ho in cor.

Marchese.

Dunque attenti.

All.

Yes, attention we'll pay!

Tutti.

Sì, attenti al cantor.

LIBIAMO NE' LIETI — *A BUMPER WE'LL DRAIN* (Alfred)

Li - bia - mo, li - bia - mo ne' lie - ti ca - li - ci che la bel - lez - za in fio - ra, e la fug - ge - vol, fug - gè - vol o - ra s'in - ne - brii a vo - lut - tà. Li - biam ne' dol - ci fre - mi - ti che su - sci - ta l'a - mo - re, poi - chè quel l'oc - chio al co - re on - ni - po - ten - te và Li - bia - mo, a - mo - re a - mor fra i ca - li - ci più cal - di ba - ci a - vrà.

A bump - er we'll drain from the wine - cup flow - ing, That fresh charms to beau - ty is lend - ing, O'er fleet - ing mo - ments, so quick - ly end - ing, Gay pleas - ure a - lone should reign. We'll drink the thrill - ing ec - sta - sies, That love ex - cites with - in us, When her bright eye doth win us, And ev - 'ry heart re - tain A bump - er to love, mid the wine - cups flow - ing, Fresh warmth will our pleas - ures re - gain.

Ah! to love, 'mid wine-cups flowing	Libiamo; amor fra i calici
New delight our joys will gain.	Più caldi baci avrà.
Violetta.	*Violetta* (s' alza).
Surrounded by you, I shall learn to lighten	Tra voi, saprò dividere
The footsteps of time with gladness;	Il tempo mio giocondo;
All of this world is but folly and madness	Tutto è follia nel monde
That is not pleasure gay	Ciò che non è piacer.
Enjoy the hour, for rapid	Godiam; fugace e rapido
The joys of life are flying—	E il gaudio dell' amore;

Like summer flow'rets dying—
Improve them while we may!
Enjoy! the present with fervor invites us,
Its flattering call obey.

All.

Enjoy then the wine-cup with songs of pleasure
That make night so cheerful and smiling,
In this charming paradise, beguiling,
That scarcely we heed the day.

Violetta
(to ALFRED).

The sum of life is pleasure.

Alfred
(to VIOLETTA).

While still unloved, unloving?

Violetta
(to ALFRED).

Experience ne'er has taught me.

Alfred
(to VIOLETTA).

And thus my fate must be.
(Music is heard in another room.)

All.

What's this?

Violetta.

Will you not join the gay group of dancers?

All.

Oh! a happy thought! We'll gladly join them.

Violetta.

Then let us enter!
(Approaching the door, VIOLETTA, seized with a sudden faintness, cries out:)

Alas!

All.

What ails thee?

Violetta.

Nothing, nothing.

All.

Why do you pause then?

Violetta.

Let's go now.
(Takes a few steps, but is obliged to re-seat herself.)

Oh, Heaven!

All.

Again still!

E un fior che nasce e muore
Nè più si può goder.
Godiam—c'invita un fervido
Accento lusinghier.

Tutti.

Godiam—la tazza e il cantico
Le notti abbella e il riso;
In questo paradiso,
Ne scuopra il nuovo dì.

Violetta
(ad ALFREDO).

La vita è nel tripudio.

Alfredo
(a VIOLETTA).

Quando non s'ami ancora.

Violetta
(ad ALFREDO).

No! dite a chi l'ignora.

Alfredo
(a VIOLETTA).

E il mio destin così.
(S' ode musica dall' altra sala.)

Tutti.

Che è cio.

Violetta.

Non gradireste ora le danze?

Tutti.

Oh, il gentile pensier!—Tutti accetiamo

Violetta.

Usciamo dunque?
(S' avviano alla porta di mezzo, ma VIOLETTA e colta d subito pallore.)

Ohimè!

Tutti.

Che avete?

Violetta.

Nulla, nulla.

Tutti.

Che mai v'arresta?

Violetta.

Usciamo.
(Fà qualche passo, ma è obbligata a nuovamente terman e sedere.)

Oh Dio!

Tutti.

Ancora!

Alfred.

Ah! you suffer—

All.

Oh, Heaven! what means this?

Violetta.

A sudden tremor seized me. Now—there, pray enter.

(Pointing to the other room.)

I will rejoin you ere long.

All.

As you desire, then.

(All pass into the other room, except ALFRED.)

SCENE III—VIOLETTA, ALFRED, afterward GASTON.

Violetta

(rises and regards herself in a mirror).

Ah me! how pale!

(Turning, she perceives ALFRED.)

You here?

Alfred.

Are you relieved from recent distress?

Violetta.

I'm better!

Alfred.

Ah, these gay revels soon will destroy thee.
Great care is needful—on this depends your being.

Violetta.

Canst thou then aid me?

Alfred.

Oh! wert thou mine now, with vigilance untiring
I'd guard thee with tenderest care.

Violetta.

What say'st thou?
Some one, perchance, then, cares for me?

Alfred

(confusedly).

No one in all the world doth love you.

Violetta.

No one?

Alfred.

I, only, love you.

Violetta.

Ah! truly!

(Laughing.)

Your great devotion I had quite forgotten.

Alfredo.

Voi soffrite.

Tutti.

Oh ciel!—ch'è questo?

Violetta.

E un tremito che provo—or là passate,

(Indicando l' altra stanza.)

Tra poco anch' io sarò.

Tutti.

Come bramate.

(Tutti passano all' altra sala, meno ALFREDO, che resta indietro.)

SCENA III—VIOLETTA, ALFREDO, e GASTONE, a tempo

Violetta

(si guarda nello specchio).

Oh, qual pallor!

Voi quì!

(Volgendosi s' accorge d' ALFREDO.)

Alfredo.

Cessata è l'ansia, che vi turbò?

Violetta.

Sto meglio.

Alfredo.

Ah, in cotal guisa v'ucciderete!
Aver v'è d'uopo cura dell' esser vostro

Violetta.

E lo potrei?

Alfredo.

Se mia foste, custode io veglierei
Pe' vostri soavi dì.

Violetta.

Che dite?
Ha forse alcuno cura di me?

Alfredo.

Perchè nessuno al mondo v'ama.

Violetta.

Nessun?

Alfredo.

Tranne sol io.

Violetta.

Gli è vero!

(Ridende.)

Si grande amor dimenticato avea.

Alfred.

Dost mock me? Have you a heart then?

Violetta.

A heart? Yes—haply—but why do you thus question?

Alfred.

Ah, if you had one you would not thus trifle with me.

Violetta.

Are you then truthful?

Alfred.

You, I deceive not.

Violetta.

'Tis long, that you have thus loved me?

Alfred.

Ah, yes; a year now.

Alfredo.

Ridete!—e in voi v' ha un core?

Violetta.

Un cor? Sì, forse—e a che lo richiedete?

Alfredo.

Oh, se ciò fosse, non potreste allora celiar.

Violetta.

Dite davvero?

Alfredo.

Io non v'inganno.

Violetta.

Di molto è che mi amate?

Alfredo.

Ah sì, da un anno.

UN DI FELICE—*ONE DAY, A RAPTURE* (Alfred)

Un di fe-li-ce e-te-re-a mi ba-le na-ste in-nan-
One day a rap-ture e-the-re-al Flash'd on my heart its bright-

te, e da quel di 'tre-man-te vis-si d'ig-no-to a-mor.
ness, And, since that day of light-ness, Life's on-ly aim has been love.

Di quell' a-mor, quell' a-mor ch'e pal-pi-to dell' u-ni-
Ah, yes, of love, of the love that pal-pi-tates Thro' all the

ver-so, dell' u-ni-ver-so in-te-ro, mi-ste-ri-o-so, mi-ste-ri-o-so al-
world, thro' cre-a-tion wide, ex-tend-ed; Oh, pow'r mys-te-rious, pow'r yet un-com-pre-

te-ro, cro-ce, cro-ce e de-li-zia, cro-ce e de-li-zia, de-li-zia al cor.
hend-ed Tor-ment, tor-ment and rap-ture, tor-ment and rap-ture, each do I prove.

Violetta.

 If this be true, ah! fly from me.
 Friendship alone I offer,
 I neither know nor suffer
 A feeling of such devotion.
 I am sincere and frank with thee;
 Look for one warmer, kinder;
 'Twill not be hard to find her,
 Then think no more of me.

Alfred.

 Oh love, sublime, yet mysterious,
 Power ne'er yet comprehended,
 Torments and raptures of love!

Gaston
    (appearing at the door).

 How now? What here employs you?

Violetta.

 Trifles and folly.

Gaston.

 Ah, that is well. Remain then.
    (Goes back.)

Violetta
    (to Alfred).

 Of love speak we no more. Is it agreed
  on?

Alfred.

 I will obey you—farewell.
    (About to depart.)

Violetta.

 Is such your pleasure?
    (Takes a flower from her bosom.)
 Then take with thee this flow'ret.

Alfred.

 And why?

Violetta.

 Soon to return it.

Alfred
    (returning).

 How soon?

Violetta.

 When its gay bloom is faded.

Alfred.

 Oh, joy! To-morrow!

Violetta.

 'Tis well—to-morrow!

Alfred.

 I am at last so happy!
    (Seizes the flower with transport.)

Violetta.

 Ah, se ciò è ver, fuggitemi—
 Pura amistade io v'offro;
 Amar non sò, nè soffro
 Di cosi eroico ardor.
 Io sono franca, ingenua;
 Altra cercar devoto—
 Non arduo troverete
 Dimentecarmi allor.

Alfredo.

 Oh amore misterioso,
 Misterioso altero,
 Croce e delizia al cor.

Gastone
    (presentandosi sulla porta di mezzo).

 Ebben?—che diavol fate?

Violetta.

 Si folleggiava.

Gastone.

 Ah, ah!—stà ben—restate.
    (Rientra.)

Violetta.

 Amor, dunque, non più—vi garba il patto?

Alfredo.

 Io v'obbedisco.—Partò.
    (Par andarsene.)

Violetta.

 A tal giungeste?
    (Si toglie un fiore dal seno.)
 Prendete questo fiore.

Alfredo.

 Perche?

Violetta.

 Per riportarlo.

Alfredo
    (tornando).

 Quando?

Violetta.

 Quando sarà appassito.

Alfredo.

 Allor domani?

Violetta.

 Ebbene domani.

Alfredo.

 Io son felice!
    (Prende con trasporto il fiore.)

Violetta.

You still declare you love me?

Alfred.

How much I love thee!

Violetta. (Going.)

You go then.

Alfred.

Yes, love! (Returns and kisses her hand.)

Violetta.

To-morrow—

Alfred.

More I will ask not.

(Exit.)

SCENE IV—VIOLETTA, and all the others, returning from the dancing-room.

All.

In the east the dawn is breaking,
And perforce we must depart,
Gentle lady, leave now taking,
Thanks we give thee from each heart.
Full the city is of pleasure,
Brief the time for love and joy,
To repose give needful measure,
Lest enjoyment we destroy!

(Exeunt.)

SCENE V—VIOLETTA, alone

How wondrous! how wondrous! those accents
Upon my heart are graven!
Will it misfortune bring me, a love in earnest?
What shall be thy resolve, my troubled spirit?
No living man hath yet enflamed thee!
Oh, rapture that I have known not, to be loved and loving.
Can my heart still disdain it
For follies dry and heartless, which now enchain me?

Violetta.

D' amarmi dite ancora?

Alfredo.

Oh, quanto v'amo!

Violetta. (Per partire.)

Partite?

Alfredo.

Parto. (Torna a lei, e le bacia la mano.)

Violetta.

Addio.

Alfredo.

Di più non bramo.

(Esce.)

SCENA IV—VIOLETTA e tutti gli altri che tornano dall sala della danza.

Tutti.

Si ridesta in ciel l' aurora,
E n' è forza ripartire;
Mercè a voi, gentil signora,
(a VIOLETTA).
Di sì splendido gioir
La città di feste è piena,
Volge il tempo del piacer;
Nel riposo omai la lena
Si ritempri per goder.

(Partono dalla destra.)

SCENA V—VIOLETTA sola.

E strano!—è strano!—In core
Scolpiti ho quegli accenti!
Saria per mia sventura un serio amore?
Che risolvi, o turbata anima mia?
Null' uomo ancora t' accendeva.—Oh, gioia
Ch'io non conobbi, esser amata amando!
E sdegnarla poss' io
Per l' aride follie del viver mio?

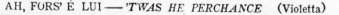

AH, FORS' È LUI — 'TWAS HE PERCHANCE (Violetta)

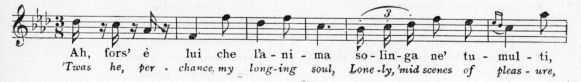

Ah, fors' è lui che l'a-ni-ma so-lin-ga ne' tu-mul-ti,
'Twas he, per-chance, my long-ing soul, Lone-ly, 'mid scenes of pleas-ure,

so - lin - ga ne' tu - mul - ti, go - dea so - ven - te pin - ge - re
lone - ly, 'mid scenes of pleas - ure, Oft loved to paint in col - ors bright,

de' suoi co - lo - ri oc - cul - ti, de' suoi co - lo - ri oc - cul - ti! Lui che, mo - des - to e
In its own gold and a - zure, In its own gold and a - zure. He, who with mod - est

vi - gi - le, all' e - gre sog - lia a - sce - se, e nuo - va feb - bre ac - ce - se
vi - gi - lance, To my sick room re - turn - ing, Kin - dled new flames, still burn - ing,

des - tan - do - mi all' a - mor! A quell a - mor, quell' a - mor che è pal - pi - to dell' u - ni -
Des - tined my heart to love! Yes! this is love, 'tis the love that pal - pi - tates Through all the

ver - so, dell' u - ni - ver - so in - te - ro, mi - ste - ri - o - so, mi - ste - ri - o - so al -
world, through cre - a - tion wide - ly ex - tend - ed, Oh, pow'r mys - te - rious, Pow'r ne'er yet com - pre -

te - ro, cro - ce, cro - ce e de - li - zia, cro - ce e de - li - zia, de - li - zia al cor.
hend - ed. Tor - ment, tor - ment and rap - ture, tor - ment and rap - ture each do we prove.

To my young heart, all guileless then,	A me, fanciulla, un candido
Filled with intrepid yearning,	E trepido desire
This dream was imaged, fair, serene,	Quest' effigiò, dolcissimo
Bright o'er my pathway burning.	Signor dell' avvenire,
When like a star from heaven,	Quando ne' cieli il raggio
Radiant he stood before me,	Di sua beltà vedea,
Visions of hope came o'er me.	E tutta me pascea
Like the fond dreams I wove.	Di quel soave error
Then beat my heart with the love that pal-	Sentia che amore è palpito
pitates	Dell' universo intero,

Through all the world, thro' creation wide
extended.

Oh! pow'r mysterious, pow'r ne'er yet comprehended.

Torment and rapture, each do we prove.

(Remains for an instant buried in thought, then says:)

What folly! All this is vain delirium!

Child of misfortune, lonely,

By all abandoned, in this gay crowded desert,

This vortex of pleasure they call Paris,

What hope remains? what must I do, then?

Surrender to pleasure's maddening whirl
again?

Misterioso, altero,

Pena e delizia al cor.

(Resta concentrata un istante poi dice.)

Follie!—follie!—delirio vano è questo!

In quai sogni mi perdo!

Povera donna, sola,

Abbandonata in questo popoloso deserto,

Che appellano Parigi,

Che spero or più?—Che far degg' io?—
gioire.

Di voluttà nei vortici finire.

SEMPRE LIBERA — *EVER FREE, SHALL I STILL WANDER* (Violetta)

la — re il mio pen - sier, dee___ vo - lar, dee___ vo
thoughts__ fly i - dly a - way, fly___ a - way, i - dly

lar   il pen-sier.
fly,   fly a - way.

(Exit on the left.)   (Parte, a sinistra.)

END OF THE FIRST ACT.   **FINE DELL' ATTO PRIMO.**

ACT II.

SCENE I—A country house near Paris. A salon on the ground floor. At the back, facing the audience, a fireplace, over which is a looking-glass. A clock hangs between two glass doors, which are closed. There are also two side doors, seats, tables, and writing materials.

(ALFRED enters, in sporting costume.)

Alfred.

Out from her presence, for me there's no enjoyment.

(Puts down his gun.)

Three months have flown already
Since my beloved Violetta
So kindly left for me her riches, admirers,
And all the haunts of pleasure,
Where she had been accustomed
To homage from all hearts, for charms transcendent,
Yet now contented in this retreat, so quiet,
She forgets all for me. Here, near my loved one,
New life springs within me;
From the trials of love restored and strengthened,
Ah! in my present rapture past sorrows are forgotten.

ATTO II.

SCENA I—Casa di Campagna presso Parigi. Salotto terreno. Nel fondo, in faccia agli Spettatori, è un camino, sopra il quale uno specchio ed un orologio, fra due porte chiuse da cristalli, che mettono ad un giardino. Al primo panno due altre porte, una di fronte all' altra. Sedie, tavolini, qualche libro, l'occorrente per scrivere.

(ALFREDO entra, in costume da caccia.)

Alfredo.

Lunge da lei per me non v' ha dilette!

(Depone il fucile.)

Volaron già tre lune
Dacchè la mia Violetta
Agi per me lascio, dovizie, onori.
E le pompose feste,
Ove agli omaggi avvezza,
Vedea schiavo ciascun di sua bellezza—
E dal suffio d'amor rigenerato
Solo esiste per me—qui presso a lei
Io rinascer mi sento,
E dal suffio d' amor rigenerato
Scordo ne' gaudj suoi tutto il passato.

DI MIEI BOLLENTI SPIRITI — *ALL MY IMPULSIVE ECSTASIES*   (Alfred)

De miei bol-len-ti spi - ri - ti   il gio-va-ni le ar - do - re,   el - la tem-prò col
All my im-pul-sive ec - sta-sies, Sprung from a youth-ful ar - dor, She hath sub-dued with

pla - ci - do sor - ri - so dell' a - mor, dell' a - mor! Dal di che dis - se:
peace - ful smiles,The smiles of hap-py love, hap-py love! Thus,since she whis-per'd,

vi - ve - re io vo - glio, io vo-glia te fe - del, dell' u - ni - ver - so im-
"Live for me, Still faith - ful, I will be true to thee." Of all the world for-

me - mo - re io vi - vo, io vi - vo qua - si, io vi - vo qua - si in
get - ful, free, The earth__ seems like heav'n to me, Yes, I seem in heav'n to

ciel. Dal di che dis - se: vi - ve - re io vo-glia te fe - del, si si,
be. Thus,since she whis-per'd "Live for me, I will be true to thee," Ah! yes,

dell' u - ni-ver-so im-me-mo - re io vi - vo,__ vi - vo qua-si, io vi-vo qua-si in
of all the world for - get - ful, free, The earth__ seems heav'n to me; now, I seem in heav'n to

ciel,   io vi - vo in ciel,   dell u - ni-ver-so im-me-mo-re   io vi-vo qua-si in
be! 'tis heav'n to me, Of all__ the world for-get-ful, now I seem in heav'n to

ciel,__ ah si, io vi - vo qua-si in cie - lo,   io vi - vo qua - si in ciel.
be,__ Ah, yes, in heav'n I seem to be, now in heav'n I seem to be.

SCENE II—The same, ANNINA, entering hastily, in a trav- elling dress.	SCENA II—Detto, ed ANNINA in arnese da viaggio.
Alfred.	*Alfredo.*
Whence have you come, Annina?	Annina! donde vieni?
Annina.	*Annina.*
From the city.	Da Parigi.
Alfred.	*Alfredo.*
By whom sent thither?	Chi tel commise!

Annina.

    My kind mistress sent me.

Alfred.

    For what purpose?

Annina.

    To sell her jewels, horses, carriages, and all that's left to her.

Alfred.

    Heard I rightly?

Annina.

    Great are the expenses of living here secluded.

Alfred.

    You ne'er told me!

Annina.

    My silence was commanded.

Alfred.

    Commanded! Much still is needed?

Annina.

    One thousand louis'!

Alfred.

    Now leave me. I go to Paris.

    Mind that your mistress knows nothing of these questions.

    Ere long I shall be able to repair all. Go—go!   (ANNINA goes out.)

SCENE III—ALFRED, alone.

Annina.

    Fu la mia signora.

Alfredo.

    Perchè?

Annina.

    Per alienar cavalli, cocchi, e quanto ancor possiede.

Alfredo.

    Che mai sento!

Annina.

    Lo spendio è grande a viver quì solinghi.

Alfredo.

    E tacevi?

Annina.

    Mi fu il silenzio imposto.

Alfredo.

    Imposto!—e v'al bisogna?—

Annina.

    Mille luigi.

Alfredo.

    Or vanne—Andrò a Parigi—

    Questo colluquio ignori la signora—

    Il tutto valgo a riparere ancora.

(ANNINA parte.)

SCENA III—ALFREDO, solo.

O MIO RIMORSO! — *OH! DARK REMORSE!* (Alfred)

O— mio ri-mor-so! oh in-fa-mia! io ___ vis-si in ta-le er - ro - re! ma il
Oh, dark re-morse! oh! in-fa-my! To ___ live in such blind ___ er - ror! From.

tur - pe son-no a fran-ge - re il ___ ver mi ba - le - no! Per
dreams so base, I wake at last To ___ truth, all now re - veal'd! One

po - co in se - no ac-que - ta - ti, o— gri-do, o gri-do dell' o' - no - re ___ m'a-
mo-ment more thy voice re-strain, Oh, cry, oh, cry of in-jured hon-or! ___ For

vrai se cu - ro - vin - de - ce, quest'___, on - ta la - ve - rò. oh, mio ros -
soon, ex-punged shall be the stain, Such___ shame-ful acts re - peal'd. Oh, blush of___

sor! oh in-fa - mia! ah si, quest' on-ta la - ve - rò si,___ la - ve -
shame! oh, base - ness! ah, yes such acts must be' re - peal'd, must be re -

rò, oh mio ros - sor! oh in-fa - mia! ah! si, quest' on-ta, sì quest'
peal'd. Oh, blush of___ shame! oh,___ base - ness!. ah, yes, this base-ness, yes, this

on - ta la - ve - rò quest' on - ta, quest' on-ta la - ve - rò.
shame must be re - peal'd, This base - ness, this act must be re - peal'd.

(Departs.)	(Esce.)
SCENE IV—VIOLETTA enters witn papers in her hand; ANNINA, JOSEPH.	SCENA IV—VIOLETTA, ch'entra con alcune carte, parlando, con ANNINA, poi GIUSEPPE a tempo.
Violetta (to ANNINA).	*Violetta.*
Alfred?	Alfredo!
Annina.	*Annina.*
He has gone to Paris, madame.	Per Parigi or or partiva.
Violetta.	*Violetta.*
When to return?	E tornerà?
Annina	*Annina.*
Before the day is ended, He bade me tell you.	Pria che tramonti il giorno—dirvel m'impose.
Violetta.	*Violetta.*
'Tis strange, this!	E strano!
Joseph (presents a letter)	*Giuseppe* (le presenta una lettera).
For you.	Per voi.
Violetta.	*Violetta* (la prende)
'Tis well. A business agent shortly will arrive here; At once admit him.	Sta bene. In breve Giungerà un uom d' affari—entri all' istante.
(Exeunt ANNINA and JOSEPH.)	(ANNINA e GIUSEPPE escono.)

SCENE V—Violetta, afterwards Germont, introduced by Joseph, who places two chairs, and goes out.

Violetta
                    (reading the letter).
  Ah! ah!
  So Flora hath my home discovered,
  And invites me to join a dance this evening!
  She'll look for me in vain!
    (Throws the letter on a table and seats herself.)

Joseph.
  A man would see you.

Violetta.
  'Tis the one I look'd for.
    (Bids Joseph show him in.)

Germont.
  Are you the lady of the house?

Violetta.
  I am, sir.

Germont.
  In me behold Alfred's father.

Violetta.
  You?
    (With surprise, invites him to be seated.)

Germont.
  Yes, of the imprudent, who goes fast to ruin,
  Led away by your follies.

Violetta
                    (rising, resentfully).
  Stay, sir, I am a lady in my own dwelling,
  And perforce I must leave you, for your
    sake more than mine.
    (About to retire.)

Germont.
  (What manners!)   But then—

Violetta.
  You have been led in error.
    (Returns to her seat.)

Germont.
  He will spend all his fortune upon you.

Violetta.
  He has not yet offered.   I should refuse.

Germont.
  How then such grandeur?
    (Looking around.)

Violetta
                    (gives him a paper).
  This deed is to all else a mystery—to you
    'twill not be

SCENA V—Violetta, quindi il Sig. Germont, introdotto da Giuseppe, che, avanza due siede, e parte.

Violetta
                    (leggendo la lettera).
  Ah, ah,
  Scuopriva Flora il mio ritiro!—
  E m'invita a danzar per questa sera!—
  In van m'aspetterà.
    (Getta il foglio sul tavolino e siede.)

Giuseppe.
  Giunse un signore.

Violetta.
  Ah! sarà lui che attendo.
    (Accenna a Giuseppe d'introd.)

Germont.
  Madamigella Valery?

Violetta.
  Son io.

Germont.
  D' Alfredo il padre in me vedete.

Violetta.
  Voi!
    (Sorpresa gli accenna di sedere.)

Germont.
  Sì, dell' incanto, che a rovina corre,
  Ammaliato da voi.
    (Sedendo.)

Violetta
                    (alzandosi risentita).
  Donna son io, signore, ed in mia casa;
  Ch'io vi lasci assentite,
  Più per voi, che per me.
    (Per uscire.)

Germont.
  (Quai modi!)   Pure—

Violetta.
  Tratto in error voi foste.
    (Torna a sedere.)

Germont.
  De' suoi beni donovuol farvi.

Violetta.
  Non l' oso finora.—Rifiuterei.

Germont.
  Pur tanto lusso—

Violetta
                    (gli da le carte)
  A tutti è mistero quest' atto.—A voi nol sia

Germont _(reads the paper)._

Heav'n, what a statement!
Have you then determined all your wealth
to dispose of?
But, your past life, ah, why must that accuse
you?

Violetta.

It does so no longer; Alfred I love now, and
Heav'n
Has cancell'd all the past with my repent
ance.

Germont.

Ah, you have noble feelings.

Violetta.

Like sweet music my ear receives your accents.

Germont _(rising)._

And of such feelings a sacrifice I ask now.

Violetta _(rising)._

Ah, no, pray do not!
A dreadful thing thou wouldst require, I'm
certain.
I foresaw it, with terror: ah, I was far too
happy!

Germont.

A father's honor requires it,
And the future of his two dear children
claims it.

Violetta.

Of two children?

Germont.

Yes.

Germont _(dopo averle scorse coll' occhio)._

D'ogni avere pensate dispogliarvi!—
Ah, il passato perchè, perchè v'accusa!

Violetta.

Più non esiste—or amo Alfredo, e Dio
Lo cancellò col pentimento mio.

Germont.

Nobile sensi invero!

Violetta.

Oh, come dolce mi suona il vostra accento!

Germont.

Ed a tai sensi un sacrifizio chieggo.

Violetta _(alzandosi)._

Ah, no, tacete—
Terribil cosa chiedereste certo—
Il predevi, v'attesi, era felice troppo.

Germont.

D'Alfredo il padre la sorte,
L'avvenir domanda or qui de' suoi due figli.

Violetta.

Di due figli?

Germont.

Sì.

PURA SICCOME UN ANGELO — _PURE AS AN ANGEL_ (Germont)

Allegro moderato

Pu - ra sic - co-me un an - ge -lo   Id - dio mi diè u-na   fi - glia,
Pure as an an - gel   from a-bove,   Kind heav'n a daugh-ter   gave   me,

se Al-fre-do nie - ga   rie - de - re   in   se no al-la fa - mi - glia,
If now Al-fre - do   to   our love Will   not   re - turn and save   me

l'a - ma-to e a-man - te   gio - vi - ne,   cui spo-sa an-dar do-
He, the be - lov'd and   lov - ing youth, Who soon should wed my

ve - - a,   or si ri - cu-sa al vin - co - lo che
daugh - - ter, Must then with-draw his plight - ed troth, With

lie - ti, lie-ti ne ren - de - va. Deh non mu-ta - te in tri - bo-li
all the joy, the joy it brought her. Then do not change love's ro - ses fair

le ro - se dell' a - mor, ah, non mu-ta - te in tri - bo-li le ro-se dell' a -
To thorns of grief and pain, Ah, do not change love's ro - ses fair To thorns of grief and

mor a' prie - ghi miei re - sis - te - re no, no, non vo-glia il vos-tro cor, no, no.
pain, Your gen - 'rous heart, to my fond pray'r, no, no, Will not op-posed re-main, no, no.

Violetta.	*Violetta.*
Ah! I see now, that I must for a season	Ah, comprendo—dovrò per alcun tempo
Be from Alfred parted. 'Twill be painful,	Da Alfredo allontanarmi—doloroso
Dreary for me, yet—	Fora per me—pur—
Germont.	*Germont.*
That will not suffice me!	Non è ciò che chiedo.
Violetta.	*Violetta.*
Heav'ns! What more dost seek for?	Cielo!—che più cercate?—offersi assai!
Enough I've offered!	
Germont.	*Germont.*
No, not quite yet.	Pur non basta.
Violetta.	*Violetta.*
You wish that I forever should renounce him?	Volete che per sempre a lui renunzi?
Germont.	*Germont.*
It must be.	E d'uopo.
Violetta.	*Violetta.*
Ah, no! I cannot—never!	Ah, no—giam no, mai!
Ah! thou know'st not what affection	Non sapete quale affetto
Burns within me, ardent, living!	Vivo, immensò in' arda il petto?

Not one kind friend or connexion
Can I number, still surviving?
But Alfred has declared it,
All in him my heart should find!
Ah! thou know'st not what dark sorrow
Mocked my being with its shadow?
All is over—how sad the morrow,
Parted thus from dear Alfred!
Ah! the trial is too cruel;
It were better far to die.

Germont.

The sacrifice is heavy;
But hear me with tranquillity.
Lovely thou art still, and youthful, too.
Hereafter—

Violetta.

No more persuade me. I know all,
But it cannot be. Him only I love and
live for!

Germont.

So be it. But the men are oft unfaithful
still—

Violetta (astounded).
Great Heaven!

Germont.

Some day, when love hath colder grown,
And time's broad gulf yawns wider;
When all the joys of life have flown,
What then will be? Consider!
No healing balm shall soothe your rest,
No warm and deep affection,
Since Heav'n your ties will ne'er have blest
With holy benediction.

Violetta.

'Tis all true!

Germont.

Then haste to dissipate the spell
Of this bright dream, controlling;
Be to my home and loved ones
Our angel, good, consoling.
Violetta, oh, consider well
While yet there may be time.
'Tis Heav'n itself that bids me speak,
'Tis Heav'n inspiring
These words in faith sublime.

Che nè amici, nè parenti
Io non conto tra' viventi?
E che Alfredo m' ha giurato
Che in lui tutto io troverò?
Non sapete che colpita
D'atro murbo è la mia vita?
Che già presso il fin ne vedo?
Ch'io mi separi da Alfredo!
Ah, il supplizio è si spietato,
Che morir preferiro.

Germont.

E grave il sacrifizio,
Ma pur, tranquilla udite.
Bella voi siete e giovane—
Col tempo—

Violetta.

Ah, più non dite—v'intendo—
M' è impossibile—Lui solo amar vogl'io.

Germont.

Sia pure—ma volubile sovente è l'uom.

Violetta (colpita).
Gran Dio!

Germont.

Un di, quando le veneri
Il tempo avrà fugate,
Fia presto il tedio a sorgere—
Che sarà allor!—pensate—
Per voi non avran balsamo
I più soavi affetti!
Da un genitor non furono
Tai nodi benedetti.

Violetta.

E vero!

Germont.

Ah, dunque, sperdasi
Tal sogno seduttore—
Siate di mia famiglia
L'angiol consolatore—
Violetta, deh pensateci,
Ne siete in tempo ancor.
E Dio che inspira, o giovane,
Tai detti a un genitor.

Violetta.

Thus, to the wretched, who falls, frail and erring,

When once again she would rise, hope is silent.

Though Heaven's indulgent, its pardon conferring,

Man unforgiving to her will be.

Say to this child of thine, young, pure and lovely,

Thou hast a victim found, whose life of sadness

Had but one single ray of rapture and gladness

Which she will yield to her, then gladly die.

Germont.

Weep on, thou hapless one,

Weep on; I witness thy trial

In what I ask of thy selfdenial.

Bear up, thou noble heart, triumph is nigh.

Violetta.

Now command me.

Germont.

Tell him that thou lovest him not.

Violetta.

He'll not believe.

Germont.

Then leave him.

Violetta.

He'll follow.

Germont.

Well, then—

Violetta.

Embrace me as thy daughter, then will my heart be strong.
(They embrace.)

Ere long, restored you'll find him; but sad beyond all telling.

Then, to console him, from the arbor approach him.
(Points to the garden and sits down to write.)

Germont.

What art thinking?

Violetta.

Cosi alla misera, ch' è un di caduta,

Di più risorgere speranza è muta!

Se pur benefico le indulga Iddio

L'uomo implacabile per lei sarà.

Dite alla giovine si bella e pura

Ch'avvi una vittima, della sventure

Cui resta un unico raggio di bene

Che a lei il sagrifica e che morrà.

Germont.

Piangi, piangi, o misera,

Supremo il veggo è il sagrifizio

Ch'orati chieggo.

Sento nell' anima già le tue pene

Coraggio, è il nobile cor vincerà.

Violetta.

Imponete.

Germont.

Non amarlo ditegli.

Violetta.

Nol crederà.

Germont.

Partite.

Violetta.

Seguirammi.

Germont.

Allor.

Violetta.

Qual figlia m'abbracciate—forte così sarò
(S'abbracciano.)

Tra breve ei vi fia reso, ma afflitto oltare ogni dire;

A suo conforto di colà volerete.
(Indicandogli il giardino, va ver iscrivere.)

Germont.

O che pensate!

Violetta.

If you my thoughts could know, you would
then oppose me.

Germont.

Generous-hearted!   How can I e'er repay
thee?

Violetta.

I shall die! let not my memory
By him be execrated,
But let my woes and trials dark
To him be all related.
This sacrifice o'erwhelming
I make of love to duty,
Will be the end of all my woe,
The last sigh of my heart.

Germont.

No, noble heart, thou still shalt live!
A bright fate shall redress thee;
These tears announce the happy day
That Heav'n will send to bless thee.
This sacrifice unbounded
You make of love to duty,
So noble is, 'twill soon a glow
Of pride to you impart.

Violetta.

Some one comes, retire now.

Germont.

Oh, how my heart is grateful!

Violetta.

We meet no more forever!
(They embrace.)

Both.

May you be happy—Heav'n bless thee!
(GERMONT goes out by the garden door.)

SCENE VI—VIOLETTA, then ANNINA, then ALFRED.

Violetta.

Oh, grant me strength, kind Heaven!
(Sits down, writes, and then rings the bell.)

Annina.

Do you require me?

Violetta.

Yes; take and deliver thou this letter.

Annina
(looks at the direction with surprise).
Oh!

Violetta.

Sapendo, v' opporreste al pensier mio

Germont.

Generosa!—e per voi che far poss' io?

Violetta
(tornando a lui).
Morrò—la mia memoria;
Non fia ch' ei maledica,
Se le mie pene orribili
Vi sia chi almen gli dica.
Conosca il sacrifizio
Ch' io consumai d'amor.
Che sarà suo fin l'ultimo
Sospiro del mio cor.

Germont.

No, generosa, vivere,
E lieto voi dovrete,
Mercè di queste lagrime
Dal cielo un giorno avrete,
Premiato il sacrifizio
Sarà del vostro cor.
D'un' opra cosi nobile
Andrete fiera allor.

Violetta.

Quì giunge alcun; partite!

Germont.

Ah, grato v' è il cor mio!

Violetta.

Non ci vedrem più, forse.
(S'abbracciano.)

A due.

Felice siate—Addio!
(GERMONT esce la porta del giardino.)

SCENA VI—VIOLETTA, poi ANNINA, quindi ALFREDO

Violetta.

Dammi tu forza, o cielo!
(Siede, scrive, poi suona il campanelle.)

Annina.

Mi chiedeste?

Violetta.

Sì, reca tu stessa questa foglio.

Annina
(ne guarda la direxione, a se na mestra sorpresa).
Oh!

Violetta.

Be silent; go directly.
(Exit Annina.)
I must write to him now. What shall I say?

Where shall I find the courage?
(Writes, then seals the letter.)

Alfred   (coming in).

What now?

Violetta   (conceals the letter).

Nothing.

Alfred.

Wert writing?

Violetta.

Yes—no—

Alfred.

What strange confusion! To whom wert writing?

Violetta.

To thee.

Alfred.

Give me the letter.

Violetta.

No—directly.

Alfred.

Forgive me; my thoughts are quite disturbed.

Violetta   (rising).

By what?

Alfred.

News from my father.

Violetta.

Hast seen him?

Alfred.

Ah no! but he hath sent a cruel letter!
I soon expect him. At a glance he will love thee.

Violetta   (with agitation).

Let him not here surprise me.
Allow me to retire now, thou wilt calm him;
Then at his feet—I'll humbly fall—
(Scarcely restraining her tears.)
He cannot will that we should part—we shall be happy—
Because thou lov'st me, Alfred—is it not so?

Violetta.

Silenzio—va all'istante.
(ANNINA parte.)
Ed or si scriva a lui—che gli dire?
Chi men darà il coraggio?
(Scrive e poi suggella.)

Alfredo.

Che fai?

Violetta   (nascendendo la lettera).

Nulla.

Alfredo.

Scrivevi?

Violetta.

No—sì—   (Confusa.)

Alfredo.

Qual turbamento?—a chi scrivevi?

Violetta.

A te.

Alfredo.

Dammi quel foglio.

Violetta.

No, per ora.

Alfredo.

Mi perdona—son io preoccupato.

Violetta   (alzandosi).

Che fu?

Alfredo.

Giunse mio padre.

Violetta.

Lo vedesti?

Alfredo.

Ah, no; un severo scritto mi lasciava—
Ma verrà—t'amerà solo in vederti.

Violetta   (molte agitata).

Ch'io quì non mi sorprenda—
Lascia che m'allontani—tu lo calma—
Ai piedi suoi mi getterò—divisi
(Mal frenande il piante.)
Ei più non è vorrà—sarem felici—
Perchè tu m'ami, Alfredo, non è vero?

Alfred.

Oh, dearly! Why dost weep thus?

Violetta.

My heart, o'ercharged, had need of weep-
ing—I now am tranquil,
Thou seest it?—Smiling on thee!
(With great effort.)
I'll be there—'mid the flow'rs, ever near
thee,—
Love me, Alfred, love me as I now love
thee.
Farewell, love!
(Runs to the garden.)

SCENE VII—ALFRED, then JOSEPH, then a MESSENGER.

Alfred.

Ah, that fond heart lives only in my de-
votion!
(Sits down and opens a book, reads a little, then rises,
and looks at the clock, which is upon the chimneypiece.)
'Tis late now! to-day it's doubtful
If I shall see my father.

Joseph
(enters hurriedly).
Sir, my lady has departed,
In a carriage that awaited,
And is already upon the road to Paris.
Annina, too, disappeared some time before
her.

Alfred.

I know—be quiet.

Joseph.

(What does this mean?)
(Retires.)

Alfred.

She goes, perhaps, to hasten
The sale of all her property.
Annina will stay all that.
(His father is seen in the distance, crossing the garden.)
Some one is in the garden!
Who's there?
(Going out.)

Messenger
(at the door).
You, sir, are Germont?

Alfred.

I am, sir.

Alfredo.

Oh, quanto!—perchè piangi?

Violetta.

Di lagrime avea duopo—or son tranquilla—
Lo vedi?—ti sorrido—
(Forzandosi.)
Sarò là, tra quei fior, presso a te sempre—
Amami, Alfredo, quant' io t'amo.—Addio.
(Corre in giardino.)

SCENA VII—ALFREDO, poi GIUSEPPE, indi un COMMIS
SIONARO, a tempo.

Alfredo.

Ah, vive sol quel core all' amor mio!

(Siede, prende a caso un libro, legge alquanto, quand
s'alza, guarda l'ora sull' orologio sovrapposto al camino.)
E tardi; ed oggi forse.
Più non verrà mio padre.

Giuseppe
(entrando frettoloso).
La signora è partita—
L' attendeva un calesse, e sulla via
Già corre di Parigi.—Annina pure
Prima di lei spariva.

Alfredo.

Il sò, ti calma.

Giuseppe
(da se).
Che vuol dir ciò!
(Esce.)

Alfredo.

Va forse d' ogni avere
Ad affrettar la perdita—
Ma Annina la impedirà.
(Si vede il Padre attraversare in lontane il giardino.)
Qualcuno è nel giardino!
Chi è là?
(Per uscire.)

Commissionaro
(alla porta).
Il Signor Germont?

Alfredo.

Son io.

Messenger.

    Sir, a lady in a coach, gave me,

    Not far from this place, a note, to you directed.

    (Gives a letter to Alfred, is paid and departs.)

SCENE VIII—ALFRED, then GERMONT, from the garden.

Alfred.

    From Violetta! ah, why am I thus moved?

    To rejoin her, perhaps she now invites me.

    I tremble.

    Oh, Heav'n! send courage!

          (Opens and reads.)

    "Alfred, at the moment this note shall reach

      you"—

    Ah!

(He utters a cry like one struck by a thunderbolt, and in turning finds himself in the presence of his father, into whose arms he throws himself, exclaiming:)

    Oh, my father!

Germont.

    My dear son!

    How thou dost suffer! restrain thy weeping,

    Return and be the glory, the pride of thy

      father.

    (ALFRED despairingly sits at a table, with his face concealed in his hands.)

Commissionaro.

    Una dama, da un cocchio, per voi,

    Di quà non lunge mi diede questo scritto.

    (Da una lettera ad ALFREDO, ne riceve qualche moneta, e parte.)

SCENA VIII—ALFREDO, poi GERMONT, ch'entra dal giardino

Alfredo.

    Di Violetta!—Perchè son io commosso?—

    A raggiungerla forse ella m' invita—

    Io tremo!—Oh ciel!—Coraggio!

          (Apre e legge.)

    "Alfredo, al giungervi di questo foglio"—

          (Come fulminato, grida.)

    (Volgendosi, si trava a fronte del padre, nelle cui braccia si abbandona. esclamando:)

    Ah!—Padre mio!

Germont.

    Mio figlio!

    Oh, quanto soffri—tergi, ah, tergi il pianto—

    Ritorna di tuo padre orgoglio e vanto.

    (ALFREDO disperato siede presso il tavolino col volte tra le mani.)

DI PROVENZA IL MAR — *FROM FAIR PROVENCE'S SOIL AND SEA*   (Germont)

Di Pro - ven-za il mar il suol chi dal cor-ti can-cel-lò? chi dal
From fair Pro-vence soil and sea, Who hath won thy heart a - way, Who hath

cor-ti can-cel-lò? di Pro-ven-za il mar il suol? al na-tio ful-gen-te sol qual de-
won thy heart a-way, From fair Pro-vence soil and sea? From thy na-tive sunny clime, What strange

sti - no ti fu-rò? qual de - sti - no ti fu-rò? al na-tio ful-gen-te sol? Oh, ram-
fate caused thee to stray, What strange fate caused thee to stray From thy na-tive sun-ny clime? Oh, re-

men -ta pur nel duol ch'i - vi gio-ja a te bril-lò, e che pa - ce co - la sol su te
mem - ber in thy woe All the joy that waits for thee, All the peace thy heart would know, On-ly

splen-de-re an-cor può, e che pa - ce co - la sol su te splen-de-re an-cor può.
there still found may be. All the peace thy heart would know, On-ly there, still found may be.

Dio mi gui - dò!_____ Dio mi gui - dò! Dio mi gui - dò!
Heav'n guid - ed me!_____ Heav'n guid - ed me! Heav'n guid - ed me!

Ah! thy father old and worn, 　What he felt, thou ne'er canst know. In thine absence, so forlorn 　Seemed his home, with grief and woe. But I find thee now again, 　If my hope doth not mislead, If yet honor doth remain 　With its voice not mute or dead, Heav'n sends me aid! Wilt not answer a father's affection? <div align="right">(Embracing him.)</div>*Alfred.* Countless furies within my heart are rag- 　ing! Go and leave me— <div align="right">(Repulses his father.)</div>*Germont.* How, leave thee? *Alfred.* (Oh, for vengeance!) *Germont.* Do not linger, let's go now, oh, haste thee! *Alfred.* (It was Dauphol!) *Germont.* Dost thou not hear? *Alfred.* No!	Oh! il tuo vecchio genitor 　Tu non sai quanto soffri— Te lontano, di squallor 　Il suo tetto si coprì— Ma se alfin ti trovo ancor 　Se in me speme non falli. Se la voce dell' onor 　In te appien non ammuti— Dio m'esaudi! Nè rispondi d'un padre all'affeto. <div align="right">(Abbracciando.)</div>*Alfredo.* Mille furie divorammi il petto— Mi lasciate— <div align="right">(Respingendolo.)</div>*Germont.* Lasciarti! *Alfredo.* (Oh, vendetta!) <div align="right">(risoluto).</div>*Germont.* Non più indugi; partiamo—t'affretta *Alfredo.* (Ah, fu Douphol!) *Germont.* M'ascolti tu? *Alfredo.* No!

Germont.

All in vain then my search will have been?
No, no, I will not chide thee now,
But hide the past forever;
The love that guides me ever
Full pardon will bestow.
Then come and drown thy cares in joy
With me again returning;
For thee loved ones are yearning;
Such hopes thou'lt not destroy!
Fond hearts at home are burning
Their soothing care to show.

Alfred

(Arousing himself; sees upon the table the letter of FLORA,
glances at its contents, and exclaims:)

Ah! She's at the fête, then!
Thither will I fly, and seek revenge.

Germont.

What say'st thou? ah, stay thee!

(ALFRED departs precipitately, followed by his father.)

SCENE IX—A salon in FLORA's palace, richly furnished
and lighted up. A door in the back scene, and two lateral
ones. On the right, a little forward, a table, on which
are cards and other implements of play. On the left a small
table, with flowers and refreshments; chairs and a settee.

(FLORA, the MARQUIS, the DOCTOR, and other guests, enter
from the left, and converse amongst themselves.)

Flora.

There'll be fun here to-night with maskers
merry;
The Count will be their leader;
Violetta and Alfred both will be here.

Marquis.

Have you not heard the news then?
Germont and Violetta are divided.

Flora.
Doctor. } Is that true?

Marquis.

Yes, and she will come with the Baron.

Doctor.

I saw them yesterday, appearing quite happy.

(A noise is heard on the right.)

Flora.

Be silent—you hear them?

All.

Yes, our friends are coming.

Germont.

Dunque invano trovoato t'avrò!
No, non udrai rimproveri;
Copriam d'oblio il passato;
L'amor che m'ha guidato
Sa tutto perdonar.
Vieni, i tuoi cari in giubilo
Con me rivedi ancora;
A chi penò finora
Tal gioja non niegar
Un padre ed una suora
T'affretta a consolar.

Alfredo

(Scuotendosi, getta a caso gli occhi sulla tavola. a vede
la lettera di FLORA, la scorre ed esclama:)

Ah!—ell' è alla festa!—volisi
L' offesa a vendicar.

Germont.

Che dice? ah ferma!

(Fugge precipitoso seguito dal padre.)

SCENA IX—Galleria nel palazzo di FLORA, riccamente
addobata ed illuminata. Una porta nel fondo e due laterali.
A destra piu avanti un tavoliere con quanto occorre pel
giuoco; a sinistra, ricco tavolino con fiori e rinfreschi, varie
sedis e un divano.

(FLORA, il MARCHESE, il DOTTORE, ed altri invitati entrano
dalla sinistra, discorrendo tra loro.)

Flora.

Avrem lieta di maschere la notte;
N' è duce il viscontino—
Violetta ed Alfredo anco invitai.

Marchese.

La novita ignorate?
Violetta e Germont son disgiunti.

Dottore.
Flora. } Fia vero.

Marchese.

Ella verrà qui col barone.

Dottore.

Li vidi jeri ancor—parean felici.

(S' ode rumore a destra.)

Flora.

Silenzio—Udite?

Tutti

(vanno verso la destra).

Giungono gli amici.

SCENE X—The same, and a number of ladies masked as GIPSIES, some of whom hold a staff in the hand, some have tambourines, with which to beat time.

SCENA X—Detti, e molte Signore mascherate da ZINGARE, che entrano dalla destra.

NOI SIAMO ZINGARELLE — *WE'RE GIPSIES GAY AND YOUTHFUL* (Chorus)

Allegro moderato

Noi sia-mo zin-ga-rel-le ve-nu-te da lon-ta-no: d'o-
We're gip-sies gay and youth-ful, From dis-tant shores ar-riv-ing: *With*

gnu-no sul-la ma-no leg-gia-mo l'av-ve-nir,   Se___
skil-ful art con-triv-ing The fu-ture to fore-tell,   *We___*

con-sul-tiam le stel-le, con-sul-tiam le stel-le null' av-vi-a noi d'os-cu-ro no, null'
read the plan-ets truth-ful, read the plan-ets truthful, Their se-crets dark un-fold-ing, all their

av-vi-a noi d'os-cu-ro, e i ca-si del fu-tu-ro pos-sia-mo al-trui pre-
se-crets dark un-fold, The realms of fate be-hold-ing, We can your for-tunes

dir. Se__con-sul-tiam le stel-le null' av-vi-a noi d'os-cur, e i ca-si del fu-
tell. We__read the plan-ets truth-ful, Their se-crets dark un-fold, The realms of fate be-

tu-ro pos-sia-mo al-trui pre-dir, e i ca-si del fu-tu-ro, e__ i ca-si del fu-
hold-ing, We can your for-tunes tell, The realms of fate be-hold-ing, We can thus your fortunes

tur e i ca-si del fu-tu-ro pos-sia-mo al-trui, pos-sia-mo al-trui pre-
tell, All the realms of fate be-hold-ing, we thus can tell, For-tunes we thus can

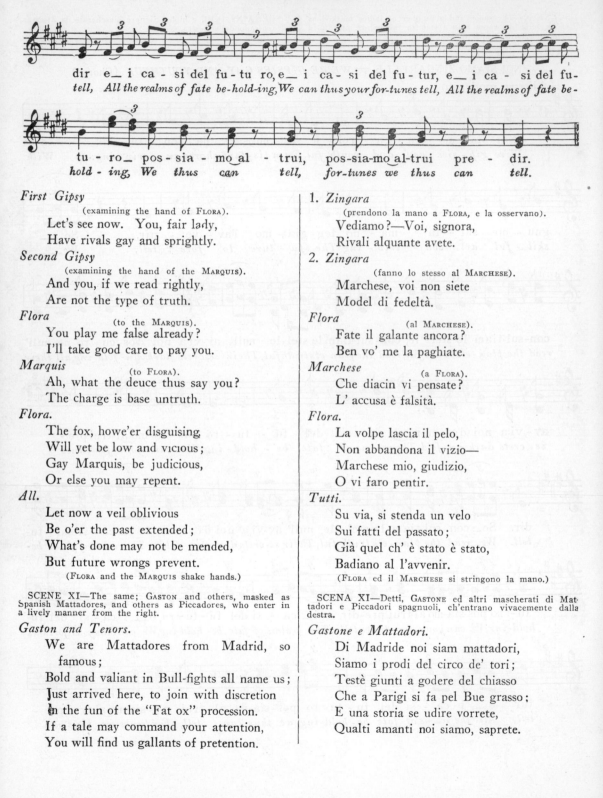

dir e_ i ca - si del fu - tu ro, e_ i ca - si del fu - tur, e_ i ca - si del fu-
tell, All the realms of fate be-hold-ing, We can thus your for-tunes tell, All the realms of fate be-

tu - ro_ pos - sia - mo al - trui, pos-sia-mo al-trui pre - dir.
hold - ing, We thus can tell, for-tunes we thus can tell.

First Gipsy (examining the hand of FLORA). Let's see now. You, fair lady, Have rivals gay and sprightly.	1. *Zingara* (prendono la mano a FLORA, e la osservano). Vediamo?—Voi, signora, Rivali alquante avete.
Second Gipsy (examining the hand of the MARQUIS). And you, if we read rightly, Are not the type of truth.	2. *Zingara* (fanno lo stesso al MARCHESE). Marchese, voi non siete Model di fedeltà.
Flora (to the MARQUIS). You play me false already? I'll take good care to pay you.	*Flora* (al MARCHESE). Fate il galante ancora? Ben vo' me la paghiate.
Marquis (to FLORA). Ah, what the deuce thus say you? The charge is base untruth.	*Marchese* (a FLORA). Che diacin vi pensate? L' accusa è falsità.
Flora. The fox, howe'er disguising, Will yet be low and vicious; Gay Marquis, be judicious, Or else you may repent.	*Flora.* La volpe lascia il pelo, Non abbandona il vizio— Marchese mio, giudizio, O vi faro pentir.
All. Let now a veil oblivious Be o'er the past extended; What's done may not be mended, But future wrongs prevent. (FLORA and the MARQUIS shake hands.)	*Tutti.* Su via, si stenda un velo Sui fatti del passato; Già quel ch' è stato è stato, Badiano al l'avvenir. (FLORA ed il MARCHESE si stringono la mano.)
SCENE XI—The same; GASTON and others, masked as Spanish Mattadores, and others as Piccadores, who enter in a lively manner from the right.	SCENA XI—Detti, GASTONE ed altri mascherati di Mattadori e Piccadori spagnuoli, ch'entrano vivacemente dalla destra.
Gaston and Tenors. We are Mattadores from Madrid, so famous; Bold and valiant in Bull-fights all name us; Just arrived here, to join with discretion In the fun of the "Fat ox" procession. If a tale may command your attention, You will find us gallants of pretention.	*Gastone e Mattadori.* Di Madride noi siam mattadori, Siamo i prodi del circo de' tori; Testè giunti a godere del chiasso Che a Parigi si fa pel Bue grasso; E una storia se udire vorrete, Qualti amanti noi siamo, saprete.

All the Others.
   Yes, yes, bravi! go on now relating.
   With much pleasure we'll listen.
Gaston and Chorus.
   Hear then.

Gli Altri.
   Sì, sì, bravi; narrate, narrate;
   Con piacere l'udremo.
Gastone e Mattadori.
   Ascoltate.

E PIQUILLO UN BEL GAGLIARDO — *YOUNG PIQUILLO* (Gaston and Chorus)

E__ Pi-quil-lo un bel__ ga-gliar-do bi - sca-gli-no mat - ta-dor,
Young Pi-quil-lo, gay__ and dar-ing, Was__ a val-iant mat - ta-dor,

for - te il brac-cio, fie - ro il guar-do, del - le gio-stre e-gli è sig - nor.
Strong his arm was, proud his bear-ing, In__ all sports, the prize he bore.

D'An - da - lu - sia gio - vi-net-ta fol - le - men - te in-na-mo-rò;
One__ of Spain's fair maids en-chant-ing, With this youth fell mad-ly in love:

ma - la bel-la ri - tro-set-ta co - sì al gio-va - ne__ par-lò:
But__ the maid, ere fa - vors grant-ing, Bade__ him thus his val - or prove—

Cin - que to - ri in un sol gior - no vo' ve - der - ti ad at - ter-rar,
"Five stout bulls, in one brief morn-ing I would see__ thee meet and slay;

e se vin - ci, al tuo ri - tor - no ma - no e cor - ti vo'__ do-nar.
If suc - cess - ful, here re - turn-ing, Hand and heart shall thee re - pay."

Si__ gli dis-se il mat - ta - do - ro al - le gio-stre mos-se il piè;
Then the mat - ta - dor__ as-sent - ed, To__ the tri-al led__ the way;

cin - que to - ri vin - ci - to - re   sull' a - re - na e - gli sten - dè,
Five fierce bulls, in turn pre - sent - ed,   His strong arm did van-quish that day,

cin - que to - ri vin - ci - to - re   sull' a - re - na e - gli sten - dè.
Five fierce bulls, in turn pre - sent - ed,   His strong arm did van-quish that day.

Flora and Others.

Bravely he with courage daring
Did his gallantry display!
While his love, with strength unsparing,
He declared in such gallant way.

Gaston and Chorus.

Then, 'mid plaudits loud, returning
To the maid, with winning grace,
Took the prize with blushes burning,
Held her fast in love's embrace.

Others of the Chorus.

Proofs we Mattadores thus render,
How we can vanquish all the fair!

Gaston.

Here, the hearts are far more tender,
We content with trifling are.

All.

Yes, let's try now to discover
All the various moods of fate;
The arena we uncover,
And for all bold players wait!

(The men take off their masks—some walk about, while
others commence playing.)

SCENE XII—The same, and ALFRED; then VIOLETTA with
the BARON; afterwards, a servant.

All.

Alfred!—you!

Alfred.

Yes, my kind friends.

Flora.

Violetta?

Alfred.

I don't know.

All.

What cool indifference! Bravo! We'll
now commence to play.

(GASTON shuffles the cards, ALFRED and others put up their
stakes. VIOLETTA enters, leaning on the arm of the BARON.)

Gli Altri.

Bravo invero il mattadore
Ben gagliardo si mostrò,
Se alla giovine l' amore
In tal guisa egli provò.

Gastone e Mattadori.

Poi, tra plausi, ritornato
Alla bella del suo cor,
Colse il premio desïato
Dal a fede, dall' amor.

Gli Altri.

Con tai prove i Mattadori
San le amanti conquistar!

Gastone e Mattadori.

Ma diù sen più miti i cori;
A noi basta folleggiar.

Tutti.

Sì, sì allegri—Or pria tentiamo
Della sorte il vario umor.
La palestra dischiudiamo
Agli audaci giuocator.

(Gli uomini si tolgono la maschera, chi passeggia e chi s
accinge a giuocare.)

SCENA XII—Detti, ed ALFREDO, quindi VIOLETTA coi
BARONE; un Servo a tempo.

Tutti.

Alfredo!—Voi!

Alfredo.

Sì, amici.

Flora.

Violetta?

Alfredo.

Non ne so.

Tutti.

Ben disinvolto!—Bravo!—Or via, giuocar
Si può.

(GASTONE si pone a tagliare: ALFREDO ed altri puntano,
VIOLETTA entra al braccia del BARONE.)

Flora

(going to meet them).

Here comes the guest most welcome.

Violetta.

To your kind wish I yielded.

Flora.

Thanks to you, also, Baron, for your polite acceptance.

Baron

(softly to VIOLETTA).

Germont is here! do you see him?

Violetta.

(Heav'n! 'tis he, truly!)   I see him.

Baron.

Let not one word escape you, addressed to this Alfred!

Violetta.

(Why, ah, why came I hither?   In mercy, Heaven, thy pity send to me!)

Flora.

Sit here beside me.   Tell me now, what new and strange is passing.

(To VIOLETTA, making her sit beside her on the settee. The DOCTOR approaches them while they are conversing in an undertone. The MARQUIS converses with the BARON. GASTON continues to play. ALFRED and others stake, and the rest walk about.)

Alfred.

A four-spot!

Gaston.

Ah! thou hast won it.

Alfred.

Unfortunate in loving, makes fortunate in gaming—

(Stakes again and wins.)

All.

Still he remains the victor.

Alfred.

O I shall gain this evening, and with my golden winnings,

To the green fields returning, I shall again be happy.

Flora.

Singly?

Alfred.

No, no.   With some one like her who once was with me, but fled and left me!

Flora.

(andandole incontro).

Qui desïata giungi.

Violetta.

Cessi al cortese invito.

Flora.

Grata vi son, Barone, d' averlo pur gradito.

Barone

(piano a VIOLETTA).

Germont è qui! il vedete?

Violetta.

Cielo!—egli è vero!

(Da sè.)

Il vedo.

Barone.

(piano a VIOLETTA).

Da voi non un sol detto si volga a questo Alfredo.

Violetta

(da sè).

Ah, perchè venni incauta!   Pieta di me, gran Dio!

Flora.

Meco t' assidi; narrami—quai novità vegg' io?

(A VIOLETTA, facendola sedere presso dis è sul divano. Il DOTTORE si avvicina ad esse, che commessamente conversano. Il MARCHESE si trattiene a parte col BARONE; GASTONE taglia; ALFREDO ed altri puntano altri passegiano.)

Alfredo.

Un quattro!

Gastone.

Ancora hai vinto!

Alfredo.

Sfortuna nell' amore vale fortuna al giuco.

(Punta e vince.)

Tutti.

E sempre vincitore!

Alfredo.

Oh, vincerò stassera; e l' oro guadagnato

Poscia a goder fra' campi ritornerò beato.

Flora.

Solo?

Alfredo.

No, no, con tale, che vi fu meco ancor,

Poi mi sfuggia.

Violetta.

(Oh, Heaven!)

Gaston

(to ALFRED, pointing to VIOLETTA)

Some pity show.

Baron

(with ill-restrained anger).

Beware!

Violetta

(softly to the BARON).

Be calm, or I must leave you.

Alfred

(carelessly).

Did you address me, Baron?

Baron

(ironically).

You are in such good fortune
I fain would try against you.

Alfred.

Yes? I accept your challenge.

Violetta.

(Who'll aid me? Death seems approaching.
O Heaven, look down and pity me!)

Baron

(staking).

Here at the right one hundred.

Alfred

(staking).

I, at the left one hundred.

Gaston

(dealing off).

An ace there, a knave, too; thou'st won it!
To ALFRED.)

Baron.

Wilt double?

Alfred.

A double be it.

Gaston

(dealing off).

A four-spot—a seven.

Alfred.

Then I'm again victorious.

All.

Bravely indeed! good fortune seems partial to Alfred!

Violetta

(da sè).

Mio Dio!

Gastone

(ad ALFREDO indic. VIOLETTA).

Pietà di lei.

Barone

(ad ALFREDO, con mal frenata ira).

Signor!

Violetta

(piano al BARONE).

Frenatevi, o vi lascio.

Alfredo

(disinvolto).

Barone, m' appellaste?

Barone

(ironico).

Siete in si gran fortuna,
Che al gioco mi tentaste.

Alfredo.

Sì!—la disfida accetto.

Violetta

(da sè).

Che fia?—morir mi sento!
Pietà, gran Dio, di me!

Barone

(punta).

Centro luigi a destra.

Alfredo

(punta).

Ed alla manca cento.

Gastone

(ad ALFREDO).

Un asso—un faute—hai vinto!

Barone.

Il doppio?

Alfredo.

Il doppio sia.

Gastone

(tagliando).

Un quattro, un sette—

Tutti.

Ancora!

Alfredo.

Pur la vittoria è mia!

Coro.

Bravo davver!—la sorte è tutta per Alfredo.

Flora.

Ah! for the rustic dwelling the **Baron** pays expenses.

Alfred
                    (to the BARON).

Now we'll go on!

Servant
                    (entering).

The banquet is ready!

Flora.

Let's go then.

All
                    (starting).

Let's go, then.

Alfred
                    (to the BARON).

Shall we our game continue?

Baron.

At present, no, we cannot;
Ere long, my losses I'll regain.

Alfred.

At any game that suits you.

Baron.

Our friends we'll follow. After—

Alfred.

Whene'er you call, you'll find me.

(All retire through a door in the centre—the stage left empty for a moment.)

SCENE XIII—VIOLETTA returns, breathless, followed by ALFRED.

Violetta.

I have asked him to come hither.
Will he do so? And will he hear me?
Yes, he will, for bitter hate
Controls him more than my sad accents.

Alfred.

Didst thou call me? What dost wish for?

Violetta.

Quickly leave this place, I pray you;
Danger o'er you is suspended.

Alfred.

Ah! you're clearly comprehended.
E'en so base you then believe me?

Violetta.

Ah no, no, never!

Alfred.

But what then fear you?

Flora.

Del villeggia la spesa farà il Baron, già ü vedo.

Alfredo
                    (al BARONE).

Seguite pur!

Serve.

La cena è pronta.

Flora.

Andiamo.

Coro
                    (avriandosi).

Andiamo.

Alfredo
                    (tra loro a parte)

Se continuar v' aggrada—

Barone.

Per ora nol possiamo.
Più tardi la rivincita.

Alfredo.

Al gioco che vorrete.

Barone.

Seguiam gli amici; poscia—

Alfredo.

Sarò qual mi vorrete.

(Tutti entrano nella porta di mezze: la scena rimane un istante vuota.)

SCENA XIII—VIOLETTA, che ritorna affannata, indi ALFREDO.

Violetta.

Invitato a qui seguirmi,
Verrà desso?—vorrà udirmi?
El verrà—chè l' odio atroce
Puote in lui più di mia voce.

Alfredo.

Mi chiamaste?—Che bramate?

Violetta.

Questi luoghi abbandonate—
Un periglio vi sovrasta.

Alfredo.

Ah, comprendo!—Basta, basta—
E si vile mi credete?

Violetta.

Ah, no, mai.

Alfredo.

Ma che temete?

Violetta.

Ah, I fear the Baron's fury.

Alfred.

An affair of death's between us;
Should this hand in death extend him,
One sole blow would then deprive thee
Both of lover and protector;
Would such losses sorrow give thee?

Violetta.

But if he should prove the victor!
There behold the sole misfortune,
That, I fear, would prove me fatal.

Alfred.

Pray, what care you for my safety?

Violetta.

Hence, depart now, this present instant!

Alfred.

I will go, but swear this moment,
Thou wilt follow now and ever,
Where I wander.

Violetta.

Ah, no; never.

Alfred.

No! and never!

Violetta.

Go, thou, unhappy! and forget me.
Thus degraded, go and leave me!
At this moment, to escape thee
I a sacred oath have taken!

Alfred.

To whom? tell me! who could claim it?

Violetta.

One who had the right to name it.

Alfred.

'Twas Dauphol?

Violetta　　　　(with great effort).

Yes.

Alfred.

Then thou lov'st him?

Violetta.

Ah, well, I love him.

Alfred
(Runs furiously, throws open the doors and cries out:)

Come hither all!

Violetta.

Tremo sempre del Barone.

Alfredo.

E tra noi mortal quistione—
S' ei cadrà per mano mia
Un sol colpo vi torria
Coll' amante il protettore—
V'atterrisce tal sciagura?

Violetta.

Ma s' ei fosse l' uccisore!—
Ecco l' unica sventura—
Ch' io pavento a me fatale!

Alfredo.

La mia morte!—Che ven cale?

Violetta.

Deh, partite, e sull' istante.

Alfredo.

Partiro, ma giura innante
Che dovunque seguirai
I miei passi.

Violetta.

Ah no, giammai.

Alfredo.

No!—giammai!

Violetta.

Va, sciagurato,
Scorda un nome ch' è infamato—
Va—mi lascia sul momento—
Di fuggirti un giuramento
Sacro io feci.

Alfredo.

E chi potea?

Violetta.

Chi diritto pien ne avea.

Alfredo.

Fu Douphol?

Violetta　　　　(con supremo sforzo).

Sì.

Alfredo.

Dunque l'ami?

Violetta.

Ebben—l'amo.

Alfredo
(corre furente sulla porta, e grida:)

Or tutti a me.

SCENE XIV—The same, and all the others, who enter in confusion.

All.

Did you call us? Now what would you?

Alfred

(pointing to VIOLETTA, who leans fainting against the table).

Know ye all this woman present?

All.

Who? Violetta?

Alfred.

Know ye, too, her base misconduct?

Violetta.

Ah! spare me!

All.

No!

Alfred.

All she possessed, this woman here
Hath for my love expended.
I blindly, basely, wretchedly,
This to accept, condescended.
But there is time to purge me yet
From stains that shame, confound me.
Bear witness all around me
That here I pay the debt.

(In a violent rage he throws a purse at VIOLETTA's feet—she faints in the arms of FLORA and the DOCTOR. At this moment Alfred's father enters.)

SCENE XV—The same, and GERMONT, the elder, who has entered at the last words.

All.

Oh, to what baseness thy passions have moved thee.
To wound thus fatally one who has loved thee!
Shameless traducer of woman defenceless,
Depart hence, speedily, scorned and despised!

Germont.

Of scorn most worthy himself doth render
Who wounds in anger a woman tender!
My son, where is he? No more I see him;
In thee, Alfred, I seek him, but in vain.

Alfred

(aside).

Ah! yes, 'twas shameful! a deed, abhorrent,
A jealous fury—love's maddening torrent

SCENA XIV—Detti, e TUTTI i precedenti, che confusamente ritornano.

Tutti.

Ne appellaste?—Che volete?

Alfredo

(additando VIOLETTA che abbattuta, si appeggia al tavolino).

Questa donna conoscete?

Tutti.

Chi? Violetta?

Alfredo.

Che facesse
Non sepete?

Violetta.

Ah, taci.

Tutti.

No.

Alfredo.

Ogni suo aver tal femina
Per amor mio sperdea.
Io cicco, vile, misero,
Tutto accettar potea,
Ma, è tempo ancora! tergermi,
Da tanta macchia bramo
Qui testimon vi chiamo,
Che quì pagato io l'ho!

(ALFREDO getta con furente sprezzo il ritratto di VIOLETTA ai piedi di lei, ed essa sviene tra le braccia di FLORA e del DOTTORE. In tal momento entra il Padre.)

SCENA XV—Detti, ed il Signor GERMONT, ch' entra all' ultime parole.

Tutti.

Oh, infamia orribile tu commettesti!—
Un cor sensibile cosi uccidesti!—
Di donne ignobile insultatore,
Di qua allontanati, ne desti orror.

Germont.

Di sprezzo degno sè stesso rende
Chi pur nell' ira la donna offende.
Dov' è mio figlio?— Più non lo vedo.
In te più Alfredo—trovar non so.

Alfredo

(da se).

Ah, sì!—che feci!—ne sento orrore!
Gelosa smania, deluso amore

Oppressed my senses, destroyed my reason;
From her, no pardon shall I obtain!
To fly and leave her, strength was denied
me,
My angry passions did hither guide me.
But now that fury is all expended,
Remorse and horror to me remain.

Germont
(aside).
I 'mid them only know what bright virtues
Dwell in that sad heart so torn and bleed-
ing.
I know she loves him, all else unheeding;
Yet must, tho' cruel, silent remain.

Gaston. ⎱Oh! thou dost suffer! but cheer thy
Flora. ⎰ heart,
Here in thy trials we all take part.
Kind friends surround thee, care o'er thee
keeping,
Cease then thy weeping, thy tears restrain.

Baron.
This shameful insult against this lady
Offends all present; behold me ready
To punish outrage! Here now declaring
Such pride o'erbearing I will restrain.

Violetta
(reviving).
Ah, loved Alfred, this heart's devotion
Thou canst not fathom yet—its fond emo-
tion!
Thou'rt still unknowing that at the meas-
ure
Of this displeasure. 'tis proved again.
But when, hereafter, the truth comes o'er
thee,
And my affection shall rise before thee,
May Heav'n in pity then spare thee re-
morse.
Ah, tho' dead, still loving, ever will I re-
main!

(GERMONT takes his son with him; the BARON follows;
VIOLETTA is taken into an adjoining room by the DOCTOR
and FLORA, and the rest disperse.

END OF THE SECOND ACT.

Mi strazian l'alma—più non ragiono—
Da lei perdono—più non avro.
Volea fuggirla—non ho potuto!—
Dall' ira spinto, son qui venuto!—
Or che lo sdegno ho disfogato.
Me sciagurato!—rimorso io n' ho.

Germont
⎝da se).
Io sol fra tutti so qual virtude
Di quella misera il sen racchiude—
Io so che l'ama, che gli è fedele;
Eppur, crudele, tacer dovrò!

Gastone. ⎱Oh quanto peni! ma pur fi cor
Flora. ⎰Quì soffre ognuno del tuo dolor;
Fracari amici quì sei soltanto,
Rascinga il pianto che t' inondò.

Barone.
A questa donna l' atroce insulto
Qui tutti offese ma non inulto
Fia tanto oltraggio! Provar vi voglio
Che il vostro orgoglio fiaccar saprò!

Violetta
(riavendosi).
Alfredo, Alfredo, di questo core
Non puoi comprendere tutto l'amore;
Tu non conosci che fino a prezzo
Del tuo disprezzo—provato io l' ho!
Ma verrà giorno, in che il saprai—
Com' io t'amassi confesserai—
Dio dai rimorsi ti salvi allora
Io penta ancora—pur t'amero.

(GERMONT trae seco il figlio; il BARONE lo segue. VIOLETTA
è condotta in altra stanza dal DOTTORE e da FLORA; gli
altri si disperdano.)

FINE DELL' ATTO SECONDO.

ACT III.

SCENE 1—VIOLETTA's bed-room. At the back a bed, with the curtains partly drawn. A window shut by inside shutters. Near the bed a table with a bottle of water, a crystal cup, and different kinds of medicine on it. In the middle of the room a toilet-table and settee; a little apart from which is another piece of furniture, upon which a night-lamp is burning. Chairs and other articles of furniture. On the left a fireplace with a fire in it.

(VIOLETTA discovered sleeping on the bed—ANNINA, seated near the fireplace, has fallen asleep.)

Violetta   (awaking).

Annina!

Annina   (waking up, confusedly).

Did you call me?

Violetta.

Poor creature, were you sleeping?

Annina.

Yes, but forgive me.

Violetta.

Bring me here some water.
          (ANNINA does so.)
Look out now—is it yet daylight?

Annina.

It is seven.

Violetta.

To a little light give access.
(ANNINA opens the blinds, and looks into the street.)

Annina.

Doctor Grenvil has come—

Violetta.

A friend most faithful!

I wish to rise, assist me!

(She rises, but falls again—then, supported by ANNINA, she walks slowly towards the settee, and the DOCTOR enters in time to assist her to sit upon it—ANNINA places cushions about her.

SCENE II—The same, and the DOCTOR

Violetta.

How kind in you thinking of me thus early.

Doctor   (feeling her pulse).

Yes, are you somewhat better?

Violetta.

With pain I suffer; but my mind is tranquil.

A priest came here last evening and brought
     me comfort.

Ah! religion is a solace to us in affliction.

Doctor.

Last night, how were you?

ATTO III.

SCENA I—Camera da letto di VIOLETTA. Nel fondo e un letto con cortine mezzo tirate; una finestra chiusa da imposte interne; presso il letto uno sgabello su cui una bottiglia d'acqua, una tazza di cristallo, diverse medicine. A metà della scena una toilette, vicino un canapè; più distante un altro mobile, su cui arde un lume da notte, varie sedie ed altri mobili. La porta è a sinistra; di fronte v' è un caminnetto con fuoco acceso.

(VIOLETTA dorme sul letto—ANNINA, seduta presso il caminetto, è pure addormita.)

Violetta   (destandosi).

Annina!

Annina   (svegliandosi confusa).

Comandate?

Violetta.

          Dormivi, poveretta?

Annina.

Sì, perdonate.

Violetta.

Dammi d' acqua un sorso.
          (ANNINA esequisce.)
Osserva, è pieno il giorno?

Annina.

Son sett' ore.

Violetta.

Dà accesso a un pò di luce.
     (Apre le imposte, e guarda nella via.)

Annina.

Il Signor Grenvil!

Violetta.

Oh, il vero amico!—

Alzar mi vo'—m'aita.

(Si alza e ricade; poi sostenuta da ANNINA va lentamente verso il canapè, ed il DOTTORE entra in tempo per assisterla ad adagiarvisi—ANNINA vi aggiunge dei cuscini.)

SCENA II—Dette, ed il DOTTORE.

Violetta.

Quanta bontà!—Pensaste a me per tempo!

Dottore   (le tocca il polso).

Or come vi sentite?

Violetta.

Soffre il mio corpo, ma tranquilla ho l'alma.

Mi confortò ier sera un pio ministro.

Religione è sollievo a' sofferenti.

Dottore.

E questa notte?

Violetta.

    Calmly I slept till morning.

Doctor.

    Then keep your courage.

    Convalescence, haply, is not far distant.

Violetta.

    Oh! that's a kind deception

    Allowed to all physicians.

Doctor
             (pressing her hand).

    Farewell now. I'll return soon.

Violetta.

    Be not forgetful.

Annina
    (in a low tone, whilst following the Doctor).

    Is her case more hopeful?

Doctor.

    But few brief hours of life are to her re-

    maining.

             (Departs.)

      SCENE III—Violetta and Annina

Annina.

    Now cheer thy heart.

Violetta.

    Is this a festal morning?

Annina.

    Paris gives up to folly—'tis carnival day.

Violetta.

    Ah, 'mid this gay rejoicing, Heav'n alone

      doth know

    How the poor are suffering! What amount

    Is there in that casket?

Annina
             (opens and counts).

    Just twenty louis'.

Violetta.

    Take from it ten, and give them to the

      needy.

Annina.

    Little you'll have remaining.

Violetta.

    Oh, 'twill for me be plenty!

             (Sighing.)

    You can bring then my letters here.

Annina.

    But you?

Violetta.

    Ebbi tranquillo il sonno.

Dottore.

    Coraggio adunque—la convalescenza

    Non è lontana.

Violetta.

    Oh, la bugia pietosa

    A' medici è concessa.

Dottore
             (stringendole la mano).

    Addio—a più tardi.

Violetta.

    Non mi scordate.

Annina
      (piano al Dottore, accompagnandolo).

    Come va, Signore?

Dottore.

    La tisi non le accorda che poch' ore.

          (Piano, e parte.)

      SCENA III—Violetta ed Annina.

Annina.

    Or fate cor.

Violetta.

    Giorno di festa è questo?

Annina.

    Tutta Parigi impazza—è carnevale.

Violetta.

    Oh, nel comun tripudio, sallo il cielo

    Quanti infelici gemon!—Quale somma

    V' ha in quello stipo?

             (Indicandolo.)

Annina
             (l'apre e conta).

    Venti luigi.

Violetta.

    Dieci ne reca ai poveri tu stessa.

Annina.

    Poco rimanvi allora.

Violetta.

    Oh, mi sarà bastante!—

             (Sospirando.)

    Cerca poscia mie lettere.

Annina.

    Ma voi?

Violetta.

Naught will occur. You need not long be absent.

(Exit ANNINA.)

SCENE IV—VIOLETTA takes a letter from her bosom and reads:

"Thou hast kept thy promise. The duel took place. The Baron was wounded, but is improving. Alfred is in foreign countries. Your sacrifice has been revealed to him by me. He will return to you for pardon. I too will return. Haste to recover, thou deservest a bright future.
"GEORGIO GERMONT."

Violetta.

'Tis too late!

Still watching and waiting, but to me they come not!

(Looking in the mirror.)

Oh, how I'm changed and faded!

But the Doctor doth exhort me to be hopeful;

Ah! thus afflicted, all hope is dead within me!

Violetta.

Nulla occorrà, sollecita, se puoi,

(ANNINA esce.)

SCENA IV—VIOLETTA, che trae dal seno una lettera, è legge

"Teneste la promessa—La disfida ebbe luogo; il Barone fu ferito, però migliora Alfredo è in stranio suolo; il vostro sacrifizio io stesso gli ho svelato. Egli a voi tornerà pel suo perdono; io pur verrò— Curatevi—mertaste un avvenir migliore.
"GIORGIO GERMONT."

Violetta.

E tardi!—

(Desolata.)

Attendo, attendo—Nè a me giungon mai?

(Si guarda nello specchio.)

Oh, come son mutata!—

Ma il Dottore a sperar pure m' esorta!—

Ah, con tal morbo ogni speranza è morta.

ADDIO DEL PASSATO — *FAREWELL TO THE BRIGHT VISIONS* (Violetta)

Ad - di - o_ dei pas - sa - to_ bei_ sog - ni ri - den - ti, le
Fare - well to_ the bright vis - ions I_ once fond - ly_ cher - ish'd, Al -

ro - se_ del_ vol - to gia_ so - no pal - len - ti l'a - mo - re d'Al -
read - y_ the_ ro - ses_ that_ deck'd me_ have_ per - ish'd, The love of Al

fre - do_ per - fi - no_ mi man - ca, con - for - to, so - ste - gno dell'
fre - do_ is lost, past_ re - gain - ing, That cheer'd me when faint - ing, my

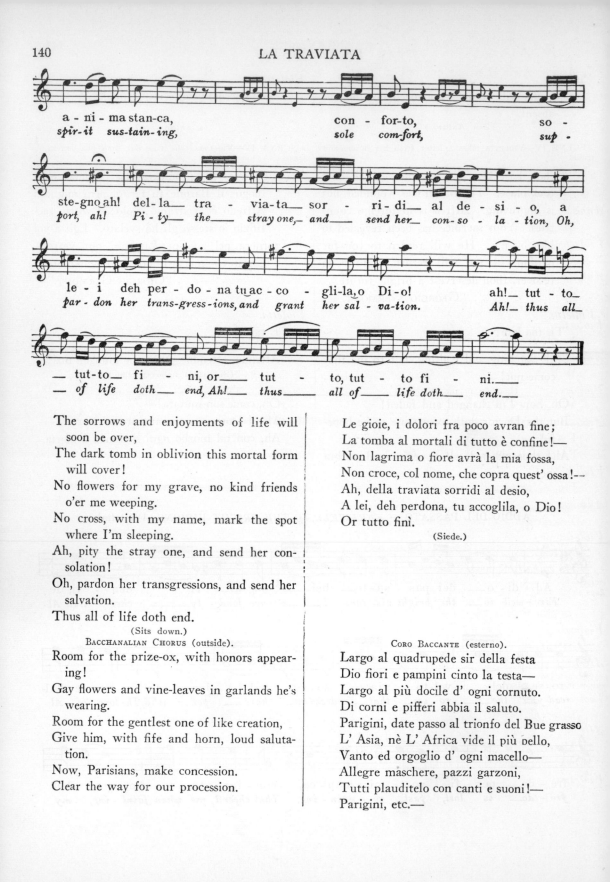

a - ni - ma stan-ca,   con - for-to,   so -
spir-it sus-tain-ing,   sole com-fort,   sup-

ste-gno ah! del-la tra - via-ta sor - ri - di al de - si - o, a
port, ah! Pi - ty the stray one,— and send her con-so - la - tion, Oh,

le - i deh per - do - na tu ac - co - gli-la, o Di-o!   ah!— tut - to
par - don her trans-gress-ions, and grant her sal - va-tion.   Ah!— thus all

— tut-to fi - ni, or— tut - to, tut - to fi - ni.—
— of life doth— end, Ah!— thus— all of— life doth— end.—

The sorrows and enjoyments of life will
soon be over,
The dark tomb in oblivion this mortal form
will cover!
No flowers for my grave, no kind friends
o'er me weeping.
No cross, with my name, mark the spot
where I'm sleeping.
Ah, pity the stray one, and send her con-
solation!
Oh, pardon her transgressions, and send her
salvation.
Thus all of life doth end.
(Sits down.)
BACCHANALIAN CHORUS (outside).
Room for the prize-ox, with honors appear-
ing!
Gay flowers and vine-leaves in garlands he's
wearing.
Room for the gentlest one of like creation,
Give him, with fife and horn, loud saluta-
tion.
Now, Parisians, make concession.
Clear the way for our procession.

Le gioie, i dolori fra poco avran fine;
La tomba al mortali di tutto è confine!—
Non lagrima o fiore avrà la mia fossa,
Non croce, col nome, che copra quest' ossa!—
Ah, della traviata sorridi al desio,
A lei, deh perdona, tu accoglila, o Dio!
Or tutto finì.
(Siede.)

CORO BACCANTE (esterno).
Largo al quadrupede sir della festa
Dio fiori e pampini cinto la testa—
Largo al più docile d' ogni cornuto.
Di corni e piffferi abbia il saluto.
Parigini, date passo al trionfo del Bue grasso
L' Asia, nè L' Africa vide il più bello,
Vanto ed orgoglio d' ogni macello—
Allegre maschere, pazzi garzoni,
Tutti plauditelo con canti e suoni!—
Parigini, etc.—

Asia or Afric ne'er saw one to beat him!

He is the proud boast of all those who meet him.

Maskers and merry boys with fun o'erflowing,

Songs in his honor raise, plaudits bestowing.

Now, Parisians, etc.

SCENE V—Violetta, and Annina, returning hastily.

Annina (hesitating).

My lady—

Violetta.

What has happened?

Annina.

This morning—'tis true then? You are really better?

Violetta.

Yes; but why?

Annina.

Will you promise to be tranquil?

Violetta.

Yes, what wouldst tell me?

Annina.

I would now prepare you

For a pleasure unexpected.

Violetta.

For a pleasure, thou sayest?

Annina.

Yes, gentle mistress.

Violetta.

Alfred! Ah, thou hast seen him?

He comes! oh, haste thee!

(ANNINA makes signs with her hand in the affirmative, and goes to open the door.)

SCENE VI—Violetta, Alfred, and Annina.

Violetta.

Alfred! (Going towards the door.)

Alfred.

(ALFRED enters, pale with emotion, and they throw themselves into each others' arms, exclaiming:)

Violetta.

Beloved Alfred!

Alfred.

My own Violetta!

Ah! I am guilty! I know all, dearest.

Violetta.

I only know, love, that thou art near me!

SCENA V—Detta, ed Annina, che torna frettolosa.

Annina (esitando).

Signora—

Violetta.

Che t' accadde?

Annina.

Quest oggi, è vero? vi sentite meglio?

Violetta.

Sì; perchè?

Annina.

D' esser calma promettete?

Violetta.

Si; che vuoi dirmi?

Annina.

Prevenir vi volli—

Una gioia improvvisa.

Violetta.

Una gioia!—dicesti?

Annina.

Si, o Signora.

Violetta.

Alfredo!—Ah, tu il vedesti!

Ei vien! l' affretta.

(ANNINA afferma col capo, e va ad aprire la porta.)

SCENA VI—Violetta, Alfredo ed Annina.

Violetta.

Alfredo?— (Andando verso l' uscio.)

Alfredo

(comparisce, pallido pella commozione, ed ambidue gettandosi le braccia al collo, esclamano:)

Violetta.

Amato Alfredo!

Alfredo.

Mia Violetta!—

Colpevol sono—so tutto, o cara—

Violetta.

Io so che alfine reso mi sei.

Alfred.

This throbbing heart will show how I still love thee.

I could no more exist, if from thee parted.

Violetta.

If thou hast found me yet with the living,

Believe that grief and woe no more can kill.

Alfred.

Forget the sorrow in love forgiving,

Both sire and son thou'lt pardon still.

Violetta.

Ask me for pardon? 'Tis I am guilty,

Thus rendered by my loving heart.

Both.

No earthly power, nor friend, beloved,

Shall tear us hence apart.

Alfredo.

Da questo palpito, s' io t'ami, impara—

Senza te esistere più non potrei.

Violetta.

Ah, s'anco in vita m' hai ritrovata,

Credi, che uccidere non può il dolor.

Alfredo.

Scorda l'affanno, donna adorata.

A me perdona e al genitor.

Violetta.

Ch' io ti perdoni?—La rea son io;

Ma solo amore tal mi rendè.

Alfredo e Violetta.

Null' uomo o demone, angelo mio.

Mai più staccarti portà da me.

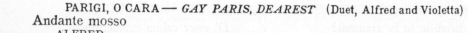

PARIGI, O CARA — *GAY PARIS, DEAREST* (Duet, Alfred and Violetta)

Andante mosso

de'_ cor si af - fan - ni com-pen-so a-vra - i la_ mia sa - lu - te
Joy_ shall re - pay_ thee for_ each dark sor - row, Thy_cheek, so fad - ed,

ri - fio - ri - rà. So - spi-ro e lu - ce tu_ mi sa - ra - i, tut - to il fu-
shall bloom a - gain. Life, light and breath from me thou shalt bor - row, O'er com-ing

ALF.

tu - ro ne ar - ri - de - Pa - ri - gi o ca - ra, noi las - ce -
years, love, bright smiles shall Gay Par - is, dear - est, we'll leave with
reign.

VIOL.

re - mo. De cor - si af-fan - ni com-pen-so a-vra - i, tut-to il cre - a - to ne ar - ri - de-
gladness, Joy shall re - pay us for each dark sor - row, O'er com-ing years, love, bright smiles shall

ALF. VIOL.

La vi ta u - ni - ti tra - scor - re - re - mo, De' cor - si af-
reign. Our lives u - nit - ed, fly we from sad - ness, Joy shall re -

fan - ni com - pen - so a - vra - i; tut - to il fu - tu - re ne ar ri - de -
pay_ thee for each dark sor - row, O'er com - ing years, love, bright smiles shall

VIOL.

rà, de' cor - si af - fan - ni com - pen - so a -
reign. For ev - 'ry dark sor - row some joy_ shall re -

ALF.

de' cor - si af - fan - ni com - pen - so a - vrai,
For all thy sor - rows thou'lt com - fort find.

vra - i, la mia sa - lu - te, la mia sa - lu - te ri-fio-ri - rà, ri-fio-ri -
pay thee, My cheek so fad - ed, My cheek so fad - ed, shall bloom a - gain, shall bloom a -

ah! si la tua sa - lu - te, la tua sa - lu - te ri-fio-ri - rà.
Ah! yes, thy cheek so fad - ed, thy cheek so fad - ed, shall bloom a - gain.

rà.   De' cor-si af - fan - ni com-pen-so a -
gain.   *Joy shall re - pay thee for ev -'ry*

Pa - ri - gio ca - ra, noi la - sce - re - mo,   si,   noi
Gay Par - is, dear - est, we'll leave with glad - ness,   Yes,   we'll

vra - i, tut-to il cre - a - to ne ar-ri-de - rà.
sor - row, O'er com - ing years, love, bright smiles shall reign.

la - sce - re - mo,   la vi-ta u - ni - ti
leave with glad - ness,   Our lives u - nit - ed,

De cor-si af - fan - ni com-pen-so a - vra - i tut-to il fu -
Joy shall re - pay thee for ev -'ry sor - row, O'er com - ing

tra - scor-re - re - mo,   noi tra - scor - re -
fly we from sad - ness,   we will fly from

so a- vra - i,   la mia sa- lu - te, ah! sì, ri - fio - ri - rà.___
re - pay thee,   my cheek, so fad - ed, ah! yes, shall bloom a - gain.___

so a- vra - i,   la mia sa- lu - te, ah! sì, ri - fio - ri - rà.___
re - pay thee,   thy cheek, so fad - ed, ah! yes, shall bloom a - gain.___

Violetta.

 Ah, no more! to church let us be going,
 Our thanks to render with hearts o'erflowing.
     (Staggers.)

Alfred.

 'Thou'rt growing pale!

Violetta.

 'Tis nothing, mark me; unlooked for pleasure can never enter
 Without disturbing a heart o'erburdened.
(She sinks on a chair fainting, and her head falls backwards.)

Alfred.

 Great Heaven!—Violetta!
   (Alarmed, and supporting her.)

Violetta.

 'Tis but the weakness
 From recent illness. Now, love, I'm
  stronger—
 See'st thou? and smiling—
    (With effort.)

Alfred.

 (Ah! cruel fortune!)

Violetta.

 'Twas nothing! Annina, a shawl bring
  hither.

Alfred.

 What now, love? but wait then—

Violetta.

 No! I will go now.
(ANNINA presents the shawl, which she makes an effort to
put on, but finds she is too weak, and exclaims:)
 Great Heav'n, I cannot.
(She throws away the shawl vexedly, and sinks again on
the chair.)

Alfred.

 Heavens, what is it!
 Go, call the Doctor.
    (To ANNINA.)

Violetta.

 Ah, non più—a un tempio—Alfredo, andiamo,
 Del tuo ritorno grazie rendiamo.
     (Vacilla.)

Alfredo.

 Tu impallidisci!

Violetta.

 E nulla, sai? Gioja improvvisa non entra
  mai,
 Senza turbarlo, in mesto core.
(S' abbandona, come sfinita, sopra una sedia. col capo
pendente all' indietro.)

Alfredo.

 Gran Dio!—Violetta!
   (Spaventato, sorreggendola.)

Violetta.

 E il mio malore.
 Fe debolezza—ora son forte—
 Vedi?—sorrido.
    (Sforzandosi.)

Alfredo.

 (Ahi, cruda sorte!)

Violetta.

 Fu nulla—Annina, dammi a vestire.

Alfredo.

 Adesso!—Attendi.

Violetta.

 No—voglio uscire.
(ANNINA le presenta una vesta ch'ella fa per indossare, e
impeditane dalla debolezza, exclama:)
 Gran Dio!—non posso!
(Getta con dispetto la veste, e ricade sulla sedia.)

Alfredo.

 Cielo, che vedo!
 Va pel Dottore.
    (Ad ANNINA.)

Violetta.

Ah, tell him—say that Alfred is now beside
me.
Return'd and faithful to my affection—
Tell him I wish still to live.
(Annina returns.)
(To Alfred.)
But though returned, love, thou hast not
saved me,
No earthly power from the tomb can shield
me.

SCENE VII—Violetta and Alfred.

Violetta.

Ah, cruel fate to die so young,
Tho' much I've borne of sorrow.
To die when hopes, to which I clung,
Reveal a brighter morrow!
Ah! then 'twas naught but madness.
The love to which I yielded!
In vain my heart was shielded,
Armed with faith, all, all in vain.

Alfred.

Oh, dearer far than breath or life,
Beloved one, fondly treasured!
My burning tears, in this dark hour,
With thine shall flow, unmeasured.
But, ah! far more than e'er before
I need thy fond devotion;
Yield not to sad emotion
While hope doth still remain!
(Violetta throws herself upon the lounge.)

SCENE THE LAST—The same, Germont, and the Doctor.

Germont
(entering)
Ah! Violetta—

Violetta.
You, my friend?

Alfred.
My father—

Violetta.
Thou'st not forgot me?

Violetta.

Digli che Alfredo
E ritornato all' amor mio—
Digli che vivere ancor vogl' io.
(Annina parte.)
(Ad Alfredo.)
Ma se tornando non m'hai salvato.
A niuno in terra salvarmi è dato.

SCENA VII—Violetta ed Alfredo.

Violetta.

Gran Dio! morir sì giovane,
Io, che penato ho tanto!
Morir si presso a tergere
Il mio si lungo pianto!
Ah, dunque fu delirio
La credula speranza;
Invano di costanza
Armato avrò il mio cor!
Alfredo—oh, il crudo termine
Serbato al nostro amor!

Alfredo.

Oh, mio sospiro,—oh, palpito
Diletto del cor mio!
Le mie colle tue lagrime
Confondere degg' io—
Or più che mai nostr' anime
Han duopo di costanza—
Ah, tutto alla speranza
Non chiudere il tuo cor!
Violetta mia, deh calmati.
M' uccide il tuo dolor.
(Violetta s'abbandona sul canapè.)

SCENA ULTIMA—Detti, Germont, ed il Dottore

Germont
(entrando).
Ah, Violetta!

Violetta.
Voi, signor!

Alfredo.
Mio padre!

Violetta.
Non mi scordaste?

Germont.

I redeem my promise—
And come, thou noble-hearted,
As my daughter to embrace thee.

Violetta.

Alas. too late thou comest!
Yet, in truth, I am grateful.
(They embrace.)
You see me, Grenvil? dying in the embrace
Of those I love most dearly!

Germont.

Ah, what say'st thou?
(Looking at her, aside.)
Oh, Heaven! 'tis true.

Alfred.

Oh, father, dost thou see her?

Germont.

Withhold! no more thus rend me;
For dark remorse devours my heart already!
Like the pealing of thunder each word con-
        founds me—
Ah! incautious old father!
The wrong accomplished, now stands be-
        fore me!

Violetta
(having opened a drawer over her toilet-table, she takes out
        a medallion, and says:)

Approach more nearly, beloved Alfred, and
        hear me;
Take this, a fair resemblance still
Of me in days of gladness;
A thought 'twill bring in sadness
Of her who loved thee well.

Alfred.

Oh, say not so, thou wilt not die,
But live, with love to bless me!
With such a dread bereavement
Kind Heav'n will not distress me.

Germont.

Oh, noble victim! noble sacrifice
To generous devotion!
Forgive me all the anguish
Thy heart has borne through me.

Violetta.

Should some young maiden, pure and fair,
Fresh as a flower, just blowing,

Germont.

La promessa adempio—
A stringervi qual figlia vengo al seno,
O generosa.

Violetta.

Ohimé! tardi giungeste!
Pure, grata ven sono—
(La abbraccia.)
Grenvil, vedete?—Tra le braccia io spiro
Di quanti ho cari al mondo.

Germont.

Che mai dite!
(Da se.)
Oh cielo!—è ver!
(La osserva.)

Alfredo.

La vedi, padre mio?

Germont.

Di più, non lacerarmi—
Troppo rimorso l'alma mi divora—
Quasi fulmin mi atterra ogni suo detto—
Oh, malcauto vegliardo!
Ah, tutto il mal che feci ora sol vedo!

Violetta
(frattanto avrà aperto a stento un ripostiglio della toilette
        e toltone un medaglione, dici:)

Prendi, quest è l' immagine
De' miei passati giorni.
A rammentar ti torni
Colei che sì t'amo.

Alfredo.

No, non morrai, non dirmelo.
Dêi vivere, amor mio—
A strazio cosi orribile
Qui non mi trasse Iddio.

Germont.

Cara, sublime vittima
D'un generoso amore
Perdonami lo strazio,
Recato al tuo bel core.

Violetta.

Se una pudica vergine
Degli anni suoi nel fiore

Love thee with heart o'erflowing,
Make her, I wish it, thy bride;
Show her this pictured likeness,
Say, 'tis a gift from me,
Who, now in heav'n, 'mid angels bright,
Prayeth for her, for thee.

Germont. ⎫ While yet these eyes have tears to
Doctor. ⎬   flow,
Annina. ⎭ I shall still weep, still weep for
                thee.
Go, join the blessed spirits now:
God calls thee heavenward, his own to be.

Violetta   (reviving).
   'Tis wondrous!

All.
   What?

Violetta
           (speaking).
   They all have ceased.
   The paroxysms that distressed me.
   Fresh life awakens within me, giving me
   A vigor new and rare!
   I am to life restored now!
   Oh, rapture!
       (She falls upon the sofa.)

All.
   Oh, heaven! Dead!

Alfred.
   Violetta!

All.
   May Heav'n her soul receive!

Doctor
      (examining the pulse).
   'Tis over!

All.
   Oh, grief and woe!

A te donasse il core—
Sposa ti sia—lo vo'
Le porgi questa effigie,
Dille che dono all' è
Di chi, nel ciel tra gli angeli
Prega per lei, per te.

Germont. ⎫ Finchè avrà il ciglio lagrime
Dottore. ⎬ Io piangerò per te.
Annina. ⎭ Vola a' beati spiriti;
            Iddio ti chiama a sè.

Violetta   (alzandosi riammata).
   E strano!

Tutti.
   Che!

Violetta.
   Cessarono
   Gli spasmi del dolore.
   In me rinasce, m'anima
   Insolito vigore!
   Ah!—io ritorno a vivere!
        (Trasalendo.)
   Oh, gio—ia!
        (Ricade sul canapè.)

Tutti.
   Oh, cielo!—muori!

Alfredo.
   Violetta!

Tutti.
   Oh, Dio!—soccorrasi.

Dottore
      (dapo averle toccato il polso).
   E spenta!

Alfredo e Tutti.
   Oh, ⎰ rio ⎱ dolor!
      ⎱ mio ⎰

LA FORZA DEL DESTINO
(THE FORCE OF DESTINY)

by

GIUSEPPE VERDI

ARGUMENT.

DONNA LEONORA has a lover, in the person of *Don Alvaro*, with whom she is on the point of eloping from the house of her father, the *Marquis of Calatrava*, when the latter enters; a scene ensues, and the *Marquis* is slain by the accidental discharge of *Don Alvaro*'s pistol.

Leonora, after the death of her father, believing that *Alvaro* has deserted her, flies, and, disguised in male attire, becomes a recluse, living in a cavern, the privacy of which is secured to her by *Father Guardiano*, the superior of a religious community. Her brother, *Don Carlos di Vargas*, becomes imbued with the belief that it is his paramount duty to hunt the world through until he finds *Leonora* and her lover, and by their deaths to avenge his father's and the dishonor brought on the name he bears.

Don Carlos and *Don Alvaro*, under assumed names, and unknown to each other, being in the camp of the Italian and Spanish armies, *Alvaro* is the means of saving the life of *Don Carlos* from assassins, and they vow lasting friendship. Soon after this *Alvaro* is wounded in battle, it is supposed mortally. *Don Carlos* finds in the wounded man's possession a portrait of *Leonora*, which confirms him in his suspicion that his new friend is none other than *Alvaro*.

Alvaro, under the name of Father Raffaello, becomes a friar in a religious establishment situated in the immediate vicinity of the cavern in which *Leonora* is secluded. *Don Carlos* agains finds and compels him to fight; *Carlos* falls—this time mortally wounded. *Leonora* enters from her cavern, and the three recognize each other. *Don Carlos* calls upon his sister to embrace him ere he dies, seizes the opportunity to stab her, and then expires. *Leonora* implores the forgiveness of Heaven for *Alvaro*, who, humbled in heart by her earnest accents, throws himself penitent at her feet, and the curtain falls at the death of *Leonora*.

CHARACTERS.

IL MARCHESE DI CALATRAVA.

DONNA LEONORA,
DON CARLO DI VARGAS, } *his Children.*

DON ALVARO, *Donna Leonora's Lover.*

PREZIOSILLA, *a Young Gipsy.*

PADRE GUARDIANO,
FRA MELITONE, } *Franciscan Friars.*

CURRA, *Waiting-Woman to Leonora.*

MASTRO TRABUCO, *A Muleteer, afterwards a Pedlar.*

Alcade, a Magistrate.

A Spanish Military Surgeon.

Muleteers, Spanish and Italian Peasants, Spanish and Italian Soldiers, Franciscan Friars, Beggars, Vivandiers, Tumblers, Host, Hostess, Servants, Pedlars, Trumpeters, etc.

Scene, — SPAIN and ITALY. Time — End of the 18th Century.

LA FORZA DEL DESTINO
[THE FORCE OF DESTINY]

ATTO I

SCENA I—Siviglia.—Una sala, tappezzata di damasco, con ritratti di famiglia, ed arme gentilizie, addobbata nello stile del secolo 18.0 pero in cattivo stato. Di fronte due finestre; quella a sinistra chiusa, l'altra a destra aperta e praticable, dalla quale si vede un cielo purissimo, illuminato dalla Luna, e cime d'alberi. Tra le finestre e un grande armadio chiuso, contenente vesti, biancherie, ecc. Ognuna delle pareti laterali ha due porte. La prima a destra della spettatore e la comune; la seconda mette alla stanza di CURRA. A sinistra in fondo e l' appartamento del MARCHESE; piu presso al proscenio quello di LEONORA. A mezza scena, alquanto a sinistra, e un tavolino coperto da tappeto di damasco, e sopra il medesimo una chitarra vasi di fiori, due candelabri d' argento accesi con paralumi, sola luce che schiarira la sala. Un seggiolone presso il tavolino; un mobile con sopra un oriuolo fra le due porte a destra; altro mobile sopra il quale e il ritratto, tutta figura, del MARCHESE, appoggiato alla parete sinistra. La sala sara parapettata.

Il MARCHESE DI CALATRAVA, con lume in mano, sta congedandosi da DONNA LEONORA preoccupata. CURRA viene dalla sinistra.

Marchese.

(Abbracciandola con affetto.)

Buona notte, mia figlia ! Addio, diletta !
Aperto ancora è quel verone !

(Va a chiuderlo.)

Leonora.

(Oh angoscia !)

Marchese.

Nulla dice il tuo amor ? Perchè si trista ?

(Tornando a lei.)

Leonora.

Padre—Signor—

Marchese.

La pura aura de' campi
Calma al tuo cor donova ;
Fuggisti lo straniero di te indegno
A me lascia la cura
Dell' avvenir. Nel padre tuo confida,
Che t' ama tanto.

Leonora.

Ah, padre !

ACT I

SCENE I.—Seville.—A room, hung with damask, family portraits, and arms of nobility, furnished in the style of the 18th century, all, however, in a shabby condition. Two windows face the audience; that on the left is closed, that on the right open and practicable, from which is seen a clear sky, and the tops of trees, with a bright moonlight? Between the windows a large wardrobe, containing clothes, etc. Each side has two doors. The first to the right of the spectator is the common door; the second leads to CURRA'S room. On the left side farthest off, is the apartment of the MARQUIS; that nearest the proscenium leads to LEONORA'S room. Halfway, a little to the left, is a table with a damask cover, and on it a guitar, vases of flowers, and two lighted silver candlesticks with shades, the only light in the room. A large chair near the table; a piece of furniture with a clock on it between the two doors on the right; other furniture on the left, above which, hung against the wall, is the full-length portrait of the MARQUIS. The room is entirely enclosed.

MARQUIS OF CALATRAVA, with a light in his hand is taking leave of DONNA LEONORA, who is thoughtful. CURRA comes from the left.

Marchese

(Embracing her affectionately.)

Good night, my child ! Adieu, my dear one!
That balcony-window still open ?

(Goes and shuts it.)

Leonora.

(Oh, anguish !)

Marchese.

Not a word of love ? Why so sad ?

(Turning to her.)

Leonora.

Father—sir—

Marchese.

The pure air of the fields
Has brought peace to thy heart,
Thou hast left a stranger unworthy of thee,
And to me leave the care
Of thy future. In thy father confide,
Who so dearly loves thee.

Leonora.

Ah, my father !

Marchese.

Ebben, che t' ange ?

Non pianger, io t'adoro !

Leonora.

(Oh, mio rimorso !)

Marchese.

Ti lascio.

Leonora

      (Gettandosi con effusione tra le braccia del padre.)

Ah, padre mio !

Marchese.

Ti benedica il cielo ! Addio !

Leonora.

Addio !

(Il MARCHESE bacia, riprende il lume, e va nelle sue stanze.)

SCENA II.—CURRA segue il MARCHESE, chiude la porta ond' e uscito, e riviene a LEONORA abbandonatasi sul seggiolone piangente)

Curra.

Temea restasse qui fino a domani !

Si riapra il veron.

      (Eseguisce.)

Tutto s'appronti. E andiamo.

Toglie dall' armadio un sacco da notte in cui ripone biancherie e vesti.)

Leonora.

E si amoroso padre avverso

Fia tanto a' voti miei ?

No, no, decidermi non so.

Curra

      (Affaccendata.)

Che dite ?

Leonora.

Quegli accenti nel cor come pugnalia

Scendevanmi. Se ancor restava, appreso

Il ver gli avrei.

Curra

      (Smette il lavoro.)

Domani allor nel sangue

Suo saria don Alvaro,

Od a Siviglia prigioniero, e forse

Al patibol poi—

Leonora.

Taci !

Marchese.

What disturbs thee ?

Do not weep—I love thee dearly.

Leonora.

(Oh, what remorse !)

Marchese.

I leave thee.

Leonora

      (Throwing herself with transport into his arms.)

Ah, dearest father !

Marchese.

Heaven bless thee ! Adieu !

Leonora.

Adieu !

(The MARQUIS kisses her, takes up a light, and goes to his room.)

SCENE II.—CURRA follows the MARQUIS, closes the door, at which he went out, and returns to LEONORA, who has thrown herself in the chair.

Curra.

I thought he would stay till daylight !

Let us re-open the balcony.

      (Opens it.)

Prepare everything and let us go.

(Takes travelling bag from the wardrobe, and fills it with linen and clothes.)

Leonora.

Can so fond a father

Oppose my dearest wishes ?

No, no, I cannot leave.

Curra

      (Very busy.)

What do you say ?

Leonora.

His loving tones struck like a dagger

To my soul. Had he remained,

The truth I should have spoken.

Curra

      (Leaving off work.)

Then to-morrow

Don Alvaro would lie weltering in his blood,

Or be a prisoner in Seville,

And perhaps on the scaffold—

Leonora.

Be silent !

Curra.

E tutto puesto
Perch' egli volle amar chi non l' amava.

Leonora.

Io non amarlo! Tu ben sai s'io l'ami!
Patria, famiglia, padre,
Per lui non abbandono!
Ahi troppo!—troppo sventurata sono!
Me pellegrina ed orfana
Lungi dal natio nido,
Un fato inesorabile
Trascina a stranio lido,
Colmo di triste immagini,
Da' suoi rimorsi affranto
E il cor di questa misera
Dannato a eterno pianto.
Ti lascio, ahimè, con lacrime,
Dolce mia terra!—Addio!
Ahimè, non avrà termine
Si gran dolore!—Addio!

Curra.

M' aiuti, signorina—
Più presto andrem.

Leonora.

S' ei non giungesse?
        (Guarda l' orologio.)
E tardi.
Mezzanotte è suonata!
        (Contenta.)
Ah no, più non verrà!

Curra.

Quale romore!
Calpestio di cavelli!

Leonora

        (Corre al verone.)
E desso!

Curra.

Era impossibil
Ch' ei non venisse!

Leonora.

Ciel!

Curra.

Bando al timore.

Curra.

And all because he loves one
Who does not return his love.

Leonora.

Does not return it?
Well thou knowest I love him!
Country, family, father, for him do I not
    leave?
Ah me!—I am indeed unhappy!
A friendless wanderer,
Far from my native land!
An inexorable fate
Drags me to a foreign country,
Overwhelmed in dire woe,
Crushed with deep remorse,
My miserable spirit
Is condemned to constant grief.
With tears, alas! I leave thee,
My own sweet native land.—Adieu!
Never, never will end
This bitter woe!—Adieu!

Curra.

Help me, signora—
We shall the sooner be ready.

Leonora.

If he should not come?
        (Looks at the clock.)
It is late—
Midnight has struck!
        (Contentedly.)
Ah no, he will not come.

Curra.

What noise is that?
It is the tread of horses!

Leonora

        (Running to balcony.)
    It is he!

Curra.

It was impossible
That he should fail to come.

Leonora.

Heavens!

Curra.

Away with fear

SCENA III. Detti.—DON ALVARO senza mantello, con giusta-cuore a maniche larghe, e sopra una giubbetta da Majo, rete sul capo, stivali, speroni, entra dal verone e si getta tra le braccia di LEONORA.

SCENE III.—The same,—DON ALVARO, without a cloak, wearing a tight vest, with large sleeves and a slashed doublet, a net on his head, boots and spurs, he enters throught the balcony, and throws himself into LEONORA'S arms.

Alvaro.

Ah, per sempre, o mio bell' angelo,
Ne congiunse il cielo adesso
L'universo in questo amplesso
Con me veggo giubilar.

Leonora.

Don Alvaro !

Alvaro.

Ciel, che t' agita ?

Leonora.

Presso è il giorno.

Alvaro.

Da lung' ora
Mille inciampi tua dimora
M'han vietato penetrar;
Ma d' amor si puro e santo
Nulla opporsi può all' incanto,
E Dio stesso il nostro palpito
In letizia tramutò.

(A CURRA.)

Quelle vesti dal verone
Getta.

Leonora

(A CURRA.)

Arresta.

Alvaro

(A CURRA.)

No, no !

(A LEONORA.)

Seguimi;
Lascia omai la tua prigiane.

Leonora.

Ciel ! risolvermi non so !

Alvaro.

Pronti destrieri di già ne attendono;
Un sacerdote ne aspetta all' ara !
Vieni, d'amore in sen ripara
Che Dio dal cielo benedirà!
E quando il sole, nume dell' India,
Di mia regale stirpe signore,
Il mondo innondi del suo splendore,
Sposi, oh diletta, ne troverà.

Alvaro.

Ah, for ever, my lovely angel,
Heaven now unites us !
All the universe is glad
With me, in this embrace.

Leonora.

Don Alvaro !

Alvaro.

Oh Heaven, why thus agitated ?

Leonora.

The dawn is nigh.

Alvaro.

For a long time
Many obstacles kept me
From reaching thy dwelling
But nought can stay the power
Of a love so pure and holy,
And Heaven itself our fears
Changes to contentment.

(To CURRA.)

Those vestments
Throw from the balcony.

Leonora

(To CURRA.)

Stay.

Alvaro

(To CURRA.)

No, no !

(To LEONORA.)

Follow me.
Leave thy prison now for ever.

Leonora.

Oh Heaven ! I cannot decide !

Alvaro.

Swift steeds are waiting,
A priest at the altar attends !
Come, shelter find in the love
Which Heaven will richly bless.
And when the sun, the god of India,
Sire of my royal race
Shall flood the earth with splendor,
Oh, beloved ! it will find us united.

Leonora.

E tarda l' ora.

Alvaro

(A CURRA.)

Su via t' affretta !

Leonora.

Ancor sospendi !

Alvaro.

Eleonora !

Leonora.

Diman.

Alvaro.

Che parli ?

Leonora.

Ten prego aspetta !

Alvaro

(Assai turbato.)

Diman.

Leonora.

Domani si partirà.
Anco una volta il padre, veder desio;
E tu contento, gli è ver, ne sei?

Sì perchè m'ami—

(Si confonde.)

Nè opporti dèi—
Oh anch' io, tu il sai— t' amo io tanto !
Ne son felice ! oh cielo, quanto !
Gonfio di gioia ho il cor ! Restiamo !

Sì, Don Alvaro, io t'amo, io t' amo !

(Piange.)

Alvaro.

Gonfio hai di gioia il core—e lagrimi!

Come un sepolcro tua mano è gelida !
Tutto comprendo—tutto, signora.

Leonora.

Alvaro !—Alvaro !

Alvaro

Eleonora !

(Lunga pausa.)

Saprò soffrire io solo. Tolga Iddio
Che i passi miei per debolezza segua—

Leonora.

The hour is late.

Alvaro

(TO CURRA.)

Away—make haste !

Leonora

(TO CURRA.)

Wait awhile !

Alvaro.

Eleonora !

Leonora.

To-morrow.

Alvaro.

What sayest thou ?

Leonora.

I pray thee, wait !

Alvaro

(Much disturbed.)

To-morrow.

Leonora.

To-morrow we will go .
Once more my father
I desire to see !
Thou art willing—is it not so ?
Yes, for thou lovest me, and wilt not refuse.
I too, thou knowest, love thee !

(Confusedly.)

Am I not happy ? O heaven !
How my heart swells with joy !—Let us wait !
Yes, Alvaro, I love thee ! I love thee !

(Weeps.)

Alvaro.

Thy heart swells with joy—then why these tears ?
Thy hand is cold as death !
I understand all, signora—all !

Leonora.

Alvaro !—Alvaro !

Alvaro.

Eleonora !

(A long pause.)

I can suffer alone. Heaven forbid
That weakly thou shouldst follow me—

Sciolgo i tuoi giuri. Le nuziali tede
Sarebbero per noi segnal di morte,
Se tu, com' io non m' ami—se pentita—

Leonora.

Son tua, son tua col core e colla vita !

I absolve thy vows. The nuptial tie
Would be for us the stroke of death,
If thou lovest not as I do—if, repenting—

Leonora.

I am thine ! thine with heart and soul !

AH! SEGUIRTI FINO — *AH! I'LL FOLLOW* Air (Leonora)

Ah! se - guir - ti fi - no a - gl'ul - ti - mi Con - fi - ni del - la
Ah! I'll fol - low ev - er in thy path To earth's far con - fines

ter - ra; Con te sfi - dar - im - pa - vi - da Di rio des - tin la
wing - ing, And bold - ly with thee I de - fy The ter - rors war is

guer - ra; Mi fia pe - ren - ne gau - di - o De te - rea vo - lut - ta. Ti
bring - ing, I'll share all dan - gers by thy side, With love and joy e - late; I'll

se - guo, an - diam di - vi - der - ci, Il fa - to, no, no, non po - tra.
fol - low thee what - e'er may be - tide, We win a hap - py fate.

Alvaro.

Sospiro, luce ed anima
Di questo cor che t' ama ;
Finchè mi batta un palpito,
Far paga ogni tua brama
Il solo ed immutabile
Desio per me sarà.
Mi segui ! Andiam, dividerci
Il mondo non potrà.

(S' avvicinano al verone, quando ad un tratto si sente a sinistra
un aprire e chiudere di porte.)

Leonora.

Quale rumor !

Curra

(Ascoltando.)

Ascendono le scale !

Alvaro.

Hope, light and life
Of the heart that adores thee !
Till my pulses beat no more
My sole desire will be
To meet thy every wish,
To cherish thee for aye.
Follow me—let us go !
The world has no power to part us.

(They approach the balcony when of a sudden is heard the
opening and shutting of a door.)

Leonora.

What is that noise ?

Curra

(Listening.)

Some one is coming up stairs !

Alvaro.

Presto, partiamo !

Leonora.

E tardi.

Alvaro.

Allor di calma
E duopo.

Curra.

Vergin santa !

Leonora

(A ALVARO.)

Colà t' ascondi !

Alvaro.

No. Degg' io difenderti.

(Traendo una pistola.)

Leonora.

Ripon quell' arma—contro ai genitore
Vorresti ?

Alvaro.

No, contro me stesso.

(Ripone la pistola.)

Leonora.

Orrore !

SCENA IV.—Dopo vari colpi apresi con istrepito la porta del
ondo a sinistra, ed il MARCHESE DI CALATRAVA entra infuriato
brandendo una spada e seguito da due servi con lume.

Marchese.

Vil seduttor !—infame figlia !

Leonora

(Correndo a' suoi piedi.)

No, padre mio !

Marchese.

Più non lo sono.

(La respinge.)

Alvaro

(AL MARCHESE.)

Il solo colpevole son io
Ferite ' vendicatevi !

(Presentandogli i' petto.)

Marchese

(Al ALVARO)

No la condotta vostra
Da troppo abbietta origine uscito vi dim-
ostra.

Alvaro.

Quick ! Let us go !

Leonora.

Too late !

Alvaro.

Well, then,
We must be calm and firm.

Curra.

Holy Virgin !

Leonora

(To ALVARO.)

Conceal thyself there !

Alvaro.

No. I must defend thee.

(Drawing out a pistol.)

Leonora.

Put back that weapon—
Wouldst use it 'gainst my father ?

Alvaro.

No, against myself.

(Replaces the pistol.)

Leonora.

Horrible !

SCENE IV.—After repeated blows the door at the back, on the
left, is burst open, and the MARQUIS OF CALATRAVA enters, enraged,
sword in hand, and followed by two servants with lights.

Marchese.

Vile seducer !—shameless daughter !

Leonora

(Rushing to his feet.)

No, father, no.

Marchese.

I am no longer thy father.

(Repulsing her.)

Alvaro

(To the MARQUIS.)

I alone am guilty.
Strike !—avenge thyself !

(Presenting himself.)

Marchese

(To ALVARO.)

No, thy conduct
Shows thee of origin too low.

Alvaro.

Signor Marchese !

(Risentito.)

Marchese

(A LEONORA.)

Scostati—

(Ai Servia.)

S' arresti l' empio !

Alvaro

(Cavando nuovamente la pistola)

Guai
Se alcun di voi si move.

(Ai Servi, che retrocedono.)

Leonora

(Currendo a lui.)

Alvaro, oh ciel, che fai !

Alvaro

(Al MARCHESE.)

Cedo a voi sol—ferite !

Marchese.

Morir per mano mia !
Per mano del cranefice tal vita estinta fia.

Alvaro.

Signor di Calatrava,
Pura siccome gli angeli è vostra figlia—
Il giuro—reo son io solo. Il dubbio
Che l' ardir mio qui desta, si tolga colla
    vita.
Eccomi inerme.

(Getta la pistola, che percuote al suolo, scarica il colpo, e
ferisce mortalmente il MARCHESE.)

Marchese.

Io muoio !

Alvaro

(Disperato.)

Arma funesta !

Leonora

(Correndo a' piedi del padre.)

Aita !

Marchese

(A LEONORA)

Lungi da me—
Contamina tua vista la mia morte !

Leonora.

Padre !

Alvaro.

Marquis !

(Excitedly.)

Marchese

(To LEONORA.)

Stand aside—

(To the Servants.)

Seize the wretch !

Alvaro

(Again taking out his pistol.)

Approach me, if you dare !

(To the Servants, who retire.)

Leonora

(Running to him.)

Alvaro, what madness is this ?

Alvaro

(To the MARQUIS.)

To thee alone I yield—strike !

Marchese.

Not by my hand you die ;
So base a life belongs only to the execu-
    tioner.

Alvaro.

Signor de Calatrava, your child
Is innocent as an angel ;
I alone am guilty.
Let the doubt which my rashness has raised
Be dispelled with my life. Behold me
    unarmed.

(Throws away the pistol, which in falling, goes off, and kills
the MARQUIS.)

Marchese.

I am dying !

Alvaro

(In despair.)

Ill-fated weapon !

Leonora

(Rushing to her father.)

Help !

Marchese

(To LEONORA.)

Begone—
Thy presence disgraces me in death!

Leonora.

Father :

Marchese.

    Ti maledico !

        (Cade tra le braccia dei Servi.)

Leonora.

    Cielo pietade !

Alvaro.

    Oh sorte !

(I Servi portano il MARCHESE alle sue stanze, mentre DON ALVARO trae seco verso il verone la sventurata LEONORA. Cade la tela.)

FINE DELL' ATTO PRIMO:

Marchese.

    My curse upon thee !

        (Falls into the Servants' arms.)

Leonora.

    Have mercy, kind Heaven !

Alvaro.

    O cruel fate !

(The Servants bear the MARQUIS to his apartments, whilst DON ALVARO drags the unhappy LEONORA towards the balcony. The Curtain falls.)

END OF THE FIRST ACT

ATTO II.

SCENA I. Villaggio d' Hornachuelos e vicinanze.—Grande cucina d'una Osteria a pian terreno. A sinistra, e la porta d' ingresso che da su la via; di fronte una finestra ed un credenzone con piatti, ecc. A destra, in fonda un gran focolare ardente con varie pentole; piu vicino alle bocca-scena breve scaletta che mette ad una stanza, la cui porta e praticabile. Da un lato gran tavola apparecchiata con sopra una lucerna accesa. L' Oste e l' Ostessa che non parlano, sono affaccendati ad ammanir la cena. L' ALCADE e seduto presso al foco; uno STUDENTE presso la tavola. Alquanti MULATTIERI, fra quali MASTRO TRABUCO, ch' e al dinanzi sopra un suo basto. Due CONTADINI. due CONTADINE, la SERVA, ed un MULATTIERE. ballano la SEGUIDILLA. Sopra altra tavola, vino, bicchieri fiaschi, una bottiglia d'acquavite.

L'ALCADE, uno STUDENTE, MASTRO TRABUCO, MULATTIERI, PAESANI FAMIGLI, PAESANE ecc. A tempo LEONORA in vesti virile.

Coro.

Hola, hola, hola !
Ben giungi, o mulattier,
La notte a riposar.
Hola, hola, hola !
  Qui devi col bicchier
  Le forze ritemprar !

(L' Ostessa mette sulla tavola una grande zuppiera.)

Alcade.

La cena è pronta.
        (Sedendosi alla mensa.)

Tutti
        (Prenendo posto presso la tavolo.)

A cena, a cena !

Studente
        (Frattanto sul d' avanti dice.)

(Ricerco invan la suora e il eduttore.)
  Perfidi !

Coro
        (All' ALCADE.)

Voi la mensa benedite ?

Alcade.

Può farlo il Licenziato.

Studente.

Di buon grado. Benedetto
E il pane che il Padre del ciel ci manda.

Tutti
        (Sedendo.)

Cosi sia.

ACT II.

SCENE I. The Village of Hornachuelos and neighborhood A large kitchen on the ground-floor of an Inn. On the left, the entrance-door leading to the road, facing the audience; a window, and a large dresser, with plates, etc. On the right, at the back, a large fireplace, with cauldrons, etc., nearer the proscenium, a short staircase, leading to a room which has a practicable door. On one side a large table, laid out, and on it a lighted lamp. The Host and Hostess, who do not speak, are busy preparing the supper. The ALCADE is seated near the fire; a STUDENT s seated near the table. Some MULETEERS, amongst others MASTER TRABUCO, who is in front, leaning on his pack saddle. Two male and two female PEASANTS, the female SERVANT and a MULETEER dance the Seguidilla. Upon another table, wine, glasses, flasks, and a bottle of brandy.

The ALCADE, a STUDENT, MASTER TRABUCO, MULETEERS, PEASANTS ATTENDANTS, FEMALE PEASANTS, etc. Later LEONORA, in male attire.

Chorus.

Hurrah, hurrah, hurrah !
Now welcome, O muleteer,
Who comes to pass the night ;
Hurrah, hurrah, hurrah !
Here is the brimming cup,
Thy strength thou canst restore.

(The Hostess places a large soup-tureen on the table.)

Alcade.

The supper is ready.
        (Seating himself at table.)

All
        (Taking their places at table.)

To supper, to supper !

Student
        (In the foreground.)

In vain my sister and her betrayer I seek !
The ingrates !

Chorus
        (To the ALCADE.)

Will you not ask a blessing ?

Alcade.

The Licentiate can do it.

Student.

With all my heart. Blessed be
The bread that Heaven sends us from
  above.

All
        (Seated.)

Amen.

Leonora

(Presentandosi alla potra della stanza a destra, che terra socchiusa

(Che vedo !—mio fratello !)

(Si ritira.)

(L' Ostessa avra gia distribuito il riso e siede cogli altri. Inseguito e servito altro piatto. TRABUCO e in disparte, sempre appoggiato al suo basto.

Alcade

(Assaggiando.)

Buono.

Studente

(Mangiando.)

Eccellente !

Mulattieri.

Par che dica mangiami.

Studente

(All' Ostessa.)

Tu das epulis accumbere divum.

Alcade.

Non sa Latino ma cucina bene.

Studente.

Viva l'Otessa !

Tutti.

Evviva !

Studente.

Non vien Mastro
Trabuco ?

Trabuco.

E Venerdi.

Studente.

Digiuna ?

Trabuco.

Appunto.

Studente.

E quella personcina con lei guinta?

SCENA II. Detti, e PREZIOSILLA, ch' entra saltellando.

Preziosilla.

Viva la guerra !

Leonora

(Appearing at the door of the room on the right, which she keeps half closed.)

What do I see !—my brother !

(She retires.)

(The Hostess has already distributed the rice, and sits down with the others. Other dishes are served up. TRABUCO on one side leans on his pack-saddle.)

Alcade

(Tasting.)

Capital !

Student

(Eating.)

Excellent !

Muleteer.

It seems to say, 'Come, eat me.'

Student

(To the Hostess.)

Tu das epulis accumbere divum.

Alcade.

She does not know Latin, but she cooks well.

Student.

Long live the Hostess !

All.

Hurrah !

Student.

Does not Master Trabuco
Come to supper ?

Trabuco.

It is Friday.

Student.

Oh, you are fasting ?

Trabuco.

Just so.

Student.

And the little person who came with you

SCENE II. The same, enter PREZIOSILLA, dancing.

Preziosilla.

Success to war !

Tutti.
> Preziosilla !—Brava !
> Brava !

All.
> Preziosilla !—Bravo !
> Bravo !

Studente.
> Qui, presso a me.

Student.
> Here, sit by me.

Tutti.
> Tu la ventura.
> Dirne potrai.

All.
> You will be able
> To tell us our fortunes.

Preziosilla.
> Chi brama far fortuna ?

Preziosilla.
> Who wishes to make his fortune ?

Tutti.
> Tutti il vogliam.

All.
> Everyone wishes it.

Preziosilla.
> Correte allor soldati.
> In Italia, dov' è rotta la guerra
> Contro al Tedesco.

Preziosilla.
> Haste, then, to Italy, as soldiers,
> Where war has broken out
> Against the Germans.

Tutti.
> Morte
> Ai Tedeschi !

All.
> Death
> To the Germans !

Preziosilla.
> Flagel d' Italia eterno
> E de' figliuoli suoi.

Preziosilla.
> Of Italy and her sons
> They are the eternal scourge.

Tutti.
> Tutti v' andremo.

All.
> We will all go.

Preziosilla.
> Ed io sarò con voi.

Preziosilla.
> And I shall be with you.

AL SUON DEL TAMBURO —*THE DRUM GAILY BEATING* (Preziosilla and Chorus)

Al suon del tam - bu - ro, Al brio del cor - sie - ro, Al nu - go-lo az-
The drum gai - ly beat - ing The hors - es swift fleet - ing, And vol - leys re-

zur - ro, Del bron - zo guer - rier! Dei cam - pi al su - sur - ro S'e-
peat - ing Give glo - ry to war! The bu - sy sounds a - bout the camp Drive

sal - ta il pen-sier! E bel - la la guer-ra, E bel - la la
anx-ious thought a - far! In bat - tle is glo - ry, In bat - tle is

guer - ra! Ev - vi - va la guer - ra, ev - vi - va!
glo - ry! Hur - rah,— then, hur - rah, hur - rah, —— hur - rah!

E so - lo ob - bli - a - to Da vi - le chi muo - re; Al bra - vo sol -
No cow - ard can ev - er Make no - ble en - deav - er, But he - roes in

da - to Al ve - 'ro va - lor E pre - mio ser - ba - to Di glo - ria d'o -
sto - ry Re - mem - ber'd will be: To them be the glo - ry By for - tune's de -

D.C. ℅ al Fine   (Turning from one to the other)

nor!   Se vie - ni, fra - tel - lo, Sa - rai ca - po - ra - le,   E
cree!   Good luck shall o'er - take you, A cor - po - ral make you,   A

tu col - lon - nel - lo, E tu ge - ne - ra - le Il di - o fur - fan - tel - lo dall'
co - lonel's place take you, A gen - 'ral you'll be; Be brave in the bat - tles When

D.C. ℅ al Fine

ar - co im - mor - ta - 'le Fa - ro— di cap - pel - lo Al bra - vo uf - fi - zial.
mus - ket - ry rat - tles, And forth in dis - or - der The foe - men will flee.

Studente.	Student.
E che riserbasi	And for the student
Allo studente ?	What is reserved ?
(Le presenta la mano.)	(Holding out his hand.)
Preziosilla	*Preziosilla*
(Osservando.)	(Observing him)
O tu miserrime	Miserable man,
Vicende avrai.	Sorrow shortly will find thee.
Studente.	*Student.*
Che di'?	What do you say ?
Preziosilla	*Preziosilla*
(Fissandolo.)	(Earnestly)

Non mente
Il labbro mai—
Ma a te—carissimo,
Non presto fè

(Poi sotto voce.)

Non sei studenti ;
Non dirò niente,
Ma, gnaffe, a me,
Non se la fa,—
No per mia fè.
Tral la la là !

SCENA III.   Detti, e PELLEGRINI, che passao da furoi.

Voci Ie.

(Lontane.)

Ah, pietade o Signor !

Voci 2e.

Pieta di noi.

Voci Ie.

Sii clemente, o Signor !

Voci 2e.

Pietà di noi.

Voci Ie.

(Piu vicine.)

Te lodiamo, o Signor !

Voci 2e.

Pietà di noi.

Voci Ie.

Deh, pietade, o Signorà!

Voci 2e.

Pietà di noi.

Tutti.

Chi sono ?

(Alzandosi e scoprendosi.)

Alcade.

Pellegrini,
Che vanno al giubileo.

Leonora

(Ricomparendo agitatissima sulla stessa porta.)

Fuggir potessi.

Coro.

Che passino attendiamo.

Alcade.

Ebben, preghiam noi pure.

My lips
Ne'er utter falsehoods,
But on thee, dear sir,
I don't much rely.

(In an undertone.)

No student art thou.
I'll say nothing,
But with me, forsooth,
The ruse has failed,
By my faith !
Tra la la la !

SCENE III.   The same, and PILGRIMS, passing outsid

1st Voice

(in the distance.)

Pardon, gracious Heaven.

2nd Voice.

Have pity on us.

1st Voice.

Grant us grace !

2nd Voice.

Have pity on us.

1st Voice

(Nearer.)

We praise thee, O Heaven !

2nd Voice.

Have pity on us.

1st Voice.

We thank thee, O Heaven !

2nd Voice.

Have pity on us.

All.

Who are these ?

(Rising and showing themselves.)

Alcade.

They are Pilgrims,
Who are going to the jubilee.

Leonora

(Appearing, in great agitation, at the same door.)

If I could only escape !

Chorus.

Let us wait till they pass.

Alcade.

And let us also pray.

Coro.

Si preghiamo.

Tutti

(Lasciando ıa mensa s' inginocchiano.)

Suo noi concordi e supplici,
Stendi la man, Signore ;
Dall' infernal malore
Ne salvi tua pietà.

Leonora.

(Ah, da un fratello salvami
Che anela il sangue mio ;
Se tu nol vuoi, gran Dio,
Nessun mi salverà !)

(Rientra nella stanza chiudendone la porta. Tutti riprendono
i loro posti. Sı passano un fiasco.)

Studente.

Viva la buona compagnia !

Tutti.

Viva !

Studente.

Salute qui, l' eterna gloria poi !

(Alzando il bicchiere)

Tutti.

Cosi sia.

(Fanno altrettanto.)

Siudente.

Già cogli angioli, Trabuco ?

Trabuco.

E che ?—con questo inferno ?

Studente.

E quella personcina con lei giunta,
Venne pel giubileo ?

Trabuco.

Nol so.

Studente.

Per altro.
E gallo, oppur gallina ?

Trabuco.

De' forastier non bado che al danaro.

Siudente.

Molto prudente !

(Poi all' ALCADE.)

Chorus.

Yes, let us pray.

All

(Leaving the table and kneeling down.)

O'er us, imploring Thee,
Extend Thy hand, O Lord,
From the power of ill
Let Thy mercy save us.
And mercy protect us.

Leonora.

Ah, from a brother save me,
Who thirsts for my blood ;
Thy hand alone, O Lord,
Can save me from his wrath.

(Re-enters the room and shuts the door. All reseat themselve
and pass the bottle.

Student.

Long live this goodly company.

All.

Hurrah !

Student.

Health here, and happiness hereafter !

(Raises the goblet.)

All.

So be it.

(They do the same.)

Student.

Already dreaming, Trabuco ?

Trabuco.

What ? in this uproar ?

Student.

And the little person who came with you
Does she go to the Jubilee ?

Trabuco.

I do not know.

Student.

By the by,
Is it man or woman ?

Trabuco.

With strangers, I only think of the money

Student.

Most prudent !

(To the ALCADE.)

Ed ella
Che giungere la vide— perchè a cena.
Non vien ?

Alcade.

L'ignoro.

Studente.

Dissero chiedesse
Acqua ed aceto.—Ah ah !—per rinfrescarsi.

Alcade.

Sara.

Studente.

E ver ch' è gentile, e senza barba ?

Alcade.

Non so nulla.

Studente.

(Parlar non vuol !) Ancora
(To TRABUCO.)
A lei.
Stava sul mulo,
Seduta o a cavalcioni ?

Trabuco
(Impazientato.)
Che noia !

Studente.

Onde veniva ?

Trabuco.

So che andrè, presto o tardi, in Paradiso.

Studente.

Perchè ?

Trabuco
(Alzandosi.)
Ella il purgatorio.
Mi fa soffrir.

Studente.

Or dove va ?

Trabuco.

In istalla,
Dormir colle mie mule,
Che non san di Latino,.
Nè sono Baccellieri.
(Prende il suo basto e parte.)

And you,
Who saw her arrive, say
Why she comes not to supper ?

Alcade.

I cannot tell.

Student.

They say she asked—ha ha !—
For vinegar and water, as refreshment.

Alcade.

May be.

Student.

Is it true that she is pretty, and has no
beard ?

Alcade.

I really do not know.

Student.

(He will not speak.)
(TO TRABUCO.)
Once more,
Was she seated on the mule,
Or rode astride ?

Trabuco
(Impatiently.)
What vexation !

Student.

Whence came she ?

Trabuco.

I know I shall go, sooner or later, to
Paradise.

Student.

Why ?

Trabuco
(Rising.)
Because you make me
Suffer purgatory here.

Student.

Where are you going now ?

Trabuco.

To the stable,
To sleep with my mules,
Who don't know Latin,
And are not Bachelors of Arts.
(Takes his pack-saddle and goes.)

SCENA IV. I Suddettie meno MASTRO TRABUCO. | SCENE IV. The same, except TRABUCO.

Tutti.

Ah ah ! è fuggito !

Studente.

Poich' è imberbe l'incognito facciamgli
Col nero du baffetti,
Doman ne rideremo.

Alcuni.

Bravo ! bravo !

Alcade.

Protegger debbo il viaggiator; m' oppongo.
Meglio farebbe dirne

D' onde venga, ove vade, e chi ella sia ?

Studente.

Lo vuol saper ?—Ecco l'istoria mia.

All.

Ha ha ! he is off !

Student.

As the unknown is a stripling,
Let us paint on him a pair of moustaches,—
That will make us all laugh to-morrow.

Some of them.

Bravo ! Bravo !

Alcade.

I am bound to protect travellers,
And therefore object.—You had better tell us

Whence you come, where going, and who you are.

Student.

You wish to know ?—This is my tale.

SON PEREDA — *I'M PEREDA* Air (Student)

Allegro

Son Pe - re - da, son ric - co d'o - no - re, Bac - cel - lie - re mi fe—Sa - la -
I'm Pe - re - da, from Sal - a - man - ca, Soon a— Doc - tor will be— my—

man - ca; Sa - ro pre - sto in u - tro - que Dot - to - re, Che di— stu - dio an - cor
ti - tle; As a stu - dent I am a— rank - er, In— my— stu - dies I

po - co mi man - ca. Di la— Var - gas mi tol - se da un an - no E a Si -
ne'er was i dle. With one— Var - gas, I went now a year,— And to Se -
cresc.

vi - glia con se— mi gui - do, Non trat - ten - ne Pe - re - da al - cun
vil - la our way— we did wend; Toil and hard-ship ne'er trou - bled Pe -

da - no, Per - l'a - mi - co il suo co - re par - lo.
re - da, For— his— heart— e'er was faith - ful to his friend.

Della suora, un amante straniero,
Colà il padre gli avea trucidato,
Onde il figlio, da pro' cavaliero,
La vendetta ne aveva giurato.
Gl' inseguimmo di Cadice in riva,
Nè la coppia fatal si trovò.
Per l' amico Pereda soffriva,
Chè l suo core per esso parlò.
Là e dovunque narrar che del pari
La sedotta col vecchio peria,

Chè a una zuffa di servi e sicari,
Solo il vil seduttore sfuggia,
Io da Vargas allor mi staccava ;
Ei seguir l' assassino giurò.
Verso America il mare solcava,
E Pereda a' suoi studi torno.

Coro.
Truce storia Pereda narrava,
Generoso il suo cor si mostrò.

Alcade.
Sta bene.

Preziosilla
         (Con finezza.)
Ucciso fu quel Marchese ?

Studente.
Ebben ?

Preziosilla.
L'amante rapia sua figlia ?

Studente.
Si.

Preziosilla.
E voi l'amico fido, cortese,
Andaste a Cadice, dopo Siviglia ?
Ah, gnaffe, a me non se la fa,
No, per mia fè—tra la la là !

Alcade
     (S' alza, e guardato l' oriuolo dice.)
Figluoli, è tardi ; poichè abbiam cenato
Si rendan grazie a Dio, e partiam

Tutti.
Partiamo.

Alcade.
Or buona notte !

A stranger, the lover of his sister,
Had there his father slain,
Wherefore his son, as true knight
Had sworn to be avenged.
We followed to the shores of Cadiz.
But ne'er o'ertook the guilty pair.
Pereda felt for his friend's distress,
Whom he most truly loved.
Here it is needful to inform you,
That the seduced one perished with her
     sire:
In a struggle 'twixt servants and assassins
The vile seducer fled alone.
From Vargas then I parted ;
For he swore to follow the assassin:
He crosses the ocean to America,
And Pereda to his studies returns.

Chorus.
A dismal story Pereda has related,
Which shows a generous soul.

Alcade.
It is well.

Preziosilla
         (Slyly.)
Slain was the Marquis ?

Studente.
What then ?

Preziosilla.
The lover carried off his daughter ?

Studente.
Yes.

Preziosilla.
And you, the friend, faithful, chivalrous
Went to Cadiz, afterwards to Seville ?
Ah, truly, such tales to me
Carry no weight, tra la !

Alcade
     (Rising and looking at the clock.)
My children, it is late, and we have supped:
Let us give thanks and go.

All.
Let us go.

Alcade.
Now good night !

Coro.

Buona notte !

Tutti.

Andiamo.

(Partono.)

SCENA V. Una piccola spianata sul declivio di scoscesa Montagna. A sinistra precipizii e rupi; di fronte la facciata della chiesa della Madonna delgi Angeli, di povera ed umile architettura, a destra la porta del Convento, in mezzo alla quale una fine strella, da un lato la corda del companello. Sopra vi e una piccola tettoia sporgente. Al di la della chiesa alti monti col villaggio d' Hornachuelos. La porta della chiesa e chiusa, ma larga, sopra dessa una finestra semicircolare lasciera vedere la luce interna. A mezza scene, un po' a sinistra, sopra quattro gradini s' erge una rozza croce ei pietra, corrosa dal tempo. La scena sara illuminata da luna chiarissima.

DONNA LEONORA giunge, ascendendo dalla destra, stanca, vestita da uomo, con pastrano a larghe maniche, largo capello e stivali.

Leonora.

Son giunta—grazie, o Dio !
Estremo asil quest' è per me—son giunta !
Io tremo ! La mia orrenda storia è nota
In quell' albergo—e mio fratel narrolla !
Se Scoperta m'avesse ! Cielo ! Ei disse
Naviga verso occaso Don Alvaro !
Nè morto cadde quella notte in cui
Io, io del sangue di mio padre intrisa,
L' ho seguito, e il perdei ! ed or mi lascia,
Mi fugge ! ohimè, non reggo a tanta ambascia !

(Cade inginocchio.)

Chorus.

Good night !

All.

Let us go.

(They depart.)

SCENE V. A small level space, on the side of a steep Mountain. On the left, precipices and rocks; facing the audience, the facade of the Church of the "Madonna degli Angeli," of simple architecture: on the right, the door of the Convent in the middle of which is a small window, on one side the cord of the bell, above which is a small projecting roof. On the other side of the church are high mountains, and the village of Hornachuelos. The door of the church is closed, but spacious; above it a semicircular window shows the light within. Half way down the stage, a little to the left, on four steps, is a rough stone cross, corroded by time. There is a bright moonlight over the whole scene.

DONNA LEONORA arrives, in male attire, ascending from the right, wearing a cloak with large sleeves, a large hat, and boots

Leonora.

I have arrived—thank Heaven !
This is my last refuge—I am here !
I tremble ! My dreadful story is known :
In that inn my brother did recount it.
Oh Heavens ! had he discovered me !
He said Don Alvaro was sailing westward,
And fell not on that fearful night
When, steeped in my father's blood,
I followed and lost him ! Now he leaves me—
Flies from me !—Ah me, I cannot bear it !

(Falls on her knees.)

MADRE, MADRE — *O HOLY MOTHER* (Leonora and Chorus)

ro - re. Pie-ta di me, pie-ta, Si-gnor, pie-ta di me, pie-ta, Si-
plete-ly, In mer-cy hear, in mer-cy hear, in mer-cy hear my fer-vent

gno - re, Deh! non m'ab-ban-do-nar, pie-ta, Pie-ta di me, Si-
plead-ing! For- - sake me not, for-sake me not, for-sake me not, O

LEONORA

gno-re! Deh! non m'ab-ban-do-nar, ah!_____ Pie-ta, pie-ta, di me, Si
Heav-en! For-sake me not, O Heav-en, Ah,_____ for-sake me not, for-sake me

CHORUS (Within)

Ve-

gnor!   Ah! que su-bli-mi can-ti-ci,
not!   Ah! how sub-lime the   an-them sounds,

nj-te,a-do-re-mus et pro-ce-da - mus   an - - te

Dell' or-ga-no i con-cen-ti, Che co-me in-cen-so as-
With sol-emn or-gan blend-ing, It floats like in-cense

De - - - - - - - - - - -

cresc.   3

cen-do-no A Dio sui fir-ma-men-ti,   In-spi-ra-no, in-
on the air, To heav-en's gate as-cend-ing,   Un - to my soul, un-

um,   plo - re - mus, plo - re - mus

spi-ra-no a quest' al - ma Fe - de, Con - for-to e cal - ma!
to my soul 'tis bring - ing Calm - ness, and faith un - sha - ken.

co - ram Do-mi-no co-rum, Do-mi-no qui fe - cit nos.

Al santo asilo accorrasi.	Let me to the sacred asylum haste.
(S' avvia.)	(Going.)
E l'oserò a quest' ora ?	But dare I, at this hour ?
(Arrestandosi.)	(Stopping.)
Ma si potria sorprendermi !	Yet I may be o'ertaken !
Oh, misera Leonora,	Oh, wretched Leonora,
Tremi ?—il pio frate accoglierti	Dost fear ?—the holy friar
No, non ricuserà.	To receive thee will not refuse.
Non mi lasciar, soccorrimi,	Have mercy, Heaven, mercy !
Pietà, Signor, pietà.	Aid me, desert me not !
(Va a suonare il campanello del Convento.)	(Rings the convent-bell.)

SCENA VI. Si apre la finestrella della porta, o n'esce la luce d'una lanterna. Che riverbera sul volto di DONNA LEONORA, la quale si arretra spaventata. FRA MELITONE parla sempre all' interno.

SCENE VI. The little window in the door opens, through which is seen a light, which is reflected in DONNA LEONORA'S face, who starts back alarmed. BROTHER MELITONE speaks from within.

Melitone.
Chi siete ?

Leonora.
Chiedo il Superiore,

Melitone.
S' apre
Alle cinque la chiesa,
Se al giubileo venite.

Leonora.
Il Superiore—
Per carità !

Melitone.
Che carità a quest' ora !

Leonora.
Mi manda il Padre Cleto.

Melitone.
Quel sant' uomo ? Il motivo ?

Leonora.
Urgente.

Melitone.
Who is it ?

Leonora.
I seek the Superior.

Melitone.
At five o'clock
The church will open,
If to the jubilee you come.

Leonora.
The Superior—
For charity's sake !

Melitone.
Charity at this hour !

Leonora.
I am sent by Father Cleto.

Melitone.
By that holy man ? The reason ?

Leonora.
Most urgent.

Melitone.

Perchè mai ?

Leonora.

Un infelice !

Melitone.

Brutta solfa—però v' apro ond' entriate.

Leonora.

Nol posso.

Melitone.

No ?   Scomunicicato siete ?
Chè strano fia aspettar a ciel sereno.
V' annuncio—e se non torno,
Buona notte.

(Chiude la finestrella.)

SCENA VII.   DONNA LEONORA, sola.

Leonora.

Ma s' ei mi respingesse !
Fama pietoso il dice,
Ei mi proteggerà;—Vergin, m'assisti !

SCENA VIII.   DONNA LONORA, il PADRE GUARDIANO. fra
MELITONE.

Guardiano.

Chi mi cerca ?

Leonora.

Son io.

Guardiano.

Dite.

Leonora.

Un segreto—

Guardiano.

Andate Melitone.

Melitone

(Partendo.)

(Sempre segreti !
E questi santi soi han da saperli !
Noi siamo tanti cavoli.)

Guardiano.

Gratello
Mormorate ?

Melitone.

Oibò, dico ch' è pesante
La porte, e fa romore.

Guardiano.

Obbedite.

Melitone.

Why so ?

Leonora.

An unfortunate creature !

Melitone.

A likely tale—however, I will let you in.

Leonora.

I cannot enter.

Melitone.

No ?   Are you excommunicated ?
'Tis strange you should prefer the open air,
I will announce you—and if I don't return,
Good night.

(Shuts the window)

SCENE VII.   DONNA LEONORA alone.

Leonora.

But if he should repulse me ?
He is reputed merciful.
He will protect me ;—Holy Virgin, aid me !

SCENE VIII.   DONNA LEONORA, the FATHER GUARDIANO
BROTHER MELITONE.

Guardiano.

Who asks for me ?

Leonora.

'Tis I.

Guardiano.

Speak on.

Leonora.

A secret—

Guardiano.

Go, Melitone.

Melitone

(Going.)

(Always secrets !
And these saints only know them !
We are nobodies !)

Guardiano.

Brother,
Are you grumbling ?

Melitone.

Oh no, I said the door
Was heavy, and creaked,

Guardiano.

Obey.

Melitone.

(Che tuon da Superiore !)

(Rientra in Convento socchiudendone la porta.)

SCENA IX. DONNA LEONORA e il PADRE GUARDIANO.

Guardiano.

Or siam soli.

Leonora.

Una donna son io.

Guardiano.

Una donna a quest' ora !—gran Dio !

Leonora.

Infelice, dulusa, rejetta,
Dalla terra, e dal ciel maledetta,
Che nel pianto prostratavi al piede,
Di sottrarla all' inferno vi chiede.

Guardiano.

Come un povero frate lo può ?

Leonora.

Padre Cleto un suo foglio v'inviò ?

Guardiano.

Ei vi manda ?

Leonora.

Sì.

Guardiano

(Sorpreso.)

Dunque voi siete
Leonora di Varges ?

Leonora.

Fremete !

Guardiano.

No: venite fidente alla croce,
Là del Cielo v' inspiri la voce.

Leonora

(S' inginocchia presso la croce, la bacia, quindi torna meno agitata al PADRE GUARDIANO.)

Ah, tranquilla l' alma sento
Dacchè premo questa terra ;
De' fantasmi lo spavento
Più non provo farmi guerra ;
Più non sorge sanguinante
Di mio padre l' ombra innante,
Nè terribile l' ascolto
La sua figlia maledir.

Melitone.

(Quite the voice of the Superior !)

(Re-enters the Convent, half-closing the door.)

SCENE IX. DONNA LEONORA and the FATHER GUARDIANO.

Guardiano.

Now, we are alone.

Leonora.

I am a woman.

Guardiano.

A woman at this hour !—good heavens !

Leonora.

Unhappy, deluded, rejected
On earth, and cursed by Heaven !
Who, prostrate at your feet, with tears
Implores you to save her from destruction.

Guardiano.

How can a poor friar do so ?

Leonora.

Father Cleto sent you a letter ?

Guardiano.

He sent you ?

Leonora.

Yes.

Guardiano

(Surprised.)

Then you must be
Leonora di Vargas ?

Leonora.

You shudder !

Guardiano.

No: in confidence approach the cross,
There may Heaven inspire you.

Leonora

(Kneeling close to the cross, kisses it, then turning with less agitation to FATHER GUARDIANO.)

Ah, my soul is calm
Now I tread this soil;
The dread forebodings
I no longer feel within me ;
Nor does there rise before me
The bleeding shade of my sire;
I do not hear with horror
His curses on his child.

Guardiano.

Sempre indarno qui rivolto
Fu di Satana l' ardir.

Leonora.

Perciò tomba qui desio,
Fa le rupi ov' altra visse.

Guardiano.

Che !—sapete —

Leonora.

Cleto il disse.

Guardiano.

E volete—

Leonora.

Darmi a Dio !

Guardiano.

Guai per chi si lascia illudere
Dal delirio d'un momento !
Più fatal per voi, si giovane,
Sorgerebbe il pentimento.
Nel futuro chi può leggere,
Chi immutabil farvi il cor.
E l' amante ?

Leonora.

Involontario
Di mio padre è l' uccisor.

Guardiano.

Il fratello ?

Leonora.

La mia morte
Di sua mano egli giurò.

Guardiano.

Meglio a voi la sante porte.
Schiuda un chiostro.

Leonora.

Un chiostro ? No.
Se voi scacciate questa pentita,
Andrò per balze gridando aita.
Ricovro ai monti ciba, alle selve,
E fin le belve ne avran pietà.
Qui, qui del ciela udii la voce:
Salvati all' ombra di questa croce—
Voi mi scacciate ?   E questo il porto;
Chi tal conforto mi toglierà ?

(*Corre ad abbracciar la croce.*)

Guardiano.

Never has Satan dared
These precincts to approach,

Leonora.

Therefore a tomb I seek
Among the rocks where one other lived.

Guardiano.

What !—do you know—

Leonora.

Cleto mentioned it,

Guardiano.

And you wish—

Leonora.

To devote myself to Heaven !

Guardiano.

Woe unto those who delude themselves
In the wild frenzy of a moment !
More wretched for you, so young,
Would repentance hereafter become.
Who can read the future,
Or make the heart steadfast ?
And thy lover ?

Leonora.

He by mischance
My father killed.

Guardiano.

Thy brother ?

Leonora.

My death he has sworn
By his own hand.

Guardiano.

For you 'twere best to seek
A cloister's holy shelter.

Leonora.

A cloister ? No.
If you reject the penitent,
Aid will I shrieking ask the rocks,
Shelter the mountains, food the woods ;
The savage beasts at least will pity me.
Here, where heaven's voice is heard
Salvation in the shadow of the Cross I seek.
You cast me out ? This is the haven
Of solace—you will tear me from it ?

(*Runs and clings to the cross.*)

Guardiano.

    (A te sia gloria, o Dio clemente,
    Padre dei miseri onnipossente,
    A qui sgabello sono le sfere !
    Il tuo volere—si compirà !)
    E fermo il voto ?

Leonora.

    E fermo,

Guardiano.

    V' accolga dunque Iddio !

Leonora.

    Bontà divina ?

Guardiano.

    Sol io saprò chi siate.
    Tra le rupi è uno speco ; ivi starete.
    Presso una fonte, al settimo, di scarso
    Cibo porrovvi io stesso.

Leonora.

    V' andiamo.

Guardiano

          (Versa la porta.)

    Melitone !

       (A MELITONE chi comparisce.)

    Tutti i fratelli con ardenti ceri,
    Dov' è l' ara maggiore,
    Nel tempio si raccolgan del Signore.

       (MELITONE rientra.)

Guardiano.

    (Thine be the glory, O merciful Heaven !
    Father of sinners, omnipotent,
    Who o'er all worlds reigns,
    Let Thy will be accomplished.)
    Thou art resolved ?

Leonora.

    I am.

Guardiano.

    Heaven accept thee !

Leonora.

    Oh, clemency divine !

Guardiano.

    I alone shall know who thou art.
    Among the rocks is a cave, thy future abode:
    Beside a spring, every seven days,
    Thy scanty food I myself will bring.

Leonora.

    Let us go.

Guardiano

          (Turning to the door.)

    Melitone !

       (To MELITONE who enters.)

    Let all the brothers, with lighted torches,
    Before the high altar assemble,
    In the temple of our Lord.

       (MELITONE withdraws.)

SULL' ALBA IL PIEDE — *TO SEEK THE LONELY HERMITAGE* Duet. (Guardiano and Leonora)
GUARDIANO
Allegro moderato

Sull' al-ba il pie-de all' e - re - mo So - lin-ga _ vol-ge - re - te, Ma
To seek the low - ly her-mit-age At dawn you _ must be stir-ring But

pria dal pa-ne an - ge - li - co Di - vin con-for-to a - vre - te, Le
first take of the sa - cra - ment, God's grace on _ you con - fer - ring, Em-

san-te la-ne a cin ge - re I - te, sia fer-mo il cor. Sul nuo-vo cal-le a
brace the cross with sim-ple faith To set your mind at rest, And Heav'n will not de -

LEONORA

Tua gra - zia, o Di - o, Sor-
My pray'rs and thanks - giv - ing To

reg-ger-vi____ V'as-sis-te - ra il Si - gnor.
ny you aid,____ You will be rich - ly___ blest.

LEONORA

ri - de al-la___ re - jet - ta! Oh, gau - dio in - so - li - to! Io
Thee on high are___ wing - ing, And hap - pi - ness un - mer - it - ed Thy

son,___ Io son ri - be - ne - det - ta! Gia sen-to in me ri - na-sce - re A
peace. to my poor heart is bring-ing, New hope once more with - in I feel, New

nuo-va vi-ta il cor; Plau - di - te, o co - ri an - ge - li - ci, Mi per-do-no___ il Si-
cour-age in my breast; Me-thinks an-gel - ic songs I hear And par - don makes me___

gnor, Mi per-do - no il Si - - gnor_____ Mi per- do-no il Si - gnor.
blest, And par-don, par-don makes me blest,_____ Thy par-don makes me blest.

SCENA X. La gran porta della Chiesa si apre. Di fronte vedesi l' altar maggiore, illuminato. L' organo suona. Dai lati del coro procedono due lunghe file di FRATI, con cerei ardenti. Piu tardi il PADRE GUARDIANO precede LEONORA in abito da FRATE. Egli la conduce fuor della chiesa, FRATI che gli si schierano intorno. LEONORA si prostra innanzi a lui, che stendendo solennemente le mani spora il suo capo intuona.	SCENE X. The great door of the Church opens. In front is seen the high altar, illuminated. The organ is sounded. From the sides of the choir proceed two long rows of FRIARS, with lighted tapers. A little later, the FATHER GUARDIANO, followed by LEONORA, in the FRIAR'S dress. He leads her out of the church, followed by the FRIARS, who range themselves around. LEONORA prostrates herself before him. he solemnly spreads his hands over her head, and chants.

Guardiano.

 Il santo nome di Dio Signore
 Sia benedetto.

Tutti.

 Sia benedetto.

Guardiano.

 The holy name of the Lord
 Be blessed.

All.

 Be blessed.

Guardiano.
  Un' alma a piangere viene l' errore,
  I queste balze chiede ricetto.
  Il santo speco noi la schiudiamo—
  V' è noto il loco ?

Tutti.
  Lo conosciamo.

Guardiano.
  A quell' asilo sacro inviolato
  Nessun si appressi.

Tutti.
  Obbediremo.

Guardiano.
  Il cinto umile non sia varcato.
  Che nel divide.

Tutti.
  Nol varcheremo.

Guardiano.
  A chi il divieto frangere osasse,
  O di quest' anima scoprir tentasse
  Nome o mistero, maledizione !

Tutti.
  Maledizione ! maledizione !
  Il cielo fulmini incenercisa
  L' empio mortale se tanto ardisca ;
  Su lui scatenisi ogni elemento,
  L' immonda cenere ne sperda il vento.

Guardiano
          (A LEONORA.)
  Alzatevi, e partite.
  Alcun vivente più non vedrete.
  Dello speco il bronzo
  Ne avverta se periglio vi sovrasti,
  O per voi giunto s'a l' estremo giorno—
  A confortarvi l' alma
  Volerem, pria ch' a Dio faccia ritorno.
  La Vergine degli angeli
  Vo copra del suo manto,
  E voi protegga vigile
  Di Dio l' angelo santo.

Tutti.
  La Vergine, ec.

(LEONORA bacia la mano del PADRE GUARDIANO s' avvia all' eremo sola. Il GUARDIANO stendendo le braccia verso di lei, la benedice. Cade la tela.)

FINE DELLA' ATTO SECONDO.

Guardiano.
  A penitent soul, to atone for errors,
  Demands a shelter in these rocks.
  The holy cave we will open—
  Do you know the place ?

All.
  We know the place.

Guardiano.
  The sacred holy asylum
  Let none approach.

All.
  We will obey.

Guardiano.
  The low boundary enclosing it
  Let none pass

All.
  We will not.

Guardiano.
  To him who dares this rule to break,
  Or of this poor soul seeks to discover
  The name or story, malediction !

All.
  Malediction ! malediction !
  May the thunderbolt reduce to ashes
  The impious mortal who dares attempt it ;
  May all the elements be loosed upon him,
  And his impure ashes be scattered by the
    wind.

Guardiano
          (To LEONORA.)
  Rise and depart. No living soul
  Will see you more. The bell in the cave
  Will give us notice if you are in danger :
  If your last hour be at hand,
  We will haste to bring absolution
  Ere thy soul to God returns.
  The Virgin of the heavenly host
  Cover you with her holy mantle,
  And the holy angels of God
  Be to you watchful guardians.

All.
  The Virgin, etc.

(LEONORA kisses the hand of FATHER GUARDIANO, and sets out alone for the hermitage. GUARDIANO, extending his arms towards her, blesses her. The curtain falls.)

END OF THE SECOND ACT.

ATTO III

In Italia. presso Velletri.

SCENA I. Bosco. Notte oscurissima. DON ALVARO in uniforme di Capitano Spagnuolo de' Granatieri del Re, si avanza lentamente dal fondo. Si sentono voci interno a destra.

1a Voce.

Attenti, gioco.—Un asso a destra.

2a Voce.

Ho vinto.

1a Voce.

Un tre alla destra—cinque a manca.

2a Voce.

Perdo !

Alvaro

(Che si sara innoltrato.)

La vita e inferno all infelice invano
Morte desio !—Siviglia !—Leonora !
Oh, rimembranze !—Oh notte !
Ch' ogni mio ben rapisti !
Sarò infelice eternamente è scritto.

Della natal sua terra il padre volle
Spezzar l' estranio giogo, el coll', unirsi ;
All' ultima degli Incas la corona
Cingerne confidò—fallì l' impresa,
In un carcere nacqui ; m' educava
Il deserto ; sol vivo per chè ignota
E mia regale stirpe. I miei parenti
Sognaro un trono e, li destò la scure !

Oh, quando fine avran le mie sventure ?

ACT III

In Italy, near Villeteri.

SCENE I. A wood. A dark night. DON ALVARO, in the uniform of a Captain of Royal Spanish Grenadiers, advances slowly from the back. Voices are heard on the right, from within.

1st Voice.

Attention, I play. An ace to the right.

2nd Voice.

I have won.

1st Voice.

A three to the right—five to the left.

2nd Voice.

I have lost.

Alvaro

(Who has come forward.)

Life has no charms for unhappy souls.
In vain I seek to die !—Seville !—Leonora !
Oh, sad memories !—Fatal night,
Which of every good deprived me !
It is decreed that I shall ever be unfortunate.

My father sought to free his native land
From foreign rule ;
United to the last of the Incas,
He hoped to obtain the crown.
He failed—and in prison I was born,
In the desert reared, and only live because
My royal birth is unknown. My parents
Dreamt of thrones, and suffered by the scaffold.

Ah, when will my sorrows end ?

OH, TU CHE IN SENO — *O SAINTED SOUL* Air. Alvaro

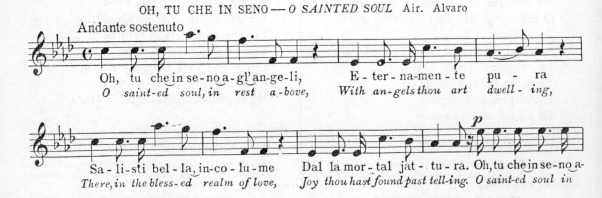

Oh, tu che in se-no a-gl' an-ge-li,   E-ter-na-men-te pu—ra
O saint-ed soul, in rest a-bove,   With an-gels thou art dwell-ing,

Sa-li-sti bel-la, in-co-lu-me   Dal la mor-tal jat-tu-ra. Oh, tu che in se-no a-
There, in the bless-ed realm of love,   Joy thou hast found past tell-ing. O saint-ed soul in

gl' an-ge-li, Sa-li-sti bel-la e pu-ra, Non i-scor-dar di
rest a-bove, With an-gels thou art dwell-ing, In pi-ty turn thy

vol-ger Lo sguar-do a me ta-pi-no, Che sen-za no-me ed
glan-ces up-on my soul in sor-row, Who wan-der here in

e-su-le, In o-dio del de-sti-no, Che sen-za no-me ed
ex- -ile And dread each com-ing mor-row, Who wan-der here in

e-sul, In o-dio del de-sti-no, Chie-do a-ne-lan-do, ahi
ex-ile, And dread each com-ing mor-row, Yes, in this war and

mi-se-ro, Chie-do a-ne-lan-do, ahi mi-se-ro, La mor-te d'in-con-
mi-se-ry, For ev-er seek-ing, ev-er seek-ing death a-mid the

trar, Leo-no-ra mia, soc-cor-ri-mi, Leo-no-ra mi-a, soc-cor-ri,
foe, Oh, Le-o-no-ra, pi-ty me, Oh, Le-o-no-ra, pi-ty, pi-ty

mi, Pie-ta, pie-ta,_____ pie-ta del mi-o pe-nar; Leo-no-ra, soc-cor-ri
me, And give me help,_____ And give me help to bear my woe; Leo-no-ra, oh, pi-ty

mi, pie-ta, del mi-o pe-nar;_ Leo-no-ra, mi- -a, pie-
me, And give me help to bear my woe;_ Oh, Le-o-no- -ra, give

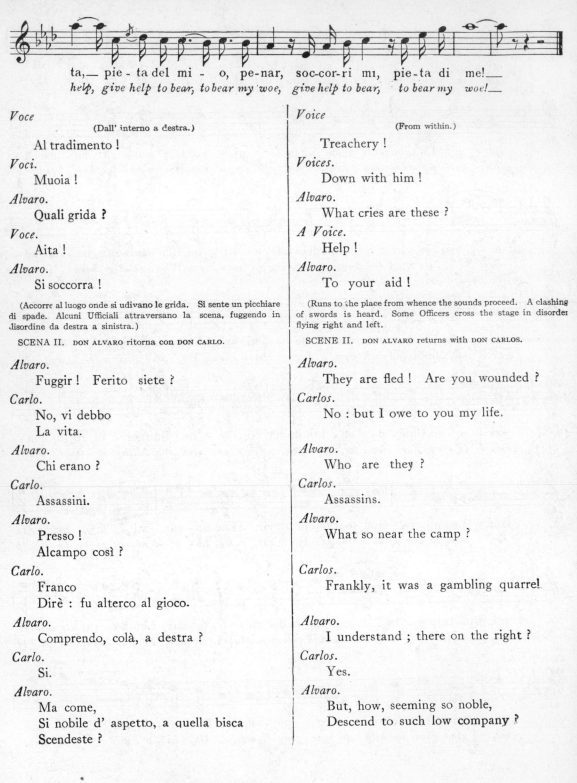

ta,— pie - ta del mi - o, pe-nar, soc-cor-ri mi, pie-ta di me!—

help, give help to bear, to bear my woe, give help to bear, to bear my woe!—

Voce	*Voice*
(Dall' interno a destra.)	(From within.)
Al tradimento !	Treachery !
Voci.	*Voices.*
Muoia !	Down with him !
Alvaro.	*Alvaro.*
Quali grida ?	What cries are these ?
Voce.	*A Voice.*
Aita !	Help !
Alvaro.	*Alvaro.*
Si soccorra !	To your aid !

(Accorre al luogo onde si udivano le grida. Si sente un picchiare di spade. Alcuni Ufficiali attraversano la scena, fuggendo in disordine da destra a sinistra.)

(Runs to the place from whence the sounds proceed. A clashing of swords is heard. Some Officers cross the stage in disorder flying right and left.

SCENA II. DON ALVARO ritorna con DON CARLO.

SCENE II. DON ALVARO returns with DON CARLOS.

Alvaro.	*Alvaro.*
Fuggir ! Ferito siete ?	They are fled ! Are you wounded ?
Carlo.	*Carlos.*
No, vi debbo La vita.	No : but I owe to you my life.
Alvaro.	*Alvaro.*
Chi erano ?	Who are they ?
Carlo.	*Carlos.*
Assassini.	Assassins.
Alvaro.	*Alvaro.*
Presso ! Alcampo così ?	What so near the camp ?
Carlo.	*Carlos.*
Franco Dirè : fu alterco al gioco.	Frankly, it was a gambling quarrel.
Alvaro.	*Alvaro.*
Comprendo, colà, a destra ?	I understand ; there on the right ?
Carlo.	*Carlos.*
Si.	Yes.
Alvaro.	*Alvaro.*
Ma come, Si nobile d' aspetto, a quella bisca Scendeste ?	But, how, seeming so noble, Descend to such low company ?

Carlo.

Nuovo sono.
Del general con ordini sol jeri
Giunsi ; senza voi morto
Sarei.   Or dite a chi miei giorni debbo ?

Alvaro.

Al caso.

Carlo.

Pria il mio nome
Dirò—(non sappia il vero)—
Don Felice de Bornos, ajutante
Del Duce.

Alvaro.

Io Capitan de' Granatieri
Don Federico Herreros !

Carlo.

La gloria dell' esercito !

Alvaro.

Signore—

Carlo.

Io l' amistà ne ambia, la chiedo, e spero.

Alvaro.

Io pure della vostra sarò fiero.

(Si stringono le destre.)

Voci

(Interne, a sinistra, e squillo di trombe.)

All' armi !

A 2.

Andiamo—all' armi !

Carlo.

Ah più gradito questo suono or parmi !
Con voi scendere al campo d' onore,
Emularne l' esempio potrò.

Alvaro.

Testimone del vostro valore,
Ammirarne le prove saprò.

SCENA III. E il Mattino. Salotto nell' abitazione d' un ufficiale superiore dell' esercito Spagnuolo in Italia non lungi da Velletri. Nel fondo sonvi due porte, quella a sinistra mette ad una stanza da letto, l' altra e la comune. A sinistra presso il proscenio a una finestra. Si sente il rumore della vicina battaglia.

Un Chirurgo Militare, ed alcuni Soldati, ordinanze dalla comune corrono alla finestra.

Soldati.

Arde la mischia !

Carlos.

I am a stranger, with orders from the general.
I yesterday arrived, and but for you I had
    died.
Say, to whom do I owe my life ?

Alvaro.

To chance.

Carlos.

I will first tell my name—
(Not my true one)—
Don Felice de Bornos,
Adjutant to the Duke.

Alvaro.

I Captain of the Grenadiers,
Don Federico Herreros !

Carlos.

The pride of the army !

Alvaro.

Signor—

Carlos.

I desire and would obtain your friendship.

Alvaro.

I shall be proud to have yours.

(They shake hands.)

Voices

(Within, to the left, with sound of a trumpet.)

To arms !

Together.

Let us go—to arms !

Carlos.

Ah, that sound is more agreeable now !
With you I will go to the field of honor,
And seek to emulate your bright example.

Alvaro.

Witness of your valor,
In future I shall know how to admire it.

SCENE III.   Morning. A small room in the house of a superior officer in the Spanish army, in Italy, not far from Velletri. At the back are two doors, one on the left leads to a bedroom, the other is the common door.   On the left, near the proscenium, is a window.   The noise is heard of the neighboring battle.

A Military Surgeon, and some common Soldiers, run to the window.

Soldiers.

The battle rages !

Chirurgo
          (Guardando con cannocchiale.)

Prodi i granatiere !

Soldati.

Li guida Herreros.

Chirurgo
          (Guardando con cannocchiale.)

Ciel ! ferito o spento
Ei cadde ! Piegano i suoi ! l'Ajutante
Li raccozza alla carica li guida !
Già fuggono i Tedeschi ! I nostril han vinto
Portan qui il Capitano.

Soldati.

Ferito !
          (Corrono ad incontrarlo.)

Voci
          (Fuori.)

A Spagna gloria !

Altre.

Viva l' Italia !

Tutti.

E nostra la vittoria !

SCENA IV   DON ALVARO, ferito e svenuto e portato in una
lettiga da quattro Granatieri. Da un lato e il Chirurgo, dall'
altro DON CARLO, coperto di polvere ed assai afflitto. Un Soldato
repone una valigia sopra un tavolino. La lettiga e collocata quasi
nel nezzo della scena.

Carlo.

Piano—qui posi—approntisi il mio letto.

Chirurgo.

Silenzio.

Carlo.

V' ha periglio ?

Chirurgo.

La palla che ha nel petto mi spaventa.

Carlo.

Deh, il salvate.

Alvaro
          (Rinviene.)

Ove son ?

Ccrlo.

Presso l' amico.

Alvaro.

Lasciatemi morire.

Surgeon
          (Looking through a telescope.)

Brave   grenadiers !

Soldier.

Herreros leads them.

Surgeon
          (Looking through a telescope.)

Heavens ! he falls
Wounded or dead ! His men give way !
The Adjutant rallies and leads them to
     the charge !
The Germans fly ! Our troops conquer !
They bring hither the Captain.

Soldier.

Wounded !
          (They run to meet him.)

Voices
          (Without.)

Glory to Spain !

Others.

Long live Italy !

All.

Ours is the victory !

SCENE IV. DON ALVARO, wounded and insensible, is borne in
on a litter by four Grenadiers. On one side the Surgeon, on the
other DON CARLOS, covered with dust and sorrowful. A Soldier
places a traveling-bag on a small table. The litter is placed nearly
in the middle of the scene.

Carlos.

Gently—lay him here—get ready my bed

Surgeon.

Silence !

Carlos.

Is there danger ?

Surgeon.

The bullet in his chest alarms me.

Carlos.

Ah, try to save him !

Alvaro
          (Recovering his senses.,

Where am I ?

Carlos.

With your friend.

Alvaro.

Leave me to die.

Carlo.

Vi salveran le nostra cure premio
L' ordine vè sarà di Calatrava.

Alvaro

(Trasalendo.)

Di Calatrava ! No—mai !

Chirurgo.

Siate calmo.

Carlo.

(Ch, ! inorridi di Calatrava al nome !)

Alvaro.

Amico—

Chirurgo.

Se parlate—

Alvaro.

Un detto sol.

Carlo

(Al Chirurgo.)

Ven prefo ne, lasciate.

(Chirurgo si ritrae al fonde.)

Carlos.

Our cares will save you.
The Order of Calatrava will be conferred
upon you.

Alvaro

(Shuddering.)

Of Calatrava ! No—never !

Surgeon.

Be calm.

Carlos.

(He shuddered at the name of Calatrava !)

Alvaro.

My friend—

Surgeon.

If you speak—

Alvaro.

Only one word.

Carlos

(To the Surgeon.)

Leave us, I pray you.

(The Surgeon retires to the back.)

SOLENNE IN QUEST' ORA — *IN THIS SOLEMN HOUR*—Duet (Don Alvaro and Don Carlo)

CARLO

me - co mor - ra.   S'ab - bru - ci me spen - to.   Lo giu - ro, sa -
die with my death.   *To burn it I pray thee.*   *On hon - or I*

Andante

ALVARO

Or muo - jo tran - quil - lo   Vi strin - go al cor
I die now con - tent - ed,   As to my heart I

CARLO

rà.
swear.

mi - o,   al co -
hold thee,   I hold

A - mi - co fi - da - te, fi - da - te nel cie - lo, fi - da - te nel
My friend, put thy faith now in Heav - en, thy faith now in Heav - en a

re, or muo - jo tran - quil - lo vi strin - go al cor mi -
thee, Con - tent - ed I die as I hold thee up - on my

ciel; a - mi - co, fi - da - te nel cie - lo, fi - da -
bove, in Heav - en a - bove, put thy faith now in Heav -

o, or muo - jo tran - quil - lo, vi strin - go al cor
heart. I die now con - tent - ed, as to my heart I

te.
en.

mi - o,
hold thee,

al co -
I hold_____

A - mi - co, fi - da - te, fi - da - te nel cie - lo, fi - da - te nel
My friend, put thy faith now in Heav - en, thy faith now in Heav - en a -

re,____ or muo - jo tran - quil - lo vi strin - go al cor mi - o! Ad -
thee,____ Con - tent - ed I die__ as I hold thee up - on my heart. Fare -

ciel;____ a - mi - co, fi - da - te nel cie - lo, fi - da - te.
bove,____ in Heav - en a - bove, put thy faith now in Heav - en.

di - o,
well____ now.

ad - di - o, ad - di - o!
fare - well__ now. for ev - er!

Ad - di - o, ad - di - o, ad - di - o!
(Fare - well now, fare - well now for ev - er!

(Il Chirurgo e le Ordinanze trasportano il ferito nella stanza da letto.)	(The Surgeon and Soldiers carry the wounded man into the bed-room.)
S ENA V. DON CARLOS, poi il Chirurgo.	SCENE V. DON CARLOS, afterwards the Surgeon.

Carlo.

 Morir ! Tremenda cosa !
 Sì intrepido, sì prode,
 Ei pur morrà ! Uom singolar costui !
 Tremò di Calatrava !
 Al nome ! A lui palese
 N' è forse il disonor ? Cielo ! qual lampo !
 S' ei fosse il seduttore ?
 Desso in mia mano, e vive !
 Se m' ingannassi ? Questa chiave il dica.

(Apre convulso la valigia, e ne trae un plicco suggellato.)

Carlos.

 Die ! How terrible !
 So fearless, so brave.
 Yet he must die ! What a strange man !
 He shuddered at the name of Calatrava !
 Does he know it has been disgraced ?
 Heavens ! a thought strikes me !
 What if he were the vile seducer ?
 In my hands, and yet alive !
 But if I should mistake ? This key will
  tell.

(He hastily opens the bag, and draws out a sealed packet.)

Ecco i fogli.
(Fa per aprirlo.)

Che tento?
(S' arresta.)

E la fè che giurai? e questa vita
Che debbo al suo valor? Anch' io l' ho
    salvo!
E s' ei fosse quell' Indo maledetto
Che macchiò il sangue mio?

(Risoluto.)

Il suggello si franga.
(Sta per eseguire.)

Niun qui mi vede; No!
(S' arresta.)

Ben mi vegg' io?
(Getta il plicco, e se ne allontana con raccapriccio.)

Urna fatale del mio destino,
Va, t' allontana, mi tenti insano;
L' onor a tergere qui venni, e insano
D' un onta nuova nol brutterò.
Un giuro è sacro per l' uom d' onore;
Que' fogli chiudano il lor mistero—
Disperso vada il mal pensiero;
Che all' atto indegno mi concitò.
E s' altra provar invenir potessi? Vediam.

(Torna a frugare nella valigia e vi trova un astuccio.)

Qui v' ha un ritratto.
(Lo esamina.)

Suggel non v' e'—nulla ei ne disse—nulla—
Promisi—s' apra dunque.
(Eseguisce.)

Ciel! Leonora!
(Con estaltazione.)

Don Alvaro e' il ferito!
Ora egli viva—
Edi mai man poi mueoia.

Chirurgo
(Si presenta lieto sulla porta della stanza.)

Lieta novella è salvo.
(Rientra.)

Carlo.
Oh gioia! oh gioia!

Here are the papers.
(About to open them.)

What am I doing?
(Stops.)

And the oath I swore? And the life
I owe to his valor?

But I have also saved him.
Yet if he were this vile Indian
Who has my named disgraced?

(Resolutely.)

The seal shall be broken.
(Is about to do it.)

None see me! No.!
(Stops.)

Do I not see myself?
(Throws away the packet, and turns from it with horror.)

Fatal urn of my destiny,
Away, in vain you tempt me;
Hither I came to clear my honor,
And will not stain it with a new disgrace.
An oath is sacred to a man of honor;
Those papers contain their own secret—
Away with the evil thought
That urged me to the base attempt.
But if other proof I might obtain;
Let me see.

(Looks into the bag, and finds a case.)

Here is a portrait.
(Examines it.)

Here is no seal—he spoke not of it—
Nothing did I promise.
(Opens it.)

Heavens! Leonora!
(Excitedly.)

The wounded man is then Alvaro!
Let him live—then, later die by my hands!

Surgeon
(Appearing at the door of the room.)

Here is the ball: he is saved!
(Retires.)

Carlos.
Oh, happiness! oh, joy!

AH! EGLI E SALVO — *OH, WHAT A JOY.* Air. (Don Carlos)

Ah! 'e - glie sal' - vo! oh gio - ja im - men - sa Che m'in - non - di il
cor, ti sen - to! Po - tro al fi - ne il tra - di - men - to Sull' in -
fa - me ven - di - car. Le - o - no - ra, ove t'a - scon - di? Di': se -
gui - sti tra le squa - dre. Chi del san - gue di tuo pa - dre, Chi del
san - gue di tuo pa - dre. Ti fe il vol - to ros - seg - giar.

Oh, what a joy my heart is know-ing That ere long my
sword shall find him! Soon his blood for ven-geance flow-ing, Shall repay me for the wrong. Where, Leo - no - ra, art thou hid - ing? If with
that vile man thou'rt bid - ing, Who did slay thy a - ged fa - ther, Who did
slay thy a - ged fa - ther, None can see thee with - out scorn.

Ah, felice appien sarei	Ah, I should be truly happy
Se potesse il brando mio,	If with my own sword,
Amendue d' averno al Dio,	And with the selfsame blow
D' un sol colpo consacrar.	I might send both to realms below.
(Parte rapidamente.)	(Exit.)

SCE A VI. Accampamento Militare presso elletri. Sul davanti a sinistra e una bottega da rigattiere; a destra altra ove si vendono cibi, bevande, frutta. All' ingiro tende militari, baracche di rivenduglioli, ecc. E notte, 1a scena e deserta. Una Patt glia entra cautamente in scena, esplorando il campo.

SCENE VI. Millitary Encampment, near Velletri. In front is a sutler's booth. To the right, others with food, fruits, bottles. Around are soldiers' tents, huxter's stalls etc. Night. he scene is vacant. The watch-guard enter cautiously, and search the camp

Coro.

Compagni, sostiamo,
Il campo esploriamo ;
Non s' ode rumore,
Non brilla un chiarore ;
In sonno profondo
Sepolto ognun sta.
Compagni, inoltriamo.

(Allontonandosi a poco a poco.)

Chorus.

Comrades, halt !
The camp explore.
No sound is heard,
No light is seen,
In sleep profound
Now all repose.
Comrades, forward !

(Go of gradually.)

Fra poco la sveglia
Suonare s' udrà.

SCENA VII. Spunta l' alba lentamente. Entra DON ALVARO pensoso.

Alvaro.
Nè gustare m' è dato
Un'.ora di quiete ; affranta è l' alma
Dalla lotta crudel.
Pace ed oblio indarno io chieggo al Cielo.

SCENA VIII. Detto e DON CARLO.

Carlo.
Capitan.

Alvaro.
Chi mi chiama ?
(Avvicinandosi e riconoscendo CARLO gli dice con affetto.)
Voi che sì larghe cure
Mi prodigaste ?

Carlo.
La ferita vostra
Sanata è appieno ?

Alvaro.
Sì.

Carlo.
Forte ?

Alvaro.
Qual prima.

Carlo.
Sosterreste un duello ?

Alvaro.
E con chi mai ?

Carlo.
Nemici non avete ?

Alvaro.
Tutti ne abbian—ma a stento
Comprendo—

Carlo.
No ?—Messaggio non v' inviava
Don Alvaro l' Indiano ?

Alvaro.
Oh tradimento !
Sleale ? il segreto fu dunque violato ?

Ere long the morning call
Will rouse them.

SCENE VII. The day slowly dawns. Enter DON ALVARO, in deep thought.

Alvaro.
Not one hour of rest
Can I enjoy. Tortured is my soul
With the cruel struggle.
Peace and oblivion I ask of Heaven in vain.

SCENE VIII. Enter DON CARLOS.

Carlos.
Captain.

Alvaro.
Who calls me ?
(Advancing recognizes CARLOS with gladness.)
Is it you who such great care
Upon me lavished ?

Carlos.
Has your wound
Healed completely ?

Alvaro.
Yes.

Carlos.
Strong ?

Alvaro.
As ever.

Carlos.
Could you fight a duel ?

Alvaro.
And with whom ?

Carlos.
Have you no enemy ?

Alvaro.
All have some—but I hardly
Understand—

Carlos.
No ?—Don Alvaro the Indian,
Did he not send you a message?

Alvaro.
Oh, treachery ! disloyal man?
The secret has been there disclosed ?

Carlo

 Fu illeso quel piego, l' effigie ha parlato ;

 Don Carlo di Vargas, tremate, io sono.

Alvaro.

 D' ardite, minaccie non m' agito al suono.

Carlo.

 Usciamo, all' istante un di noi dee morire.

Alvaro.

 La morte disprezzo, ma duolmi inveire

 Contr' uom che per primo amistade m' offria.

Carlo.

 No, no profanato tal nome non sia.

Alvaro.

 Non io, fu il destino, che il padre v' ha ucciso ;

 Non io che sedussi quell' angiol d' amore—

 Ne guardano entrambi, e dal paradiso

 Ch' io sono innocente vi dicono al core—

Carlo.

 Adunque colei ?

Alvaro.

 La notte fatale

 Io caddi per doppia ferita mortale ;

 Guaritone, un anno in traccia ne andai—

 Ahimè, ch' era spenta Leonora trovai.

Carlo.

 Menzogna, menzogna !

 La suora—ospitavala antica parente ;

 Vi giunsi, ma tardi—

Alvaro
> (Con ansia.)

 Ed ella—

Carlo.

 E fuggente.

Alvaro
> (Trasalendo.)

 E vive ! o amico, il fremito

 Ch' ogni mia fibra scuote,

 Vi dica che quest' anima

 Infame esser non puote—

 Vive ! gran Dio, quell' angelo !

Carlos.

 Unopened was the packet, but the portrait spoke ;

 Tremble, for I am Don Calros di Vargas.

Alvaro.

 Threats disturb me not.

Carlos.

 Come, on the instant one of us must die !

Alvaro.

 Death I despise, but it grieves me to injure

 Him who first offered me friendship.

Carlos.

 Profane not the word.

Alvaro.

 Not I, but fate, your father slew ;

 I ne'er seduced that lovely angel ;

 Both look on us, and from heaven

 Tell your heart I am innocent.

Carlos.

 And she ?

Alvaro.

 That fatal night I fell,

 Through many mortal wounds ;

 Then, cured, I sought her for a year.

 And found Leonora dead.

Carlos.

 False, false !

 My sister found refuge with a relative ;

 I arrived too late.

Alvaro
> (With anxiety,)

 And she ?

Carlos.

 Has fled.

Alvaro
> (Joyously.)

 She lives ! Ah, my friend.

 The trembling which my frame pervades

 Will tell you that my soul

 Cannot be so debased.

 She lives ! thank God !

Carlo.
  Ma in breve morirà.

Alvaro.
  No, d' un imene il vincolo
  Stringa fra noi la speme ;
  E s'ella vive, insieme
  Cerchiamo ove fuggì.
  Giuro che illustre origine
  Eguale a voi mi rende,
  E che il mio stemma splende
  Come rifulge il dì.

Carlo.
  Stolto ! fra noi dischiudesi
  Insanguinato avello ;
  Come chiamar fratello
  Chi tutto mi rapì ?
  D' eccelsa o vile origine,
  E duopo ch' io vio spegna,
  E dopo voi l' indegna
  Che il sangue suo tradì.

Alvaro.
  Che dite ?

Carlo.
  Ella morrà.

Alvaro.
  Tacete !

Carlo.
  Il giuoro
  A Dio ; cadrà l' infame.

Alvaro.
  Voi pria cadretc nel fatal certame.

Carlo.
  Morte ! ov 'io non cada esangue
  Leonora   giungerò.
  Tinto àncor del vostro sangue
  Questo acciar le immergerò.

Alvaro.
  Morte, sì !—col drando mio.
  Un sicario ucciderò ;
  Il pensier volgete a Dio,
  L' ora vostra alfin suonò.

  (Sguainano le spade e si battono furiosamente.)

Carlos.
  But she will shortly die.

Alvaro.
  No, by the fond nuptial tie
  Soon may we be united ;
  If yet she lives, together
  Let us seek her abode.
  I swear that rank as noble
  Even as thine, I own,
  And that my birth is pure,
  Unstained, as light of day.

Carlos.
  Madman ! rising between us
  A river of blood is flowing ;
  How can I call him brother,
  Who did my hopes efface ?
  Whate'er may be thy origin,
  I live but to destroy thee ;
  Then too shall die the unworthy one
  Who did her race betray.

Alvaro.
  What sayest thou ?

Carlos.
  She shall die !

Alvaro.
  Hold !

Carlos.
  I swear to heaven
  The infamous wretch shall die !

Alvaro.
  Thou shalt first die thyself in mortal combat.

Carlos.
  But ere I fall, Leonora shall perish!
  This sword, with your blood dyed red
  Will I plunge into her heart.

Alvaro.
  Die thou ! with my steel
  Will I slay the assassin ;
  Turn your thoughts to heaven,
  For your last hour is nigh.

  (They draw swords and fight furiously.)

SCENA IX. Accore la Pattuglia del campo per separati.)

Coro.

Fermi, arrestate !

Carlo

(Furente.)

No. La sua vita.

Coro.

Lunge di qua si tragga.

Alvaro.

(Forse—del ciel l' aita a me soccorre.)

Carlo.

Colui morrà !

Coro

(A CARLO che cerca svincolarsi.)

Vieni   .

Carlo.

Carnefice del padre mio !

(A DON ALVARO viene trascinato altrove dalla pattuglia.)

Alvaro.

Or che mi resta ! Pietoso Iddio

Tu inspira, illumina il mio pensier.

(Gettando la spada.)

Al chiostro, all' eremo, ai santi altari

L'obblio, la pace chiegga il guerrier.

(Esce.)

SCENA X. Spunta il sole.—il rullo dei tamburi e lo squillo delle trombe danno il segnale della sveglia. La scena va animandosi a poco a poco. Soldati Spagnuoli ed Italiani di tutte le armi sortono dalle tende ripulendo schioppi, spade, uniformi, ecc., ecc. Ragazzi militari giuocano ai dadi sui tamburi. Vivandiere che vendono liquori, frutta, pane, ecc., PREZIOSILLA dall' alto d' una baracca predice la buona ventura. Scena animatissima.

Coro.

Lorchè pifferi e tamburi

Par che assordino la terra,

Siam felici, ch' è la guerra

Gioja e vita al militar.

Vita gaia, avventurosa,

Cui non cal doman nè jeri,

Ch' ama tutti i suoi pensieri

Sol nell' oggi concentrar.

Preziosilla

(Alle Donne.)

Venìte all' indovina.

Ch' è giunta di lontano,

E puote a voi l' arcano.

SCENE IX. The Sentries of the Camp run to part them

Chorus.

Hold ! stay !

Carlos

(Raging.)

No : his life !

Chorus.

Drag him hence !

Alvaro.

(Heaven has sent me aid.)

Carlos.

He shall die.

Chorus

(To DON CARLOS, who tries to fight him.)

Come away.

Carlos.

Murderer of my father !

(To DON ALVARO, as he is dragged off by the Sentries.)

Alvaro.

What now remains for me ? Merciful Heaven,

A thought from above inspires me.

(Throws down the swor.d)

To the cloister I go and at the holy altar,

Peace and oblivion will the warrior seek.

(Exit.)

SCENE X. Sunrise. The roll of drums and call of trumpets give the signal for waking. The scene gradually becomes full of life. Spanish and Italian soldiers emerge from their tents, cleaning muskets, swords, uniforms, etc. etc. Young recruits play at dice on the drum heads. Vivandiers sell liquors, fruit, bread, etc. PREZIOSILLA, mounted on a stand, tells fortunes. Great animation

Chorus.

When fife and drums

Deafen the world,

We rejoice, for war to the soldier

Is life and full delight.

A life of joy and adventure

To him who cares naught for the morrow;

Who loves in his thoughts to dwell

On the bright hopes of to-day.

Preziosilla

(To the Women.)

Come to the fortune-teller,

Who has come from distant parts ;

She to you can reveal

Futuro decifrar.
(Ai Soldati.)
   Corrette a lei d' intorno,
La mano le porgete.
Le amanti apprenaerete
Se fide vi restar.

Coro.
   Corriamo all' indovina
La mano le porgiamo,
Le belle udir possiamo
Se fide vi restar.

Preziosilla.
   Chi vuole il paradiso
Si accendo di valore,
E il barbaro invasore
S' accenga a debellar.
Avanti, avanti, avanti.
Predirvi sentirete
Qual premio coglierete
Dal vostro battagliar.
(Molti la circondano.)

Coro.
   Avanti, ec.

Soldati.
   Qua, vivandiere, un sorso.
(La Vivandiere versano loro.)

Uno.
   Alla salute nostra !

Tutti
(Bevendo.)
   Viva !

Altro.
   A Spagna ! ed all' Italia unite !

Tutti.
   Evviva !

Preziosilla.
   Al nostro eroe, Don Federico Herreros.

Tutti.
   Viva ! Viva !

Uno.
   Ed al suo degno amico
Don Felice de Bornos.

Tutti.
   Viva ! viva !

What the future will bring.
(To the Soldiers.)
   Come around her,
And hold out your hands ;
So all you can learn
If your maidens be true.

Chorus.
   Let us haste to the teller of fortunes,
And show her our hands,
Thus we all can learn
If our fair ones are true.

Preziosilla.
   He who longs for Paradise
Must show himself brave,
Prepare to subdue
The savage horde of invaders,
Come on, come on, come on,
And you shall hear foretold
What the prize you shall win
In the war that you wage.
(Many surround her.)

Chorus.
   Come on, etc.

Soldiers.
   Here, vivandiers, give us to drink.
(The vivandiers give them drink.)

A Soldier.
   To our own health we drink !

All
(Drinking.)
   Hurrah !

Another.
   To Spain and Italy united !

All.
   Hurrah !

Preziosilla.
   To our hero, Don Federico Herreros !

All.
   Hurrah ! hurrah !

A Soldier.
   And to his noble friend,
Don Felice de Bornos !

All.
   Hurrah ! Hurrah !

SCENA XI L' attenzione e attirata da TRABUCO. rivendugilolo, che dalla bottega a sinistra viene con una cassetta al colla portante vari oggetti di meschino valore?.

Trabuco.

A buon mercato chi vuol comprare ?
Forbici, spille, sapon perfetto !
(Lo attorniano.)
Io vendo e compero qualunque oggetto,
Concludo a pronti qualunque affare.

Soldato 1.

Ho qui un monile, quanto mi dai ?
(Lo mostra.)

Soldato 2.

Ve' una collana ? Se vuoi la vendo.
(Lo mostra.)

Soldato 3.

Questi orecchini li pagherai ?
(Lo mostra.)

Coro.

Vogliamo vendere ?
(Mostrando orologi, anelli, ecc.)

Trabuco.

Ma quanto vedo
Tutto è robaccia, brutta robaccia !

Coro.

Tale, o furfante, è la tua faccia.

Trabuco.

Pure aggiustiamoci ; per ogni pezzo
Do trenta soldi.

Tutti

(Tumultuando.)
Da ladro è il prezzo.

Trabuco.

Ih ! quanta furia ! c' intenderemo,
Qualch' altro soldo v' aggiungeremo—
Date qua, subito !

Coro.

Purchè all' istante
Venga il danaro bello e sonante.

Trabuco.

Prima la merce—qua—colle buone.

Soldati.

A te.
(Dandogli gli affetti.)

Altri.

A te.
(Dandogli gli affetti.)

SCENE XI. TRABUCO, the Pedlar, attracts their attention, who, from the shop on the left, comes with a box at his waist, carrying various objects of small value.

Trabuco.

Who will buy at a bargain?
Scissors, pins, scented soap !
(They surround him.)
I buy and sell all sorts of things
And quickly conclude my bargains.

1st Soldier.

Here is a necklace—what will you give ?
(Showing it.)

2nd Soldier.

Here is another—I will sell it.
(Showing it.)

3rd Soldier.

Wilt pay the price of these earrings ?
(Showing them.)

Chorus.

We'll sell ?
(Showing watches, rings, etc.)

Trabuco.

But what you show me
Is all rubbish, mere rubbish !

Chorus.

Just like yourself, you rogue !

Trabuco.

However, we may agree: for each article
I will give thirty soldi.

All

(Enraged.)
'Tis the price of a thief !

Trabuco.

Eh ! what a fuss ! we shall agree,—
Another soldo we will add:
Give them here—quick.!

Chorus.

Provided on the instant
We see the money sound and shining.

Trabuco.

The merchandise first—here—fair play.

Soldiers.

There's for thee.
(Giving the things.)

Others.

For thee.
(Giving things.)

Altri.

  A te.

      (Dandogli gli affetti.)

Trabuco

      (Ritira le robe e paga.)

  A voi, a voi, benone !

Coro.

  Al diavol vattene !

      (Cacciandolo.)

Trabuco

      (Da se contento.)

  (Che buon affare !)

  A buon mercato chi vuol comprare ?

      (Avviandosi ad altro lato del compo.)

SCENA XII. Detti, e Contadini questuanti, con Ragazzi a mano

Contadini.

  Pane, pan per caritò!

  Tetti e campi devastati

  N' ha la guerra, ed affamati,

  Cerchiam pane per pietà.

SCENA XIII. Detti, ed alcuni RECLUTE, piangenti, che giungono scortate.

Reclute.

  Povere madri deserte nel pianto !

  Per dura forza dovemmo lasciar.

  Della beltà n' han rapiti all' incanto,

  A' nostre case vogliamo tornar.

Vivandiere

    (Accostandosi gaiamente alle RECLUTE. e offerendo loro da bere.)

  Non piangete, giovanotti,

  Per le madri e per la belle ;

  V' ameremo quai sorelle,

  Vi sapremo confortar.

  Certo il diavolo non siamo ;

  Quelle lacrime tergette.

  Al passato, ben vedete,

  Ora è inutile pensar.

Preziosilla

    (Entrando fra le RECLUTE. ne prende alcune pel braccio, e dice loro burlescamente.)

  Che vergogna !—Su coraggio !

  Bei figliuoli, siete pazzi ?

  Sè piangete quai ragazzi,

  Vi farete corbellar.

Others.

  For thee.

      (Giving things.)

Trabuco

      (Taking the things and paying.)

  To you, to you, very good !

Chorus.

  Go to the devil !

      (They drive him away.)

Trabuco

      (Highly pleased.)

  (What good luck !)

  Who will buy everything cheap ?

      (Goes to the other side of the camp.)

SCENE XII. The same, and PEASANTS begging and leading Children

Peasants.

  Bread, for charity's sake !

  The war has destroyed

  Our homes and our fields ;

  Starving we ask for bread !

SCENE XIII. The same, and some RECRUITS, weeping, with an escort.

Recruits.

  Our poor mothers are deserted in their grief !

  By force we were made to leave,

  And from our lovers' arms torn away.

  To our homes we wish to return.

Vivandiers

    (Approaching gaily the RECRUITS, and offering them drink.)

  Do not repine, O young men,

  For your mothers and your lovers ;

  Like sisters we will love you,

  And seek to console you.

  Truly fiends we are not,

  Then dry your tears

  And cease to think

  Upon the happy past.

Preziosilla

    (Mixing with the RECRUITS, takes some of them by the arm, and says, jeeringly.)

  Shame on you !—Show more courage !

  Great babies, are you mad ?

  If you wail like little children

  You will be jeered and hooted.

Un' occhiata a voi d' intorno,
E scommetto che indovino ;
Ci sarà più d' un visino,
Che sapravvi consolar.

Tutti.

Nella guerra è la follia
Che dee il campo rallegrar.
Viva ! viva la pazzia,
Che qui sola ha da regnar !

(Le Vivandiere prendono francamente le RECLUTE pel braccio, e s' incominica vivacissima danza generale. Ben presto la confusione e lo schiamazzo giungono al como.)

SCENA XIV. Detti e Fra MELITONE, che preso nel vortice della danza, e per un momento costretto a ballare colle Vivandiere. Finalmente, riuscito a fermarsi, esclama:

Melitone.

Toh, toh ! poffare il mondo ! oh che tempone !
Corre ben l' aventura !—Anch' io ci sono !
Venni di Spagna a medicar ferite,
Ed alme a medicar. Che vedo ! è questo
Un campo di Christiani, o siete Turchi ?
Dove s' è visto berteggiar la santa
Domenica cosi ? Ben più faccenda

Le *bottiglie* vi dan che le *battaglie* !
E invece di vestir *cenere* e *sacco*
Qui si tresca con *Venere*, con *Bacco* ?
Il mondo è fatto una casa di pianto ;
Ogni convento, o qual profanazione !
Or è *covo del vento* ! I *Santuari*
Spelonche diventàr di sanguinari
E perfino i *tabernacoli di Cristo*
Fatti son *ricettacoli del tristo.*
Tutto è soqquadro.
E la ragion ? pe' vostri
Peccati

Soldati.

Ah, frate ! frate !

Melitone.

Voi le feste
Calpestate, rubate, bestemmiate—

Soldati Italiano.

Togone infame !

Soldato Spag.

Segui pur, padruccio.

Cast your eyes around,
And I'll wager you can find
More than one face here
To console your vain regrets.

All.

In war it is folly only
That makes the camp resound.
Hurrah ! long life to folly.
That alone has a right to reign !

(The Vivandiers boldly sieze the RECRUITS by the arm, and commence a dance all around. Soon the noise and confusion reach its height.)

SCENE XIV. The same, and BROTHER MELITONE, who, seized in the whirl of the dance, is obliged to dance with the Vivandiers. At last, managing to release himself, he exclaims:

Melitone.

Oh, oh ! good heaven ! what a wild life !
Adventures are coming fast !—I am in for it !
I came from Spain wounds to heal,
And souls to cure. What do I see ?
Is this a camp of Christians or of Turks ?
Where do people make such a mockery
Of the holy Sabbath ? You have more to do
With bottles than with battles !
And instead of putting on sackcloth and ashes,
You play tricks with Venus and Bacchus.
The world is made a place of tears ;
Every convent—oh, what profanation—
Is open to the winds. The sanctuaries
Are become dens of murderers !
And, to crown all, the most sainted shrines
Made refuges for rascals.
All is upset ; and wherefore ?
Through your sins.

Soldiers.

Ah, friar ! friar !

Melitone.

You despise the feasts of the Church,
You rob, you swear—

Italian Soldier.

Infernal friar !

Spanish Soldier.

Go on, old fellow.

Melitone.

E membra e capi siete d' una stampa ;
Tutti eretici.

Italiano.

Or or l' aggiustiam noi.

Melitone.

Tutti, tutti, cloaca di peccati,
E finchè il mondo puzzi di tal *pece*
Non isperi mai la terra alcuna *pace*.

Italiano.

Dàlle, dàlli !

(Serrandolo intorno)

Spagno

(Difendendolo.)

Scappa ! scappa !

Italiano.

Dàlli, dàlli sulla cappa !

(Cercano picchiarlo, ma egli se la svigna, declamando sempre.)

Preziosilla

(Ai Soldati che lo inseguono uscendo di scena.)

Lasciatelo, ch' ei vada.

Far guerra ad un cappuccio!—bella impresa !

Non m' odon?—sia il tamburo sua difesa.

(Prende a caso un tamburo, e imitata da qualche Tamburino, lo suona. I Soldati accorrono tosto a circondarla seguiti da tutta la turba.)

Melitone.

And chiefs and soldiers all of a stamp,
All heretics.

Italian.

We will soon settle you.

Melitone.

All, all, sinks of iniquity ;
And until the world is smothered with tar,
The earth cannot hope for peace.

Italian.

Give it him!

(Crowding round him)

Spanish

(Defending him)

Escape ! be off !

Italian.

Give it him—knock him on the head !

(They try to beat him, but he avoids them, continuing to exclaim.)

Preziosilla.

(To the Soldiers, who follow him off the stage.)

Let him alone, let him go.

Make war upon a friar !—a fine affair !

They hear me not—the drum shall defend him.

(Takes up a drum, and, imitated by a little Drummer, sounds it.) The Soldiers immediately surround her, followed by the whole throng.)

RATAPLAN, DELLA GLORIA — *RATAPLAN, SONGS OF GLORY* (Preziosilla and Chorus)

plan,   ra - ta - plan,   ra - ta - plan,   ra - ta - plan,   ra - ta -

plan, ra - ta - plan, plan, plan,   ra - ta - plan, ra - ta - plan, plan, plan.

Rataplan, si raccolgon le schiere,	Rataplan, the troops assemble,
Rataplan, son guidate a pugnar.	Rataplan, are led to the fight,
Rataplan, rataplan, le bandiere	Rataplan, rataplan, the banners
Del nemico si veggon piegar !	Of the enemy give way before us.
Rataplan, pim, pum, pam, inseguite	Rataplan, pim, pum, pam, pursue
Chi le terga, fuggendo, voltò.	The coward who flees from the foe.
Rataplan, le gloriose ferite	Rataplan, the wounds of the brave
Col trionfo il destin coronò.	Are with triumph crowned by fate.
Rataplan, della patria la gloria,	Rataplan, the glory of the country
Più rifulge de' fili al valor !	Shines forth in the valor of her sons
Rataplan, rataplan, la vittoria	Rataplan, rataplan, victory
Al guerriero conquista ogni cor.	Has won each warrior's heart.
FINE DELL' ATTO TERZO.	END OF THE THIRD ACT.

ATTO IV

SCENA I. Vicinanze d' Hornachuelos. Interno del Convento della Madonna degli Angeli. Meschino porticato circonda una Corticella con aranci, oleandri, gelsomini. Alla sinistra dello spettatore, e la porta che mette alla via; a destra altra porta, sopra la quale si legge 'Clausura.'

Il PADRE GUARDIANO passeggia gravemente leggendo il breviario. Dalla sinistra entrano molt Pezzenti, d' ogni eta e sesso, con rozze scodelle, alla mano pignatte o piatti.

Coro.

Fate la carità,
E un' ora che aspettiamo !
Andarcene dobbiamo,
Fate la carità.

SCENA II. Detti e FRA MELITONE, che viene dalla destra, caperto il ventre d' ampio grembiale bianco ed ajutato da altro Laico, porta una grande caldaja a due manichi, che depongono nel centro; il Laico riparte.

Melitone.

Che ! siete all' osteria ! Quieti.

(Incomincia a distribuire col ramaiuolo la ministra.)

Donne
(Spingendosi fra loro.)

Qui, presto a me.

Vecchi.

Quante porzioni a loro.

Altri.

Tutti vorrian per sè.

Tutti.

N' ebbe già tre Maria.

Una
(A MELITONE.)

Quattro a me.

Tutti.

Quattro a lei !

Detti.

Sì, perchè ho sei figliuolì.

Melitone.

Perchè ne avete sei ?

Detta.

Perchè li mandò Iddio.

Melitone.

Sì, sì, Dio—non li avreste
Se al par di me voi pure la schiena per-
cotèste
Con aspra disciplina, e più le notti intere
Passaste recitando rosari e miserere.

ACT IV

SCENE I. The neighborhood of Hornachuelos. Interior of the Convent of the 'Madonna degli Angeli.' A simple Colonnade surrounds a small Court, filled with orange trees, oleanders, and jessamines. On left of the spectator, a door opening on the road; on the right another door, on which is written 'Clausura.'

The FATHER GUARDIANO walks about, seriously reading his breviary. From the left enter many Beggars, of each sex, with rough porringers, pipkins, or plates in their hands.

Chorus.

Alms we beg of you.
An hour we have waited,
And soon we must go.
Alms ! Alms !

SCENE II. The above and BROTHER MELITONE, who comes from the right, with a large white apron in front, and, aided by another Lay-brother, carries a great cauldron with two handles, which they place in the middle; the Lay-brother goes away.

Melitone.

What ! do you take this for an inn ? Be silent.

(Begins to distribute the minestra with a ladle.)

Women
(Pushing forward.)

Quick, give me some.

Old Men.

What a quantity for them.

Others.

Each wants for it himself.

All.

Maria has already had three.

A Woman
(To MELITONE.)

Four for me.

All.

Four for her !

Woman.

Yes, for I have six children.

Melitone.

Why have you six ?

Woman.

Because Heaven sent them to me.

Melitone.

Ay, ay, Heaven—you would not have them
If, like me, you scourged your back
With a sharp scourge, and spent the night
In reciting rosaries and misereres.

Guardiano.

Fratel—

Melitone.

Ma tai pezzenti son di fecondità.

Davvero spaventosa.

Guardiano.

Abbiate carità.

Vecchi.

Un po' di quel fondaccio ancora ne donate.

Melitone.

Il ben di Dio, briccóni, fondaccio voi chiamate ?

Alcuni.

A me padre !

(Presentando le scodelle.)

Altri.

A me.

(Presentando le scodelle.)

Melitone.

Oh andatene in malora,

O il ramajuol sul capo v' aggiusto bene or ora !

Io perdo la pazienza !

Guardiano.

Oh, carità, fratello !

Donne.

Più carità ne usava il padre Raffaello.

Melitone.

Sì, sì ma in otto giorni, avutone abbastanza.

Di poveri e ministra, restò nella sua stanza.

E scaricò la soma sul dosso a Melitone,

E poi con tal canaglia usar dovrò le buone ?

Guardiano.

Soffrono tanto i poveri : la carità è un dovere.

Melitone.

Carità con costoro che il fanno per mestiere?

Che un campanile abbattere co' pugni sarien buoni,

Che dicono fondaccio il ben di Dio?

Briccóni!

Alcuni.

Oh, il padre Raffaele—

Guardiano.

Brother—

Melitone.

But these beggars are prolific

To such a wonderful degree.

Guardiano.

Be merciful.

Old Men.

Give us a little more of these dregs.

Melitone.

A godsend, you rogues, and you call it dregs !

Some.

To me, Father !

(Presenting their porringers.)

Others.

To me?

(Presenting theirs.)

Melitone.

Go to Jericho,

Or I will lay the ladle about your heads !

I lose all patience !

Guardiano.

Be merciful, brother !

Women.

Father Raffaello was more kind.

Melitone.

True, true, but after a week of soup and beggars

He had enough and took to his bed.

He left his burden on the back of Melitone.

And how can I be gentle with such rabble ?

Guardiano.

They suffer much : charity toward them is a duty.

Melitone.

Charity to those who make it their trade ?

Who could fell a steeple with their fists ?

Who call this godsend dregs ? The rogues !

Some.

Oh, Father Raffaello—

Altri.

Era un angelo.

Altri.

Un santo !

Tutti.

Se il padre Raffaele—

Melitone.

Non m'annojate tanto !

(Distribuisce in f-etta il residuo, dicendo—

Il resto, a voi, prendetevi,
Non voglio più parole !

(Fa rotolare la caldaia con un calcio.)

Fuori di qua, lasciatemi,
Sì fuori, al sole, al sole :
Pezzenti più di Lazzaro,
Sacchi di pravità,
Via, via, bricconi, al diavolo !
Toglietevi di qua !

(Indispettito le scaccia, confusamente, percuotendoli col grembiale che si sara tolto, e chiude la porta, restandone assai adirato e stanco.)

SCENA III.   Il padre guardaino e melitone.

Melitone

(Asciugandosi il sudore con un fazzoletto bianco che avara cavato da una manica.)

Auf ! pazienza non v'ha che basti !

Guardiano.

Troppa
Dal Signor non ne aveste :
Facendo carità un dover s' adempie
Da render fiero un angiol.

Melitone

(Prendendo tabacco.)

Che al mio posto
In tre dì finerebbe
Col ministrar de' schiaffi.

Guardiano.

Tacete ; umil sia Meliton, nè soffra
Se veda preferirsi Raffaele.

Melitone.

Io? no—amico gli son, ma ha certi gesti.
Parla da sè—ha cert' occhi.

Others.

Was an angel !

Others.

A saint !

All.

Yes, Father Raffaello—

Melitone.

Don't bother me so !

(Hastily distributing what remains, saying—)

Take what is left.

(Makes the cauldron roll over with a kick.)

I will have no more words—go ?
Out of here—leave me !
Yes, go and warm yourselves in the sun ;
Beggars greater than Lazarus.
Bags of depravity,
Go, rascals, go to the devil !
Be off from here !

(He angrily drives them out, striking them with the apron he has taken off, and shuts the door, remaining very angry and tired.)

SCENE III.   FATHER GUARDIANO and MELITONE.

Melitone

(Wiping off the perspiration with a white handkerchief, which he takes from his sleeve.)

Ouf ! I have no more patience !

Guardiano.

Truly Heaven has not
Blessed you with over much ;
Giving charity is fulfilling a duty
Which might rejoice an angel.

Melitone

(Taking snuff.)

Who would be done for in my place
In three days.

Guardiano.

Silence : be humble, Melitone, not be
   vexed.
Though Raffaello be preferred.

Melitone.

I? no—I am his friend : but he has such
   ways.
He talks to himself—has such looks.

Guardiano.

Son le preci,
Il digiun.

Melitone.

Jer nell' orto lavorava
Cotanto stralunato, che scherzando,

Dissi : Padre, un mulatto
Parmi–Guardommi bieco,
Strinse le pugna, e—

Guardiano.

Ebbene ?

Melitone.

Quando cadde
Sul campanil la fulgore, ed usciva
Fra la tempesta gli gridai : Mi sembra
Indo selvaggio un urlo
Cacciò che mi gelava.

Guardiano.

Che v' ha a ridir ?

Melitone.

Nulla, ma il guardo e penso
Che il demonio, narraste,
Qui stette un tempo in abito da frate,
Gli fosse il padre Raffael parente ?

Guardiano.

Giudizzii temerarii.   Il ver narrai ;
Ma n' ebbe il superior revilazione
Allora.   Io, no.

Melitone.

Ciò è vero !
Ma strano è molto il padre !   La ragione ?

Guardiano.

Del mondo i disinganni,
L' assidua penitenza.
Le veglie, l' astinenza
Quell' anima turbar.

Melitone.

Saranno i disinganni
Adunque e l'astinenza.
L' assidua penitenza,
Che il capo gli guastar !

(suona con forza il campanello alla porta.)

Guardiano.

It is through his praying
And fasting.

Melitone.

Yesterday, as he worked in the orchard.
His eyes seemed so starting out, that
jestingly
I said, 'Father, you look like a mulatto !'
He turned an angry glance on me,
Clenched his fist, and—

Guardiano.

What then ?

Melitone.

When the lightning struck the steeple,
As he went out into the storm, I cried,
'You look to me like a wild Indian !'
Whereupon he uttered a howl
That froze my blood.

Guardiano.

What followed ?

Melitone.

Nothing ; but I looked at him, and thought
That the demon you told us of,
Who once lived here in a friar's dress,
Might be a relative of Father Raffaello.

Guardiano.

A rash judgment. I told the tale ;
But to the superior 'twas revealed,
And not to me.

Melitone.

That is true ;
But the father is most strange ! What is
the cause ?

Guardiano.

Finding out the deceit of the world,
Constantly performing penance,
Vigils and abstinence,
Have disturbed his mind.

Melitone.

Discovering the world's deceit,
The various abstinences,
And the frequent penances,
Have upset his brain !

(The bell at the door is rung violently.)

Guardiano.

Giunge qualcuno—aprite.

(Parte.)

SCENA IV.   FRA MELITONE e DON CARLO, che avviluppato in un grande mantello, entra francamente.

Carlo

(Alteramente.)

Siete voi il portiere ?

Melitone.

(E goffo ben costui !)
S' ora v' apersi, parmi.

Carlo.

Il padre Raffaele ?

Melitone.

(Un altro !) Due ne abbiamo ;
L' un di Porcuna, grasso,
Sordo come una talpa, l' altro scarno,
Bruno, occhi (ciel quali occhi !) voi chiedete ?

Carlo.

Quell dell' inferno.

Melitone.

(E desso !)   E chi gli annuncio ?

Carlo.

Un cavalier.

Melitone.

(Qual boria ! è un mal arnese.)

(Parte.)

SCENA V.   DON CARLOS, poi DON ALVARO in abito da frate.

Carlo.

Invano Alvaro ti celasti al mondo

E d'ipocrita veste
Scudo fecesti alla viltà. Del chiostro

Ove t' ascondi m' additàr la via
L'odio e la sete di vendetta ; alcuno
Qui non sarà che ne divida ;
Solo il tuo sangue può lavar l' oltraggio
Che macchiò l' onor mio ;
E tutto il verserò, lo giuro a Dio.

Guardiano.

Someone has arrived—open.

(Exit.)

SCENE IV.—FATHER MELITONE, and DON CARLOS, who enters boldly, wrapped in a great cloak.

Carlos

(Haughtily.)

Are you the porter ?

Melitone.

(The man must be a fool !)
It appears to me I just let you in.

Carlos.

Father Raffaello?

Melitone.

(Another !) We have two of them ;
One from Porcuna, fat,
Deaf as a post ; the other lean, dark eyes,
(Heavens, what eyes !) Which do you want ?

Carlos.

The fiend.

Melitone.

('Tis he !)   And whom shall I announce ?

Carlos.

A cavalier.

Melitone.

(What arrogance ! an ill-bred fellow.)

(Exit.)

SCENE V.   DON CARLOS, after him DON ALVARO, in a monk's habit.

Carlos.

In vain, Alvaro, from the world thou hidest,

And with hypocrite's garb
Wouldst shield thy villainy. To the cloister
Which concealed thee, hate
And vengeance pointed out the way.
None here shall hold me from thee ;
Thy blood alone can cleanse the stain
From my outraged honour :
And before heaven I swear to shed it !

Alvaro.

Fratello—

Carlo.

Riconoscimi.

Alvaro.

Don Carlo! Voi vivente!

Carlo.

Da un lustro ne vo' in traccia,
Ti trovo finalmente :
Col sangue sol cancellasi
L' infamia ed il delitto.
Ch' io ti punisca è scritto
Sul libro del destin.
Tu prode fosti, or monaco,
Un' arma qui non hai ;
Deggio il tuo sangue spargere,
Scegli, due ne portai.

Alvaro.

Vissi nel mondo—intendo ;
Or queste vesti l' eremo,
Dicon che i falli ammendo,
Ah ! cessi il sangue alfin !
Lasciateme.

Carlo.

Difendere
Quel sajo, nè il deserto.
Codardo, non ti possono.

Alvaro
(Trasalendo.)

Codardo ! tale asserto—
(Poi frenandosi.)

(Ah no !—assistima, Signore !)
(A DON CARLO.)

La minaccie, i fieri accenti,
Portin seco in preda i venti;
Perdonatemi, pietà.
A che offendere cotanto
Chi fu solo sventurato !
Deh chiniam la fronte al fato :
O fratel, pietà, pietà !

Carlo.

Tu contamini tal nome.
Una suora mi lasciasti
Chi tradita abbandonasti
All' infamia, al disonor.

Alvaro.

Brother—

Carlos.

Behold and know me.

Alvaro.

Don Carlos ! Alive !

Carlos.

For five years I have been on thy track,
At length I find thee :
With blood alone, can thy imfamy
And misdeeds be blotted out.
'Tis written in the book of fate
That I shall punish thee.
Thou wert then valiant, now a monk ;
Thou hast no weapon here ;
As I must shed thy blood,
Two have I brought : choose.

Alvaro.

In the world I have lived—I understand ;
The garments I wear, this desert place,
Proclaim my errors reformed,
Ah ! at least cease this strife ;—
Leave me.

Carlos.

Coward,
Neither the cassock, or the desert,
Can protect thee !

Alvaro
(Shrinking.)

Coward ! that assertion—
(Restraining himself.)

(Ah no !—help me, Heaven !)
(To DON CARLOS.)

Threats, fierce and angry tones
Are cast to the winds ;
Pardon and pity me.
Wherefore goad so far
Him who was only unfortunate ?
Let us yield to fate :
Brother, mercy, mercy !

Carlos.

Thou dost contaminate the name.
Thou hast left me a sister
Whom thou didst betray, and then abandon
To infamy and dishonour !

Alvaro.

No, non fu disonorata,
Ve lo giura un sacerdote !
Sulla terra l'.ho adorata
Come in cielo amar si puote.
L'amo ancora, e s' ella m' ama
Più non brama questo cor.

Carlo.

Non si placa il mio furore
Per mendace e vile accento ;
L' arme impugna, ed al cimento
Scendi meco, o traditor.

Alvaro.

Se i rimorsi, il pianto omni.
Non vi parlano per me,
Qual nessun mi vide mai,
Io mi prostoro al vostro piè !

(Eseguisce.)

Carlo.

Ah, la macchia del tuo stemma
Or provasti con quest' atto !

Alvaro

(Balzando in piedi furente.)

Desso splende piucchè gemma.

Carlo.

Sangue il tinge di mulatto.

Alvaro

(Non potendo piu frenarsi.)

Per la gola voi mentite !
A me un brando .

(Glielo strappa di mano.)

Un brando—uscite !

Carlo

(Avviandosi.)

Finalmente !

Alvaro

(Ricomponendosi.)

No; l' inferno
Non trionfi. Va—riparti.

(Getta la spada.)

Carlo.

Ti fai dunque di me scherno ?
S' ora meco misurarti,
O vigliacco, non hai core,
Ti consacro al disonore !

(Gli da uno schiaffo.)

Alvaro.

No, she was not dishonoured,
It is a priest who swears it !
On earth I have adored her.
As only in Heaven they can love.
I love her still, and if she love me,
My heart has no other wish.

Carlos.

My rage will not be quelled
By base and lying words ;
Take the weapon, and to the combat
I challenge thee, O villain.

Alvaro.

If my remorse and tears
Speak not to you in my favour,
I will do what none have ever seen—
Prostrate myself at your feet !

(Kneels.)

Carlos.

Ah, the baseness of thy birth
Thou hast now proved by this act !

Alvaro

(Rising up furiously.)

That is more than jewels resplendent.

Carlos.

It is tinged with the blood of the mulatto

Alvaro

(No longer able to restrain himself.)

I cast the lie in your teeth !
Give me a sword !

(Snatches one from his hand.)

A weapon—lead on !

Carlos

(Moving on.)

Al !ast !

Alvaro

(Recovering himself.)

No ; the fiend shall not
Prevail. Go—away !

(Throws away the sword.)

Carlos.

What, dost thou make a jest of me ?
If to measure weapons with me
Thou hast not courage, coward,
Thus I disgrace thee !

(Gives him a blow.)

Alvaro

(Furente.)

Ah, seguasti la tua sorte !
Morte a entrambi !

(Raccogliendo la spada.)

Carlo.

A entrambi morte !

A 2.

Paga l' ira alfin sarà.
Te l' inferno ingoierà !

(Escono currendo dalla sinistra.)

SCENA VI. Valle tra rupi inaccessibili, attraversata da un ruscello. Nel fondo, a sinistra dello spetattore, e una Grotta con porta practicabile, e sopra una campana che si potra suonare dall' interno. E il tramonto. La scena si oscura lentamente; la luna apparisce splendidissima.

DONNA LEONORA pallida, sfigurata, esce dalla grotta agitatissima.

Leonora.

Pace, pace, mio Dio ! cruda sventura
M' astringe, ahimè, a languir ;

Come il dì primo da tant' anni dura
Profondo il mio soffrir.
L'amai, gli è ver ! ma di beltà e valore
Cotando Iddio l' ornò.
Che l' amo ancor, nè togliermi dal core
L' imagine saprò.
Fatalità ! fatalità !—un delitto
Disgiunti n' ha quaggiù !
Alvaro, io t' amo, e su mel cielo è scritto ;

Non ti vedrò mai più !
Oh, Dio, Dio fa ch' io muoja ; chè la calma
Può darmi morte sol.
Invan la pace qui sperò quest' alma
In preda a lungo duol.

(Va ad un sasso, ove sono alcune provigione deposte da lPADRE GUARDIANO.)

Misero pane, a prolungarmi vieni
La sconsolata vita—ma chi giunge ?
Profanare che ardisce il sacro loco ?
Maledizione ! maledizione !

(Torna rapidamente alla Grotta, e vi si rinchiude)

SCENA VII. Si ode dentro la scena un cozzar di spade.

Carlo

(Dal' interno.)

Io muojo !—Confession!—

Alvaro

(Furiously.)

Thy death warrant is sealed !
Death to both !

(Picks up the sword.)

Carlos.

Death to both !

Both.

Wrong shall at last be avenged,
And hell shall receive thee !

(They rush out towards the left.)

SCENE VI. A valley amongst inaccessible rocks, traversed by a stream. At the back, on the left of the spectator, is a Grotto with a practicable door, and above it a bell, which can be sounded from within. The sun has set. The scene darkens gradually; The moon rises brightiy.

DONNA LEONORA, pale, wan, enters agitated from the grotto.

Leonora.

Peace, grant me peace, O Lord ;
By dire misfortune I'm condemned to languish ;
As on the first day, during so many years,
Profound has been my grief.
I loved him ! with beauty and courage
Heaven had so endowed him.
I love him still, nor can I from my heart
Banish his image.
O cruel fate !—a crime
Has parted us forever here below !
Alvaro, I love thee, and in heaven 'tis decreed
That I shall never see thee more !
O Lord, suffer me to die, for peace
To my soul comes only in death.
Here in vain I hope for peace,
A prey to lingering woe.

(She goes to a stone, on which are some provisions, placed there by FATHER GUARDIANO.)

Miserable food, thou comest to prolong
A wretched life—but who approaches ?
Who dares profane this sacred spot ?
Malediction ! malediction !

(Returns quickly to the Grotto and shuts herself in.)

SCENE VII. A clashing of swords is heard close at hand.

Carlos

(Without.)

I am slain !—Absolution !

L'alma salvate.

(ALVARO entra in scena colla spada sguainata.)

E questo ancor sangue d'un Vargas.

Carlo

(Sempre dall' interno.)

Padre. Confession.

Alvaro

(Getta la spada.)

Maledetto io son ; ma è presso
Un eremita.

(Corre alla grotta e batte alla porto.)

A confortar correte
Un uom che muor.

Leonora

(Dall' interno)

Nol posso.

Alvaro.

Fratello ! in nome del Signor.

Leonora.

Nol posso.

Alvaro

(Batte con piu forza.)

E d' uopo.

Leonora

(Dall' interno suonando la campana.)

Ajuto ! Ajuto !

Alvaro.

Deh venite.

SCENA VIII.   Detto e LEONORA che si presenta sulla porta.

Leonora.

Temerarii, del ciel l' ira fuggite !

Alvaro.

Una donna ! qual voce—ah no—uno
spettro.

Leonora

(Riconoscendo DON ALVARO.)

Che miro ?

Alvaro.

Tu—Leonora !

Leonora.

Egli è ben desso.

(Avvicinandosi ad ALVARO.)

Io ti riveggo ancora.

Save my soul.

(ALVARO enters, with unsheathed sword.)

Again is the blood of Vargas shed.

Carlos

(Still without.)

A priest—absolution.

Alvaro

(Throwing down the sword.)

I am accursed :
But here dwells a hermit.

(Runs to cave, and beats at the door.)

Hasten to aid.
A dying man.

Leonora

(From the cave.)

I cannot.

Alvaro.

Brother, in the name of heaven !

Leonora.

I cannot come.

Alvaro

(Beating furiously.)

His last moments are near.

Leonora

(Ringing the bell in the cave.)

Help ! help !

Alvaro.

Come quickly !

SCENE VIII.   LEONORA appears at the door of the cave.

Leonora.

Rash one, fly from the wrath of heaven !

Alvaro.

A woman ! that voice ! ah, no—'tis a
vision !

Leonora

(Recognizing DON ALVARO.)

What do I see !

Alvaro.

Leonora !

Leonora.

'Tis he.

(Advancing to ALVARO)

Again I see thee !

Alvaro.

Lungi—lungi da me— queste mie mani
Grondano sangue. Indietro !

Leonora.

Che mai parli ?

Alvaro
(Accennando.)

Là giace spento un uom.

Leonora.

Tu l'uccidesti ?

Alvaro.

Tutto tentai per evitar la pugna.
Chiusi i meie dì nel chiostro.

Ei mi raggiunse—m' insultò—l'uccisi.

Leonora.

Ed era ?

Alvaro.

Tuo fratello !

Leonora.

Gran Dio ?
(Corre ansante verso il bosco.)

Alvaro.

Destino avverso
Come a scherno mi prendi !
Vive Leonora e ritrovarla deggio
Or che versai di suo fratello il sangue !

Leonora
(Dall' interno. mette un grido.)

Ah !

Alvaro.

Qual grido !—che avvenne ?

SCENA IX. LEONORA ferita entra sostenuta dal GUARDIANO e detto.

Alvaro.

Ella—ferita !

Leonora
(Morente.)

Nell' ora estrema perdonar non seppe.
E l'onta vendicò nel sangue mio.

Alvaro.

E tu paga non eri
O vendetta di Dio !—Maledizione !

Alvaro.

Away, away from me, my hands
Are stained with blood. Look yonder.

Leonora.

What meanest thou ?

Alvaro
(Pointing.)

See, there lies a dying man.

Leonora.

Thou has killed him ?

Alvaro.

Vainly I tried to evade this fray.
Within the cloister's shelter passed my
life !
He sought me out there—insulted me,—
I slew him.

Leonora.

And he was ?

Alvaro.

Thy brother !

Leonora.

Great heaven !
(Runs breathlessly towards the wood.)

Alvaro.

Relentless destiny
Thus mocks me ever !
Leonora lives, and I meet her
With her brother's blood upon me.

Leonora
(Shrieks without.)

Ah !

Alvaro.

That cry ! what has happened.

SCENE IX. LEONORA enters, wounded, supported by GUARD-IANO.

Alvaro.

'Tis she—wounded !

Leonora
(Dying)

In his last hour he pardoned not ;
And with my blood revenged his shame.

Alvaro.

And thou art thus repaid,
Oh, vengeance of heaven ! malediction. !

Guardiano
(Solenne.)

Non imprecare ; umiliati
A lui ch'è giusto e santo—
Che adduce a eterni gaudii
Per una via di pianto.
D'ira e furor sacrilego.
Non profferir parola,
Mentre quest' angiol vola
Al trono del Signor.

Leonora
(Con voce morente.)

Sì, piangi— e prega.

Alvaro.

Un reprobe, un maledetto io sono.
Flutto di sangue inalzasi.
Fra noi.

Leonora.

Di Dio il perdono io ti prometto.

Guardiano.

Prostrati !

Leonora.

Alvaro.

Alvaro.

A quell' accento
Più non poss' io resistere.
(Gettandosi ai piedi di LEONORA.)

Leonora, io son redento,
Dal ciel son perdonato !

Leonora e Guardiano.

Sia lode a te Signor.

Leonora.
(Ad ALVARO.)

Lieta or poss' io precederti.
Alla promessa terra.
Là cesserà guerra.
Santo l'amor sarà.

Alvaro.

Tu mi condanni a vivere,
E mi abbandoni intanto !
Il reo, il reo soltanto.
Dunque impunito andrà !

Guardiano
(Solemnly.)

Curse thou not. Humble thyself
Before Him who is just and holy ;
Who by a path of tears
To eternal joys conducts thee.
Pour not forth words.
Of ire and sacrilegious fury.
While this angel ascends
To the heavenly throne.

Leonora
(With dying accents.)

Yes,—weep and pray.

Alvaro.

Reprobate, accursed am I.
Barriers of blood between us
Have arisen.

Leonora.

Heaven grants me power to pardon thee.

Guardiano.

Kneel.

Leonora.

Alvaro—

Alvaro.

Those loved tones
No more can I resist.
(Throwing himself at LEONORA'S feet.)

Leonora, I am saved,
Heaven has forgiven my sins.

Leonora & Guardiano.

Power eternal, praise be to Thy name !

Leonora
(To ALVARO.)

Gladly now can I precede thee
To the promised land ;
There strife shall cease.
And holy love shall reign.

Alvaro.

Thou condemnest me to live
While thus forsaking me ;
I, the guilty one,
Alone go unpunished.

Guardiano.

 Santa del suo màrtirio
 Ella al Signore ascenda.
 E il suo morir ti apprenda
 La fede e la pieta !

Leonora.

 O Ciel ti attendo, addio !
 Io ti precedo Alvaro.

Alvaro.

 Morta !

Guardiano.

 Salita a Dio.

    (Cala lentamente la tela.)

    FINE DELL' OPERA.

Guardiano.

 Holy in her martyrdom,
 She now departs to heaven ;
 And piety and faith
 Her death will teach thee.

Leonora.

 Oh, heaven, I await thee ; farewell,
 I do but precede thee, Alvaro.

Alvaro.

 Dead !

Guardiano.

 Ascended to heaven !

    (Curtain slowly falls.)

    END OF THE OPERA.

AÏDA

by

GIUSEPPE VERDI

LIBRETTO BY ANTONIO GHISLANZONI

THE STORY OF THE ACTION

Aïda, daughter of Amonasro, King of Ethiopia, has been led into captivity by the Egyptians. While in bondage sne conceives a tender passion for Radames, a young Egyptian warrior, who warmly responds to her affection. The opening incidents of the opera disclose these facts, and set forth, besides, the choice of Radames as leader of an expedition against the invading forces of Ethiopia, and the love, still unrevealed, of Amneris, daughter of Egypt's sovereign, for the fortune-favored chieftain. Amneris suspects the existence of a rival, but does not learn the truth until Radames returns victorious. The second act commences with a scene between the Princess and the slave. Amneris wrests from Aïda the secret she longs and yet dreads to fathom, and dire hate at once possesses her. Radames comes back, laden with spoils. Among his prisoners—his rank being unknown to his captors—is Amonasro, father of Aïda. Radames asks of his sovereign that the captives be freed. The King consents to releasing all of them except Aïda and Amonasro. The monarch then bestows upon the unwilling Radames the hand of Amneris, and amid songs of jubilation the act terminates. In the third act the marriage of Amneris and Radames is on the eve of celebration. Radames, however, is devotedly attached to Aïda, and the maiden, urged thereunto by Amonasro, seeks to persuade the soldier to flee to Ethiopia and turn his sword against his native land. Without resolving upon the act of treachery, Radames lends an ear to her supplications. The party is about to take to flight, when the High Priest, Ramphis, and Amneris, both of whom have overheard the lovers, appear. Aïda and Amonasro, on the advice of Radames, escape. Radames remains to await his fate. This is speedily decided. Radames, in act the fourth, is tried on a charge of treason. Amneris, repentant, vainly endeavors to save his life,—foɪ the lover of Aïda scorns to renounce her,—and he is deaf to the entreaties of the daughter of the King, whose jealousy, as Amneris herself is aware, has brought about his downfall. The dénouement is not long delayed. The final picture shows the interior of the Temple of Vulcan. Above is the hall of worship; below, the vault in which Radames, doomed to die, is interred alive by the priests. As the stone is sealed over his head, Aïda, who has awaited Radames in the tomb, rises before him. The lovers are locked in a last embrace as Amneris, heart-broken, kneels in prayer on the marble which parts from the living the couple now united in death.

AÏDA

ACT I.

SCENE I.—Hall in the Palace of the King at Memphis; to the right and left a colonnade with statues and flowering shrubs; at the back a grand gate, from which may be seen the temples and palaces of Memphis and the Pyramids.

(RADAMES and RAMPHIS.)

Ramphis.

Yes, a report runs that the Ethiopian dares
Again defy us, and the Valley of the Nile
And Thebes to threaten.—A messenger shortly
Will bring the truth.

Radames.

The sacred Isis
Didst thou consult?

Ramphis.

She has named
Of the Egyptian phalanxes
The supreme leader.

Radames.

Oh! happy man!

Ramphis
(with meaning, gazing at RADAMES).

Young and brave is he. Now to the king
I convey the decrees of the goddess.
(Exit.)

Radames
(alone).

If that warrior I were! If my dream
Should be verified! An army of brave men
Led by me—victory—the applause
Of all Memphis! And to thee, my sweet Aïda,
To return, crowned with laurels!
To say to thee,—for thee I have fought, and for thee conquered!

ATTO I.

SCENA I.—Sala nel Palazza del Re a Menfi. A destra e a sinistra una colonnata con statue e arbusti in flori—Grande porta nel fondo, de cui appariccone i tempii, i palazzi di Menfi e le Piramidi.

(RADAMES e RAMFIS.)

Ramfis.

Sì: corre voce che l'Etiope ardisca
Sfidarci ancora, e del Nilo la valle
E Tebe miniacciar—Fra breve un messo
Recherà il ver.

Radames.

La sacra
Iside consultasti?

Ramfis.

Ella ha nomato
Delle Egizie falangi
El condottier supremo.

Radames.

Oh lui felice!

Ramfis
(con intenzione, fissando RADAMES).

Giovine e prode è desso—Ora, del Nume
Reco i decreti al Re.
(Esce.)

Radames
(solo).

Se quel guerrier
Io fossi! se il mio sogno
Si avverasse!... Un esercito di prodi
Da me guidato... e la vittoria... e il plauso
Di Menfi tutta!—E a te, mia dolce Aïda,
Tornar di lauri cinto...
Dirti: per te ho pugnato e per te ho vinto!

AÏDA

CELESTE AÏDA—*RADIANT AÏDA*   Air (Radames)

Andantino

Ce - les-te A - i - da,   for - ma di - vi - na,   Mi - sti - co ser - to
Heav'n-ly_ A - i - da,   beau - ty_ re - splen-dent,   Mys - te - rious blend - ing

di lu - ce e fior,   del mio pen - sie - ro,   tu sei re - gi - na, tu di mia
of flow'rs and light,   Queen of_ my   soul thou reign-est tran-scen-dent, Thou of my

vi - ta sei lo splen-dor,   Il tuo bel   cie - lo vor-rei ri -
life art the splen-dor bright.)   To thy bright   skies once more I'd re -

dar - ti, le dol-ci brez-ze del pa - tria suol, un re-gal ser - to sul crin po -
store thee, To the soft   air of thy na - tive   land, Gar-lands im - pe - rial I would wreathe

sar - ti, er - ger-ti un tro - no vi-ci-no al sol, ah!_   Ce - les-te A - i - da,_
o'er thee, Raise thee a   throne_ near the sun to stand! ah!_   Heav'n - ly A - i - da,_

for - ma_ di - vi - na,_   mi - sti - co rag-gio   di lu - ce e fior;
beau - ty_ re - splen - dent,_   Mys - te - rious blend-ing   of flow'rs and light;

del mio pen-sie - ro   tu sei re - gi - na, tu di mia vi - ta sei lo splen-dor.
Queen of_ my soul thou reign-est tran-scen-dent, Thou of my   life art the splen-dor bright.

Il tuo bel cie - lo vor-rei ri - dar - ti; le dol - ci brez - ze del pa-tria
To thy bright skies once more I'd re - store thee, To the soft air of thy na-tive

suol; un re-gal ser-to sul crin po-sar-ti, er-ger-ti un tro-no vi-ci-no al
land, Gar-lands im-pe-rial I would wreathe o'er thee, Raise thee a throne e-ter-nal to

sol, un tro-no vi-ci-no al sol, un tro-no vi-ci-no al sol. ___
stand; A throne near the sun to stand, A throne near the sun to stand. ___

Amneris. (Enter AMNERIS.)

What unwonted fire in thy glance!
With what noble pride glows thy face.
Worthy of envy—oh, how much—
Would be the woman whose beloved aspect
Should awaken in thee this light of joy!

Radames.

With an adventurous dream
My heart was blessed. To-day the goddess
Declared the name of the warrior who to the
    field
The Egyptian troops shall lead. If I were
To such honor destined!

Amneris.

Has not another dream
More gentle, more sweet,
Spoken to thy heart? Hast thou not in
    Memphis
Desires—hopes?

Radames.

I! (What a question!
Perhaps—the hidden love
Which burns my heart she has discovered—
The name of her slave
She reads in my thoughts!)

Amneris.

(Oh! woe if another love
Should burn in his heart;
Woe, if my search should penetrate
This fatal mystery!)

Radames (Enter AÏDA.)
    (seeing AÏDA).
She!

Amneris. (AMNERIS e detto.)

Quale insolita givia
Nel tuo sguardo! Di quale
Nobil fierezza ti balena il volto!
Degna di invidia oh! quanto
Saria la donna il cui bramato aspetto
Tanta luce di gaudio in te destasse!

Radames.

D'un sogno avventuroso
Si beava il mio cuore—Oggi, la diva
Profferse il nome del guerrier che al campo
Le schìere Egizie condurrà... S'io fossi
A tale onor prescelto...

Amneris.

Nè un altro sogno mai
Più gentil... più soave...
Al cuore ti parlò?... Non hai tu in Menfi
Desiderii... speranze?

Radames.

Io!... (quale inchiesta!)
Forse... l'arcano amore
Scoprì che m' arde in core...
Della sua schiava il nome
Mi lesse nel pensier!)

Amneris.

(Oh! guai se un altro amore
Ardesse a lui nel core!...
Guai se il mio sguardo penetra
Questo fatal mister!)

Radames (AÏDA e detto.)
    (vedendo AÏDA).
Dessa!

Amneris.

(He is moved! And what
A glance he turns to her!
Aïda!—My rival—
Perhaps is she?)

(After a short silence turning to AïDA.)

Amneris.

(Ei si turba... e quale
Sguardo rivolse a lei!
Aïda!... a me rivale...
Forse saria costei?)

(Dopo breve silenzio volgendois ad AïDA.)

VIENI, O DILETTA—*COME, DEAREST FRIEND* Trio (Amneris, Aïda and Radames)

Andante mosso   AMNERIS

Vie— ni, o di - let - ta ap-pres-sa-ti   schia - va non sei ne an -
Come, dear-est friend, come near to me,   Slave— I no long-er

cel - la,   Qui— do-ve in dol - ce fa - - sci-no   Io ti chia-mai so -
name— thee;   Here— in af-fec-tion's ten- - der bonds, My sis-ter I pro-

rel - la   Pian - gi?   del - le tue la - cri-me sve - la il se -
claim thee,   Weep'st thou?   Why are these tears flow-ing, tell me thy

AIDA *Più mosso*

gre - to,— sve-la il se - gre-to a me. Ohi-mè! di guer-ra fre-me-re   l'a-
se - cret,— thy se-cret tell to me. A-las! the din of strife re-sounds, The

tro - ce gri-do io sen - to Per l'in-fe-li - ce pa-tri-a,   per me, per voi pa-
war-like hosts as - sem-ble, For my un-hap-py na-tive land, For me, for thee, I

AMN

ven - to.   Fa-vel-li il ver?   nè s'a-gi-ta più gra-ve cu-ra in te?
trem-ble.   Dost tru-ly speak?   no grav-er care dis-turbs thy gen-tle heart?

Allegro   RADAMES

Tre-ma,   o re - a schia-va,   Nel vel-
Trem-ble,   O slave dis- sem-bling!   Up - on—

- to a lei ba - le - na   Ah! tre - ma,   rea schia - va
— her face is gleam-ing.   Ah! trem-ble,   Oh! slave dis-

tre - ma,   Lo sde-gno ed il so-spet-to Chio nel tu - o cor di-scen-da!
sem-bling!   Dis - dain and dark sus - pi-cion Could I — in thy heart de-scend-ing,

                                   Tre - ma che il ver — m'ap - pren - da quel
                                   Learn the truth of thy — of - fend - ing, The

pian-to e quel ros -   sor   Ah! ___ no,   Sul - la mia pa - tria,   Non
                                             Ah! ___ no,
tear - ful blush that   starts   Oh! land be - lov - ed,   Thy

— ge - me il cor, il cor sol-tan-to,   Quel - lo ch'io —
— sor - row my heart, my heart's not griev-ing, These — tears my —

ver - so è pian - to,   È ___ pian - to, ___ pian - to ___ di
lone heart re - liev - ing,   Are ___ flow - ing, — flow - ing on

sven - tu - ra to a - mor!   Ah! ___ è pian - to ___ pian - to di
love's — un - hap - py part!   Ah! ___ are flow - ing, — flow ing from

sven - tu - ra to a - mor!   Pian - to   Di sven-tu-
love's un - hap - py smart!   Flow - ing   From love's un-

220   *AÏDA*

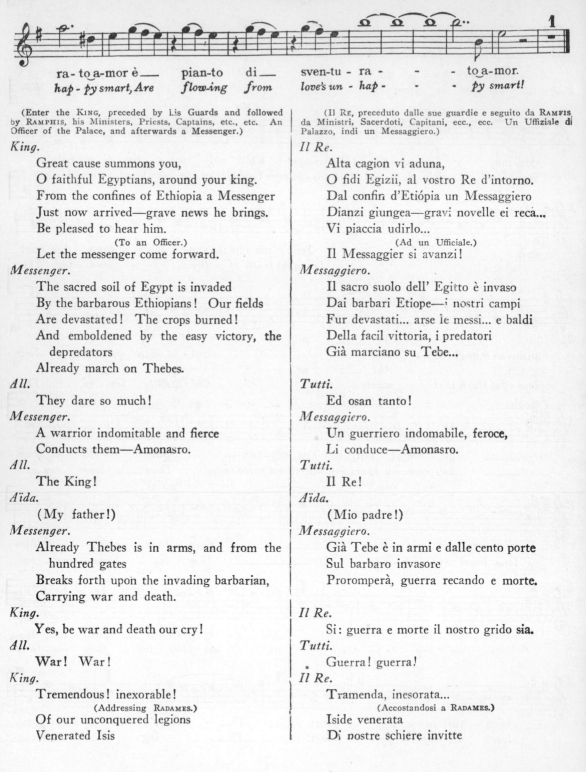

ra-to a-mor è—— pian-to di—— sven-tu - ra - - - to a-mor.
hap - py smart, Are flow-ing from love's un - hap - - - py smart!

(Enter the KING, preceded by his Guards and followed by RAMPHIS, his Ministers, Priests, Captains, etc., etc. An Officer of the Palace, and afterwards a Messenger.)	(Il RE, preceduto dalle sue guardie e seguito da RAMFIS, da Ministri, Sacerdoti, Capitani, ecc., ecc. Un Uffiziale di Palazzo, indi un Messaggiero.)

King.

Great cause summons you,
O faithful Egyptians, around your king.
From the confines of Ethiopia a Messenger
Just now arrived—grave news he brings.
Be pleased to hear him.
(To an Officer.)
Let the messenger come forward.

Messenger.

The sacred soil of Egypt is invaded
By the barbarous Ethiopians! Our fields
Are devastated! The crops burned!
And emboldened by the easy victory, the depredators
Already march on Thebes.

All.

They dare so much!

Messenger.

A warrior indomitable and fierce
Conducts them—Amonasro.

All.

The King!

Aïda.

(My father!)

Messenger.

Already Thebes is in arms, and from the hundred gates
Breaks forth upon the invading barbarian,
Carrying war and death.

King.

Yes, be war and death our cry!

All.

War! War!

King.

Tremendous! inexorable!
(Addressing RADAMES.)
Of our unconquered legions
Venerated Isis

Il Re.

Alta cagion vi aduna,
O fidi Egizii, al vostro Re d'intorno.
Dal confin d'Etiópia un Messaggiero
Dianzi giungea—gravi novelle ei reca...
Vi piaccia udirlo...
(Ad un Ufficiale.)
Il Messaggier si avanzi!

Messaggiero.

Il sacro suolo dell' Egitto è invaso
Dai barbari Etiope—i nostri campi
Fur devastati... arse le messi... e baldi
Della facil vittoria, i predatori
Già marciano su Tebe...

Tutti.

Ed osan tanto!

Messaggiero.

Un guerriero indomabile, feroce,
Li conduce—Amonasro.

Tutti.

Il Re!

Aïda.

(Mio padre!)

Messaggiero.

Già Tebe è in armi e dalle cento porte
Sul barbaro invasore
Proromperà, guerra recando e morte.

Il Re.

Sì: guerra e morte il nostro grido sia.

Tutti.

Guerra! guerra!

Il Re.

Tramenda, inesorata...
(Accostandosi a RADAMES.)
Iside venerata
Di nostre schiere invitte

Has already designated the supreme leader—
Radames.

All.

Radames!

Radames.

Thanks be to the gods!
My prayers are answered.

Amneris.

(He leader!)

Aïda.

(I tremble!)

King.

Now move, O warrior,
To the temple of Vulcan. Gird thee
With the sacred arms, and fly to victory.
Up! To the sacred bank of the Nile
Hasten, Egyptian heroes;
From every heart let burst the cry,
War and death to the foreigner!

Ramphis and Priests.

Glory to the gods! Remember all
That they rule events;
That in the power of the gods alone
Lies the fate of warriors.

Ministers and Captains.

Up! Of the Nile's sacred shore
Be our breasts the barrier;
Let but one cry resound:
War and death to the foreigner!

Radames.

Holy rage of glory
Fills all my soul.
Up! Let us rush to victory:
War and death to the foreigner!

Amneris
(bringing a banner and consigning it to RADAMES).

From my hand receive, O leader,
The glorious standard.
Be it thy guide, be it thy light,
On the path of glory.

Aïda.

(For whom do I weep? For whom pray?
What power binds me to him!
I must love him! And this man
Is an enemy—an alien!)

Già designava il condottier supremo:
Radames.

Tutti.

Radames.

Radames.

Sien grazie ai Numi!
I miei voti fur paghi.

Amneris.

(Ei duce!)

Aïda.

(Io tremo!)

Il Re.

Or, di Vulcano al tempio
Muovi, o guerrier—Le sacre
Armi ti cingi e alla vittoria vola.
Su! del Nilo al sacro lido
Accorrete, Egizii eroi;
Da ogni cor prorompa il grido.
Guerra e morte allo stranier!

Ramfis e Sacerdoti.

Gloria ai Numi! ognun rammenti
Ch'essi reggono gli eventi—
Che in poter d'e Numi solo
Stan le sorti guerrier.

Ministri e Capitani.

Su! del Nilo al sacro lido
Sien barriera i nostri petti;
Non echeggi che un sol grido:
Guerra e morte allo stranier!

Radames.

Sacro fremito di gloria
Tutta l'anima mi investe—
Su! corriamo alla vittoria!
Guerra e morte allo stranier!

Amneris
(recando una bandiera e consegnandota a RADAMES).

Di mia man ricevi, o duce,
Il vessillo glorioso;
Ti sia guida, ti sia luce
Della gloria sul sentier.

Aïda.

(Per chi piango? per chi prego?...
Qual poter m'avvince a lui!
Deggio amarlo... ed è costui
Un nemico... uno stranier!)

III.

War! War! Extermination to the invader!
Go, Radames, return conqueror!
                    (Exeunt all but AÏDA.)

Aida.

Return victorious! And from thy lips
Went forth the impious word! Conqueror
Of my father—of him who takes arms
For me—to give me again
A country, a kingdom; and the illustrious
    name
Which here I am forced to conceal! Con-
    queror
Of my brothers, with whose dear blood
I see him stained, triumphant in the ap-
    plause
Of the Egyptian hosts; and behind the
    chariot
A king!—my father—bound with chains!
The insane word
Forget, O gods!
Return the daughter
To the bosom of her father;
Destroy the squadrons
Of our oppressors!
Unhappy one! What did I say?—And my
    love
Can I ever forget,
This fervid love which oppresses and en-
    slaves,
As the sun's ray which now blesses me?
Shall I call death
On Radames?—On him whom I love so
    much?
Ah! Never on earth was heart torn
By more cruel agonies.
The sacred names of father, of lover,
I can neither utter, nor remember—
For the one—for the other—confused—
    trembling—
I would weep—I would pray;
But my prayer changes to blasphemy.
My tears are a crime—my sighs a wrong—
In dense night the mind is lost—
And in the cruel anguish I would die.

Tutti.

Guerra! guerra! sterminio all' invasor!
Va, Radames, ritorna vincitor!
                    (Escono tutti meno AÏDA.)

Aida.

Ritorna vincitor!... E dal mio labbro
Uscì l'empi parola!—Vincitore
Del padre mio... di lui che impugna l'armi
Per me... per ridonarmi
Una patria, una reggia! e il nome illustre
Che qui celar mie è forza—Vincitore
De' miei fratelli... ond' io lo vegga, tinto
Del sangue amato, trionfar nel plauso
Dell' Egizie coorti!... E dietro il carro,
Un Re... mio padre... di catene avvinto!...

L'insana parola,
O Numi, sperdete!
Al seno d'un padre
La figlia rendete;
Struggete le squadre
Dei nostri oppressor!
Sventurata! che dissi?... e l'amor mio?...
Dunque scordar poss' io
Questo fervido amor che oppressa e schiava
Come raggio di sol qui mi beava?
Imprecherò la morte
A Radames... a lui che amo pur tanto!
Ah! non fu in terra mai
Da più crudeli angoscie un core affranto.
I sacri nomi di padre... di amante
Nè profferir poss' lo, nè ricordar...
Per l'un... per l'altro... confusa... tremante...
Io piangere vorrei... vorrei pregar.
Ma la mia prece inbestemmia si muta...
Delitto è il pianto a me... colna il sospir...
In notte cupa la mente è perduta...
E nell' ansia crudel vorrei morir.

NUMI, PIETÀ!—*PITY, KIND HEAVEN* Air (Aïda)

Nu-mi, pie - tà— Del mio sof - frir! Spe - me non v'ha pel mio do-
Pi - ty, kind Heav'n, To Thee I fly; Hope there is none in this my

lor. A - mor fa - tal, Tre - men-do a - ror Spez - za— mi il
woe. Oh! fa - tal love, Thy pow'r I know, Break thou, my

cor,— fam-mi mo - rir! Nu-mi,— pie - tà del mio— sof-
heart,— cause me to die. Pi - ty,— kind Heav'n, Thy pow'r I

frir, Ah!— pie - tà, Nu-mi, pie - tà,— del mio— sof - frir,— Nu-mi, pie-
know. Oh,— kind Heav'n, pi - ty my woe, Thy mer - cy show,— pi - ty, kind

tà del mio— sof - frir, pie - tà, pie - tà, del mio sof - frir
Heav'n, re - lieve— my— woe: re - lieve my woe, re - lieve my woe.

SCENE II.—Interior of the Temple of Vulcan at Memphis. A mysterious light descends from above; a long row of columns one behind another is lost in the darkness; Statues of various deities; in the middle of the scene, above a platform covered with carpet, rises the altar, surmounted by sacred emblems; from golden tripods rises the smoke of incense.

PRIESTS and PRIESTESSES—RAMPHIS at the foot of the altar, afterwards RADAMES—The song of the PRIESTESSES accompanied by harps, is heard from the interior.

Priestesses (in the interior).

Infinite Phthah, of the world
Animating spirit,
We invoke thee!

Infinite Phthah, of the world
The fructifying spirit,
We invoke thee!

SCENA II.—Interno del Tempio di Vulcano a Menfi. Una luce misteriosa scende dal' alto.—Uno lunga fila di colonne l'una all' altra addossate, si perde fra le tenebre. Statue di varie Divinità. Nel mezzo della scena, sovra un palco coperto da tappeti, sorge l'altare sormontato da emblemi sacri. Dai tripedi d'oro si innalza il fumo degli incensi.

SACERDOTI e SACERDOTESSE—RAMFIS ai piedi dell' altare—A suo tempo, RADAMES—Si sente dall' interno il canto delle SACERDOTESSE accompagnato dalle arpe.

Sacerdotesse (nell' interno).

Immenso Fthà, del mondo
Spirito animator,
Noi ti invochiamo!

Immenso Fthà, del mondo
Spirito fecondator,
Noi ti invochiamo!

Fire uncreate, eternal,
Whence the sun has light,
We invoke thee!

Priests.

Thou who from nothing hast made
The waters, the earth and the heavens,
We invoke thee!

God, who of thy spirit
Art son and father,
We invoke thee!

Life of the Universe
Gift of eternal love,
We invoke thee.

(Enter RADAMES, introduced unarmed—While he goes to the altar the PRIESTESSES execute the sacred dance—On the head of RADAMES is placed a silver veil.)

Ramphis.

Mortal, beloved of the gods, to thee
Is confided the fate of Egypt. Let the holy sword
Tempered by the gods, in thy hand become
To the enemy, terror—a thunderbolt—death.
              (Turning himself to the gods.)
God, guardian and avenger
Of this sacred land,
Spread thy hand
Over the Egyptian soil.

Radames.

God, who art leader and arbiter
Of every human war,
Protect thou and defend
The sacred soil of Egypt.

(While RADAMES is being invested with the consecrated armor, the PRIESTS and PRIESTESSES resume the religious hymn and mystic dance.)

END OF THE FIRST ACT.

Fuoco increato, eterno,
Onde ebbe luce il sol,
Noi ti invochiamo!

Sacerdoti.

Tu che dal nulla hai tratto
L'onde, la terra e il ciel,
Noi ti invochiamo!

Nume che del tuo spirito
Sei figlio e genitor,
Noi ti invochiamo!

Vita dell' Universo,
Mito di eterno amor,
Noi ti invochiamo!

(RADAMES viene introdotto senz' armi—Montre va all' altare, le SACERDOTESSE eseguiscono la danza sacra—Sul capo di RADAMES vien steso un velo d'argento.)

Ramfis.

Mortal, diletto ai Numi—A te fidate
Son d'Egitto le sorti,—Il sacro brando
Dal Dio temprato, per tua man diventi
Ai nemici terror, folgore, morte.
              (Volgendozi al Nume.)
Nume, custode e vindice
Di questa sacra terra,
La mano tua distendi
Sovra l'Egizio suol.

Radames.

Nume, che duce ed arbitro
Sei d'ogni umana guerra,
Proteggi tu, difendi
D'Egitto il sacro suol!

(Mentre RADAMES viene investito delle armi sacre, le SACERDOTESSE e SACERDOTI riprendono l'inno religioso e la mistica danza.)

FINE DELL' ATTO PRIMO.

ACT II.

SCENE I.

A Hall in the Apartments of AMNERIS.
AMNERIS surrounded by female SLAVES, who are adorning her for the triumphal festival. From tripods arise aromatic perfumes. Moorish Slave Boys dancing and agitating feather fans.

Slave Girls.

Thou who amidst hymns and plaudits
Raisest thy flight to glory
Terrible even as a god!
Effulgent as the sun,
Come, on thy tresses rain
Laurels and flowers interwoven;
Let sound the songs of glory
With the songs of love.

Amneris.

(Come, my love, intoxicate me;
Make my heart blessed!)

Slave Girls.

Now where are the barbarian
Hordes of the foreigner?
Like a mist they scatter
At the breath of the warrior.
Come: gather the reward
Of glory, O conqueror;
Victory smiled upon thee—
Love shall smile upon thee.

Amneris.

(Come, my love, revive me
Again with thy dear voice!)
Silence! Aïda approaches us;
Daughter of the vanquished, her grief to me
is sacred.

(At a sign from AMNERIS all withdraw to a distance.)

In seeing her again, the fearful doubt
Awakens itself within me.
Let the fatal mystery be at last rent.

(Enter AÏDA.)

Amneris

(to AÏDA, with feigned affection).

The fate of arms was deadly to thy people,
Poor Aïda. The grief
Which weighs down thy heart I share with
thee.
I am thy friend:
Thou shalt have all from me—thou shalt live
happy.

ATTO II.

SCENA I.

Una Sala nell' Appartamento di AMNERIS.
AMNERIS circondata dalle SCHIAVE che li abbigliano per la festa trionfale. Dai tripodi si eleva il profumo degli aromi. Giovani schiavi mori denzando agitano i ventagli di piume.

Schiave.

Chi mai fra gli inni e i plausi
Erge alla gloria il vol,
Al par di un Dio terribile,
Fulgente al par del sol?
Vieni; sul crin ti piovano
Conteste ai lauri i fior;
Suonin di gloria i cantici
Coi cantici d'amor.

Amneris.

(Vieni, amor mio, mi inebria...
Fammi beato il cor!)

Schiave.

Or, dove son le barbare
Orde dello stranier?
Siccome nebbia sparvero
Al soffio del guerrier.
Vieni: di gloria il premio
Raccogli, o vincitor;
T'arrise la vittoria,
T'arriderà l'amor.

Amneris.

(Vieni, amor mio, ravvivami
D'un caro accento ancor!)
Silenzio! Aïda verso noi si avanza...
Figlia dei vinti, il suo dolor mi è sacro.

(Ad un cenno di AMNERIS tutti allontanano.)

Nel rivederla, il dubbio
Atroce in me si desta...
Il mistero fatal si squarci alfine!

(AMNERIS ed AÏDA.)

Amneris

(ad AÏDA con simulata amorevolezza).

Fu la sorte dell' armi a' tuoi funesta,
Povera Aïda!—Il lutto
Che ti pesa sul cor teco divido.
Io son l'amica tua...
Tutto da me tu avrai—vivrai felice!

Aïda.

  Can I be happy,

  Far from my native land; here where unknown

  To me is the fate of father and brothers?

Amneris.

  Deeply do I pity thee! Nevertheless they have an end,

  The ills of this world. Time will heal

  The anguish of thy heart.

  And more than time—a powerful god—love.

Aïda.

  Felice esser poss' io

  Lungi dal suol natio... qui dove ignota

  M'è la sorte del padre e dei fratelli?

Amneris.

  Ben ti compiango; pure hanno un confine

  I mali di quaggiù... Sanerà il tempo

  Le angosce del tuo core...

  E più che il tempo, un Dio possente...

  Amore.

AMORE, AMORE!—*O LOVE IMMORTAL!* Duet (Aïda and Amneris)

ri - so mi ___ schiu-de il ciel, _____ Ne' tuoi do - lo - ri la vi-ta io
rap - ture thy ___ smiles dis - close, _____ As in thy tri-als new life I

D'in-ter-ro-gar-la qua-si hò sgo-men-to,
Her will I ques-tion— feign-ing com - mo - tion,

sen - to un tuo sor - ri - so mi schiu-de il ciel.
bor - row, A heav'n of rap-ture thy smiles dis - close.

Di - vi - do l'an-sie del su - - o ter - ror.
As if her trou-ble to share _____ or re - move.

AMNERIS

Eb-ben qual nuo - vo fer-mi-to t'as-sai,gen-til A - ï - da?
What new a - larm dis - turbs thee now, my gen-tle friend, A - ï - da?

I tuoi se-gre - ti sve-la-mi, al - l'a-mor mi - o, al - l'a-mor mio t'af-
Thy se-cret thoughts un-veil to me, trust my ___ af - fec-tion, to my fond love con-

fi - da, Tra i for-ti che pu-gna-ro-no del-la tua pa-tria a dan-ne, quel-
fide thee! A-mong the braves who fought so well, lost in their coun-try's ser-vice, Has

AIDA

cu - no un dol-ce af-fan-no for-se a te in cor de-stò? Che
some one a ten-der sor-row hap-ly wak-en'd in your heart? What

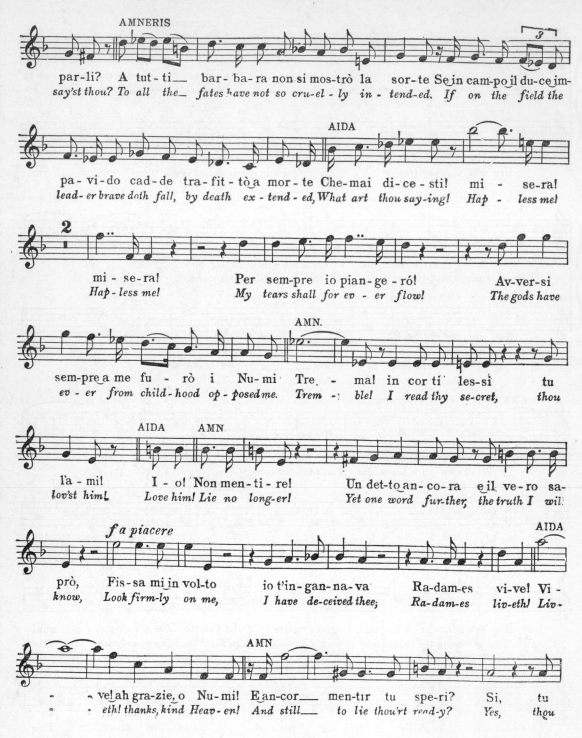

AMNERIS

par-li? A tut-ti___ bar-ba-ra non si mos-trò la sor-te Se in cam-po il du-ce im-
say'st thou? To all the___ fates have not so cru-el-ly in-tend-ed. If on the field the

AIDA

pa-vi-do cad-de tra-fit-tò a mor-te Che-mai di-ce-sti! mi - se-ra!
lead-er brave doth fall, by death ex-tend-ed, What art thou say-ing! Hap - less me!

mi - se-ra!   Per sem-pre io pian-ge - ró!   Av-ver-si
Hap - less me!   My tears shall for ev - er flow!   The gods have

AMN.

sem-pre a me fu - rò i Nu-mi Tre - ma! in cor ti les-si   tu
ev - er from child-hood op-posed me. Trem - ble! I read thy se-cret,   thou

AIDA   AMN.

l'a - mi!   I - o! Non men-ti - re!   Un det-to an-co-ra e il ve-ro sa-
lov'st him!   Love him! Lie no long-er!   Yet one word fur-ther, the truth I will

f a piacere   AIDA

prò, Fis-sa mi in vol-to   io t'in-gan-na-va   Ra-dam-es vi-ve! Vi-
know, Look firm-ly on me,   I have de-ceived thee;   Ra-dam-es liv-eth! Liv-

AMN

ve! ah gra-zie, o Nu-mi! E an-cor___ men-tir tu spe-ri? Si,   tu
eth! thanks, kind Heav-en! And still___ to lie thou'rt read-y? Yes,   thou

l'a - mi— Ma l'a-mo_an-ch'io in - ten - di tu? son tua ri -
lov'st him— I love him too, dost thou not hear? I am thy

AIDA

val-le fi - glia de' Fa - ra - o - ni Mia ri - va-le! eb-ben sia
ri - val, daugh - - ter of kings E - gyp-tian, Thou my ri - val! 'tis well, so

pu - re An-ch'io son tal Ah! Che dis - si mai? pie-
be it! And I am too— Ah! What have I said? for-

Adagio

tà! per - do - no! Ah!____ pie-tà! ti pren-da del mio do-
give, and pit - y, Ah! Let this my) sor-row thy warm heart

lor! È ve - ro, io l'a-mo d'im-men-so_a - mor. Tu sei fe - li - ce, tu sei pos-
move. 'Tis true I a-dore him with bound-less love Thou art so hap-py, thou art so

AMN

sen - te io__ vi - vo so - lo__ per que-sto_a - mor! Tre - ma, vil
might - y, I__ can - not live hence from love a - part! Trem - ble, vile

schia - va! spez-za_il tuo co - re! Se - gnar tuo mor - te, pùo que-st'a -
min - ion! be__ ye heart - bro-ken, War - rant of death__ this love shall be

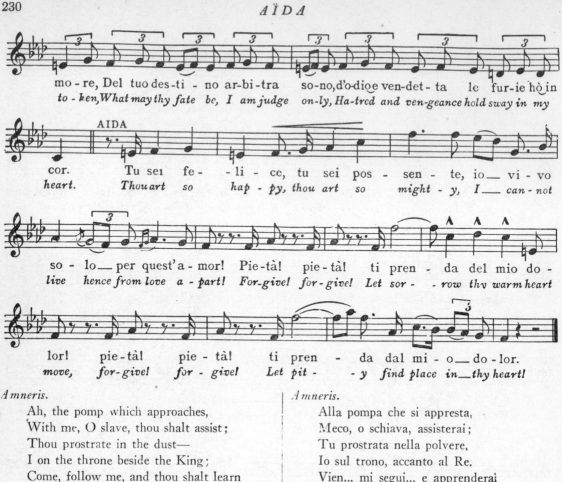

mo - re, Del tuo des-ti - no ar-bi-tra so-no, d'o-di, e ven-det - ta le fur-ie hò in
to - ken, What may thy fate be, I am judge on-ly, Ha-tred and ven-geance hold sway in my

cor. Tu sei fe - li - ce, tu sei pos - sen - te, io - vi - vo
heart. Thou art so hap - py, thou art so might - y, I__ can-not

so - lo__ per quest' a - mor! Pie-tà! pie - tà! ti pren - da del mio do -
live hence from love a - part! For-give! for - give! Let sor - - row thy warm heart

lor! pie-tà! pie - tà! ti pren - da dal mi - o__ do-lor.
move, for-give! for - give! Let pit - - y find place in__ thy heart!

Amneris.	Amneris.
Ah, the pomp which approaches,	Alla pompa che si appresta,
With me, O slave, thou shalt assist;	Meco, o schiava, assisterai;
Thou prostrate in the dust—	Tu prostrata nella polvere,
I on the throne beside the King;	Io sul trono, accanto al Re.
Come, follow me, and thou shalt learn	Vien... mi segui... e apprenderai
If thou canst contend with me.	Se lottar tu puoi con me.

Aïda.	Aïda.
Ah, pity! What more remains to me?	Ah! pietà!... che più mi resta?
My life is a desert;	Un deserto è la mia vita:
Live and reign, thy rage	Vivi e regna, il tuo furore
I will quickly appease.	Io tra breve placherò.
This love which angers thee	Questo amore che ti irrita
In the tomb I will extinguish.	Nella tomba spegnerò.

SCENE II.

An entrance to the City of Thebes. In front a group of palms; to the right the Temple of Ammon; to the left a throne surmounted by a purple canopy; at the back a triumphal gate. The scene is crowded with people.

Enter the KING, followed by Ministers, Priests, Captains, Fan-Bearers, Ensign-Bearers, etc., etc. Afterwards AMNERIS, with AÏDA and SLAVES. The KING seats himself on the throne; AMNERIS places herself to the left of the KING.

SCENA II.

Uno degli ingressi della Città di Tebe. Sul davanti un gruppo di palme; a destra il Tempio di Ammone; a sinistra un trono sormontato da un baldacchino di porpora; nel fondo una porta trionfale; la scena è ingombra di popolo.

Entra il RE, seguito dai Ministri, Sacerdoti, Capitani, Flabelliferi, Porta-Insegne, ecc., ecc. Quindi AMNERIS con AÏDA e SCHIAVE. Il RE va a sedere sul trono. AMNERIS prende posto alla sinistra del RE.

People.	Popolo.
Glory to Egypt, and to Isis,	Gloria all Egitto e ad Iside
Who the sacred soil protects;	Che il sacro suol protegge;

To the king who rules the Delta
Festal hymns let us raise.
Come, O champion warrior,
Come to rejoice with us;
In the path of the heroes,
Laurels and flowers let us strew.

Women.

Weave the lotus with the laurel
On the hair of the conqueror
A sweet shower of the flowers,
Spread on their arms a veil.
Let us dance, daughters of Egypt,
The mystic dances,
As around the sun
Dance the stars of heaven!

Priests.

To the supreme arbiters of victory
Raise your eyes;
Render thanks to the gods
On the happy day.
Thus for us with glory
May the future be marked,
Nor may that fate seize us
That struck the barbarians.

(The Egyptian troops, preceded by trumpets, defile before the KING—the chariots of war follow—the ensigns—the sacred vases and statues of the gods—troops of Dancing GIRLS who carry the treasures of the defeated—and lastly RADAMES, under a canopy borne by twelve Officers.)

King

(who descends from the throne to embrace RADAMES).

Saviour of thy country, I salute thee.

Come, and let my daughter with her own hand
Place upon you the triumphal crown.

(RADAMES bows before AMNERIS, who places the crown upon him.)

King

(to RADAMES).

Now ask of me
What thou most wishest. Nothing denied to thee
On such a day shall be—I swear it
By my crown, by the sacred gods.

Radames.

Deign first to let the prisoners
Be drawn up before thee.

(Enter between the Guards the Ethiopian prisoners, AMONASRO last, dressed as an Officer.)

Al Re che il Delta ragge
Inni festosi alziam!
Vieni, o guerriero vindice,
Vieni a gioir con noi;
Sul passo degli eroi
I lauri e i fior versiam!

Donne.

S'intrecci il loto al lauro
Sul crin dei vincitori;
Nembo gentil di fiori
Stenda sull' armi un vel.
Danziam, fanciulle Egizie,
Le mistiche carole,
Come d'intorno al sole
Donzano gli astri in ciel!

Sacerdoti.

Della vittoria agli arbitri
Supremi il guarde ergete;
Grazie agli Dei rendete
Nel forsunato dì.
Così per noi di gloria
Sia l'avvenir segnato,
Nè mai ci colga il fato
Che i barbari colpi.

(Le truppe Egizie precedute dalle fanfare sfilano dinanzi al RE—Seguono i carri di guerra, le insegne i vasi sacri, le statue degli Dei—Un drapello di danzatrici che recano i tesori dei vinti—Da ultimo, RADAMES, sotto un baldacchino portato da dodici Ufficiali.)

Il Re

(che scende dal trono per abbracciare RADAMES).

Salvator della patria, io ti saluto.

Vieni, e mia figlia di sua man ti porga
Il serto trionfale.

(RADAMES si inchina davanti AMNERIS che gli porge la corona.)

Il Re

(a RADAMES).

Ora, a me chiedi
Quanto più brami. Nulla a te negato
Sarà in tal dì—lo giuro
Per la corono mia, pei sacri Numi.

Radames.

Concedi in pria che innanzi a te sien tratti
I prigionier...

Entrano fra le guardie i prigionieri Etiopi, ultimo, AMONASRO, vestito da Uffiziale

Aïda.

What do I see? He!—my father!

All.

Her father!

Amneris.

In our power!

Aïda

(embracing her father).

Thou prisoner!

Amonasro

(softly to AÏDA).

Betray me not!

King

(to AMONASRO).

Draw thou near—
Then—thou art?

Amonasro.

Her father.—I also fought—
Was conquered, and death I sought in vain.
(Pointing to the uniform in which he is dressed.)
This livery that I wear may tell you
That I have defended my king and my country.
Fate was hostile to our arms;
Vain was the courage of the brave.
At my feet in the dust extended
Lay the king, transfixed by many wounds;
If the love of country is a crime
We are all criminals—all ready to die!
(Turning to the KING with a supplicating motion.)
But thou, O king, thou puissant lord,
Be merciful to those men.
To-day we are stricken by Fate,
To-morrow Fate may smite you.

Aïda, Prisoners and Female Slaves.

Yes; by the gods we are stricken;
Thy pity, thy mercy we implore;
Ah! May you never have to suffer
What is now given to us to suffer.

Ramphis and Priests.

Destroy, O king, these savage hordes,
Close your heart to their perfidious voices,
By the gods they were doomed to death,
Let the will of the gods be accomplished.

People.

Priests, your anger soften,

Aïda.

Che veggo?... Egli!... mia padre!

Tutti.

Suo padre!

Amneris.

In poter nostro!...

Aïda

(abbracciando il padre).

Tu! Prigionier!

Amneris

(piano ad AÏDA).

Non mi tradir!

Il Re

(ad AMONASRO).

Ti appressa...
Dunque... tu sei?...

Amonasro.

Suo padre—Anch' io pugnai...
Vinti noi fummo e morte invancercai.
(Accennando alla divisa che lo veste.)
Questa assisa ch'io vesto vi dica
Che il mio Re, la mia patria ho difeso:
Fu la sorte a nostr' armi nemica...
Tornò vano dei forti l'ardir.
Al mio piè nella polve disteso
Giacque il Re da più colpi traffito;
Se l'amor della patria è delitto
Siam rei tutti, siam pronti a morir!
(Volgendosi al RE con accento supplichevole.)
Ma tu, o Re, tu signore possente,
A costoro ti volgi clemente...
Oggi noi siam percossi dal fato
Doman voi potria il fato colpir.

Aïda, Prigionieri e Schiava.

Sî: dal Numi percossi non siamo;
Tua pietà, tua clemenza imploriamo;
Ah! giammai di soffrir vi sia dato
Ciò che in oggi n'è dato soffrir!

Ramfis e Sacerdoti.

Struggi, o Re, queste ciurme feroci,
Chiudi il core alle perfide voci,
Fur dai Numi votati alla morte,
Si compisca dei Numi il voler!

Popolo.

Sacerdoti, gli sdegni placate,

The humble prayer of the conquered hear,
And thou, O king, powerful and strong,
Open thy thoughts to mercy.

Radames

(fixing his eyes on AïDA).

(The sorrow which speaks in that face
Renders it more beautiful to my sight;
Every drop of the beloved tears
Reanimates love in my breast.)

Amneris.

(What glances on her he turns!
With what flame their faces flash!
To such a fate as this am I destined?
Revenge groans in my heart.)

King.

Now that events smile favor upon us,
To these people let us show ourselves mer-
    ciful;
Pity ascends grateful to the gods,
And confirms the power of princes.

Radames

(to the KING).

O King! by the sacred gods,
By the splendor of thy crown,
Thou sworest to fulfill my vow?

King.

I swore.

Radames.

Well; of thee for the Ethiopian prisoners,
Life I demand and liberty.

Amneris.

(For all!)

Priests.

Death to the enemies of the country!

People.

Grace
For the unhappy.

Ramphis.

Listen, O King,

(To RADAMES.)

Even thou,
Young hero, listen to wise counsel:
They are enemies and they are warriors—
They have revenge in their hearts.
Emboldened by thy pardon
They will run to arms again.

L'umil prece dei vinti ascoltate;
E tu, o Re, tu possente, tu forte,
A clemenza dischiudi il pensier.

Radames

(fissando AïDA).

(Il dolor che in quel volte favella
Al mio sguardo la rende più bella;
Ogni stilla del pianto adorato
Nel mio petto ravviva l'amor.)

Amneris

(Quali sguardi sovr' essa ha rivolti!
Di qual fiamma balenano i volti!
E a tal sorte serbata son io?...
La vendetta mi rugge nel cor.)

Il Re.

Or che fausti ne arridon gli eventi
A costoro mostriamci clementi:
La pietà sale ai Numi gradita
E rafferma dei Prenci il poter.

Radames

(al RE).

O Re: pei sacri Numi,
Per lo splendore della tua corona.
Compier giurasti il voto mio...

Il Re.

Giurai.

Radames.

Ebbene: a te pei prigionieri Etiopi
Vita domando e libertà.

Amneris.

(Per tutti!)

Sacerdoti.

Morte ai nemici della patria!

Popolo.

Grazie
Per gli infelici!

Ramfis.

Ascolta, o Re—

(A RADAMES.)

Tu pure
Giovine eroe, saggio consiglio ascolta:
Son nemici e prodi sono...
La vendetta hanno nel cor,
Fatti audaci dal perdono
Correranno all' armi ancor!

Radames.

Amonasro, the warrior king slain,
No hope remains to the vanquished.

Ramphis.

At least
As an earnest of peace and security, among us
With her father let Aïda remain.
Let the rest be free.

King.

To thy counsel I yield.
Of security and peace a better pledge
I will now give: Radames, the country
Owes all to thee. The hand of Amneris
Be thy reward. Over Egypt one day
With her shalt thou reign.

Amneris.

(Now let the slave come—
Let her come to take my love from me—if
she dares!)

King.

Glory to Egypt and to Isis,
Who the sacred soil defends,
Weave the lotus with the laurel
On the hair of the victors.

Priests.

Hymns let us raise to Isis,
Who the sacred soil defends;
Let us pray that the Fates may ever smile
Propitious on our country.

Aïda.

(What hope more remains to me?
To him glory and the throne.
To me, oblivion—the tears
Of hopeless love.)

Prisoners.

Glory to the merciful Egyptian
Who has unloosed our fetters,
Who restores us to the free
Paths of our native land!

Radames.

(The Thunder of the adverse gods
On my head descends—
Ah! no, the throne of Egypt
Is not worth the heart of Aïda.)

Radames.

Spento Amonasro il re guerrier, non resta
Speranza ai vinti.

Ramfis.

Almeno,
Arra di pace e securtà fra noi
Resti col padre Aïda...
Gli altri sien sciolti...

Il Re.

Al tuo consiglio io cedo.
Di securità, di pace un miglior pegno
Or io vuo' darvi—Radames, la patria
Tutto a te deve—D'Amneris la mano
Premio ti sia. Sovra l'Egitto un giorno
Con essa regnerai...

Amneris.

(Venga or la schiava,
Venga a rapirmi l'amor mio... se l'osa!)

Il Re.

Gloria all' Egitto e ad Iside
Che il sacro suol difende,
S'intrecci il loto al lauro
Sul crin del vincitor!

Sacerdoti.

Inni leviamo ad Iside
Che il sacro suol difende;
Preghiam che i fati arridano
Fausti alla patria ognor.

Aïda.

(Qual speme omai più restami?
A lui la gloria e il trono...
A me l'oblio... le lacrime
Di disperato amor.)

Prigionieri

Gloria al clemente Egizio
Che i nostri ceppi ha sciolto,
Che ci ridona ai liberi
Solchi del patrio suol!

Radames.

(D'avverso Nume il folgore
Sul capo mio discende...
Ah no! d'Egitto il soglio
Non val d'Aïda il cor.)

Amneris.

(By the unexpected joy
I am intoxicated;
All in one day are fulfilled
The dreams of my heart.)

Amonasro (to AÏDA).

Take heart, for thy country
Expects happy events;
For us the dawn of vengeance
Is already near.

People.

Glory to Egypt and to Isis,
Who the sacred soil defends.
Weave the lotus with the laurel
On the hair of the victors!

END OF THE SECOND ACT.

Amneris.

(Dall' inatteso giubilo
Inebbriata io sono:
Tutti in un dì si compiono
I sogni del mio cor.)

Amonasro (ad AÏDA).

Fa cor: della tua patria
I lieti eventi aspetta;
Per noi della vendetta
Già prossimo è l'albor.

Popolo.

Gloria all' Egitto e ad Iside
Che il sacro suol difende!
S'intrecci il loto al lauro
Sul crin del vincitor!

FINE DELL' ATTO SECONDO.

ACT III.

SCENE.—The Banks of the Nile. Rocks of granite, among which grow palm trees; on the top of the rocks the Temple of Isis, half concealed among the foliage; it is starlight and bright moonlight.

Chorus (in the temple).

O Thou who art of Osiris,
Mother immortal and spouse,
Goddess who awakenest the beatings
In the heart of human creatures,
Come piteous to our help,
Mother of eternal love.

(From a boat, which approaches the shore, descend AMNERIS, RAMPHIS, some Women closely veiled, and Guards.)

Ramphis (to AMNERIS)

Come to the Temple of Isis,
On the eve of thy nuptials implore
The favor of the goddess. Isis rules
The heart of mortals; every mystery
Of mankind to her is known.

Amneris.

Yes: I will pray that Radames may give
me
His whole heart, as mine to him
Is consecrated forever.

Ramphis.

Let us enter.
Thou shalt pray till dawn. I shall be with
thee.

(All enter the temple. The Chorus repeat the sacred song.)

ATTO III.

SCENA.—Le Rive del Nilo. Roccie di granito fra cui crescono dei palmizii. Sul vertice delle roccie il Tempio d'Iside per metà nascosto tra le fronde. E notte stellata Splendore di luna.

Coro (nel tempio).

O tu che sei d'Osiride
Madre immortale e sposa,
Diva che i casti palpiti
Desti agli amani in cor;
Soccorri a noi pietosa,
Madre d'eterno amor.

(Da una barca che approda alla riva, discendono AMNERIS, RAMFIS, alcune donne coperte da fitto velo e Guardie.)

Ramfis (ad AMNERIS).

Vieni d'Iside al Tempio—alla vigilia
Della tue nozze, implora
Della Diva il favore—Iside legge
Dei mortali nel cuore—ogni mistero
Degli umani è a lei noto.

Amneris.

Sì: pregherò che Radames mi doni
Tutto il suo cor, come il mio core a lui
Sacro è per sempre.

Ramfis.

Pregherai fino all' alba—io sarò teco.

(Tutti entrano nel tempio. Il Coro ripete il canto sacro.)

Aida   (entering cautiously, covered with a veil).

Here Radames will come. What would he
  say to me?
I tremble—ah, if thou comest
To give me, O cruel one, the last farewell,
The deep water of the Nile
Shall give me a tomb—and peace perhaps—
  and oblivion.

Aïda   (entra cautamente coperta da un velo).

Qui Radamès verrà... Che vorrà dirmi?
Io tremo... Ah! se tu vieni
A recarmi, o crudel, l'ultimo addio,
Del Nilo i cupi vortici
Mi daran tomba... e pace forse... e oblio.

OH! CIELI AZZURI—*O SKIES OF TENDER BLUE*   Air (Aïda)

Andante mosso

Oh pa-tria mia, mai più, mai più ti ri-ve-dro!
O na-tive land, no more to thee—shall I re-turn!

mai più!   mai più! ti ri-ve-dro!
no more!   *no more to thee re-turn!*

Lo stesso movimento

O cie-li az - zur-ri,o dol-ci au - re na-ti - - ve, do-ve se-
O skies of ten-der blue, O soft airs blow - -ing, Where calm and

re - no il mio mat-tin bril - lò, o ver-di col-li o pro-fu-ma-te
peace-ful my dawn of life pass'd o'er, O hills of ver-dure, O per-fumed wa-ters

ri - ve, o pa-tria mi-a, mai più ti ri-ve-drò!   Oh pa-tria
flow-ing, O home be-lov-ed, I ne'er shall see thee more!   *O home be-*

mi-a,   mai più, ah — mai più ma - i — più — ti ri-ve-
lov-ed, no more, ah,— no more, nev-er — more — shall I re-

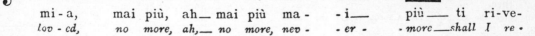

Aïda.   (Enter Amonasro.)

Heaven! My father!

Amonasro.

Grave occasion
Leads me to thee, Aïda. Nothing escapes
My sight; thou art destroying thyself with
    love
For Radames. He loves thee, and here thou
    awaitest him,
The daughter of the Pharaohs is thy rival—
An infamous race, abhorred and fatal to us.

Aïda.

And I am in her power!—I, the daughter
Of Amonasro.

Amonasro.

In her power! No! If thou wishest,
This powerful rival thou shalt defeat,
And country, and throne, and love all shall
    be thine.
Thou shalt see again the balmy forests,
The fresh valleys, our temples of gold!

Aïda   (with transport).

I shall see again the balmy forests,
Our valleys, our temples of gold!

Amonasro.

Happy bride of him whom thou lovest so
    much,
Great jubilee thence shall be thine.

Aïda   (with transport).

One day only of such sweet enchantment,
One hour of such joy—and then to die!

Amonasro.

Nevertheless thou rememberest that the
    merciless Egyptian
Profaned our houses, temples, and altars;
He drew in fetters the ravished virgins—
Mothers, old men and children he has slain.

Aïda.

Ah! well I remember those unhappy days.
I remember the grief that my heart suffered.
Ah! make return to us, O gods,
The longed-for dawn of peaceful days.

Amonasro.

Delay not. In arms now are roused
Our people—everything is ready—

Aïda.   (Amonasro e Aïda.)

Cielo! mio padre!

Amonasro.

A te grave cagione
Mi adduce, Aïda. Nulla sfugge al mio
Sguardo—D'amor ti struggi
Per Radames... ei t'ama... e qui lo attendi,
Dei Faraon la figlia è tua rivale...
Razza infame, aborrita e a noi fatale!

Aïda.

E in suo potere io sto!... Io d'Amonasro
Figlia!...

Amonasro.

In poter di lei!... No!... se lo brami
La possente rival tu vincerai,
E patria, e trono, e amor, tutto avrai.
Rivedrai le foreste imbalsamate,
Le fresche valli, i nostri templi d'ôr...

Aïda   (con trasporto).

Rivedrò le foreste imbalsamate...
Le nostre valli... i nostri tempii d'ôr!

Amonasro.

Sposa felice a lui che amasti tanto,
Tripudii immensi ivi potrai gioir...

Aïda   (con trasporto)

Un'giorno solo di sì dolce incanto.
Un'ora di tal gaudio.. e poi morir!

Amonasro.

Pur rammenti che a noi l'Egizio immite,
Le case, i tempii e l'are profanò..
Trasse in ceppi le vergini rapite..
Madri, vecchi e fanciulli ei trucidè.

Aïda.

Ah! ben rammento quegli infausti giorni
Rammento i lutti che il mio cor soffrì..
Deh! fate o Numi che per noi ritorni
L'alba invocata dei sereni dì.

Amonasro.

Non fia che tardi—In armi ora si desta
Il popol nostro—tutto e pronto già..

Victory we shall have. It only remains for
  me to know
What path the enemy will follow.

Aïda.

Who will be able to discover it? Who?

Amonasro.

Thyself!

Aïda.

I?

Amonasro.

Radames will come here soon—he loves
  thee—
He leads the Egyptians. Dost thou understand?

Aïda.

Horror!
What dost thou counsel me? No, no! Never!

Amonasro (with savage fury).

Up, then! Rise,
Egyptian legions!
With fire destroy
Our cities—
Spread terror,
Carnage and death.
To your fury
There is no longer check.

Aïda.

Ah, father!

Amonasro (repulsing her).

My daughter
Dost thou call thyself?

Aïda (terrified and beseeching).

Pity!

Amonasro.

Rivers of blood pour
On the cities of the vanquished—
Seest thou?—From the black gulfs
The dead are raised—
To thee they point and cry:
"For thee the country dies."

Aïda.

Pity!

Amonasro.

A horrible ghost
Among the shadows to us approaches—

Vittoria avrem.. Solo a saper mi resta
Qual sentier il nemico seguirà..

Aïda.

Chi scoprirlo potria? chi mai?

Amonasro.

Tu stessa!

Aïda.

Io!..

Amonasro.

Radamès so che qui attendi.. Ei t'ama..
Ei conduce gli Egizii.. Intendi?

Aïda.

Orrore!
Che mi consigli tu? No, no, giammai!

Amonasro (con impeto selvaggio).

Su, dunque! sorgete
Egizie coorti!
Col fuoco struggete
Le nostre città..
Spargete il terrore,
Le stragi' le morti..
Al vostro furore
Più freno non v'ha.

Aïda.

Ah padre!

Amonasro (respingendola).

Mia figlia
Ti chiami!..

Aïda (atterrita e supplichevole).

Pietà!

Amonasro.

Flutti di sangue scorrono
Sulle città dei vinti..
Vedi?..dai negri vortici
Si levano gli estinti..
Ti additan essi e gridano:
"Per te la patria muor."

Aïda.

Pietà!..

Amonastro.

Una larva orribile
Fra l'ombre a moi s'affaccia..

Tremble! the fleshless arms
Over thy head it raised—
It is thy mother—recognize her—
She curses thee.

Aïda   (in the greatest terror).
Ah, no!
Father.

Amonasro   (repulsing her).
Go, unworthy one! Thou'rt not my off-
spring—
Thou art the slave of the Pharaohs!

Aïda.
Father, their slave I am not—
Reproach me not—curse me not;
Thy daughter again thou canst call me—
Of my country I will be worthy.

Amonasro.
Think that a people conquered, torn to
pieces,
Through thee alone can arise—

Aïda.
O my country, O my country—how much
thou costest me!

Amonasro.
Courage! he comes—there I shall hear all.
(Conceals himself among the palm trees.)
(Enter RADAMES.)

Radames.
I see thee again, my sweet Aïda.

Aïda.
Stop! begone. What, hopest thou still?

Radames.
Love guided me to thee.

Aïda.
The rites of another love await thee,
Spouse of Amneris.

Radames.
What sayest thou?
Thee alone, Aïda, must I love.
Hear me, gods!—Thou shalt be mine!

Aïda.
Stain not thyself with perjury.
Valiant I loved thee; foresworn I should not
love thee.

Radames.
Doubtest thou my love, Aïda?

Trema! le scarne braccia
Sul capo tuo levò..
Tua madre ell'è..ravvisala.
Ti maledice..

Aïda   (nel massimo terrore).
Ah, no!..
Padre.

Amonasro   (respingendola).
Va, indegna! non sei mia figlia!
Dei Faraoni tu sei la schiava.

Aïda.
Padre, a costoro schiava io non sono.
Non maledirmi.. non imprecarmi..
Tua figlia ancora potrai chiamarmi..
Della mia patria degna sarò.

Amonasro.
Pensa che un popolo, vinto, straziato
Per te soltanto risorger può..

Aïda.
O patria! o patria.. quanto mi costi!

Amonasro.
Corraggio! ei giunge.. là tutto udrò..
(Si nasconde fra i palmizii.)
(RADAMES e AÏDA.)

Radames.
Pur ti riveggo, mia dolce Aïda...

Aïda.
Ti arresta, vanne... che speri ancor?

Radames.
A te dappresso l'amor mi guida.

Aïda.
Te i riti attendono d'un altro amor.
D'Amneris sposo...

Radames.
Che parli mai?
Te sola, Aïda, te deggio amar.
Gli Dei mi ascoltano... tu mia sarsi...

Aïda.
D'uno spergiuro non ti machiar?
Prode t'amai, non t'amerei spergiuro.

Radames.
Dell' amor mio dubiti, Aïda?

Aïda.

And how

Hopest thou to free thyself from the love of Amneris,

From the King's will, from the vows of thy people,

From the wrath of the priests?

Radames.

Hear me, Aïda.

To the fierce pant of a new war

The land of Ethiopia has re-awakened—

Thy people already invade our country.

I shall be leader of the Egyptians.

Amid the fame, the applause of victory,

I prostrate myself before the King, I unveil to him my heart.

Thou shalt be the reward of my glory,

We shall live blessed by eternal love.

Aïda.

Nor fearest thou Amneris and

Her vindictive fury? Her revenge,

Like a dreadful thunderbolt,

Will fall on me, on my father, on all.

Radames.

I protect thee.

Aïda.

In vain! Thou couldst not—

Still—if thou lovest me—again a way

Of escape opens to us.

Radames.

Which?

Aïda.

To fly!

Radames.

To fly!

Aïda.

E come

Speri sottrarti d'Amneris ai vezzi,

Del Re al voler, del tuo popolo ai voti,

Dei sacerdoti all' ira?

Radames.

Odimi, Aïda.

Nel fiero anelito di nuova guerra

Il suolo Etiope si ridestò...

I tuoi già invadono la nostra terra,

Io degli Egizii duce sarò.

Fra il suon, fra i plausi della vittoria,

Al re mi prostro, gli svelo il cor...

Sarai tu il serto della mia gloria,

Vivrem beati d'eterno amor.

Aïda.

Nè d'Amneris paventi

Il vindice furor? la sua vendetta,

Come folgor tremenda

Cadrà su me, sul padre mio, su tutti.

Radames.

Io vi difendo.

Aïda.

Invan tu nol potresti..

Pur... se tu m'ami... ancor s'apre una vìa

Di scampo a noi...

Radames.

Quale?

Aïda.

Fuggire...

Radames.

Fuggire!

FUGGIAM GLI ARDORI—*AH! FLY WITH ME* Duet (Aïda and Radames)

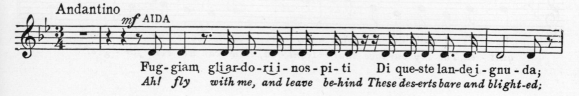

U - na no-vel-la pa - tri - a,   al no-stro a-mor si schiu - de.
Some coun-try, new and fresh to find, Where we may love u - nit - ed.

dolciss

Là - tra fo - re - ste ver - gi - ni,   Di fio - ri pro - fu - ma - te, in
There 'mid the vir - gin for - est groves,   By fair and sweet flow'rs scent - ed, In

pp

e - sta - si be - a - te la ter - ra scor - de - rem, in e - sta - si,
qui - et joy con - tent - ed, The world will we for - get, in qui - et joy,

_ in e _ sta - si la _ ter - _ ra _ scor - de -
_ in qui - et _ joy, The _ world _ will _ we for -

RADAMES

rem, So - vra u - na ter - ra e - stra - nia te - co fug - gir do - vrei! ab - ban - do - nar la
get, To some strange land far dis - tant Must I then with you fly! Our home and coun - try

pa - tria l'a - re de' no - stri Dei! il suol dov' io rac - col - si di glo - ria i pri - mi al -
leav - ing, Our gods and al - tars high! The soil where first I gath - er'd The bays that deeds re -

lo - ri; il ciel de no - stri a - mo - ri   co - me scor - dar po - trem?
quit - ed, The sky our love that light - ed, How can we e'er for - get?

AIDA

Là tra for-es-ti ver-gi-ni, di fio-ri pro-fu-ma-te, in
There 'neath the vir-gin for-est groves; By fair and sweet flow'rs scent-ed, In

e-sta-si be-a-te la ter-ra scor-de-rem, in e-
qui-et joy con-tent-ed The world will we for-get, In qui-

-sta-si,— in è-sta-si la— ter—ra scor-de-
et joy,— in qui-et joy The— world———— will we for-

RADAMES   AIDA

rem   Il ciel di nos-tria-mo-ri co-me scor-dar po-trem? Sot-to il mio ciel, più
get,   The sky our love that-light-ed. How can we e'er for-get? Be-neath my sky more

li-be-re là-mor ne fia con-ces-so, i-vi nel tem-pio i
light and free Love's gen-'rous aid con-fid-ing; In tem-ples there a

stes-so gli stes-si Nu-mia-vrem, i-vi nel tem-pio i
bid-ing, Gods like your own we'll find, In tem-ples there a-

stes-so gli stes-si Nu-mia-vrem; I-vi nel tem-pio i
bid-ing, The self-same gods we'll find, In tem-ples there a-

stes-so gli stes-si Nu-mia-vrem; fug-giam, fug-giam!
bid-ing the self-same gods we'll find, then fly! ah! fly!

Radames (hesitating).

Aïda!

Aïda.

Thou lovest me not—go!

Radames.

I love thee not?
Never mortal, nor god,
Burnt with love so powerful as mine!

Aïda.

Go, go! Amneris awaits thee
At the altar.

Radames.

No, never!

Aïda.

Never, saidst thou?
Then falls the axe
On me, on my father.

Radames.

Ah, no, let us fly!
(With impassioned resolution.)
Yes; let us fly from these walls,
To the desert let us fly together;
Here misfortune reigns alone.
There opens to us a heaven of love.
The boundless deserts
Shall be our nuptial couch,
On us the stars will shine
With a more limpid effulgence.

Aïda.

In the happy land
Of my fathers heaven awaits us;
There the air is perfumed,
There the ground is fragrant with flowers.
Fresh valleys and green fields
Shall be our nuptial couch,
On us the stars will shine
With a more limpid effulgence.

Aïda and Radames.

Come with me—together let us fly
This land of grief.
Come with me—I love thee, I love thee:
Love shall be our leader.

Aïda (They go rapidly aside.)
(stopping suddenly).
But tell me by what road
Shall we avoid the armed hosts?

Radames (esitante).

Aïda!

Aïda.

Tu non m'ami... Va!—

Radames.

Non t'amo!
Mortal giammi nè Dio
Arse d'amore al par del mio possente.

Aïda.

Va... va... ti attende all' ara
Amneris...

Radames.

No!... giammai!...

Aïda.

Giammai, dicesti?
Allor piombi la scure
Su me, sul padre mio...

Radames.

Ah no! fuggiamo!
(Con appassionata risoluzione.)
Sì: fuggiamo da queste mura,
Al deserto insiem fuggiamo;
Qui sol regna la sventura,
Là si schiude un ciel d'amor.
I deserti interminati
A noi talamo saranno,
Su noi gli astri brilleranno.
Di più limpido fulgor.

Aïda.

Nella terra avventurata
De' miei padri, il ciel ne attende;
Ivi l'aura è imbalsamata,
Ivi il suolo è aromi e fior.
Fresche valli e verdi prati
A noi talamo saranno,
Su noi gli astri brilleranno.
Di più limpido fulgor.

Aïda e Radames.

Vieni meco—insiem fuggiamo
Questa terra di dolor—
Vieni meco—io t'amo, io t'amo!
A noi duce fia l'amor!

Aïda (Si allontanano rapidamente.)
(arrestandosi all' improvviso).
Ma, dimmi; per qual via
Eviterem le schiere
Degli armati?

Radames.

    The path chosen by our troops
    To fall on the enemy will be deserted
    Until to-morrow.

Aïda.

    And that path?

Radames.

    The Pass
    Of Napata.

(Enter AMONASRO.)

Amonasro.

    The Pass of Napata!
    There shall be my people.

Radames.

    Oh! who hears us?

Amonasro.

    The father of Aïda and King of the Ethiopians.

Radames

(greatly agitated).

    Thou, Amonasro! Thou, che King! Gods, what said I?
    No! It is not true!—I dream—this is dilirium.

Aïda.

    Ah, no! calm thyself—listen to me,
    Trust thyself in my love.

Amonasro.

    Aïda's love shall raise thee
    To a throne.

Radames.

    For thee to betray my country!
    I am dishonored.

Amonasro.

    No; Thou art not guilty—
    It was the will of fate.
    Come; beyond the Nile await us
    The brave men devoted to us;
    There the vows of thy heart
    Shall be crowned with love.

(Enter AMNERIS from the Temple, then RAMPHIS, PRIESTS and GUARDS.)

Amneris.

    Traitor!

Aïda.

    My rival!

Radames.

    Il sentier scelto dai nostri
    A piombar sul nemico fia deserto
    Fino a domani...

Aïda.

    E quel sentier?...

Radames.

    Le gole
    Di Nàpata?

(AMONASRO e AÏDA e RADAMES.)

Amonasro.

    Di Nàpata le gole!
    Ivi saranno i miei...

Radames.

    Oh! chi ci ascolta?

Amonasro.

    D'Aida il padre e degli Etiopi il Re.

Radames

(agitatissimo).

    Tu! Amonasro!... Tu il Re?
    Numi! che dissi?
    No!..non è ver!..sogno... delirio è questo..

Aïda.

    Ah, no! ti calma. .ascoltami,
    All' amor mio t'affida.

Amonasro.

    A te l'amor d'Aïda
    Un soglio innalzerà!

Radames.

    Per te tradii la patria!
    Io son disonorato..

Amonasro.

    No: tu non sei colpevole—
    Era voler del fato.
    Vieni: oltra il Nil ne attendono
    I prodi a noi devoti,
    Là del tuo core i voti
    Coronerà l'amor.

(AMNERIS, dal tempio, indi RAMFIS, SACERDOTI, GUARDIE e detti.)

Amneris.

    Traditor!

Aïda.

    La mia rivale!..

Amonasro
      (rushing upon AMNERIS with a dagger).
Comest thou to destroy my work?
Die!

Radames   (interposing himself).
Stop, madman!

Amonasro.
Oh, fury!

Ramphis.
Guards, hither!

Radames   (to AÏDA and AMONASRO).
Haste!—fly!

Amonasro   (drawing AÏDA away).
Come, O daughter!

Ramphis   (to the GUARDS).
Follow them!

Radames   (to RAMPHIS).
Priest, I remain with thee.

      END OF THE THIRD ACT.

ACT IV.
SCENE I.

Hall in the King's Palace; to the left a grand gate, which opens on the subterranean hall of judgment; passage to the right which leads to the prison of RADAMES.

Amneris
    (in a sad attitude before the gate of the hall).
My abhorred rival escapes me—
Radames awaits from the priests
The punishment of a traitor. Traitor
He is not, though he revealed
The high secret of war. He wished to fly—
To fly with her—traitors all!
To death, to death! Oh, what did I say? I
    love him—
I love him always—desperate, mad
Is this love which destroys my life.
Oh! if he could love me!
I would save him—and how?
Let me try. Guards: Radames comes.
    (Enter RADAMES, guarded.)

Amneris.
Already the priests assemble.
Arbiters of thy fate; —
Of the horrible crime however

Amonasro
      (avventandosi ad AMNERIS con un pugnale)
Vieni a strugger l'opre mia!
Muori!

Radames   (frapponendosi).
Arresta, insano!..

Amonasro.
Oh rabbia!

Ramfis.
Guardie, olà.

Radames   (ad AÏDA e AMONASRO)
Presto! fuggite!..

Amonasro   (transciando AÏDA).
Vieni, o figlia!..

Ramfis   (alle GUARDIE).
Li inseguite!

Radames   (a RAMFIS).
Sacerdote, io resto a te.

      FINE DELL' ATTO TERZO.

ATTO IV.
SCENA I.

Sala nel Palazzo del Re. Alla sinistra, una gran porta che mette alla sala sotterranea della sentenze.—Andito a destra che conduce alla prigione di RADAMES.

Amneris
    (mestamente atteggiata davanti la porta del sotterraneo).
L'abborrita rivale a me sfuggia..
Dai sacerdoti Radamès attende
Dei traditor la pena,—Traditore
Egli non è..Pur rivelò di guerra
L'alto segreto..egli fuggir volea..
Con lei fuggire.. Traditori tutti!
A morte! A morte!..Oh! che mai parlo?
    Io l'amo,
Io l'amo sempre..Disperato, insano
E quest' amor che la mia vita strugge.
Oh! s'ei potesse amarmi!..
Vorrei salvarlo.. E come?
Si tenti!.. Guardie: Radamès qui venga
    (RADAMES condotto dalle guardie, e AMNERIS.)

Amneris.
Già i sacerdoti adunansi
Arbitri del tuo fato;
Pur della accusa orribile

Still it is given thee to exculpate thyself.
Exculpate thyself, and grace for thee
I will beg from the throne;
And a messenger of pardon—
Of life, to thee I will be.

Radames.

Of my exculpation the judges
Will never hear the sound.
Before gods and men
Neither vile nor guilty do I feel.
My incautious lips
Uttered the fatal secret, it is **true,**
But pure my thought
And my honor remained.

Amneris.

Then save and exculpate thyself.

Radames.

No.

Amneris.

Thou wilt die.

Radames.

Life
I abhor; the font
Of every joy dried up,
Every hope vanished,
I wish only to die.

Amneris.

To die! Ah; thou shouldst live!
Yes, for my love thou shalt live;
For thee I have undergone
The dreadful anguish of death.
I loved thee—I suffered so much—
I watched through the **nights in tears.**
Country and throne and life—
All I would give for thee.

Radames.

For her I too betrayed
The country and my honor.

Amneris.

Of her no more——

Radames.

Infamy
Awaits me, and thou wishest that I live?
Utterly wretched thou madest me;
Aïda thou hast taken from me;

Scolparti ancor ti è dato:
Ti scolpa, e la tua grazia
Io pregherò dal trono,
E nunzia di perdono,
Di vita, a te sarò.

Radames.

Di mie discolpe i giudici
Mai non udran l'accento:
Dinanzi ai Numi e agli uomini
Nè vil, nè reo mi sento.
Profferse il labbro incauto
Fatal segreto, è vero.
Ma puro il mio pensiero
E 'l onore mio restò.

Amneris.

Salvati dunque e scolpati.

Radames.

No.

Amneris.

Tu morrai..

Radames.

La vita
Abhorro; d'ogni gaudio
La fonte inaridita,
Svanita ogni speranza,
Sol bramo di morir.

Amneris.

Morire!..ah!..tu dei vivere!..
Si, all' amor mio vivrai;
Per te le angoscie orribili
Di morte io già provai;
T'amai..soffersi tanto..
Vegliai le notti in pianto..
E patria, e trono, e vita
Tutto darei per te.

Radames.

Per essa anch' io la **patria**
E l'onor mio tradiva...

Amneris.

Di lei non più!...

Radames.

L'infamia
Mi attende e vuoi che io **viva?...**
Misero appien mi festi,
Aïda a me **togliesti.**

Killed her perhaps! And for gift
Thou offerest life to me?

Amneris.

I—the cause of her death?
No! Aïda lives!

Radames.

Lives?

Amneris.

In the desperate struggle
Of the fugitive hordes
Fell her father alone——

Radames.

And she?——

Amneris.

She disappeared, nor more news
Had we.

Radames.

May the gods lead her
Safe to her native walls,
And let her not know the unhappy fate
Of him who will die for her.

Amneris.

Now, if I save thee, swear to me
That thou wilt not see her more.

Radames.

I cannot do it!

Amneris.

Renounce her
Forever, and thou shalt live!

Radames.

I cannot do it!

Amneris.

Yet, once more;
Renounce her!

Radames.

It is in vain!

Amneris.

Wouldst thou die, then, madman?

Radames.

I am ready to die.

Amneris.

Who saves thee, O wretch,
From the fate that awaits thee?
To fury hast thou changed
A love that had no equal.

Spenta l' hai forse... e in dono
Offri la vita a me?

Amneris.

Io...di sua morte origine!
No!... vive Aïda...

Radames.

Vive!

Amneris.

Nei disperati aneliti
Dell' orde fuggitive
Sol cadde il padre..

Radames.

Ed ella?

Amneris.

Sparve, nè più novella
S'ebbe...

Radames.

Gli Dei l'adducano
Salve alle patrie mura,
E ignori la sventura
Di chi per lei morrà!

Amneris.

Or, s'io ti salvo, giurami
Che più non la vedrai..

Radames.

Nol posso!

Amneris.

A lei rinunzia
Per sempre...e tu vivra!...

Radames.

Nol posso!

Amneris.

Anco una volta
A lei rinunzia..

Radames.

E vano..

Amneris.

Morir vuoi dunque, insano?

Radames.

Pronto a morir son già.

Amneris.

Chi ti salva, o sciagurato,
Dalla sorte che ti aspetta?
In furore hai tu cangiato
Un amor ch' equel non ha.

Revenge for my tears
Heaven will now consummate.

Radames.

Death is a supreme blessing,
If for her it is given me to die;
In undergoing the last extremity
My heart will feel great joy.
Human anger I fear no more,
I fear only thy pity.

(Exit RADAMES, surrounded by Guards.)

Amneris (falls desolate on a seat).

Ah me! I feel myself dying. Oh! who will
save him?
And in their power
I myself threw him. Now I curse thee,
Atrocious jealousy, who didst cause his death
And the eternal grief of my heart!

(Turns and sees the PRIESTS, who cross the stage to enter
the subterranean hall.)

What do I see? Behold the fatal,
The merciless ministers of death!
Oh, that I might not see those white ghosts!

(Covers her face in her hands.)

Priests (in the subterranean hall).

Spirit of the gods descend upon us!
Awaken us to the ray of thy eternal light:
By our lips make thy justice known.

Amneris.

Gods, pity my torn heart.
He is innocent; save him, O gods!
Desperate, tremendous is my sorrow!

(RADAMES, between Guards, crosses the stage and descends
to the subterranean hall—AMNERIS on seeing him utters a
cry.)

Ramphis (in the subterranean hall).

Radames, Radames: thou didst reveal
The country's secrets to the foreigner.

Priests.

Defend thyself!

Ramphis.

He is silent.

All.

Traitor!

Ramphis.

Radames, Radames: thou didst desert
From the camp the day preceding the battle.

De'miei pianti la vendetta
Ora il cielo compirà.

Radames.

E la morte un ben supremo
Se per lei morir m' è dato:
Nel subir l'estremo fato
Gaudii immensi il core avrà;
L'ira umana io più non temo,
Temo sol la tua pietà.

(RADAMES parte circondato dalle Guardis.)

Amneris (cade desolata su un sedile).

Ohimè!.. Morir mi sento.. Oh! chi lo
salva?
E in poter di costoro
Io stessa lo gettai!...Ora, a te impreco
Atroce gelosia, che la sua morte
E il lutto eterno del mio cor segnasti!

(Si volge e vede i SACERDOTI che attraversano la scena per
entrare nel sotterraneo.)

Che veggo! Ecco i fatali
Gli inesorati ministri di morte...
Oh! ch' io non veggo quelle bianche larve!

(Si copre il volto colle mani.)

Sacerdoti (nel sotterraneo).

Spirito de l'Nume sovra noi discendi!
Ne avviva al raggio dell' eterna luce;
Pel labbro nostro tua giustizia apprendi.

Amneris.

Numi, pietà del mio straziato core...
Egli è innocente, lo salvate, o Numi!
Disperato, tremendo è il mio dolore!

(RADAMES, fra le Guardie, attraversa la scena e scende
nel sotterraneo—AMNERIS al vederlo, mette un grido.)

Ramfis (nel sotterraneo).

Radamès—Radamès: tu rivelasti
Della patria i segretti allo straniero...

Sacerdoti.

Discólpati!

Ramfis.

Egli tace..

Tutti.

Traditor!

Ramfis.

Radamès, Radamès: tu disertasti
Dal campo il dì che precedea la pugna.

Priests.

Defend thyself!

Ramphis.

He is silent.

All.

Traitor!

Ramphis.

Radames, Radames: thou brokest thy faith,
Foresworn to thy country, king and honor.

Priests.

Defend thyself!

Ramphis.

He is silent.

All.

Traitor!
Radames thy fate is decided:
Thou shalt die the death of the infamous.
Under the altar of the angered god
To thee alive be opened the tomb.

Amneris.

To him alive—the tomb! Oh the infamous
wretches!
Never satisfied with blood:
And then call themselves ministers of
heaven!

(Attacking the PRIESTS, who issue from the subterranean hall.)

Priests, you have done a wicked deed—
Infamous tigers! thirsting for blood;
You outrage earth and gods.
You punish him who has done no wrong.

Priests.

He is a traitor! he shall die.

Amneris

(to RAMPHIS).

Priest, this man whom thou slayest—
Thou knowest it—was loved by me.
The curse of a broken heart,
With his blood, will recoil on thee!

Priests.

He is a traitor! He shall die!

(They withdraw slowly.)

Amneris.

Impious band—anathema! On you
The vengeance of heaven will fall!

(Exit in despair.)

Sacerdoti.

Discólpati!

Ramfis.

Egli tace..

Tutti.

Traditor!

Ramfis.

Radamès, Radamès: tua fè violasti,
Alla patria spergiuro, al Re, all' onor.

Sacerdoti.

Discólpati!

Ramfis.

Egli tace..

Tutti.

Traditor!
Radamès è deciso il tuo fato;
Degli infami la morte tu avrai;
Sotto l'ara del Nume sdegnato
A te vivo fia schiuso l'avel.

Amneris.

A lui vivo..la tomba..Oh! gli infami!
Nè di sangue son paghi giammai..
E si chiaman ministri del ciel!

(Investendo i SACERDOTI che escono die sotterraneo.)

Sacerdoti: compiste un delitto..
Tigri infami di sangue assetate..
Voi le terra ed i Numi eltraggiate..
Voi punite chi colpa non ha.

Sacerdoti.

E traditor! morrà.

Amneris

(a RAMFIS).

Sacerdote! quest' uomo che uccidi,
Tu io sai.. da me un giorno fu amato..
L'anatéma d'un core straziato
Col suo sangue su te ricardrà!

Sacerdoti.

E traditor! morrà.

(Si allontanano lentamente.)

Amneris.

Empia razza! anatéma! su voi!
La vendetta del ciel scenderà!

(Esce disperata.)

SCENE II.

The Scene is divided into two floors. The upper floor represents the Interior of the Temple of Vulcan, resplendent with light and gold; the lower floor a subterranean hall; long rows of arcades which are lost in the darkness; colossal statue of Osiris, with the hands crossed, sustains the pilasters of the vault.

RADAMES is in the subterranean hall, on the steps of the staircase by which he has descended; above, two PRIESTS, engaged in closing the stone over the subterranean entrance.

Radames.

The fatal stone is closed above me—
Behold my tomb. The light of day
I shall see no more. I shall no more see
    Aïda.
Aïda, where art thou? May thou at least
Live happy, and my dreadful fate
Never know. What a groan! A ghost!
A vision—No, it is a human shape—
Heavens! Aïda!

Aïda.

It is I.

Radames.

Thou—in this tomb?

Aïda.

My heart, prophetic of thy sentence,
Into this tomb which opened itself for thee
I furtive made my way.
And here afar from every human glance
In thy arms I wished to die.

Radames.

To die! So pure and beautiful!
To die for love of me;
In the flower of thy youth
To fly from life!
Heaven created thee for love,
And I kill thee by having loved thee!
No, thou shalt not die!
Too much I loved thee—
Too beautiful art thou.

Aïda

      (raving).

Seest thou the angel of death
Radiant to us approaches?
He takes us to eternal joys
Under his golden pinions.
Above us heaven has already opened;
There every grief ceases;

SCENA II.

La Scena è divisa in due piani. Il piano superiore rap presenta l'interno del Tempio di Vulcano splendente d'oro e di luce; il piano inferiore un sotterraneo. Lunghe file d'arcate si perdono nell' oscurità. Statue colossali d'Osiride colle mani incrociate sostengono i pilastri della volta.

RADAMES è nel sotterraneo sui gradini della scala per cui è disceso—Al di sopra, due SACERDOTI intenti a chiudere la pietra del sotterraneo.

Radames.

La fatal pietra sovra me si chiuse..
Ecco la tomba mia.—Del dì la luce
Più non vedrò..Non rivedò più Aïda...
—Aïda, ove sei tu? Possa tu almeno
Viver felice e la mia sorte orrenda
Sempre ignorar!—Qual gemito!—Una
    larva..
Una vision..No; forma umana è questa.
Cielo!..Aïda!

Aïda.

Son io..

Radames.

Tu.. in questa tomba!

Aïda.

Presago il core della tua condanna,
In questa tomba che per te si apriva
Io penetrai furtiva..
E qui lontana da ogni umano sguardo
Nelle tue braccia desiair morire.

Radames.

Morir! si pura e bella!
Morir per me d'amore..
Degli anni tuoi nel fiore
Fuggir la vita!
T'aveva il cielo per l'amor creata,
Ed io t'uccido per averti amata!
No, non morrai!
Troppo io t'amai!..
Troppo sei bella!..

Aïda

      (vaneggiando).

Vedi?..di morte l'angelo
Radiante a noi si appressa..
Ne adduce a eterni gaudii
Sovra i suoi vanni d'ôr.
Su noi già il ciel dischiudersi..
Ivi ogni affanno cessa..

There begins the ecstasy
Of an immortal love.

(Songs and dances of the PRIESTESSES in the Temple.)

Aïda.

Sad song!

Radames.

The jubilee
Of the priests!

Aïda.

Our hymn of death . . . .

Radames

(trying to move the stone of the vault).

My strong arms
Cannot move thee, O fatal stone!

Aïda.

It is vain—all is over
For us on earth.

Radames

(with desperate resignation).

It is true—it is true!

(Goes to AÏDA and supports her.)

Aïda and Radames.

O earth, farewell! Farewell, vale of
tears—
Dream of joy which vanished in grief.
Heaven opens itself to us, and the wander-
ing souls
Fly to the rays of eternal day.

(AÏDA falls gently into the arms of RADAMES.)
(AMNERIS in mourning robes appears in the temple, and
goes to prostrate herself on the stone which closes the vault.)

Amneris.

Peace I pray for thee, O adored corse;
Isis appeased, may she unclose heaven to
thee!

Ivi comincia l'estasi
D'un immortale amor.

(Canti e danze della SACERDOTESSE nel Tempio.)

Aïda.

Triste canto!..

Radames.

Il tripudio
Dei Sacerdoti..

Aïda.

Il nostro inno di morte..

Radames

(cercando di smuovere la pietra del sotteraneo).

Nè le mie forti braccia
Smuovere ti potranno o fatal pietra!

Aïda.

Invan!..tutto è finito
Sulla terra per noi..

Radames

(con desolata rassegnazione).

E vero! è vero!

(Si avvicina ad AÏDA e la sorrege.)

Aïda e Radames.

O terra, addio; addio valle di pianti..
Sogno di gaudio che in dolor svani..
A noi si schiude il cielo, e l'alme erranti
Volano al raggio dell' eterno di.

(AÏDA cade dolcemente fra le braccia di RADAMES.)
(AMNERIS in abito di lutto apparisce nel Tempio e va a
prostrarsi sulla pietra che chiude il sotterraneo.)

Amneris.

Pace t'imploro—salma adorata..
Isi placata—ti schiuda il ciel!

THE END.

LUCIA DI LAMMERMOOR

by

GAETANO DONIZETTI

THE STORY OF
"LUCIA DI LAMMERMOOR"

LORD HENRY ASHTON, of Lammer moor, brother of Lucy, in order to retrieve his fallen fortunes, and extricate himself from a perilous position in which his participation in political movements, directed against the reigning dynasty, has placed him, arranged a marriage between his sister and Lord Arthur Bucklaw.

He (Lord Henry) is at this time ignorant of an attachment which exists between his sister Lucy and Sir Edgar Ravenswood, whose family has long been in a state of deadly enmity with his own.

Sir Edgar, absent on an embassy to France to look to the interests of his native country, Scotland, despatches many letters to his beloved Lucy. These letters are intercepted, and a forged paper tending to show the infidelity of Sir Edgar, is shown to the bewildered maiden.

Maddened by disappointed love, and urged by the necessities of her brother, Lucy unwillingly consents to become the bride of Lord Arthur Bucklaw, who is already at the gates of the castle, invited by Lord Ashton, who never doubts of his success in bending her to his schemes. When Lucy had signed the marriage contract, Edgar of Ravenswood suddenly appeared among the assemblage. Having just returned from France, he had come to claim the hand of Lucy. He was too late. Henry and his partisans repulsed the intruder with bitter words; swords were drawn, and but for the timely interference of the old Chaplain of the house of Ashton blood would have been spilt. Edgar yielded reluctantly to the entreaties of the Chaplain to quit the scene, but not before he had hurled the fiercest curses upon the hated house of Lammermoor. At night he was sought out in his retreat by the infuriated Henry, and the foes agreed upon a meeting on the ensuing morning, when Edgar, weary of life, would have thrown himself on his adversary's weapon, the last of a doomed race.

But Fate had willed it otherwise. The burden of woe heaped upon Lucy was too much for the mind of the unfortunate maiden. She had heard Edgar's reproaches with stupor, and remained absent-minded during the remainder of the ceremonies. At night, after the newly married pair had retired, and the inhabitants of the Castle were noisy with revels and mirth, groans were heard from the nuptial chamber, like those of a dying man. The Chaplain immediately burst the door open. On entering the room, Lord Bucklaw is discovered bleeding to death, while Lucy, in a fit of insanity, brandishes the sword of her victim, reeking with his blood. Her senses return, but she sinks under the horror of her situation, and dies the victim of disappointed love.

Edgar was meanwhile waiting for his enemy in the churchyard of Ravenswood; but Ashton came not. Struck with remorse at the scene of misery which his selfishness had wrought, he had fled. But Edgar's solitude was interrupted by a train of mourners coming from the Castle. They reported Lucy dying, and while they yet stayed, her decease was announced by the funeral-bell from the Castle. Edgar, upon hearing this, plunged his dagger into his breast, and sank down lifeless among the tombstones of his ancestors.

LUCIA DI LAMMERMOOR

ACT I.

SCENE I—A Vestibule. NORMAN and Chorus.

Norman and Chorus.

Search ye well through the neighboring valley,

Through the ruins of yon gloomy tower.

This dark mystery that round us doth lower,

It concerneth our honor to clear.

As the lightning the stormcloud uprendeth,

So asunder this veil we will tear.

(Exeunt Chorus.)

SCENE II—Enter HENRY and RAYMOND.

Norman.

Thou seemest troubled?

Henry.

And 'tis with reason;

Thou knowest that of my destiny

Darkly the star declineth;

This hated Edgar, to my race

Bearing enmity deep and deadly,

From his rockbound tower laughing

To scorn my vows of vengeance, doth brave me!

One hand alone can prop my falling fortune!

There is but one thing now can save me. Yet Lucy

To Arthur still her hand refuseth! Ah! sister

She is no longer.

Raymond.

A sorrowing

Maiden, who mourns o'er the tomb of a parent,

A dear loved mother, say how canst thou suppose

She'll yet think of marriage? Ah, respect that heart

Which, enslaved of grief, dreams not of love.

ATTO I.

SCENA I—Vestibulo. NORMANDO e Coro.

Normando e Coro.

Percorrete ⎰ le spiagge vicine—

Percorriamo ⎱

Della torre le vaste rovine.

Cada il vel di sì turpe mistero;

Lo domanda, lo impone l'onor!

Fia che splenda il terribile vero,

Come lampo fra nubi d'orror!

SCENA II—ENRICO, RAIMONDO.

Normando.

Tu sei turbato?

Enrico.

E n'ho ben d'onde.

Il sai, del mio destin

Si ottenebrò la stella; intanto Edgardo

Quel mortale nemico

Di mia prosapia, dalle sue rovine

Erge la fronte baldanzosa, e ride.

Sola una mano raffermar mi puote

Nel vacillante mio poter: Lucia

Osa respinger quella mano! Ah! suora

Non m'è colei!

Raimondo.

Dolente

Vergin, che geme sull' urna recente

Di cara madre, al talamo potria

Volger io sguardo? Ah! rispettiam quel core

Che, traffitto dal duol, schivo è d'amore.

Norman.

> Dreams not of love?
> Thou'rt fearfully mistaken.

Henry.

> What sayest thou?

Raymond.

> (I tremble.)

Norman.

> But hearken. Lucy some few weeks since
> Was walking home alone thro' the park.
> As near her mother's tomb she was passing,
> Furious a bull pursued her;
> Death at that time seemed certain,
> When thro' the still air came the short,
>   sharp ring
> Of a rifle; the ball sped truly;
> The bull fell lifeless.

Henry.

> And who was he that saved her?

Norman.

> One who in mystery still himself enshroud-
>   eth.

Henry.

> And think'st thou Lucy—

Norman.

> She loves him!

Henry.

> Then they have met since?

Norman.

> Each morning.

Henry.

> Say where?

Norman.

> By yonder fountain.

Henry.

> I tremble;
> Dost know the vile seducer's name?

Norman.

> Shrewdly
> I have suspicions—

Henry.

> Proceed! speak!

Norman.

> That 'tis an enemy!

Normando.

> Schivo d' amor! Lucia
> D' amore avvampa!

Enrico.

> Che favelli?

Raimondo.

> (Oh, detto!)

Normando.

> M'ascolta. Ella sen gia colà
> Del parco nel solingo vial
> Dove la madre giace sepolta—
> Impetuoso toro
> Ecco su lor s'avventa—
> Quando per l'aria sibilar si sente
> Un colpo, e al suol repente
> Cade la belva—

Enrico.

> E chi vibrò quel colpo?

Normando.

> Tal—che il suo nome ricopri d'un velo.

Enrico.

> Lucia, forse—

Normando.

> L' amò!

Enrico.

> Dunque il rivide?

Normando.

> Ogni alba!

Enrico.

> E dove?

Normando.

> In quel viale.

Enrico.

> Io fremo!
> Nè tu scopristi il seduttor?

Normando.

> Sospetto
> Io n'ho soltanto—

Enrico.

> Ah, parla!

Normando.

> E tuo nemico!

Raymond.	Raimondo.
(Oh, heaven!)	(Oh, Ciel!)
Norman.	Normando.
One thou detestest!	Tu lo detesti!
Henry.	Enrico.
Say whom thou meanest. Is't Edgar?	Esser potrebbe—Edgardo?
Norman.	Normando.
Ah! thou hast named him!	Ah, lo dicesti!

CRUDA, FUNESTA — *EACH NERVE WITH FURY* (Enrico)

Larghetto

Cru - da, fu - ne-sta sma-nia__ tu m'hai sve - glia-to in pet - - to! è
Each nerve with fu - ry trem - bleth__ at these dark thoughts thou wak - est! 'Tis

trop-po, è trop-poor-ri-bi-le, ques-to fa-tal sos-pet - to! Mi fa ge-la-re e
too fright-ful! 'tis too hor-ri-ble! Say but that thou mis-tak - est! My blood con-geal'd with

fre - me - re! sol - le - va in fron-te il crin, ah!___ mi fa ge-la - re e
rage doth freeze, And stag-nant stands each vein, ah!___ My ve - ry blood con-

fre - me - re sol - le - va in fron-te, sol - le - va in fron-te il crin! Col-ma di tan-to ob
geal'd with rage doth freeze, and stag-nant, and stag-nant stands each vein! Broth-er's coun-sel

bro-brio chi suo-ra a me nas - ce - a! Ah! pria che d'a-mor si per-fi-do
slight-ed, A sis-ter's hon-or blight-ed! Ah! thy black and match-less per-fi-dy

a me sve-lar-ti re - a se ti col-pis-se un ful-mi-ne, se ti col-pis-se un
full soon shall be re-quit-ed, On his head fall heav'n's thun-der-bolt, On his head fall heav'n's

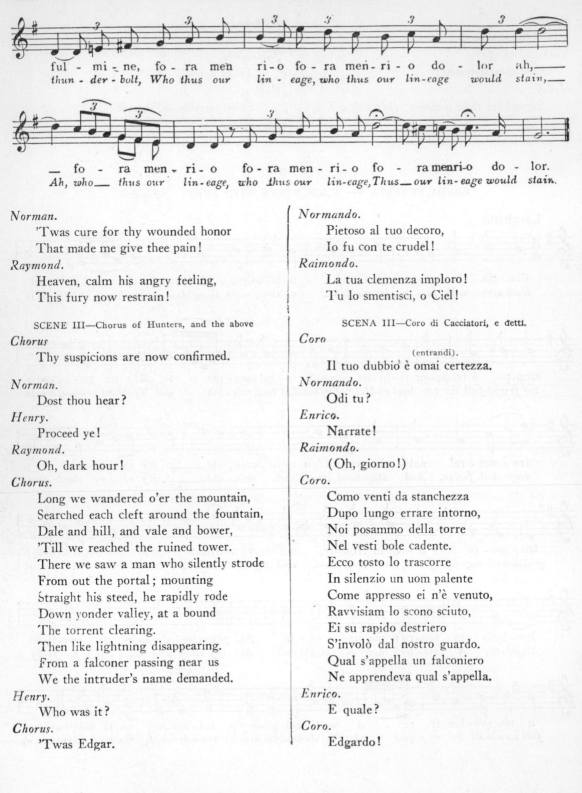

ful - mi - ne, fo - ra men ri - o fo - ra men - ri - o do - lor ah,___
thun - der - bolt, Who thus our lin - eage, who thus our lin - eage would stain,___

___ fo - ra men - ri - o fo - ra men - ri - o fo - ra menri - o do - lor.
Ah, who___ thus our lin - eage, who thus our lin - eage, Thus___ our lin - eage would stain.

Norman.	*Normando.*
'Twas cure for thy wounded honor	Pietoso al tuo decoro,
That made me give thee pain!	Io fu con te crudel!
Raymond.	*Raimondo.*
Heaven, calm his angry feeling,	La tua clemenza imploro!
This fury now restrain!	Tu lo smentisci, o Ciel!
SCENE III—Chorus of Hunters, and the above	SCENA III—Coro di Cacciatori, e detti.
Chorus	*Coro*
	(entrandi).
Thy suspicions are now confirmed.	Il tuo dubbio è omai certezza.
Norman.	*Normando.*
Dost thou hear?	Odi tu?
Henry.	*Enrico.*
Proceed ye!	Narrate!
Raymond.	*Raimondo.*
Oh, dark hour!	(Oh, giorno!)
Chorus.	*Coro.*
Long we wandered o'er the mountain,	Como venti da stanchezza
Searched each cleft around the fountain,	Dupo lungo errare intorno,
Dale and hill, and vale and bower,	Noi posammo della torre
'Till we reached the ruined tower.	Nel vesti bole cadente.
There we saw a man who silently strode	Ecco tosto lo trascorre
From out the portal; mounting	In silenzio un uom palente
Straight his steed, he rapidly rode	Come appresso ei n'è venuto,
Down yonder valley, at a bound	Ravvisiam lo scono sciuto,
The torrent clearing.	Ei su rapido destriero
Then like lightning disappearing.	S'involò dal nostro guardo.
From a falconer passing near us	Qual s'appella un falconiero
We the intruder's name demanded.	Ne apprendeva qual s'appella.
Henry.	*Enrico.*
Who was it?	E quale?
Chorus.	*Coro.*
'Twas Edgar.	Edgardo!

Henry.

Edgar? Ah, vengeance! What deadly fury
fires me.
Thus to brave me doth he dare!

Raymond.

Ah, not believe it yet—
Suspend your anger—Lucy—

Henry.

No, no!

Raymond.

Hear me!

Henry.

I'll hear no more!

Enrico.

Egli? Oh rabbia che m'accendi!
Contenerti un cor non può!

Raimondo.

Ah no, non credere! no, no—
Deh sospendi—Ma—

Enrico.

No, no!

Raimondo.

M'odi!

Enrico.

Udir non vuò.

LA PIETADE — *FROM MY BOSOM* (Enrico and Chorus)

La pie-ta - de in suo fa-vo-re mi ti sen-si in-van mi
From my bos - om all fear I ban-ish, From my breast now mer-cy doth

det - ta Se mi par - li di ven-det - ta so - lo in
an - ish, For the wrongs this man hath wrought me, Nought but

ten-der - ti po-trò! Scia-gu-ra - ti! il mi - o fu-
his blood can re - pay! Ev -'ry pulse for re - venge wild-ly

ro - re già su voi tre-men-do rug - ge, l'em-pia fiam - ma che vi
bound - ing, Ev -'ry nerve is strung to mad-ness, And de - spair, with dead-ly

strug - ge io col - san-gue spe - gne-ro, io col san - gue, io col san -
fu - ry, Now to ven-geance points the way, now to ven - geance, now to ven -

gue l'em-pia fiam-ma che vi strug-ge spe - gne-rò, spe - gne -
geance, now to ven-geance, now to ven - geance points the way, vengeance points the

rò, col san - gue spe-gne-rò, l'em-pia fiam - ma chei vi strug-
way, to ven-geance points the way. Nought, nought but blood my hate can al-

ge, l'em-pia fiam-ma che vi strug-ge io col san-gue spe - gne-rò, sì,
lay, And de-spair with dead-ly fu-ry un-to ven-geance points the way, Yes,

spe-gne - rò, sì, sì, col san-gue spe-gne - rò, sì, spe-gne - rò, sì,
points the way, Yes, yes, to ven-geance points the way, De-spair to ven-geance

spe-gne - rò, spe-gne - rò, spe-gne - rò, col san - gue spe-gne-rò.
points the way, Yes, de-spair points the way, de-spair doth point the way.

Norman and Chorus.	*Normando e Coro.*
He thy foe can ne'er escape thee,	Quell' indegno al nuovo albore
Let that thought thy rage allay.	L'ira tua fuggir non può.
(O'er thy house dark clouds do lower	(Ahi! qual nube di terrore
On this inauspicious day.)	Questa casa circondò!)
<div align="center">(Exeunt.)</div>	<div align="center">(Partone.)</div>
<div align="center">SCENE IV—A park. Enter Lucy and Alice.</div>	<div align="center">SCENA IV—Parco. Lucia ed Alisa.</div>
Lucy.	*Lucia.*
Still, still he comes not!	Ancor non giunse!
Alice.	*Alisa.*
Thou darest much in hither venturing;	Incauta a che mi traggi?
Think, should thy brother suspect, or aught discover,	Avventurarti or che il fratel qui venne
Dark were thy doom.	E folle ardir!
Lucy.	*Lucia.*
'Tis too true! Ah, Edgar knoweth not	Ben parli. Edgardo sappia
What fearful perils, what dangers circle round me!	Qual ne circonda orribile periglio!
Alice.	*Alisa.*
Why turn'st thou toward yon fountain	Perchè d' intorno il ciglio
That glance of terror!	Volgi alterrita?
Lucy.	*Lucia.*
Yonder fountain! ah! Alice,	Quella fonte, ah!
Whenever I behold it	Mai senza temar non veggo.
Dark fears oppress me! A Ravenswood here	Ah tu lo sai; un Ravenswood ardende
By jealousy with mad fury inspired,	Di geloso furor, l'amata donna

His dear loved lady most foully murdered,
And she unhappy in those dark waters
Was cast, and there did find a sepulchre.
Her shade hath once appeared to me.

Alice.

What say'st thou?

Lucy.

Dear Alice, ah, listen.

Colà trafisse; e l' infelice cadde
Nell' onda ed ivi rimanca sepolta.
M'apparve l'ombra sua.

Alisa.

Che dici?

Lucia.

Ascolta.

REGNAVA NEL SILENZIO —— *SILENCE O'ER ALL* (Lucia)

Reg—na—va nel si—len—zio al—ta la not—te bru—na,
Si—lence o'er all_ was reign—ing, Dark was the night and low—'ring,

col—pia la fon—te un pal—li—do rag—gio_ di te—tra Lu—na,
And o'er yon foun—tain her pal—lid ray Yon—der_ pale moon was pour—ing,

quan—do un som—mes—so ge—mi—to fra l'au—reu—dir si fè,____ ed
Faint—ly a sharp but sti—fled sigh Fell on my star—tled ear,____ And

ec—co, ec—co su_quel mar—gi—ne_____ l'om—bra mostrar—si, l'om—bra mo—strar—si a
straight—way up—on that same foun—tain's brink,____ The spec—tre did ap—pear, spec—tre did_ ap—

me, ah! qual di chi par—la muo—ver—si il lab—bro su—o ve—
pear, ah!. Fast fixed it kept its blood—less lip, No fur—ther sound e_—

de——a, e con la ma—no e—sa—ni—me chia—mar—mi a se—pa—
mit——ting, But slow on high its phan tom hand, Threat—'ning it did up—

re—a; stet—te un mo—men——to im—mo—bi—le, poi rat—ta di—le—
rear, Stood for a mo—ment im—mov—a—ble, Then van—ish'd from my

gnò_____ e l'on-da pria si lim-pi - - da di_____ san-gue ros - seg -
view,_____ While that pure and lim-pid_____ stream to_____ blood had_____changed its_____

giò, si, pria si, lim-pi-da di san-gue ros - seg-gio, si, pria si,
hue, While that pure lim-pid stream to_ blood had changed its hue, While that pure

lim-pi - da, ah,_____ di ros - seg - gio.
lim-pid stream. ah,_____ had changed its hue.

Oh, what horrid presage	Ah, il pressagio orenda
Is this? I ought to banish	E questa cancellar,
From my heart the fatal,	Dovrei dal petto
Loved object, but I cannot,	Il fatale amato oggnetto ma nol posso,
No, I cannot; it is my life,	Egli è una luce e conforto al mio penar.
And comfort to my suffering.	

QUANDO RAPITA — *THEN SWIFT AS THOUGHT*   (Lucia)

Quan - do ra - pi - ta in e - sta - si del più co - cen - te ar - do - re
Then swift as thought up - clear'd the sky, Out shone the stars with ~ brilliance,

col fa - vel - lar del co - - re mi giu - ra é - ter - na
Soft sigh'd the breeze, and from on high The moon poured forth her

fe gli af - fan - ni miei_ di - men - ti - co gio - ja di - vie - ne il
*light, All na - ture seem'd in_ smiles to sleep, Un - to my wan - d'ring_*

pian - to, par - mi, che a lui d'ac - can - - - to si
sight, And hea - ven, in_ ten - fold_ splen - - - - dor En-

schiu - da il — ciel per - me _____ si _____
robed __ then the wan - ing night, _____ in __

schiu - da il — ciel — per - me _____ si _____
splen - dor en - robed the — night, _____ in __

schiu - da il ciel _____ per me a lui d'ac - - can - to si
splen - dor en - robed — the night, En - robed then _____ the night, Heav'n

schiu - da _____ il ciel _____ per - me ah! _____
robed then _____ the wan - ing _____ night, ah! _____

_____ si _____ schiu - da il ciel, il ciel per me, si, si, a
_____ in _____ ten - fold splen - dor robed the night, Ah, yes, in

lui d'ac - can - to par - che si schiu - da il ciel — per — me.
splen - dor robed the night, Heav'n in splen - dor — robed — the — night.

Alice.	*Alisa.*
At length he comes! Concealed behind the foliage	Egli s'avanza! La vicina soglia
A careful watch I'll keep.	Io cauta veglierò.
(Exit ALICE.)	
SCENE V—EDGAR and LUCY.	SCENA V—EDGARDO e LUCIA.
Edgar.	*Edgardo.*
My Lucy, your pardon	Lucia perdona
That past the hour appointed	Se ad ora inusitata
I've delayed thus our meeting.	Io vederti chiedea—
Most powerful reasons from thee detained me!	Ragion possente a ciò mi trasse.
On the coming morn, love,	Pria che in Ciel biancheggi
Ere breaks the dawn, from my home and country	L'alba novella, delle patrie sponde
I must depart.	Lungi sarò.

Lucy.

What say'st thou?

Edgar.

To France I bend my steps, love!
Business of moment calls me thus early from thee.
'Tis Scotland needs my service!

Lucy.

And unto misery
Thou thus abandonest me!

Edgar.

Yet ere I leave thee
I'll seek thy brother; to him in truth and friendship
This hand I'll tender, and as a pledge of peace
'Twixt our houses I'll ask of him thine!

Lucy.

What hear I?
Ah, no, I pray thee—In secrecy and silence
Still let our loves concealed be!

Edgar.

I comprehend thee. Thy fell brother,
My dark, relentless foe, for blood
Still yearneth, nor vengeance will forego.
He killed my father,
He hath ta'en away my heritage! What more?
What seeks he more? That heart
Ferocious, what would it?
My entire utter ruin? He'd take my life!
Yes, he hates me!

Lucy.

Ah, no!

Edgar.

Abhors me!

Lucy.

Calm, oh, calm this fearful passion!

Edgar.

Deadly fury my heart inflameth!
Hear me!

Lucy.

My Edgar!

Edgar.

Hear me, and tremble!

Lucia.

Che dici?

Edgardo.

Pe' Franchi lidi amici
Sciolgo le vele—ivi trattar m'è dato
Le sorti della Scozia.

Lucia.

E me nel pianto
Abbandoni così?

Edgardo.

Pria di lasciarti
Ashton mi vegga—stenderò placato
A lui la destra, e la tua destra, pegno
Fra noi di pace, chiederò.

Lucia.

Che ascolto?
Ah, no! Rimanga nel silenzio avvolto
Per or l'arcano affetto.

Edgardo.

Intendo. Di mia stirpe
Il reo persecutore
Ancor pago non è. Mi tolse il padre,
Il mio retaggio avito—nè basta?
Che brama ancor?
Quel cor feroce e rio?
La mia perdita intera? il sangue mio
Ei m'odia!

Lucia.

Ah, no!

Edgardo.

M'abborre!

Lucia.

Calma! Oh, Ciel, quell' ira estrema!

Edgardo.

Fiamma ardente in sen mi corre!
M'odi.

Lucia.

Edgardo!

Edgardo.

M'odi, e trema!

By this lone tomb, o'er the cold grave
Where my father's bones lie moulding,
With thy kindred eternal warfare
To the death I swore to wage.
Ah! when I saw thee my heart relented
Of my dark vow I half repented;
But my oath remains unbroken,
Still I've power to redeem my gage.

Lucy.

Ah! pray calm thee, ah, restrain thee;
Think what misery will soon enthral me;
I can scarce from fear sustain me;
Would'st thou have me die with terror?
Yield thee, yield thee to the dictates of af-
    fection.
'Tis a nobler, purer passion,
Let that thought thy wrath assuage!

Edgar.

Here, then! here in the eye of heaven
Swear, thy true faith to me now is given;
Him above, who sees and hears us,
Witness these mutual vows of love!
Thy fate forever to mine united!
Thou art mine, love!

Lucy.

Yes, I am thine, love.
Thou who see'st us, Thou who hearest us,
Witness these our vows of love!
Power eternal, oh, grant Thy blessing,
Look down kindly from above.

Edgar.

Now at length we must part, love!

Lucy.

Heavy falleth that word on my heart, love,
Thou with thee this heart wilt bear—

Edgar.

Mine with thee will stay forever!

Lucy.

Ah! thou wilt not fail to write me?
Each dear letter thou dost send me,
Each fond word thou dost indite me,
Many a lonely hour will cheer.

Edgar.

A cherished memory of thee,
Dearest, shall ever treasured be!

Sulla tomba che rinserra
Il tradito genitore,
Al tuo sangue eterna guerra
Io giurai nel mio furore!
Ma ti vidi, in cor mi nacque
Altro affetto, e l'ira tacque.
Pur quel voto non è infranto—
Io potrei compirlo ancor!

Lucia.

Deh, ti placa! deh, ti frena!
Può tradirne un solo accento!
Non ti basti la mia pena?
Vuoi ch'io mora di spavento?
Ceda, ceda ogn' altro affetto,
Solo amor t'infiammi il petto!
Ah, il più nobile, il più santo
De tuoi voti è un puro amor!

Edgardo.

Quì, di sposa eterna fede
Quì mi giura, al Cielo innante!
Dio ci ascolta, Dio ci vede!
Tempio ed ara è un core amante.
Al tuo fato unisco il mio:
Son tuo sposo!

Lucia.

E tua son io!
A' miei voti amore invoco!
A' miei voti invoco il Ciel!
Ah soltanto il nostro foco
Spegnerà di morte il gel.

Edgardo.

Separarci omai conviene.

Lucia.

Oh, parola a me funesta!
Il mio cor con te ne viene!

Edgardo.

Il mio cor con te quì resta!

Lucia.

Ah, talor del tuo pensiero
Venga un foglio messaggiero
E la vita fuggitiva
Di speranza nudrirò!

Edgardo.

Io di te memoria viva
Sempre, o cara, serberò!

VERRANNO LA SULL' AURE — *MY SIGHS SHALL ON THE BALMY* Duet (Lucia and Edgardo)

ah!_ si,_ su quel peg-no al-lor, Ed — gar-do.
Ah!_ with_ ma-ny a bit - ter tear,_ Ed - gar.

lor, ah!_ sú_ ques-to peg-no al-lor,_ ah,_ su quel peg-no al-lor.
tear, Ah!_ with_ ma-ny a bit - ter tear! Ah!_ ma-ny a bit - ter tear.

Il tuo scrit-to sem-pre vi-va la me-mo-ria in me ter - rà!
Ah! thou wilt not fail to write me, ma-ny a lone-ly hour 'twill cheer;

Ah! si! si, si, Lu - ci - a, si,
Fear not! Have no fear, thou shalt

ah! _____ ver-ran-no a te sull' au — re i tuoi sos-
Ah! _____ my sighs shall on the balm-y breeze that hith - er

si! ah! _____ ver-ran-no a te sull' au — re i miei sos-
hear! Ah! _____ my sighs shall on the balm-y breeze that hith - er

pi - ri ar-den - ti, u-dro nel mar che mor-mo-ra_ l'e-co de tuoi la-
wafts thee be borne, love; Each mur-m'ring wave shall e - cho make how I thy ab-sence do

pi - ri ar-den - ti, u-drai nel mar che mor-mo-ra_ l'e-co de miei la-
wafts thee be borne, love; Each mur-m'ring wave shall e - cho make how I thy ab-sence do

men - ti pen-san-do che di ge - mi-ti mi pas-coe di do-
mourn,_ love! Ah! think of me when far_ a - way, with nought my heart to

men - ti!
mourn, love!

lor_
cheer;_

spar - gi su ques - to pe-gnoal-
Ah! dear love! with ma-nya bit - ter

spar-gi un a - ma - ra la-gri - ma su ques - to pe-gnoal-
I shall be - dew each thought of thee with ma - ny a bit - ter

lor, ah!_ su_ ques-to pe - gnoal-lor, ah!_ su_ ques -
tear, Ah!_ with_ ma-nya bit - ter tear, ah!_ with_ ma-nya

lor, ah!_ su_ ques-to pe - gnoal-lor, ah!_ su_ ques -
tear, Ah!_ with_ ma-nya bit - ter tear, ah,_ with_ ma-nya

to pe-gnoal - lor,_ ah!_ ques-to pe - gnoal-lor.
bit - ter tear, ah,_ ah,_ ma-nya bit - ter tear!

to pe-gnoal - lor,_ ah!_ ques-to pe - gnoal-lor.
bit - ter tear, ah,_ ah,_ ma-nya bit - ter tear!

 END OF THE FIRST ACT.

ACT II.

SCENE I—An Apartment. HENRY and NORMAN.

Norman.

Thy sister will shortly now be here.

Henry.

I tremble
To meet her. The nuptial guests are fast assembling!
Within the castle my noble friends and kinsmen
Wait now to greet the bridegroom: for Arthur only
We tarry! Should she still pertinaciously persist
In opposing—

Norman.

Have no fear! The long absence
Of him she mourneth, the letters
We've intercepted, and the false news thou'lt tell her,
Will quench all hope that yet may linger.
Believing Edgar faithless, from her bosom love will vanish!

Henry.

See, she approaches! Thou hast that forged letter,
Give it me—Now haste thee to the northern entrance,
There keep watch, and wait
The approach of Arthur, and with all speed, on his arrival
Conduct him hither!

(Exit NORMAN.)

SCENE II—HENRY and LUCY.

Henry.

Draw nearer, my Lucy,
On this fair morn accept a brother's greeting!
May this glad day, sacred to love and Hymen,
Auspicious prove to thee. Thou hearest me?
Thou'rt silent!

ATTO II.

SCENA I—Sala. ENRICO e NORMANDO.

Normando.

Lucia fra poco a te verrà.

Enrico.

Tremante
L'aspetto. A festeggiar le nozze illustri
Già nel castello i nobili congiunti
Di mia famiglia accolsi; in breve Arturo
Quì volge; e s'ella pertinace osasse
D'opporsi—

Normando.

Non temer; la lunga assenza
Del tuo nemico—i fogli
Da noi rapiti e la bugiarda nuova
Ch'egli s'accese di altra fiamma—in core
Di Lucia spegneranno il cieco amore.

Enrico.

Ella s'avanza! Il simulato foglio
Porgimi; ed esci sulla via che tragge
Alla città regina
Di Scozia; e quì fra plausi e liete grida
Conduci Arturo.

(Parte NORMANDO.)

SCENA II—ENRICO e LUCIA.

Enrico.

Appressati, Lucia.
Sperai più lieta in questo dì vederti,
In questo dì, che d'imeneo le faci
Si accendono per te. Mi guardi e taci?

IL PALLOR FUNESTO — *SEE THESE CHEEKS* (Lucia)

Henry.

Cease this wild recrimination,
Both to thee and me degrading.
Of the past be thou but silent!
I thy brother will no further make complaint!

Enrico.

A ragion mi fe' spietato,
Quel che t'arse indegno affetto;—
Ma si taccia del passato—
Tuo fratello io sono ancor;
Spenta è l'ira nel mio petto—

Flown has my anger! Banish thy dejection,
Buried be all that thine honor could taint.
A noble husband—

Lucy.

Cease to urge me!
To another true faith I have sworn!

Henry.

To another!

Lucy.

My brother!

Henry.

'Tis well!
By this letter thou may'st see
How he keeps his faith with thee!
Read it!   (Hands her a letter.)

Lucy.

How beats my fluttering heart!

Henry.

Thou dost falter—

Lucy.

Ah! great Heaven!
          (Reads.)
Break, poor heart!

Spegni tu l'insano amor.
Nobil sposo—

Lucia.

Cessa! ah, cessa!
Ad altr' uom giurai la fè.

Enrico.

Nol potevi.

Lucia.

Enrico!

Enrico.

Basti!
Questo foglio appien ti dice,
Qual crudel, qual empio amasti
Leggi!

Lucia.

Il core mi balzò!

Enrico.

Tu vacilli!

Lucia.

Me infelice!
          (Legge.)
Ahi! la folgore piombò!

SOFFRIVA NEL PIANTO — *MY SUFF'RINGS* (Lucia and Enrico)

LUCIA

Sof-fri-va nel pian-to, lan-gui-a nel do-lo-re, la
My suf-f'rings and sor-rows I've borne with-out re-pin-ing, I

spe-me la vi-ta ri-po-si in un cor l'i-stan-te di
hoped that the mor-row some com-fort might dawn! All's lost now, for-

mor-te e giun-to per me quel co-re in-fe-
sa ken, de-sert-ed, for-lorn, My last hope de-

de-le ad al-tra ad al-tra si die! Un fol-le t'ac-
part-ed, my true love, my love turn'd to scorn. Thy name thou dis-

ENRICO

-reinfe-de - le quel co-re infe-de-le ad al-tra si
_____ hope de -part - ed, My love treat-ed with scorn, Ah, my love turn'd to

-reinfe-de - le quel co-re in-fe-de-le ad al-tra si
- ce's dark foe-man, Thy ra-ce's dark foe-man doth treat thee with

diè! ad al - tra si diè, ad al - tra, ad
scorn! De-sert - ed, for - lorn, de-sert - ed, for-

diè, ad al - tra si diè, si, si, si diè, ad al - tra, ad
scorn, He treats thee with scorn, Yes, yes, with scorn, he treats thee, he

al - - tra, ad al - tra sì diè.
sa - - ken, de-sert - ed, for - lorn.

al - - tra, ad al - tra si diè.
treats _____ thee, he treats __ thee __ with __ scornL

(Noise heard without.)   (Gridi al di fuori.)

Lucy.	*Lucia.*
What hear I?	Che fia?
Henry.	*Enrico.*
Those sounds of gladness	Suonar di giubilio
Tell the arrival—	Odi la riva?
Lucy.	*Lucia.*
Of whom?	Ebbene?
Henry.	*Enrico.*
Thy destined husband.	Giunge il tuo sposo!
Lucy.	*Lucia.*
Through every vein	Un brivido
My blood doth seem congealing.	Mi corse per le vene!
I tremble!	Tremo!

Henry.
> The marriage rites await thee now!

Lucy.
> The dark grave be my refuge rather!

Henry.
> Oh, fatal hour of dark despair!
> Hear me. The late rebellion
> I was one who secretly abetted;
> To Arthur, for my present safety
> I'm alone indebted!
> He from a foul, a traitor's doom,
> Alone hath power to save me.

Lucy.
> And I then?

Henry.
> Thou must
> Wed him.

Lucy.
> My brother!

Henry.
> Come to the altar.

Lucy.
> I love another.

Henry.
> Still dost thou falter?

Lucy.
> But—

Henry.
> To the altar!

Lucy.
> Oh, heaven!

Henry.
> I'm thy guardian, darest thou brave me?
> I'm thy brother—wilt thou save me?
> From the hands of thee, my sister,
> Must I meet a traitor's doom?
>
> See the axe, by one thread hanging;
> Hark; the deep-toned deathbell clanging.
> Hath affection lost all power?
> Wilt consign me unto the tomb?

Lucy.
> I'm thy sister, dost thou love me!
> I am dying, will that move thee!
> From the hands of thee, my brother,
> Must I meet now this dreadful doom!

Enrico.
> A te appresta il talamo.

Lucia.
> La tomba a me s'appresta!

Enrico.
> Ora fatale è questa!
> Spento è Guglielmo ascendere
> Vedremo il tron Maria.
> Prostrata è nella polvere
> La parte ch'io seguia;
> Dal precipizio solo
> Arturo può salvarmi sol egli.

Lucia.
> Ed Io—

Enrico.
> Salvarmi
> Devi—

Lucia.
> Enrico!

Enrico.
> Vieni allo sposo.

Enrico.
> Ad altri giurai.

Enrico.
> Devi salvarmi?

Lucia.
> Ma—

Enrico.
> Il devi!

Lucia.
> Oh, Ciel!

Enrico.
> Se tradirmi tu potrai,
> La mia sorte è già compita
> Tu m' involi onore e vita:
> Tu la scure appresti a me!
>
> Ne' tuoi sogni mi vedrai
> Ombra irata e minacciosa.
> Quella scure sanguinosa
> Starà sempre innanzi a te.

Lucia.
> Tu, che vedi il pianto mio,—
> Tu, che leggi in questo core,—
> Se respinto il mie dolore,
> Come in terra, in Ciel non è!

Hopeless misery all surrounding,
E'en while the marriage bell is sounding;
Fear and hate will be my dower;
Better had I wed the tomb.

(Exeunt.)

SCENE III—Corridor. LUCY and RAYMOND.

Lucy.

Thy news?

Raymond.

Hope hath departed,
Even the last faint ray hath **fled**!
Believing as thou suspectest,
That perchance thy brother,
His ends to answer, thy notes had **inter-
cepted**,
And bared all correspondence
Between thee and young Edgar,
I took thy letter! To France I sent it,
By secure conveyance. He did receive it
Five weeks since! Still is he silent!
'Tis too certain that he to thee hath proved
unfaithful.

Lucy.

What dost thou counsel?

Raymond.

To submit to thy destiny.

Lucy.

The oath I pledged him?

Raymond.

Thou talkest wildly—
The holy nuptial vow
Through the priest can alone be sworn, at
the altar,
Nor heaven nor man holds aught else bind-
ing.

Lucy.

Ah, cease, pray; tho' my mind thou con-
vincest,
Still deaf to reason's voice my heart re-
sisteth!

Raymond.

Be firm and conquer!

Lucy.

What utter misery awaits me!

Tu mi togli, eterno Iddio!
Questa vita disperata!
Io son tanta sventurata,
Che la morte è un ben per me!

(Partone.)

SCENA III—LUCIA e RAIMONDO.

Lucia.

Ebben?

Raimondo

Di tua speranza
L'ultimo raggio tramontò.
Credei al tuo sospetto
Che il fratel chiudesse
Tutte le strade, onde sul Franco suolo,
All uom che amar giurasti
Non guingesser tue nuove;
Io stesso un foglio date vergato,
Per secura mano; recarglifeci
In vano! Tace mai sempre—
Quel silenzio assai d'infideltà ti parlà!

Lucia.

E me consigli?

Raimondo.

Di piegarti al destino.

Lucia.

E il giuramento?

Raimondo.

Tu pur veneggi!
I nuziati voti
Che il ministro di Dio non bene,
Nè il ciel nè il mondo riconosce.

Lucia.

Ah! cede persuasa la mente,
Ma sordo alla ragion resisto il core.

Raimondo.

Vincerlo è forza.

Lucia.

Oh sventurato amore!

Raymond.

Ah, to thy destiny calmly resign thee!
Horrors greater far will else befall thee;
To the voice of affection incline thee!
From her grave thy mother doth call thee.
From this peril save thy brother!
'Tis a parent doth implore.
See yon angry shade uprise before thee,
Mark yon blood-stained scaffold drenched
     with gore.

Lucy.

Cease—

Raymond.

Save him!

Lucy.

Thou hast conquered!
I will act as thou requirest.

Raymond.

O what rapture! In me confide thee.
Every cloud now disappeareth!
This thy heroic sacrifice,
Laid on the shrine of duty,
Shall be by holy angels
Recorded in heaven above.
Tho' man may not regard it,
Tho' earth may not reward it,
Thy Maker who ruleth thy destiny
Doth mark this deed of love.

Lucy.

Guide thou me, support me,
Thou hast conquered, I confide in thee!

Raimondo.

Ah, cedi, o più sciagure
Ti sovra stanti infelice,
Per te venere mie cure
Per l'estinta genitrice,
Il periglio d' un fratello
Deh ti muova e cangi il cor!
O la madre nell' avello
Fremerà per te d'orror.

Lucia.

Taci—

Raimondo.

Cedi—

Lucia.

Ah, vincerti.
Non son tanto suatuarata.

Raimondo

Oh! qual giosa; in me tu desti.
Oh qual nube hai dissipata!
Al ben de' tuoi vittima
Offri, Lucia, te stessa,
E tanto sagrifizio
Scritto nel ceil sarà.
Se la pietà degli uomini
A te non fia concessa,
V' è un Dio, che tergere
Il pianto tuo saprà.

Lucia.

Guidami tu, tu reggime
Son fuori, di me stessa!

SCENE IV—Henry, Arthur, Norman; Knights and Ladies related to Ashton; Pages, Squires; Inhabitants of Lammermoor, and Domestics.

SCENA IV—Enrico, Arturo, Normando; Cavaiieri c Dame congiunti di Ashton; Paggi, Armigeri; Abitanti di Lammermoor, e Domestici.

PER TE IMMENSO — *HOPE BRIGHTLY* (Chorus)

Per te d'im-men-so giu-bi-lo   tut-to s'av-vi-va in-tor-no, · per te veg-giam ri-
Hope bright-ly beams be-fore thee now,   *Ah, day of joy and glad-ness, Heav'n sheds its sun-light*

na-sce-ra del-la spe-ran-za il gior-no, qui l'a-mis-tà ti
o'er thee now, No more of grief or sad-ness. Dark tho' the clouds did

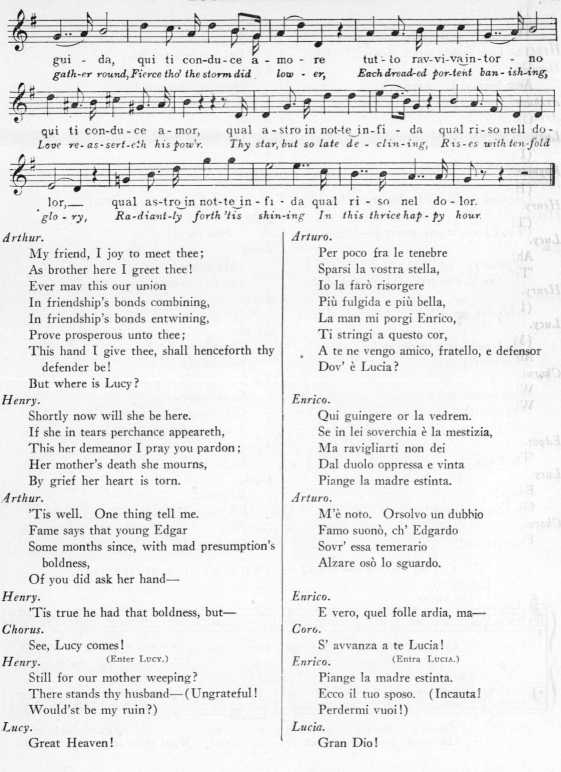

gui - da, qui ti con-du-ce a - mo - re tut-to rav-vi-va in-tor - no
gath-er round, Fierce tho' the storm did low - er, Each dread-ed por-tent ban-ish-ing,

qui ti con-du-ce a - mor, qual a-stro in not-te in-fi - da qual ri-so nell do-
Love re-as-sert-eth his pow'r. Thy star, but so late de-clin-ing, Ris-es with ten-fold

lor,— qual as-tro in not-te in-fi - da qual ri - so nel do-lor.
glo - ry, Ra-diant-ly forth 'tis shin-ing In this thrice hap-py hour.

Arthur.

My friend, I joy to meet thee;
As brother here I greet thee!
Ever may this our union
In friendship's bonds combining,
In friendship's bonds entwining,
Prove prosperous unto thee;
This hand I give thee, shall henceforth thy
    defender be!
But where is Lucy?

Henry.

Shortly now will she be here.
If she in tears perchance appeareth,
This her demeanor I pray you pardon;
Her mother's death she mourns,
By grief her heart is torn.

Arthur.

'Tis well. One thing tell me.
Fame says that young Edgar
Some months since, with mad presumption's
    boldness,
Of you did ask her hand—

Henry.

'Tis true he had that boldness, but—

Chorus.

See, Lucy comes!

Henry. (Enter LUCY.)

Still for our mother weeping?
There stands thy husband—(Ungrateful!
Would'st be my ruin?)

Lucy.

Great Heaven!

Arturo.

Per poco fra le tenebre
Sparsi la vostra stella,
Io la farò risorgere
Più fulgida e più bella,
La man mi porgi Enrico,
Ti stringi a questo cor,
A te ne vengo amico, fratello, e defensor
Dov' è Lucia?

Enrico.

Qui guingere or la vedrem.
Se in lei soverchia è la mestizia,
Ma ravigliarti non dei
Dal duolo oppressa e vinta
Piange la madre estinta.

Arturo.

M'è noto. Orsolvo un dubbio
Famo suonò, ch' Edgardo
Sovr' essa temerario
Alzare osò lo sguardo.

Enrico.

E vero, quel folle ardia, ma—

Coro.

S' avvanza a te Lucia!

Enrico. (Entra LUCIA.)

Piange la madre estinta.
Ecco il tuo sposo. (Incauta!
Perdermi vuoi!)

Lucia.

Gran Dio!

Arthur.
>Thus lowly at thy feet, fair maid,
>Thy lover kneels before thee.

Henry.
>Dost hear, girl? Approach,
>And sign thy dower. We wait thee.

Arthur.
>Oh, blissful hour!

Lucy.
>(I go to the sacrifice!)

Raymond.
>(Heaven shield her in this trying hour.)

Henry.
>(Thou know'st my power.)—Sign it!

Lucy.
>Ah, misery!   (She signs.)
>'Tis done! I've writ I have signed it.

Henry.
>(I breathe again!)

Lucy.
>(My blood seems turned to ice.
>All is over!)

Chorus.
>What means this?
>Who cometh?

SCENE V—EDGAR and the above.

Edgar.
>'Tis Edgar!

Lucy.
>Edgar!
>Oh, hide me, earth!

Chorus.
>Fearful hour!

Arturo.
>Ti piaccia i voti accogliere
>Del tenero amor mio!

Enrico.
>Omai si compia il rito—
>T'appressa!

Arturo.
>Oh dolce invito!

Lucia.
>(Io vado al sacrifizio!)

Raimondo.
>(Reggi, buon Dio, l'afflitta!)

Enrico.
>Non esitar!

Lucia.
>(Me misera!
>La mia condanna ho scritta!)

Enrico.
>(Respiro!)

Lucia.
>(Io gelo ed ardo!
>Io manco!)

Tutti.
>Qual fragor!
>Chi giunge?

SCENA V—EDGARDO, LUCIA, servi e detti.

Edgardo.
>Edgardo!

Lucia.
>Edgardo!
>Oh, fulmine!

Gli Altri.
>Oh, terror!

CHI MI FRENA —— *WHAT RESTRAINS ME* (Edgardo and Enrico)

Larghetto

cor - so? il suo duo - lo il suo spa - ven - to son la
scab - bard? Is't af - fec - tion that still re - main - eth. And each

cor - so? del - la mi - se - ra in fa - vo - re nel mio
scab - bard? Is't af - fec - tion still re - main - eth And each

pro - va, son la pro - va d'un ri - mor - so! ma qual ro - sai na ri
an - gry thought, each an - gry thought en - chain - eth. Of thine own___ blood thou'rt be -

pet - to un gri - do cor - se! è mio san - gue! l'ho tra
an - gry, dark thought en - chain - eth. Of mine own___ blood I'm be -

di - ta, el - la sta___ fra mor - te e vi - ta! io son vin - to son com -
tray - er! Now, 'twixt life___ and death she stand - eth! Ah! de - spair, my heart doth

di - ta, el - la sta___ fra mor - te e vi - ta! ah! che spe - gne - re non
tray - er! Now, 'twixt life___ and death she stand - eth! Ah! de - spair her heart doth

mos - so! t'a - mo, in - gra - ta, t'a - mo, t'a - mo in - gra - ta, t'a - mo an - cor!___
with - er, Yet, un - grate - ful one, I love thee, yes, I love thee still!___

pos - so i ri - mor - si del mio co - re, del mio cor!___
with - er, And re - morse my breast doth fill, my breast doth fill!___

Lucy.	Lucia.
(I had hoped that death had found me,	(Io sperai che e me la vita
And in his drear fetters bound me,	Tronca avesse il mio spavento;

But he comes not to relieve me!
Ah! of life will none bereave me?
Still in dark despair I languish,
Nought to hope but ceaseless anguish;
Even tears mine eyes abandon,
My cup of woe to fill.)

Raymond.

(Time, thou hast wrought thy worst, terrible moment,
No longer sense hath mastery over words;
Dense and impervious clouds of fear are seen,
As threatening e'en the brilliance of the sun.
Ah! like a rose that withers on the stem,
She now is hovering 'twixt death and life!
He who for her by pity is not moved,
Has of a tiger in his breast the heart.)

Henry, Arthur, Norman and Chorus.

Hence, thou traitor, hence betake thee.
Ere our rage o'erwhelm thee.

Edgar.

Dare advance one single step,
And other blood with mine shall flow!

Raymond.

Stay, ye rash, ye impious men,
Your sinful purposes forego.
Heaven's servant now here stand I!
In your Maker's name, command I.
Sheathe your weapons! Know that the murderer
He abhorreth! What saith His word?
"He that wieldeth the sword in anger
By the sword shall be laid low."

Henry.

Vile intruder, say what within these walls
Thou seekest?

Edgar.

Hither came I
For my bride. Thy sister
Unto me her faith hath sworn!

Raymond.

Thou must all hope of her relinquish;
She's another's!

Edgar.

Another's? no!

Ma la morte non m' aita—
Vivo ancor per mio tormento!
Da' miei lumi cadde il velo—
Mi tradì la terra e il Cielo!
Vorrei pianger, ma non posso:
Ah! mi manca il pianto ancor!)

Raimondo.

(Qual terribile momento!
Più formar non so parole;
Densa nube di spavento
Par che copra i rai del sole.
Come rosa inaridita
Ella sta fra morte e vita!
Chi per lei non è commosso
Ha di tigre in petto il cor.)

Enrico, Arturo, Normando e Cavalieri.

T' allontana! sciagurato,
O il tuo sangue fia versato.

Edgardo.

Morirò; ma insiem col mio
Altro sangue scorrerà.

Raimondo.

Rispettate in me di Dio
La tremenda maestà!
In suo nome io vel comando,
Deponete l'ira e il brando.
Pace, pace;—egli abborrisce
L'omicida, e scritto sta—
Chi di ferro altrui ferisce,
Pur di ferro perirà.

Enrico.

Ravenswood in queste porte
Chi ti guida?

Edgardo.

La mia sorte!
Il mio dritto; sì, Lucia
La sua fede a me giurò!

Raimondo.

Questo amor per sempre obblia
Alla è d'altri.

Edgardo.

D'altri! ah, no!

Raymond.
> Read!

Edgar   (to LUCY).
> Tremblest? Art confounded?
> Didst thou write this? I wait thy answer!
> Didst thou write this?

Lucy.
> Yes.

Edgar.
> Beholdest thou
> This token? Perfidious heart!
> I return it.

Lucy.
> Ah, no—

Edgar.
> Receive it—
> Thou fallen traitress to heaven, to Love,
> Accursed forever be the day on which I saw
> thee!
> Blotted from time be that dark hour when
> first I met thee!
> For thy shameless, base desertion,
> Pardon vainly thou'lt ask above.
> Despair and anguish grant thy heart
> May desolation!

Henry and Chorus.
> No further dare.
> Hence away, ere our fury o'erwhelm thee;
> Hence away, if thy life thou regardest.
> But a moment the blow is suspended;
> Tempt us no longer, we bid thee beware!

Edgar.
> Strike, the frail strings of life now dividing,
> At her nuptials my pale corpse presiding.
> Drain my heart's blood at thy wedding ban-
> quet.
> Strike! why pause ye? I'm ready; prepare.

Lucy.
> Heaven, in mercy, oh save him, protect him,
> And through this fearful danger direct him!
> By the woe thou hast now heaped upon me,
> I do implore for him thy kindly care.
> Since to me thou hast doomed a life of
> misery,
> Ah, refuse not my last, my dying prayer.

Raimondo.
> Mira!

Edgardo.
> Tremi, ti confondi!
> Son tue ciffre? A me rispondi!
> Son tue ciffre?

Lucia.
> Sì!

Edgardo.
> Riprendi
> Il tuo pegno, infido cor!
> Il mio dammi.

Lucia.
> Almen—

Edgardo.
> Lo rendi!
> Hai tradito il Cielo e amor!
> Maledetto sia l'istante
> Che di te mi resi amante!
> Stirpe iniqua, abbominata—
> Io dovea da te fuggir!
> Ah, di Dio la mano irata
> Ti desperda!

Tutti
> Insano ardir!
> Esci, fuggi il furor che m' accende.
> Solo un punto i suoi colpi sospende,
> Ma fra poco più atroce più fiero,
> Sul tuo capo abborrito cadrà!

Edgardo.
> Trucidatemi! e pronubo al rito
> Sia lo scempio d'un core tradito!
> Del mio sangue bagnata la soglia,
> Dolce vista per l'empia sarà:
> Calpestando l'e sangue mia spoglia
> All' altare più lieta ne andrà.

Lucia.
> Dio, lo salva! in sì fiero momento
> D' una misera ascolta l' accento.
> E la prece d' immenso dolore
> Che più in terra speranza non ha:
> E l'estrema domanda del core,
> Che sul labbro spirando mi sta!

Raymond, Alice and Ladies.

Unhappy man, fly hence—let prudence haste
thee;
Thy life, the claims of station, rank, respect.
Live! it may be thy grief may find an end;
All woes must end by never-ending pity,
How often is it to a single torture
A thousand joys have in their turn suc-
ceeded!

END OF ACT II.

ACT III.

SCENE I—A Room in the Tower of Wolf's Crag.

Edgar.

Darkly the night is lowering,
Even as is my destiny. Yes! roll on, thou
thunders!
Flash, ye fierce forked lightning; convulsion,
Shake the vast womb of nature, the world
o'erwhelming!
Ah! Is't deception? On the hard earth
beating
A horse's hoof I hear! It stops—
Who is it that thro' the tempest
With fierce and threatening gesture
Comes at this hour to meet me!

SCENE II—Enter HENRY.

Henry.
'Tis I.
Edgar.
Ha! what boldness! Ashton!
Henry.
Yes.
Edgar.
Within these drear walls
Darest thou thus at this hour present thee?
Henry.
Doth my presence not content thee?
I do but return thy visit!
Edgar.
See my father's shade uprising,
For his wrongs revenge demanding!
Death is in the air thou breathest;

Raimondo, Alisia e Dame.

Infelice, t'invola—t'affretta:
I tuoi giorni, il suo stato rispetta.
Vivi! e forse il tuo duolo fia spento
Tutto è lieve all' eterna pietà.
Quante volte ad un solo tormento
Mille gioje succeder non fa!

FINE DELL' ATTO II.

ATTO III.

SCENA I—Sala terreno nella terre di Volfureng.

Edgardo.

Orrida è questa notte
Come il destino mio! Sì, tuona, o cielo—
Imperversate, o turbini—sconvolto
Sia l'ardin di natura, e pera il mondo—
Io non m' inganno! scalpitar d' appresso
Odo un destrier—s' arresta—
Chi mai della tempesta
Fra le minaccie e l'ire,
Chi puote a me venire?

SCENA II—Entra ENRICO.

Enrico.
Io.
Edgardo.
Quale ardire!—Ashton!
Enrico.
Sì.
Edgardo.
Fra queste mura
Osi offrirti al mio cospetto?
Enrico.
Io vi sto per tua sciagura.
Non venisti nel mio tetto!
Edgardo.
Quì del padre ancor s' aggira
L'ombra inulta—e par che frema!
Morte ogn' aura a te quì spira!

E'en the earth shaketh, trembleth, where
  thou'rt standing,
When thou didst cross the threshold
Did thy heart not quake with fear,
As a living man descending
To thy tomb with no help near?

Henry.
Even now the bridal chamber
Opens for the blooming bride!

Edgar.
Ah, infuriating thought this!
Oh, what torments! what torture!

Henry.
But hearken. Tho' the sounds of mirth and
  gladness
Echoed far and wide around me,
Stronger far than ties of pleasure
Are the bonds in which hate for thee hath
  bound me,
Friends, relations, guests forsaking,
Flew I straight to meet thee here,
While the mad and furious tempest
Shouted vengeance in my ear.

Edgar.
What here hath brought thee?

Henry.
Thou now shalt hear.
Think of the wrongs thou hast done me,
And dare not to falter or shun me;
Words were too poor to express them—
This arm alone can redress them!
I give thee defiance to death—
Nought else can wipe away the stain.

Edgar.
By my dead father's ashes,
Thy heart's blood I will drain!

Henry.
Thou!

Edgar.
When meet we?

Henry.
At earliest dawning of the next approaching day.

Edgar.
Where?

Il terren per te qui trema!—
Nel varcar la soglia orrenda
Ben dovesti palpitar,
Come un uom che vivo scenda
La sua tomba ad albergar!

Enrico.
Fu condutta al sacra rito,
Quindi al talamo Lucia.

Edgardo.
(Ei più squarcia il cor ferito!
Oh tormento!—oh gelosia!)

Enrico.
Ascolta. Di letizia il mio soggiorno,
E di plausi rimbombava;
Ma più forte al cor d'intorno
La vendetta a me parlava!
Quì mi trassi—in mezzo ai venti
Le sua voce udia tuttor,
E il furor degli elementi
Rispondeva al mio furor.

Edgardo.
Da me che brami?

Enrico.
Ascoltami:
Onde punir l'offessa,
De' miei la spada vindice
Pende su te sospesa—
Onde punir l'offessa,
Ch'altri to spenga? Ah! mai—
Chi dee svenarti il sai!

Edgardo.
So che al paterno cenere
Giurai strapparti il core.

Enrico.
Tu!

Edgardo.
Quando?

Enrico.
Al primo sorgere del mattutino albore.

Edgardo.
Ove?

Henry.
> By the icy tombs
> Of Ravenswood.

Edgar.
> Agreed.

Henry.
> There shalt thou join thy ancestors.

Edgar.
> There too thyself shalt fall.

Enrico.
> Fra l' urne gelide
> De Ravenswood.

Edgardo.
> Verrò.

Enrico.
> Ivi a restar preparati.

Edgardo.
> Ivi t'ucciderò.

O SOLE PIÙ RATTO — *OH, HASTE, CRIMSON MORNING* (Edgardo and Enrico)

Allegro moderato

O so-le più rat-to a sor-ger t'ap-pres-ta ti cin-ga di
Oh, haste, crim-son morn-ing, Bright sun of the mor-row, Let red clouds give

O so-le più rat-to a sor-ger t'ap-pres-ta ti cin-ga di
Oh, haste, crim-son morn-ing, Bright sun of the mor-row, Let red clouds give

san-gue ghir-lan-da fu-nes-ta con quel-la ris-chia-ra, l'or-
warn-ing, A-round thee of sor-row. Like snails how ye lin-ger, slow

san-gue ghir-lan-da fu-nes-ta con quol-la ris-chia-ra, l'or-
warn-ing, A-round thee of sor-row. Like snails how ye lin-ger, slow

ri-bi-le ga-ra d'un o-dio mor-ta-le d'un cie-co fu-
mo-ments de-lay-ing, That long the a-ven-ger from ven-geance are

ri-bi-le ga-ra d'un o-dio mor-ta-le d'un cie-co fu-
mo-ments de-lay-ing, That long the a-ven-ger from ven-geance are

ro - re, O so - le più rat - to ri - sor-gi è ris - chia-ra d'un o - dio mor-
stay - ing, Oh, haste, crim-son morn-ing, Bright sun of the mor-row, Let the red

ro - re, O so - le più rat - to ri - sor-gi è ris - chia-ra d'un
stay - ing, Oh, haste, crim-son morn-ing, Bright sun of the mor-row, Let

ta - - - le il, cie-co, il cie-co fu - ror.
clouds give the warn-ing Of sor-row a - round.

o - dio mor - ta - le il cie-co, il cie-co fu - ror.
the red clouds give warn-ing, give warn-ing Of sor-row a - round.

SCENE III—Hall in Henry's Castle. Peasants and Domestics of the Castle.	SCENA III—Sala.
Chorus.	*Coro.*
Ah, happy, happy day,	D'immenzo giubilo
Swell high the choral lay	S'innalzi un grido
Through all Scotland,	Corra di Scozia
To all her shores	Per ogni lido,
Tell the wretches,	È avverta i perfidi
Our enemies,	Nostri nemici,
That more terrible,	Che più terribili,
As more happy,	Che più felici
The presence renders us	Ne rende l'aura
Of our great joy.	D'alto favor;
Ah! e'en the stars themselves	Ch' a noi sorridono
Smile happily down on us.	Le stelle ancor.
SCENE IV—Raymond, Norman, and the above.	SCENA IV—Raimondo, Normando, e detti.
Raymond.	*Raimondo.*
Cease, ah, cease these sounds of gladness!	Cessi, ah cessi quel contento!
Chorus.	*Coro.*
Thou dost seem aghast with fear!	Sei cosparso di pallore!
What has chanced?	Ciel, che rechi?
Raymond.	*Raimondo.*
Horrible event!	Un fiero evento!
Chorus.	*Coro.*
Thou freezest our souls with terror.	Tu ne agghiacci di terrore!

Raymond.

To their chamber the bride and bridegroom
Scarce a moment had departed,
When a shriek came, a cry of anguish!
As a man in death throes did languish.
Straight I forced the door; trembling entered;
Moment terrible! sight of horror!
There poor Arthur, upon the floor, lay
Pale and deathlike, besmeared with blood,
While Lucy, brandishing a sword,
Like some fell demon, threatening stood!
Then on me her eyes fast fixing,
"Where's the bridegroom?" she cried.
And a smile across her pallid face
With ghastly splendor shone.
Ah, unhappy maid! thy reason
From thee had forever flown!

Chorus.

Ah, dreadful moment, dire deed of horror;
Omen portentous, dark fears confound us.
Night, thy dark mantle throw close around us;
Cover this deed with thy densest veil.
Ah, let not the hand that this did compass
Upon her kindred thy wrath entail.

Raymond.

Ah! she comes!

SCENE V—LUCY, ALICE, and the above.

Lucy.

How sweetly, gently
Steals thy voice on mine ear. Ah, those dear accents
Once more, once more I hear.
My Edgar, at length I'm safe with thee,
To thee I've flown from all thine enemies.
—What coldness
Shoots like ice through my veins! Each fibre trembleth;
My foot doth fail! Here, at the fountain,
Once more I'm at thy side, love. Oh, Heaven, see'st thou
Yon dark, fearful phantom! Ah! it would part us!—

Raimondo.

Dalle stanze ove Lucia
Trassi già col suo consorte,
Un lamento, un grido uscia,
Come d'uom vicino a morte.
Corsi ratto in quelle mura:
Ahi! terribile sciagura!
Steso Arturo al suol giaceva
Muto, freddo, insanguinato;
E Lucia l'acciar stringeva—
Che fu già dei trucidato.
Ella in me le luci affisse:
"Il mio sposo ov' è?" mi disse;
E nel volto suo pallente
Un sorriso balenò.
Infelice! della mente
La virtude a lei mancò!

Tutti

Oh! qual funesto avvenimento!
Tutti ne ingombra cupo spavento!
Notte, ricopri la ria sventura
Col tenebroso tuo denso vel!
Ah, quella destra di sangue impura
L'ira non chiami su noi del Ciel!

Raimondo.

Eccolà!

SCENA V—LUCIA, ALISA, e detti.

Lucia.

Il dolce suono
Mi colpì di sua voce. Ah! quella voce
M' è qui nel cor discesa!
Edgardo, io ti son resa—
Fuggita lo son da' tuoi nemici. Un gelo
Mi serpeggia nel sen—trema ogni fibbra
Vacilla il piè, presso la fonte meco
T'assidi alquanto. Ahimè! sorge il tremendo
Fantasma e ne separa!
Un serto io voglio. Un armonia celeste
Di, non ascolti? Ah! l'inno
Suona di nozze. Il rito
Per noi s'appressa! oh! me felice!
Oh! gioia che si sente e non si dice!

Hark, thro' the dark air heavenly harmony
 swelleth!
Say! dost thou hear it? Ah, 'tis the hymn
Of our nuptials! They wait us
At the altar; oh, I am happy
The joy that fills my bosom words cannot
 tell thee.
They light the incense! See now
The sacred tapers brightly are burning;
The priest approaches. Place thy hand
In mine now! oh, blissful moment,
At length thou'rt mine, love, and I am
 thine;
What rapture boundless for me is now pre-
 paring!
Each pleasure doubly sharing.
Yes! doubly enjoying, if 'tis shared with
 thee,
Thanks, bounteous Heaven!
Thou hast given new life to me!

Raymond.
 Here comes her brother!

SCENE VI—HENRY and the above.

Henry.
 Answer me,
 Can this dark deed be real?
Raymond.
 But too surely.
Henry.
 Abandoned one,
 Thy punishment condign shall be!
All.
 Stay thee, oh, heaven!
Raymond.
 Seest thou not
 Her fearful state?
Lucy.
 What say'st thou?
Henry.
 What death-like paleness!
Lucy.
 Ah, what misery!
Raymond.
 Her reason has for ever fled from her!

Ardon gl'incensi—splendono
Le sacre facì intorno!—
Ecco il ministro! Porgini
La destra—oh! lièto giorno!
Alfin son tua, alfin sei mio,
A me ti dona un Dio
Ogni piacer più grato
Sì ogni piacere mi fia conte diviso.
Del ciel demente un riso
La vita a noi sarà.

Raimondo.
 S' avanza Enrico!

SCENA VI—ENRICO, e detti

Enrico.
 Ditemi,
 Vera è l'atroce scena?
Raimondo.
 Vera, pur troppo!
Enrico.
 Ah! perfida!
 Ne avrai condegna pena—
Alisa, Raimondo e Coro.
 T'arresta! oh, Ciel!
Raimondo.
 Non vedi
 Lo stato suo?
Lucia.
 Che chiedi?
Enrico.
 O qual pallor!
Lucia.
 Me misera!
Raimondo.
 Ha la ragion smarrita!

Henry.
Great Heaven!—
Raymond.
Tremble, heartless man,
Thou should'st, for her life.
Lucy.
Frown not so harshly on me,
Although 'tis true I signed it;
Ah, look not, love, so fearfully,
Break not the ring I gave thee;
And do not curse me; I was the victim
Of a cruel brother.
I love but thee, my Edgar!
Whom did'st thou name? was't Arthur?
Ah! fly me not; have mercy, pray!

Enrico.
Gran Dio!—
Raimondo.
Tremare, o barbaro!
Tu dei per la sua vita.
Lucia.
Non mi guardar sì fiero;
Segnai quel foglio è vero;
Nell' ira sua terribile
Calpesta, oh Dio! l'anello—
Mi maledice! Ah! vittima
Fui d'un crudel fratello!
Ma ognor t'amai—lo giuro.
Chi mi nomasti—Arturo?
Ah, non fuggir! perdone!

SPARGI D' AMARO PIANTO — *SHED THOU ONE TEAR* (Lucia)

Spar-gi d'a-ma-ro pian-to   il mio ter-res-tre
Shed thou one tear of sor-row   O'er my un-time-ly

ve—lo   men-tre las-sù nel cie-lo io pre-ghe-
grave,——   love: While there, a-bove, in heav-en I pray for

ro, pre-ghe-ro per te al giun-ge tu-o sol-tan-to
thee! yes, I'll pray for thee! E'en heav'n, if thou, love, art ab-sent,

fia bel-lo il ciel—per me, per me, ah, si! ah, si! per me!
No joy will bring un-to me! no joy, ah, no! ah, no! ah! no,

fia—bel-lo il ciel, il—ciel per—me, ah, si! ah, si! per me, per
E'en heav-en will bring no—joy to—me! ah, no! ah, no! ah, no! E'en

me,————————————— si, per———— me,
heav'n,——————————————— heav'n will———— bring

per_____ me,_____ per_____ me.
no_____ joy_____ to_____ me

Henry.

(Bitter remorse and misery
Ever my lot will be.)
With care remove her! Alice, kinsmen and
    friends,
I pray you with gentlest kindness treat her;
Remorse is henceforth my earthly portion!

Raymond.

Man of blood, in this thy work now exult
    thee!

Norman.

What meanest thou?

Raymond.

Thou broughtest the brand that this dire
    flame engendered,
'Twas thy fell hand that fired it!
Each spark that kindled, thou didst fan to a
    blaze.

Norman.

But I believed not—

Raymond.

Thou of this crime art author. Traitor!
    E'en now
His blood cries for vengeance! At heaven's
    bar
It doth accuse thee and there the hand su-
    preme
Thine awful sentence signeth! Depart hence
    and tremble.

(Exeunt.)

SCENE VII—Exterior part of the Castle. Night.

Edgar.

Tombs of my far-famed ancestors, open wide
    your portal,
And the last fated scion
Of your doomed race receive ye!
My hate has vanished! Past is resentment.
On his vengeful blade now

Enrico.

(Giorni d'amaro pianto
Serba il rimorso a me.)
Si tragga altrove! Alisa, pietoso amico,
Deh! voi la misera vegliate
Io più me stesso in me non trovo!

Raimondo.

Delator! gioisci dell' opra tuo!

Normando.

Che parli?

Raimondo.

Sì, dell' incendio che divampa e strugge
Questa casa infelice,
Hai tu destata la primiera favilla.

Normando.

Io non credei—

Raimondo.

Tu del versato sangue, impio! tu sei
La ria cagion!—Quel sangue
Al ciel t'accusa, e già la man suprema
Segna la tua sentenza—or vanne, e trema.

(Parte.)

SCENA VII—Parte esterna del Castello. Notte.

Edgardo.

Tombe degli avi miei, l'ultimo avanzo
D'una stirpe infelice,
Deh! raccogliete voi!
Cessò dell' ira il breve foco—
Sul nemico acciaro
Abbandonar mi vo'. Per me la vita

How gladly would I fall. This life of
   misery,
I cannot bear it! The vast universe
Is but one desert, unless with her I share it!
The sounds of mirth and feasting
Echo around me. Ah, swiftly
Flies the night mid their revelry. Ungrate-
   ful woman,
While here I struggle, desperate in mine
   anguish.
With mockery thou deridest me!
Thou most false, thou most shameless!
Thy heart with rapture boundeth,
While death me surroundeth.

E orrendo peso—l' universo intero
E un deserto per me senza Lucia!
Di faci tutta via
Splende il castello! Ah! scarsa
Fu la notte al tripudio! Ingrata donna!
Mentr' io mi struggo in disperato pianto,
Tu ridi,—esulti accanto
Al felice consorte!
Tu delle gioje in seno,
Io—della morte!

FRA POCO A ME — *WILD FLOWERS SOON* (Edgardo)

Larghetto

Fra po-co a me ri - co-ve - ro   da - rà ne-glet-to a vel - lo,—
The wild flow'rs soon will shed their bloom   A - round my sad and lone - ly tomb;

u - na pie-to - sa la-gri-ma non scen-de - rà su quel - lo, ah!
No kind-ly tear shall bless the spot Where blight-ed love's for - got - ten Ah!

fin de-gli e-stin-ti, ahi mi - se - ro!— man-ca il con-for-to a - me.   Tu
my wear - y wound-ed soul to heav'n Shall wing its rap'-id flight   Oh!

pur, tu pur di - men-ti - ca   quel mar-mo dis-preg-gia - to:
Lu - cy, should you with your spouse Roam near the tomb you've here — made,

mai non pas-sar-vi o bar-ba-ra, del— tuo con-sor-te a la-to, ah! ris-
In si - lence pass, a word of love Would— rouse my sleep-ing shade: Oh! re

pet-ta al-men le ce - ne-ri di chi mo-ria per te, ri-spet-ta al-men le
spect at least, thou faith-less girl, The dust of him who died for thee, Re - spect at

ce - ne - ri di chi mo-ria per te! Mai non pas-sar-vi, tu lo di-
least the dust of him who died for thee. In si - lence pass then; a word of

men - ti - ca, ri - spet-ta al - me - no chi muo-re per te, maï non pas-
hap - py love Would rouse, would wak - en my sleep-ing shade. In si - lence

sar - vi, tu lo di - men-ti-ca ris-pet-ta al-me - no chi
pass then; Re - spect, re - spect at least, thou faith-less girl The dust of

muo - re, chi muo - re per te, o bar - ba-ra, io mo -ro per te.
him, of him who died for thee, of him who died, who died for thee.

SCENE VIII—Inhabitants of Lammermoor coming from the Castle, and EDGAR.	SCENA VIII—Abitanti di Lammermoor dal Castello e detto.
Chorus.	**Coro.**
Poor forlorn one! oh, fate most fearful,	Oh meschina! oh, caso orrendo!
Hope of life at length hath vanished,	Più sperar non giova omai.
Ere on this dark night of sorrow	Questo dì che sta sorgendo,
Morning dawns she'll be no more.	Tramontar tu non vedrai!
Edgar.	**Edgardo.**
Gracious heaven! say, what mean ye?	Giusto Cielo! ah, rispondete!
What doth mean this wailing cry?	Di chi mai, di chi piangete?
Chorus.	**Coro.**
'Tis for Lucy.	Di Lucia!
Edgar.	**Edgardo.**
Say ye for Lucy?	Lucia diceste?
Chorus.	**Coro.**
She, alas, is surely dying.	Sì; la misera sen muore.

FUR LE NOZZE — *THIS UNHAPPY, FATAL MARRIAGE* (Chorus)

Fur le noz-ze a lei fu - nes-te di ra-gion la tras-se a - mo - re s'av-vi-
This un-hap-py, fa-tal mar-riage Hath of rea-son quite de - prived her, All'for-

ci - na_all'ore es - tre - me e te chie-de per te ge - me. Ques - to
lorn and bro - ken - heart-ed, Life hath from her nigh de - part - ed; Death his

di, ques-to sol che-stà sor - gen - do tra-mon-tar, tra-mon-tar piu non ve-
vic-tim, his vic-tim sure-ly claim-eth; Ere the morn-ing, the morn-ing sun doth

dra! di ra - gion le tras-se_a - mo - re, e te chie-de per te ge - me.
rise. E'en while mad-ness sense en - thrall-eth, Still on thee for aid she call-eth.

Edgar.	**Edgardo.**
Ah! Lucy, Lucy!	Ah Lucia! Lucia!
(A bell sounds without.)	
Chorus.	**Coro.**
That sad	Rimbomba
And solemn bell her end doth tell.	Già la squilla in suon di morte!
Edgar.	**Edgardo.**
It rings both hers and my knell!	Ahi! quel suono al cor mi piomba!
Yes, my fate is now decided!	E decisa la mia sorte:
In death we will not be divided.	Rivederla ancor vogl' io;
Soon I'll join thee, dearest Lucy!	Rivederla, e poscia—
Chorus.	**Coro.**
Oh, heaven! Whither goest thou?	Oh Dio!
O calm thee, nought can now the past recall.	Qual trasporto sconsigliato!
	Ah, desisti! ah, riedi in te!
SCENE THE LAST—Raymond and the above.	SCENA ULTIMA—Raimondo, e detti.
Raymond.	**Raimondo.**
Stay, rash man, what seekest thou further?	Ove corri, sventurato?
She's forever lost to thee.	Ella in terra più non è.
Edgar.	**Edgardo.**
My Lucy.	Lucia!
Raymond.	**Raimondo.**
All is over.	Sventurata.
Edgar.	**Edgardo.**
Forever lost to me!	In terra più non è.
She hath departed—	Ella dunque—

Raymond.
To heaven!

Raimondo.
E in cielo.

TU CHE A DIO — *THO' FROM EARTH THOU'ST FLOWN* (Edgardo)

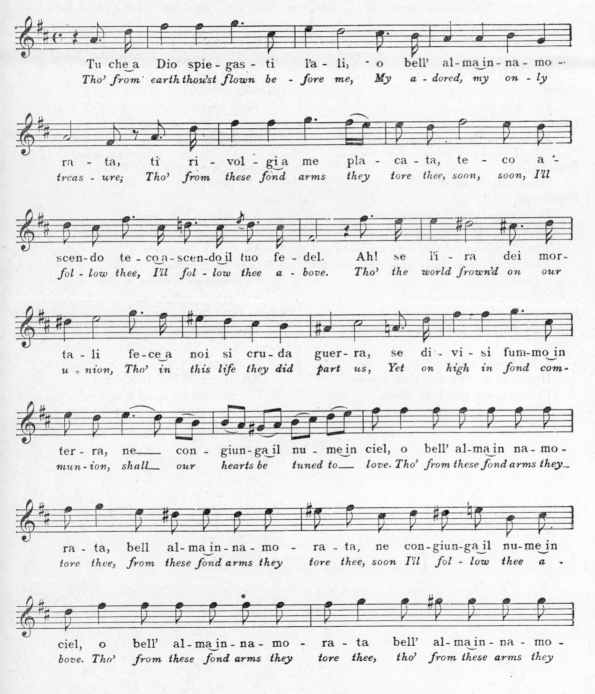

Tu che a Dio spie - gas - ti l'a - li, o bell' al - ma in - na - mo -
Tho' from earth thou'st flown be - fore me, My a - dored, my on - ly

ra - ta, ti ri - vol - gia me pla - ca - ta, te - co a -
treas - ure; Tho' from these fond arms they tore thee, soon, soon, I'll

scen - do te - co a - scen - do il tuo fe - del. Ah! se l'i - ra dei mor -
fol - low thee, I'll fol - low thee a - bove. Tho' the world frown'd on our

ta - li fe - ce a noi si cru - da guer - ra, se di - vi - si fum - mo in
u - nion, Tho' in this life they did part us, Yet on high in fond com -

ter - ra, ne con - giun - ga il nu - me in ciel, o bell' al - ma in na - mo -
mun - ion, shall our hearts be tuned to love. Tho' from these fond arms they

ra - ta, bell al - ma in - na - mo - ra - ta, ne con - giun - ga il nu - me in
tore thee, from these fond arms they tore thee, soon I'll fol - low thee a -

ciel, o bell' al - ma in - na - mo - ra - ta bell' al - ma in - na - mo -
bove. Tho' from these fond arms they tore thee, tho' from these arms they

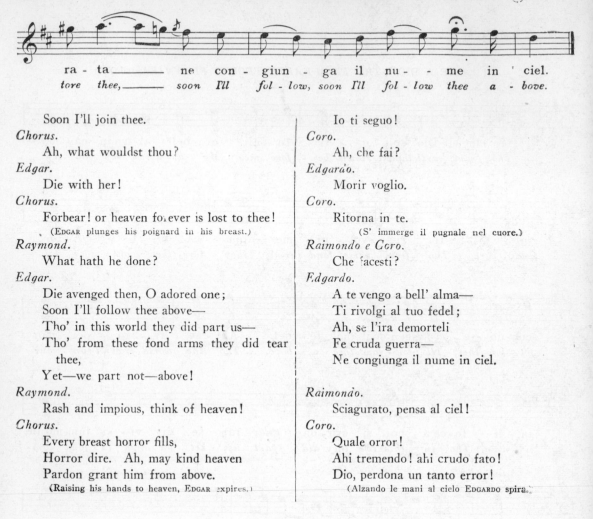

ra - ta_____ ne con - giun - ga il nu - - me in ciel.
tore thee,_____ soon I'll fol - low, soon I'll fol - low thee a - bove.

Soon I'll join thee.

Chorus.

Ah, what wouldst thou?

Edgar.

Die with her!

Chorus.

Forbear! or heaven forever is lost to thee!

(EDGAR plunges his poignard in his breast.)

Raymond.

What hath he done?

Edgar.

Die avenged then, O adored one;
Soon I'll follow thee above—
Tho' in this world they did part us—
Tho' from these fond arms they did tear thee,
Yet—we part not—above!

Raymond.

Rash and impious, think of heaven!

Chorus.

Every breast horror fills,
Horror dire. Ah, may kind heaven
Pardon grant him from above.

(Raising his hands to heaven, EDGAR expires.)

Io ti seguo!

Coro.

Ah, che fai?

Edgardo.

Morir voglio.

Coro.

Ritorna in te.

(S' immerge il pugnale nel cuore.)

Raimondo e Coro.

Che facesti?

Edgardo.

A te vengo a bell' alma—
Ti rivolgi al tuo fedel;
Ah, se l'ira demorteli
Fe cruda guerra—
Ne congiunga il nume in ciel.

Raimondo.

Sciagurato, pensa al ciel!

Coro.

Quale orror!
Ahi tremendo! ahi crudo fato!
Dio, perdona un tanto error!

(Alzando le mani al cielo EDGARDO spira.)

THE END.

LA GIOCONDA

by

AMILCARE PONCHIELLI

DRAMATIS PERSONÆ.

LA GIOCONDA, *a ballad-singer.*
            Mme. Christine Nilsson.
LA CIECA, *her blind mother.*   Mme. Scalchi.
LAURA, *wife of* ALVISE.   Mme. Fursch-Madi.
BARNABA, *a spy of the Inquisition.* Signor Del Puente.
ALVISE BADOÈRO, *one of the heads of the State In-*
    quisition.   Signor Novara.

ZUANE, *a boatman.*   Signor Augier
ISÈPO, *a public letter-writer.*   Signor Grazzi.
ENZO, *a Genoese noble.*   Signor Stagno
A PILOT.   Signor Barberis.
Monks, Senators, Sailors, Shipwrights, Ladies, Gentlemen,
    Populace, Masquers, etc.

The action takes place in Venice in the 17th Century.

First produced in America at the Metropolitan Opera House, New York, Dec. 20, 1883, under the direction of Signor Vianesi.

ARGUMENT.

Act. I. The place and time are Venice in the seventeenth century. Act I. opens with a festal chorus of the people — monks, sailors, masquers, etc., gathered in the courtyard of the ducal palace. *Barnaba*, a spy of the Council of Ten, comments on their gayety, and begins his plans to capture the affections of *Gioconda*, a ballad-singer, with whom he is deeply in love. *Gioconda* enters, leading and comforting her blind mother, *Cieca*. The former is in love with *Enzo*, a Genoese noble, originally the betrothed of *Laura*, who is now the wife of *Alvise*, chief of the Council of Ten. *Gioconda* repulses *Barnaba's* advances, and the latter determines to get the girl's mother in his power to further his designs. When the people return from the regatta, *Barnaba* persuades the defeated boatman *Zuàne* that *Cieca* has caused his disappointment by witchcraft, and the fate of the old woman hangs in the balance, when *Enzo* enters and saves her life. *Alvise* and *Laura* appear upon the scene, and the latter secures the pardon of *Cieca*, who gives her deliverer a rosary. *Laura* and *Enzo* recognize each other, and when *Barnaba*, bent upon getting *Enzo* out of the way so that he may have *Gioconda* to himself, tells him that *Laura* will be on his ship at nightfall, the rapture of the lover is boundless. *Barnaba's* real designs are not suspected. He then warns *Alvise* that his wife is about to elope with *Enzo*, and *Gioconda*, learning this, laments the perfidy of *Enzo*, while the monks and people are singing the vesper hymn.

Act II. takes place on board *Enzo's* vessel, and on the bank of the Fusina Lagoon. The sailors are carousing. *Barnaba* arrives with *Isèpo*, both disguised as fishermen, and the spy despatches *Isèpo* to summon three war galleys. He then departs; *Enzo* comes on deck, and sends the crew below, leaving him on deck, waiting for *Laura*, who presently arrives. The reunited lovers determine to set sail during the night; *Enzo* goes below to complete his preparations, and *Laura* prays to the Virgin for aid. *Gioconda* rushes upon her and is about to slay her, but on *Laura* lifting up the rosary remembers it was the grateful gift of *La Cieca*; gives her own mask to *Laura*, calls up two boatmen, and sends *Laura* away in safety before the arrival of *Alvise* and *Barnaba*. The Venetian galleys bear down on the "Hecate," which is set on fire by *Enzo* as the curtain falls.

Act III. opens on the following night, in *Alvise's* residence. He has resolved to poison *Laura*, and when she comes, at his summons, he tells her that she must drink the phial of poison he places on the table, before the last note shall be sung of a Serenata which is being chanted by some passing gondoliers. He no sooner quits the room than *Gioconda* enters. She brings a flask containing a powerful narcotic; makes *Laura* drink it; pours into the empty flask the poison contained in the phial, and departs to mingle with the masquers. *Alvise* enters; finds the phial empty, and believes his revenge complete. The scene changes to a grand fête, in which the ballet of "The Hours" is introduced. *Barnaba* drags in *La Cieca*, whom he has found in one of the reserved apartments. She declares that she was "praying for her, just dead," and the guests are dismayed. *Alvise* asks who has the right to be gloomy when *Alvise Badoèro* is gay? *Enzo*, who has learned from *Barnaba* that it is *Laura* who lies dead, rushes forward, throws off his mask, denounces *Alvise*, and is seized by the guards. *Gioconda* promises *Barnaba* to become his if he will obtain *Enzo's* liberty, and he accepts this compact. The grand finale is brought to a close by *Alvise* opening the curtain of the funeral chamber, and showing *Laura*, extended on her bier. He proudly avows that he has taken her life, to avenge his outraged honor, and the curtain falls on a scene of fearful interest.

In Act IV. the sleeping *Laura* is brought to the dwelling of *Gioconda*, who meditates suicide; then is tempted to destroy her rival. While she is hesitating, *Enzo* arrives, grateful to her for obtaining his freedom, but resolved to end his life. *Laura*—waking from her trance—calls out "Enzo!" and presently comes from behind the screen which had concealed her. The two lovers offer grateful thanks to their deliverer, and escape in a boat provided by her. Left alone, she remembers her compact with *Barnaba*, and resolves to fly. She prays to the Virgin for deliverance "from the foul demon," and her prayer is overheard, through the half-open door, by *Barnaba*, who confronts her as she is about to come forth. Summoning all her courage, she tells him gayly that she means to keep her word, but must put on her gayest ornaments, to do him honor, and while — to his delight — adorning herself with trinkets, contrives to seize a dagger, with which she stabs herself to the heart, saying, "I have sworn to be thine. Take me. I am thine!"

LA GIOCONDA.

ATTO I.	ACT I.

LA BOCCA DEI LEONI.

Il cortile del Palazzo Ducale parato a festa. Nel fondo la SCALA DEI GIGANTI e il PORTICO DELLA CARTA colla porta che adduce nell' interno della chiesa di S. Marco. A sinistra lo scrittoio d' uno scrivano pubblico. Sopra una parete del cortile si vedrà una fra le storiche bocche dei leoni colla seguente scritta incisa sul marmo a caratteri neri :

DENONTIE SECRETE PER VIA
D' INQVISITIONE CONTRA CADA
VNA PERSONA CON L' IMPVNITA
SEGRETEZA ET BENEFITTI
GIVSTO ALLE LEGI.

È uno splendido meriggio di primavera. La scena è ingombra di popolo festante. BARNABOTTI, ARSENALOTTI, MARINAI, maschere d' ogni sorta, ARLECCHINI, PANTALONI, BAUTTE, e in mezzo a questa turba vivace alcuni DALMATI ed alcuni MORI. BARNABA addossato ad una colonna, sta osservando il popolo; ha una piccola chitarra ad armacollo.

THE LION'S MOUTH.

Scene. — The Grand Courtyard of the Ducal Palace, decorated for festivities. At back, the Giant's Staircase and the Portico della Carta, with doorway leading to the interior of the Church of St. Mark. On the left, the writing-table of a public letter-writer. On one side of the court-yard is seen one of the historical Lion's Mouths, with the following inscription cut in black letters into the wall :

FOR SECRET DENUNCIATIONS
TO THE INQUISITION
AGAINST ANY PERSON,
WITH IMPUNITY, SECRECY, AND
BENEFIT TO THE STATE.

It is a splendid afternoon in spring. The stage is filled with holiday folks, Monks, Sailors, Shipwrights, Masquers, etc., and amidst the busy crowd are seen some Dalmatians and Moors. BARNABA, leaning his back against a column, is watching the people. He has a small guitar, slung around his neck.

SCENA I.

Marinai, Popolo e BARNABA.

Coro di Marinai e Popolo.
Feste e pane! la Repubblica
Domerà le schiatte umane
Finche avran le ciurme e i popoli
　　Feste e pane.
L'allegria disarma i fulmini
Ed infrange le ritorte.
Noi cantiam! chi canta è libero,
Noi ridiam! chi ride è forte.
Quel sereno Iddio lo vuol
Che allegrò questa laguna
Coll' argento della luna
È la porpora del sol.
　　[campane a distesa, squilli di trombe.
Feste e pane! a gioia suonano
Di San Marco le campane.
Viva il Doge e la Repubblica!
　　Feste e pane!

SCENE I.

BARNABA, Sailors, and People.
Opening Chorus.
Sports and feasting! Feasting and sports
　　Our Republic wise,
That rules the world from farthest East to
　　West,
Provides us — galley-slaves and populace —
　　　　Sports and feasts.
Joy disarms the angry thunderbolt,
And breaks the fetters forged by sinners!
Let us sing! for free are they who sing:
Let us laugh! for they who laugh are winners!
Calmly, brightly, the heavens are shining!
Pouring joy o'er yon lagoon!
While rays, sent from the rising moon,
Blend with the sunset glow declining.
　　[pealing of bells in the distance, sound of trumpets
But hark! the joyous bells of St. Mark are
　　loudly pealing!
Cheers for our Republic and our Doge!

BAR. (*si muove dal posto. Dominando il frastuono festosamente*).
　　Compari! già le trombe
　　V' annuncian la regata.
Marinai (*correndo a sinistra*). Alla regata!
Popolo. Alla regata!
　　[gridando e saltando, il popolo esce dal cortile. Il
　　tumulto s' allontana.

BAR. (*coming forward*).
　　The Regatta now commences! The trumpets loud are pealing!

People. To the Regatta let us hasten. *[exeunt*

SCENA II.

BARNABA (solo).

BAR. (accennando gli spiragli delle prigioni sotterranee).
E danzan su lor tombe !
E la morte li guata!   [cupamente.
E mentre s' erge il ceppo o la cuccagna,
Fra due colonne tesse la sua ragna,
Barnaba, il cantastorie; e le sue file
                    [Guarda e tocca la sua chitarra.
Sono le corde di questo apparecchio.
Con lavorio sottile
E di mano e d' orecchio
Colgo i tanfani al volo
Per conto dello Stato.   E mai non falla
L' udito mio.   Coglier potessi solo
Per le mie brame e tosto
Una certa vaghissima farfalla!

SCENA III.

LA GIOCONDA colla CIECA entrando da destra, e detto.
La vecchia ha il volto coperto fin sotto gliocchi da un
severo zendado.

... (conducendo per mano la madre e avviandosi alla
chiesa lentamente) Madre adorata, vieni.
BAR. (scorge la GIO. e si ritrae accanto alla colonna.)
                    (Eccola ! al posto.)
CIECA. Figlia, che reggi il tremulo
Piè che all' avel già piega,
Beata è questa tenebra
Che alla tua man mi lega.
Tu canti agli uomini
Le tue canzoni,
Io canto agli angeli
Le mie orazioni
Benedicendo
L' ora e il destin,
E sorridendo
Sul mio cammin,
" Io per la tua bell' anima
" Prego chinata al suol,
" E tu per me coi vividi
" Sguardi contempli il sol.
GIO. Vien ! per securo tramite
Da me tu sei guidata.
Vien ! ricomincia il placido
Corso la tua giornata.
Tu canti agli angeli
Le tue orazioni
Io canto agli uomini
Le mie canzoni,
Benedicendo
L' ora e il destin,
E sorridendo
Sul mio cammin.
" Ed io pel tuo dimane
" A te guadagno il pane ;
" Tu col pregar fedel
" A me guadagni il ciel.

SCENE II.

BARNABA (alone)

BAR. (moodily, pointing to the gratings of the
subterranean prisons).
Above their graves they 're dancing!
Death upon them is stealing !
And while the reckless victims seek their
pleasure,
Here will I weave my nets for them at
leisure.
Stories, and songs, and legends, are attractions
Whose power no mortal e'er thinks of
denying!
I watch the listening gadflies, — note all
their actions,
And catch them while they 're flying.
Woe to them thereafter! — My ear, unfailing, has
worked their ruin!   Ah! how I am longing
to make my captive, at once and securely
the wayward Gioconda.

SCENE III.

Enter LA GIOCONDA, with LA CIECA.

GIO. (leading her mother by the hand, and advancing slowly toward the church).
This way, dear mother!
BAR. (aside).   She is here!
GIO. (to CIECA).   This way.
BAR. (aside).   I 'll hide me!
                    [Hides behind a column
CIECA. Daughter, in thee my faltering steps
Find guidance and protection;
I gratefully bless my loss of sight,
That heightens thy affection!
While thou into mankind thy songs art
singing,
To Heav'n my ceaseless pray'rs their flight
are winging,
For thee I pray, and render thanks to Fate
That left me sightless, — but not desolate

GIO. Place thy dear hand once more in mine
Thy steps I 'm safely guiding;
Here recommence thy daily life,
In calm contentment gliding.

BAR. (*in desparte*). (Sovr' essa stendere
La man grifagna!
Amarla e coglierla
Nella mia ragna!
Terribil estasi
Dell' alma mia!
Sta in guardia! l' agile
Farfalla spia!)

GIO. L' ora non giunse ancor del vespro sante!
Qui ti riposa appie del tempio ; intanto
Io vado a rintracciar l' angelo mio.

BAR. (*Derision!*)

GIO.   Torno con Enzo.

CIECA.   Iddio
Ti benedica.

GIO.   Taciturna ed erma.
Pace qui spira.

CIECA (*estrae da tasca un rosario*) Addio figliuola.

BAR. (*sbucando e sbarrando la via a* GIO., *che fa per escire da destra*).
                  Ferma.

GIO. Che ?

BAR. Un uom che t' ama, e che la via ti sbarra.

GIO Al diavol vanne colla tua chitarra !
        [*Vivacemente.*
Già l' altra volta tel dissi : funesta
M' è la tua faccia da mistero.
        [*Per andarsene.*

BAR. (*trattenendola e ironicamente*). Resta.
Enzo attender potrà.

GIO.   Va, ti disprezzo.

BAR. (*inculzando*). Ancor m' ascolterai.

GIO   Mi fai ribrezzo !

BAR Resta . . t' adoro, o vaga creatura.

GIO. Vanne !

BAR.   Non fuggirai ! [*Slandiandosi su*
         essa.

GIO.   Mi fai paura !
Ah !   [*Fugge.*

CIECA (*alzandosi spaventata*).
        Qual grido ! mia figlia ! Aita ! aita!
La voce sua !

BAR   (La farfalla è sparita. . .)

CIECA (*brancolando*).
Figliuola ! o raggio della mia pupilla,
Dove sei ? dove sei ?

BAR (*ridendo*). La Cieca strilla;
Lasciamola strillar.)

CIECA (*lentamente e protendendo le palme ritorna a sedersi sui gradini*). Tenebre orrende!

BAR. (*osservandola pensieroso*).
(Pur quella larva che la man protende.
Potrebbe agevolar la meta mia . .
Se la madre e in mia man . .

CIECA (*rigirando con fervore le Ave Marie del suo rosario*). Ave Maria.

BAR. (*sempre meditando*).
Tengo il cor della figlia incatenato . .

CIECA Ave Maria . .

BAR   . . con laccio inesorato.
L' angiol m' aiuti dell' amor materno,
E la Gioconda è mia ! Giuro all' Averno!)

BAR. (*aside*). With fiercest joy my soul would be enraptured
If in my net she were securely captured!
The wildest ecstasies within me waken!
Beware thee, moth, if in my net thou 't taken !

GIO. Erelong the vesper chimes will loud be ringing;
Here rest thee near the sacred shrine while — singing —
I seek him I love tenderly and truly

BAR. (Silly fool!)

GIO.   I 'll return with Enzo.

CIECA.   Heaven duly
Will bless thy footsteps! Adieu, my daughter! [*Takes rosary from her pocket*

BAR. (*quitting his hiding place and stopping* GIO.). Stay thee!

GIO. How?

BAR.   A man who loves thee, and bars thy onward progress.

GIO. Go thou to the devil, thou and thy guitar too!
Stand thou aside from my pathway! Away!
I love not faces full of myst'ry.

BAR.   Stay!
Enzo yonder can wait.

GIO.   Go! go! I despise thee.

BAR. Once more ; — say, wilt thou listen?

GIO. (*trying to pass* BAR.) At thee I shudder!

BAR. Stay, I adore thee, angelic creature!

GIO. Quit me.

BAR.   Ah no, thou shalt not fly me!

GIO. I hate and fear thee.
Ah!   [*Escapes from the grasp of* BAR.

CIECA. My daughter in danger. Help! No one hears me!
It was her voice.

BAR.   So the moth has escaped me!

CIECA. My daughter, sole ray o'er my existence beaming,
Where art thou? Where art thou?

BAR.   La Cieca is screaming,
Well let her scream her best!

CIECA.   O darkness fearful!

BAR. Yet may this spectral creature, weak and tearful,
Aid me to conquer thee, *Gioconda mia!*
(CIECA *has seated herself again by the church door.*)
Once the mother is mine —

CIECA. (*praying*).   Ave Maria!

BAR. Then the daughter to foil me in vain will endeavor.

CIECA. Ave Maria!

BAR.   She 's fettered fast forever!
Thanks to thine aid, angel of love maternal,
She shall be mine ; I swear it, powers infernal!

SCENA IV.

SCENE IV.

BARNABA, LA CIECA, ISÈPO, ZUÀNE, *Coro. Indi sei sgherri.* LA GIOCONDA, ENZO, *più tardi* LAURA, ALVISE. *Il Popolo porta in trionfo il* VINCITORE DELLA REGATA, *il quale tien alto il pallio verde (la bandiera del premio). Donne, Marinai, Fanciulli con fiori e ghirlande,* ZUÀNE *triste in disparte.*

Enter ISÈPO, ZUÀNE, LA GIODONDA, and ENZA, *afterwards* LAURA *and* ALVISE. *Chorus People, &c. bringing in triumph the victor in the regatta.*

Arsenalotti (al vincitore).   Polso di cerro!

Barnabotti (idem).   Occhio di lince!

Arsenalotti.   Remo di ferro!

Donne.   Gagliardo cor!

Tutti.   Gloria a chi vince
Il pallio verde!

Donne (guardando ZUÀ.).   Beffe a chi perde!

Tutti.   Lieta brigata,
Per lieto calle
Portiamo a spalle
Il vincitor
Della regata,
Fra canti e fior.
Gli sguardi avvince,
I flutti ei sperde!
Gloria a chi vince!
Beffe a chi perde!

[*Quasi tutti affluiscono verso la* SCALA DEI GIGANTI, *ove depongono il vincitore.*

Chorus.   Hail to the victor!
Wrists that are oaken!   Eyes of lynx!
Sinews of iron ! the victor hail !
Hail to the winner of the green banner !
Laugh at the losers !   Why did they fail,
Merry, light-hearted, onward we go,
With songs and with flowers our path to
    cheer;
Bearing the victor in the regatta
High on our shoulders — see him here !
[*They carry the victor to the foot of the Giant's Staircase.*
All eyes beheld him the waves dispersing;
Hail to the winner of the green banner !
Laugh at the losers !   Why did they fail ?

BAR. (*che gia da qualche tempo avrà osservato* ZUÀ. *lo arresta*).
(Questi è l' uomo ch' io cerco.   Non m' ingannc)
Patron Zuàne, hai faccia da malanno.
Si direbbe davver che alla regata
Non hai fatto bandiera.

ZUÀ.   T' inforchi Satanasso!

BAR.   E se la vera
Cagione io ti dicessi del tuo danno?

ZUÀ.   Lo so, la prora ho greve ed arrembata.

BAR.   Baje!

ZUÀ.   E che dunque?

BAR. (con mistero).   T' avvicina. — O lasso!
(sottovoce) Hai la barca stregata,

ZUÀ. (inorridito).   Vergine santa!

BAR.   Una malìa bieca
Sta sul tuo cap.   Osserva quella cieca . .

Coro (Accanto alla Scala dei Giganti.)

Arsenalotti.   Dadi e bambàra!
Cuccagne e corse!

Barnabotti.   Giuochiamo a zara
Le nostre borse!

Tutti.   Tentiam la mobile
Fortuna a gara.
Ginochiamo a zara.

[*alcuni estraggono dei dadi, molti si siedono sui gradini, e intavolano un giuoco di zara.*

BAR. (continuando e sempre facendo fissare CIECA a ZUÀ.). (La vidi stamani gittar sul tuo legno
Un segno maliardo, un magico segno.

ZUÀ.   Orror!

BAR.   La tua barca sarà la tua bara.
Sta in guardia, fratello!)

Arsenalotti.   Sei!

Barnabotti.   Cinque!

Arsenalotti.   Tre!

Tutti.   Zar

CIECA (pregando).   Turris eburnea...
Mistica rosa

BAR. (*who has been observing* ZUÀ.).
'T is he whom I was seeking.   I 'm ne'er
   mistaken.
How now, Zuàne? by fortune you 're forsaken.
If 't is true, as I 'm told, that in the race
You never once were seen leading ?

ZUÀ.   May Satan send you torments !

BAR.   Suppose the case
That I explained what cause has hindered
   your succeeding ?

ZUÀ.   I know; my boat was sadly overweighted.

BAR.   Nonsense.

ZUÀ.   What mean you ?

BAR.   Draw nearer.   'T was fated
'T was the spell of a sorceress.   Wherever
   you wander,
Witchcraft enfolds you.   Observe the blind
   woman yonder.

Chorus.   Dice and *Bambara!*
Races and frisking !
We 'll play at *Zara,*
Our purses risking.

BAR. (to ZUÀ.).
I saw her this morning throw over your
   line
Some foul spell of her witchcraft — a magical sign.

ZUÀ.   Alas!

BAR. (to ZUÀ.).
Lest thy barque be thy bier — through thy
   cara,
Be watchful, Zuàne. [*points to* CIECA

Chorus.   Six! Five! Three — Zara.

BAR. (*a* ZUÀ.). La vidi tre volte scagliar su tuoi remi
    Parole tremende —lugùbri anatèmi.

ZUÀ. *e* ISÈ. (ISÈ. *sarà mosso verso* BAR. *e ascoil'* *a curioso*). Gran Die!

BAR.   La tua barca sarà la tua bara.
    Sta in guardia, fratello . . .

Arsenalotti.   Sette!
Barnabotti.   Otto!
Arsenalotti.   Tre!
Tutti.   Zara.

CIECA (*come sopra*).   Turris Davidica. .
    Mater gloriosa..

BAR. (*come sopra*).
    Suo covo è un tugurio—laggiù alla Giudeca,
    Tien sempre quell' orrido zendado, ed è cieca. .
    Ha vuote le occhiaie — ma pure (e chi il crede ? !)
    La Cieca ci guarda — la Cieca ci vede!

4 *Marinai* (*che si saranno aggiunti al gruppo*). Ci vede !

ISÈ.   Oh spavento !

3 *Arsenalotti* (*aggiunto anch' essi al gruppo*).
    Che avvenne ?

ZUÀ.   Oh maliarda !

3 *Barnabotti.* Che avvenne? che mormori ?. .

BAR., ZUÀ., ISÈ.   La Cieca ci guarda !
    [*il gruppo si fa sempre più numeroso.*

Coro. Addosso ! accoppiamola !

ISÈ.   Coraggio. .

ZUÀ (*per avventarsi alla* CIECA, *poi retrocede*)
    Ho paura.

BAR. Badate, può cogliervi la sua jettatura.

Coro. Al rogo l' eretica !

ZUÀ.   Davver, più l'addocchio,
    Più i rai le balenano,

BAR. (*ridendo*). La Cieca ha il mal occhio.

Coro. Ah ! ah ! qual facezia !

ZUÀ.   (*ad* ISÈ. *che si sarà avvicinato pianamente alla* CIECA, *che gira sempre il rosario*)
    Che brontola ?

ISÈ.   Prega.

1 a. *parte del Coro.* Addosso alla strega !

2 a. *parte* (*si scagliano sulla* CIECA). Addosso alla strega !

BAR. (Già l' aure s' annuvolano,
    Già i nembi s' accumulano.
    Ah ! ah ! greggie umana !
    Scagliato ho il mio ciottolo,
    Or fuggo la frana !)

CIECA (*afferrata dal popolo e trascinata in mezzo al palco*). Aiuto !

Coro.   Mandràgora !

CIECA.   Ah ! chi mi trascina !
    Son Cieca !

Donne.   Vediamola salir la berlina !

Uomini. Ai piombi !

CIECA.   Soccorso ! soccorso !

Donne   Ai marrani !

Uomini. Ai pozzi !

Donne.   Fra Todero e Marco !

BAR. (*to* ZUÀ.). I heard her three times curse thy oars and thy rudder,
    In accents infernal, that made my soul shudder

ZUÀ. Great Heaven !

BAR. Lest thy barque be thy bier, through la cara,
    Be watchful, Zuàne!

Chorus.   Seven! Eight! Six! — Zara !

BAR. (*to* ZUÀ. *and* ISÈ.).
    Her den is a cabin, hard by the Giudeca;
    And there with the demons, her companions, dwells la Cieca.
    Her eye-sockets are empty, yet that will not free you.
    La Cieca is watchful, la Cieca can see you.

Sailors. (*who have drawn nigh*). Can see us !

ISÈ. Hateful monster !

Laborers. What has happened?

ZUÀ.   Heaven free us !

4 *Monks.* What has happened? What mean these cries?

BAR., ZUÀ. *and* ISÈ. La Cieca can see us !

Chorus. Upon her! Let us bind her fast!

ZUÀ. (*venturing toward* CIECA).
    Now, courage! Ah! I fear her!

BAR. Be careful! Lest she bewitch ye, if ye go near her.

Chorus. We 'll burn the old heretic !

ZUÀ.   The more I look at her
    More spiteful her glances seem!

BAR. (*mockingly*). The evil-eyed Cieca !

Chorus. The evil-eyed Cieca? — ha, ha!
    A blind woman's glances? — ha, ha!

BAR. (*aside*). (Already the clouds gather fast.)

ZUÀ. (*to* ISÈ.). What 's she about ?

ISÈ.   Praying.

ZUÀ. *and Chorus.* Her pray'rs she 's backward saying.

CIECA. (*seized by the populace, and dragged into the middle of the stage*).
    O, help me! I 'm sightless! Have mercy! Help!

BARN. (*aside*). (The ball I 've sent rolling, now on let it wander.)

(*To the Guards.*)

    Friends, there lodge her in prison

BAR. (*ad una pattuglia di sgherri in disparte*).
Sgherrani,
Sia tratta nel carcere.
Uomini. Al rogo!
Donne. Alla pira
Tutti (*sghignazzando*). Ah! ah!
CIECA. Santa Vergine!
Donne. Martira!
Tutti. Martira!
BAR. (Ho in man la mia vittima, ho in man due destini.)
Tutti. A morte la strega!
GIO. (*rientrando e slanciandosi*). Mia madre!
ENZO. (*vestito da marinaio dalmato, rompendo la calca con uno scoppio d' ira*). Assassini!
Assassini! quel crin venerando
Rispettate! o ch' io snudo il mio brando
Contro un' egra rejetta dal sole
Generosa è la vostra tenzon!
Vituperio! è cresciuta una prole
Di codardi all' alato leon!

Coro. Iddio vuol ciò che il popolo vuole;
No, la strega non merta perdon.
CIECA. Ah! su me si scatena l' averno!
GIO. Niun mi tolga all' amplesso materno!
CIECA. Figlia. .

Coro. A morte!
ENZO. (*con impeto far per togliere i ceppi alla CIECA, ma è impedito dal popolo*). Quel ceppo la strazia.
Sciolta sia.
Coro. La vogliam giudicare.
Spenta sia!
ENZO. (*correndo all' ingresso della riva furiosa mente ed esce*). Su, fratelli del mare!
Alla lotta!
Coro. Al patibolo!
[*Intanto sull' alto della scata saranno apparsi ALV. e LAU., che avranno assistito al tumulto*
LAU. (*dall' alto della scala, scendendo. Il lembo della sua veste sarà sostenuto da due paggi. Ha una maschera di velluto nero sul volto.*)

(*Aside*). Ha, ha! the fools yonder!
Chorus. The pillory steps she will soon be ascending!
To the Piombi! the Pozzi! The sorceress shall suffer! [*Enter* GIO. *with* ENZO
CIECA. Mercy! I 'm sightless! Help!
Chorus. We 'll destroy her, we 'll burn her!

GIO. (*rushes toward* LA CIECA). My mother!
ENZO. Base assassins!
Base assassins! these locks, gray and scattered,
Harm no longer! My sword shall protect them!
'Gainst a woman, old, feeble, and sightless
It is noble and safe to contend!
Ye are monsters! Descendants or heroes
All are cowards, yon wing'd lion disgracing
Chorus. No! Heav'n wills what the populace wills
The sorceress' life now must end.
ENZO. Let me free her! these fetters will kill her
GIO. Mother, darling!
ENZO. Quick release her, base assassins!
Quick release her.
Chorus. We will bring her to trial.
ENZO (*calling out at the back of the stage*).
Rise, comrades, rise, for mercy meets denial.
Now for fighting, for fighting!
CIECA. On me hell's fury is lighting.
Chorus. Burn her! destroy her!
[LAU. *and* ALV. *are seen at the head of the staircase about to descend.* LAU. *wearing a black mask descends the staircase, while* LA CIECA *is struggling with her persecutors.*
Chorus Destroy her!
LAU. Mercy!

SCENA V.

LA CIECA, GIOCONDA, ALVISE, LAURA, BAR-
NABA, Coro, poi ENZO.

ALV. (alteramente e con gravità).
Ribellion! che? la plebe or qui si arroga
Fra le ducali mure
I dritti della toga
E della scure
[Movimento di rispetto nella folla.
Parla, o captiva!
Perchè stai china là fra quelle squadre?
Coro. È una strega!
GIO. E mia madre!
LAU. (la CIECA alza ta testa).
È Cieca! o mio signor! fa ch' essa viva!

ALV. (freddamente a BAR.). Barnaba! è rea
costei?
BAR. (assai sottovoce all' orecchio d' ALV.). Di male-
fizio.
GIO. (a BAR.). T' ho udito! . . menti!
ALV. Sia tratta in giudizio.
GIO. (gettasi ai piedi di ALV.).
Pietà . . ch' io parli attendete ora infrango
Il gel che m' impietrava . . e sgorga l' onda
Del cor . . Costei della mia infanzia bionda
L' angelo fu . . Sempre ho sorriso . . or
piango.
Mi chiaman . . la Gioconda.
Viviam cantando ed io
Canto a chi vuol le mie liete canzoni,
Ed essa santa a Dio
Le sue sante orazioni. . .
ENZO (che sarà ritornato da qualche tempo seguito dai
marinai dalmati). Salviamo l' innocente.
LAU. (scorgendo ENZO). Qual volto!
GIO. (alzandosi e trattenendo ENZO).
Ah! no! ti ferma! Quel possente
La salverà!
BAR. (osservando LAU., poi ENZO).
(Come lo guarda fiso!)
LAU. (ad ALV. in disparte).
("Concedi, o mio signor, se non ti duole,
"Ch' io mi levi la maschera dal viso.")
ALV. "No, madonna, nemmen l' occhio del sole
"Non dee mirarti.")
GIO. (ad ALV.). Dalle tue parole
La vita attendo.
BAR. (ad ALV. sottovoce). È una strega, il nefario
Suo silenzio tel dica.
LAU. Essa ha un rosario!
No, l' inferno non è con quella pia.
ENZO. (Qual voce!)
BAR. Muoia!
LAU. (ad ALV. supplichevole). La salva!
ALV. E salva sia.

BAR. (Furore!!)
GIO. Gioia!!
CIECA (liberata da LAU. che l' allontana dagli
Sgherri).

SCENE V.

LA CIECA, GIOCONDA, ALVISE, LAURA, BAR-
NABA, and Chorus, afterward ENZO.

ALV. (imperiously). Rebellion? What? the popu-
lace can venture here, near our Ducal
Palace — to claim to act as judges? — and
as executioners? (To CIECA.) Answer me,
captive. Why art thou kneeling to yonder
people?
Chorus. She 's a sorceress.
LAU. (toward whom LA CIECA has turned her face).
She 's sightless, see, signor! save her from
outrage!
ALV. (aside to BAR.). Barnaba, has she been
guilty?
BAR. (aside to ALV.). Guilty of witchcraft.
GIO. (to BAR.). I heard thee! Thou liest!
ALV. To trial conduct her
GIO. (kneeling to ALV.).
Mercy! ah, hear me one moment! I break
The ice that in fetters my soul was keeping!
She of my life has been the angel bright,
I once was ever smiling, now I 'm weeping
" La Gioconda " they call me.
We are always singing; to all comers
I sing my gay songs till day 's ending;
While gentle strains of pious rapture
Are from her pure lips ascending.

ENZO (to his Sailors).
We will save the innocent victim.
LAU. (observing him). (Those features?)
GIO. (to ENZO). Ah, no! have patience! The
Duke will protect La Cieca.

BAR. (aside, watching ENZO and LAU.).
(His gaze is fixed upon her.)

GIO. (to ALV.).
Thou alone hast power to save my mother.
BAR. She is a sorceress! her guilty silence be-
trays her.
LAU. She bears a rosary. Satan has naught to
do with this pious woman.
ENZO (observing LAU.). (Those accents!)
BAR. Burn her!
LAU. (to ALV.). O save her!
ALV. She is saved, and pardoned!
GIO. Ah, joy!
BAR. (They foil me!)
GIO. What rapture!
CIECA (to LAU.)

CIECA'S SONG.

English version by L. M. UNDERWOOD.

Andante sostenuto.
p dolciss espress.

CIECA. Light to my dark soul bring-est me, Thy voice that's an-gel-ic, yet hu-man;
Vo-ce di don-na o d'an-ge-lo, le mi-e ca-te-ne ha sciol-to;

allarg.

Oh, could thy bless-ed coun-te-nance My poor blind eyes, my poor blind eyes il-lu-mine!
Mi vie-tan le mie te-ne-bre Di quel-la san-ta, di quel-la san-ta il vol-to,
affrett.

rall.

Now ere we part, thou'lt mer-ci-ful, Yes, thou wilt mer-ci-ful grant me this one re-
Pu-re da me non par-ta-si, Da me non par-ta-si, sen-za un pie-to-so
in tempo.

-quest: Ah! Ah! I'd give to thee this ro-sa-ry,
don, No! No! A te que-sto ro-sa-ri-o,

With all my pray'rs con-nect-ed. Take it: thy fu-ture hap-pi-ness Shall be there
Che le pre-ghie-re a-du-na, Io te lo par-go, ac-cett-a-lo, Ti por-te-

-by pro-tect-ed, And o'er thee watching ten-der-ly, My blessing on thee
ra for-tu-na Sul-la tua te-sta vi-gi-li la mia be-ne-di-
espandendosi. *allarg molto.* *a tempo.*

rest,...... Yes, o'er the watch-ing, yes o'er thee watch-ing ten-der-ly....... My
zion,...... Sul-la tua te-sta, sul-la tua te-sta vi-gi-li......... La

blessing shall on thee..... rest, My bless-ing on thee
mi-a be-ne-di-- zion, La mia be-ne-di-

rest, Ten-der-ly,...... ten-der-ly. Ah! yes, o'er thee watching
zion, Vi-gi-li,...... vi-gi-li. Ah! sul-la tua te-sta

ten-der-ly, my bless-ing shall on thee rest..........
vi-gi-li la mi-a be-ne-di-- zion........

ALV. (a BAR   damente mentre canta la CIECA).
(Barnaba!)
BAR.   Mio padron.
ALV.   Facesti buona caccia
Quest' oggi?
BAR.   Sulla traccia
Cammino d' un leon.
LAU. ed ENZO.   Ascolti il dette pio
L' onnipossente Iddio!
GIO.   O madre mia, ti guarda
Un angelo fedel.
Coro.   Protegge la vegliarda
Visibilmente il ciel!
[LAU. s' avvicina alla CIECA e prende il rosario, la
CIECA stende le mani come per benedirla, LAU. fa
per i´ginocchiarsi, ALV. vede e afferra il braccio di
LAU. sforzandola a rialzarsi.
ALV. (a LAU.).   Che fai? vaneggi?
[Gettando una borsa a GIO.
Bella cantatrice,
Quest' oro a te.
GIO. (raccoglie e s' inchina).   Sia grazia a voi,
Mesere. (a LAU.)   Acciò ch' io l' abbia
nelle mie preghiere.   Dimmi il tuo nome,
o ignota salvatrice.

LAU. (guardando ENZO).   Laura.
ENZO (colpito).   (È dessa!)
ALV. (a LAU. assorta).   Ti scuoti! al tempio andiamo!
GIO. Madre! — Enzo adorato! Ah! come t' amo!
[Tutti si dirigono al tempio. ALV. e LAU. primi, i due
paggi dopo, indi tutto il Coro, e GIO. fra la madre ed
ENZO. Giunto alla porta della chiesa, ENZO s'
arresta, e rimane indietro assorto profondamente ne'
suoi pensieri. BAR. lo sta fissando. La scena si
vuota.

GIO.   Ah, mother,'t was an angel, sent down from
yonder heaven!
LAU. and ENZO.   The pious pray'rs she utters,
may they be heard in heaven!
Chorus.   'T is evident unto her celestial aid is
given.
ALV. (to BAR.).   Barnaba!
BAR.   Signor!
ALV.   Say, have you had good hunting to-day?
BAR.   I'm in chase of a lion, gone astray.

[LAU. approaches LA CIECA, and takes the rosary. LA
CIECA extends her hands as if to bless LAU., who
kneels before her. ALV. abruptly seizes the arm
of LAU., and compels her to rise.
ALV. (to LAU.).   What now?   'T is folly.
(To GIO.)   Pretty singing maiden.
This gold is thine. [Giving purse to GIO.
GIO.   Thanks, signor !
(To LAU.)   That I may never in my prayers for-
get it,
Tell me thy name, unknown, generous
benefactress.
LAU. (looking at ENZO).   Laura.
ENZO (aside).   'T is she!
ALV. (to LAU.).   Arouse thee.   To church let us
hasten.
GIO.   Beloved mother! Enzo, how I love thee!
[Exeunt all into the church, except ENZO, who stands ab
sorbed in thought, and BAR., who watches him intently

SCENA VI.

ENZO e BARNABA.

BAR. (avvicinandosi ad ENZO).
Enzo Grimaldo, Principe di Santaflor, che
pensi?
ENZO.   (Scoperton son.)
BAR.   Qual magico stupor t' invade i sensi?
Pensi a Madonna Laura d' Alvise Badoèro.

ENZO. (scosso).   Chi sei?
BAR. So tutto: e penetro in fondo al tuo pensiero.
Avesti culla in Genova. .

ENZO   Prence non son, sui flutti
Guido un vascel, son dalmato: Enzo Gior-
dan. .
BAR.   Per tutti
Ma non per me.   Venezia t' ha proscritto,
ma un forte
Disio qui ancor ti trasse ad affrontar la
morte.
Amasti un dì una vergine — là, sul tuo mar
beato,
A estranio imene vittima — la condannava
il fato.

SCENE VI.

ENZO and BARNABA.

BAR. (approaching ENZO).   Enzo Grimaldo,
Prince of Santa Fior, thou art pensive.
ENZO (aside).   (I am discovered.)
BAR.   What magic stupor steals away thy senses?
'T is of the Lady Laura, Alvise's wife.
thou 'rt thinking.
ENZO.   Who art thou?
BAR.   I know all; can penetrate
Thy thoughts, however secret.   Thy birth-
place was Genoa!
ENZO.   Prince I am not, but sailor.   Yonder's
my ship.
I am Dalmatian, Enzo Giordan.
BAR.   For others.
But not for me.   Proscribed thou wert by
Venice,   [pulse,
Yet hither thou art led, by chainless im-
Thy life to peril.   Thou didst love a maiden
Yonder, in thine own Genoa, but she
Another's bride became.   Fate to ye both
was cruel.

ENZO. Giurai fede a Gioconda.
BAR. (*sorridendo*).   La cantatrice errante
Ami come sorella, e Laura come amante.
Già disperavi in terra di riveder quel volto,
E l' amor di Gioconda hai per pietà raccolto,
Ed or, sotto la maschera l' angelo tuo t' apparve. .
Ti riconobbe. .

ENZO.   (Oh giubilo!)
BAR.   L' amor passa le larve.
Sulla sua sposa vigila con cuor geloso, il tetro
Inquisitor, nell' aurea prigione io sol penetro,
E spesso fra le lagrime io la sorpresi, e muto
Lo sguardo suo mestissimo al ciel chiedeva aiuto.
Badoër questa notte — veglia al dogale ostello
Col Gran Consiglio, Laura sarà sul tuo vascello.

ENZO. Dio di pietà!
BAR.   'Le angosce dell' amor tuo soccorro.
ENZO. O grido di quest' anima, scoppia dal gonfio core!
Ho ritrovato l' angelo del mio celeste amore.)
Ma alfin ch' sei? mio lugubre benefattor?

BAR.   T' abborro.
[*Apre il suo mantello e la giubba e mostra sul giustacuore queste lettere in argento* "C. X."
Sono il possente démone del *Consiglio dei Dieci*
Leggi.
ENZO.   Infamia!
BAR.   Al supplizio trarti potea, nol feci.
Gioconda amo, essa m' odia. . giurai schiantarle il cor.
Enzo morto era poco — ti volli traditor.

ENZO. "O sàtana furente, lordo di sangue e fiel.
" Coll' ira tua demente tu m' hai scagliato in ciel.
(Gran Dio! la togli all' orrida condanna di dolor,
L' idolatrata Laura a me ridona ancor.)
BAR. Va: corri al tuo desio: spiega le vele in mar,
Tutto il trionfo mio negli occhi tuoi m' appar.
Ebbene?
ENZO.   A notte bruna sul brigantino aspetto Laura.
BAR. (*inchinandosi e sogghignando*). Buona fortuna!
ENZO (*sul limitare della scena*). E tu sia maledetto!
[*Esce.*

ENZO. I have pledged my faith to Gioconda.
BAR. Poor wand'ring ballad-singer!
Her thou dost love as sister, but Laura as thy mistress.
Thou hadst all hope abandoned, dreamed not to see her features,
But here, under her velvet mask, thy beauteous angel saw thee,
And recognized thee.

ENZO.   O happiness!
BAR.   Love sees through disguises.
All this night will her husband stay at the Doge's palace,
With the Great Council. Laura shall be on board thy vessel.

ENZO. Powers divine!
BAR.   Love's sweetest consolations await thee.
ENZO. Ah, with what joy my heart is filled,
Fortune at last is kind!
Soon shall I clasp the angel-form
In this fond heart enshrined.
But who art thou, O gloomy messenger of joy?
BAR. I hate thee! I am the demon-in-chief
Of the Council of Ten. Read this Beware thee!
[*Opens his dress, and shews the letters* "C.X." (*Council of Ten*) *embroidered in silver on his vest.*

ENZO. Oh horror!   [spare thee
BAR. To thy doom at once I could bring thee.
Gioconda loves thee, hates me fiercely;
I have sworn to crush her heart.
Enzo's death would little serve me;
She must learn how false thou art.
ENZO (*aside*). Kind heaven, to her thy mercy show,
Save her from grief and pain;
But ah, sweet Laura, my adored,
Bring to my arms again!
BAR. (*to* ENZO). Go! not a moment lose,
Spread thy white sails to the skies,
I can my triumph read
In each glad glance of thine eyes.
Well?
ENZO. When the dark night falls, on board my ship I shall wait my Laura.
BAR. (*sneeringly*). Good luck attend you!
NZO. And thou — be thou accursed! [*Exit*

SCENA VII.

BARNABA, *poscia* ISÈPO, *indi per un instante* LA GIO-
CONDA *e* LA CIECA.

BAR. Maledici? sta ben . . l' amor t' accieca.
Compiam l' opra bieca,
L' idolo di Gioconda sia distrutto . .
S' annienti tutto.
[*Va nel fondo, apre una porta accanto le prigioni.*
Isèpo!
ISÈPO (*escendo*). Padron barnaba . .
BAR. Scrivano,
L' anima m' hai venduto e la contenna
Fin che tu vivi; [*lo conduce al banco.*
In son la mano
E tu la penna.
Scrivi. [*dettando.*
AL CAPO OCCULTO DELL' INQUISIZIONE.
[Isèpo *scrive. Intanto alla porta del tempio apparis-
cono* GIOCONDA *e* LA CIECA.
GIO. (Ti nascondi, c'è Barnaba.)
[*Alla madre ritraendola e sta spiando nascosta dal
pilastro.*
BAR. LA TUA SPOSA CON ENZO IL MARINAR.
GIO. (Oh ciel!)
STA NOTTE IN MAR
TI FUGGIRÀ SUL BRIGANTINO DALMATO.
GIO. Ah! [*Disperatamente e scompare in chiesa.*
BAR. Più sotto: LA BOCCA DEL LEONE.
Qua, porgi, taci, vanne.
[*Prende il foglio,* ISÈPO *esce.*

SCENA VIII.

BARNABA *solo.*

BAR. (*col piego in mano contemplando la scena*).
O monumento!
Regia e bolgia dogale! Atro portento!
Gloria di questa e delle età future;
Ergi fra due torture
Il porfido cruento.
Tua base i *pozzi*, tuo fastigio i *piombe*
Sulla tua fronte il volo dei palombi,
I marmi e l'ôr.
Gioia tu alterni e orror con vece occulta.
Quivi un popolo esulta,
Quivi un popolo muor.
Là il Doge, un muto scheletro
Coll' acidaro in testa,
Sovr' esso il Gran Consiglio,
La Signoria funesta;
Sovra la Signoria
Più possente di tutti, un re ; la spia.
O monumento! Apri le tue latèbre,
[*Vicino alla bocca del leone.*
Spalanca la tua fauce di lenèbre,
S' anco il sangue giungesse a soffocarla!
Io son l' orecchio e tu la bocca: Parla!
[*Getta il piego nella bocca del leone ed esce.*

SCENE VII.

BARNABA, ISÈPO, LA GIOCONDA, *and* LA CIECA.

BAR. Accursed? We shall see. 'T is love that
blinds thee.
Should my dark plots be successful,
This idol of Gioconda's will be shattered.
And dashed to pieces. Isèpo!
[*Calling at a door near the prison. Enter* Isa.
ISA. Padron Barnaba!
BAR. Now, penman, long since thy soul to me
thou didst sell;
Thy skin also, to save thy life.
I am the hand, and thou art **the pen.**
Write! [*Enter* GIO. *and* CIECA *from the
church.*
BAR. (*to* ISA.).
" Unto the secret chief of the inquisition—
GIO. (*to* CIECA). Quick conceal thee. 'T is Bar-
naba.
[*They hide behind a column.* GIO. *listens*
BAR. "Thy wife will with Enzo, the young
sailor,
This night elope; will sail away from thee
On board his vessel."
GIO Ah! [*Exeunt* GIO *and* CIECA *into the churc.*
BAR Now, lower down,
" The Mouth of the Lion." Give it me
Silence! Go! [*Exit* Isa

SCENE VIII.

BARNABA, *alone.*

BAR. (*contemplating the palace*).
O mighty monument, palace and den of the
Doges!
Gloomy and wondrous, glory of this age
And of the ages yet unborn,
Between twin tortures glistens
Thy porphyry ensanguined!
Below are the Pozzi, 'neath thy roof the
Piombi;
Thy front is gay, with its fearless flocks of
pigeons.
Its marble and gold.
Joy thou dost alternate with woe, in work
ings secret.
Here is a nation exulting; there a nation
dies.
There the Doge, an ancient skeleton,
Sits in state, in his headdress quaint;
Above him, the Great Council — sinister
oligarchy!
Over the oligarchs, far more powerful than
they,
A King — the Spy!
O mighty monument, open thy jaws capa-
cious!
Spread wide thy throat, that waits in sullen
darkness,
Until blood, poured in torrents, shall choke
it forever!
I am the ear, and thou the mouth-piece
Speak!
[*Throws the letter into the Lion's Mouth, and ex-*

SCENA IX.

Entra nel cortile una Mascherata; la segue il popolo cantando e danzando. Poscia un Barnabotto, GIOCONDA e LA CIECA.

Coreo e Danza.   Viva il Doge e la Repubblica!
    La baldoria e el carnevale!
    Baccanale! Baccanale!!
    Gaia turba popolana
    Su! correte al torneamento!
    Su! danzate la *furlana!*
    Chiome al sol! zendadi al vento!
    Fate un chiasso da demóni
    Colle palme e coi talloni!
    Tuoni il portico ducale
    Sovra il pazzo baccanale!
    si odono alcuni tocchi di campana.

Voci interne (dalla chiesa). Angelus Domini . . .
    cessa la danza.

Un Barnabotto (schiudendo la tenda che copre la porta della basilica).   Tramonta il sol.

    Udite il canto
    Del vespro santo
    Prostrati al suol.
    [tutti si prostrano rivolti verso il fondo.

LA GIOCONDA e LA CIECA attraversano la folla inginocchiata mentre dura l'orazione.

GIO. (*con passo vacillante, lentissimo, appoggiandosi alla CIECA*).
    Tradita?.. Ahimè!.. soccombo.. il fianco mio
    Vacilla.. o madre.. mi soreggi.   O Dio!
    Cuore! dono funesto!
    Retaggio di dolor!
    Il mio destino è questo!
    O Morte o Amor!

CIECA. Dimmi dov' è il tuo cor! la man vi guida..
    Ch' io lo posi sul mio!
    Vieni e facciamo un sol di due dolor!

GIO. (*prendendo la mano della CIECA e portandosela al cuore*). Ah sì! la mano tua sovra il mio cor!
    Senti e comprendi, o madre, il mio dolor!
    si slancia fra le braccia della CIECA.

Voci interne. Angelus Domini ..
La Folla (inginocchiata). Glor a al Signor
    E pace agli uomini!   [*cala lentamente la tela.*

        FINE DELL' ATTO I.

SCENE IX.

Enter Masquers and Populace, dancing and singing

Chorus. Carnival! Baccanal!
    Day's last beams are o'er as glancing,
    Let us pass our time in dancing
    La Furlana!

BALLET.

Chorus (inside the church). Angele Dei.
Chorus (on the stage).   Glory to God!

A Monk (to the people, drawing aside the curtain from before the door of the church).
    The sun sinks low, the vesper hymn is pealing;
    Now listen to the holy strain, devoutly kneeling.

Chorus. Angele Dei, qui custos es mei,
    Me, tibi commissum, nocte illumina,
    Rege, custodi et rege,
    Rege et guberna, custodi,
    Angele Dei, qui custos es mei.

[*While the vesper prayer is being sung, enter GIO. and LA CIECA from the church. GIO. is supported by LA CIECA.*

GIO.   Forsaken! Betrayed! All is over! In every limb
    I am trembling. Thou must support me dear mother.
    O heart, gone is thy gladness!
    Thy heritage is sadness!
    My doom was framed by pow'rs above:
    To die! to die, if robbed of love!
    Upon my heart, dear mother,
    Place thy hand, and thou 'lt know,
    The while it throbs so wildly,
    How great, alas, my woe!

CIECA.   Ah, come, my child, my darling,
    Hand in hand let us go,
    One grief of two griefs making.
    Sharing each other's woe!

Chorus. Angele Dei, qui custos es mei. etc.

        END OF ACT I.

ATTO II

IL ROSARIO.

Notte. Un brigantino visto di fianco. Sul davanti una riva deserta d' isola disabitata nelle acque di Fusina. Nell' estremo fondo il cielo in qualche parte stellato, e la laguna; a destra la luna tramonta dietro una nube. Sul davanti un altarino della Vergine con una lampada rossa accesa. "HECATE," il nome del brigantino, sta scritto a prua. Alcune lanterne sul ponte.

All' alzarsi della tela alcuni Marinai sono seduti sulla tolda, altri in piedi aggruppati; tutti hanno un portavoce in mano; molti Mozzi sono arrampicati, o seduti, o sospesi alle sartie degli alberi e stanno cantando una marinaresca.

SCENA I.

MARINARESCA.

Primi Marinai (a destra sul ponte cantando attraverso il portavoce).
Ha! He! Ha! He!
Fissa il timone!
Secondi Marinai (a sinistra col portavoce).
Fissa!
Ha! He! Ha! He!
Issa artimone!
Primi Marinai. Issa!
La ciurma ov' è?
Primi e Secondi Marinai.
Ha! He! Ha! He!
Mozzi (ragazzi sulle antenne).
Siam qui sui culmini,
Siam sulla borda,
Siam sulle tremule
Scale di corda.
Guardate gli agili
Mozzi saltar:
Noi gli scoiattoli
Siamo del mar.
Marinai (sotto la tolda, nel cassero).
Siam nel fondo più profondo
Della nave, della cala,
Dove il vento furibondo
Spreca i fischi e infrange l' ala
Siam nel fondo più profondo
Della nave, della cala.
Primi Marinai (sul ponte).
Ha! Ho! Ha! Ho!
Vele a babordo!
Secondi Marinai. Issa!
Ha! Ho! Ha! Ho!
Remi a tribordo!
Primi Marinai. Issa!
Il ciel tuonò!
Ha! Ho! Ha! Ho!
Mozzi (sulle antenne).
In mezzo ai fulmini
Delle tempesta,
Noi tra le nuvole

ACT II.

THE ROSARY.

Night. A brigantine, showing its starboard side. In front, the deserted bank of an uninhabited island in the Fusina Lagoon. In the farthest distance, the sky and the lagoon. A few stars visible On the right, a cloud, above which the moon is rising. In front, a small altar of the Virgin, lighted by a red lamp. The name of the brigantine — "Hecate" — painted on the prow. Lanterns on deck.

At the rising of the curtain Sailors are discovered; some seated on the deck, others standing in groups each with a speaking-trumpet. Several Midshipmen are seen; some clinging to the shrouds, some seated. Remaining thus grouped, they sing a Marinaresca.

SCENE I.

Sailors (on deck, singing through speaking-trumpets)
Ho, he! ho, he!
Look to the rudder!
Ho, he! ho, he!

1st Sailor.   Look well!

2d Sailor.   Look well!
Ho, he! ho, he!
Up with the mainsail!
Up with it!
Where are the rowers?

1st Sailor.   Ay! where?

All.   Ho, he! ho, he!
Rowers, reply!

Basses (under the deck in the hold).
Here are we, in depths profoundest
Of the vessel; in the hold,
While angry winds, in fury howling
Shriek, while rending sails to tatters
Here are we, in depths profoundest

Tuffiam la testa
Come sugli alberi
D' una foresta,
Osiam le pendule
Sartie scalar.
Noi gli scoiattoli
Siaom del mar.

Marinai (*sotto il ponte*).

Sotto prora, sotto poppa
È una placida dimora,
Qui vuotiam l' ardente coppa
Del liquor che inganna l' ora.
Sotto poppa, sotto prora.

Mozzi (*sulle antenne*).

Il mar mugghiante,
Il ciel furente,
Greco a Levante,
Bora a Ponente,
Scioni e turbini
Sappiam sfidar.
Noi gli scoiattoli
Siamo del mar !

Una Voce Sola (*di dentro*).

BAR.   Pescator, affonda l' esca,
E sia l' onda a te fedel,
Lieta sera e buona pesca
Ti promette il mare e il ciel.

Midshipmen and Boys.

We 're here ; some perched aloft, some on the
      gunwale,
Some to the tremulous rope-ladders clinging
See how the nimble midshipmen can climb !
Behold in us the squirrels of the sea !

1st Midshipman.   Ho, he ! ho, he !

BAR. (*from behind*).

Fisher-boy, thy bait now lower ;
May the waves prove true to thee !

                              [*He enters*

Now good night !   May luck attend thee !

SCENA II.

Coro, BARNABA, ISEPO.

BARNABA *è vestito da pescatore con una rete in mano.*

Il Pilota.   Chi va là?

BAR.   La canzon ve lo dicea :

Un pescator che attende la marea.

Ho la barca laggiù nell' acqua bassa.

È tempora domani, e si digiuna,

(Per mia fortuna)

La mensa magra il pescatore ingrassa.

Marinai (*ridendo*).   Ha ! Ha !

BAR. (*ad* ISE.).   (Siam   salvi !   Han riso.   Sono
      ottanta

Fra marinari e mozzi.   Han tre decine

Di remi e nulla più ; due colubrine

Di piccolo calibro.   Or va, con quanta

Lena ti resta, e disponi le scolte

Colà dove le macchie son più folte.

Io qui rimango a far l' ufficio mio.

Vanne con Dio.)   [*Ise esce.*

SCENE II.

Chorus, BARNABA, ISEPO.

A Pilot.   Who goes there?

BAR.   My song itself will tell you.
I am a fisher ; for the tide I am waiting,
And my boat waits for me
In yon deep waters.
To-morrow is a fast day.   When people fast
They bring me good fortune :
And but for fast days, fishermen ne'er would
      fatten.

Sailors (*laughing*).   Ha ! Ha !

BAR. (*to* ISE.).   We are safe now !   They 're laugh
      ing.   They, in all,
Number eighty, men and boys.   They have
      three ranks
Of ten oars each, and no more ; only two cul-
      verins,
Both of small calibre.   Now go, with all
The breath that is left thee, and place out
      the scouts
Down yonder, where the bushes are thickest
I here remain, till the moment comes for
      action.
Heaven go with thee.   [*Exit Ise.*

"FISHER-BOYS, YOUR BOATS MAKE READY."

English adaptation by THEO. T. BARKER.

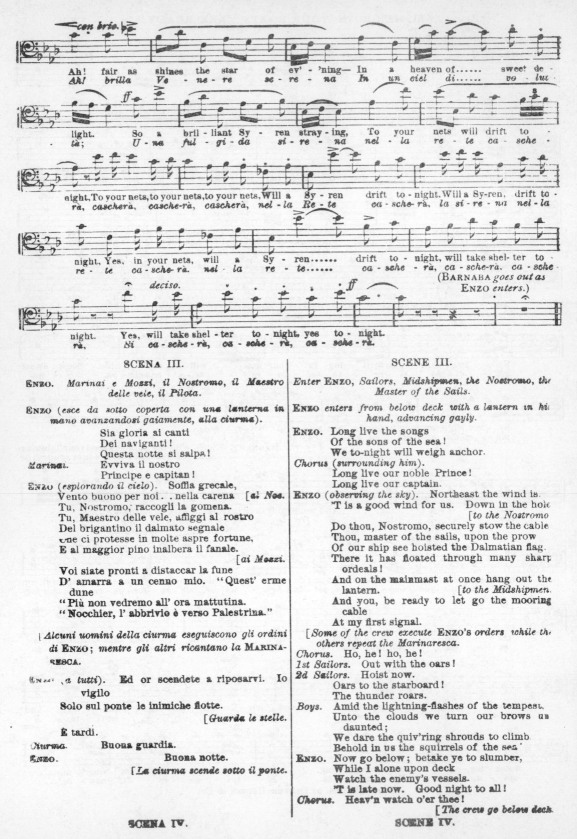

Ah! fair as shines the star of ev'-'ning— In a heaven of...... sweet de-
Ah! brilla Ve-ne-re se-re-na In un ciel di...... vo-lut-

light. So a bril-liant Sy-ren stray-ing, To your nets will drift to-
tà; U-na ful-gi-da si-re-na nel-la re-te ca-sche-

night, To your nets, to your nets, to your nets, Will a Sy-ren drift to-night. Will a Sy-ren, drift to-
rà, caschera, casche-rà, caschera, nel-la Re-te ca-sche-rà, la si-re-na nel-la

night, Yes, in your nets, will a Sy-ren...... drift to-night, will take shel-ter to-
re-te ca-sche-rà. nel-la re-te...... ca-sche-rà, ca-sche-rà, ca-sche-

(BARNABA *goes out as* ENZO *enters.*)

night. Yes, will take shel-ter to-night, yes to-night.
rà, Si ca-sche-rà, ca-sche-rà, ca-sche-rà.

SCENA III.	SCENE III.
ENZO. *Marinai e Mozzi, il Nostromo, il Maestro delle vele, il Pilota.*	Enter ENZO, *Sailors, Midshipmen, the Nostromo, the Master of the Sails.*
ENZO (*esce da sotto coperta con una lanterna in mano avanzandosi gaiamente, alla ciurma*).	ENZO *enters from below deck with a lantern in his hand, advancing gayly.*

Sia gloria ai canti
  Dei naviganti!
  Questa notte si salpa!
	ENZO. Long live the songs
	  Of the sons of the sea!
	  We to-night will weigh anchor.

Marinai. Evviva il nostro
  Principe e capitan!
	Chorus (*surrounding him*).
	  Long live our noble Prince!
	  Long live our captain.

ENZO (*esplorando il cielo*). Soffia grecale,
 Vento buono per noi . . nella carena [*ai Nos.*
 Tu, Nostromo, raccogli la gomena.
 Tu, Maestro delle vele, affiggi al rostro
 Del brigantino il dalmato segnale
 Che ci protesse in molte aspre fortune,
 E al maggior pino inalbera il fanale.
        [*ai Mozzi.*
 Voi siate pronti a distaccar la fune
 D' amarra a un cenno mio. "Quest' erme dune
 "Più non vedremo all' ora mattutina.
 "Nocchier, l' abbrivio è verso Palestrina."
	ENZO (*observing the sky*). Northeast the wind is.
	 'T is a good wind for us. Down in the hold
	        [*to the Nostromo*
	 Do thou, Nostromo, securely stow the cable
	 Thou, master of the sails, upon the prow
	 Of our ship see hoisted the Dalmatian flag.
	 There it has floated through many sharp ordeals!
	 And on the mainmast at once hang out the lantern. [*to the Midshipmen.*
	 And you, be ready to let go the mooring cable
	 At my first signal.

[*Alcuni uomini della ciurma eseguiscono gli ordini di* ENZO; *mentre gli altri ricantano la* MARINA-RESCA.	[*Some of the crew execute* ENZO'S *orders while the others repeat the Marinaresca.*

ENZO (*a tutti*). Ed or scendete a riposarvi. Io vigilo
 Solo sul ponte le inimiche flotte.
      [*Guarda le stelle.*
 È tardi.
	Chorus. Ho, he! ho, he!
	1st Sailors. Out with the oars!
	2d Sailors. Hoist now.
	  Oars to the starboard!
	  The thunder roars.
	Boys. Amid the lightning-flashes of the tempest,
	  Unto the clouds we turn our brows un daunted;
	  We dare the quiv'ring shrouds to climb
	  Behold in us the squirrels of the sea!

Ciurma. Buona guardia.	ENZO. Now go below; betake ye to slumber,
	  While I alone upon deck
	  Watch the enemy's vessels.

ENZO.   Buona notte.
   [*La ciurma scende sotto il ponte.*
	'T is late now. Good night to all!
	Chorus. Heav'n watch o'er thee!
	    [*The crew go below deck.*

SCENA IV.   SCENE IV.

English adaptation by THEO. T. BARKER.

Andante con calma.   *a tempo.*
Maestoso a piacere.

O - cean, and sky! The blue vault e - the - rial, Like a ho - ly al - tar shines.
Cie - lo! e mar! l'e - te - re o ve - lo splende co - me un santo al - tar.

Will my an - gel come from Heaven? Will she come from o-cean's billow's? Here !
L'angiol mio ver - rà dal cie - lo? l'angiol mio verrà dal ma - re?   Qui l'at

wait her; for warm - ly blows the breeze to - day, that love doth hold. Ah! what heart,
ten - do; ar - den - te spi - ra og-gi il ven - to dell' a - mor.   Ah! quel - l'uom,
animando

for you out - reach - ing.... Would dis - turb you, O bright dream, O dream of gold! Ah! what
che vi so - spi - ra.... vi con - qui - de o so - gni, o so - gni d'or! ah! quell'
fa tempo allarg.

heart for you out - reach - ing, would dis - turb you,........ O bright dream, O dream of
uom che vi so - spi - ra vi con - qui - de,........ o so - gni, o so - gni
molto rall.

gold! O vision, O vi - sion of gold! Thro' the mist's glooming, There's no land, no mountain
d'or! o so - gni, o so - gni d'or! Per l'au - ra fon - da non appar nè suol, nè

loom - ing, Wavelets kiss the pale ho - ri - zon! Wavelets kiss the pale ho - ri - zon!
mon - te, L'o - rizzon - te ba - cia l'on - da! l'on - da ba - cia l'o - rizzonte!

On the bil - low where I am wait - ing with a pulse that scarce doth move,
Qui nell' on - da, ov'io mi gia - cio coll' a - ne - li - to del cor,

Come, O my dar - ling, Come take the kiss - es, Life's sweet bliss - es,......
vie - ni, o do - nna, vie - ni al ba - cio del la vi - te,.....

poco piu mosso.

sweetest boon of life and love, Come, oh! dear-est, here I wait thee, with a pulse that scarce doth
del-la vi-ta e dell' a-mor, vie-ni,o don-na, qui t'at-ten-do, coll' a-ne-li-to del

cres. con passione.   *string. animatiss.*

move, Come, O darl-ing, and take my kiss-es, Come love, Come love, Come, O my
cor, vie-ni,o don-na, ah vie-ni al ba-cio, vie-ni, vie-ni, vie-ni al

ff   *allarg.*

darl-ing, take my kiss-es, the sweet-est boon of life and love, ah!........
ba-cio del-la vi-ta e dell' a-mo-re, dell' a-mor, ah!........

come! ah! come!....................
vien! ah! vien!....................

[*fissando il mare.*	[*gazing at the sea.*
Ah! chi è là? non è uno spetro	But who comes? 'T is not a phantom
Del pensier! quella è una barca.	Of my brain? A boat approaches!
Odo già de' remi il metro,	I already hear the rowers;
Verso me volando varca . . .	They towards me are swiftly steering.
La voce di BAR. (*dietro il brigantino*).	BAR. (*from behind*). Signor Captain, on board
Capitano! a bordo!	there?
ENZO (*sclamando verso la direzione della voce di*	ENZO. Come this way.
BAR.).	(*Aside.*) (Heaven aid me to bear the fulness
Avanti!!	Of this rapture!) Now then, boatmen,
(Dio! sostieni ancor la piena	Keep on this side of the vessel.
Della gioia!) O naviganti,	[*throws a rope over the side*
Costeggiate la carena!	There! the guide rope hold tightly.
[*prende una fune e la getta al di là della sponda.*	Now tie it, keep from falling. Mount
Qua la fune . . . aggrappa . . . annoda	quickly!
Le tue mani . . un passo ancor . . .	
Non cadere! approda! approda! . . .	

SCENA V.   **SCENE V.**

ENZO, LAURA.   *Enter* LAURA.

LAU. (*nelle braccia di* ENZO). Enzo!	ENZO. Laura! Laura! dearest, I am thine!
ENZO. Laura! Amore! Amor!	LAU. Enzo, my ENZO! Ah, dearest, I am thine!
La voce di BAR. (*sinistramente, allontanandosi*).	BAR. (*departing*). Good luck attend ye!
Buona fortuna!	
LAU. Oh! la sinistra voce!	LAU. Ah! at that voice I shudder!
Fuggiam! fuggiam!	
ENZO S' ei fu che ti salvò! . . .	ENZO. It is by him thou 'rt saved.
LAU. Pur sorridea d'un infernal sorriso! . . .	LAU. Yet, when he smiles, his smile appears in-fernal.

ENZO. E l' uomo che ci aperse il paradiso!
Deh! non turbare — con ree paure
Di questo istante — le ebbrezze pure;
D' amor soltanto — con me ragiona,
E il cielo, o cara — che schiudi a me!

LAU. Ah! del tuo bacio — nel dolce incanto
Celeste gioia — diventa il pianto,
A umano strazio — Dio non perdona,
Se perdonato — amor non è!

ENZO. Ma dimmi come, — angelo mio,
Mi ravvisasti?
LAU. — Nel marinar
Enzo conobbi. —
ENZO. Al pari anch' io
Te al primo suono — della parola . . .
LAU. Enzo adorato! — ma il tempo vola.
All' erta! all' erta! —
ENZO. Deh! non tremar!
Siamo in un' isola — tutta deserta,
Tra mare e cielo — tra cielo e mar!
Vedrem pur ora tramontar la luna . . .
Quando sarà corcata, all' aura bruna
Noi salperem; cogli occhi al firmamento,
Coi baci in fronte e colle vele al vento!

(*La luna bassa si svolve dalle nuvole, il suo disco s'
asconderà dietro il vascello.*

» 2. Laggiù nelle nebbie remote,
Laggiù nelle tenebre ignote,
Sta il segno del nostro cammin.
Nell' onde, nell' ombre, nei venti,
Fidenti, ridenti, fuggenti,
Gittiamo la vitae il destin.
La luna discende, discende
Ricinta di roride bende,
Siccome una sposa all' altar.
E asconde — la spenta — parvenza
Nell' onde; — con lenta — cadenza,
La luna è discesa nel mar!

ENZO (*staccandosi*). E il tuo nocchiere
Or la fuga t' appresta — O amata donna,
Tu qui resta.   [*scende sotto il ponte.*

SCENA VI.

LAURA *sola, poi* GIOCONDA.

LAU. Ho il cuor pieno di preghiere.
Quel lume! Ah! una Madonna!
(*Davanti all' immagine della Madonna orando con pas-
sione; mentre ch' essa prega, GIO. mascherata uscirà
da un nascondiglio sotto prora, e s' avanzerà lenta.*
Stella del marinar! Vergine Santa,
Tu mi difendi in quest' ora suprema,
Tu vedi quanta passione e quanta
Fede mi trasse a tale audacia estrema!
Sotto il tuo velo che i prostrati ammanta
Ricovera costei che prega e trema,
Scenda per questa fervida orazion
Sul capo mio, Madonna del perdon,
Una benedizion.

ENZO. 'T is he who for us opens Paradise.
Ah! cloud not, dearest, with fears and
doubtings
The pure enjoyment of these blessed mo-
ments.
Of love, love only, let our discourse be!
Love is the heaven unveil'd to-night.
LAU. Ah, love, thy kisses, with sweet enchant-
ment,
Change ev'ry sorrow to rapture celestial
No human frailty will heaven pardon.
If 't will not pardon love's delight.
ENZO. But tell me how, my angel,
Thou didst recognize me?
LAU. The sailor's dress hid not my Enzo.

ENZO. 'T was thus with me, love. Soon as thy voice
Bless'd the air with its music.
LAU. Enzo, beloved!
(*Starting.*) But time is flying — be watchful!
ENZO. Fear not, my love!
This is an island wholly deserted,
'Mid sky and ocean, ocean and sky.
We soon shall see yonder the moon de-
scending,
And when she sinks to slumber, favor'd by
darkness,
We will set sail, with kisses on our fore
heads,
And fav'ring winds our sails filling.

Ensemble.

Down yonder, amid the dim far-off mists,
Down yonder, amid the dark, unknown
clouds,
Our goal will, erelong, be espied.
To the billows, the shadows, the breezes,
Both faithful, and smiling, and flying,
Our lives and our fate we confide.
The moon is descending, descending,
Surrounded and veiled by the night dews,
Like bride for the altar attired;
And, hiding her fast fading lustre,
Sinks under the waves in slow cadence;
The moon 'neath the sea has retired.
ENZO. It is thy pilot.
For flight now prepare thee. O my beloved
Rest here awhile.   [*descends below deck*

SCENE VI.

LAURA, *alone; then* GIOCONDA.

LAU. My heart is full of happy tears.
[*Throws herself at the foot of the altar, and prays ear-
nestly. While she is praying, GIO., masked, comes
from her hiding-place, under the prow of the ship, and
advances slowly toward LAU.*
Star of the mariner, Virgin most holy!
Be my defender in this hour of trial!
Thou seest by how much ardor, by how
much faith,
I am led to adventure this audacious step!
Under thy mantle, kneeling sinners shel-
t'ring,
Find refuge for one who is praying and trem-
bling.
Send down, in answer to my fervent prayer,
Upon my head, O Virgin, full of mercy,
A blessing from on high!

GIOCONDA and LAURA.

English adaptation by THEO. T. BARKER.

GIOCONDA.

Curs - es at - tend you, Who am I, ask you? I'm your
E un a - na - tè - ma! Chi son tu chia - mi? So - no

LAURA. *(with a cry of terror.)*

Ah! Who are you?
Ah! chi sei?

prestissimo.

shadow in at - tend-ance! All the world thro' My name is Vengeance. And I love the man you love, too.
un' om-bra che t'a - spet - ta! Il mio no - me è la Vendet - ta. A - mo l'uo-mo che tu a - mi.

Heaven!
Ciel!

(with suppressed anger, pointing at the prow.)

cres.

There, his time and chance he's bid - ing, Like a beast of prey in hiding, Ah! with
Là at - te - sie il tem - po col - si co - me bel - va nel - la ta - na, ah! la

a piacere poco. ten.

ff   *a tempo.*

force past hu - man show - ing, Fu - ry in my heart is glow - ing! Would you
for - za so - vru - ma - na del fu - ror m'invade i pol - si! Vuoi fug-

fly? Is't love de - lays you? Would you fly from here, hap - py riv - al? Well, the
gir? D'amor ti struggi? Vuoi fug - gi - re? lie - ta ri - va - le? Si, l'an

f   *ff*

sails and rud - der still your pleas - ure wait, 'Tis well, 'tis well, go, go! N'angh
ten - na e il go - ver - na - le pron - ti son, sta ben, sta ben, va, va, Va

LA GIOCONDA.

GIO. Il mio braccio t' afferra!
Vien ch' io ti scorga in viso! a terra a
terra.
Presso a quel lume . . o i lagrimosi rai . .
Or più scampo non hai!
Questo pugnale . .
Ma no . . tu avrai per sorte
Un fulmin più fatale . .
In quella barca bruna . .

LAU. O ciel!
GIO.　　　　　Là è il tuo consorte!

LAU. Perduta io son!
GIO.　　　　　La morte
Voga sulla laguna.
Ecco! oramai nè un nume, nè un santuario
Salvar ti può.
LAU. (alzando il rosario). M' aita!

GIO.　　　　　Ah! quel rosario!
Esso è per te benedizione e schermo.
[la trascina verso la riva.

LAU. Che fai?
GIO. Ti salvo! Olá, il mio palischermo!
[appariscono due Marinai con una barca.
Fuggi! . . a te . . questa maschera ti asconda!
[stacca la maschera e la pone sul volto a LAU.
LAU. Ma mi dirai chi sei?
GIO.　　　　　Son la Gioconda!
[GIO. spinge quasi a forza LAU. nella barca che si
allontana rapidamente. GIO. scomparisce un istante
dietro al brigantino, come per assicurarsi della fuga
di LAU.

BAR. (dalla riva, osservando i movimenti della barca che
porta LAU. e scorgendo in distanza la gondola
D' ALVISE).
Maledizione! Ha preso il vol! Padron!
Nel canal morto . . là . . forza di remi!
[scomparisce.
GIO. È salva! O madre mia, quanto mi costi! . .

SCENA VIII.

GIOCONDA, ENZO.

ENZO (scendendo dal ponte). Laura, Laura! ove sei?

GIO. (avanzandosi verso ENZO fieramente).
Laura è scomparsa!
ENZO. Gioconda! o ciel! che avvenne?
GIO.　　　　　Invano a' rei
Baci sognati il tuo sospir la chiama . . .
ENZO. Menti, menti, o crudel!
GIO.　　　　　No! più non t' ama!
[trascinandolo verso la riva.
Vedi là, nel canal morto,
Un navil che forza il corso?
Essa fugge! il suo rimorso
Fu più forte dell' amor!
Questo lido è a lei funesto,
Chè la morte intorno sta . .
Essa fugge ed io qui resto! . .
Chi di noi più amato avrà?
ENZO. Taci! ahimè! da che t' ho scòrto,
Sospettai nefando agguato,
Non mi dir d' avermi amato.

GIO. In my grasp now I hold thee!
Come, let me see thy features! Kneel down!
No escape for thee now!
Soon shall this poniard—
[about to strike, stops suddenly
But no! for thee approaches
A punishment more fatal!
[holding her tightly with one hand, and with the other
pointing to the sea, on which a boat is seen approach-
ing.
There! look there!
LAU. Heaven!
GIO. There in yonder boat,
There 's thy husband!
LAU. Heaven! I am lost.
GIO. My curse is now accomplished.
No one on earth, nor even in Heaven,
Can save thee now.

LAU. (lifting up the Rosary).
Virgin, oh aid me! grant thine aid!
GIO. (struck at recognition of the Rosary).
What! 't is the Rosary!
[takes off her mask, and places it over the face of
LAU.
LAU. What dost thou?
GIO. I save thee! Ho there! my boat bring
quickly!
[a boat arrives with two Sailors.

LAU. But tell me first, who art thou?
GIO. I am La Gioconda.
[hurries to the boat. Exeunt behind vessel.

Enter BARNABA.

BAR. (looking on all sides). May they be curst!
They have taken flight. Signor!
[makes signs to ALV., who is seen in his boat at back
of stage.
By the canal, out there— (pointing) there!
Urge on the rowers, urge them! [Exit
GIO. (entering again).
I 've sav'd her. Alas, dear mother,
How much thou dost cost me!

SCENE VIII.

GIOCONDA, ENZO.

ENZO (entering from below deck).
Laura, Laura! where art thou?
GIO. (advancing haughtily toward ENZO).
Laura has vanish'd.
ENZO. Gioconda! oh heaven! what has happened?
GIO. In vain, to taste dreamy soft guilty kisses
Thy sighs may seek to recall her.
ENZO. Falsehood! cruel! 't is false!
GIO. No more she loves thee!
See out there, in yonder channel,
Fast a boat its way is making.
She flies from thee: the pangs of conscience
Were far stronger than her love.
From these shores, to her ill-omened,
Where pale death reigns all around,
She is flying; I am here remaining;
Which of us shows truest love?

ENZO. Silence! alas! since first I met thee,
I have evil plots suspected.
Tell me not that thou hast loved me!

Odio sol tu porti in cor!
Ma al suo barbaro consorte
L' angiol mio saprò strappar! . .
Là è la vita!   [*slanciandosi verso la riva.*

GIO.   Là è la morte!

ENZO.   Che di' tu?

GIO.   Riguarda al mar!
Tu sei tradito!   Un infame, un crudele
Al Gran Consiglio il tuo nome svelò
Rompi gli indugi, — fa forza di vele,
Il cielo ancora salvare ti pùo!

ENZO.   Taci! è un insulto dei vili il consiglio.
Dove è la morte, là impavido io sto!
Noto m' è il rombo del fiero naviglio,
Fuga od arresa che sieno non so!

[*si ode un culpo di cannone. Alcuni Marinai dell'*
HECATE *sbucano dal ponte altri irrompono dalla scena
alcuni con fiaccole in mano.*]

Marinai.   Le galèe! le galèe! Salvi chi può!

ENZO (*strappando la fiaccola ad uno dei Marinai*).
Sin ch' io sia vivo, no!
Al nemico darem cenere e brage!
Incendio!   [*dà fuoco all'* HECATE.   La nave
arde.

Tutti.   Incendio! guerra! morte! strage!
Fuggiam! fuggiam! piu speranza non v' ha!

ENZO (*dalla tolda slanciandosi in mare*).
O Laura, addio!

GIO (*dalla riva*).
E sempre Laura! oh almeno con te morir
poss io!

[*La nave si sprofonda.   Cade la tela.*

FINE DELL' ATTO II.

Hate alone thy heart doth nourish.
But from thy detested consort,
Dearest love, I 'll bear thee away!
Life is yonder.   [*rushing toward the water*

GIO   Death is yonder!

ENZO.   What say'st thou?

GIO.   Look out to sea.

Sailors (*entering*).   See the galleys! your safety
seek!

GIO. (*to* ENZO).
Thou art betrayed by a wretch vile and cruel
To the Council thy name was revealed.
Delay not a moment, hoist every sail,
And heav'n may yet spare thy life.

ENZO.   Silence! 't is an insult to give such vile
counsels;
Where death is nearest I fearless will stand.
Well do I know how to steer a tight vessel,
Flight and surrender I ne'er understand.
          [*enter Sailors in confusion*

Sailors.   No hope is left us.   Ah, fly!

ENZO (*taking a lighted torch from a Sailor*).
While I 'm living, no!
To the enemy we 'll give ashes and embers!
          [*sets fire to ship, flames break out*
We 'll burn her!

Sailors.   We 'll burn her!   Fight them! kill them

ENZO.   Adieu, my Laura.

GIO. (*aside*).   'T is ever Laura! Yet I, at least, may
die with thee!

          [*The burning vessel sinks*

END OF ACT II.

ATTO III.

CÀ D'ORO.

Una camera nella CÀ D'ORO. *Sera; lampada accesa. Da un lato un' armatura antica.*

SCENA I.

ALVISE *entrando in preda a violenta agitazione.*

ALV. Sì! morir ella de'! Sul nome mio
Scritta l' infamia impunemente avrà?
Chi un Badoèr tradì
Non può sperar pietà!..
Se ier non la ghermì
Nell' isola fatal questa mia mano,
L'espïazion non fia tremenda meno!
Ieri un pugnal le avria squarciato il seno,
Oggi.. un ferro non è.. sarà un veleno!
[*accennando alle sale contigue*
Là turbini e farnetichi
La gaia baraonda,
Dell' agonia col gemito
Qui l' orgia si confonda!
Ombre di mia prosapia
Non arrossite ancor!
Tutto la morte vendica,
Anche il tradito amor!
Là del patrizio veneto
Si compia il largo invito,
Quivi il feral marito
Provveda al proprio onor!
Fremete, o danze, o cantici!
È una infedel che muor!

SCENA II.

LAURA, ALVISE.

LAU. (*entra in ricca veste da ballo, con perle e gemme; ad* ALV.).
Qui chiamata m' avete?
ALV. (*con affettata cortesia*). Pur che vi piaccia...
LAU. Mio signor...
ALV. Sedete!
[*siedono ai due lati di un ampio tavolo.*
Bella così, madonna, — io non v' ho mai veduta;
Pur il sorriso è languido; — perchè ristarvi muta?
Dite: un gentil mistero — v' è grave a me svelar,
O un qualche velo nero — dovrò da me strappar?
LAU. Dal vestro accento insolito — cruda ironia traspira,
Il labro a grazia atteggiasi — e fuor ne scopia l'ira...
Mio nobile consorte, — non vi comprendo ancora!

ACT III

THE HOUSE OF GOLD.

A Chamber in the House of Gold. Night; a lamp lighted. On one side of the stage, a suit of ancient armor.

SCENE I.

ALVISE.

ALV. *(in violent agitation)*.
Yes, to die is her doom! My name in honor,
Shall not with impunity be disgraced.
From Badoers, when betrayed,
Pity 't were vain to hope.
Though yesterday upon the fatal isle
She 'scaped this vengeful hand,
She shall not escape a fearful expiation.
Last night a sharp poniard should have pierced her bosom;
This night no poniard I 'll use; she dies by poison! [*pointing to the adjoining room*
While there the dancers sing and laugh,
In giddy movements flying,
Their mirthful tones shall blend with groans,
Breath'd by a sinner dying.
Shades of my honor'd forefathers!
Soon shall your blushes disappear;
Soon shall a deadly vengeance prove
Honor to me is dear.
While dance the giddy crowd,
In mirthul movements flying,
Here shall be heard the bitter groans
The sinner breathes in dying.
Yonder, the nobles of the nation
Are gathered at my invitation;
Here, an insulted husband
For signal vengeance cries!
Exult, in dances and in songs,
While here a faithless one dies!

SCENE II.

LAURA, ALVISE.

Enter LAURA, *in a rich ball dress.*

LAU. You have summon'd me hither?
ALV. (*with an affectation of courtesy*).
Hoping to please you.
LAU. My lord— [*slowly seating herself*
ALV. Be seated.
[*they sit at opposite sides of large table*
Lovely as this, signora, I never yet have seen you;
Yet faint and languid your smiles appear
Why thus do you sit speechless?
Tell me, is some gentle secret
About to be revealed?
Or will some veil of blackest dye
From sin at once be torn?
LAU. Throughout these accents unusual
Irony still is breathing;
Your lips may kindness simulate,
Yet they are white with anger.
My noble lord and consort,
I do not understand you

322   LA GIOCONDA.

ALV (concitato). Pur d'abbassar la maschera, —
madonna, è giunta l' ora.
           [alzandosi con violenza.
Giunta è l' ora! — ad altr' uomo rivolto,
Donna impura, è il tuo primo sospir...
LAU. Ad altr' uomo? Che dite? Che ascolto!
           [fra sè.
(Cielo! orrendo m' imponi martir.)
ALV. Ieri quasi t' ho côlta in peccato,
Pur potesti salvarti e fuggir...
Col mio guanto t' ho oggi afferrato,
Più non fuggi, — ti è d' uopo morir!
   [la atterra violentemente. LAU. getta un grido.

LAU. (a piedi di ALV.).
Morir! è troppo orribile!
Aver davanti il ciel...
E scender nelle tenebre
D' un desolato avel!
Senti! di sangue tiepido
In sen mi scorre un rivo...
Perchè, se piango e vivo,
Dirmi: tu dêi morir?
La morte e pena infame
Anche a più gran fallir!
ALV. Invan tu piangi — invan tu speri,
Dio non ti può esaudir!
In lui raccogli — i tuoi pensieri;
Preparati a morir!
E già che ai nuovi imeni
L' anima tua sospira,
Indocil sposa, ten vieni
E mira!

LAU.   Ahimè!
Ove m' adduci?
ALV. (con forza sollevando la drapperia della ca-
mera attigua e indicando un catafalco. Si
vedrà il riverbero dei ceri). Vieni!
LAU. (inorridita). Ah! orribil cosa!
Serenata interna (sulla laguna).
Ten va serenata,
Per l' aura serena,
Ten va, cantilena,
Per l' onda incantata.

*Entra GIOCONDA e s' appiatta in fondo. La serenata
cessa per un momento.*
ALV. (estraendo una fiala).
Prendi questo velen; e gia che   *Serenata interna.*
    forte
Tanto mi sembri ne' tuoi detti   —
    audaci,   La gaia canzon
Con quelle labbra che succhi-
    aro i baci,   Fa l' eco languir,
Suggi la morte.
' La tua condanna confido a te   E l' ilare suon
    stessa;
'' Non far che mal securo
'' Voler t' arresti la mano per-   Si muta in sospir.
    plessa,
' Non far che il mio pugnale ti   Con vago miraggie
    percota
'' E insozzi i lari del tuo san-   Riflette la luna
    gue impuro.
Scampo non hai,   *[vrai.*
Odi questa canzon? *Morir do-*   L' argenteo suo raggie
Pria ch' essa giunga all' ultima sua
meta.   *[esce.*   Sull' ampia laguna

ALV. (with sudden violence).
Well, then, to tear away the mask.
The hour has come, signora;
This is the moment. To another was given
Shameless woman, thy first loving sigh!
LAU. To another? What mean you?

ALV. Yes, vilest of women.
I last night had nigh caught thee when
    sinning,
But from me thou wert able to fly!
In my grasp I to-day have enchained thee,
Ne'er to fly me; for now thou must die.
         [throws her down violently
LAU. To die! alas, 't is a fate too horrible!
To quit a smiling sky,
And, 'mid the deepest, darkest gloom.
In desolation die!
Lo! here, my life-blood's rapid stream
Its onward course is keeping;
Yet life for me means weeping!
Why say'st thou I must die?
Death is the shameful punishment
For crimes of deepest dye!

ALV. In vain thou weepest, in vain thou hopest,
Heav'n will not heed thy pray'r.
To yonder heav'n thy thoughts directing,
For death at once prepare.
And now that for fresh nuptials
Fondly thy soul is sighing,
Unfaithful consort, come hither;
Admire this!
      [drags her towards the curtained doo
LAU. (terrified). Where wouldst thou lead me?

ALV. (violently uplifting the draperies of the adjoining
chamber, and pointing to a funereal bier).
Nearer! 'T is thy bridal bed.
LAU. (horrified). Ah!
Serenade behind (far off on the Lagoon).
Enter GIOCONDA, who conceals herself.
Chorus. Our gay songs are ending;
The soft echoes die,
And blithe, careless laughter
Is chang'd to a sigh.

ALV. (producing a flask).   *Chorus*
This poison thou must take.
Thou hast dar'd   Our gay songs are
                      ending,
To utter words that seem to
me audacious,   The soft echoes die,
Now let the lips that spoke   And blithe, careless
them, that drank kisses,   laughter
Drink in thy death. No hope   Is chang'd to a sigh.
is left thee.   The wavelets and
Dost thou hear yonder song?   moonbeams
Thy life must cease   Together are blending.
Ere of that song the last note has   The bright rays of sil-
sounded!   ver
         [exit ALV. On ocean descending.

SCENA III.

LAURA e GIOCONDA.

Gio. (accorrendo verso Lau., afferra il veleno che Lau. ha tra le
mani e le porge un' ampolla).
   A me quel filtro! a te codesto!
   bevi!

Lau. Gioconda, qui?
Gio.   Previdi la tua sorte.
   Per salvarti mi armai, ti rassicura.
   Quel narcotico è tal, che della
   morte
   Finge il letargo... Angosciosi,
   brevi
   Sono gl' istanti... bevi... ame
   la cura
   Lascia dell' opra. — Or via!!

Lau. Mi fai paura!
Gio. S' ei qui torna t' uccide.

Lau.   Atra agonia!
Gio. Prega per te quaggiù la
   madre mia,
   Nell' oratorio, i miei fidi cantori
   Son presso.. ascolta.

Lau.   Orror!
   Già la canzone muor!

Gio. Con essa muori!
   La condanna t' è nota:
   Pria ch' essa giunga all' ultima
   sua nota...

Lau. Porgi! ho bevuto.
   [prende la fiala dalle mani di
   Gio. poi scompare dietro le
   cortine della camera mortuaria

Gio. La fiala a me! oh gran Dio!
   [travasa il veleno d' Alv. nella
   fiala del sonnifero e lascia l'
   ampolla del veleno vuota sul tavolo. Esce precipitosa

E in quei si sublima
Riverbere pio,
Patetica rima
Creata da Dio.
—
Ten va, cantilena,
Per l' aura serena,
Ten va, serenata,
Per l' onda incantata,
Udite le blande
Canzoni vagar.
Il remo ci scande
Gli accordi sui mar.
Ten va, serenata,
Sull' onda incantata.
—
Il canto è la vita,
Di sogni si pasce,
Ai sogni c' invita,
Dai sogni rinasce,
D' un' anima ignota
E l' eco fedel;
L' estrema sua nota
Si perde nel ciel.

SCENE III.

LAURA and GIOCONDA.

Enter Gioconda, who runs to Lau-
ra, from whose hand she takes the
poison, and gives her a phial.
Gio. Give me that phial, and
   take this quickly! Drink it.
Lau. Gioconda here?
Gio. Thy cruel doom foreseeing,
   I came hither to save thee.
   All fear now banish.
   This narcotic is such, that in a
   trance
   Like death it will plunge thee.
   Drink it, drink it!
   Full of anguish, yet brief
   Are the moments now left thee.
Lau. Of thee I am fearful.
Gio. He who returns here will
   kill thee.
Lau. O dark despair!
Gio. For thy safety my mother
   in yon oratory
   Is praying, and some stanch
   friends are nigh.
   Their singing thou hearest.
Lau. Alas! slowly the song dies
   out.
Gio. Drink, then. With it, thy
   life was to cease!
   This was the sentence:
   "Ere of that song the last note has
   sounded."
Lau. Give me.
            [drinks the narcotic.
   I have drained it.
   [rushes behind the curtains of the
   funereal chamber.
Gio. Give me the flask.
   [pours the poison into the flask
   which had contained the narcotic,
   and leaves the empty flask on the
   table.
Great heaven!
   [exit precipitately.

Sublime is the mes-
   sage
By nature now given,
In tenderest cadence.
Created in Heaven!
—
Our gay songs are
   ending,
The soft echoes die,
And blithe, careless
   laughter
Is chang'd to a sigh.
We listen to songs
Full of innocent glee,
Our oars keeping time
As we float o'er the
   sea.
Float on, serenade!
Heaven soft air is
   granting;
In harmony float
O'er the waters so
   chanting.
—
We listen to songs
Full of innocent glee,
Our oars keeping time
As we float o'er the
   sea.
From some unknown
   soul
Comes Echo's reply,
The last note, ascend-
   ing,
Is lost in the sky.

SCENA IV.

Alvise solo, mentre la cadenza della serenata è alle
ultime sue note. Osserva l' ampolla vuota sul tavolo.

Alv.   Tutto è compiuto!
   Vuoto è il cristal.
   [entra nella cella funeraria, vi rimane un momen to.,
   torna in scena.
   Vola su lei la morte.
   La morte è il nulla e vecchia fola è il ciel!
            [esce lentamente.

SCENE IV.

Enter Alvise; he observes the flask empty on the table.

Alv.   All now is over!
   Empty is the flask.
   [enters the funereal chamber for a moment, then re-
   enters.
   Death has forever claim'd her!   [exit.

SCENA V.

GIOCONDA sola.

GIO. *(ricomparisce dal lato opposto a quello donde è uscito*
ALV. *Si guarda intorno, solleva la cortina*
della cella, voi, vistasi sola, esclama:
O madre mia, nell' isola fatale
Frenai per te la sanguinaria brama
Di rejetta rival. Or più tremendo
E il sacrifizio mio . . .
Io la salvo per lui, per lui che l' ama!

[*esce precipitosamente.*

SCENE V.

Re-enter GIOCONDA *from her hiding-place.*

GIO. O dearest mother, on yonder fatal island,
For thy dear sake, I check'd the burning
frenzy
Of a passion disdain'd. Now, more tremendous
The sacrifice I'm making!
I save her; but for his sake, who loves her.

[*exit precipitately*

SCENA VI.

Sontuosissima sala attigua alla cella funeraria, splendidamente parata a festa. Ampio portone nel fondo a sinistra, un consimile a destra, ma questo tutto chiuso da una drapperia. Una terza porta nella parete a sinistra.

Entrano Cavalieri, Dame, Maschere. ALVISE *moverà loro incontro ricevendo e complimentando chi entra. Il Paggio gli sta accanto.* GIOCONDA.

ALV. Benvenuti messeri! Andrea Sagredo!
Erizzo, Lordan! Venier! Chi vedo?
Isèpo Barbarigo, a noi tornato
Dalla pallida China! e il ben amato
Cugino mio Partecipazio! O quanti
Bei cavalieri! . . . Belle dame! Avanti,
Avanti! e voi, vispi cantori e maschere,
Presto sciogliete le carole e i canti.

Coro. S' inneggi alla *Cà d' Oro*
Che intreccia in rami d' òr
Della virtù l' alloro
Col mirto dell' amor.

ALV. Grazie vi rendo per le vostre laudi,
Cortesi amici. A più leggiadri gaudi
Ora v' invito. Ecco una mascherata
Di vaghe danzatrici. — Ognuna è ornata
Di bellezza e fulgore
E tutte in cerchio rappresentan l' ore.
Incomincia la danza.

SCENE VI.

A magnificent hall, adjoining the funereal chamber, and splendidly adorned for a festivity. At back, wide entrance door. A similar door, completely closed by curtains. A third door, opening from the side.

Enter Cavaliers, Ladies and Masquers. ALVISE *advances to meet them, and exchanges compliments with all who arrive. A Page stands behind him.* GIOCONDA *enters unobserved.*

ALV. *(receiving the Guests).*
Worthy friends, you are welcome! Andrea
Sagredo!
Erizzo, Loredan, Venier! Whom see I?
Isèpo Barbarigo, to us returning
From pale, far-distant China?
And here my much lov'd cousin comes,
Partecipazio!
Of splendid knights what a concourse!
Pass onward, charming ladies, pass onward,
Ye signors, too, are welcome, and ye, cavaliers,
And ye, merry young singers, and masquers
too.
Brighten the revelry with songs and dances!

Chorus. We sing in praise of the House of Gold,
Where twine, in golden chaplets,
With virtue's laurel leaves,
The myrtles of true love.

ALV. Thanks let me offer ye for these kind praises,
These accents courteous. And now, to
gayer spectacles
Let me invite ye. Hither come the masqueraders,
A troop of lovely dancers. Each one is
glowing
With beauty and ardor. In graceful movements
The Hours representing;
And their dance now commences.

DANZA DELLE ORE.

La Ore del Mattino — del Giorno — della Sera — della Notte.

DANCE OF THE HOURS.

The Hours of the Daybreak. — The Hours of the Day. — The Hours of the Evening. — The Hours of the Night.

DANCE OF THE HOURS.

DANCE OF THE HOURS. Concluded.

SCENA VII.

i precedenti, BARNABA, LA CIECA, ENZO.

BAR. (*trascinando* LA CIECA *che invano cerca svincolarsi dalle sue strette*). Vieni!

CIECA. Lasciami! Ahimè!

Coro e ALV. La Cieca!

GIO. (*accorrendo*). O madre!

ALV. (*alla* CIECA). Qui che fai tu?

BAR. Nelle vietate stanze
Io la sorpresi al maleficio intenta!

CIECA. Pregavo per chi muor!

Coro. Per chi muor? che di' tu?

[*si odono i lenti rintocchi della campana degli agonizzanti.*

Qual suon funèbre!

ENZO (*a* BAR.). Un' agonia! per chi?

BAR. (*sottovoce ad* ENZO). Per Laura!

ENZO. Orror!
Che più mi resta se quell' angiol muor?

ALV. (*avanzandosi tra la folla atterrita e confusa*).
E che? la gioia sparve!
Se gaio è Badoèro.
Chi ha fra gli ospiti suoi dritto al dolor?

ENZO. Io l' ho più ch' altri.

ALV. Tu? ma tu chi sei?

ENZO (*gettando la maschera*).
Il tuo proscritto io sono, Enzo Grimaldo,
Prence di Santaflor! Patria ed amore
Tu m' hai rubato un dì . . .
Or compi il tuo delitto!

Tutti. Audacia!

CIECA e GIO. Orror!

ALV. Sul capo tuo rispondi,
Barnaba, del codardo insultator!

Coro. D' un vampiro fatal — l' ala fredda passò
E in teda funeral — ogni face mutò.
Un sinistro baglior — le fronti illuminò,
Più la gioia regnar — nella festa non può!

ENZO (*fra sè*).
(O mia stella d' amor, — o mio Nume fedel,
Se rapita a me sei, — ti raggiungo nel ciel!)

GIO. (*fra sè*). (Oh tortura crudel! — inaudito martir!
Quanto ei l' ama! è per lei — qui venuto a morir!)

CIECA (*a* BAR.). O fatal delator, — se trafitte alcun fu,
Riconosco la man, — l' assassino sei tu!

BAR. (*alla* CIECA).
Giuro al cielo, se ier — quella rea ti salvò,
La vendetta oggimai — più sfuggirmi non può!

ENZO (*fra sè*). (Già ti vedo immota e smorta
Tutta avvolta in bianco vel,
Tu se morta, tu sei morta,
Angiol mio dolce e fedel!
Su di me piombi la scure,
S' apra il baratro fatal,
E mi guidin le torture
All' imene celestial.)

SCENE VII

Enter BARNABA, ENZO, *and* LA CIECA.

BAR. (*dragging in* CIECA). Come on!

CIECA. Let me go! Ah me!

Chorus. La Cieca!

GIO. (*running*). My mother!

ALV. (*to* CIECA). What dost thou here?

BAR. In the forbidden chambers
I just now caught her, intent upon some malice.

CIECA. For her, just dead, I prayed.

[*the passing bell for the dying and dead is heard slowly tolling.*

Chorus. Her, just dead! What say'st thou?
Ah! That sound funereal!

ENZO (*in an undertone to* BAR.).
The knell of death! For whom?

BAR. (*aside to* ENZO). For Laura.

ENZO. For Laura? O Heaven!
What now remains for me, if she be dead?

ALV. (*with sudden animation*).
What now? Joy is immortal!
If gay is Badoèro,
Who, amongst all his guests, has the right to be gloomy?

ENZO (*advancing*). I, of all others!

ALV. Thou! But who art thou?

ENZO (*unmasking*).
By thee proscribed; Enzo Grimaldo,
Prince of Santaflor. My country, my beloved,
Were stolen from me by thee.
Of crime thou may'st now fill up the measure!

ALV. Audacious!

Chorus. Audacious! He dies!

ALV. Barnaba, thy head for him shall answer,
Should the vile insulter escape.

Chorus. As if over our brows a vampire's wing had passed,
A shudder takes the place of the smiles that each wore;
With a sinister gleam our foreheads are illum'd,
And gay, light-hearted joy at the feast reigns no more.

ENZO (*aside*).
O bright star of my soul, ever constant and sweet,
Though from me thou art torn, we in Heaven shall meet!

GIO. (*aside*).
Cruel tortures are mine, evil fated am I!
True love's martyr is he; he for her came to die!

CIECA (*to* BAR.).
O vile, hated spy! I too well know thee, now!
If a death wound was given, the assassin — 't was thou!

BAR. (*to* CIECA).
Ah, hear me swear! If last night thou wert sav'd,
I 'll to-day be reveng'd, too long I 've been brav'd!

ENZO (*aside*). I behold thee motionless, pallid,
Shrouded in thy snowy veil!
Thou art dead, love! thou art dead, love!
Ah! my darling, hopeless I wail
The sharp axe for me is waiting,
Opens wide a dark abyss;
But to thee shall torture guide me,
Soon we 'll share celestial bliss!

GIO. (Scorre il pianto a stilla a stilla
Nel silenzio del dolor.
Piangi, o turgida pupilla,
Mentre sanguina il mio cor.)

BAR. (a GIO.).
Cedi alfin, della mia mano
Vedi qui l' opra fatal.
Mi paventa! un genio arcano
Mi trascina verso il mal.

GIO. (sottovoce, a BAR.).
Se lo salvi e adduci al lido,
Laggiù presso all Redentor,
Il mio corpo t' abbandono,
O terribile cantor.

BAR. (come sopra, a GIO.).
Disperato è questo dono,
Pur lo accetta il tuo cantor.
Al destin spietato irrido,
Pur d' averti sul mio cor.

CIECA (a GIO.).
Le tue lagrime, o Gioconda,
Che non versi sul mio cor?
Un amor non ti circonda
Che sia pari a questo amor!

ALV. (cupamente guardando ENZO).
Nel fulgor di questa festa
Mal venisti, o cavalier,
Par che sia per te funesta
L' allegria dei Badoèr!
Ma già appresto a' tuoi sgomenti
Nuova scena di terror!
Tu saprai, se invan si attenti
Del mio nome al puro onor!

Coro. Tristi eventi! Audacie orrende!
Spaventevole festin!
Come rapida discende
La valanga del destin!

ALV. (avanzandosi in mezzo della scena, con atto di suprema dignità).
Or tutti a me! La donna che fu mia
L' estremo oltraggio al nome mio recò!

(Va verso la cella funeraria ed alza le cortine. LAU. apparisce vestita di bianco stesa sul suo letto di morte. La cella è rischiarata da molti doppieri.
Miratela! Son io che spenta l' ho!

ENZO (si slancia brandendo il pugnale ma è trattenuto dalle guardie). Carnefice!

GIO., CIECA.   Sventura!

Coro.   Orror! orror!

[GIO. corre verso ENZO che viene trascinato dalle guardie. BAR. afferra per la mano CIECA e, giovandosi della confusione la spinge entro una porta segreta. ALV. resta immobile presso la cella funeraria, additando il cadavere di LAU. Gli invitati si atteggiano ad espressioni di raccapriccio, di sdegno e di pietà. Quadro. Cala la tela.

GIO. Sadly fall the tear-drops,
In the silence of despair;
Break, oh heart! sad eyes, rain torrents
Fate, thy sharpest doom prepare!

BAR. (aside to GIO.).
Yield thee, yield thee! all around thee
See what pow'r I have for ill!
Well may'st thou fear me; pow'rs infernal
To ill deeds attract me still!

GIO. (aside to BAR.).
Do thou save him, bring him safe out there
Close by the Redentor, and then
Myself I will surrender
To thee, fearfullest of men.

BAR. (to GIO.).
Though despair may prompt thy offer
I accept it for my part,
And the bitterest fate will welcome.
Once to press thee to this heart.

CIECA. Thou art weeping, O Gioconda,
Let me fold thee to my breast.
Never love, like love maternal,
Can encounter ev'ry test.

ALV. 'Mid the splendor this fête surrounding
Thou art unwelcome, cavalier;
But, erelong, new scenes of horror
Shall from thee attention claim.
Thou shalt soon see if I am watchful
Of the honor of my name.

Chorus. Mournful feasting, fearful horrors
Mournful feast, soon desolate!
Ah! how rapidly descending,
Falls the avalanche of fate!

ALV. (proudly glancing around).
Now, all draw nigh! A woman, once my wife,
The foulest outrage brought upon my name.

[Opens the curtain of the funereal chamber, and points to LAU. extended on her bier.
Behold her now! 'T was I who took her life!

ENZO (brandishing a poniard, rushes on ALV., but is seized by the Guards).
Base murderer!

Chorus. Horror! despair! woe!

ATTO IV.

IL CANAL ORFANO.

L' atrio di un palazzo diroccato nell' isola della GIUDECCA. — *Nell' angolo di destra un para-vento disteso, dietro il quale sta un letto. — Un gran portone di riva nel fondo da cui si vedrà la laguna e la piazzetta di San Marco illuminata a festa. — Una immagine della* Madonna *ed una croce appesa al muro. — Un tavolo, un canapè, sul tavolo una lucerna ed una lanterna accese, un' ampolla di veleno, un pugnale. — Sul canapè varii adornamenti scenici di* GIOCONDA. *A destra della scena una lunga e buia calle.*

SCENA I.

GIOCONDA *sola, cupamente assorta ne' suoi pen-sieri.*

(Intanto dal fondo della calle si avanzano due uomini che portano in braccio LAURA *avvolta in un mantello nero. Battono all' uscio.* GIOCONDA *si scuote e va ad aprire. Entrano.)*

GIO. Nessun v' ha visto?
Primo Cantore.   Nessuno.
GIO.   Sul letto
     La deponete.
     [GIO. *va al paravento.* LAU. *deposta sul letto.*
Cantore.   " Ad un' occulta riva
     " Sbarcati siam per evitar gl' incontri.
GIO. " Sta ben. E quando fu sepolta?
Cantore.   " A vespro.
GIO. " E quanto tempo giacque?
Cantore.   " In circa un' ora.
GIO. " Era vasto l' avel?
Cantore.   " Vasto.
GIO.   I compagni
     Verranno questa notte?
Cantore.   Si.
GIO.   Ecco l' oro
     Che vi promisi.
Cantore.   Nol vogliam . . . gli amici
     Prestan opra da amici.
GIO. *(mutando accento e supplicando).* O
     pietosi,
     Per quell' amor che v' ha creati, un' altra
     Grazia vi chiedo. Nella scorso notte
     Mi scompariva la mia cieca madre,
     Già disperata la cercai ma invano.
     Deh! scorrete le vie, le piazze e l' orme
     Della mia vecchierella Iddio v' insegni.
     Doman, se la trovate, a Canareggio
     V' aspetterò, Quest' antro di Giudecca
     Fra brev'ora abbandono.

ACT IV.

THE ORFANO CANAL.

SCENE. — *The vestibule of a palace in ruins, on the island of Giudeca. In the right-hand corner an opened screen, behind which is a bed. Large porch at back, through which are seen the Lagoon, and the square of St. Mark, brilliantly illuminated. A picture of the Virgin, and a crucifix, hang against the wall. Table and couch; on the table a lamp and a lighted lantern, a flask of poison, and a dagger; on the couch various scenic orna-ments belonging to* GIOCONDA. *On the right of the scene, a long, dimly lighted street.*

SCENE I.

GIOCONDO, *sola, gloomily buried in thought.*

From the end of the street two men advance. carrying in their arms LAURA, *who is en-veloped in a black cloak. The two Cantori (street singers) knock at the door, which is opened by* GIOCONDA.

GIO. No one has seen you?
1st Cant.   No one.
GIO.   Upon yonder bed
     Now place her.
     [*the Cantori carry* LAU. *behind the screen*
                         Our companions?
     Will they to-night be ready?
Cant.   Yes.
GIO.   Here 's the gold
     That to you I promised.
Cant. Take it back; true friends
     Willingly help one another.

GIO. O have pity! By the love of those who
     bore ye,
     For further aid I implore ye. During
     yesternight
     From my blind mother I was separated
     Since then despairingly have sought her
     but vainly.
     Ah, then, search ev'ry highway and
     piazza!
     To the traces of my blind angel mother
     Kind heaven will guide ye.
     To-morrow, if ye find her, at Cana
     reggio
     I shall be found. This den. th's for
     Giudeca,
     I erelong shall abandon.

Cantori.   A noi t' affida.

[GIO. *stringe ad essi la mano; escono da dove sono entrati.*

SCENA II.

GIOCONDA *sola presso il tavolo guarda il pugnale, la tocca, poi prende l' ampolla del veleno.*

GIO.
Suicidio ! . . . in questi
Fieri momenti
Tu sol mi resti,
Tu sol mi tenti.
Ultima voce
Del mio destin,
Ultima croce
Del mio cammin.
E un dì leggiadre
Volavan l' ore ;
Smarrii la madre,
Perdei l' amore,
Vinsi l' infausta
Gelosa febre !
Or piombo esausta
Fra le tenebre ! . . .
Tocco alla mèta . . .
Domando al ciel
Di dormir queta
Dentro l' avel.

[*guardando ancora l' ampolla.*

Ecco, il velen di Laura, a un' altra vittima
Era serbato ! io lo berrò ! — Quand' esso
Questa notte qui giunga, io non vedrò
Il loro immenso amplesso ;
Ma chi provvede alla lor fuga ? ah ! no !

[*getta il veleno sul tavolo.*

No, tentator, lungi da me ! conforta,
Anima mia, le tue divine posse !
Laura è là . . . là sul letto . . . viva . . .
morta . . .
Nol so . . . se spenta fosse ! ! !
Io salvarla volea, mio Dio lo sai !
Pur, s' ella è spenta !? . . . un indistinto
raggio
Mi balena nel cor . . . vediam . . . coraggio.

prende la lanterna, fa per avviarsi al letto e poi si pente.

No . . . no . . . giammai, giammai !
No, non mi sfugga questo dubbio arcano '

Cant.   On us rely

[GIO. *clasps the hands of the Cantori, who depart through the porch by which they had entered.*

SCENE II.

GIOCONDA *sola.   She approaches the table, and looks fixedly at the dagger, which she examines, and then takes up the flask of poison.*

GIO.
Yes, suicide ! the sole
Resource now left me !
Stern fate forever
Of hope has bereft me.
I the last accents
Of destiny hear,
Bear my last cross ;
Know the end draweth near
Bright is the day,
The hours gayly flying !
Lost is my mother ;
Love lies a-dying.
Conquer'd by jealousy's
Terrible fever,
I sink exhausted ;
Sink down forever !
Nigh draws the end now !
If Heav'n prove kind,
Erelong in the grave
Repose I may find.

[*again contemplating the flask of poison*

The poison, meant for Laura, to another
victim
Soon will be fatal.   Let me drink it !
When *he*
Shall to-night hither come, I shall not see
How fervent their embraces.
But who for their escape will answer ?
Ah, no !

[*throwing the poison on the table.*

Tempter, away ! out of my sight !
Take comfort,
O my soul, in thy divine endurance !

[*with ferocious joy.*

Laura is there ! yonder lying : dead ?
— or living ?
None knows.   She 's in my power —
I to save her endeavor'd, great Heav'n,
thou knowest !
Still, were she dead ?   An indistinct
suggestion,
Like a lightning-flash comes.   Let 's
see !   Now, courage !

[*takes up the lantern, and is about to approach the bed, but stops.*

Ah, no ! no, never !   No, never !
And yet — and yet the gloomy doubt
still haunts me.

Ma s' ella vive? ebben. . . Laura è in mia
mano.   .   [biecamente.
Siam soli — E notte — Nè persona alcuna
Saper potrìa . . . profonda è la laguna . . .

Una voce lontana sull' acqua.
  Ehi! dalla gondola,
  Che nuove porti?
Altra voce piu lontana.   Nel Canal Orfano Ci.
  son de' morti.
Gio.   Orrore! orrore!! orrore!!!
  Sinistre voce! illuminata a festa
  Splende Venezia nel lontano . . . in core
  Già si ridesta
  La mia tempesta
  Immane! furibonda!
  O amore! amore!!
  Enzo! pietà! . . .
*al culmine della disperazione si getta accanto
a tavolo.*

SCENA III.

Intanto si vedrà Enzo *venir dalla calle, trova
la porta socchiusa, entra.*

Enzo.   Gioconda!
Gio.   Enzo! . . . sei tu!
Enzo (*cupamente*).   Dal carcere
  M' hai tratto; e i miei legami
  Sciogliesti, e armato e libero
  Qui son. Da me che brami?

Gio. (*con accento d' esaltazione straziante*)
  Da te che bramo? ahi! misera!
  Ridarti il sol, la vita!
  La libertà infinita!
  La gioia e l' avvenir!
  L' estatico sorriso,
  L' estatico sospir!
  L' amor . . . il paradiso!
  (Gran Dio! fammi morir!)
o Donna! col tuo delirio
  Tu irridi a un moribondo,
  Per me non ha più balsami
  L' amor, nè raggi il mondo.
  Addio. .
Gio.   Che fai?
Enzo.   Non chiedere.
Gio. (*afferrandolo*).   Resta. . . M' ascolta.
Enzo (*svincolandosi*).   Cessa.
Gio.   Tu vuoi morir per essa!
Enzo.   Sì, sul suo santo avel
  Baciare anco una volta
  La povera sepolta

But — were she living? Well, then,
we are alone —
Without witness; 'tis night, and no
human being
Could know when 'twas over. And
deep is yon Lagoon.
A voice (in the distance).
  Ho! gondolier! hast thou any fresh
  tidings?
Other voice in the distance.
  In the Orfano Canal there are corpses.
Gio.   Ah me! ah me! oh horror!
  O sinister voices! Illuminated brightly,
  Resplendent Venice shines out yonder!
  My heart
  Is thus illumined
  By flames of vengeance,
  Relentless, unforgiving.
  O Love! O Love!
  Enzo, have pity! Have pity, love, on
  me!
*in despair throws herself down, weeping and
exhausted, near the table.*

SCENE III.

Enter Enzo.

Enzo. Gioconda!
Gio.   Enzo! — 'tis thou!
Enzo.   From prison
  Thou hast freed me: by thee my chains
  Have been unfastened, and armed and
  free
  Behold me here. Of me what wouldst
  thou?
Gio. (*in accents of passionate exaltation*).
  Of thee what would I? Alas!
  With smiles thy life is surrounded,
  Thy liberty unbounded,
  Bright joys in thy pathway lie.
  The smiles that speak love's yearning
  The sighs of rapture burning,
  This earth to Eden turning!
(*Aside.*)   Great Heaven, now let me die!
Enzo.   Woman, thy frenzied passion calm
  My days will soon be over:
  New life, new love, no balm can bring
  A broken-hearted lover.
  Adieu now!
Gio.   What dost thou?
Enzo.   Seek not to know
Gio.   Stay here, and listen?
Enzo.   Cease!
Gio.   Thou wilt then die for Laura?
Enzo.   Yes, unto Laura's tomb I go,
  Once more to kiss, while dying,
  My lost love, lifeless lying.

GIO. (*con possente ironia*). Ebben, corri al
    tuo voto,
    Eroe mesto e fedel !
    L' avel di Laura è vuoto ;
    Io l' ho rapita !
ENZO.   O ciel !   [*con un grido.*
    No, menti, menti. . .
GIO. (*accennando alla croce appesa al muro*).
        Giuro,
    Giuro su quella croce.
ENZO. No : la bestemmia atroce
    Tergi dal labbro impuro !
    Di' che hai mentito !
GIO. (*con fierezza, poi supplichevole*). Il vero
    Dissi ! il furor . . . deh ! frena !
ENZO. O furibonda jena
    Che frughi il cimitero !
    O maledetta Eumènide,
    Gelosa della morte,
    Dimmi ove celi l' angelo
    Mio dalle guance smorte.
    Parla ! o in quest' ora lùgubre
    Convien che qui tu muoia. . .
    Vedi ! già brilla il fulmine
    Del mio pugnal. . .
    [*sguainando il suo pugnale e afferrando*
    GIO.

GIO.   (Oh gioia !
    M' uccide !)
ENZO   Il tuo mister saprò.
    Parla. . .

GIO.   No.
ENZO.   Parla.
GIO.   No.
ENZO. Ebben. . . infame. . . muori !
    [*per ferirla.*

GIO. (*mockingly*).
    'T is well ; fulfil thy purpose,
    O faithful hero, but know,
    The tomb of Laura is vacant.
ENZO. Heaven !
GIO.   I have remov'd her.
ENZO. No ! Falsehood ! falsehood !
GIO. (*pointing to the crucifix on the wall*). I
    swear it !
    Swear it by yon Redeemer.
ENZO. No ! thou art a blasphemer ;
    Yon crucifix profaning.
    No ! thou art perjur'd !
GIO.   No !
    No ! the truth I have sworn.
ENZO. O furious hyena,
    The sepulchre despoiling !
    O worse than the Eumenides !
    For thou of the dead art jealous.
    Say, where hast thou my angel con
    cealed ?
    Where doth she lie with cheeks cold
    and faded ?
    Answer ! or in this fatal hour
    Thy life shall pay the forfeit !
    See with gleam-like lightning flash
    Shines my keen poniard !
    [*drawing his dagger and grasping* GIO
GIO. (*aside*).   (O joy,
    He will kill me !)
ENZO. Thy mystery unfold !
GIO.   No !
ENZO. Answer !
GIO.   No !
ENZO.   Answer !
GIO.   No !
ENZO. Then thou thy life shall forfeit.
    [*about to stab* s.

SCENA IV.

LAURA, GIOCONDA, ENZO.

LAU. (*dall' alcova*). Enzo !
ENZO.   Chi è là !
GIO. (*atterrita*).   Mio Dio !

LAU. (*comparendo*). Enzo ! amor mio !
    Ah ! il cor mi si ravviva . . .
    Respiro all' aura . . .
    [ENZO, *immobile, trasognato.*
    Enzo. vieni . . . sei tu, vieni . . . son
    viva !
ENZO (*slanciandosi, abbracciando* LAU.).
    Laura ! ciel ! non deliro ! Ah ! Laura !
    Laura !
GIO. (*avviluppandosi la testa nel suo manto*).
    (Nascondili, o tenèbra !)

SCENE IV.

LAURA, GIOCONDA, ENZO.

LAU. (*from the alcove*). Enzo !
ENZO.   Who 's there ?
GIO.   (Great Heaven
    Enter LAURA.
LAU. Enzo ! my beloved !
    My strength is fast reviving —
    I breathe the pure balmy air —
ENZO. I 'm not dreaming ?
LAU. Enzo ! Come, love ! I 'm living !
ENZO. I 'm not dreaming ! — Heaven ! — Liv
    ing !
    [*he rushes forward and embraces* LAU
GIO. (*covering her face with her mantle*).
    (Let darkness hide them from me.)

Lau. (*guardando verso* Gio.). Ahimè! quell' ombra
È Alvise . . . fuggi . . .

Enzo. No, il terror disgombra.

Lau. (*avvicinandosi riconosce* Gio. *che si sarà scoperta*).
Sei tu? costei salvò la vita a me.

Enzo. Fanciulla santa!
Ch' io mi ti prostri ai piè!
[Lau. *ed* Enzo *cadono in ginocchio davanti a* Gio. — *Quadro.*

Voci lontane. Ten va, serenata,
Per l' aura serena,
Ten va cantilena,
Per l' onda incantata.
Ud.te le blande
Canzoni vagar,
Il remo ci scande
Gli accordi sul mar.
Il canto è la vita,
Di sogni si pasce,
Ai sogni c' invita,
Nei sogni rinasce,
D' un' anima ignota
È l' eco fedel,
L' estrema sua nota
Si perde nel ciel.

Gio. (*con calma dolcissima*).
Questa canzone ti rammenti o Laura?
È la canzone della tua fortuna.
Essa viene, vêr noi. Attenti udite,
Fratelli miei, quei rematori in salvo
V' addurran questa notte. Per la fuga
Tutto provvidi cautamente. "Alzate
" Le vostre fronti, ch' io veda il sorriso
" Ch' io vi creai. No, d' attristar Gio-
" conda
" Più non temete. . . amatevi. . .
" Ho il cuore rassegnato.
" Nessuno è qui colpevole,
" So che l' amore è un fato!

Enzo e Lau. (*al colmo della commozione*).
Oh! benedetta!

Gio. (*sempre con maggior fretta*).
Basta! il tempo fugge!
La barca s' avvicina. . . i miei compagni
Vi condurran prima dell' alba al lido
Dei Tre Porti. . . " ed appena giunti a
terra
" Domanderete due corsieri e lesti."
Verso Aquileja drizzerete il volo,
E di là poco lunge il sol d' Illiria
Vi splenderà liberamente in viso.
" Tu per lenir il trepido vïaggio [*a* Lau.
" Gli narrerai la tua ventura. Addio. .
Ecco la barca. . . il mio mantel t' asconda.

Lau. (*looking toward* Gio.). Ah, me! your shadow in mantle shrouded! Alvise! Fly!

Enzo. Dearest, have no fear!

Lau. (*approaching and recognizing* Gio., *who has uncovered her face*).
'T is thou! 'T is she by whose aid my life was sav'd.

Enzo (*to* Gio.). Angelic maiden,
Ah, let me kiss thy feet!

Chorus (*at a great distance off*).
Float on, serenade!
Heaven soft airs is granting;
Float on, serenade,
O'er the waters enchanting!
We listen to songs
Full of innocent glee,
Our oars keeping time
As we float o'er the sea.
A song is Existence,
On dreams it has flourished.
To dream we 're invited,
By dreams we are nourished.
From some unknown soul,
Comes echo's reply;
The last note, ascending,
Is lost in the sky.

Gio. Dost thou remember yonder song, O Laura?
It is the song with which was linked thy fortunes.
'T is for us it is sung. Attentively listen!
Dearest companions, yon rowers shall in safety
Place ye both, ere morning dawns. For your flight
All is provided, with due caution.
The barque is fast approaching: my companions
Will arrive, just before daybreak, abreast
Of the Three Gates: swiftly
Towards Aquileja then your flight directing,
You from thence (not far off) will see Illyria
Smiling a welcome to the wand'ring lovers.
Here are the boatmen. (*To* Lau.) My cloak will serve to hide thee.

[Si vede la barca dei cantori che s' arresta alla riva. GIO. si toglie il mantello di dosso e copre LAU.; poi scorge al collo di LAU. il rosario.

Che vedo là ! Il rosario ! oh sommo Dio !
Così dicea la profezia profonda :
A te questo rosario
Che le preghiere aduna.
Io te lo porgo, accettalo,
Ti porterà fortuna. . .
E così sia ! quest' ultimo
Bacio che il pianto innonda
V' abbiate in fronte, è il povero
Bacio del labbro mio.
Talor nei vostri mèmori
pensieri alla Gioconda
Date un ricordo.   Amatevi. . .
Lieti vivete. . . Addio !

ENZO *e* LAU.   Sulle tue mani l' anima
Tutta stempriamo in pianto.
No, mai su queste lagrime
Non scenderà l' oblio.
Ricorderem la vittima
Del sacrificio santo.
Ti benedican gli angeli
Addio. . . Gioconda — Addio.
[Sull' ultimo verso LAU. ed ENZO avranno già un piede sulla barca.—Quadro.—Partono. — Pausa.

SCENA V.

GIOCONDA *sola, poi* BARNABA *nella calle.*

GIO. (*afferra l' ampolla del veleno*).
Ora posso morir.   Tutto è compiuto
Ah no ! mia madre ! aiuto !
Aiuto, o santa Vergine !
Troppi dolori sovra un solo cuore !
Vo' ricercar mia madre ! . . . Oh ! mio
terrore !
[côlta da un pensiero improvviso.
Il patto or mi rammento ! Ah ! la paura
Di Barnaba m' agghiaccia !
Qui riveder l' orribile sua faccia !
[corre all' immagine della Madonna e si prostra.
Vergine Santa, allontana il Demonio ! !
BAR. (*viene dalla calle, si ferma alla porta socchiusa e sta spiando*).
Il ciel s' oscura.   [*scompare la luna.*
' ed essa non sa qual testimonio.
la guarda.

[The barque of the Cantori arrives, and stops at the bank. GIO. takes off her mantle which she places on LAU., then sees the rosary on LAU.'s breast.

What do I see? 'T is the rosary
Eternal Heaven !
Thus did my mother speak in tones
prophetic :
" *This rosary I offer,*
No richer prize possessing ;
Deign to accept the humble gift !
'*T will bring to thee a blessing.*"
It brings thee blessing ; this last gentle
kiss,
By my tears inundated,
I place on thy forehead ; the last kiss
That my lips will proffer.
Recall sometimes to memory
Kind thoughts of La Gioconda ill-fated
Keep me in memory, and love each
other :
May ye both be happy !   Farewell !

ENZO *and* LAU.
Upon thy hands thy generous tears
Of sympathy are falling.
These mournful parting tears of thine
Shall be forgotten never
Thy memory we 'll cherish aye,
Thy sacrifice recalling ;
May angels bring thee bliss divine.
Adieu, Gioconda, adieu !
       [*Exeunt LAU. and ENZO*

SCENE V.

GIOCONDA, *alone, then* BARNABA.

GIO. (*clutching the flask of poison*).
Now I can die.   All is over.
Ah, no ! — my mother !   O aid me,
Aid me, O Holy Virgin !
Too heavy is for one sad heart this
anguish ;
I go to seek my mother. Oh, woe is me !
That compact I remember.   Ah me !
the terror
     [*struck with a sudden thought*
Of Barnaba o'erwhelms me :
Here to behold again those hellish fea
tures

Gio. Vergine Santa, allontana il Demonio..
Ebben, perchè son così affranta e tarda,
La fuga è il mio riscatto!
Bar. (Ah! vuol fuggir . . .)
[*mentre* Gio. *fa per fuggire s'incontra con*
Bar. *che spalanca l'uscio ed entra.*

SCENA ULTIMA.

Gioconda e Barnaba.

Bar. (*terribilmente*). Così mantieni il patto?

Gio. (*prima atterrita, poi con coraggio supremo
sino alla fine*).

Sì, il patto mantengo — lo abbiamo
giurato,

Gioconda none deve — quel giuro tradir.

Che Iddio mi perdoni — l'immenso
peccato

Che sto per compir!

Bar. (*fra sè*).

Ebbrezza? delirio! — Mio sogno supremo!

Ti colgo e repente — quest'arido cuor

S'innonda di gioia! — già palpito e
tremo

Ai rai dell'amor!

Gio. (*a* Bar. *che fa per avvicinarsi*).

Raffrena il selvaggio—delirio! t'arresta.

Vo' farmi più gaia, — più fulgida ancor.

Per te voglio ornare — le bionda mia
testa

Di porpora e d'ôr!
[*va ad ornarsi.*

Con tutti gli orpelli — sacrati alla scena

Dei pazzi teatri — coperta già son.

Ascolta di questa — sapiente sirena

L'ardente canzon.

T'arresta, che temi? — mantengo il
mio detto,

Non mento, non fuggo, — tradirti non
vo'.

Volesti il mio corpo, — dimon maledetto?

E il corpo ti do!

*si trafigge nel cuore col pugnale che avrà
raccolto furtivamente nelle resti adornan-
tosi e piomba a terra come fulmine -*

[*flies to the image of the Virgin and kneels before it.*
O Holy Virgin ! keep away the foul demon

SCENE THE LAST

Enter Barnaba. *He comes down the street, and
stops at the half-opened door.*

Bar. (*watching* Gio.). The sky is cloudy.
[*the moon disappears.*
Praying! but she little knows what witness here unto her pray'rs is list'ning.

Gio. .O Holy Virgin, keep away the foul
demon!
And now, why am I thus exhausted. 'T is
late.

Bar. (*aside*). (Ah! she would fly!)

Gio In flight is my only safety
[Gio., *when about to fly, meets* Bar. *who
throws the door wide open, and enters*

Bar. (*in terrible tones*) Thy compact thus
thou keepest?

Gio. (*at first terrified, recovers her courage
and retains it to the end*).
Yes, I keep to my compact : we both
swore to keep it,
And ne'er will Gioconda be false to her
oath.
May Heaven in mercy withhold condem
nation.
And pardon us both !

Bar. O rapture ecstatic ! O dream of
Elysium !
Thou 'rt mine now! and swift, from
this desolate heart,
Expell'd by love's rays, sombre shadows
depart.

Gio. (*to* Bar., *who is approaching her*).
Restrain awhile thy ardent passion !
Thou soon shalt in splendor Gioconda
behold ;
For thee, I am braiding my clustering
tresses
With purple and gold.
[*begins to adorn herself*
With glittering jewels, the gay jewels
worn nightly
By madcaps theatrical, cover'd I 'll be
Now list to the song that this ardent
young siren
Will sing unto thee !
I keep to my compact ; no false oath
was mine ;
Thou claimest Gioconda ? Now, demon
accursed,
Gioconda is thine

BAR. Ah! ferma! irrisïon ... ebben ... or tu
         ... M' odi ... e muori dannata:
      [*curvandosi sul cadavere di* GIO. *e gridandogli
      al l' orecchio con voce furibonda.*

         Ier tua madre m' ha offeso! Io l' ho
      affogata!

                Non ode più!!

      [*esce precipitosamente e scompare nelle tene-
      bre della calle.*

                        [*Cade la tela.*

           FINE DELL' OPERA.

      [*stabs herself to the heart with the dagge
      that she had furtively secreted whil
      adorning herself, and falls dead, as y
      lightning-struck.*
BAR. Ah, stay thee! 'Tis a jest! Well
         then, thou shalt hear this,
         And die ever damned!
      [*bending over the corpse of* GIO., *and scream
      ing furiously into her ear.*
         Last night thy mother did offend me:
         I have strangled her!
         She hears me not!
      [*with a cry of half-choked rage, rushes dow
      the street.*   [*Curtain*

           END OF THE OPERA

CAVALLERIA RUSTICANA
(Rustic Chivalry)

by

PIETRO MASCAGNI

RUSTIC CHIVALRY.

TURIDDU. (Behind the scenes.)

O Lo - la, fair as flow'rs in beau - ty smil - ing, . . Love from thy soul - lit
O Lo - la, bian - ca co - me fior di spi - no, . . quan - do t'af - fac - ci

eyes Soft - ly is glow - ing; . . He who would kiss thy lips, red and be -
te s'affac - cia il so - le; . . Chi t'ha ba - cia - to il lab - bro por - po

guil - ing . . Bliss - ful and fa-vor'd were he, Such heav - en know - ing! . .
ri - no . . Gra - zia più bel - la a Di - o chie-dernon vô - le

Tho' thy thresh - old blood, crim - son, is stain - ing, . . Car - ing for naught, I
C'è scrit - to san - gue so - pra la tua por - ta; . . Ma di re - star - cia

seek thee, scorning to hide me; . . What tho' I for - feit life, thy pres - ence
me non me n'in - por - ta; . . Se per te mo - jo e va - do in pa - ra

gain - ing? What were the joy of heav'n, wert thou de - nied me!
di - so, Non c'en - tro se . . non ve - do il tuo bel vi . so,

(3)

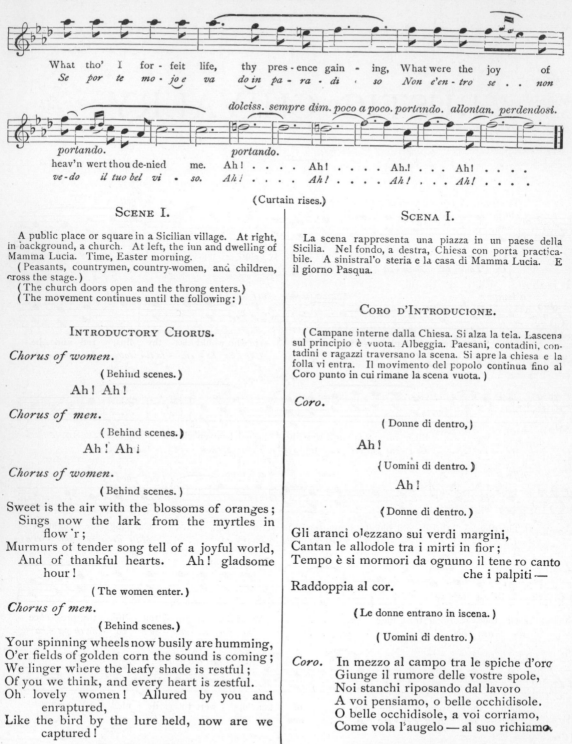

What tho' I for-feit life,   thy pres-ence gain - ing,   What were the joy   of
Se   por te   mo - jo e   va   do in pa - ra - di so   Non e'en-tro se . . non

dolciss. sempre dim. poco a poco. portando. allontan. perdendosi.

portando.   *portando.*

heav'n wert thou de-nied   me.   Ah! . . . .   Ah! . . . . Ah.! . . . Ah! . . . .
ve-do   il tuo bel vi • so.   Ah! . . . .   Ah! . . . . Ah! . . . Ah! . . . .

(Curtain rises.)

SCENE I.

A public place or square in a Sicilian village. At right, in background, a church. At left, the inn and dwelling of Mamma Lucia. Time, Easter morning.

(Peasants, countrymen, country-women, and children, cross the stage.)

(The church doors open and the throng enters.)

(The movement continues until the following:)

INTRODUCTORY CHORUS.

Chorus of women.

(Behind scenes.)

Ah! Ah!

Chorus of men.

(Behind scenes.)

Ah! Ah!

Chorus of women.

(Behind scenes.)

Sweet is the air with the blossoms of oranges;
  Sings now the lark from the myrtles in
    flow'r;
Murmurs of tender song tell of a joyful world,
  And of thankful hearts.   Ah! gladsome
    hour!

(The women enter.)

Chorus of men.

(Behind scenes.)

Your spinning wheels now busily are humming,
O'er fields of golden corn the sound is coming;
We linger where the leafy shade is restful;
Of you we think, and every heart is zestful.
Oh lovely women! Allured by you and
    enraptured,
Like the bird by the lure held, now are we
    captured!

(The men enter.)

SCENA I.

La scena rappresenta una piazza in un paese della Sicilia. Nel fondo, a destra, Chiesa con porta practicabile. A sinistral'o steria e la casa di Mamma Lucia.   E il giorno Pasqua.

CORO D'INTRODUCIONE.

(Campane interne dalla Chiesa. Si alza la tela. Lascena sul principio è vuota. Albeggia. Paesani, contadini, contadini e ragazzi traversano la scena. Si apre la chiesa e la folla vi entra.   Il movimento del popolo continua fino al Coro punto in cui rimane la scena vuota.)

Coro.

(Donne di dentro,)

Ah!

(Uomini di dentro.)

Ah!

(Donne di dentro.)

Gli aranci olezzano sui verdi margini,
Cantan le allodole tra i mirti in fior;
Tempo è si mormori da ognuno il tene ro canto
                              che i palpiti—
Raddoppia al cor.

(Le donne entrano in iscena.)

(Uomini di dentro.)

Coro.   In mezzo al campo tra le spiche d'oro
Giunge il rumore delle vostre spole,
Noi stanchi riposando dal lavoro
A voi pensiamo, o belle occhidisole.
O belle occhidisole, a voi corriamo,
Come vola l'augelo—al suo richiamo.

(Gli uomini entrano in iscena.)

Women.
Work in the field now is ended; —
    The Holy Mother mild
    In ecstasy fondles the Child.

All.

(Withdrawing from stage.)
Murmurs of tender song tell of a joyful world,
And of thankful hearts.
Ah! gladsome hour!

(Enter, Santuzza, approaching Lucia's dwelling.)

SCENE II.

(Santuzza, Lucia, Alfio, and chorus.)

Santuzza.   Tell me, mother Lucia —

Lucia.
    (Coming from house.)
It is thou? What wilt thou?

Sant.   Where is Turiddu?

Lucia.   For him you ask? For him, my son
    Turiddu!

Sant.   Only for him I ask you. Pardon, but
    answer!   Where is Turiddu?

Lucia.   Ask me not! I know not; I want no
    trouble.

Sant.   Mamma Lucia, with weeping do I pray
    you!
Even as spake the Saviour to the Magdalen,
Say, in pity say, where is Turiddu!

Lucia.   He 's gone to bring some wine from
    Francofonte.

Sant.   No! Last night some within the village
    saw him.

Lucia.   What says't thou? Who told it?
    Nay, he hath not yet returned.
    Enter!

Sant.   I may not step across your threshold,
    I cannot pass it, I, most unhappy out-
    cast!
    Excommunicated!

Lucia.   What of my son? What hast thou to
    tell me?

Sant.   Ah! the torture, the heart-pain.

[Cracking of whips and jingling of bells behind scenes.)
(Chorus enters, followed soon by Alfio.)

Donne.   Cessin le rustiche opre: [tor;
    La Virgine serena allietasi del Salva-
    Tempo è si mormori da ognuno il
        tenero canto che i palpiti —
    Raddoppia al cor.

Uomini.

(Allontanandosi.)
In mezzo al campo, etc.

Donne.

(Allontanandosi.)
Gli aranci olezzano, etc.

SCENA II.

Sortita di Alfio.

Santuzza.

(Entra e si dirige alla casa di Lucia.)
Dite, Mamma Lucia —

Lucia.

(Sortendo.)
Sei tu? che vuoi?

Santuzza.   Turiddu ov'è?

Lucia.   Fin qui vieni a cercare il figlio mio?

Santuzza.   Voglio saper soltanto,
    Perdonatemi voi, dove trovarlo.

Lucia.   Non lo so, non lo so, non voglio
        brighe!

Santuzza.   Mamma Lucia, vi supplico pian-
        gendo,
    Fate come il Signore a Maddalena,
    Ditemi per pietà, dov' è Turiddu.

Lucia.   E andato per il vino a Francofonte.

Santuzza.   No! l'hanvisto in paese ad alta
        notte.

Lucia.   Che dici? che dici? se non è tornato
        casa!   Entra!

Santuzza.   Non posso entrare in casa vostra.
    Sono scomunicata!

Lucia.   E che ne sai del mio figliuolo?

Santuzza.   Quale spina ho in core!

(Dall' interno schiocchi di frusta e tintinnio di sonagli
    Entrano in iscena i coristi indi Alfio.)

Andante rit.
ALFIO.

My lov-ing Lo-la calls me! Her gen-tle grace en-thralls me, Ah!
M'a spet-ta a ca-sa Lo-la che m'a ma e mi con-so-la, ch'è

.. faith-ful-ly she calls..... My lov-ing Lo-la calls me, Her
tut-ta fe-del-tà...... M'a spet-ta a ca-sa Lo-la! che

gen-tle grace en-thralls me, Ah! fond-ly I re-ply........
m'ama e mi con-so-la, ch'è tut-ta fe-del-tà.......

Tempo 1.

Gay-ly moves the tramping horse, Joy-ful sound the ring-ing bells; 'Tis Eas-ter and home come
Il ca-val-lo scal pi-ti, i so-na-gli squil-li-no, è Pas-qua, ed io son

(Women of the chorus enter the scene.)

I!... 'Tis Eas-ter and home come I!... come I!...
quà,... è Pas-qua ed io son quà... son quà!..

ALFIO.

A - hi! A - hi! Snap, now, the
Ehi-là! Ehi-là! schioc-chi la

Who hath call-ing mer-rier, Than the life of car-rier, Where is a
O che bei me-stie-re fa-re il car-ret-tie-re an-dar di

lash goes, a-hi! Snap, now, the lash goes, Snap, now, the lash goes
fru-sta, Ehi-là! schioc-chi la fru-sta, schioc-chi la fru-sta

jol-lier man? Where is a jol-lier man? Where
quà e di là, an-dar di quà e di là! an-

Snap, now, the lash goes,
schioc-chi la fru-sta,

is a jol-lier man?
dar - di quà e di là,

Where is a jol-lier man, a jol-lier
an - dar di quà e di là, di quà e di

{ come!　　I'm the mer-ry car - rier!　I'm the mer-ry car - rier, Who hath call-ing
Son quà!　　Oh che bel me - stie - re　fa - re il car - ret - tie - re, oh che bel me-

man? . . .
là, ...

mer - rier than the life, the life of car - rier, than the life, this life of mine,　A
stier, an - dar di quà, an - dar di là, an - dar di quà, an - dar di là!

hap-pier man than I? . . .　　Where is a jol - lier man, where is a jol - lier man? 'T is
Pasqua ed io son quà, . .　　an - dar di quà e di là, an - dar di quà e di là,　E

Eas - ter, home come I, ...　　come I! . . . . .
Pas - qua ed io son qua, . . .　　sou qua! . . . .

(Chorus withdraws into the church ; others separate in various directions.)

(Il Coro esce, alcuni entrano in chiesa, altri prendono direzioni diverse.)

SCENE III.

SCENE AND PRAYER.

Lucia.　Blest are you, friendly Alfio !
　　　So favored, ever thus to be gay !

Alfio.　Mamma Lucia, have you that rare old wine,
　　　The same as ever ?

SCENA III.

Lucia.　Beato voi, compar Alfio,
　　　Che siete sempre allegro così !

Alfio.

(Spigliato.)

Mamma Lucia,
N'avete ancora di quel vecchio vino ?

Lucia. Not now; Turiddu has gone to buy a plenty.

Alfio. No; he is here! I saw him here this morning;
He lingered near my cottage.

Lucia.

(Surprised.)

What now!

Santuzza.

(Rapidly, to Lucia.)

Be silent!

Alfio. I will not tarry,
You will to church devotedly?

(Exit.)

Chorus.

(In church.)

Queen of the Heavens, sorrow flieth!

People.

(External chorus.)

Hallelujah!

Chorus.

(In church.)

Thy holy Son lives, nor dieth!

People. Hallelujah!

Chorus.

(within.)

From the dead He now hath risen,
Truly hath He risen.

People. Hallelujah.

Chorus.

(External. Grouping in devotional attitudes.)

We will sing of the Lord now victorious!
All the terrors of death were in vain!
Let us sing of the Christ ever glorious;
He is risen, in glory to reign!

Santuzza. We will sing of the Lord now victorious;
We will sing of the Christ ever glorious;
Pow'r of death was in vain.
Unto heaven the Lord now riseth,
Now riseth in glory to reign.

Lucia. Non so; Turiddu è andato a provvederne.

Alfio. Se è sempre qui!
L'ho visto stamattina vicino a casa mia

Lucia.

(Sorpresa.)

Come?

Santuzza.

(A Lucia rapidamente.)

Tacete.

Alfio. Io me ne vado, ite voi altre in chiesa

(Esce.)

Coro.

(Interno.)

Regina Cœli, lætare —

Alleluja!

Quia, quem meruisti potare —

Alleluja!

Resusrexit sicut dixit —

Alleluja!

Coro.

(Esterno.)

(Uomini e donne entrano e si schierano innanzi alla Chiesa in atteggiamento devoto.)

Inneggiamo, il Signor non è morto!
Ei fulgente ha dischiuso l'avel,
Inneggiamo al Signore risorto
Oggi asceso alla gloria del ciel!

Chorus. We will sing, of the Lord now victorious !
            All the terrors of death were in
vain !
            Let us sing of the Christ ever
glorious ;
            He is risen, in glory to reign.
            Praise the Lord.

(All enter the church, except Santuzza and Lucia.)

Inneggiamo, il Signor non è morto !
Ei fulgente ha dischiuso l'avel,
Inneggiamo al Signore risorto
Oggi asceso alla gloria del ciel !

(Tutti entrano in chiesa tranne Santuzza e Lucia.)

Scene IV.

ROMANZA.

Lucia

(To Santuzza.)

  And why with signals would you gain
  my silence?

Santuzza. Now shall you know, kind mother :
  Ere he went forth as a soldier,
  Turiddu pledged his love to Lola,
      All his faithfulness renewing
  But ; ah ! homeward returning,
  Married he found his Lola !
  And, her falsity shaming —
      All the old love subduing —
      Loved *me !*
  And I loved *him !*
  With jealousy, hatefully, and
with madness,
      Scorning wifely duty, envious of
my gladness,
      Lola, in malice shameful, re-
gains Turiddu !
  Fate disgraceful o'ertakes me,
  My own Turiddu forsakes me !
  Lola and he in joy remain,
  Having each other's love again !
  Ah me ! alone I weep, I weep !

Lucia. Grief is upon us !
  Such dire and woeful tidings to hear
this holy morning.

Santuzza. I am accursed ! I am accursed !
  Good mother, go pray for me unto
the Saviour !
  Thou 'lt beseech Him for me !
  I 'll seek Turiddu, and pray to him
  That he again may love me !

Lucia. Holy Mary be with thee — the blessed
  Mary !

(Lucia enters the church)

Scena IV.

Lucia. Perchè m'hai fatto segno di tacere?

Santuzza. Voi lo sapete, o mamma, prima
  d'andar soldato
  Turiddu aveva a Lola eterna fè
  giurato.
  Tornò, la seppe sposa ; e con un
  nuovo amore
  Volle spegner la fiamma che gli
  bruciava il core
  M'amò, l'amai, l'amai, ah !
  Quell' invida d'ogni delizia mia,
  Del suo spcso dimentica, arse di
  gelosia.
  Me l'ha rapito. Priva dell' onor
  mio,
  Dell' onor mio rimango :
  Lola e Turiddu s'amano, io piango !

Lucia. Miseri noi, che cosa vieni a dirmi
  In questo santo giorno?

Santuzza. Io son dannata.
  Andate, o mamma, ad implorar
  Iddio,
  E pregate per me. Verrà Turiddu,
  Vo' supplicarlo un' altra voltra
  ancora !

Lucia. Ajutatela voi, Santa Maria !

(Lucia entra in chiesa.)

SCENE V.

DUET. SANTUZZA AND TURIDDU.

Turiddu.

(*Entering.*)

Thou here, Santuzza!

Santuzza. Here I await thee.

Turiddu. Attending not the service of Easter?

Santuzza. Not now! Thee would I speak with.

Turiddu. I seek my mother.

Santuzza. Thee would I speak with!

Turiddu. Not here, not here!

Santuzza. From whence dost thou come?

Turiddu. Why dost thou ask me? —
From Francofonte.

Santuzza. Ah, that is false!

Turiddu. Santuzza, believe me!

Santuzza. No! thou art lying!
Over yon path I beheld thee approach:
And thou wert seen to-day returning homeward
From the dwelling of Lola!

Turiddu. Ah! thou wert spying!

Santuzza. No, I do swear it!
Her husband, Alfio, saw thee
Here within the town, and told it me!

Turiddu. So thou rewardest the love I gave thee,
What though he slay me!

Santuzza. Ah! Tell me not of murder!

Turiddu. Leave me, I tell thee! leave me!
The rage within me burning —
My righteous wrath, thou cast not assuage!

SCENA V.

Turiddu.

(*Entrando.*)

Tu qui Santuzza?

Santuzza. Qui t'aspettavo

Turiddu. È Pasqua in chiesa non vai?

Santuzza. Non vo. Debbo parlarti.

Turiddu. Mamma cercavo.

Santuzza. Debbo parlarti.

Turiddu. Qui no! qui no!

Santuzza.

(*Parlato.*)

Dove sei stato?

Turiddu.

(*Parlato.*)

Che vuoi tu dire? A Francofonte.

Santuzza. No, non è ver.

Turiddu. Santuzza credimi.

Santuzza. No, non mentire
Ti vidi volgere giù dal sentir.
E stamattina all' alba t'hanno
Scorto presso l'uscio di Lola.

Turiddu. Ah! mi hai spiato!

Santuzza. No! te lo giuro, a noi l'ha raccontato
Campar Alfio il marito poco fa.

Turiddu. Cosi ricambi l'amor che ti porto?
Vuoi che m'uccida?

Santuzza. Oh! questo non lo dire.

Turiddu. Lasciami dunque, lasciami invan tenti sopire
Il giusto sdegno colla tua pietà.

Santuzza. Then, thou dost love her!
More fair than I is Lola!
False friend! Oh, curses on her!

Turiddu. Santuzza!

Santuzza. She — vilest woman, steals the love that should be mine!

Turiddu. Heed thou!
I am no slave to thy envy
Scornfully showing, jealously showing

Santuzza. Insult and punishment I am unheeding!
Yet do I love thee,
Even though anguish my heart is rending,
E'en though in sorrow my life is ending.

SCENE VI.

LOLA'S DITTY.

Lola.

(Behind scenes.)

Bright flower, so radiant!
Angelic thousands stand arrayed in heaven,
Yet none so fair as thou hath yet been given!

(Enters. Pauses suddenly.)

Oh! Turiddu, hast thou seen Alfio?

Turiddu. I came but this moment: I have not.

Lola. Then at the forge perchance he awaiteth.
Here I must not linger.
And thou?
Is't here in public thou art praying?

Turiddu.

(Confusedly.)

Santuzza here was telling —

Santuzza.

I was saying this is Easter!

(Meaningly.)

And the Lord all things beholdeth!

Lola.

(To Santuzza.)

Thou wilt not go to the service?

Santuzza. Tu l'ami dunque?

Turiddu. No!

Santuzza. Assai più bella è Lola!

Turiddu. Taci, non l'amo.

Santuzza. L'ami, l'ami, Oh! maledetto!

Turiddu. Santuzza!

Santuzza. Quella cattiva femmina ti tolse a me!

Turiddu. Bada, Santuzza, schiavo non sono
Di questa vana tua gelosia.

Santuzza.

(Con angoscia.)

Battimi, insultami, t'amo e perdono
Ma è troppo forte l'angoscia mia.

(Troncando nel sentire avvicinarsi Lola.)

SCENA VI.

Lola.

(Dentra alla scena.)

Fior di giaggiolo
Gli angeli belli stanc
A mille in cielo
Ma belli come lui
Ce n'è uno solo.

(Entra in scena e s'interrompe.)

Oh! Turiddu, è passato Alfio?

Turiddu. Son giunto ora in piazza non so.

Lola. Forse è rimasto dal maniscalco ma non può tardare!
E voi sentite le funzioni in piazza?

Turiddu.

(Confuso affret.)

Santuzza mi narrava -

Santuzza. Gli dicevo che oggi è Pasqua
E il Signor vede ogni cosa.

Lola. Non venite alla messa?

Santuzza.

No, no!   None shall attend but those
Who know they are not guilty!

Lola.

(Vehemently.)

In the grace of the Saviour
I bow before thee!

Santuzza.

(Bitterly.)

O, well thou speakest! —
Lola!

Turiddu.

(Embarrassed.)
(To Lola.)

Away then! Come, Lola;
Here there is naught to hold us.

Lola.

(Ironically.)

Oh, stay thou with *her!*

Santuzza.

(To Turiddu.)

Yes, stay thou!

(Firmly.)

I have something yet to tell thee:

Lola.

(Mockingly.)

May the Saviour assist thee!

(Going.)

So, I will leave thee.

(Enters the church.)

SCENE VII.

CONTINUATION OF THE DUET.

Turiddu.

(To Sant.)

Ah! how foolish! naught availing!

Santuzza.

(Coldly.)

I have spoken; 't is well — 't is the truth.

Santuzza.

(Subito.)

Io no, ci deve andar chi sa

(Con intensione.)

Di non aver peccato!

Lola.

(Con forza.)

Io ringrazio il Signore, e bacio in terra!

Santuzza.

(Esprimendosi.)

Oh! fate bene, fate bene,

(Con amarezza.)

Lola!

Turiddu.

(A Lola.)
(Impacciato.)

Andiamo, andiamo, Oni non abbiam
che fare.

Lola.

(A Turiddu.)

Oh!

(Con ironia.)

Rimanete.

Santuzza.

(A Turiddu con fermezza.)

Si, resta, resta,
Ho da parlarti ancora.

Lola.

(Sempre ironica.)

E v'assista il Signore,

(Con caricatura.)

Io me ne vado.

(Entra in chiesa.)

SCENA VII.

Turiddu.

(Con ironia.)

Ah! lo vedi, che hai tu detto?

Santuzza.

(Fredda.)

L'hai voluto e ben ti sta!

Turiddu.

        (Threateningly.)

  Ah ! by heaven !

Santuzza.   My heart is breaking !

Turiddu.

        (Approaching her.)

  No !

Santuzza.

        (Warding him away.)

  Turiddu, ah ! hear me !

Turiddu.

  Go !

      (Turns from her.)

Turiddu.

        (S'avventa.)

  Ah ! per Dio !

Santuzza.   Squarciami il petto.

Turiddu.

        (S'avvia.)

  No !

Santuzza.

        (Trattenendolo.)

  Turiddu, ascolta !

Turiddu. Va !

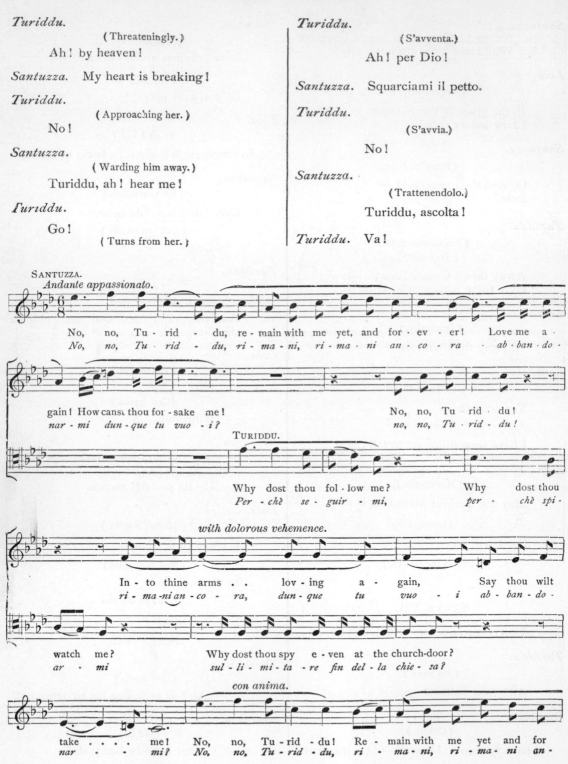

con disperazione.

Wilt thou leave me thus? Ah! . Then dost thou leave me, Then dost thou
tu puo - i co - si Ah! . dun - que tu vuo - i ab - ban - do -

I re - peat it, Go! Ah! . Go! I re - peat it, Go! I re -
ti - ri pe - to va! ah! . va ti ri - pe - to, va, non te -

Maestoso.
ff con suprema passione.

leave . . . . me? Ah! No! Tu - rid - du! Re - main with me yet and for -
nàr - - mi? ah! no! Tu - rid - du! ri - ma - ni, ri - ma - ni an -

peat - - it! Go! . . Go! Vain were re - pent - ance for thine of -
diar - - mi va! . . Pen - tir - si e va - no do - po - l'of -

sempre animando.

ev - er! I im - plore thee, do not for - sake me, Tu - rid - du!
co - ra, dun - que vuo - i ab - ban - do - nar - mi. Tu - rid - du!

fend - ing! Once more do I tell thee, go! And, for - ev - - er!
fe - sa, pen - tir - si è va - no do - po l'of - fe - - sa.

Santuzza.	**Santuzza.**
(Threateningly.)	(Minacciosa.)
False! false!	Bada!
Turiddu.	**Turiddu.**
(With increased rage.)	(Con moltissima forza.)
Thus I reward thee in my anger.	Dell' ira tua non mi curo!
(Throws her down, and hastens into the church.)	(La getta a terra e fugge in chiesa.)
Santuzza.	**Santuzza.**
(In the height of fury.)	(Nel colmo dell' ira.)
Accurs'd! accurs'd at Easter, thou false one.	A te la mala Pasqua, spergiuro!
(Falls, despairingly.)	(Cade affranta ed angosciata.)

SCENE VIII.

DUET, SANTUZZA AND ALFIO.

(Enter, Alfio.)

Santuzza.

(Calming herself.)

Oh! doth the Saviour send thee, neighbor Alfio?

Alfio. At what point is the service?

Santuzza. 'T is now at closing.
But I tell thee Lola has gone with Turiddu!

Alfio.

('Surprised.)

What are you saying?

Santuzza. While thou dost labor to earn an honest living,
Lola unfaithfully her love is giving.

Alfio. Ah! in the name of heaven, Santuzza, what sayest thou?

Santuzza. The truth!
Turiddu forsakes me — and he hath betrayed me!
'T was your wife who enticed him away from me!

Alfio.

(Threateningly.)

And if thou art lying
I'll have thy heart's blood!

Santuzza. Lies, as yet, my lips have never uttered.
Prone to be truthful am I.

Alfio.

(After a pause.)

Santuzza, I am thankful that you have spoken.

Santuzza. But ah! what shame!
And I have told it thee!

Alfio.

(Suddenly, in fury.)

T 'is they who are shameful!
Revenge I'll have upon them!
This day and hour my wrath
Shall fall upon them!

SCENA VIII.

(Sorte Alfio e s'incontra con Santuzza.)

Santuzza.

(Ad Alfio rianimandosi.)

Oh! Il Signore vi manda, compar Alfio.

Alfio.

(Tranquillo.)

A che punto è la messa?

Santuzza.

È tardi ormai, ma per voi

(Con intenzione.)

Lola è andata con Turiddu!

Alfio.

(Sorpreso.)

Che avete detto?

Santuzza. Che mentre correte
All' acqua e al vento a guadagnarvi il pane,
Lola v'adorna il tetto in malo modo!

Alfio. Ah! nel nome di Dio, Santa che dite?

Santuzza. Il ver. Turiddu mi tolse, mi tolse l'onore,
E vostra moglie lui rapiva a me!

Alfio.

(Minaccioso.)

Se voi mentite, vo' schiantarvi il core.

Santuzza. Uso a mentire il labbro mio, il labbro mio non è!
Per la vergogna mia, pel mio dolore
La trista verità — vi dissi, ahimè!

Alfio.

(Dopo un poco di pausa.)

Comare Santa, allor grato vi sono.

Santuzza. Infame io son che vi partai così!

Alfio. Infami loro, ad essi non perdono
Vendetta avrò pria che tra monti il dì!
Io sangue vo glio, all'ira m'abbandono,
In odio tutto l'amor mio finì!

(Escono.)

INTERMEZZO.

SCENE IX.

CHORUS AND BRINDISI.

(The people enter from the church. Lucia crosses and enters the inn.)

Chorus of men.

(sotto voce.)

Now homeward, now homeward ye
neighhors,
Good cheer is awaiting there;
And wives our joy will share,
Now Easter day shall be for all a time
of rest,
Without sorrow or care.

Chorus of women.

(Lola and Turiddu come from the church.)

Turiddu. My pretty Lola! Have you not a
greeting,
When honest people we are meeting?

Lola. I must leave thee.
I must go and welcome Alfio!

Turiddu. Here he will seek thee.
Do not hasten!
(To the people.)
Meanwhile, good friends, come hither.
(All come forward.)
We'll try the merry wine!

(All take cups from the bar of the inn.)

SCENA IX.

(Tutti escono di chiesa. Lucia attraversa ia scena de entra in casa. A gruppi soto voce fra loro.)

Coro.

(Uomini.)

A casa, a casa, amici, ove ci aspettano
Le nostre donne, andiam,
Or che letizia rasserena gli animi.

Coro.

(Donne.)

A casa, a casa, amiche, ecc.

[Lola e Turiddu escono dalla chiesa.]

Turiddu. Comare Lola, ve ne andante via
Senza nemmeno salutare?

Lola. Vado a casa; Non ho visto compar
Alfio!

Turiddu. Non ci pensate, verrà in piazza.

(Rivolgendosi al Coro che s'avvia.)

Intanto, amici, qua,
Beviamone un bicchiere.

(Tutti si avvicinano alla tavola dell' osteria e prendono in mano i bicchieri.)

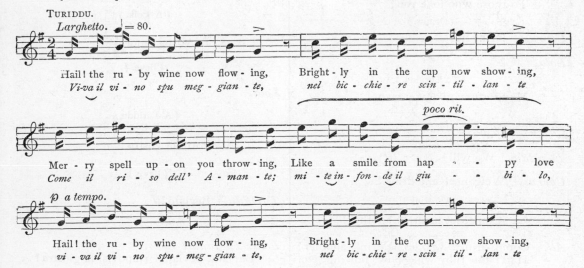

TURIDDU.
Larghetto. ♩ = 80.

Hail! the ru - by wine now flow - ing, Bright - ly in the cup now show - ing,
Vi-va il vi - no spu meg - gian - te, nel bic - chie - re scin - til - lan - te

poco rit.

Mer - ry spell up - on you throw - ing, Like a smile from hap - py love
Come il ri - so dell' A - man - te; mi - te in - fon - de il giu - bi - lo,

p a tempo.

Hail! the ru - by wine now flow - ing, Bright - ly in the cup now show - ing,
vi - va il vi - no spu - meg - gian - te, nel bic - chie - re - scin - til - lan - te

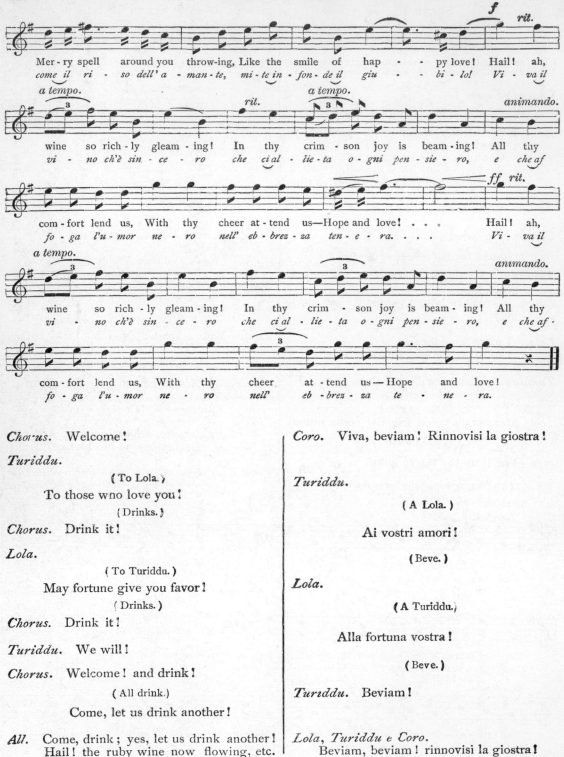

Mer - ry spell around you throw-ing, Like the smile of hap - - py love! Hail! ah,
come il ri - so dell' a - man - te, mi - te in - fon - de il giu - - bi - lo! Vi - va il

wine so rich - ly gleam - ing! In thy crim - son joy is beam-ing! All thy
vi - no ch'è sin - ce - ro che ci al - lie - ta o - gni pen - sie - ro, e che af

com - fort lend us, With thy cheer at - tend us—Hope and love! . . . Hail! ah,
fo - ga l'u - mor ne - ro nell' eb - brez - za ten - e - ra. . . . Vi - va il

wine so rich - ly gleam - ing! In thy crim - son joy is beam - ing! All thy
vi - no ch'è sin - ce - ro che ci al - lie - ta o - gni pen - sie - ro, e che af -

com - fort lend us, With thy cheer at - tend us — Hope and love!
fo - ga l'u - mor ne - ro nell' eb - brez - za te - ne - ra.

Chorus. Welcome!	*Coro.* Viva, beviam! Rinnovisi la giostra!
Turiddu.	
(To Lola.)	*Turiddu.*
To those who love you!	
(Drinks.)	(A Lola.)
Chorus. Drink it!	Ai vostri amori!
Lola.	(Beve.)
(To Turiddu.)	
May fortune give you favor!	*Lola.*
(Drinks.)	
Chorus. Drink it!	(A Turiddu.)
Turiddu. We will!	Alla fortuna vostra!
Chorus. Welcome! and drink!	(Beve.)
(All drink.)	
Come, let us drink another!	*Turiddu.* Beviam!
All. Come, drink; yes, let us drink another!	*Lola, Turiddu e Coro.*
Hail! the ruby wine now flowing, etc.	Beviam, beviam! rinnovisi la giostra!

FINALE.

Alfio. Unto all of you, greeting!

Chorus. Neighbor Alfio, greeting!

Turiddu.

(To Alfio.)

Hearty welcome!
Now join with us in revel.

(Fills a glass for him.)

Look you! drink you this measure!

Alfio. Thank you! but I must refuse the
offer!
A cup of deadly poison perhaps you
proffer!

Turiddu. Then suit your pleasure!
(Throws away the wine.)

Lola. Ah me! what now befalls!

(Some of the women consult together, and then approach
Lola, saying:)

Neighbor Lola, come, haste away from
here!

(Exit, all the women, with LOLA.)

Turiddu.

(To Alfio.)

Perhaps you have something to tell me!

Alfio. I? nothing!

Turiddu. Then hear me!
You will find me at your service!

Alfio. This moment?

Turiddu. This moment!

(They embrace, Turiddu bites Alfio's ear, viciously.)

Alfio. Neighbor Turiddu, you give a ready
challenge!
And I accept it! you understand me!

Turiddu. Neighbor Alfio!
I own thou shouldst have vengeance,
And I admit, in the name that is
holy,
That I should be dealt with as a
dog, by thee!
But, shouldst thou kill me — if I
perish

FINALE.

(Entra Alfio.)

Alfio. A voi tutti salute.

Coro. Compar Alfio, salute.

Turiddu. Benvenuto! con noi dovete bere,

(Empie un bicchiere.)

Ecco pieno e il bicchiere.

(Troncando.)

Alfio. Grazie, ma il vostro vino io non l'accetto,
Diverrebbe veleno entro il mio petto!

Turiddu.

(Parlato.)

A piacer vostro.

(Getto il vino.)

Lola. Ahimè che mai sarà?

(Alcune donne nel Coro si consigliano fra loro poi si a-
vicinano a Lola dicendole sotto voce.)

Coro. Comare Lola, andiamo via di qua.

(Tutte le donne escono conducendo Lola.)

Turiddu. Avete altro a dirmi?

Alfio. Io nulla.

Turiddu. Allota sono agli ordini vostri —

Alfio. Or ora?

Turiddu. Or ora!

(Si abbracciano. Turiddu morde l'orecchio destro d
Alfio.)

Alfio. Compar Turiddu, a vete morso, a buono

(Con intenzione.)

Cintenderemo bene a quel che pare!

Turiddu. Compar Alfio.
Lo so che il torto è mio;
E ve lo giuro nel nome di Dio
Che al par d'un cane mi fare!
sgozzar —
Ma s'io non vivo,

(Dolorosamente.)

By thine arm — yes, if I perish, —
Unhappy Santa, she whom I have cherished —
Lone, unhappy Santa, my dagger
Will embed within thy heart!

Alfio. Good neighbor, act upon it as may suit you!
You will find me yonder in the orchard.

(Exit.)

Turiddu.

(Calling.)

My mother!

(Enter LUCIA.)

Mother! the wine-cup too freely passes!
Exciting, crazing!
Too many cups I have been drinking!
—— I must leave you, good mother!

But first let me ask for a kindly blessing,
As on that day when I became a soldier.
And, mother, hear me — and heed it:
If I return not, thou unto my Santa
Must be a kindly mother!
Santa, whom I promised I would lead
to the altar!
—If I return —

Lucia. Why say you this to me?
What is it? tell me!

Turiddu. Ha — nothing!
'T is wine — that I have drunk so freely.
—For me oh! pray to heaven,
That I may be forgiven!
One kiss, one kiss, my mother!
And yet — and yet another!
Farewell!

(Rushes off, desperately.)

Lucia. Turiddu! Ah!

(Retires to back of stage, crying.)
(Enter, Santuzza.)

Santuzza!

Santuzza. Ah! good mother!

(Throws her arms around Lucia's neck.)

(People crowd upon the stage.)

(Excitement and agitation.)

(Enter a woman in the distance crying. "Neighbor Turiddi is murdered.")

Resta abbandonata povera Santa!
Lei che mi s'è data!

(Con impeto.)

Vi saprò in core il ferro mio piantar!

Alfio.

(Freddamente.)

Compare fate come più vi piace,
Io v'aspetto qui fuori dietro l'orto.

Esce.

Turiddu.

(Chiamando.)

Mamma —

(Entra Lucia.)

Mamma — quel vino è generoso,
E certo oggi troppi bicchier
Ne ho traccannati —
Vado fuori all' aperto —
Ma prima voglio che mi benedite—
Come quel giorno che partii soldato:
E poi mamma,
Sentite, s'io non tornassi —
Voi dovrete fare da madre a Santa,
Ch'io le avea giurato di condurla all' altare.

Lucia. Perche parli cosi, figliolo mio?

Turiddu.

(Con disinvoltura.)

Oh! nulla, è il vino che m'ha suggerito!
M'ha suggerito il vino —
Perme pregate Iddio,
Un bacio mamma! un altro bacio
Addio!

(Fugge disperatamente.)

Lucia. Turiddu! che vuoi dire!

(Va in fondo alla scena a disperatamente chiama.)

Turiddu! Turiddu! ah!

(Entra Santuzza.)

Santuzza.

Santuzza. Oh! madre mia!

(Le getta le braccia al collo. La scena si popolo. L'agitazione si scorge sul volto di tutti. Che scambievolmente s'interrogano con terrore. Si ode un mormorio confuso da lontano. Una donna sola, assai lontano, gridando.)

Hanno ammazzato compare Turiddu!

Several women hastily enter, terrified. One of them shrieks —

" Neighbor Turiddu is murdered."

(All rush upon the stage.)

All. Ah !

(Santuzza falls ; swooning. Lucia faints, and is supported by some of the women.)

THE CURTAIN FALLS RAPIDLY.

(Si sentono delle voci confuse piu vicine. Alcune donne entrano atterite correndo, ed una di esse grida disperatamente.)

Hanno ammazzato compare Turiddu !

(Tutti si precipitano sulla scena.)

Santuzza, Lucia e Coro.

(Gridando.)
Ah !

(Santuzza cade priva di sensi, Lucia sviene ed è sorretta dalle donne del Coro. Tutti restano atterriti.)

CALA RAPIDAMENTE LA TELA.

I PAGLIACCI
(Punchinello)

by

RUGGIERO LEONCAVALLO

PREFATORY NOTE.

RUGGIERO LEONCAVALLO, who wrote both the book and music of *Pagliacci*, belongs to the feverish neo-Italian school of composers for the theatre, whose other leading lights are his contemporaries, Puccini, Mascagni, and Giordano. *Pagliacci* was written at about the same time as Mascagni's *Cavalleria Rusticana*, and was likewise submitted to the prize competition of the publisher Sonzogno, in which Mascagni's opera was the successful work; but there is a credible story that *Pagliacci* would have received the award, but for the fact of its being in two acts instead of one, which placed it outside the conditions. The astute publisher, however, secured and issued both operas; and *Pagliacci* made a sensation only second to that of the triumphant *Cavalleria*. It was first produced, May 21, 1892, at the Dal Verme Theatre, Milan, with the following cast:

CANIO	GERAUD.
TONIO	MAUREL.
SILVIO	ANCONA.
BEPPE	DODDI.
NEDDA	MME. STEHLE.

It soon made its way into the leading Italian and German theatres, scored a season's success in London, and was heard the following year in New York. Now the work holds a permanent place in the repertory of the great opera-houses.

Leoncavallo asserts that the tragedy on which he founded his libretto actually took place in the mountains of Calabria at a given date; but the idea is not a new one in stage-literature, having been previously used in somewhat similar form by both Spanish and French dramatists. The nearest approach to the opera is found in "La Femme du Tabarin," a tragi-parade by Catulle Mendès, which was performed, in 1887, at the *Theatre Libre* in Paris.[1] In fact, Mendès attempted to enjoin the performance of *Pagliacci* at Brussels, on the ground that Leoncavallo had stolen his plot; but the latter was able to demonstrate that the same story had been used long before.

In his treatment of the tragedy, Leoncavallo has made both text and music poignantly effective. The one purpose of the music is to vivify the dramatic significance of the text in every detail; the raw passions and brute impulses of a crude people are dealt with swiftly and directly, and the ironic contrasts which the action invites are seized and brought surely home to the spectator.

THE ARGUMENT.

THE scene of the story is laid in Calabria at the time of the Feast of the Virgin di Mezzagosto. During the prelude Tonio comes forward, as in the Prologue of ancient Greek tragedy, and explains that the subject of the play is taken from real life, and that the composer has devoted himself to expressing the sentiment, good or bad, but always human, of the characters he introduces, without commenting on their social condition. He then makes a sign for the curtain to rise.

The first act shows the meeting of two roads at the entrance of a village; at the right a travelling theatre. Villagers greet the arrival of a troupe of strolling players. Canio, the *Punchinello*, and chief of the little troupe, invites the crowd to attend the performance at seven o'clock, and then goes off with Beppe (the *Harlequin*) and several peasants to drink at the tavern. Tonio the *Clown* remains behind to care for the donkey, but takes advantage of Canio's absence to declare his love to Nedda, who is the *Columbine* of the troupe, and also Canio's wife. Upon being pressed for a kiss, she strikes Tonio with a whip, and he goes off vowing to be revenged. Then Silvio, a rich young villager, joins Nedda and tries to induce her to leave her husband, and the forlorn life of a stroller, which she loathes, to run away with him. Tonio espies

[1] The play has had at least one performance in New York, in which George Fawcett played the part of Tabarin.

2

the lovers, and runs to fetch Canio the husband. They return in time to hear Nedda's parting words to Silvio in which she appoints to meet him at night. Canio breaks from the restraining hands of Tonio to attack Silvio, but the latter succeeds in escaping over the wall without being recognized. Canio, baffled and jealous, orders Nedda to tell the name of her lover; but she refuses, and Canio is about to stab her, when Beppe interferes, persuades Nedda to go to the theatre to dress for her part, and induces Canio to be calm and prepare for the performance. The act closes with a cry of despair from Canio, who is obliged to act a comedy with death in his very soul.

In the second act the peasants arrive to witness the performance. By chance this proves to be a burlesque of all that has taken place in the first act. Tonio, who plays the part of the idiot servant, makes a declaration of love to *Columbine* (Nedda), which she receives with scorn. *Harle-*

quin (Beppe), in love with *Columbine*, then appears, but after a short interview is nearly surprised by the *Pagliaccio* (Canio), who arrives just as *Columbine* is helping *Harlequin* to run away, and hears her repeat to him the very words which she had used to Silvio when she bade him meet her after the play that night. At this Canio loses his head, forgets his part, and furiously demands the name of her lover. Nedda laughs in order to put the public off the scent, and they, failing to grasp the truth, are much amused. Suddenly, however, Canio, beside himself with rage and jealousy, seizes the knife on the table and stabs Nedda to the heart, declaring that she will reveal the name of her lover with her last despairing cry. She calls to Silvio for help, and he attempts to reach her, but is attacked by Canio, who slays him also. The peasants disarm Canio, who says, stupefied, " The comedy is finished."

CHARACTERS.

NEDDA (in the play, Columbine), a strolling player, wife of Canio . . *Soprano.*

CANIO (in the play, Punchinello), master of the troupe . . . . . *Tenor.*

TONIO, the clown, (in the play, Taddeo), *Baritone.*

BEPPE (in the play, Harlequin) . . *Tenor.*

SILVIO, villager . . . . . . *Baritone.*

Villagers.

The scene is laid in Calabria, near Montalto, on the Feast of the Assumption.

Period between 1865 and 1870.

PERSONAGGI.

NEDDA (nella commedia Colombina), attrice da fiera, moglie di . . *Soprano.*

CANIO (nella commedia Pagliaccio), capo della compagnia . . . *Tenore.*

TONIO, lo scemo (nella commedia Taddeo) commediante . . *Baritono.*

PEPPE (nella commedia Arlecchino), commediante . . . . . . *Tenore.*

SILVIO, campagnuolo . . . . . *Baritono.*

Contadini e Contadine.

La Scena si passa in Calabria presso Montalto, il giorno della festa di Mezzagosto.

Epoca presente, fra il 1865 e il 1870.

PAGLIACCI.

PROLOGUE.

Tonio, dressed as Taddeo of the Comedy, comes in front of the curtain.

Tonio. A word — allow me! (*bowing*) sweet
    ladies and gentlemen,
I pray you, hear, why alone I appear,
I am the Prologue!
Our author loves the custom of a prologue
    to his story,
And as he would revive for you the ancient
    glory,
He sends me before you to speak the pro-
    logue!
But not to prate, as once of old,
That the tears of the actor are false, unreal,
That his sighs and cries, and the pain that
    is told,
— He has no heart to feel!
No! No! Our author to-night a chapter will
    borrow
From life with its laughter and sorrow.
Is not the actor a man with a heart like you?
So 'tis for men that our author has written,
And the story he tells you is — true!

A song of tender memories deep in his lis-
    tening heart
One day was ringing; with trembling heart,
    he wrote it,
And marked the time with sighs and
    tears. . . . Come then,
Here on the stage you shall behold us, in
    human fashion,
And see the sad fruits of love and passion!
Hearts that weep and languish, cries of rage
    and anguish,
And bitter laughter. . . . Ah, think then
    — sweet people,
When ye look on us, clad in our motley and
    tinsel,
Ours are human hearts, beating with passion,
We all are men like you, for gladness or
    sorrow.
'Tis the same broad Heav'n above us,
The same wide lonely world before us!

Will ye hear then the story, how it unfolds
    itself, surely and certain?
Come then! ring up the curtain!

(*Exit. The curtain rises.*)

PROLOGO.

Tonio, in costume da Taddeo come nella commedia, passando a traverso al telone.

Tonio. Si può? . . . (*poi salutando*) Signore!
Signori! . . . Scusatemi se solo mi presento. —
Io sono il Prologo. Poichè in iscena ancor le
antiche maschere mette l' autore, in parte ei
vuol riprendere le vecchie usanze, e a voi di
nuovo inviami. Ma non per dirvi come pria:
" Le lagrime che noi versiam son false: Degli
spasimi e dei nostri martir non allarmatevi!"
No: L'autore ha cercato invece pingervi uno
squarcio di vita. Egli ha per massima sol che
l' artista è un uomo e che per gli uomini scrivere ei deve. — Ed al vero ispiravasi.

Un nido di memorie in fondo a l' anima cantava
un giorno, ed ei con vere lacrime sorisse, e i
singhiozzi il tempo gli battevano! Dunque,
vedrete amar sì come s' amano gli esseri umani;
vedrete de l' odio i tristi frutti. Del dolor gli
spasimi, urli di rabbia, udrete, e risa ciniche!

E voi, pruttosto che le nostre povere gabbane d'
istrioni, le nostr' anime considerate, poichè noi
siam uomini di carne e d' ossa, e che di quest'
orfano mondo all pari di voi spiriamo l' aere!

Il concetto vi dissi. — Or ascoltate com' egli è
svolto. (*Gridando verso la scena.*) Andiamo.
Incominciate!

(*Rientra e la tela si teva.*)

5

ACT I.

SCENE I.

SCENE: The entrance of a village,—where two roads meet. On right, a travelling theatre. As the curtain rises, sounds of a trumpet out of tune and a drum are heard. Laughing, shouting, whistling voices approaching. Enter Villagers in holiday attire. TONIO looks up road on left. Then, worried by the crowd which stares at him, lies down in front of the theatre.

Time 3 o'clock. — Bright sunlight.

Men and Women

(entering one by one).

This way they come
With pipe and drum,
This way they come,
This way they come.
Here's a pretty Columbine
And Punchinello,
A merry fellow.
With laugh and jest
They come, they come.
Look how sedately
He smiles and passes,
Beating his drum
With a nod to the lasses.

Boys

(behind).

Hi there! Harlequin!
Whip up your donkey!

Canio

(behind).

Go to the devil!

Beppe

(behind).

Take that, you monkey!

(Crowd of boys run on from left.)

Keep back! They're coming now,
The wagon's coming!
Oh what an awful row!
Oh what a drumming!

(Enter BEPPE, dressed as harlequin leading donkey, which draws a gaily painted cart, in which NEDDA is lying. Behind her, the drum, and CANIO dressed as Punchinello in back of cart, trumpet in his right hand, drumsticks in left. The villagers surround the cart.)

Villagers.

Hail, Punchinello!
Long live the merry king,
Who keeps us mellow!
He is the blithest fellow!
Long life to him we sing,
Hail, Punchinello!

ATTO PRIMO.

SCENA I.

La scena rappresenta un bivio di strada in compagna, al l' entrata di un villaggio. La destra occupata obliquamente da un teatro di fiera. All' alzarsi della tela si sen ono squilli di tromba stonata alternantisi con dei colpi di cassa, ed insieme risa e, grida allegre, fischi di monelli e vociare che vanno appressandosi. — Attirati dal suono e dal frastuono i contadini di ambo i sessi, in abito da fes a, accorrono a frotte dal viale, mentre TONIO il gobbo, va a guardare verso la strada a sinistra, poi, annojato dalla folla che arriva, si sdraia, ainanzi al teatro. Son tre ore dopo mezzogiorno; il sole di agosto splende cocente.

Coro di Contadini, NEDDA. CANIO, TONIO, e PEPPE.

Coro di uomini e donne

(arrivando a poco a poco).

— Son quà!
— Ritornano . . .
— Pagliaccio è là.
— Tutti lo seguono
    grandi e ragazzi
    e ognuno applaude
    ai motti, ai lazzi.
— Ed egli serio
    saluta e passa
    e torna a battere
    su la gran cassa
— In aria gittano
    i lor cappelli,
    fra strida e sibili,
    tutti i monelli.

Ragazzi

(di dentro).

Ehi, sferza l' asino, bravo Arlecchino!

Canio

(di dentro).

Itene al diavolo!

Peppe

(di dentro).

To, birichino!

(Un gruppo di monelli entra, correndo, in iscena dalla sinistra.)

— Indietro, arrivano . . .
— Ecco il carretto . . .
— Che diavolerio
    Dio benedetto!

(Arriva una pittoresca carretta dipinta a varî colori e tirata da un asino che PEPPE, in abito da Arlecchino, guida a mano camminando, mentre collo scudiscio allontana i ragazzi. Sulla carretta sul davanti e sdrajata NEDDA in un costume tra la zingara e l' acrobata. Dietro ad essaiè piazzata la gran cassa. Sul di dietro della carretta è CANIO in piedi, in costume di Pagliaccio, tenendo nella destra una tromba e nella sinistra la mazza della gran cassa. — I contadini e le contadine attorniano festosamente la carretta.)

Tutti.

Evviva! il principe
se' dei pagliacci
Tu i guai discacci
co 'l lieto umor.
Evviva!

Canio. Thank you !

Villagers. Bravo !

Canio. Allow me.

Villagers. Now then begin the play !

Canio
(beating drum)
Gentlemen all.
(Drowning the voices of the crowd.)

Villagers
(stopping their ears).
You deafen us. Do stop, I say !

Canio
(politely).
A word, a word, I pray !
(Taking off his cap and bowing.)

Villagers.

Hush ! Hush ! be quiet, pray,
Begin and say your say !

Canio. This evening at seven of the clock I
invite you
To see our performance, I know 'twill
delight you.
We'll show you the troubles of poor
Punchinello
And the vengeance he wreaked on a
treacherous fellow ;
And Tony the clown with his big cor-
poration,
And strange combination of love and of
hate.
O come then, and honor us,
You'll all be delighted,
At seven you're invited,
At seven you're invited !

Villagers. With pleasure, with pleasure !
We all are delighted.
At seven we're invited !
At seven we're invited !

(Tonio advances to help Nedda down from the cart, but Canio,
who has already alighted, boxes his ears.)

Canio. Get away !
(Takes Nedda by the arms and lifts her down.)

Women
(laughing at Tonio).
How d'you like it, pretty lover !

Boys
(whistling).
How d'you like it ?

(Tonio shakes his fists at the boys, who run away, and goes off,
grumbling, right of theatre.)

Canio. Grazie . . .

Coro. Bravo !

Canio. Vorrei . . .

Coro. E lo spettacolo ?

Canio
(picchiando forte e ripetutamente sulla cassa per dominar le voci)
Signori miei !

Tutti
(scostandosi e turandosi le orecchie).
Uh ! ci assorda ! . . . finiscila.

Canio
(affettando cortesia e togliendosi il berretto con un gesto comico).
Mi accordan di parlar ?

La Folla
(ridendo).
Oh ! con lui si dee cedere.
tacere ed ascoltar.

Canio. Un grande spettacolo
a ventitrè ore
prepara il vostr' umile
e buon servitore.   (*Riverenza.*)
Vedrete le smanie
del bravo Pagliaccio ;
e come ei si vendica
e tende un bel laccio.
Vedrete di Tonio
tremar la carcassa,
e quale matassa
d' intrighi ordirà.
Venite, onorateci
Signori e Signore.
A ventitrè ore !
A ventitrè ore !

La Folla. Verremo, e tu serbaci
il tuo buon umore.
A ventitrè ore !
A ventitrè ore !

(Tonio si avanza per ajutar Nedda a discendere dal carretto, ma
Canio, che è già saltato giù, gl' dà un ceffone dicendo.)

Canio. Via da lì.
(Poi prende fra le braccia Nedda e la depone a terra.)

Le Donne
(ridendo, a Tonio).
Prendi questo, bel galante !

I Ragazzi
(fischiando).
Con salute !

(Tonio mostra il pugno ai monelli cne scappano, poi si allontana
bron olando e scompare setto la tenda a destra del teatro.)

Tonio

(aside).

Oh, he shall pay me, you'll discover !

(BEPPE leads off donkey and cart behind theatre.)

Villager

(to CANIO).

Say ! wilt drink with me a measure ?
They sell good liquor at the tavern yonder.

Canio. With pleasure !

(BEPPE reappears, and throws down his whip in front of theatre.)

Beppe. I say ! Wait, you two !
I'll come with you !

(Enters theatre to change his dress.)

Canio

(calling towards theatre).

Hi ! Tonio, art thou coming ?

Tonio

(behind).

I've got to clean the donkey.
I'll soon be after you.

Villager

(laughing to CANIO).

Take care, my master. He waits till you're
departed, to go a-courting Nedda !

Canio

(smiling and frowning).

You think so ?

Canio

(half in earnest, half ironically).

Such a game, believe me, friends, is hardly
worth the playing.
Let Tonio ponder what I am saying.
For the Stage and Life are different, you'll
discover ;
For if up there

(pointing to the theatre)

I caught her — my lady, with a lover,
I'd preach a little sermon, and get into a
passion,
Then calmly I would seat me there,
And let her lover beat me there,
While the people would applaud me in the
usual silly fashion !
But if Nedda — in earnest should deceive
me,
The ending would be different, believe me.
Mark the words that I am saying,
Such a game, believe me, friends, is hardly
worth the playing !

Tonio

(a parte).

La pagherai ! . . . brigante.

(Intanto PEPPE conduce l' asino col carretto dietro al teatro.)

Un Contadino

(a CANIO).

Di', con noi vuo' tu bevere
un buon bicchiere sulla crocevia ?

Canio. Con piacere.

Peppe

(ricompare di dietro al teatro ; gitta la frusta, che ha ancora in mano, dinanzi alla scena e dice).

Aspettatemi . . .
Anch' io ci sto !

(Poi entra dall' altro lato del teatro per cambian costume.)

Canio

(gridando verso il fondo).

Di Tonio, vieni via ?

Tonio

(di dentro).

Io netto il somarello.
Precedetemi.

Un Contadino

(ridendo).

Bada, Pagliaccio, ei solo vuol restare
per far la corte a Nedda.

Canio

(ghignando, ma con cipiglio).

Eh ! Eh ! vi pare ?

Canio

(tra il serio e l' ironico).

Un tal gioco, credetemi, è meglio non gio-
carlo.
con me, miei cari ; e a Tonio . . . e un poco
a tutti or parlo.
Il teatro e la vita non son la stessa cosa ;
e se lassù Pagliaccio sorprende la sua sposa
col bel galante in camera, fa un comico
sermone,
poi si calma od arrendesi ai colpi di bas-
tone ! . . .
Ed il pubblico applaude, ridendo allegramente.
Ma se Nedda sul serio sorprendessi . . .
altramente
finirebbe la storia, com' è ver che vi parlo . . .
Un tal gioco, credetemi, è meglio non gio-
carlo.

Nedda
                    (aside).
        What can he mean?

Villagers. But surely you cannot suspect her?

Canio
                    (slightly moved).
        No, no, of course not.   That could not be.
        I love her and respect her!

        (Kisses NEDDA on her forehead.)

        (Bagpipes heard from within.   The villagers ran to the left and look off.)

Boys. Hark! hark the bagpipes! The pipers
        are coming!

Men. See where the people churchward are
        going!

Old People. Hark to the bagpipes so merrily
        blowing!
        Gaily the couples to vespers are going!

Women Come away!
        The gray twilight falleth,
        The Angelus calleth!

Canio. Yes, but remember, pray,
        At seven you're invited!

        (Enter bagpipe Players from left, in holiday attire.   A troop of villagers follows.   Villagers on stage greet them.   All disperse in couples, and at close of chorus go off singing, down road behind theatre.)

Chorus. Ding, dong! the shadows fall,
        Then come, one and all!
        To the church come away,
        Ding, dong! we roam along,
        In love's dream so fair.
        But mothers have watchful eyes,
        Beware! oh beware!
        Soon in the twilight
        Love will be told;
        But the old folks are watching,
        Be not too bold!
        Ding, dong! all above,
        All around, is bright with love.
        Ding, dong! the shadows fall,
        Come one and all!

        (During the above, CANIO goes into theatre, and after taking off his Punchinello's dress, returns, nods good-bye to NEDDA with a smile, and goes off with BEPPE and several villagers, left.   NEDDA remains.)

Nedda
                    (a parte).
        Confusa io son! . . .

Alcuni Contadini.   Sul serio pigli dunque la cosa?

Canio
                    (un po' commosso).
        Io? . . . Vi pare! . . . Scusatemi . . .
        Adoro la mia sposa!

        (CANIO va a baciar NEDDA in fronte.   Un suono di cornamusa si fa sentire all' interno; tutti si precipitano verso la sinistra, guardando fra le quinte.)

I Monelli
                    (gridando).
        I zampognari! . . . I zampognari! . . .

Gli Uomini.   Verso la chiesa vanno i compari

        (Le campane suonano a vespero da lontano.)

I Vecchi.   Essi accompagnano la comitiva
        che a coppie al vespero sen va giuliva.

Le Donne.   Andiam. — La campana
        ci appella al signore.

Canio.   Ma poi .. ricordatevi,
        A ventitrè ore.

        (I zampognari arrivano dalla sinistra in abito da festa con nastri dai colori vivaci e fiori ai cappelli acuminati.   Li seguono una frotta di contadini e contadine anch' essi parati a festa.   Il coro, che è sulla scena, scambia con questi saluti e sorrisi, poi tutti si dispongono a coppie ed a gruppi, si uniscono alla comitiva e si allontanano, cantando, pel viale del fondo, dietro al teatro)

Coro Generale.   Din, don, — suona vespero,
        ragazze e garzon,
        a coppie affrettiamoci,
        al tempio — din, don!
        Il sol diggia i culmini,
        Din, don, vuol baciar;
        Le mamme ci adocchiano,
        attenti, compar.
        Din, don. — Tutto irradiasi
        di luce, d'amor;
        Ma i vecchi sorvegliano,
        gli arditi amador.
        Din, don, — suona vespero,
        ragazze e garzon,
        Le squille ci appellano
        al tempio — din, don!

        (Durante il coro, CANIO entra dietro al teatro e va a lasciar la sua giubba da Pagliaccio, poi ritorna, e dopo aver fatto, sorridendo, un cenno d' addio a NEDDA, parte con PEPPE e cinque o sei contadini per la sinistra. — NEDDA resta sola.)

SCENE II.

NEDDA, alone, then TONIO.

Nedda

(musing).

How fierce he looked and watched me !
I hung my head, fearing lest he should
discover
My secret thoughts of my lover.
Heav'ns ! if he should suspect me,
With all his brutal ways ! No matter ! I fear
not,
These are but empty dreams and idle fancies.
Shine, oh thou glorious sun, upon me !
Every pulse is throbbing, glowing,
Like the tide, my passion flowing,
Oh my heart, my restless heart, where art
thou going ?

(Looking to the sky.)

Ah, ye beautiful song-birds ! I hear your
pinions.
What seek ye ? Whither going ? Who knows ?
My mother knew the meaning of your sweet
voices,
And the song she sang me in happy child-
hood
Comes back for ever ! High ! high aloft they
fly,
Through Heaven's blue ether launched in
their flight,
Like arrows of light, in the sky,
The storm clouds and the tempest and the
sunlight defying,
For ever flying, — through the boundless
sky !
Afar, ever they journey ! on, upward for
ever !
On ! wearying never, their fetterless wings
unfold.
They have their visions, their tender, beauti-
ful visions,
They soar for ever through clouds of gold.
What though the wind howls, and night is
dark above them,
Spreading their pinions by planet and star,
No night dismays them, no storm delays
them,
They soar for ever o'er sea and scar.
Far ! oh so far they fly on wings untiring,
Seeking sweet regions they may never know,
For what can bar their dreams and their
desiring?
'Tis fate that leads them ; — still on they go !

SCENA II.

NEDDA sola, poi TONIO

Nedda

(pensierosa).

Qual fiamma avea nel guardo !
Gli occhi abbassai per tema ch' ei leggesse
il mio pensier segreto.
Oh ! s'ei mi sorprendesse . . .
brutale come egli è . . . Ma basti, orvia.
Son questi sogni paurosi e fole !
    O che bel sole
di mezz' agosto ! Io son piena di vita, e
tutta illanguidita
per arcano desio, non so che bramo !

(Guardando in cielo.)

Oh ! che volo d' augelli, e quante strida ! . . .
Che chiedon ? dove van ? chissà . . La
mamma
mia, che la buona ventura annonciava,
comprendeva il lor canto e a me bambina
così cantava :
Hui ! stridono lassù, liberamente
lanciati a vol come frecce, gli augel.
Disfidano le nubi e 'l sol cocente,
e vanno, e vanno per le vie del ciel.
Lasciateli vagar per l' atmosfera
questi assetati d' azzurro e splendor :
seguono anch' essi un sogno, una chimera,
e vanno, e vanno fra le nubi d'or.
Che incalzi il vento e latri la tempesta,
con l' ali aperte san tutto sfidar ;
la pioggia, i lampi, nulla mai li arresta,
e vanno, e vanno, sugli abissi e i mar.
Vanno laggiù verso un paese strano,
che sognan forse e che cercano invan.
Ma i boëmi del ciel seguon l'arcano
poter che li sospinge . . . e vanno . . e van

(During the song, Tonio comes from behind theatre, leans against tree listening. As Nedda moves to go off, she sees him.)

Nedda

(crossly).

What! thou? I thought that thou wast gone to market!

Tonio

(coming forward).

The fault lies in thy singing.

(Caressingly.)

The song bewitched me,
And I could not leave thee.

Nedda

(laughing scornfully).

Ha! ha! How very poetical.

Tonio. Do not laugh, Nedda.

Nedda. Go to the tavern!

Tonio. I know that you hate me and laugh in derision,
For what is the Clown? he plays but a part.
Yet he has his dream, and his hope and his vision,
     The Clown has a heart.
And ah when you pass me, uncaring, unseeing,
You know not my sorrow, so cruel and sweet.
I give you my spirit, my life, and my being,
     I die at your feet.

(Approaching her.)

Ah, hear me then, hear me then,
Let me tell thee—

Nedda

(interrupting and scoffing at him).

     — You love me.
'Tis time enough to tell me this evening,
To-night when you're playing the fool,
With sighs and grimaces.
Why not postpone the confession till then?

Tonio

(passionately).

No, 'tis now I will tell it thee,
And thou shalt hear me now.
I love thee, worship and long for thee.
To make thee mine for ever.

(Tonio durante la canzone sarà uscito di dietro al teatro e sarà ito ad appoggiarsi all' albero, ascoltando beato. — Nedda, finito il canto, fa per rientrare e lo scorge.)

Nedda

(bruscamente contrariata).

Sei là? credea che te ne fossi andato.

Tonio

(ridiscendendo, con dolcezza).

E colpa del tuo canto. Affascinato
io mi beava!

Nedda

(ridendo con scherno).

Oh! quanta poesia!...

Tonio. Non rider, Nedda...

Nedda. Va, va all' osteria.

Tonio. So ben che difforme, contorto son io;
che desto soltanto lo scherno o l' orror.
Eppure ha 'l pensiero un sogno, un desio,
     e un palpito il cor!
Allor che sdegnosa mi passi d' accanto
non sai tu che pianto mi spreme il dolor,
perchè, mio malgrado, subito ho l' incanto,
     m' ha vinto l' amor!

(Appressandosi.)

Oh! lasciami, lasciami
or dirti...

Nedda

(interrompendolo e beffeggiandolo).

che m'ami?
Hai tempo a ridirmelo
stasera, se il brami,
facendo le smorfie
colà, sulla scena.
Intanto risparmiati
per ora la pena.

Tonio

(delirante con impeto).

No, è qui che voglio dirtelo,
e tu m' ascolterai.
che t' amo ti desidero,
e che tu mia sarai!

Nedda

(with studied insolence)

Tell me, thou silly varlet,
Do thy shoulders itch for a drubbing?
Or do thy ears want a rubbing?
How shall I teach thee
    To cool thy love?

Tonio. You mock me? Too long I've borne it.
By the cross of the Saviour, I'll make thee pay,
I've sworn it!

Nedda. You threaten?
Must I then call Canio to thee?

Tonio

(moving towards her).

But not before I kiss thee!

Nedda

(drawing back).

Hands off!

Tonio

(advancing and putting out his arms to embrace her).

No! No! thou shalt be mine.

(NEDDA goes up stage backwards, sees whip left by BEPPE, takes it
up and strikes TONIO in the face.)

Nedda. Unhand me, wretch!

Tonio

(screaming and drawing back).

By the Holy Virgin of the Assumption, Nedda,
I swear it, I'll be revenged upon thee.

(Exit left, with threatening gestures.)

Nedda. Viper, begone! Thou hast revealed thy nature.
Tonio—the Fool! Thou hast a heart as foul
And ugly as thy body, ay! fouler still!

SCENE III.

SILVIO, NEDDA; then TONIO.

SILVIO leans half over wall, right, and calls in a low voice.

Silvio. Nedda!

Nedda

(hurrying towards him).

Silvio! at this hour. What madness!

Nedda

(seria ed insolente).

Eh! dite, mastro Tonio!
La schiena oggi vi prude, o una tirata
    d' orecchi è necessaria
al vostro ardor?

Tonio. Ti beffi? sciagurata!
Per la croce di Dio, bada che puoi
pagarla cara!...

Nedaa. Tu minacci?... Vuoi
che vada a chiamar Canio?

Tonio

(movendo verso di lei).

Non prima chio ti baci

Nedda

(retrocedendo).

Bada!

Tonio

(s' avanza ancora aprendo le braccia per ghermirla).

Oh, tosto sarai mia!...

Nedda

(sale retrocedendo verso il teatrino, vede la frusta lasciata da
PEPPE, l' afferra e dà un colpo faccia a TONIO, dicendo).

Miserabile!...

Tonio

(dà un urlo e retrocede).

Ah! Per la vergin pia di mezz' agosto
Nedda, lo giuro... me la pagherai!...

(Esce minacciando dalla sinistra.)

Nedda

(immobile guardandolo allontanarsi).

Aspide! va. — Ti sei svelato ormai
Tonio lo scemo! — Hai l' animo
Siccome il corpo tuo difforme... lurido!...

SCENA III.

SILVIO, NEDDA, e poi TONIO.

Silvio

(sporgendo la metà del corpo arrampicandosi dal muretto a destra,
e chiama a bassa voce).

Nedda!

Nedda

(affrettandosi verso di lui).

Silvio! a quest' ora... che imprudenza.

Silvio

(jumping over and coming towards her).

Bah! Bah! No danger, dear, I'm thinking.
Canio I left at yonder tavern drinking.
By the pathway that we love, through the
bushes, I came hither.

Nedda.   A moment sooner and Tonio would
have caught thee.

Silvio

(laughing).

Ha! ha! The fool!

Nedda.   The fool is to be feared.   He loves me,
Just now he told me.
With burning words and brutal fire,
He tried to kiss me in his mad desire.

Silvio.   By Heaven!

Nedda.   Nay, be not anxious!   For such a
passion,
A whip's the fashion.

(Pointing to BEPPE'S whip.)

Silvio.   Why wilt thou live, then, for ever like
this, Nedda?
My fate is in thy hands.
Nedda, pity my sorrow.
To-night the fair is o'er,
Thou wilt be gone to-morrow.
Ah, what of me, when thou art departed?
How shall I live apart from thee
And broken-hearted?

Nedda

(deeply moved).

Silvio!

Silvio.   Nedda, hear, I implore thee!
If for thy husband no passion inspires thee,
If all this roving life sickens and tires thee,
If this great love of thine is not empty de-
light,
Fly with me, fly with me, dearest, to-night!

Nedda.   Ah, tempt me not!   Has not life enough
of sadness?
Silvio, tempt me no more.   'Tis folly, 'tis
madness!
Have I not given thee my heart?   Thou
hast my love for aye.
Then say good-bye and part.   Thou wilt
not then betray.
Ah, tempt me not, for pity's sake, my heart
will break!

Silvio

(saltando allegramente e venendo verso di lei).

Ah bah! sapea che non
rischiavo nulla.
Canio e Peppe da lunge a la taverna
ho scorto con gli amici!... Ma prudente
per la macchia a me nota qui ne venni.

Nedda.   E ancora un poco in Tonio t' imbattevi.

Silvio

(ridendo).

Oh! Tonio il gobbo!

Nedda.   Il gobbo è da temersi.
M' ama...Ora qui mel! disse...e nel bestiale
delirio suo, baci chiedendo, ardiva
correr su me...

Silvio.   Per Dio!

Nedda.   Ma con la frusta
del cane immondo la foga calmai.

Silvio.   E fra quest' ansie in eterno vivrai?
Decidi il mio destin,
Nedda, Nedda rimani!
Tu il sai; la festa ha fin
e parte ognun dimani.
E quando tu di qui sarai partita
che addiverrà di me... de la mia vita?...

Nedda

(commossa).

Silvio!

Silvio.   Nedda, rispondimi.
Se è ver che Canio non amasti mai,
se è vero che t' è in odio
il ramingare e il mestier che tu fai,
se l'immenso amor tuo fola non è
questa notte partiam!... fuggi con me.

Nedda.   Non mi tentar!... Vuoi tu — perder la
vita mia?
Taci Silvio, non piu... — E deliro... è
follìa!...
Io mi confido a te — a te cui diedi il cor
Non abusar di me — de 'l mio febbrile
amor!...
Non mi tentar!... E poi... — Chissà!
meglio è partir

Who knows, dear heart, 'tis best to part!
Tears are vain, all is vain; we must not meet
again.
And yet remembering all our love, since first
I met thee,
I shall dream of thee, live for thee, never
forget thee.

(TONIO appears at back, left.)

Silvio.   No! you do not love me!

Tonio

(aside, watching).

I've caught thee, thou baggage!

(Runs down pathway, with threatening gestures.)

Nedda.   I love thee, love thee!

Silvio.   And yet you leave me to-morrow.

(Lovingly, trying to move her.)

Why hast thou taught me Love's magic
story,
If thou wilt leave me, hopeless, alone?
Why press to mine thy lips in their glory,
Why fold thy heart unto mine own?
If thou forgettest all our caresses,
I still remember that dream divine,
I want thy heart, thy passionate kisses,
I want thy spirit to melt in mine!

Nedda

(overcome and yielding).

Can I forget, as I see thee before me,
The spell of love thy heart has woven o'er
me?
By the words thou hast spoken, the ties that
have bound me,
All I want is thy love, folded around me.
Ah, do not leave me! wherefore must we
sever?
Thou hast my heart, and I am thine for-
ever!

Silvio

(clasping her in his arms).

Wilt come?

Nedda.   Yes! Kiss me, love!

Silvio.   Forget the past, think not of to-morrow!

Nedda.   Look in mine eyes, and kiss away my
sorrow.

Silvio.   In thy dear eyes, I kiss away my sorrow.

Sta il destin contro noi. — E vano il nostro
dir.
Eppure da 'l mio cor — strapparti non poss'
io,
Vivrò sol de l' amor — ch' hai destato al cor
mio.

(TONIO appare dal fondo a sinistra.)

Silvio.   No, più non m' ami!

Tonio

(scorgendoli, a parte).

T' ho colta, sgualdrina!

(Fugge dal sentiero minacciando.)

Nedda.   Sì, t' amo! t' amo!

Silvio.   E parti domattina?...

(Amorosamente, cercando ammaliarla.)

E allor perchè, di', tu m' hai stregato
se vuoi lasciarmi senza pietà?
Quel bacio tuo perchè me l' hai dato
fra spasimi ardenti di voluttà?
Se tu scordasti l' ore fugaci
io non lo posso, e voglio ancor
que' spasmi ardenti, que' caldi baci
che tanta febbre m' han messo in cor!

Nedda

(vinta e smarrita).

Nulla scordai — m' ha sconvolta e turbata
questo amor che ne 'l guardo ti sfavilla.
Viver voglio a te avvinta, affascinata
una vita d' amor calma e tranquilla.
A te mi dono; su me solo impera.
Ed io ti prendo e m' abbandono intera.

Silvio

(stringendola fra le braccia).

Verrai?...

Nedda.   Sì — Baciami!...

Silvio.   Tutto scordiamo...

Nedda.   Negli occhi guardami!

Silvio.   Sì, ti guardo e ti bacio, t' amo... t' amo!

SCENE IV.

The same. CANIO, **and then** BEPPE.

As NEDDA and SILVIO go off towards the wall, talking, CANIO and TONIO come stealthily by the short path.

Tonio

(holding CANIO back).

Tread lightly, lightly, and you will catch them so !

(CANIO advances cautiously, still held back by TONIO ; they cannot see SILVIO getting over the wall.)

Silvio

(half over the wall).

At midnight, dearest, I wait thee below !
Come to me, love, when the starbeams shine.

(SILVIO disappears, and CANIO approaches the corner of the theatre.)

Nedda. To-night, love, and for-ever I am thine !

Canio

(who overhears).

Ha !

Nedda.

(turns round, frightened, and calls towards the wall).

Fly, love !

(CANIO with one bound reaches the wall ; NEDDA places herself in front of him. After a short struggle he pushes her into a corner, gets over the wall and disappears. TONIO remains on left, watching NEDDA, who, as if pinned to the wall, tries to hear whether they are fighting.)

Nedda. Ah, Heav'n, preserve him now !

Tonio

(laughing ironically).

Ha ! ha !

Canio

(outside).

Coward ! where art thou ?

Nedda

(turning at TONIO's laugh, looking with disgust at him).

Well done, well done, then, Tonio.

Tonio. Yes — yes, I did it.

Nedda. Just like you, you coward !

Tonio. But next time, I expect to do better !

Nedda. You make me hate and loathe you.

Tonio. Love me, or hate me ! 'Tis naught to me.

SCENA IV.

I precedenti, CANIO e poi PEPPE.

Mentre SILVIO e NEDDA s' avviano parlando verso il muricciuolo, arrivano, camminando furtivamente dalla scorciatoia, CANIO e TONIO.

Tonio

(ritenendo CANIO).

Cammina adagio e li sorprenderai.

(CANIO s' avanza cautamente sempre ritenuto da TONIO, non potendo vedere, dal punto ove si trova, SILVIO che scavalca il muricciuolo.)

Silvio

(che ha già la metà del corpo dall' altro lato ritenendosi al muro)

Ad alta notte laggiù mi terrò.
Cauta discendi e mi ritroverai.

(SILVIO scompare e CANIO si appressa all' angolo del teatro.)

Nedda

(a SILVIO che sarà scomparso di sotto).

A stanotte — e per sempre tua sarò !

Canio

(che dal punto ove si trova ode queste parole, dà un urlo).

Oh ! . . .

Nedda

(si volge spaventata e grida verso il muro).

Fuggi !

(D' un balzo CANIO arriva anch' esso al muro ; NEDDA gli si para dinante ma dopo breve lotta egli la spinge da un canto, scavalca il muro e scompare. — TONIO resta a sinistra guardando NEDDA che come inchiodata presso il muro cerca sentire se si ode rumore di lotta mormorando.)

Nedda. Aitalo . . . Signor ! . . .

Tonio

(ridendo cinicamente).

Ah ! . . . ah !

La Voce di Canio

(di dentro).

Vile ! t' ascondi !

Nedda

(al riso di TONIO si è voltata e dice con disprezzo fissandolo)

Bravo ! Bravo il mio Tonio !

Tonio. Fo quel che posso !

Nedda. E quello che pensavo !

Tonio. Ma di far assai meglio non dispero.

Nedda. Mi fai schifo e ribrezzo.

Tonio. Oh, non sai come lieto ne sono !

(CANIO re-enters, over the wall, pale, and wiping the perspiration from his forehead.)

Canio. So again, she's fooled me. Baffled again!
He knows the path too well.
But no matter. This moment you shall tell me
Your lover's name.

Nedda (turning in confusion).
Who?

Canio (furiously).
You. by Heav'n eternal!
And if here now this moment, I have not cut your throat,
(drawing dagger from his belt)
'Tis because before I kill thee, and thy blood stains my dagger,
Thou shameless woman, thou shalt tell me
Who is thy lover. Tell me!

Nedda. Vain are thy insults. My lips are sealed for ever.

Canio (shouting).
His name, I tell thee. This moment, thou shalt tell me.

Nedda. No! No! Never will I tell thee.

Canio (rushing on her furiously with dagger raised).
By Heav'n, I'll kill thee.

(BEPPE, entering left, hearing NEDDA's answer, snatches dagger from CANIO and throws it away among the trees.)

Beppe. Ah, stay, good master, for the love of Heav'n!
The people! see! they're coming.
Look, where they come from church, to see the play.
Come away. Be calm, I pray.

Canio. (struggling).
Leave me. I tell thee. His name, then, his name!

Beppe. Tonio, come here and hold him.
The people come this way. Don't let them see you.

(TONIO takes CANIO by the hand, while BEPPE turns to NEDDA.)

Canio (con rabbia concentrata).
Derisione e scherno!
Nulla! Ei ben lo conosce quel sentiero
Fa lo stesso; poichè del drudo il nome
or mi dirai.

Nedda (volgendosi turbata).
Chi?

Canio (furente).
Tu, pel padre eterno!...
(Cavando dalla cinta lo stiletto.)
E se in questo momento quì scannata
non t' ho già, gli è perchè pria di lordarla
nel tuo fetido sangue, o svergognata,
codesta lama, io vo' il suo nome. — Parla.

Nedda. Vano è l' insulto. — E muto il labbro mio.

Canio (urlando).
Il nome, il nome, non tardare o donna!

Nedda. No, nol dirò giammai ...

Canio (slanciandosi furente col pugnale alzato).
Per la madonna!...

(PEPPE, che sarà entrato dalla sinistra, sulla risposta di NEDDA corre a CANIO e gli strappa il pugnale che gitta via tra gli alberi.)

Peppe. Padron! che fate!... Per l' amor di Dio ...
La gente esce di chiesa e a lo spettacolo
qui muovo ... andiamo Canio, via, calmatevi!

Canio (dibattendosi).
Lasciami Peppe — Il nome, il nome.

Peppe. Tonio
vieni a tenerlo. Andiamo arriva il pubblico.

(TONIO prende CANIO per la mano mentre PEPPE si volge a NEDDA.)

And Nedda, you go hence, I say.
Go hence and dress yourself. You know
  well, Canio
Is hasty but tender.

(Pushes Nedda under the curtain and exit with her.)

Canio
(holding his head in both hands).

'Tis shameful, shameful !

Tonio.
(in a low voice to Canio, pushing him towards front of stage).

Ah ! calm thyself, my master. 'Tis best to
  make believe !
The gallant will return. I am convinced
  of it.
Trust me to watch her. Now it is time the
  play began.

(Canio makes a fierce gesture, but Tonio, pushing him by the
elbow, comes forward slowly.)

Who knows ? Haply the lover will be here
  to-night,
And will betray it. Come, then, we must
  dissemble,
If we would win.

Beppe
(entering, to Canio).

Come, come, go dress yourself, I pray you.

(To Tonio.)

And you play up your drum there, Tonio !

(Tonio goes behind, Beppe re-enters theatre. Canio, worn out
with emotion, walks slowly towards the curtain.)

Canio. To act, with my heart maddened with
  sorrow.
I know not what I'm saying or what I'm
  doing.
Yet I must face it. Courage, my heart !
Thou art not a man ; thou'rt but a jester !
On with the motley, the paint and the
  powder,
The people pay thee, and want their laugh,
  you know.
If Harlequin thy Columbine has stolen,
Laugh, Punchinello ! The world will cry
  " Bravo ! "
Go hide with laughter thy tears and thy
  sorrow,
Sing and be merry, playing thy part,
Laugh, Punchinello, for the love that is
  ended,
Laugh for the sorrow that is eating thy heart.

(Passes under the curtain of the stage theatre, while the curtain
slowly falls.)

(End of the first act.)

Vi spiegherete. — E voi di lì tiratevi.
Andatevi a vestir, — Sapete, Canio,
è violento, ma buono . . .

(Spinge Nedda sotto la tenda e scompare con essa.)

Canio
(stringendo il capo fra le mani).

Infamia ! infamia !

Tonio
(piano a Canio, spingendolo sul davanti della scena).

Calmatevi padrone. — E meglio fingere;
il ganzo tornerà. — Di me fidatevi.

(Canio ha un gesto disperato, ma Tonio spingendolo col gomito
prosegue piano.)

Io la sorveglio — Ora facciam la recita.
Chissà ch' egli non venga a lo spettacolo
e si tradisca !   Or via. — Bisogna fingere
per riuscir . . .

Peppe
(uscendo dalle scene).

Andiamo, via, vestitevi
padrone. — E tu batti la cassa, Tonio.

(Tonio va di dietro al e teatro Peppe anch esso ritorna all'
interno, mentre Canio accasciato si avvia lentamente verso la cortina.

Canio.   Recitar ! . . . mentre preso dal delirio
non so più quel che dico e quel che faccio !
Eppur . . . è d' uopo . . . sforzati !
Bah, se' tu forse un uom ? Tu se' Pag
  liaccio !
Vesti la giubba e la faccia infarina.
La gente paga e rider vuole quà.
E se Arlecchin t' invola Colombina,
ridi, Pagliaccio . . . e ognuno applaudirà !
Tramuta in lazzi lo spasmo ed il pianto;
in una smorfia il singhiozzo e 'l dolor . . .
Ridi Pagliaccio, sul tuo amore infranto !
Ridi del duol che t' avvelena il cor !

(Entra commosso sotto la tenda, mentre la tela cade lentamente.)

(Fine del' atto primo.)

ACT II.

Scene as in Act I.

SCENE I.

Tonio appears with big drum and takes up his position at the left angle of the theatre. People come from different directions for the performance. Beppe places benches for the women.

Women
(arriving).

Quickly, sweet gossips come,
  The show's beginning,
Hark, how they beat the drum,
  Oh, what a dinning !
Come, quickly, come, I say,
  Let's get good places.

Tonio
(beating drum).

Walk up and see the play,
All take your places

Men. Look how they rush and run,
  Ribbons and laces,
Come here and see the fun,
  My pretty faces !
Oh, what a crush and rush,
  Just for first places !

(Silvio comes from back, and takes his place in front, left, nodding to his friends.)

Tonio. Walk up, walk up, I say,
All take your places !

Women
(sitting down, pushing each other).

Why are you pushing, you ?
I'm nearly baking ;
Help, Beppe, help us, do !
Our places taking.

(Nedda enters dressed as Columbine, holding plate to receive money. Beppe tries to settle the women. Tonio re-enters theatre, carrying away the drum.)

Som of the Crowd
(to Beppe).

Now, then, begin the play,
Have done your prating !
Why keep us waiting ?
We all are here !

Beppe. Keep back, keep back, I say !
First you must pay, please,
This way, this way, please !

ATTO SECONDO.

La stessa scena dell' atio primo.

SCENA PRIMA.

Tonio compare dall' altro lato del teatro colla gran cassa e ra a piazzarsi sull' angolo sinistro del proscenio del teatrino. Intanto la gente arriva da tutte le parti per lo spettacolo e Beppe viene a mettere nei banchi per le donne.

Donne, Uomini, Tonio, Nedda, Silvio, Peppe, Canio e Coro.

Donne
(arrivando).

Presto, affrettiamoci
svelto, compare,
chè lo spettacolo
dee cominciare.
Cerchiam di metterci
ben sul davanti.

Tonio
(picchiando la cassa).

Si dà principio ;
avanti ! avanti !

Uomini. Veh, come corrono
le bricconcelle !
Accomodatevi
comari belle.
O Dio, che correre
per giunger tosto !

(Silvio arriva dal fondo e va a pigliar posto sul davanti a sinistra salutando gli amici.)

Tonio. Si dà principio
pigliate posto !

Le Donne
(cervando sedersi, spingendosi).

— Ma non pigiatevi,
fa caldo tanto !
— Su ; Peppe ajutaci.
V' è posto accanto !

(Nedda esce vestita da Colombina col piatto per incassare posti. — Peppe cerca di mettere a posto le donne. — Tonio rientra nel teatro portando via la gran cassa.)

Una Parte del Coro (a *Peppe*). Suvvia, spiccia tevi
incominciate.
Perchè tardate ?
Siam tutti là.

Peppe. Che furia, diavolo !
Prima pagate.
Nedda, incassate.

All
    (trying to pay at once).
This way !
This way !

Others. See how they fight their way
To get between us !
You, there ! sit down, I say,
Take care, take care !

Silvio
    (in a low voice to NEDDA as he pays for his seat).
Nedda !

Nedda. Be careful,
He has not seen us !

Silvio. To-night, remember, love !
I shall be there !

(NEDDA, leaving SILVIO, takes money for more seats, and then re-enters theatre with BEPPE.)

Full Chorus. Now, then, begin the play,
Have done your prating !
Why keep us waiting ?
Begin, I say !
Time to begin ! —
Let's make a din !
It's seven o'clock, that's certain !
Ring up the curtain !
Time to begin ! We all are in.

(Bell rung loudly.)

Ring up the curtain.
Silence, you there !
Begin ! Begin !

(Some of the women sit on benches placed obliquely towards the stage of theatre, others stand with the men on rising ground under tree. Others at wing, left. SILVIO among them.)

SCENE II.

The Play.

NEDDA (Columbine), BEPPE (Harlequin), CANIO (Punchinello), TONIO (Taddeo), and SILVIO.

Curtain of the theatre rises. SCENE: a small room with two side doors, practicable window at back. NEDDA as Columbine is walking about anxiously.

Columbine. My husband Punchinello
Comes not till morning ; empty lies the street !
Taddeo's at the market — lazy fellow !
All is safe and sweet !

(A guitar is heard, off COLUMBINE runs to window, with signs of love and impatience.)

Tutti
    (volendo pagare nello stesso tempo).
Di qua — di qua !

Un' altra Parte del Coro. Veh, si accapigliano ! .
chiamano ajuto ! . . .
Ma via, sedetevi
senza gridar.

Silvio
    (piano a NEDDA, pagando il posto).
Nedda !

Nedda. Sii cauto !
Non t' ha veduto.

Silvio. Verrò ad attenderti
Non obliar ! . . .

(NEDDA dopo aver lasciato SILVIO riceve ancora il prezzo delle sedie da altri, e poi rientra anch' essa nel teatro con PEPPE.)

Coro Generale. Questa commedia
incominciate.
Perchè tardate ?
Perchè indugiar ?
Facciamo strepito,
facciam rumore,
ventitrè ore
suonaron già.
Allo spettacolo
ognuno anela ! . . .

(Si ode una lunga e forte scampanellata.)

S' alza la tela !
Silenzio. — Olà.

(Le donne sono parte sedute sui banchi, situati obliquamente, volgendo la faccia alla scena del teatrino ; parte in piedi formano gruppe cogli uomini sui rialzo di terra ov' è il grosso albero. Altri uomini in piedi lungo le prime quinte a sinistra. SILVIO è innanzi ad essi.)

SCENA II.

Commedia.

NEDDA (Colombina), PEPPE (Arlecchino), CANIO (PAGLIACCIO), TONIO (Taddeo), e SILVIO.

La tela del teatrino si alza. — La scena, mal dipinta, rappresenta una stanzetta con due porte laterali ed una finestra praticabile in fondo. Un tavolo e due sedie rozze di paglia son sulla destra del teatrino. — NEDDA in costume da COLOMBINA passeggia ansiosa.

Colombina. Pagliaccio, mio marito,
a tar la notte sol ritornerà.
E quello scimunito
di Taddeo perchè ancora non è quà !

(Si ode un pizzicar di chitarra all' interno ; COLOMBINA corre alla finestra e dà segni d' amorosa impazienza.)

Harlequin

(behind the scene).

O Columbine, unbar to me
Thy lattice high.
I watch and sigh,
Longing to hear thee,
And be near thee, as the hours go by.
Ah, show thy little face to me.
So dear thou art,
Thou hast my heart.
Ah, do not vex me,
Tease and perplex me! how can I live
Without thy loving heart?
O Columbine, then list to me,
Thy door unbar,
Come down, my star!
Come down, and love me,
See, where alone I sigh!
For if thou lov'st me not,
Then let me die!

Columbine

(returning anxiously to front).

Ah, yes! 'tis now love's hour entrancing!
The moment's advancing!
And Harlequin is waiting there!

(Seats herself, with troubled looks, with her back to door on right, through which TONIO, dressed as TADDEO, enters with basket on left arm. He stops, and gazes at NEDDA with exaggerated expression of love.)

Taddeo. Behold her!

(Suddenly raising his hands and the basket to ceiling.)

Ah! how surpassing fair!

(The audience laugh.)

Ah! just to tell her, rebellious maiden,
Just to tell her the love with which I'm
    laden!
All safe and clear, now!
No husband near, now!
Why should I fear, now!
There's no one to suspect me.
Come, Love! Direct me!

(Loud and exaggerated sigh. The audience laugh.)

Columbine

(turning).

Well, fool? Is't thou?

Taddeo

(without moving).

Yes, 'tis I.

Columbine. Hast thou seen Punchinello?

La Voce di Arlecchino

(PEPPE, di dentro).

O Colombina, il tenero
fido Arlecchin
è a te vicin!
Ver te chiamando,
e sospirando — aspetta il poverin!..
La tua faccetta mostrami,
ch' io vo' baciar
senza tardar
la tua boccuccia.
Amor mi cruccia— e mi sta a tormentar!
O Colombina schiudimi
il finestrin,
che a te vicin
ver te chiamando
e sospirando — è il povero Arlecchin!

Colombina

(ritornando ansiosa sul davanti).

Di fare il segno convenuto appressa
l' istante, ed Arlecchino aspetta!...

(Siede ansiosa volgendo le spalle alla porta di destra. Questa si apre e TONIO entra sotto le spoglie del servo TADDEO, con un paniere infilato al braccio sinis tro. Egli si arresta a contemplare NEDDA con aria esageratamente iragica, dicendo.)

Taddeo. E dessa!

(Poi levando bruscamente al cielo le mani ed il paniere.)

Dei, com' è bel a!

(Il pubblico sul teatro ride.)

Se a la rubella
io disvelassi
l' amor mio che commuove sino i sassi!
Lungi è lo sposo.
Perchè non oso?
Soli noi stamo
e senza alcun sospetto! Ors . Proviamo!

(Sospiro lungo, esagerato.)

Oh!...

(Il pubblico ride.)

Colombina

(volgendosi).

Sei tu, bestia?

Taddeo

(immobile).

Quell' io sono, sì!

Colombina. E Pagliaccio è partito?

Taddeo
(as before).

He went just now.

Columbine.   Come, then, what were you sent for?
Where is the fowl you went for?

Taddeo
[throwing himself on his knees before COLUMBINE and offering basket as he approaches).

Low at thy feet it is lying,
See us both.
(Pointing to fowl in basket.)
Ah! I implore thee,
Luckless couple here before thee,
O Columbine — be mine, be mine!
Hear, O maiden tender!
From the day —

(COLUMBINE opens window and makes signal.)

Columbine
(turning to TADDEO).

How much, I say?
(Snatching basket.)
Your reck'ning render!

Taddeo.   (Just one and threepence!) —
Hear me say
How I love thee and adore thee!

Columbine
(near to table).

Get away, get away!

(HARLEQUIN enters by window, places bottle which he is carrying under his arm on floor, and goes towards TADDEO, who pretends not to see him.)

Taddeo
(to COLUMBINE pointedly).

Pure!   Yes, I know thou art,
Pure as the snowflake falling.
Why wilt thou close thy heart
Unto my calling?
Must I leave thee and forsake thee?

Harlequin
(taking him by the ear and kicking him up).

Yes, or I'll make thee!

(The audience laugh.)

Taddeo
(retiring comically to door, right; to HARLEQUIN).

Heav'ns!   You love her!
Then I must hand her over!
(Raising his hands.)
Bless you, my children!
(Retiring to door.)
Yonder I will watch o'er you!

(The audience laugh and applaud.)

Taddeo
(come sopra).

Egl partì!

Colombina.   Che fai così impalato?
Il pollo hai tu comprato?

Taddeo.   Eccolo, vergin divina!
(Precipitandosi in ginocchio, offrendo colle due mani il paniere?
COLOMBINA che si appressa.)

Ed anzi eccoci entrambi ai piedi tuoi.
Poichè l' ora è suonata, o Colombina,
di svelarti il mio cor.   Di', udirmi vuoi?
Dal dì . . .

(COLOMBINA va alla finestra la schiude e fa un segno; poi va verso
TADDEO.)

Colombina
(strappandogli il paniere).

Quanto spendesti dal trattore?

Taddeo.   Una e cinquanta.   Da quel dì il mio
core . . .

Colombina
(presso alla tavola).

Non seccarmi Taddeo!

ARLECCHINO scavalca la finestra, depone a terra una bottiglia che ha
(sotto il braccio, e poi va verso TADDEO mentre questi finge non vederlo.)

Taddeo
(a COLOMBINA, con intenzione).

So che sei pura
E casta al par di neve!   E ben che dura
Ti mostri, ad obliarti non riesco!

Arlecchino
(lo piglia per l' orecchio dandogli un calcio e lo obbliga a levarsi)
Va a pigliar fresco! . . .

(Il pubblico ride.)

Taddeo
(retrocedendo comicamente verso la porta a destra).

Numi! s' aman! m' arrendo ai detti tuoi.

(Ad ARLECCHINO.)

Vi benedico! . . . là . . . veglio su voi!

(TADDEO esce.   Il pubblico ride ed applaude.)

Columbine. Dear Harlequin!

Harlequin
> (in exaggerated style).

Sweet Columbine! Ah, how we've prayed, dear,
And Love has heard our prayer.

Columbine
> (pointing to the table on which she has placed the fowl, knives, and forks, etc.).

The supper's laid, dear!
See here, see here, my dearest dear,
The supper that I've bought you!

Harlequin
> (pointing to the wine which he places on the table).

See here, my love, my dainty dove,
The splendid wine I've brought you!

Both
> (sitting down opposite each other).

For love is very fond of wine,
And partial to the kitchen.

Harlequin. My greedy little Columbine!

Columbine. My toper most bewitchin'!

Harlequin
> (taking a phial from his breast).

Take then this little philtre fine,
Give it to thy husband,
Pour it in his wine,
And then let's fly, my dear!

Columbine. Yes — give it me!

Taddeo
> (entering by door, on right, crosses stage, trembling in exaggerated style).

Beware! Thy husband is here!
For weapons seeking, with anger stamping,
All's discovered! I'd better be decamping.

> (Exit hurriedly through door, left. The audience laugh.)

Columbine
> (to HARLEQUIN).

Fly, then.

Harlequin
> (getting through window).

Pour the philtre in his wine, love!

> (Disappears.)
> (CANIO, dressed as PUNCHINELLO, appears at door, right.)

Columbine. To-night and for ever, I am thine, love!

Colombina. Arlecchin!

Arlecchino
> (con affetto esagerato).

Colombina! Alfin s'arrenda
Ai nostri prieghi amor!

Colombina. Facciam merenda!

> (COLOMBINA prende dal tiretto due posate e due coltelli ARLECCHINO va a prender labottiglia, poi entrambi sieaono a tavola uno in faccia all altro.)

Colombina. Guarda, mio ben, che splendida cenetta preparai!

Arlecchino. Guarda, amor mio, che nettare divino t'apportai!

> (A due.)

L'amor ama gli effluvii
del vin, de la cucina!

Arlecchino. Mia ghiotta Colombina

Colombina. Amabile beon!

Arlecchino
> (prendendo un'ampolletta che ha nella tunica).

Prendi questo narcotico,
dallo a Pagliaccio pria che s'addormenti,
e poi fuggiamo insiem.

Colombina. Sì, porgi.

Taddeo
> (spalanca la porta a destra e traversa la scena tremando esageratamente).

Attenti! . . .
Pagliaccio è là tutto stravolto . . . ed armi cerca! Ei sa tutto. Io corro a barricarmi!

> (Entra precipitoso a sinistra e chiude la porta. Il pubblico ride.)

Colombina
> (ad ARLECCHINO).

Via!

Arlecchino
> (scavalcando la finestra).

Versa il filtro ne la tazza sua.

> (Scompare.)
> (CANIO in costume da PAGLIACCIO, compare sulla porta a destra.)

Colombina
> (alla finestra).

A stanotte. — E per sempre sarò tua!

Canio

(with his hand to his heart, aside).

God! am I dreaming? What she said this
morning!
Courage!

(Advancing for his part.)

Some one was with you here!

Nedda. What nonsense! You've been drinking.

Canio

(looking at her).

Been drinking!... I think so!

Nedda

(resuming the play).

You're back too early.

Sanio

(pointedly).

Too early! Thou fearest!
Art sorry, my sweetest, my dearest?

(Resuming the play.)

Ah, nay, thou wast not lonely.

(Pointing to the table.)

Who has been with thee here?

Nedda. The Fool Taddeo — only!
In fact, he's in the cupboard hiding!

(Pointing to door, left.)

Come out!... explain!

Tonio

(from within).

Believe me, sir, thy wife is true. She'd
never grieve thee!

(Pretending to be afraid, pointedly.)

Those pious lips of hers would ne'er deceive thee.

(The audience laugh.)

Canio. Do not trifle, false woman,
Dost thou forget that I am also human?
Tell me his name!

Nedda. Whose name?

Canio. Tell me, then, by God who made me,
Within whose shameless arms thou hast
betrayed me?

Canio

(porta la mano al cuore e mormora a parte).

Nome di Dio!... quelle stesse parole!.

(Avanzandosi per dir la sua parte.)

coraggio!

(Forte.)

Un uomo era con te.

Nedda. Che fole!
Ser briaco?

Canio

(fissandola).

Briaco! sì .. da un' ora!...

Nedda

(riprendendo la commedia).

Tornasti presto.

Canio

(con intenzione).

Ma in tempo!
T' accora dolce sposina.

(Riprende la commedia.)

Ah! sola ti credea

(mostrando la tavola)

e due posti son là.

Nedda. Con me sedea
Taddeo che là si chiuse per paura.

(Verso la porta a sinistra.)

Orsù, parla!...

Tonio

(di dentro fingendo tremare ma con intenzione).

Credetela. Essa è pura!...
E abborre dal mentir quel labbro pio!

(Il pubblico ride forte.)

Canio

(rabbioso al pubblico).

Per la morte!

(Poi a Nedda sordamente.)

Smettiamo. Ho Dritto anch' io
d' agir come ogni altr' uomo. Il nome suo.

Nedda

(fredda e sorridente).

Di chi?

Canio. Vo' il nome de i' amante tuo,
del drudo infame a cui ti desti in braccio
O turpe donna!

Nedda
(continuing the play).

Punchinello! Punchinello!

Canio. No! Punchinello no more! I am a man again,
With aching heart and anguish deep and human,
Calling for blood to wash away the stain,
Thy foul dishonor, thou shameless woman!
No! Punchinello no more! Fool that I sheltered thee!
And made thee mine by every tender token!
Of the love that I gave thee, what is there left to me?
What have I now, but a heart that is broken?

(Falls on chair, overcome.)

Women
(aside to each other).

Sweet gossip, ah, it makes me weep,
So true it all is seeming.

Men. Silence, down there. Quiet keep.

Silvio
(aside).

Ah, can it be I'm dreaming?

Canio
(recovering himself, and becoming gradually more excited).

I hoped in my passion so blindly confiding,
If not for love, for pity sweet.
I loved thee more than God in heav'n abiding,
All my life and my being I laid at thy faithless feet!
I dreamt thou wast true! I would I ne'er had met thee!
I thought of thee pure and stainless as the morn.
Thou hast broken my heart, I live but to forget thee.
Thou hadst my love, but now thou hast my hate and scorn!

Audience
(with enthusiasm).

Bravo!

Nedda
(coldly, and in earnest).

Well, then, if thou deem'st me so unworthy,
Come, let me go and leave thee.

Nedda
(sempre recitando la commedia).

Pagliaccio! Pagliaccio!

Canio. No, Pagliaccio non son; se il viso è pallido
è di vergogna, e smania di vendetta!
L' uom riprende i suoi dritti, e il cor che sanguina
vuol sangue a lavar l' onta, o maledetta! . . .
No, Pagliaccio non son! . . . Son quei che stolido
ti raccolse orfanella in su la via
quasi morta di fame, e un nome offriati
ed un amor ch' era febbre e follìa! . . .

(Cade come affranto sulla seggiola.)

Gruppi di Donne a Parte. Comare, mi fa piangere!
— Par vera questa scena!

Un Gruppo di Uomini. Zitte laggiù. — Che diamine!

Silvio
(a parte).

Io mi ritengo appena!

Canio
(riprendendosi ed animandosi a poco a poco).

Sperai, tanto il delirio accecato m' aveva,
se non amor, pietà . . . mercè!
Ed ogni sacrifizio
al cor, lieto, imponeva,
e fidente credeva,
più che in Dio stesso, in te!
Ma il vizio alberga sol ne l' alma tua negletta;
tu viscere non hai . . . sol legge è 'l senso a te . . .
Va, non merti il mio duol, o meretrice abbietta,
vo' ne lo sprezzo mio schiacciarti sotto i piè! . . .

La Folla
(entusiasta).

Bravo! . . .

Nedda
(fredda, ma seria).

Ebben se mi giudichi
Di te indegna, mi scaccia in questo istante

Canio
(laughing).
No doubt ! no doubt ! and set thee free,
And let thy lover's arms receive thee !
No !   Thou shalt remain, I swear it.
I want thy lover's name — Come, then — declare it !

Nedda
(trying to resume the play, with forced smile).
I never knew, my dear, that you
   Were such a tragic fellow !
You here will see no tragedy,
   My dearest Punchinello !
The man who's been to sup with me,
   And caused you all this bother,
Was only Harlequin, you see,
   Poor Harlequin, no other !
(Stops laughing, seeing CANIO's attitude.)

Canio
(in fury).
Ah ! dost thou mock me ? My rage thou still defiest.
Say who's thy lover — this moment — or thou diest !

Nedda. No ! By my mother's soul, unworthy though thou call me,
I will not tell thee, whatever fate befall me !

Voices in the Crowd. Are they in earnest ? What are they doing ?
(BEPPE tries to pass through door on left ; TONIO detains him.)

Beppe. Let us be going, Tonio !

Tonio. Silence, fool !

Beppe. I am afraid !

Silvio
(aside).
Oh, the play is a strange one.
I can bear it no more !

Nedda. For thine anger, I care not. Love is a weapon stronger !
Thus I defy thee ! I fear thee no longer !

Canio
(yelling, takes knife from table).
His name !   His name !

Canio
(sogghignando).
Ah ! ah ! di meglio chiedere
Non dèi che correr testo al caro amante.
Sei furba ! — No, per Dio. tu resterai
E 'l nome del tuo ganzo mi dirai.

Nedda
(cercando riprendere la commedia sorridendo forzatamente).
Suvvia, così terribile
davver non ti credeo !
Qui nulla v' ha di tragico.
(Verso la porta a sinistra.)
Vieni a dirgli, o Taddeo,
che l' uom seduto or dianzi a me vicino
era . . . il pauroso ed innocuo Arlecchino !
(Risa tosta represse dall' attitudine di CANIO.)

Canio
(terribile).
Ah ! tu mi sfidi !   E ancor non l' hai capita
Ch' io non ti cedo ?   Il nome, o la tua vita !
(Assieme.)

Nedda
(prorompendo).
No, per mia madre !   Indegna esser poss' io,
quello che vuoi, ma vil non son, per Dio !
Di quel tuo sdegno è l'amor mio più forte . . .
Non parlerò. No . . . A costo de la morte ! . . .

Voci tra la Folla. Fanno davvero ? Sembrami seria la cosa e scura !
(PEPPE vuol uscire dalla porta a sinistra, ma TONIO lo ritiene.)

Peppe. Bisogna uscire, Tonio.

Tonio. Taci sciocco ! . . .

Peppe. Ho paura ! . . .

Silvio
(a parte).
Oh la strana commedia !
Io non resisto più ! . . .

Canio
(urlando dà di piglio a un coltello sul tavolo).
Il nome ! Il nome !

Nedda

No !   *(defiantly).*

Silvio

(drawing his dagger).

What in the devil's name ! . . . He's in
earnest !

(The women draw back frightened, overturning the benches, preventing the men from getting to the front. SILVIO struggles to get
clear. Meantime CANIO has seized NEDDA, and stabbed her from
behind, as she tries to escape to the audience.)

Canio.   Take that, and that !
In thy last dying agony thou'lt tell !

Voices in Audience.   Stop him !

Nedda.   Ah !   Help me, Silvio !

(Dies.)

Silvio

(nearly reaching her).

Nedda !

(At the voice of SILVIO, CANIO turns savagely, leaps at him, and
stabs him.)

Canio.   So !   'Tis you, then ?   'Tis well !

(SILVIO falls dead.)

Men.   Help ! help ! arrest him !

Women

(screaming).

Father of pity !

(Several of the audience throw themselves on CANIO to disarm
and arrest him ; he stands stupefied and drops the knife.)

Canio.   The comedy is ended.

CURTAIN.

Nedda

(sfidandolo).

No !

Silvio

(snudando il pugnale).

Santo diavolo ! . . .
Fa davvero . .

(Le donne che indietreggiano spaventate, rovesciano i banchi ed
impediscono agli uomini di avanzare, ciò che obbliga SILVIO a lottare
per arrivare alla scena.   Intanto CANIO al parossismo della collera, ha
afferrata NEDDA in un attimo e la colpisce per di dietro mentre essa
cerca di correre verso il pubblico.)

Canio (a Nedda).   Di morte negli spasimi
Lo dirai !

La Folla e Peppe

(che cerca svincolarsi da TONIO).

Ferma !

Canio.   A te !

Nedda

(cadendo agonizzando).

Soccorso . . . Silvio !

Silvio

(che e quasi arrivato alla scena).

Nedda !

(Alla voce di SILVIO, CANIO si volge come una belva, balza presse
di lui è in un attimo lo ferisce, dicendo.)

Canio.   Ah ! sei tu ?   Ben venga !

(SILVIO cade come fulminato.)

Gli Uomini del Coro.   Arresta aïta !

Le Donne

(urlano).

Gesummaria ! . . .

(Mentre parecchi si precipitano verso CANIO per disarmarlo ed
arrestarlo, egli, immobile, istupidito lascia cadere il coltello dicendo.)

Canio.   La commedia è finita ! . . .

(La tela cade.)

FINE.

DON GIOVANNI
(DON JUAN)

by

WOLFGANG AMADEUS MOZART

LIBRETTO BY LORENZO DA PONTE

THE STORY OF "DON GIOVANNI"

DON GIOVANNI, a young Spanish nobleman, at a late hour of the day, under cover of darkness, entered the apartments of Donna Anna, who had not yet retired for the night, but sat musing on the divan. Donna Anna, supposing the intruder to be her betrothed, Don Ottavio, did not, at first, repulse this advance; when discovering her mistake, however, she cried for help. Don Giovanni ran out into the street, closely followed by Donna Anna, who held on to his mantle, repeating her cries, and trying to get a look at the features of the stranger, which Giovanni concealed with his mantle. Donna Anna's aged father, Don Pedro, the Commandant, at this juncture made his appearance from one of the side doors of the palace, carrying a sword in one hand and a lighted candle in the other. Donna Anna ran back, to call out others to assist her father. Don Giovanni, after striking the candle from the hand of the Commandant, was attacked by the latter, and, after only parrying his assailant's passes for a while, he, at last, getting exasperated, dealt him a death blow. Calling, then, his servant Leporello, who had been watching the above proceedings from a distance, both made off in haste. Donna Anna, returning with Ottavio and servants with torches, found the corpse of her father on the ground, and the murderer flown. To discover the perpetrator of this bloody deed and punish him, she declares shall henceforth be the object of her life. Ottavio vows his cooperation.

Happening to be outside of the walls of Seville, on the ensuing morning, Don Giovanni and Leporello fall in with Donna Elvira, a young lady from the city of Burgos, in pursuit of Giovanni, who had gained her affections and then left her. Giovanni, in order to escape from this unpleasant encounter, referred her to Leporello for the reasons which prompted his actions, and, while her attention was thus engaged by the valet for a few moments, the master slipped off. Leporello made merry with the grief of poor Elvira; he showed her a long catalog of the victims of the gay lord, and assuring her that she is neither the first of them, nor will be the last, he too departed.

A few days afterwords a rural wedding was celebrated in a village near Giovanni's country seat. While the peasants were in the midst of the festivities, the Don and his *valet-de-chambre* made their appearance among them. The pretty bride, Zerlina, struck the eye of the libertine, and led by her coquettishness of manner to consider her an easy conquest, he forthwith invited the whole party into his palace, whither they proceeded, led by Leporello, who had some trouble to allay the jealous fears of the bridegroom, Masetto, who saw his affianced detained by the handsome cavalier. Giovanni had nearly succeeded in fascinating the young peasant girl when Donna Elvira came in, aroused her suspicions, and conducted her from his presence. Scarcely had they left him when from the other side Donna Anna entered, accompanied by Don Ottavio. They asked for his assistance in discovering the murderer of the Commandant, which Giovanni readily promised, at the same time extending an invitation to join in the festivities, which were about to begin in the palace in honor of the peasant couple. While he was gallantly conversing with Donna Anna, Elvira returned, and seeing in her a new victim, began to denounce her former paramour vehemently. Giovanni gave his friends to understand that the fair stranger was out of her mind, but the others, struck by the earnestness of Elvira and the good sense of her speech, distrusted his assurances. Elvira left, overcome by her emotions; Giovanni, under the pretext of following her, and seeing to her safety, also quitted the scene. Just then Donna Anna, by something in the manner and speech of Giovanni, recognized in him the midnight assassin, under whose sword her father had fallen. She immediately communicated her discovery to her lover, and they resolved to visit the house of Giovanni, masked, in accordance with the custom of the country.

The gay festival in the palace had been interrupted by the entrance of Zerlina, led by Elvira, the latter denouncing the master of the mansion in the hardest terms, and creating thereby not a little disturbance. At length the wily Leporello succeeded in locking Elvira out into the street, and then hastened to inform his patron of the state of matters. Zerlina had made peace with Masetto, who, however, harbored still many misgivings as to the real condition of the heart of his affianced, and consequently exercised a close watch over her. They repaired to the ball room, which had a most brilliant look. Among the throng were to be noticed Anna, Elvira, and Ottavio, all in dominoes, and wearing masks. Everything went on harmoniously, until Giovanni, while unobserved by the jealous Masetto, led his unsuspecting victim, Zerlina, into an adjoining apartment, whence presently piercing shrieks were heard. Upon bursting the door open, Zerlina, pale and frightened, hurried out into the arms of Masetto. After her appeared Don Giovanni, sword in hand, and dragging Leporello with him. He tried to pass off Leporello as the real criminal, but when Donna Anna, Elvira, and Ottavio dropped their masks and confronted him, he made no stand on this pretext, but taking to the sword and making a resolute attack upon the exasperated crowd, he escaped into the garden.

Scarcely out of this predicament, Don Giovanni was again enamored. This time it was the chambermaid of Donna Elvira who had excited his passions. He considered that fine clothes would hardly secure him a good reception with the fair one; accordingly he changed mantle and cap with Leporello, when, at nightfall, both reconnoitered about Elvira's residence. Elvira just then sat down at the window, which Don Giovanni no sooner discovered, than, pushing Leporello towards the window, and himself crouching behind him, he commenced to implore Elvira's forgiveness, and asked her to come down into his loving embrace. Elvira consented, and Giovanni left his servant to act in his place, observing from a short distance how Leporello carried out the joke. The couple got along swimmingly, until Giovanni, assuming a rough voice and heavy gait, frightened them away. When thus the coast was cleared, he took his guitar and serenaded the object of his passion. But hardly had he concluded the second stanza of his song, when he heard footsteps approaching. Hearing Masetto call out to some others with him, Don Giovanni was put on his guard, and when discovered by the other party passed himself off for Leporello. He managed to send all of Masetto's comrades off, making them believe that they are put upon the track of Don Giovanni, to whom they were hired to administer a good thrashing. The simple-minded Masetto confidentially communicated to the disguised Giovanni that he was going to kill him, and handed him over his weapons to examine. Giovanni, once in possession of these, gave the simpleton a good cudgeling and left him on the ground, crying lustily. It was not long before Zerlina came, attracted to the spot by his voice, and led him away.

Elvira and Leporello, in their precipitate flight, had accidentally got into a court-yard, upon which a side wing of Donna Anna's palace opened. Leporello, now feeling uncomfortable, tried to get away from his fair companion. Anna and Ottavio entered, scaring the fugitives to remote corners of the square. Leporello slowly wends his way to the middle door; but when he was about to make his escape, it was opened from the outside, and admitted the enraged Masetto, armed with a heavy stick, followed by peasants. He seized the unfortunate Leporello (still disguised in his master's clothes) and led him before Donna Anna. Pressed closely, and fairly aroused to a fear for his ultimate personal safety, Leporello discovered himself, and, amid the confusion which followed this unexpected *denouement*, succeeded in giving the company the slip.

After a hot flight, climbing over walls and fences, Leporello suddenly found himself in the presence of his master, who had just come down from the wall opposite, and there terminated a flight similar to Leporello's. They were before the Cathedral of Seville. The full moon shone bright upon the marble statue of the Commandant, in the middle of the vast and desolate square. Giovanni, observing that the sight of the statue excited fear in Leporello, bade him go and read the inscription. Leporello, after much coaxing and threatening, read as follows :—

"I here await that vengeance decreed by Heaven Unto the wretch who slew me."

Of course this only tended to increase Leporello's fright. Moreover he had seen the eyes of the statue glare at his master. Giovanni, who was highly amused at the fears of his servant, now ordered him to go and invite the statue to supper. Leporello did as he was bidden, and the statue nodded his head in token of assent. Don Giovanni's curiosity was now awakened by what his valet claimed to have seen. He stepped up to the statue himself, repeated the invitation, and received a loud "Yes" for an answer.

On the following evening, when Giovanni sat down at table, he had already forgotten that he was to have a guest for supper. While he was enjoying a bountiful repast, Donna Elvira made her appearance, venturing a last effort to bring the sinner to repentance. But Giovanni treated her with the most cruel indifference, mocked her earnest appeals, invited her to a seat at the table, and thus fairly drove her out of the room. Presently she returned, uttering a piercing shriek, rushed across the apartment and fled by another door. Giovanni bade his valet to see what the matter was. Leporello went out, but returned immediately, thoroughly frightened, and unable to tell what he had seen. Giovanni, seizing his sword, and taking a candle from the table, now went out to see for himself. On the corridor he encountered the statue of the Com-

mandant, walking towards the supper room. He backed before it and regained the room; the statue following. Giovanni ordered Leporello to fetch another supper, but the statue stopped him, saying that he could not partake of food for mortals, and in his turn invited his host to sup with him. Giovanni accepted the invitation, and gave his hand to the spectre as earnest. But once in his grasp, the statue never released his hold of him. Three times it asked of Giovanni to repent; three times the latter refused. "Down to thy doom then pass!" were the last words of the statue. It sank, and from the abyss emerged a herd of demons, who seized Giovanni and hurled him down into the fiery gulf.

DRAMATIS PERSONÆ

DON PEDRO, THE COMMANDANT . . . . . . BASS

DONNA ANNA, HIS DAUGHTER . . . . . . SOPRANO

DON OTTAVIO, BETROTHED TO DONNA ANNA . . . . TENOR

DON GIOVANNI, A YOUNG NOBLEMAN . . . . . BARITONE

LEPORELLO, HIS VALET-DE-CHAMBRE . . . . . BASS

DONNA ELVIRA, A YOUNG LADY FROM THE CITY OF BURGOS . SOPRANO

ZERLINA, A PEASANT GIRL . . . . . . SOPRANO

MASETTO, BETROTHED TO ZERLINA . . . . . . TENOR

PEASANTS, MASKS, MUSICIANS, ETC.

THE SCENE IS LAID IN AND ABOUT THE SPANISH CITY OF SEVILLE

THE LIBRETTO IS BY LORENZO DA PONTE. THE OPERA WAS COMPOSED AND PER-
FORMED FOR THE FIRST TIME (IN PRAGUE) IN THE YEAR 1787

DON GIOVANNI.

(DON JUAN.)

ACT I.

SCENE I —*The stage represents an angle in the court-yard of the Palace of the Commandant at Seville: on the right hand stands a wing of the Palace, a window of which is seen with the jalousie partly open, and a door below it gives entrance into the court. In the middle distance stands the entrance—a handsome arch with pierced bronze gates, a dwarf wall extending from it on either side, surmounted by a richly ornamented iron railing; on the left hand tall trees are seen; beyond the railing are perceived the city of Seville, a bend of the Guadalquivir, the fortifications, the convent of San Fran-cisco, and rising above all, the lofty steeple of the Cathedral. It is night; the whole scene is illuminated by the moon, which is, however, from time to time dimmed by heavy scudding clouds; an universal stillness reigns, and the numerous lights of the distant town are calmly reflected in the river; all betokens the deepest and most solemn hour of the night.*

At the rising of the curtain, Leporello is discovered half asleep on a stone settle near the door on the right hand; his cloak is thrown over a pocket lantern standing beside him, so as to conceal it; he rouses himself, yawns, and comes forward, lantern in hand, his whole demeanor expressing lassitude and fatigue.

LEPORELLO, *solus.*

NOTTE E GIORNO FATICAR—NIGHT OR DAY. LEPORELLO.

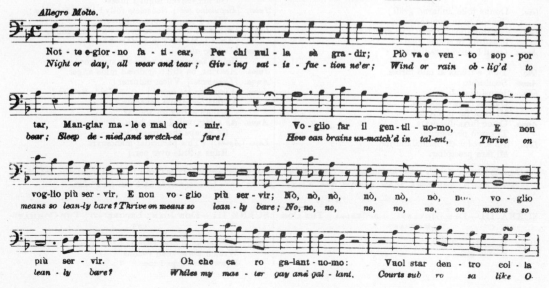

Not-te e gior-no fa-ti-car, Per chi nul-la sà gra-dir; Piò va e ven-to sop-por
Night or day, all wear and tear; Giv-ing sat-is-fac-tion ne'er; Wind or rain ob-lig'd to

tar, Man-giar ma-le e mal dor-mir. Vo-glio far il gen-til-uo-mo, E non
bear; Sleep de-nied, and wretch-ed fare! How can brains un-match'd in tal-ent, Thrive on

vog-lio più ser-vir, E non vo-glio più ser-vir; Nò, nò, nò, nò, nò, nò, Don vo-glio
means so lean-ly bare? Thrive on means so lean-ly bare; No, no, no, no, no, no, on means so

più ser-vir. Oh che ca-ro ga-lant-uo-mo: Vuol star den-tro col-la
lean-ly bare? Whiles my mas-ter gay and gal-lant. Courts sub ro sa like O-

bel - la Ed io far la sen - ti - nel - la, la sen - ti - nel - la, la sen - ti - nel - la! Vo - glio
thel - lo, I keep watch to shield the fel - low, to shield the fel - low, to shield the fel - low! Can my

far il gen-til-uo-mo, E non vo-glio più ser - vir, e non vo - glio più ser-vir, Nò, nò, nò,
brains unmatch'd in talent, Thrive on means so lean-ly bare? Thrive on means so lean - ly bare! No, no, no,

nò, nò, nò, non vo - glio più ser - vir. Ma - mi par, che ven - ga gen - te, Ma - mi
no, no, no, on means so lean - ly bare? Yet me-thinks we catch a foot-step, Yet me-

par, che ven - ga gen - te, Non mi vo - glio far sen - tir, ah! Non mi vo - glio far sen - tir. Non mi
thinks we catch a foot - step, So, for be - ing scarce pre-pare, And so for be - ing scarce pre-pare, So for

vo - glio far sen - tir, Nò, nò, nò, nò, nò, non mi vo - glio far sen - tir.
be - ing scarce pre - pare, No, no, no, no, no, So for be - ing scarce pre - pare.

[*The noise of approaching steps is heard. Don Juan rushes from the Palace sword in hand; he has endeavored to conceal his features by a large slouch hat, and his person by a great cloak; Donna Anna, in her robe-de-nuit, her hair all disheveled, pursues him and tries to tear off his disguise. Don Juan, in preventing this, struggles with her. Leporello pockets his lantern and withdraws quickly to the back as they approach.*]

SCENA II.—DONNA ANNA; DON GIOVANNI; *a detto.* | **SCENE II.**—*The same;* DONNA ANNA; DON JUAN.

Anna. Non sperar, se non m' uccidi,
    Ch' io ti lascio fuggir mai.

Gio. Donna folle, indarno gridi;
    Chi son io tu non saprai.
Lep. Che tumulto, oh ciel! che gridi!
    Il padron in nuovi guai!
Anna. Genti! servi! traditore!

Gio. Taci, e trema al mio furore.
Anna. Scollorato!
Gio. Sconsigliata!
    Questa furia disperata
    Mi vuol far precipitar.
Anna. Come furia disperata
    Ti saprò perseguitar.
Lep. Sta a veder ch' il malandrino
    Mi farà precipitar.

Anna. [*Clinging frantically to Don Juan.*]
    Villain, yield thy double seeming!
    On thy craven flight I press.
Juan. [*Repulsing her.*] Senseless folly! idle dreaming!
    Who I am, to hope to guess.
Lep. (What an uproar! ye gods, what screaming!—
    [*Aside.*] Master's in *another* mess.)
Anna. [*Calling aloud.*]
    Help! assistance! seize the stranger!
Juan. Heav'ns, be still! or dread mine anger.
Anna. [*Desperate.*] Vilest monster!
Juan. [*Fingering his sword.*]   Hold, Señora!
    At this bedlamite behavior
    I shall surely go too far.
Anna. As a fury will I rave here,
    Of escape the firmest bar.
Lep. [*Aside.*] (This particular manœuvre
    Runs a little over par.)

[*Hearing Donna Anna's cries, her father, the Commandant, comes to her assistance; he rushes in in his night robe, with drawn sword and a lamp which he has snatched from a table. Donna Anna escapes hastily back into the Palace.*]

SCENA III.—DON GIOVANNI; LEPORELLA; THE COMMANDANT. | **SCENE III.**—DON JUAN; LEPORELLO; THE COMMANDANT.

Com. Lasciala, indegno,
    Battiti meco

Com. [*Advancing to Don Juan.*]
    Wretch worse than vicious
    Draw, and defend thee!

Gio. Va, non mi degno di pugnar teco.

Juan. [*With nonchalance, striking the lamp from the Commandant's hand with his sword, so that they are in darkness.*]
Steel were too precious—
Words would offend thee—

Com. Così pretendi da me fuggir?

Com. Ye shuffle sadly ;
My sword's from sheath !

Lep. Potessi almeno di quà partir.

Lep. [*Aside.*] (I'd stand excus'd here,
In very faith.)

Gio. Misero ! attendi, se vuoi morir, *si battono.*

Juan. [*On his defence.*] Fool ! learn how madly
You rush on death.

[*They cross swords : the Commandant, tremulous and hasty, makes several desperate passes at Don Juan, which the latter coolly parries ; at last, watching his opportunity, Don Juan makes one home thrust, and wounds the Commandant mortally. Leporello, all the while, keeping out of the way at the back.*]

Com. Ah soccorso ! son tradito. L' assassino m' ha ferito, e dal seno palpitante sento l' anima partir.

Com. [*His accents choked by approaching death.*]
Lost were succor ; vain, assistance,
Soldier still,—I yield existence :—
Yet—if sav'd—a daughter's honor,
Life—its price—proves none too dear.
[*He falls and dies.*

Gio. Ah già cade il sciagurato, affannoso e agonizzante,
Già dal seno palpitante veggio l' anima partir.

Juan. Ah, the weakling dotard falleth,
And a brawl ill-sought, ignoble,
Bids yon haughty hasty noble
Basely end a brave career.
[*As he coolly wipes his sword, and returns it to the sheath.*

Lep. (Qual misfatto ! qual eccesso ! Entro il sen dalle spavento palpitar il cor mi sento, io non so che far che dir.)

Lep. [*Aside.*] (This completes him ; what excesses !
With such dying in real earnest,
My poor brain, so swift thou turnest.
I am twice as dead, I fear.)

SCENA IV.—Don Giovanni ; Leporello.

SCENE IV.—Don Juan ; Leporello.

Gio. [*Sotto voce.*] Leporello, ove sei ?
Lep. Son quì per mia disgrazia, e voi ?

Juan. [*In a semi-whisper.*] Leporello, where are ye ?
Lep. [*From the back, in the same tone.*] Still here, to my great scandal ; and you, Sir ?

Gio. Son quì.
Lep. Chi è morto ? voi, o il vecchio ?
Gio. Che domanda da bestia ! il vecchio.

Juan. Here, too.
Lep. Who's dead there, you—or th' old man ?
Juan. [*Laughing.*] O ye saints, *what* a question !—the old man.

Lep. Bravo !
Due imprese leggiadre,
Sforzar la figlia, ed ammazzar il padre.
Gio. L' ha voluto suo danno.
Lep. Ma Don Anna cos' ha voluto !
Gio. Taci.
Non mi seccar vien meco, se non vuoi.
Qualche cosa ancor tu.

Lep. [*Rubbing his hands.*]
Bravo ! just two birds of a feather :
To force the daughter ; next, to kill the father .
Juan. Was the deed not his seeking ?
Lep. Donna Anna, *she also* sought it ?
Juan. [*Haughtily, and wrapping his mantle around him.*]
Silence ; annoy me not !
And follow—[*raising his hand, as if about to strike Leporello*]—unless you seek a sound drubbing too.

Lep. Non vo' nulla, Signor, non parlo più. [*Partono.*

Lep. [*Crouching to avoid the blow, and picking up his cloak and lantern.*] My remarks on each point need thence be few.
[*Don Juan and Leporello make their escape by the trees on the left.*

SCENA V.—*Entra* Donna Anna, Don Ottavio, *servi con fiaccole.*

SCENE V.—Donna Anna ; Don Octavio ; *Attendants bearing torches.*

Anna. Ah del padre in periglio
In soccorso voliam !

Anna. [*Heard within, as she is entering hastily and in alarm, followed by Don Octavio with his sword drawn, and escorted by Attendants bearing torches.*] Ah ! my father endanger'd ; to his help ! to his aid !

Otta. Tutto il mio sangue verserò, se bisogno :
Ma dov' è il scelerato ?
Anna. In questo loco. Ma qual mai s' offre,
Oh Dei, spettacolo funesto agli occhi miei !
Padre mio ! mio caro padre !

Oct. [*With warmth.*] Freely this life-blood forth shall flow
n service, an ye show me the villain—
Ann As they enter.] Yet one step further—[*she perceives dead body of the Commandant extended upon the ground and bleeding ; his sword lying by his side.*]
But what horror, O God, now bursts upon my vision
A ghastly presence !
[*Falling in frantic grief upon the corse*
My father ! father dearest ! thou, mine own father !

Jtta. Signore!

Anna Ah! l' assassino mel trucidò,
Quel sangue, quella piaga—
Quel volto tinto e coperto del color di morte,
Ei non respira più—
Fredde le membra,
Padre mio! caro padre!
Padre amato! io manco—
Io moro.

Otta. Ah soccorrete, amici, il mio tesoro.
Cercatemi, recatemi qualche odor,
Qualche spirto, ah non tardate!

[Two of the Attendants depart at his order. To Donna Anna, as he tenderly lifts her, and parts the hair from her forehead.]

Donn' Anna! sposa! amica!
Il duolo estremo la meschinella uccide.

Anna. Ahi!
Otta. Già riviene. Datele nuovi ajuti.

Anna. Padre mio!
Otta. Celate, allontanate agli occhi
Suoi quell' oggetto d' orrore!

[The Attendants bear off the body. To Anna, whom he has lifted from the ground, and who reclines back in his embrace.]

Anima mia, consolati, fa core.

SCENA VI.—Donna Anna; Don Ottavia.

Anna. Fuggi, crudele, fuggi;
Lascia che mora anch' io,
Ora ch' è morto, oh Dio!
Chi a me la vita diè.

Otta. Senti cor mio, deh senti!
Guardami un solo istante!
Ti parla il caro amante,
Che vive sol per te.

Anna. Tu sei—perdon—mio bene—
L'affanno mio—le pene—
Ah! il padre mio dov'è?

Otta. Il padre! lascia, o cara
La rimembranza amara;
Hai sposo e padre in me.

Anna. Ah! vendicar, s' il puoi
Giura quel sangue ognor.

Otta. Lo giuro agli occhi tuoi
Lo giuro al nostro amor.

Anna and Otta. Che giuramento oh Dei!
Che barbaro momento! Tra cento affetti e cento
Vammi ondeggiando il cor.
              [Partono.

Oct. [*Stooping, feeling, and addressing the body to see if any life be still left in it.*] Don Pedro—
Anna. [*Weeping.*]
Too well the monster hath done his work!
This wound here—this damp pallor—these cold cheeks
Foully incarnadine with once their beauty!
[*Musingly.*] Yet Angels kiss'd his soul forth from its dwelling.   [*Unable to control herself*
O my father! dearest father! more than existence!
I falter—I follow—   [*Falls fainting upon the body*
Oct. [*To the Attendants, as he stoops to raise her.*]
Friends, an immediate succor for this my treasure!
Procure me now, obtain me now, cooling scent,
Purest balsam, with speed of lightning.

Mine Anna!—darling!—beloved.
        [*The Servants re-enter*
This deep extremest grief cannot prove but fatal.
[*As he applies the restoratives with which the Servants return*
Anna. [*Faintly.*] Ah!
Oct. She reviveth! [*To the Attendants.*] Help us with fresh assistance.
        [*They hand him other restoratives.*
Anna. [*Recovering, as he applies them.*] Father! father!
Oct. [*To the Attendants, pointing to the body.*]
    Be speedy, to remove
That thing of terror from her sight far apart now.

Hope of my being; console thyself, take heart now!

SCENE VI.—Donna Anna; Don Octavio.

Anna [*Aroused to the misery of her bereavement, breaks wildly from Don Octavio.*]
Fly me, unkind one, fly me!
Hence! since for death I hunger;
Life becomes loathsome, longer,
Now more than life is ta'en.

Oct. [*Tenderly.*]
Hear, then; and turn upon me
Thy lucid eye's reflection:
This heart's divine affection
That life can give again.

Anna. [*Coming to herself more.*]
By thought thro' grief distracted
Wert thou one moment neglected.
My father still is slain.   [*Relapsing*

Oct. Lull, dearest, thine emotion;
And in my deep devotion
As husband, a father retain.

Anna. [*Impressively.*] Up! this ill deed's requiting
Swear by the stars above!

Oct. [*Solemnly.*] I swear it by our plighting,
I swear it by our love!

Anna and Oct. [*Raising their eyes.*]
Record the oath, O Heaven!
May righteous Justice, gracing
The cause we are embracing,
Soon its achievement prove!
    [*Donna Anna is led off by Don Octavio*

[The scene changes. The stage represents a rather desolate spot without the walls of Seville; an entrance road to the city leads down a mountain; on one side, the court-yard of an Inn. It is daylight.]

SCENA VII.—*Strada.*—*Entra* DON GIOVANNI, LEPO-
RELLO.

Gio. Orsù spicciati presto, cosa vuoi ?

Lep. L' affar di cui si tratta
E importante.

Gio. Lo credo, e importantissimo.
Meglio ancora. Finiscila.

Lep. Ma giurate di non andar in collera.

Gio. Lo giuro sul mio onore,
Purchè non parli del commendatore.

Lep. Siamo soli ?

Gio. Lo vedo.

Lep. Nessun ci sente ?

Gio. Via ?

Lep. Vi posso dire tutto liberamente ?

Gio. Tutto sì.

Lep. Dunque quand' è così.
Caro signor padrone, la vita che menate è da briccone.

Gio. Temerario, in tal guisa !

Lep. E il giuramento ?

Gio. Zitto ! non si parli
Di giuramento ; taci, o ch' io.

Lep. Non parlo più, non fiato, padron mio.

Gio. Così saremo amici. Or odi un poco :
Sai tu perchè son qui ?

Lep. Non ne so nulla.
Ma essendo l' alba chiara,
Non sarebbe qualche nuova conquista ?
Io lo devo saper per porla in lista.

Gio. Va là che sei l' grand' uom ; sappi ch' io sono
Innamorato d'una bella dama, e son certo che
m'ama ;
La vidi, le parli i meco al casino
Questa notte verrà—zitto mi pare
Sentir odor di femina.

Lep. Cospetto ! Che odorato perfetto.

Gio. All' aria mi par bella.

Lep. E che occhia, dico !

Gio. Ritiriamoci un poco, e scopriamo terren.

Lep. Già prese foco.
                                        [*Partono.*

SCENA VIII.—*Entra* DONNA ELVIRA DON GIOVANNI
e LEPORELLO, *in disparte*

Elv. Ah chi mi dice mai
Quel barbaro dov' è ?
Che per mio scorno amai,
Che mi mancò di fè ?
Ah se ritrovo l' empio,
E a me non torna ancor,

SCENE VII.—DON JUAN ; LEPORELLO.

Juan. [*As he enters, adjusting his dress ; to Leporello, who follows.*] Well, well, now to the point, man ;—what, your matter ?

Lep. Far too important, master, to be sloven'd.

Juan. [*Ironically.*] Most doubtless, as much as usual :—to the best part, come finish it.

Lep. First swear you will not fly out in a passion.

Juan. I swear it on mine honor ; so be't, ye say not aught of yon Commander.

Lep. [*Mysteriously, looking round.*] Are we soli ?

Juan. I hope so.

Lep. [*Whispering.*] With not a fly near ?

Juan. [*Staring at him.*] Well ?—

Lep. And I can speak my mind out excellent freely ?

Juan. Yes—

Lep. [*Pompously.*] Courage, then, for here goes—
Master mine, imp of evil,
The life ye lead will take ye straight to the devil !

Juan. [*Angrily, laying his hand to his sword.*] Forward rascal ! this shall punish—

Lep. [*Making a movement back, and putting up his hand.*] Your oath, Don Juan !—

Juan. Oaths are merely made for convenience ; silence, or I—

Lep. [*Making an obeisance.*] I will not dare to even breathe, Sir Patron.

Juan. So do, and we are friends still ; your ear one moment ! know you my purpose here ?

Lep. I ne'er know *nothing* ; but since the day commences, we conjecture *you* commence some new conquest ; this I ought now to know, who keep the record. [*Significantly tapping his jacket pocket.*]

Juan. See shells, and thou'lt guess eggs, wondrous diviner ! I am enamor'd of a glorious beauty, and am certain she loves me : have seen her, have convers'd, and at the Casino sure shall meet her to-night. [*He stops short, and snuffs the air for a moment or two.*] Gently ! the zephyr wafts me an odor feminine—

Lep. [*Aside, astonished.*] (By Janus, his olfactories perfect !—)

Juan. [*Looking to one side ; his tone heightened.*] Her taille proclaims her lovely.

Lep. [*Aside.*] (And what an eye to match them !)

Juan. [*Pulling Leporello aside.*]
Let us watch the young lady,
Just in hearing and sight.

Lep. [*Aside, as he conceals himself with Don Juan behind a bush.*] (On fire already !)

SCENE VIII.—*The same* ; DONNA ELVIRA.

Elv. [*Entering in a travelling equipment.*]
Mem'ried, his passion lingers
With still delusive sway,
Tho' Truth's relentless fingers
Long dash'd the dream away.
Wild in despairing anger,
I seek the wretch ; to prove

Vò farne orrendo scempio,
Gli vò cavar il cor.

Gio. *A Lep.*] Udisti? Qualche bella
Dal vago abbandonata.
Poverina! poverina!
Cerchiam di consolar
Il suo tormento.

Lep. Così ne consola
Mille e ottocento.

Gio. Signorina! signorina!

Elv. Chi è là?

Gio. Stella! che vedo!

Lep. Oh bella! Donna Elvira

Elv. Don Giovanni!
Sei quì! mostro, fellon, nido d' inganni?

Lep. Che titoli cruscanti! manco male,
Che lo conosce bene.

Gio. Via, cara Donna Elvira,
Calmate quella collera ;—
Sentite—lasciate mi parlar.

Elv. Cosa puoi dire dopo azion sì nera? In casa mia
entri furtivamento, a forza d' arte, di giuramenti, e
di lusinghe, arrivi a sedurre il cor mio ; m' innamori,
o crudele! mi dichiari tua sposa, e poi, mancando della
terra e del ciel al santo dritto con enorme delitto doppo
trè di Burgos d' allontani, m' abbandoni, mi fuggi, e
lasci in preda al rimorso ed al pianto per pena for se
che t' amai cotanto.

Lep. (Pare un libro stampato!)

Gio. Oh, in quanto a questo ebbi le mie ragioni! [*A Lep.*]
E vero?

Lep. E vero, e che ragioni forti.

Elv. E quali sono, se non la tua perfidia, la leggerezza
tua : ma il giusto cielo volle ch' io ti trovassi prefar le
sue, le mie vendette.

Gio. Eh via, siate più ragionevole. Mi pone a cimento
costei. Se non credete al labbro mio, credete aquesto
galantuomo.

Lep. Salvo il vero.

Gio. Via dille un poco.

Lep. [*Piano.*] E cosa devo dirle?

Gio. [*Forte partendo.*] Sì sì, dille pur tutto.

SCENA IX.—Donna Elvira ; Leporello

Elv. [*A Lep.*] Ebben, fa presto.

Lep. Madame—veramente, in questo mondo
Concio, sia cosa quando—fosse—che—
Il quadro non è tondo—

Elv. Sciagurata!
Così del mio dolor gioco ti prendi?
    [*Versa Don G. che non crede partito.*
Ah voi—stelle! l' iniquo
Fuggì! misera me! dove? in qual parte?

Lep. Eh, lasciate che vada ; egli non merta ch' a lui voi
più pensate.

Elv. Il scelerato m' inganno, mi tradi—

Lep. Eh consolatevi! non siete voi, non foste, e non sarete
nè la prima, nè l' ultima ; guardate questo non picciol
libro ; è tutto pieno dei nomi di sue belle ; ogni villa,
ogni borgo ogni paese, è testimon di sue donne che
imprese.
    Madamina! il catalogo è questo
    Delle belle ch' amò il padron mio
    Un catalogo egli è ch' ho fatt' io.
    Osservate, leggete con me,

How woman can avenge her,
    When stung by outrag'd love.

Juan. [*Aside to Leporello.*] (You hear that? 'tis a name.
Abandon'd by her lover.
Poor young creature! poor young creature!
To quickly then console
A heart so sunder'd!)

Lep. (He hath " consol'd " thus
Fully eighteen hundred.)

Juan. Fair Señora!

Elv. That voice!

Juan. Gracious, whom see I?

Lep. (Delicious ; 'tis Elvira!)

Elv. So, Don Juan, thou'rt here, monster of vice prince
of deceivers!

Lep. (Compliments with a vengeance! Faith the girl hath
some little knowledge of him.)

Juan. I prithee, dear Elvira, to be, at least, more mod
erate ;—just listen—and suffer me to speak—

Elv. Lips of an angel could not clear thy baseness
Within my dwelling entering as a stranger, perforce of
cos'nings of honied falsehood, and of passion, ye triumph'd
in seducing my affections, till, enamor'd to madness, ye de
clared ye mine husband ; and then a recreant to the sacred
est ties of earth or heaven, an enormous delinquent, now
for three days from Burgos hast been absent, hast abandon
ed, has fled me, *me* left a prey to remorse and weary weep
ings, mine ineffectual penalty for folly.

Lep. (She has learnt it by heart, pat!)

Juan. For all you touch on, I had my own good reasons.
[*To Leporello.*] Is't not so?

Lep. Aye, aye, Sir ; reasons most truly cogent.

Elv. What other reasons, except that ye *must* gratify an
inborn lust for evil : but Heaven shares mine anger, and
bids Elvira become its instrument of vengeance.

Juan. If so, be but a little sensible. [*Aside.*] (She'll
worry the soul from my skin.) [*To Elvira.*] Since *my* tale
cannot gain you credence, pray credit this good, honest fel
low. [*Pointing out Leporello.*]

Lep. (" Good !"—at lying.)

Juan. [*To Leporello.*] Explain the matter—

Lep. (Explain *what* explanation?)

Juan. Yes, yes ; tell the whole truth. [*He pushes Leporello up to Donna Elvira ; and so, attracting her attention, he
slips away.*]

SCENE IX.—Donna Elvira ; Leporello.

Elv. Proceed, I prithee.

Lep. Fair lady, in old Euclid exists an axiom—which
goes-about-for-to-have-used-to was ; a square is not a circle—

Elv. Senseless ribald! to make a jest of grief ; mocking
my sorrows : [*turning, as if toward Don Juan, whom she still
believes near her,*] and you—[*not seeing him*]—heavens! the
cruel wretch hath fled ; woe is my lot! whither? in what
direction?

Lep. Eh, just suffer him? " gang his gate," he is worth
less ; thought were wasted upon such—

Elv. But then the villain hath deceiv'd, hath betray'd—

Lep. Madam, console thyself ; you will not be, nor are
not, nor further have been, either the first one, or last of
'em. [*Taking a book from his pocket.*] Look, here s a—not
unextensive volume, and cramm'd chuck full of the names
of each his mistress ;
    Ev'ry country, ev'ry township, fully confesses
    Those of the sex whom to his ranks he presses
    Gentle lady, this my catalogue numbers
    All whose charms lent my master beguiling

In Italia, sei cento e quaranta,
In Almagna, duecento trent' una,
Cento in Francia, in Turchia novant' una ;
Ma in Ispagna son già mille e tre !
V' han fra queste, contadine,
Cameriere, cittadine
V' han contesse, Baronesse,
Marchesane, principesse
E v' han donne d' ogni grado,
D' ogni forma, d' ogni età.
Nelle bionda, egli ha l usanza
Di lodar la gentilezza,
Nella bruna la costanza,
Nella bianca la dolcezza ;
Vuol d' inverno la grassotta,
Vuol d' estate la magrotta ;
E la grande, maestosa,
La piccina, ognor vezzosa ;
Delle vecchie fa conquista
Per piacer di porle in lista :
Sua passion predominante
E la giovin princi piante ;
Non si picca, se sia ricca,
Se sia brutta, se sia bella !
Purchè porti la gonnella,
Voi sapete quel che fa.

[*Parte.*

'Tis a document of my compiling,
An it please ye, peruse it with me.
In Italia,—six hundred and forty ;
Then in Germany,—ten score and twenty
As for France,—double fifty seem plenty :
Whiles in old Spain here,—we count *thousands three*
Some, you see, are country damsels,
Waiting-maids, and city ma'amselles,
Countess'—duchess'—baron-esses,
Viscount'—ev'ry kind of *'esses.*
Womenfolk of all conditions,
Ev'ry form, and ev'ry state !
First, the fair one's unthinking blindness
He would dazzle with honied speeches ;
Toward the dark-ey'd all pure kindness,
With the blue-ey'd, he beseeches ;
Winter, he prefers the fatter,
Summer, thin girls suit him better ;
Toward the tallest, bold and haughty,
With the little, he's sly and naughty ;
Old maids' fancies he makes mistier,
Just to swell this scanty list here ;
But he chiefly loves the gender
Budding, young, and ripely tender ;
Rich, or poor, or fair, or hideous,
He, nor dainty nor invidious,
Is with woman most insidious :
You the sequel can relate.

[*He presses the book to his lips with a significant gesture
then, pocketing the list, runs off.*

SCENA X.—Donna Elvira, *sola.*

Elv. In questa forma dunque mi tradì il scelerato ! è questo il premio che quel barbaro rende all' amor mio ! ah, vendicar volg' io l' ingannato mio cor ; pria ch' ei mi fugga, si ricorra—si vada—io sento in petto sol vendetta parlar, rabbia, e dispetto. [*Parte.*

SCENE X.—Donna Elvira, *sola.*

Elv. And after such vile fashion hath the libertine us'd me ! with such a guerdon, doth this barbarian recompense my passion ! Gods, I will have rich justice ; he who stabs at my heart, pays for the mischief ! [*Exit*

The scene changes. The stage represents a beautiful rural prospect among the mountains surrounding Seville ; to the right is seen, amidst its rich gardens, the Palace of Don Giovanni, backed by woods of dark trees ; the Guadalquivir is perceived winding through a valley in the distance.
Zerlina and Masetto, attended by a troop of male and female Peasants, enter, all merrily dancing and singing , they bear wreaths and baskets of flowers, and in their dancing form pretty and appropriate figures and groupings.

SCENA XI.—*Il Contado, con veduta del Palazzo di Don Giovanni.*

Zerlina ; Masetto ; *Contadini e Contadine.*

SCENE XI.—Zerlina ; Masetto ; *Chorus of Peasants.*

GIOVINETTE, QUE FATTE—PRETTY MAIDENS. Chorus.

ZERLINA. Allegro.

Gio- ve- net- te, che fa- te all'a- mo- re, che fa- te, all'a-mo-re, Non la-scia-te, che pas si l'e-
Pret-ty maidens, it lies in your pow-er, it lies in your pow-er, With the summer of life still in

tà, che pas-si l'e-tà, che pas-si l'e-tà; Se nel se-no vi bu-li-cail co-re, vi bu-li-ca il
bloom, with life still in bloom, with life still in bloom, To preserve in each bo-som Love's flower, in each bo-som

co- re, Il ri-me-dio ve-de-te-lo quà! La la la, la la la! Che pia-cer, che piacer che sa- rà.
Love's fiow'r, And be cheer'd by its dain-ty per-fume! Tra la, la, Tra la la! For then all will a sunshine assume.

CHORUS.

Ah,.................. Che pia-cer, che pia- cer che sa-rà, la la la le ra, la la la le-ra.
Ah,.................. For then all will a sun-shine assume ! la la la li-ra, la la la li-ra

Mas. Giovinetti leggieri di testa,
    Non andate girando di quà
    Poco dura dei matti la festa,
    Ma per me cominciato non ha!
        Lera, lera la!
    Che piacer, che piacer, che sarà!
        Lera la, lera la!
Coro. Che piacer! La, la, lera!
Zer. ⎰ Vieni, vieni, carino godiamo,
Mas. ⎱ carina
    E cantiamo, e balliamo, e suoniamo!
    Che piacer, che piacer, che sarà!
Coro. Che piacer! La, la lera!

Mas. Gentle lads, flying hither and thither,
    Like a shuttle despatch'd thro' a loom
    Just behold me, and ponder it, whether
    Any joy near my pleasure can come.
    What a sunshine doth all now assume!
Cho.   La la la! Lala la!
    What a sunshine doth all now assume!
        La la la, lera!
Zer. & ⎰ Then, my love, with our dancing and singing.
Mas. ⎱ Let the wide-spreading echo be ringing,
    An eternal adieu to all gloom!
Cho. An eternal adieu to all gloom!
      La la, la lera, la la la, la lera!

SCENA XII.—*Entra* Don Giovanni *e* Leporello.

Gio. (Manco male è partita;) ah guarda, guarda chè bella gioventù! che belle donne!
Lep. (Tra tanete per mia fè, vi sarà qualche cosa anchè per me.)
Gio. Cari amici, buon giorno! seguitate a star' allegramente; seguitate a suonar, o buona gente. C' è qualche sposalizio?
Zer. Sì signore, e la sposa son io.
Gio. Mene consolo. Lo sposo?
Mas. Io, per servirla.
Gio. Oh bravo? per servirmi. Questo è vero parlar di galantuomo.
Lep. (Basta, che sia marito.)
Zer. Oh, il mio Masetto è un uom d' ottimo core.
Gio. Oh anch' io, vedete! Voglio che siamo amici; il vostro nome?
Zer. Zerlina.
Gio. E il tuo?
Mas. Masetto.
Gio. Oh, caro il mio Masetto! Cara la mia Zerlina, v' esibisco la mia protezione. Leporello!—Cosa fai lì, birbone?
Lep. Anch' io, caro padrone, esibisco la mia protezione.
Gio. Presto va non costor; nel mio palazzo conducili sul fatto; ordina ch' abbiano cioccolatte, caffè, vini, presciutti; cerca, divertir tutti; mostra loro il giardino la galeria, le camere; (in effetto fa che resti contento il mio Masetto. Hai capito?)

Lep. (Ho capito;) andiam.

Mas. Signore!
Gio. Cosa c' è?
Mas. La Zerlina senza me non può star.
Lep. In vostro loco ci sarà sua eccellenza, e saprà bene fare le vostre parti.
Gio. Oh, la Zerlina è in man d' un cavalier; va pur; fra poco ella meco verrà.
Zer. Và, non temere; nelle mani son io d' un cavaliere.

Mas. E per questo?
Lep. E per questo non c' è da dubitar.
Mas. Ed io, cospetto!
Gio. Olà. Finiam le dispute; se subito senz' altro replicar, non te ne vai, Masetto. guarda ben, ti pentirai.

Mas. Hò capito, Signor, si!
    Chino il capo, e mene vò,
    Giacchè piace a voi cosi,
    Altre repliche non fò.
    "Cavalier," voi siete già
    Dubitar non posso affè.

SCENE XII.—*The same;* Don Juan; Leporello

Juan. So the pest has departed. O, look here! look here what appetizing youth! what lovely women!
Lep. (Egad, amongst so many, I hope to pick pickings for myself.)
Juan. Dearest friends, a good morning! nay, stand not check'd thus of your joyful purpose; pray continue the dance, my worthy people: surely this is a wedding?
Zer. Truly Señor, and the bride is before you.
Juan. Gladly I learn it—thy bridegroom?
Mas. Here, at your service.
Juan. O bravo! "at *my* service," that bespeaks ye in truth a gallant fellow.
Lep. (Husbands that serve *him*, are so.)
Zer. Sir, my Masetto's a lad of ev'ry goodness.
Juan. That am I also; let us be friends *instanter:* your name, my darling?
Zer. Zerlina.
Juan. And thine, friend?
Mas. Masetto.
Juan. My very dear Masetto, dearest mine own Zerlina, let this give an earnest of my protection. Leporello! what art thou after, varlet?
Lep. What after! my good master: giving earnest of my protection, truly.
Juan. Pray postpone your intent: conduct these gentlefolk straightway to my palace; order them chocolate, give them coffee, with wine, cake, and preserves too; mind, amuse the whole bevy; show them right round the garden, explain the pictures, the galleries; (yet, in fact, make chief endeavor to occupy Masetto; do you take, man?

Lep. (Like a leech.) [*To the Peasants, placing himself between Masetto and Zerlina, and pushing the former before him.*] Away!
Mas. [*To Don Juan.*] But, Señor?
Juan. What wouldst say?
Mas. That Zerlina cannot stop here without me.
Lep. Good fellow, you must yield in place to his lordship, who doubtless knoweth well how to act in *your* part.
Juan. O, your Zerlina stays with a cavalier; proceed, you shortly will see her again.
Zer. Go, dreading nothing; in a gentleman's hands I fear no evil.

Mas. For which reason—
Zer. For which reason I will not suffer doubt.
Mas. Nor I, by Pluto!—
Juan. What ho! cut short this quarrelling! Suppressing further syllables, if ye do not absent it, (*pointing to his sword,*) Masetto, have a care; ye may repent it!

Mas. O, I take you; Señor, see,
    Making reverence, I go;
    My removal hath a plea,
    Guessing which, I am not slow;
    "Cavalier" you well are nam'd,
    Could a doubt one moment be?

Me lo dice la b .ntà
Che volete aver per me
[A Zer.] (Bricconaccia, malandrina,
Fosti ognor la mia ruina.)
[A Lep.] Vengo, vengo! [A Zer!] resta, resta
E' una cosa molta onesta,
Faccia il nostr. Cavaliere,
Cavaliere anco a te.

[Parte con Leporello.

Since the title is proclaim'd
In this good design'd for me.
(Ugh, you hussey! born to ruin
Viper! bred to breed undoing.)
[To Lep.] Coming, coming! [To Zerlina.] Stay behind me
Artful slut, you cannot blind me;
Stay, and let your "cavalier" there
Have a leer again at thee!
[Pushed off unwillingly by Leporello, Masetto follows the Peasants, who depart as Don Juan has directed.]

SCENA XIII.—ZERLINA, GIOVANNI.

Gio. Alfin siam liberati, Zerlinetta gentil, da qual scioc-
cone. Che ne dite, mio ben, so far pulito ?

Zer. Signore, è mio marito.

Gio. Chi ? colui ? vi par ch' un' onest' uomo, un nobil
cavalier, qual io mi vanto, possa soffrir che qual visetto
d' oro, quel viso inzuccherato da un bifolcaccio vil sia
strapazzato ?

Zer. Ma, signore, io gli diedi parola di sposarlo.

Gio. Tal parola non vale un zero · voi non siete fatta per
esser paesana ; un' altro sorte vi procuran quegli occhi
bricconelli. Quei labretti si belli quelle dituccia can-
dide, e odorose ; parmi toccar giuncata, e fiutar rose.

Zer. Ah non vorrei !
Gio. Che non vorreste ?
Zer. Alfine ingannata restar ; io so che rado colle donne
voi altri cavalieri siete onesti e sinceri.

Gio. E un' impostura della gente plebea. La nobiltà ha
dipinta negli occhi l' onestà. Orsù non perdiam tempo ; in quest' instante io voglio sposar.

Zer. Voi ?
Gio. Certo : io. Qual casinetto e mio ; soli saremo e là,
giojello mio, ci sposeremo.

SCENE XIII.—ZERLINA, DON JUAN.

Juan. Now are we liberated, Zerlinetta my love, from that
great baby ; and is mine not, in truth, first-rate con-
trivance ?

Zer. Señor he's my affianc'd.

Juan. He ? your spouse ? think you an honest gentle, a
noble cavalier, (the which I hold me,) ever can suffer
such enchanting beauty, such ravishing demeanors, to
waste their sweetness on a clownish clod-pole ?

Zer. Soft ! fair master ; I have given my promise to espouse him.

Juan. Such promise is written on water ; thou wert
not created merely to live a peasant ; far other be
it ! O those glances that glow in light like lode-stars,
O those lips of a Hebe, that voice whose whisper
breathes more music than a nightingale's soul, must
win thee a daintier fortune.

Zer. Ah, but I dare not—
Juan. You dare not, what, child ?—
Zer. Be flatter'd,—then deceiv'd and betray'd · we know
you gentlefolk are strangely dishonest with us women
in the fashions of virtue.

Juan. That vulgar notion is too *ultra*-plebeian ; for learn
that honesty e'er was co-nate with noble birth ; the
hour is most propitious,—this very moment will I
make thee my wife.

Zer. [Astonished.] You ?
Juan. Of a surety : Yonder secluded villa, snugly shall house
And there, joy of my being, will I espouse thee ! [thee.

LA CI DAREM—NAY, BID ME NOT. DUET.

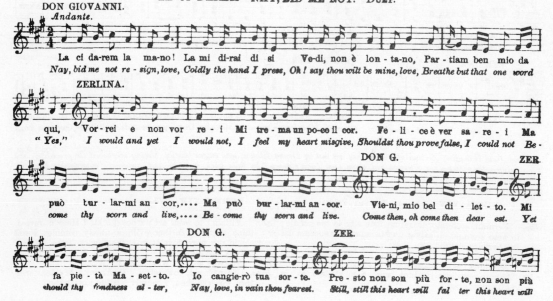

forte, non son più forte. Vieni vieni! La ci darem la mano. Vorrei e non vorrei i.
falter, this heart will falter. Come then, come then! Nay, bid me not resign, love. I would, and yet I would not

DON G.   ZER.   DON G.   ZER.
La mi dirai di sì.   Mi trema un poco il cor.   Partiam ben mio, da qui.   Ma.... può burlarmi an
Oh say thou wilt be mine.   I feel my heart mis-give.   Nay, love, in vain thou fear'st.   I.... feel my heart   mis

ZERLINA.
cor,   Mi fa pie-ta Ma-set-to,   Pre-sto non son più
give.   Yet should thy fond-ness al-tar,   Still,... still this heart will

DON GIOVANNI.
Vie-ni mio bel di-let-te,   Io cange-rò tua sor-te.
Come then, oh come then dear-est,   Nay, love in vain thou fear-est.

DON GIOVANNI.   ZERLINA.
forte non son più forte non son più forte.   An-diam, an-diam.   An-diam.
falter, this heart will fal-ter, this heart will fal-ter.   Oh come, then come.   I come.

Allegro.
Andim, andiam mio be-ne,   A ri-sto-rar le pe-ne   D'un in-no-cen-te a-mor.
Yes, hand and heart u-nit-ing,   Each other's cause re-quit-ing,   Our joy no bound shall know

DON G.
Andiam andiam mio be-ne   A ri-sto-rar le pe-ne   D'un in-no-cen-te amor.   Andiam.
Yes, hand and heart u-nit-ing,   Each other's vows requit-ing,   Our joy no bounds shall know.   Oh come.

ZERLINA.   DON G. ZER.
                                               DON G.
Andiam,   Andiam,   Andiam. Andiam mio be-ne andiam Le pene a ristorar D'un in-no-cen-te amor
I come,   I come.   Oh come. Our joy no bounds shall know, Our joy no bounds shall know, Our joy, &c.

[Don Juan is leading Zerlina off, when they are met by Donna Elvira, who enters hastily, having overheard the preceding, and
indignantly snatches the Peasant-girl from Don Juan's grasp; he falls back angrily and annoyed, placing his hand in-
stinctively to his sword.]

SCENA XIV.—DONNA ELVIRA, e detto.   SCENE XIV.—The same; DONNA ELVIRA.

Elv. Fermati, scelerato, il ciel mi fede udir le tue pefidie;   Elv. Villain! to what art purpos'd? kind Heav'n reveal
io sono a tempo di salvar questa misera, innocente dal   thine hest for further evil; a timely coming, I will
tuo barbaro artiglio.   shield this pure dovelet from the fowler, from his bar-
                                                                barous snarings.
Zer. Meschina! cosa sento!   Zer. Ah, woe is me! what hear I?
Gio. (Amor, consiglio.) Idol mio, non v'adete ch' io   Juan. (Now Cupid, counsel!) [To Elvira.] My dear crea-
vuglio divertirmi?   ture, observe then, I merely wish to amuse me.

Elv. Divertirti, è vero, divertirti ? io so crudele, come tu diverti

Zer. Ma, signor cavaliere, è ver quel ch' ella dice ?

Gio. La provera infelice è di me innamorata e per pietà deggio fingere amore, ch' io son per mia disgrazia uom di buon core.　　　　　　　　　　[*Don G. parte.*

Elv. Ah, fuggi il traditor ,
Non lo lascia più dir ;
Il labbro è mentitor,
Fallace il ciglio.
Da miei tormenti impara,
A creder a quel cor,
E nasca il tuo timor
Dal mio periglio!

　　　　　　　　　　　　　[*Partono.*

SCENA XV.—*Entra* DON GIOVANNI, DON OTTAVIO *e* DONNA ANNA.

Gio. Mi par ch' oggi il demonio si diverta, d' opporsi a miei piace voli progressi, vanno mal tutti quanti.

Otta. Ah ! ch' ora, idolo mio, son vani i pianti. Di vendetta si parli. Oh ! Don Giovanni !

Gio. (Mancava questo intoppo.)

Anna. Amico, a tempo vi ritroviam ; avete core, avete anima generosa ?

Gio. (Sta a vedere, ch' il diavolo gli ha detto qualche cosa ?) Che domanda ! perche ?

Anna. Bisogno abbiamo della vostra amicizia.

Gio. (Mi torna il fiato in corpo,) Comandate congiunti, i parenti, questa man, questo ferro, i beni, il sangue spenderò per servirvi. Ma voi, bella Donn' Anna, perchè cosi piangete ? Il crudelle che fi ? che osa la calma turbar del viver vostro ?

SCENA XVI.—*Entra* DONNA ELVIRA

Elv. [*A Giov.*] Ah ti ritrovo ancor, perfido mostre !
[*A Donna Anna.*] Non ti fidar, o misera,
Di quel ribaldo cor !
Me gia tradi quel barbaro,
Te vuol tradir ancor.

Otta e Anna. Cieli ! che aspetto nobile !
Che dolce maestà !
Il suo dolor, le lagrime
M' empiono di pietà.

Gio. La povera ragazza
E pazza, amici miei ;
Lasciatemi con lei,
Forse si calmera.

Elv. Ah non credete al perfido !

Gio. E pazza, non badate !

Elv. Restate, oh Dei ! restate.

Anna e Otta. A chi si crederà !

Gio., Anna e Otta. Certo moto d' ignoto tormento
Dentro l' alma girare mi sento,
Che mi dice per quella infelice
Cento cose ch' intender non sà.

Gio. (Certo moto d' ignoto tormento
D' entro l' alma girare mi sento,
Che mi dice per quella infelice
Cento cose che intender non sa.)

Elv. Sdegno, rabbia, dispetto, pavente,
Dentro l' alma giraremi sento,
Ch' mi dice di quel traditore
Cento cose che intender non sà.

Otta. Io di quà non vado via,
Se non so son com' è l' affar.

Elv. "*To amuse*" ye, an't please you ! "*to amuse*" ye ! too clear acquaintance bear I, of thine *amusements*.

Zer. But Señor Cavalier now, haply her words are truth some ?

Juan. Really she's mad about me, the unfortunate female ;
From sheerest pity, I bend to her blindness,
My heart's chief failing, being too much of kindness

Elv. A lie is on his lip,　　　　　　　　[*Exit*
Deceit behind his smile ;
Their poison do not sip,
Else woe is ensuing.
His crimes are vast as ocean ;
The trust I bade to sleep
Upon their treach'rous deep,
Did wake to ruin.

　　　　[*Donna Elvira retreats, leading Zerlina.*

SCENE XV.—DON JUAN ; *then* DONNA ANNA *and* DON OCTAVIO.

Juan. Beelzebub's self hath made my plans his foot-ball ;
I will that things should take a fixed progression, and they fly *vice versâ*.

Oct. Ah, fain would I assure thee how vain are weepings ;
let all speech be of vengeance : welcome, Don Juan !

Juan. (This new hindrance gives the finish.)

Anna. Don Juan, most opportunely we meet ; and have ye courage ? and hast a generous noble spirit ?

Juan. (Hath the foul fiend then set her scent right on that ugly mischief ?) Strange your questions ! and why ?

Anna. We much have need, Sir, of your kindly assistance.

Juan. (Ouf ! I take breath more freely !) Speak the mandate, mine adherents, my relations, this my hand, this my weapon, my poor wealth, life, and existence, stand at your service. Alas, loveliest Anna, why thus the child of sorrow ? hath thy peace been assailed ?
What vile occurrence hath basely ventur'd *this* deed ?—

SCENE XVI.—*The same ;* DONNA ELVIRA.

Elv. [*To Don Juan.*] *Thee* do I find again ? monster ri misdeed !
[*To Donna Anna.*] Rather repose thy faith on air,
Than in that viper-tongue ;
Lest it destroy thine own pure heart,
Even as mine it stung.

Anna & Oct. Surely ; there, pure nobility
Maintains undoubted sway :
This mien of woe, this mournful plaint,
Much in her favor say.

Juan. A poor demented lady,
A source of frequent sadness ;
If left to me, her madness
Haply I calm away.

Elv. Ah, credit not the foe to Truth.

Juan. Pray go ; she's quite insane too.

Elv. Remain ! O God, remain now !

Anna & Oct. (Each point a devious way ;
An unutter'd expression of feeling
Is a watchful suspicion concealing
In my breast, where, for eloquent sorrow,
Thousand *thousand* kind sympathies lay.)

Juan. (An unutter'd expression of feeling
Is a watchful suspicion concealing,
Lest this woman run rampant in sorrow,
Half a hint at the real truth essay.)

Elv. Anger, fury, distractions, despairing
Ev'ry chord thro' my being are tearing :
Language lingers for passion and power,
True in color the villain to lay.

Oct. I would scan the matter clearly
Ere from this affair we part.

Anna　Non ha l' aria di pazza,
　　　Il suo tratto, il suo parlar.
Gio.　(Se men vado, si potrai,
　　　Qualche cosa sospettar.)
Elv.　Da quel ceffo si dovria
　　　La ner' alma giudicar.
Otta.　Dunque quella?　　　　　[A Don Giovanni.
Gio.　E pazzarella.
Anna.　Dunque quegli?　　　　[A Donna Elvira.
Elv.　E un traditore.
Gio.　Infelice!
Elv.　Mentitore!
Anna e Otta.　(Incomincio a dubitar.)
Gio.　Zitto, zitto! che la gente
　　　Si raduna à noi d' intorno;
　　　Siate un poco piu prudente
　　　Vi farete criticar.
Elv.　Non sperarlo, o scelerato!
　　　Ho perduta la prudenza;
　　　Le tue colpe ed il mio stato
　　　Voglio a tutti palesar.
Otta e Anna.　Quegli accenti sì sommessi,
　　　Quel cangiar sì di colore,
　　　Sono indizj troppo espressi
　　　Che mi fan determinar.

[Elvira parte.

SCENA XVII.—DONNA ANNA; DON OTTAVIO; DON GIOVANNI.

Gio.　Povera sventurata! i passi suoi voglio seguir; non voglio che faccia un precipizio; perdonate, bellissima Donn' Anna: se servirvi poss' io, in mia casa v' aspetto. Amici, addio.

[Parte.

SCENA XVIII.—DONNA ANNA, DON OTTAVIO.

Anna.　Don Ottavio, son morta!
Otta.　Cos' è stato?
Anna.　Per pietà soccorretemi!
Otta.　Mio ben, fate coraggio.
Anna.　Oh Dei! quegli è il carnefice
　　　Del padre mio.
Otta.　Che dite?
Anna.　Non dubitate più;
　　　Gli ultimi accenti che l' empio proferi,
　　　Tutta la voce richiamar nel cor mio
　　　Di quell' indegno che nel mio appartamento—
Otta.　Oh, Ciel! possibile, che sotto
　　　Il sacro manto d' amicizia—
　　　Ma come fu?—Narratemi lo strano avvenimento.
Anna.　Era già alquanto avanzata la notte
　　　Quando, nelle mie stanze, (ove soletta
　　　Mi trovai per sventura,) entrar io vidi
　　　In un mantello avvolto un uom,
　　　Ch' al primo istante avea preso per voi:
　　　Ma riconobbi poi ch' un inganno era il mio.

Otta.　Stelle! seguite.
Anna.　Tacito a me s' appressa,
　　　E m' vuol abbracciar; sciogliermi cerco,
　　　E più mi stringe, io grido! non viene alcun,
　　　Con una mano cerca d' impedire la voce,
　　　E coll' altra m' afferra stretta così,
　　　Che gia mi credo vinta.

Otta.　Perfido! e alfin?
Anna.　Alfine il duol, l' orrore
　　　Dell' infame attentato accrebbe sì la lena mia,
　　　Che a forza di svincolarmi, torcermi,
　　　E piegarmi, da lui mi sciolsi

Anna.　She hath spoken sure, sincerely;
　　　Sane her mind, tho' bruis'd the heart
Juan.　(To conceal things, very nearly
　　　Conquers my consummate art.)
Elv.　O, observe that glance! how really
　　　It depicts his cold dark heart.
Oct.　These, are fancies?—
Juan.　　　　　She's lost her senses.
Anna.　So, Don Juan?—
Elv.　　　　　Would now deceive him
Juan.　Poor lost creature!
Elv.　　　　　Ne'er believe him!
Anna & Oct.　(Doubts, our various judgment part
Juan.　Gently, gently, this mad gabble
　　　May excite a crowd's attention;
　　　Somewhat roughly, too, your rabble
　　　Exercise the critic art.
Elv.　That my weakling voice were thunder!
　　　That my throat were throat of iron!
　　　I, to Earth all mute with wonder
　　　Would thy myriad crimes impart.
Anna & Oct.　(These her accents, so impressive,
　　　His attempt to treat them coolly,
　　　Are an index too expressive
　　　Of the shoals that throng the chart.)

[Donna Elvira quits the scene

SCENE XVII.—DONNA ANNA, DON OCTAVIO; DON JUAN.

Juan.　[To them.] Wretched afflicted woman! with ev'ry haste I follow her steps; I would not she did herself some rashness: an my poor service suit ye, Donna Anna, of its aid freely borrow. 'Neath my roof I expect ye, 'till when friends, good morrow!

[He runs off unconcernedly towards his Palace

SCENE XVIII.—DONNA ANNA; DON OCTAV

Anna.　Don Octavio, I perish!
Oct.　What hath happen'd?
Anna.　'Tend me help, give me ev'ry aid!
Oct.　Take courage, courage, fair mourner.
Anna.　O Heavens! O Heavens! that is the murderer
　　　Who slew my father.
Oct.　　　　　How say you?
Anna.　Without a shade of doubt:
　　　Every accent his glozing lies gave birth,
　　　Ev'ry demeanor doth proclaim him the wretch
　　　Who dar'd to violate my secluded chamber—
Oct.　O God! could he beneath the sacred cloak of early
　　　friendship?　　　　　[attempting
　　　The sequel, pray; give me acquaintance of this dart
Anna.　Slumber and midnight held the rein of all Nature,
　　　When, within mine apartment (where passing lonely
　　　I sate buried in dreamings) behold there enter'd
　　　Envelop'd in a mantle, a man,
　　　Whom for the moment I did think to be thee, love
　　　That too delicious hope was destroyed in its budding.
Oct.　Heavens! continue—
Anna.　　　　　Tacitly drew he near me
　　　With intent to embrace, back I repuls'd him;
　　　He presses on me, I shriek aloud; none aid is nigh—
　　　Now with one impious hand quite enhindering utterance
　　　He constrain'd with its fellow, so tight his grasp
　　　I fear'd me all o'erpower'd—
Oct.　　　　　Terrible! and then?—
Anna.　Grief, shame, and dread, worst horror　　[Samson
　　　Of the villainous purpose did nerve my frame into
　　　Perforce of the subtlest writhings, tortuous and elusive
　　　From him I broke loose—

Ohimè ! respiro.

sa. Allora rinforzo i stridi miei,
Chiamo soccorso ; fugge il fellcn,
Arditamente il seguo fin nella strada per fermarlo,
E sono assalatrice d' assalita ;
Il padre v' accorre, vuol conoscerlo, e l' indegno,
Che del povero vecchio era più forte,
Compie il misfatta suo col dargli morte !
 Or sai chi l' onore
 Rapir' a me volse,
 Chi fù il traditore,
 Ch' il padre mi tolse.
 Vendetta ti chieggio,
 La chiede il tuo cor,
 Rammenta la piaga,
 Del misero seno ;
 Rimira di sangue
 Coperto il terreno,
 Se l' ira in te langue
 D' un giusto furor.   [Parts.

Oct. This heart again beats.
Anna. And then were my shrieks for help redoubled—
Dreading their upshot, he sought escape ;
With lightning-speed I follow down the court-yard
 to prevent him :
Becoming of mine assailant the assailer !
My father would rescue, straight doth challenge him ,
 and the felon
Overcoming those grey hairs 'neath our own portal,
Fulfill'd his lust for evil, with blow too mortal !
 Now know the betrayer
 Who aim'd at mine honor,
 Now learn who was slayer
 Of this life's dear donor !
 To Vengeance I call thee,
  Need Love call for more ?
 Remember, o'er sorrow
 In mis'ry I've ponder'd ;
 Bethink thee with anguish
 Whose blood hath been squander'd ;
 Nor tarry, nor languish
 Till Justice shall soar !   [Exit.

SCENA XIX.—Don Ottavio, solo.

Otta Come mai creder deggio
 Di si nero delitto
 Capace un cavaliere !
 Ah di scoprire il vero
 Ogni mezzo si cerchi, io sento in petto
 E di sposo, e d' amico
 Il dover che mi parla,
 Disingannarla voglio, o vendicarla.

SCENE XIX.—Don Octavio, solus.

Oct. How can credence accept it ? than the blackest de
linquent yon cavalier were viler : so be the truth dis-
covr'd, not a means shall be lacking ; within this
bosom
 Both Affection and my Friendship are the heralds to
 action,
 He who achiev'd this guilt,—yieldeth satisfaction !

DALLA SUA PACE—ON HER APPEASING. Don Ottavio.

Quel che le in-cre - sce, mor-te mi dà, mor - te, mor-te mi da, Dal-la sua pa-ce la mia di -
There her last grievings mor-tal-ly wound, Griev - ings mor-tal-ly wound. On her appeasing, all peace de-

pen - de, Quel ch' a lei pia-ce vi-ta mi ren de Quel che le in-cre - sce mor-te mi
pendeth, To that sweet pleasing all ef-fort tend-eth, Here her last griev-ings mor-tal-ly

dà, mor - te, mor-te mi dà, mor-te mi dà, quel che le in-cre - sce mor-te mi da.
wound, Griev - ings mor-tal-ly wound, mor-tal-ly wound, Here, her last griev-ings mor-tal-ly wound.

SCENA XX.—*Entra* LEPORELLO *e* DON GIOVANNI.

Lep. Io deggio ad ogni patto per sempre abbandonar questo belmatto. Eccolo qui; guardate con qual indifferenzza se ne viene.
Gio. Leporellino mio, va tutto bene ?
Lep. Don Giovannino mio, va tutto male.
Gio. Come, va tutto male ?
Lep. Vado a casa, come voi m' ordinaste, con tutta quella gente.
Gio. Bravo!
Lep. A forza di chiacchere, di vezzi, e di bugie, ch' ho imparato si bene a star con voi, cero d' intrattenerli.
Gio. Bravo !
Lep. Dico mille cose a Masetto per placarlo, per trargli dal pensier la gelosia.
Gio. Ma bravo, in fede mia !
Lep. Faccio che bevano e gli uomini e le donne : son già mezzo ubbriacchi ; altri canta, altri scherza, altra seguita a ber ; in sul più bello chi credete che capiti ?
Gio. Zerlina.
Lep. Bravo ! e con lei chi venne ?
Gio. Donna Elvira.
Lep. Bravo ! e disse di voi—
Gio. Tutto quel mal ch' in bocca le venia.
Lep. Ma bravo in fede mia.

Gio. E tu, cosa facesti ?
Lep. Tacqui.
Gio. Ed ella ?
Lep. Segui a gridar.
Gio. E tu ?
Lep. Quando mi parve che già fosse sfogata, dolcemente fuor dell' orto la trassi, e con bell' arte chiusa la porta a chiave io me n' andai, e sulla via soletta io la lasciai.

Gio. Bravo, bravo, arcibravo ! l' affar non può andar meglio, incominciasti, io saprò terminar ; troppo mi premono queste contadinotte ; le voglio divertir finchè vien notte

SCENE XX.—LEPORELLO ; *then* DON JUAN.

Lep. Now comes the tug of battle, for I must close accounts with this fine madman ! ah, here he is ; only just mark his cucumber-indiff'rence.
Juan. Good little Leporello ; hath all gone rightly ?
Lep. Good little Juanetto ; the rather—wrongly !
Juan. What do you mean by " wrongly ?"
Lep. All those people I conducted straightway up to your saintship's palace—
Juan. Bravo !
Lep. Perforce of much chattering, caressing, and such humbug, which I learnt, by the bye, in your sweet service, sought I to entertain them—
Juan. Bravo !
Lep. I then fudge up all I could think of to Masetto, to scour his cranium of that jealous nonsense.—
Juan. Bravo ! on my very conscience.
Lep. Then do I set about a-feasting men and women, 'till the best half are tipsy : some are jesting, some singing, some continue to drink ;—when, just guess ; who comes tumbling in ?
Juan. Zerlina.
Lep. Bravo ! and now, who came with her ?
Juan. Why, Elvira !
Lep. Bravo ! and expressing toward you—
Juan. Ev'ry foul epithet her mouth could muster !
Lep. [*Rubbing his hands.*] Bravo too ! upon my very conscience.
Juan. And what were you amidst all ?—
Lep. Mum, Sir.
Juan. The lady ?—
Lep. Kick'd up a row.
Juan. And then ?—
Lep. When it appear'd she'd fizz'd the whole of her rage off, I did lead her passing gently, forth from the garden, and having ooz'd her gradually quite through the wicket, double-lock'd it : and she did find her shut out on the roadway.
Juan. Bravo ! bravo ! extra bravo ! th' affair could not go better ; your good beginning, I now know how to end
     With these young country-girls, fain would I pass some slight time,
   Amuse them therefore well, until the night time

FIN CH' HAN DAL VINO—WINE, FLOW A FOUNTAIN! Don Juan.

Fin ch'han dal vi - no, Cal - da la tes - ta, U - na gran fes - ta Fa pre - pa - rar, Se trovi in piazza;
Wine, flow a foun - tain! Ev - e - ry ves - tal, Bid to the fes - tal, Quickly re - pair, Home, by the ci - ty,

Qual - che ra - gaz - za, Te - co ancor quel - la Cer - ca me - nar, Teco an - cor quel - la Cer - ca me
All that are pret - ty, Take them beneath Thine ex - cel - lent care, Take them beneath Thine ex - cel - lent

nar; cer - ca me - nar, cer - ca me - nar. Sen - z'al - cun or - di - ne, La danza si - a, Ch'il min - u - et - to,
care, ex - cel - lent care, ex - cel - lent care, Then, set them tripping it, Wilful or willing; Those min - u - etting,

Chi la fo - li - a— Chi l'A - le - ma - na; Fa - rai bal - lar; Ch'il mi - nu - et - to Fa - rai bal - lar, Chi
Those segui - dilling, Some a Bo - le - ro On - ly may care. Those se - gue - dill - ing On - ly may care, Some

.... la fol - li - a Fa - rai bal - lar; Chi l'A - le - ma - na, Fa - rai bal - lar; Ed io frattan - to, Dall' al - tro
.... a bo - le - ro On - ly may care, Some a bo - le - ro On - ly may care; I shall en - joy in Si - ly de

can - to, Con ques - ta e quel - la, Vo' amo - reg - giar, Vo' amo - reg - giar, Vo' amo - reg - giar............
coy - ing One or a - noth - er, Love to de - clare, Love to de - clare, Love to de - clare.........

Ah la mia li - sta, Do - man mat - ti - na, D'u - na de - ci - na de - vi aumen - tar.
My list a - dorn - ing, Long ere the morn - ing, Ful - ly with twen - ty Names of the fair.

[*The scene changes. The stage represents the garden of Don Juan's Palace: on one side is a wing of that building, the open windows and colonades of which show, during the progress of the scene, the illuminations preparing within for the ball: a window has a balcony which projects; thick rose-bushes are scattered about: the valley of the Guadalquivir is seen in the distance. It is evening, and the new moon's crescent just peeps over the distant Sierra Nevada. Zerlina enters following Masetto, who appears cross and out of humor with her.*]

SCENA XXI.—Zerlina, Masetto	SCENE XXI.—Zerlina; Masetto
Zer. Masetto! senti un pò; Masetto, dico.	*Zer.* Masetto! list awhile; Masetto dearest—
Mas. Non mi toccar	*Mas.* Go, go away!
Zer. Perchè?	*Zer.* And why?
Mas. Perchè mi chiedi? Perfida! il tutto sopportar dovrei d' una mano infedele?	*Mas.* And why dost ask me? traitoress! to what condi- tions of distraction hath thy faithlessness brought me?
Zer. Ah no! taci, crudele, io non merto Da te tal trattamento.	*Zer.* No, no; silence, unkind one; do I merit from thee so harsh a treatment?
Mas. Come! ed hai l' ardimento di scusarti? star sola con un uom, abbandonarmi il dì delle mie nozze, porre in fronte a un villano d' onore questa marca d' infamia! ah se non fosse, se non fosse lo scandalo, vorrei—	*Mas.* How now? and have ye the face to dream excuses? to stay here with a man—and thus abandon me the day of our nuptials—and to chequer a peasant's rough honor with this mark of ill-favor! Ah, if it were not —if were not too scandalous—I fain would—
Zer. Ma se colpa io non ho, ma se da lui ingannata rim- asi: e poi che temi? tranquillati, mia vita, non mi toccò la punta delle dita. Non me lo credi ingrato? Vien qui, sfogati, ammazzami, fa tutto di me quel che ti piace; ma poi, Masetto poi, ma poi fa pace.	*Zer.* If the fault be no more, if so his brilliancy dazzled one moment, what further fear, love? be tranquil, mine existence: for in his speech there nothing lay to harm me. [*Masetto turns away.*] Ah, give me credit, ungrate- ful! [*Putting her arms around his neck.*] Come here; beat me, love; destroy me, love; E'en do to me as it best may please thee, Do all, Masetto dearest, so it appease thee

BATTI, BATTI--CHIDE ME, CHIDE ME. ZERLINA.

Andante Grazioso.

Bat - ti, bat - ti, o bel Ma - set-to, La tua po-ve-ra Zer - li-na; Sta-rò quì come agnel - li - na, Le tua
Chide me, chide me, dear Ma - set-to, Chide Zer-li - na at your will; Like the patient lamb I'll suffer Meek and

botte ad a spet - tar.   Bat - ti, bat - ti, la tua Zer - li na; Sta-rò quì sta - rò
mute, and lov - ing still.   Chide me, chide me, oh! chide Zer - li - na; Like the pa - tient lamb I'll

quì, Le tue botte ad as - pet - tar.   Las - cie - rò strac-ciar-mi il cri - ne;
suffer, Meek and mute and lov - ing still.   Rend those locks you prais'd so high-ly;

Las - cie - rò strac-ciar-mi gli occhi; E le ca - re tue ma - ni - ne— Lie - ta
From thine arms Zer-li - na cast These fond eyes in rage ex - tin - guish, Fond - ly

poi sa - prò ba - ciar; sa - prò ba - ciar; ba - ciar; sa - prò sa prò ba -
still they'll look their last; they'll look their last, their last; they'll fond - ly look their

ciar. Bat - ti, bat - ti, o, bel Ma - set-to, La tua po - ve - ra Zer - li-na; Sta-rò
last. Chide me, chide me, dear Ma - set-to, Chide Zer - li - na at your will; Like the

quì co - me-aguel-li-na, Le tue bot - te ad as - pet - tar.   Ah! lo ve - do, non hai
pa-tient lamb I'll suf-fer, Meek and mute, and lov-ing still.   Ah! I see, love, you're re

co - re— Ah, non hai co - re, ah, lo ve - do non hai co - re!   Pa-ce, pace, o vi - ta
lent - ing,   Par - don, kneeling, I im-plore ye! I implore ye!   Ah! I see, love, you're re-

Allegro.

mia! Pa - ce, pace, o vi - ta mia: In con-ten-ti, ed al - le - gri - a, Notte e dì vo - gliam pas
lenting—Pardon, kneeling, I implore: Night and day, to thee, de - vot - ed, Here I vow to err no

sar;.................. Notte e dì vo - gliam pas - sar;..................
more;.................. Here I vow to err no more,..................

...... Not-te e dì vo - gliam pas - sar;.......................... Not-te e dì vo-gliam pas-sar. Pa - ce.
...... Here I vow to err no more;.......................... Here I vow to err no more. Ah! I

pace, o vi - ta mi - a; Pa-ce, pa-ce, o vi - ta mia; In con-ten-ti, ed al - le - gri - a Notte e
see, love, you're re lent - ing; Pardon, kneeling I im plore; Night and day to thee de - vot - ed. Here I

di vog-liam pas-sar; sì, sì, sì, sì, sì, sì; Not-te e di vog-liam pas-sar; sì, sì, sì, sì, sì,
vow to err no more; no, no, no, no, no more; Here I vow to err no more; no, no, no, no, no

sì; Notte e di vogliam pas-sar; vogliam, vog-liam pas-sar, vog-liam, vog-liam passar.
more: Here I vow 'o err no more; to err, to err no more; to err, to err no more.

SCENA XXII.—ZERLINA, MASETTO, DON GIOVANNI.	**SCENE XXII.**—*The same ; DON JUAN, within.*

Mas. Guarda un pò, come seppe questa strega sedurmi! Siamo pure i deboli di testa.

Gio. Sia preparato tutto a una gran festa. [*E dentro.*

Zer. Ah! Masetto! odi la voce del monsù cavaliero!

Mas. Ebben, che c' è?
Zer. Verrà.
Mas. Lascia che venga.
Zer. Ah! se vi fosse un buco da fuggir—
Mas. Di cosa temi? perchè diventi pallida! ah capisco, capisco, bricconcella; hai timor, ch' io comprenda com' è tra voi passata la faccenda. Presto! presto! pria ch' ei venga por mi vo da qualche lato: c' è una nicchia, qui celato cheto cheto mi vò star.

Zer. Senti, senti! dove vai? non t' asconder, o Masetto, se ti trova, poveretto, tu non sai quel che può far.

Mas. Faccia, dica quel che vuole.
Zer. Ah! non giovan le parole.
Mas. Parla forte, e quì t' arresta.
Zer. Che capriccio ha nella testa?
Mas Capriò se m' è fedele, e in qual modo andò l' affar.

Zer. Quell' ingrato, quel crudele oggi vuol precipitar.

Mas. Look you now, how this gipsy hath the clue to seduce me! O, a man is the weakest thing in Nature.

Juan. [*Within.*] Cause that the entertainment be truly splendid.

Zer. Ah Masetto, Masetto, hark to the accents of Monsieur your late rival!

Mas. What's that to me?
Zer. He comes.
Mas. Let him! and welcome.
Zer. Were there a nut-shell within which I could creep!
Mas. And why thus fearful? why quits the rose thy pallid cheek? so; I spy it! I spy the truth, sly hussey!
Wouldst deceive me, and mean you
I should not see the what hath pass'd between you!
Presto, presto, ere he enter;
Since, a shade or so suspicious,
To a niche here quite propitious,
Coyly, coyly I repair.

Zer. But a whisper! why for hiding!
Do not leave me, O Masetto;
If he seek well where you get to,
For a sequel too, prepare.

Mas. Let him do or say his willing.
Zer. My worst fear will gain fulfilling—
Mas. Speak aloud; I fain would test thee.
Zer. W‸ ‸price hath so possess'd thee?
Mas. (Now to know, if she be faithful,
And the truth of this affair.)
[*He conceals himself in a niche of the pavilion*

Zer. (Yon my lover, over wrathful,
Just to-day should act with care.)

[*At this moment Don Juan enters, attired for the ball he is about to give; followed by a crowd of Peasants gaily dressed with masks and dominoes, and escorted by Attendants; lights begin to appear in the Palace. Zerlina steps out of his sight behind a rose-bush.*]

SCENA XXIII.—*Entra DON GIOVANNI e Contadine.*	**SCENE XXIII.**—*The same; DON JUAN; Chorus of Peasants.*

Gio. Su svegliatevi da bravi
Su coraggio, o buonà gente
Vogliam star allegramente,
Vogliam ridere e scherzar.
Alla stanza della danza
Conducete tutti quanti:
Ed a tutti in abbondanza
Gran rinfreschi fate dar.

[*Partono Contadine.*

Juan. [*To the Peasants and the Maskers, whom he motions on towards the ball-room.*]
Ye have hence but *dream'd* of Pleasure;
Hail the night of joy before us
With a shout in whirlwind-chorus
Rousing earth, and rending air!
All shall dance who swell the palace,
Liber bleed to fill the chalice,
Plenty's self shall welcome plenty,
Rich refreshment then to share!
[*Peasants and Maskers depart*

SCENA XXIV.—ZERLINA; DON GIOVANNI; MASETTO	**SCENE XXIV.**—ZERLINA; DON JUAN; MASETTO, *a first concealed.*

Zer. Tra quest' alboricelata,
Si può dar che non mi veda.

Zer. [*Running from beside the rose-bush, and endeavoring, unseen by Don Juan, to conceal herself behind the tall trees on the right.*]
Friendly grove, thy shady distance
May protect the timid maiden.

Gio. Zerlinetta mia garbata,
　　　T' ho già visto, non scappas

Zer. Ah ! lasciatemi andar via.
Gio. No, no, resta gioja mia !
Zer. Se pietade avete in core.
Gio. Sì, ben mio, son tutto amore.
　　　Vieni un poco—in questo loco,
　　　Fortunata io ti vò far.
Zer. (Ah ! sei vele il sposo mio,
　　　So ben io quel che può far.)

Juan. [*Perceiving her.*] Zerlinetta, mine existence　*thun*
　　　ning after her, and catching her.]
　　　I can spy thee, gentle fair !
Zer. Ah, pray leave me to my duty—
Juan. No, no, stay ; thou joy ! thou beauty
Zer. Bear'st a heart within thy bosom ?
Juan. One all sunshine, thou its blossom !
　　　Let that heart in yonder bower
　　　Passion's golden light declare.
Zer. [*Aside to Masetto.*]
　　　(See me now, though weak unwilling ;
　　　So, my love, quell thy despair.)

[*As Don Juan is pressing her toward the pavilion, Masetto confronts him ; Don Juan falls back ; Zerlina slips away from him.*]

Gio. Masetto !
Mas. Sì, Masetto.
Gio. E chiuso e perchè ?
　　　La bella tua Zerlina—
　　　Non può la poverina
　　　Piu star senza di te.
Mas. Capisco, sì Signore.
Gio. Adesso fate core ; o suonatori udite,
　　　Venite omai con me.

Zer. e Mas. Sì, sì, facciamo core
　　　Ed a ballar cogli altri
　　　Andiamo tutti tre.　　　　　　[*Partono.*

Juan. Masetto ?
Mas. 　　　　Aye, Masetto !
Juan. Secluded why dost stay ?
　　　Thine angel-bride Zerlina
　　　Will not so much demean her
　　　As dance, her spouse away.
Mas. I credit, Señor, truly.
Juan. Be wise, nor thus unruly ;
　　　But hear that noble music,
　　　It calls, and all obey !
Zer. & Mas. See, see ; we take it coolly,
　　　To trip it with our comrades
　　　We gladly will essay.　　　　　　[*Exeunt*

[*Don Juan gives both an arm, and gallantly leads them into his Palace. Donna Anna and Donna Elvira then enter the garden, escorted by Don Octavio ; all three are disguised in black dominoes, and wear half-masks to conceal their features ; the night darkens deeper and deeper.*]

SCENA XXV.—*Entra* DONNA ANNA, DONNA ELVIRA *e* DON OTTAVIO.

SCENE XXV.—DONNA ANNA ; DONNA ELVIRA : DON OCTAVIO.

Elv. Bisogna aver coraggio,
　　　O cari amici miei,
　　　E i suoi misfatti rei
　　　Scoprir potremo.
Otta. L' amica dice bene ;
　　　Coraggio aver conviene.
　　　[*A Donna Anna.*] Discaccia, a vita mia,
　　　L' affanno ed il timor.
Anna. Il passo è periglioso,
　　　Può nascer qualche imbroglio ;
　　　Temo pel caro sposo,
　　　E per noi temo ancor.

Elv. Let one united purpose
　　　Thus nerve us to expose him,
　　　Lay bare his guilt, disclose him
　　　The angry world before.
Oct. [*To Elvira.*] A column'd strength is rising
　　　From such sweet sage advising,
　　　[*To Anna.*] Take heart ! thy lover knoweth
　　　T' avenge, as to adore
Anna. The step is one of danger,
　　　For who may tell its issue ?
　　　[*To Octavio.*] Tho' trembling for this fair stranger,
　　　I fear for thee still more.

[*The music within the Palace is again heard ; they turn to and fro in the garden ; the window opens, and Leporello appears in the balcony with Don Juan.*]

SCENA XXVI.—*Entra* DON GIOVANNI *e* LEPORELLO.

SCENE XXVI.—*The same ;* LEPORELLO *and* DON JUAN *at the window.*

Lep. [*Dalla finestra.*] Signor guardate un poco
　　　Che maschere galanti.
Gio. Falle passar avanti,
　　　Di che ci fanno onor.

Anna, Elv. e Otta. Al volto, ed alla voce,
　　　Si scopre il traditore.
Lep. Zi ! zi ! signore maschere !

Anna e Elv. Vis rispondete.

Otta. Cosa chiedete ?
Lep. Al ballo, se vi piace,
　　　V' invita il mio signor.

Lep. Master, I pray observe now
　　　Yon gentle-folk retreating.
Juan. Bid them a hearty greeting
　　　Unto our humble door.
　　　[*Don Juan retires from the window.*
Anna, Elv. & Oct. The voice and mien proclaim him
　　　That traitor we would punish.
Lep. [*From the window, calling to them.*]
　　　Ps ! ps ! my dainty masks below—

Anna, Elv. & Oct. [*To Leporello.*] Of what desirous
Lep. Ps ! ps !
Oct. Do you require us ?
Lep. To grace a ball we hold here.
　　　So, pleasing our Señor

<table>
<tr><td>Zerl.</td><td>Grazie, di tanto onore.
Andiam, compagne belle.</td><td>Oct.</td><td>Thanks for the noble honor;
[To Anna and Elvira.] Then come, my fair companions.</td></tr>
<tr><td>Lep.</td><td>(L' amico anche su quelle
Prova farà d' amor.)</td><td>Lep.</td><td>[Aside.] ('Tis plain, its noble donor
Looks to obtain two more.)
[He retires and closes the window; Donna Anna, Donna Elvira and Don Octavio advance forward, and remove their masks.]</td></tr>
</table>

PROTEGGA IL GIUSTO CIELO—OH, GUARD ALL BOUNTEOUS HEAV'N. TRIO.

teg - ga il giu - - - sto cie lo   il   ze - - - - -
guard all boun - - teous Heav - en!   the   love.............

Ven-dichi il giu-sto cielo il mio tra - di - to a-mor!   il   mio, il
Forth be the trait-or driven From virtue's haunts a - part,   From   vir-tue's

pro-teg - ga il   giu-sto   cielo il ze - lo, del mio cor;   il   zelo il
O guard all   bounteous Heaven, the love that binds each heart,   the   love that

- lo   del   mio   cor!   pro - teg - gu il   giu - sto
...........that   binds   each   heart!   Be   Thy   pro - tec - tion

mio tra-di - - to a-mor! vendi chi, vendi chi il giusto   cie - lo
vir - tue's haunts   a - part. Aid me, O aid me, now pitying hea - ven!

ze - lo del   mio cor!   pro - teg   ga il   giu - sto
bind,   that binds   each heart!   Be   thy   pro - tec - tion

cie - lo,   il   ze - - lo   del............. mio cor!
giv - en,   Or   e'er............. our   hopes............. de - part.

il mio tra - di - to, tra - di - to a - mor,   tra - di - - to a - mor!
a - venge, a - venge this   in - jur'd heart,   this in - - jur'd heart.

cie - lo,   il   ze - - le   del   mio cor!
giv - en,   or   e'er   our   hopes   de   part.

The scene changes.   The stage represents a magnificent suite of apartments in the Palace of Don Juan : beyond a saloon in the foreground, two more are observed leading one into the other ; in each is a raised Orchestra, containing a band of Musicians : in the principal saloon in front, side galleries are seen, illuminated with candelabra and lustres, and decorated with statuary ; to the right is the door of a cabinet ; beyond the farthest saloon is seen an open terrace, giving admission to or from the garden, amidst the distant trees of which colored lamps and illuminations may be perceived.

The stage is thronged with maskers, who pass to and fro through the various apartments ; numerous servants hand about refreshments ; Don Juan enters, leading Zerlina and Masetto, Leporello following ; the whole scene is brilliantly illuminated and is altogether one of the greatest festivity ; a dance has just concluded.

SCENA XXVII.—*Entra* ZERLINA, DON GIOVANNI, LE-
PORELLO, MASETTO, *Contadini, Contadine, Servi, con
rinfreschi, Suonatori.*

Gio.   Riposate, vezzose ragazze.
Lep.   Rinfrescatevi, vei giovinetti.
Gio. e Lep.   Tornerete a far presto le pazze,
         Tornerete a scherzar, e ballar.

SCENE XXVII.—ZERLINA, DON JUAN, MASETTO, LE-
PORELLO ; *Chorus of Peasants, Musicians, and Attendants.*

Juan.   Pause a moment, from joy too exciting—
Lep.   And partake of our luscious abundance ;
Juan. & Lep.   Ere the mazy quadrille be inviting
         In a new glow of pleasure to share.

Otta. Ehi caffè !

Juan. [*Leading Zerlina to one of the tables.*] Hey ! some coffee !

Lep. Cioccolatte !

Lep. [*Leading some couples also.*] Hand the chocolate

Mas. [*A Zer.*] Ah ! Zerlina, giudizie !

Mas. (Pray Zerlina, be careful !)

Gio. Sorbetti !

Juan. The spices !

Lep. Confetti !

Lep. Some ices !

Mas. e Zer. Troppo dolce comincia la scena
In amaro potria terminar.

Zer. & Mas. (Not unoften, a sunshine as brilliant
Will a showery future declare.)

Gio. Sei pur vaga, brillante, Zerlina.

Juan. Thy pure glances are music Zerlina !

Zer. Sua bontà.

Zer. Nay, my lord !

Mas La briccona fa festa.

Mas. Why, the girl is coquetting !

Lep. Sei pur cara, Giannotta, Sandrine

Lep. [*To one of the Peasant-girls, imitating his master.*]
Thy sour answers are physic, Sandrina !

Mas. Tocca pur, che ti cada la testa.
La briccona mi fa disperar.

Mas. His impertinence she is abetting,
I am smothered in rage and despair !

Zer. Quel Masetto mi par stralunato,
Brutto, brutto si fa quest' affar.

Zer. (Poor Masetto appears in a passion,
This is truly an awkward affair.)

Gio. e Lep. Quel Masetto mi par stralunato,
Qui bisogna cervello adoprar.

Juan & Lep. (Yon Masetto must bend to the fashion ;
Now for action our talents prepare !)

SCENA XXVIII.—*Entra* DONNA ANNA, DONNA ELVIRA
e DON OTTAVIO.

SCENE XXVIII.—*The same ;* DONNA ANNA, DONNA
ELVIRA, DON OCTAVIO.

Lep. Venite pur avanti
Vezzose mascherette !

Lep. Amid the throng advancing
Each gentle mask is welcome !

Gio. E aperto a tutti quanti,
"Viva la Liberta."

Juan. All Seville, join our dancing !
Pleasure, allow no bar !

Anna., Elv. e Otta. Siam grati a tanti segni
Di generosità.

Anna, Elv. & Oct. We grateful, thank your kindness
In truth without a par !

Anna, Elv., Otta, Gio. & Lep Viva la libertà !
Gio. Ricominciate il suono.
[*A Lep.*] Tu accoppia i ballerini.

Anna, Elv., Oct., Juan & Lep. Pleasure, allow no bar !
Juan. Strike up a stirring music !
Find ev'ry girl a partner.

[*The orchestra in the foremost saloon commences a minuet ; Leporello forms the dance, in which several couples join.*]

Meco tu dei ballare,
Zerlina, vien pur quà.

Really, a dainty dancer,
Zerlina love, you are. [*They dance*

Lep. Da bravi via ballate.

Lep. Right *bravi !* swell the gambol.

Elv. Quell' è la contadina.

Elv. That is the peasant-maiden.

Anna. Io moro !

Anna. I perish !

Otta. Simulate.

Oct. Still dissemble.

Gio. e Lep. Va bene, in verità !

Juan. Lep. (Our course receives no jar.)

Gio. [*A Lep.*] A bada tien Masetto.

Juan. [*To Leporello.*] Just occupy Masetto.

[*The orchestra in the next saloon strikes up another dance, (a gavotte,) in which other couples join ; Leporello advances u Masetto.*]

Lep. Non balli poveretto ?
Vien quà, Masetto caro,
Facciam quel ch' altri fa.

Lep. [*To Mas.*] Why not dance ? where wouldst get to ?
Come here, Masetto dearest,
You from the mark fly far.

Gio. Il tuo compagno io sono,
Zerlina, vien pur quà.

Juan. Unto such deep affection,
Zerlina, place no bar !

Mas. No, no, ballar non voglio.

Mas. No, no ! I want no *dancing.*

Lep. Eh balla, amico mio !
Facciam quel ch' altri fa.

Lep. Jump high my friend ; what aileth ?
You from the mark fly far !

Mas. No.

Mas. No.

Lep. Sì, caro Masetto.

Lep. Aye, dear Masetto.

Mas. Ballare no, non voglio.

Mas. No, I want no dancing.

Anna. Resister non poss' io.

Anna. Resistance nearly faileth !

Otta. e Elv. Fingete, per pietà.

Elv. & Oct. Discov'ry all would mar.

[*A third dance (a waltz) commences in the farthest saloon*

Gio. e Zer. Vieni con me, mia vita.

Juan. [*Dancing to the gavotte, having led Zerlina to the door of the cabinet on the right, forces her to enter it.*]
Passion and love nigh slay me !

Mas [*A Lep.*] Lasciami, ah no ! Zerlina.

Mas. [*Breaking loose from Leporello.*] Let me be !
Ah no !—Zerlina !

Gio. Vieni, vieni.

Juan. Zerlina ! come then !

Zer. Oh numi ! son tradita !

Zer. O monster ! wilt betray me ?

[*Juan and Zerlina disappear through the door of the side chamber.*]

Lep. Qui nasce una rovina.   [*Si nasconde.*

Anna., Elv. e Otta. L' iniquo da se stesse
    Nel laccio se ne va.
Zer. Gente! ajuto, gente!   [*Di dentro.*]

Anna., Elv. e Otta. Soccoriamo l' innocente!

Mas. Ah Zerlina!
Zer. [*Di dentro.*] Scellerato'
Anna. e Otta. Ora grida da quel lato
    Ah gittiamo giù la porta.

Zer. [*Tornando.*] Soccorretemi! son morta
Gli Altri Siamo qui per tua difesa.

[*Don Juan follows Zerlina from the cabinet; in coming thence he encounters Leporello running in to warn him; he re-enters the ball-room, his drawn sword in his hand, pale, and dragging in Leporello, half dead with fright and astonishment.*]

Gio. [*Tornando e verso Lep.*] Ecco il birbo! che t' ha off-
    essa! ma da me la pena avrà. Mori, iniquo!

Lep. An cosa fate!
Gio. Mori, dico.
Otta., Anna e Elv. Nol sperate, nol sperate.
    L' empio crede con tal frode.
    Di nasconder l' empietà.

Gio. Donna Elvira!
Elv. Sì, malvaggio.
Gio. Don Ottavio!
Otta. Sì, signore!
Gio. Ah, credete!

Anna, Elv., Otta., Zer. e Mas. Traditore! traditore!
    Tutto, tutto già si sa;
    Trema, scelerato!
    Sapra tosto il mondo intero
    Il misfatto orrendo e nero,
    La tua fiera crudeltà.

    Odi il tuon della vendetta,
    Che ti fischia intorno interno,
    Sul tuo capo in questo giorno
    Il suo fulmine cadrà.

Gio. e Lep. E confusa la mia testa,
    Non so più quel ch' io mi faccia;
    E un' orribile tempesta
    Minacciando oh mi va.

    Ma non manca in mi coraggio,
    Non mi perdo, o mi confondo;
    Se cadesse ancora il mondo,
    Nulla mai temer mi fa.

Lep. (The devil! hath he seen her?)
    [*Masetto runs about amongst the groups of dancers, half dis-
    tracted, Leporello is entering the cabinet to warn Don Juan.*

Anna, Elv. & Oct. Iniquity fulfilling,
    Now falls his evil star!
Zer. [*Within the cabinet.*] Help! give aid! give aid! as-
        sistance!

Anna, Elv. & Oct. Rescue more than her existence'
    [*They all move from side to side, uncertain which way to go*
Mas. Ah, Zerlina!
Zer. [*In the cabinet.*] Hideous villain!
Anna, Elv. & Oct. [*Running to the door of the cabinet.*]
    Ha; her cry is through me thrilling!
    Break the lock! or force the portal!
    [*They dash in the door; Zerlina rushes from it*
Zer. O his guilt fulfill'd, 'twere mortal!
Anna, Elv., Oct. & Mas. [*To Zerlina.*] Our protections shall
    defend ye.

Juan. See! what scoundrel sought t' offend ye;
    Wrath condign thus cuts him down'
    [*Passing with his sword at Leporello*
    Die, base varlet!

Lep. [*On his knees.*] Ah, gracious goodness!
Juan. Die, I tell thee!
Oct., with Anna & Elv. [*To Don Juan.*]
    This pretence were too fallacious:
    View the pit that thou hast digged!
    Let the mask aside be thrown!
    [*They take off their masks*

Juan. How? Elvira!
Elv. Aye, thou Satan!
Juan. Don Octavio?
Oct.   Base betrayer!
Juan. Give some credence—
Anna.   Midnight slayer!
Anna, Elv., Zer., Oct. & Mas. [*To Don Juan.*]
    All thy *thousand* crimes are known!
    [*All advance, hemming in Don Juan and Leporello*.
    Tremble, tremble! more than tremble!
    Farthest Universe shall learn thee,
    Hell, alike as Heaven, spurn thee,
    Nature, thee her curse, disown!
    [*Thunder is heard, and a storm seen in the distance.*
    Hear our all-appalling vengeance
    Tear Creation's vault asunder,
    'Till its wrath, a mightier thunder,
    Hurl annihilation down!

Juan, (*his sword in hand,*) *& Lep.*
    In confusion, do my senses
    Little know what point to weather;
    I perceive the storm to gather
    With a too portentous frown.

    These positions give me/him courage;
    Earth might lose her path in error
    Ere my/his heart could dream of terror
    Or the slightest tremor own!

[*Striking right and left with his weapon, Don Juan makes his way through the crowds that menace him, and escapes with Leporello into the garden at the back, as the curtain falls.*

END OF THE FIRST ACT.

ACT II

The stage represents an open plaza in the city of Seville · to the left is a large mansion with projecting windows and balconies, in which Donna Elvira has taken up her residence.

It is evening; the moon is just perceived above the house-tops. Don Juan enters, with a mantle thrown over his shoulders, and carrying a mandoline; he is followed by Leporello.]

SCENA I—*Entra* Don Giovanni *e* Leporello.

Gio.   Eh via, buffone, non mi seccar.

Lep.   No no, padrone, non vò restar.

Gio.   Sentimi, amico—
Lep.   Vò andar, vi dico.
Gio.   Ma che ti ho fatto,
       Che vuoi lasciarmi!
Lep.   Oh niente affatto!
       Quasi ammazzarmi.
Gio.   Va, che sei matto,
       Fù per burlar.
Lep.   Ed io non burlo
       Ma voglio andar!
Gio.   Leporello!
Lep.   Signore.
Gio.   Vien quì, facciamo pace.   Prendi.

Lep.   Cosa?
Gio.   Quattro doppie.
Lep.   Oh sentite! per questa volta ancora la cerimonia accetto; ma non vi ci avvezzaste, non credeste di sedurre i miei pari, come le donne, a forza di denari.

Gio.   Non parliam più di ciò; ti basta l' animo di far quel ch' io ti dico?
Lep.   Purchè lasciam le donne.
Gio.   Lasciar le donne! Pazzo! lasciar le donne! Sai ch' esse per me son necessarie più del pan che mangio, più dell' aria che spiro?
Lep.   E avete core d' ingannarle poi tutte?

Gio.   E tutto amore. Chi a una sola è fedele, verso l' altra è crudele; io, ch' in me sento sì estesso sentimento, vo bene a tutte quante; le donne, poi che calcolar non sanno, il mio buon natural chiamano inganno.
Lep.   Non ho veduto mai naturale più vasto, e più benigno. Orsù cosa vorreste?

Gio.   Odi; vedesta tu la cameriera di donna Elvira?

Lep.   Io no.
Gio.   Non hai veduto qualche cosa di bello, caro il mio Leporello; ora io con lei vò tentar la mia sorte, ed ho pensato, giacchè siam verso sera, per aguzzarle meglio l' appetito, di presentarmi a lei col tuo vestito.

Lep.   E perchè non potreste presentarvi col vostro?

Gio.   Han poco credito con gente di tal rango gli abiti signorili. Sbrigati, via

Lep.   Signor—per più ragioni—
Gio.   Finiscila, non soffrò opposizioni.

SCENE I.—Don Juan, Leporello

Juan.   How now, Sir Stupid?
        Tease me no more.
Lep.   No, no, Don Cupid;
        Our union is o'er!
Juan.   Friend, state your grievance—
Lep.   I, Sir, would leave hence.
Juan.   Cause for this loathing
        Pray you to tell me?
Lep.   O, a mere nothing—
        You sought to kill me!
Juan.   Why, this is folly,
        'Twas but a joke.
Lep.   For which, I duly
        Throw off the yoke.
Juan.   Leporello!
Lep.   Don Juan!
Juan.   [*Taking a purse from his pocket.*] Here's *that* will make us friends yet, catch them.
Lep.   What, Sir?
Juan.   Fifteen ducats.
Lep.   [*Slipping the purse into his pouch.*] Oh,—now hear me; for this last once will I excuse such untoward joking: but make it not your practice, nor affect to gull a man of my firmness, as ye trap lasses, perforce of petty pelf, Sir.
Juan.   On to something less trite: and have ye courage, friend, to do my present pleasure?
Lep.   If you forsake the women.
Juan.   "Forsake the women!" jackass! "forsake the women!" to me they are necessary far more than the bread that feeds me, than the air I am breathing.
Lep.   And have you stomach to deceive the whole sex, then?
Juan.   'Tis all for love, child! he that's faithful to one girl, is unkind to the others; I own a heart so philanthropic, it loves the wholesale bevey; and women, whose calculating powers grasp not this *vast* idea, call it "deceiving."
Lep.   My puny comprehensions cannot grapple with feelings of such extent, Sir! pray you, explain your purpose.
Juan.   Hear me; hast ever seen the fair Elvira's enchanting servant?
Lep.   Not I.
Juan.   Then thy twin optics never scann'd what is lovely untutor'd Leporello: with this same damsel will I hazard my venture; and it has struck me, since day droops down toward evening, to lend the jest a happier complexion, I'll introduce myself in these thy garments.
Lep.   Surely are not your own, Sir, more at home in these matters?
Juan.   Too little credit, man, greets a genteel exterior from people in her station:
        Whip them off quickly!
Lep.   Señor—but my position—
Juan.   Have done at once, I brook no opposition!

[Leporello unbuttons his mantle and takes off his hat, Don Juan does the same; they exchange; while Leporello is in the act of assisting his master to put on the other cloak, a jalousie in an upper story of a mansion on the left is thrown open, and Donna Elvira appears at the window; taking her seat there, she leans her head upon her hand, and looks out pensively into the twilight, without perceiving Don Juan and Leporello in the street below.]

SCENA II.—Donna Elvira, e detto.

Elv. Ah taci, ingiusto core,
Non palpitarmi in seno !
E un empio, è un traditore,
E colpa aver pietà.
Lep. [*A Don Gio.*] Z   i donna Elvira,
Signor, ia voce io   to.
Gio. Cogliere io vò il momento,
Tu fermati un pò là—

[*He pushes the disguised Leper   ward under the window, and crouches behind him, to make Elvira, when she hears his (Don Juan's) voice, take Lep   to be the former.*]

Elvira, idolo mio !
Elv. Non è costui l' ingrato ?
Gio. Sì, vita mia, son io,
E chieggo carità.
Elv. (Numi ! Che strano affetto
Mi si risveglia in petto.)
Lep. State a veder la pazza,
Ch' ancor gli crederà.
Gio. Discendi, o gioja bella,
Vedrai che tu sei quella,
Che adora l' alma mia,
Pentito io sono già !
Elv. No, non ti credo, o barbaro.
Gio. Ah ! credimi, o m' uccide.
Lep. Se seguitate, io rido.
Gio. Idolo mio vien quà !
Elv. Dei, che cimento è questo ?
Non so s' io vado o resto—
Ah proteggete voi
La mia credulità.
Gio. Spero che cada presto ;
Che bel colpetto è questo !
Più fertile talento
Del mio no non si da.
Lep. Già quel mendace labbro
Torna a sedur costei ;
Deh proteggete, o Dei,
La sua credulità.

[*Elvira parte.*]

SCENA III.—Don Juan, Leporello.

Gio. Amico, che ti par ?
Lep. Mi par ch' abbiate un' anima di bronzo.

Gio. Va là, che sè il gran gonzo. Ascolta bene—quando costei al viene, tu corri ad abbracciarla, falle quattro Carezze, finge la voce mia ; poi con bell' arte cerca teco condurla in altra parte.

Lep. Ma signore.
Gio. Non più repliche.
Lep. E se poi mi conosce ?
Gio. Non ti conoscerà se tu non vuoi
Zitto, ell' apre ; ehi, giudizio.

'*He runs off to the side, leaving Leporello alone ; Donna Elvira enters from the house ; she advances to meet Leporello. Don Juan watches their movements from the side.*]

SCENA IV.—Donna Elvira, e detto.

Elv. Eccomi a voi.
Gio. (Veggiamo che farà.)
Lep. (Che bell' imbroglio !)
Elv. Dunque creder potrò, ch' i pianti miei abbian Vinto quel cor ? dunque pentito l' amato Don Giovanni al suo dovere, e all' amor mio ritorna ?

SCENE II.—*The same ; Donna Elvira*

Elv. [*At the window.*] Ah, lull thy rebel yearning
Fond heart, far too confiding ;—
The traitor but merits spurning,
'Twere more than crime to grieve.
Lep. Softly, I hear Elvira,
If sound be no false prophet.
Juan. Haply this turn may profit
Our purpose to achieve.

Elvira, thou mine idol !
Elv. Is this not the deceiver !
Juan. Aye ; grant a kindlier title
To one who would retrieve.
Elv. (Long dead within my bosom
Hope bids her bud re-blossom.)
Lep. (Now, ten to one, this ninny
Will actually believe.)
Juan. Descend, my joy ! my beauty !
A truant lost to duty,
Adoring still his treasure,
As penitent here receive.
Elv. No ; all is false, barbarian ;
Juan. First, credit me ; slay me, after.
Lep. (I die of smother'd laughter.)
Juan. Yon cruel casement leave.
Elv. (O, 'twere too keen a trial
Giving his pray'r denial ;
Forbid it, guardian angels,
That he *this* time deceive !)
Juan. (If she but yield, 'tis glorious,
Wit, be thou then victorious ;
For more consummate movement.
I never did conceive.
Lep. (Jove ! this amount of lying
Fram'd in with vile pretences,
Slips through her foolish senses
Like water through a sieve.)

[*Donna Elvira leaves the window above*

SCENE III.—Don Juan, Leporello.

Juan. Well, your opinion, friend.
Lep. That you're a substance of adamant and bronze, Sir !
Juan. Tut, tut, you gaby-gapeface ! now pay attention ; when the young lady comes out, run and embrace her quickly, give her twenty caresses, imitate all my manner ; and then, with dexterous seeming, try to conduct her to a distance.
Lep. Nay—good master—
Juan. Dare ye contradict !—
Lep. But suppose she should know me ?
Juan. That will she surely not, if you so will it. [*He turns.*] Gently ; she's coming : now, be careful !

SCENE IV.—Donna Elvira ; Leporello ; Don Juan at the back.

Elv. [*To Leporello.*) Love, I am with you.
Juan. (Let us see what he'll do.)
Lep. (Here's a pickle !)
Elv. I at last may believe my frequent weepings quite have melted thy heart ? deeply repentant, doth now Don Juan unto his duty, and my pure faith return him

Si, carinà!

Elv. Crudele! se sapeste quante lagrime, e quanti sospiri oi mi costate.
Lep. Io, vita mia!
Elv. Voi.
Lep. Poverina! quanto mi dispiace!
Elv. Mi fuggiste più?
Lep. No, muso bello.
Elv. Sarete sempre mio?
Lep. Sempre.
Elv. Carissimo!
Lep. Carissima! (La burla mi dà gusto.)

Elv. Mio tesoro!
Lep. Mia venere!
Elv. Son per voi tutto foco.
Lep. Io tutto cenere.
Gio. Il birbo si riscalda.
Elv. E non m' ingannerete?
Lep. Nò, sicuro.
Elv. Giuratelo.
Lep. Lo giuro a questa mano, che bacio con trasporto, E a quei bei lumi—
Gio. Ih, eh, ah, ih, sei morto.

Elv. Oh Numi! Fuggono.

Lep. [Putting his arm around Elvira's waist, and concealing his face with the cloak, while he endeavors to imitate Don Juan's voice.] Yes, my duckey!
Elv. Unkind one, if you knew how many heart-breakings and how many sighings ye have cost me!
Lep. I; precious pet-lamb!
Elv. You, love.
Lep. Pretty poppet! I am very sorry.
Elv. Wilt leave me e'er again?
Lep. No; ducksey-darling!
Elv. And thou art mine for ever?
Lep. Ever!
Elv. Caress me then!
Lep. Caress me too! [Aside.] (This is becoming pleasant.)
Elv. All my treasure!
Lep. My precious one!
Elv. I am fir'd with affection!
Lep. I am burnt up with it.
Juan. (He warms him toward the business.)
Elv. You no more will deceive me?
Lep. O, indeed no!
Elv. Dost promise me?
Lep. I swear it by this fair hand the which I kiss with transport: by those twin lode-stars—
Juan. [Calling out in a rough voice.] Ih, eh, ah, ih, ye're both dead!
Elv. & Lep. [Alarmed.] O heaven!

[Leporello throws his cloak around Elvira; they both run away for fear. Don Juan leaves his place of concealment.]

SCENA V.—Don Juan, solus

Gio. Ih, eh, ah, ih! par che la sorte mi secondi, veggiamo; le finestre son queste; ora cantiamo.

SCENE V.—Don Juan, solus.

Juan. [Running toward the side by which they have fled, and still calling out.] Ih, eh, ih, eh, ah, ih! [He turns back, and fetches his mandoline.]
Her luckiest changes that jade fortune is ringing;
So so, this is the window, now for our singing.

DEH VIENI ALLA FINESTRA—OPE, OPE THY CASEMENT. Don Juan.

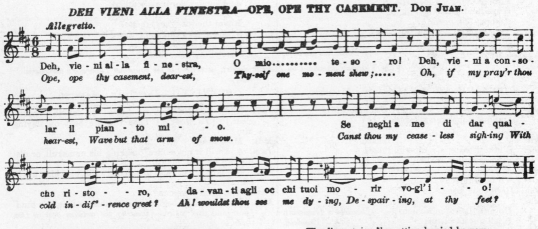

Tu ch' hai la bocca dolce più ch' del miele,
Tu ch' il zucchero posti in mezzo al core,
Non esser, gioja mio, con me crudele;
Lasciati almen veder, mio bell' amore.
Vè gente alla finestra.
Forse è dessa. Ps. ps!

Thy lip outvies Hymettian-honied bowers;
Virtue worthy an angel, thy heart doth cherish;
Thy sigh were balm amid a heav'n of flowers;
O, for one kiss, one word, this soul would perish!
[He approaches nearer the house.] Some one is at the window It's her perhaps! ps, ps! [He is interrupted by Masetto, who enters, accompanied by several Villagers, all armed with muskets Masetto also carries a pistol in his belt.]

SCENA VI.—Don Giovanni; Masetto, con seguito di Contadini armati.

SCENE VI.—The same; Masetto; some Villagers

Mas. Non ci stanchiamo;—il cor mi dice
Che trovarlo dobbiamo.

Gio. [*Aparte.*] Qualcuno parla,

Mas. Fermatevi—mi pare
Ch' alcuno quì si muova.

Gio. [*Aparte.*] Se non fallo, è Masetto.

Mas. Chi va là? Non risponde?
Animo, schioppo al muso:
Chi va là?

Gio. [*Aparte.*] Non è solo;
Ci vuol giudizio. [*Forte.*] Amici,
Non mi voglio scoprir. Sei tu, Masetto?

Mas Appunto quello; e tu?

Gio. Non mi conosci? Il servo
Son io di Don Giovanni—

Mas. Leporello!
Servo di quell' indegno cavaliere?

Gio. Certo, di quel briccone.

Mas. Di quell' uom senz' onore, ah dimmi un poco,
Dove possiam trovarlo:
Lo cerco con costor per trucidarlo.

Gio. [*Aparte.*] Bagatelle! [*Forte.*] Bravissimo Masetto,
Anch' io con voi m' unisco
Per fargliela a quel birbo di padrone;
Ma udite un pò qual è la mia intenzione:
Metà di voi quà vadano
E gli altri vadantà;
E pian' pianin' lo cerchino,
Lontan non sia di qua.
Se un uom' e una ragazza
Passeggian par la piazza,
Se sotto a una finistra
Fare all' amor sentite
Ferite, pur ferite,
Il mio patron sara!
In testo egli ha un cappello
Con canai pennachini
Addosso un gran mantelle,
E spada al fianco egli hà!
Andate, fate presto!
Tu sol verrai con me,
Noi far dobbiamo il resto
E già vedrai cos' è.
[*I Contadini partono.*]

Mas. Come on, my hearties; I feel assured we *must* fall in with his track.

Juan. (A man's voice spake then?)

Mas. But stop a bit; I'm certain that something passes yonder.

Juan. (Surely that is Masetto!)

Mas. Who goes there? [*A pause.*] Give an answer, or we present and fire, lad! who goes there?

Juan. (He has friends, too; this calls for prudence.) [*Assuming Leporello's voice.*] My masters, don't ye know an old chum? Is that Masetto?

Mas. A piece of him, Sir;—and you?

Juan. *Again* that question? the servant unto my lord Don Juan.

Mas. Leporello! servant of that dishonorable scoundrel!

Juan. Certes; of that same "scoundrel."

Mas. Lost to shame, feeling, and honor: ah, give acquaintance where we may hope to find him; we're seeking through the town intent to kill him.

Juan. (Very pretty.) Bravissimo, Masetto!
Now list me in your reg'ment, I share a like dislike and wise intention,
And here dispense the fruit of my invention.
Do you pursue the right-hand path,
You by the left repair;
And then advancing cautiously,
You'll find your man, somewhere.
Should ye spy cloak and hat, Sirs,
Or in the streets, or piazzas,
And aught of love proceeding
'Twixt two close-muffled figures,—
Present, and pull your triggers,
My *darling* master's there!
New doeskin upper-leathers,
Toledo, a scarlet mantle,
And sundry borrow'd feathers
This dainty bird doth bear.
About the job: hey, *presto!*
Friend *I* take charge of thee;
And, prophet-like, profess to
Foretell how it will be.

[*The Villagers attendant on Masetto depart, according to the supposed Leporello's directions.*]

SCENA VII.—Il Don Giovanni; Masetto.

SCENE VII.—Don Juan: Masetto.

Gio. (Zitte! lascia ch' io senta. Ottimamente!)
Dunque dobbiamo ucciderlo?

Mas. Sicuro.

Gio. E non ti basteria rompergli l' ossa,
Fracassargli le spalle?

Mas. No, no! voglio ammazzarlo!
Vò farlo in cento brani.

Gio. Hai buone arme?

Mas. Cospetto!
Ho pria questo moschetto; \Dandole a Giovanni.
E poi questa pistola. [*Dandola.*]

Gio. E poi?

Mas. Non basta?

Gio. En, basta certo. Or prendi
Questa per la pistola, [*Battendole.*]
Questa per il moschetto.

Mas. Ahi! ahi! La testa mia—

Gio. Taci, o t' uccido. [*Battendolo ancora.*]
Questa per l' ammazzarlo.

Juan. (Softly, whiles that we listen; so far the coast's clear.) [*To Masetto.*] Then you are bent on slaying him?

Mas. Most surely.

Juan. And will it not suffice, breaking his numskull, or displacing his ribs, man?

Mas. No, no; I *will* his life-blood; I'll cut him up to mince-meat!

Juan. Hast good weapons?

Mas. Just hav'nt I! beginning with this musket, this bludgeon, and this pistol—[*handing the articles over to Don Juan.*]

Juan. [*Holding out his hand for more.*] Go on, friend—

Mas. Too few then?

Juan. Nay; pretty tidy! we'll prove them. [*He gives Masetto a violent blow from behind with the bludgeon. Masetto falls to the ground, uttering loud cries.*] That, for your cur-ship's pistol—[*another blow*]—that, for your cur-ship's musket—

Mas. Ah! eh! ih! murder! murder!

Juan. Hush, or I'll kill ye! [*Gives him another and another blow.*]

Questa per farso in brani ;—
Villano, mascalzon, ceffo da cani !　　　　　　　[Parte.]

This, for your promis'd beating ; this for your prom
ised killing ;
Mean coward ! poltroon knave ! dog of a villain !

[*Administering one or two final blows, and catching up his mandoline, Don Juan steals off. Masetto lays half-dead with the beating and fright upon the ground. Zerlina, hearing his cries, comes to his assistance from the house ; she bears a cloak over her arm, and a small street-lantern in her hand.*]

SCENA VIII.—MASETTO ; *indi* ZERLINA.

Mas. [*Gridando forte.*] Ahi ! ahi ! La testa mia !
　　　Ahi, ahi, le spalle ! E il petto !
Zer. Mi parvo di sentire la voce di Masetto.
Mas. Oh, Dio ! Zerlina ! Zerlina mia, soccorso !
Zer. Cos' è stato ?
Mas. L' iniquo, il scellerato mi ruppe l' ossa, e i nervi.

Zer. O poveretta me ! chi ?
Mas. 　　　　　Leporello,
　　　O qualche diavol che somiglia à lui.
Zer. Crudel ! non tel diss' io,
　　　Che con questa tua pazza gelosia
　　　Ti ridurresti a qualche brutto passo ?
　　　Dove ti duole ?
Mas. 　　　　　Quì.
Zer. E poi ?
Mas. 　　　　Quì, e ancora quì.

Zer. E poi non ti duol altro ?
Mas. Duolmi un poco
　　　Questo piè, questo braccio, e questa mano.
Zer. Via, via, non è gran mal, s' il resto è sano.
　　　Vien tene meco a casa.
　　　Purchè tu mi prometta
　　　D' essere men geloso,
　　　Io. io ti guarirò, caro il mio sposo.

SCENE VIII.—MASETTO ; ZERLINA.

Mas. Ah ! ih ! I'm mash'd to jelly ; ih ! ah ! my back
bone ! my breast-bone !—
Zer. It would seem that I heard the voice of my Masetto.
Mas. O heav'n, Zerlina—Zerlina dearest, give aid here !
Zer. What has happen'd ?
Mas. The monster has surely broken,—aye, every bone
about me.
Zer. O, my darling pet ! who ?
Mas. Leporello ! or some infernal fiend exactly like him.

Zer. The brute !—have I not told thee, giving way to thy
stupid jealous fancies would bring upon thee the very
worst mischances ? where has he hurt you ?

Mas. [*Pointing to his head.*] Here—
Zer. Where else, dear ?
Mas. [*Pointing to his back and shoulders.*] Here—and also
here—
Zer. Do you not suffer elsewhere ?
Mas. There's a pain in this my foot, in my elbow, and in
my hand too—
Zer. Come, come ; it is not much ; the rest is unhurt
back with me home to supper,
　　　If you will truly promise next time to be less jealous
I have a cure, thou most foolish of fellows.

VEDRAI CARINO—LIST, AND I'LL FIND, LOVE. SOLO. ZERLINA.

Andante.

Ve-drai ca-ri-no, Se sei buo-ni-ne, Che bel ri-me-dio,—Ti vog-lio dar.
List, and I'll find, love, If you are kind, love, Balm for your mind, love,—Patient but be.

E na-tu-ra-le, Non da dis-gus-to, E lo spe-zia-le, Non lo sa far, nò—
This balm so pure, love, Sim-ple and sure, love, Sweet to en-dure, love, None know but me.

Non lo sa far, nò— Non lo sa far........ E un cer-to bal-samo, Che por-to a-dos-so.
None know but me, None know but me........ Thrilling and heal-ing, O-ver thee steal-ing.

Da-re tel pos-so, S' il vuoi pro-var. Sa-per vor-res-ti ? Do-ve mi stà, do-ve
Ex-qui-site feel-ing, Meant but for thee. Ex-qui-site feel-ing. Ex-qui-site feel-ing

do-ve, do-ve mi sta ?... Sen-ti-lo bat-te-re Toc ca-mi quà, Sen ti lo
Meant but for thee ... To thy en-treat-ing, I'll yield it, dear ! Feel how ti

bat - te - re, Sen-ti-lo bat-te-re;   Toc-ca-mi quà,   Sen-ti-lo bat-te-re, Sen-ti-lo
beat - ing, beat-ing just here,.......   beat-ing just here ; Feel how 'tis beat - ing, Feel how 'tis

bat-te - re, Sen-ti-lo bat-te-re, Toc-ca-mi quà. quà, quà!   Sen - ti - lo bat-te - re,
beat - ing, Feel how 'tis beat - ing, beating just here, here, here!   Feel how 'tis beat - ing, Feel

Toc-ca - mi quà, quà,   Toc-ca-mi quà, quà!   Toc-ca - mi quà, quà,   Toc - ca - mi quà!
how 'tis beating,   beat-ing just here!   Feel how 'tis beat - ing,   beat ing just here!

[*Placing the cloak round Masetto's shoulders, taking his arm, and gently showing him the way with her lantern, she leads him from the scene.*]

The scene changes. The stage represents a retired court-yard in the Palace of the Commandant, now that of Donna Anna Donna Elvira and Leporello enter by one of the doors in the wall ; the latter is still disguised in Don Juan's dress.

SCENA IX.—*Cortile Interno. Entra LEPORELLO e DONNA ELVIRA.*

Lep. Di molte faci il lume s' avvicina o mio ben! stiamo qui un poco, finchè da noi si scosta.

Elv. Ma che temi, adorato mio sposo?
Lep. Nulla, certi riguardi. Io vò veder, S' il lume è già lontano. (Ah come da costei Liberarmi?) Rimanti, anima bella.

Elv. Ah non lasciarmi!
Sola, sola in bujo loco,
Palpitar il cor mi sento,
E m' assale un tal spavento,
Che mi sembra di morir.
Lep. Piu che cerco men ritrovo
Questa porta sciagurata;
Piano piano l' ho trovata,
Ecco il tempo di fuggir.

SCENE IX.—*DONNA ELVIRA ; LEPORELLO.*

Lep. [*Still imitating his master's voice.*] Surely advancing torches track our path, O my love? then stand aside here, lest that they should perceive us.
Elv. Why this tremor? do you fear aught, ador'd one?
Lep. Nothing, nothing—tho' somewhat cautious—I wish to see if now the lights are far off. (From this appendage how to relieve me!)
Remain here, my existence!—
Elv. [*In a piteous tone.*] Ah, do not leave me!
In the solemn hush of darkness
Wilt forsake and leave me lonely;
Spurn'd in loving, the bosom only
Knows a woe no pow'r can cheer.
Lep. More I seek it, more it fails me
Where the deuce the door is lying;
Soft, I have it! now for flying,
Coast and conscience both are clear.

[*In endeavoring to find the door by which he entered with Elvira, he takes the other, and is just about to use it, when it is opened from the other side, and Donna Anna with Don Octavio, escorted by Attendants bearing torches, enter from it. Leporello slips aside unseen by them, and at their approach both he and Donna Elvira conceal themselves in different angles of the court-yard. Don Octavio advances, leading Donna Anna, and endeavoring to comfort her.*]

SCENA X.—*Entra DON OTTAVIO e DONNA ANNA.*

Otta. Tergi il ciglio, o vita mia,
E dà calma al tuo dolore,
L' ombra omai del genitore
Pena avrà de tuoi martir.
Anna. Lascia almen alla mia pena,
Questo piccolo ristoro.
Sol la morte, o mio tesoro,
Il mio pianto può finir.
Elv. Ah! dov' è, lo sposo mio.
Lep. Se mi trova, son perduto!
Elv. Una porta la vegg' io,
Cheto che io vò partir.

SCENE X.—*The same; DONNA ANNA ; DON OCTAVIO ; Attendants.*

Oct. Let the beam of consolation
Pour its balm on those that suffer;
Hence, toward the honor'd manes, offer
Hallow'd love,—not tribute tear.
Anna. Grief like mine alone hath comfort
In the soothing calm of weeping,
Till the tomb's unsorrow'd sleeping
Bring the peace denied us here.
Elv. Thinks the wretch again to slight me?
Lep. (Should they find me, I am done for.)
Elv. & Lep. [*Aside, unseen by each other, trying to reach the same door.*] (Yonder portal doth invite me
Gently now to disappear.)

[*They both meet at the door, which is opened at the same instant from the other side by Masetto and Zerlina, escorted by Peasants with clubs and torches ; Masetto bears a thick stick in his hands—perceiving Don Juan as he supposes, he drags forward the disguised Leporello to the front ; the latter all the while manages to conceal his face.*]

SCENA XI.—Entra ZERLINA e MASETTO.

Zer. e Mas. Ferma briccone,
Dove ten vai?

Anna e Ott. Ecco il fellone.
Come era quà?

A 4. Ah! mora il perfido,
Che m' ha tradito!

Elv. E mio marito,
Pietà! pietà!

Tutti. E Donna Elvira
Quella ch' io vedo!
Appena io credo;
No, morirà.

Lep. Perdon, perdono,
Signori miei,
Quello io non sono,
Sbaglia costei;
Viver lasciatemi
Per carità.

Tutti. E Leporello!
Che inganno è questo!
Stupido resto
Che mai sarà!

Lep. Mille torbidi pensieri
Mi s' aggiran per la testa;
Se mi salvo in tal tempesta,
E un prodigio in verità.

Tutti. Mille torbidi pensieri
Mi s' aggiran per la testa;
Che giornata, o stelle, è questa!
Che impensata novità!

[Donna Anna parte.

SCENE XI.—The same; MASETTO; ZERLINA; other Attendants.

Mas. [Dragging Leporello forward.]
Luck ne'er was greater,
He cannot 'scape us.

Anna & Oct. How came the traitor
Here in this place?

Anna, Oct., Mas. & Zer. Villain! thy perfidies
Henceforth are over.

Elv. He is my lover,
Ah, shew him grace!

Anna, Oct., Mas. & Zer. The fair Elvira?
Such intercedence
Barely gains credence!
No, no; he dies!

Lep. O Sirs, forgive me
For all this bother,
Since I'm myself, Sirs,
And not another; [Taking off his hat and showing
Spare me my little life [himself]
To grow more wise.

The others. Heav'n! Leporello!
Most strange of fancies!
Scarcely our senses
Believe our eyes.

Lep. Million turbulent vagaries
In mine addled brain do gather;
To avoid the coming weather
Were prodigious, in very truth.

Anna, Elv., Oct. & Mas. Million turbulent distractions
In my brain arise and gather;
Who could count on, or credit either,
This dénouement so uncouth!

[Donna Anna leaves the scene, escorted by her Attendants.

SCENA XII.—ZERLINA, ELVIRA, OTTAVIO, MASETTO, LEPORELLO.

Zer. Dunque quello sei tu che il mio Masetto poco fà, crudelmente mal tratastì!

Elv. [A Lep.] Dunque tu m' ingannasti, o scellerato, spacciandoti con me da Don Giovanni!

Otta. [A Lep.] Dunque tu in questi panni venisti quà per qualche tradimento!

Elv. A me tocca punirti.

Zer. Alzi a me.

Otta. No, no, a me.

Mas. Accopatelo meco tutti tre.

Lep. Ah, pietà! Signori miei!
Pietà, pietà di me!
Dò ragione a voi, a lei,
Ma il delitto mio non è.
Il padron con prepotenza
L' innocenza mi rubò.
Donna Elvira! compatite!
Voi capite come andò!
Di Masetto non sò nulla
Vel dirà questa fanciulla!
E' un oretta circa in circa,
Che con lei girando vò,
[A Oct.] A voi, Signore! non dico niente;
Certo timore, certo accidente,
Di fuori chiaro, di dentro oscuro,
Non c' è riparo la porta, il muro,
Vò da quel latto, poi qui celato;
L' affar si sà.
Ma s' io sapea, fuggia per qua.

[Leporello parte.

SCENE XII.—ZERLINA, ELVIRA, OCTAVIO, MASETTO, LEPORELLO.

Zer. [To Leporello.] It was then at thy hands that my Masetto did receive such a scandalous mal-treatment.

Elv. [To Leporello.] Then 'twas thy senseless jesting, heartless ribald, assumed the port and 'havior of Don Juan'

Oct. [To Leporello.] And in this sacred Palace is not thy presence fraught with purpos'd mischief?

Elv. With me rests thy chastisement.

Zer. Or with me.

Oct. Nay, nay; with me.

Mas. Lend a hand to his thrashing all ye three.

Lep. Tongue or blows I merit neither;
In grace to me incline;
With due def'rence to each and either,
Learn how the real fault was not mine.
Our gay Don a clean deception
On mine innocence did throw.
Fair Elvira, bear me witness;
How the matter went, you know.
You, Masetto, mis-state sadly,
And o'ershoot the mark most madly;
Some wild phrensy circumcurrent
Through each brain begins to flow.
Now, gentle Señor, I crave your pardon,
But sorely frighten'd I 'spied the garden,
Without, 'twas lamplight—within, obscure, Sir,
That door stood open, inviting and sure, Sir—
Whiles lurking cosey
Came this exposé:
The rest is clear, O, quite clear!
Would I had known it, and slipp'd off here!
Edging himself gradually up to the door, he takes to his heels and makes off.

SCENA XIII.—Zerlina, Elvira, Ottavio, Masetto.

Elv.   Ferma, perfido, ferma!
Mas.   Il birbo ha l' ali si piedi.
Zer.   Con qual arte
     Si sottrasse l' iniquo !
Otta   Amici miei
     Dopo eccessi sì enormi,
     Dubitar non possiam, che Don Giovanni
     Non sìa l' empio uccisore
     Del padre di Donn' Anna. In questa casa
     Per poche ore fermatevi : un ricorso
     Vò far a chi si deve ; e in pochi istanti
     Vendicarvi prometto :
     Così vuole dover, pietade, affetto.

SCENE XIII.—Zerlina. Elvira, Octavio Masetto

Elv.   Stay thee ! wicked one, stay thee !—
Mas.   His pace would baffle lightning—
Zer.   And how neatly he escaped further question—

Oct.   I claim your audience ; after crime so enormous there is no shade of doubt but that Don Juan was the midnight assassin of Anna's aged father : repair awhile within this Palace to comfort her—I will seek out the ministers of Justice,
     And work my Vengeance 'neath that mighty protection
     'Tis the duty of Love ! the proof of Affection !

IL MIO TESORO—FLY THEN, MY LOVE. Octavio.

Il mio te-so-ro in tan-te, An-da-te, an-da-te a con-so-lar!
Fly then, my love, en-treat-ing, To calm,.... to calm........ her anx-ious fears;

E del bel cig-lio il pian-to, Cer-ca-te di a sciu-gar,.............. cer-ca-te, cer-
Oh, still her heart's wild beat-ing, And wipe a way her tears,.............. and wipe a-way, and

ca-te, cer-ca-te di a-sciu-gar, Cer-ca-te
wipe away, and wipe.... a way her tears, And wipe................ a-

di a-sciu-gar. Di-te le che i suoi tor-ti A ven-di-car io va-do; A ven-di-car io
way her tears. Tell her I'll vengeance take On him who slew her sire, On him who slew her

va-do. Che sol di stra-gi e mor-ti Nun-zio vogl' io tor-nar, Nun-zio vogl' io tor-
sire; This arm his grave shall make, Or I'll by his ex-pire, Or I'll by his ex-

nar— Sì, Nunzio vogl' io tor nar.................
pire— Yes, Or I'll by his ex-pire.

[Exeunt Don Octavio, Zerlina, Donna Elvira and Masetto

The scene changes. The stage represents an open square or plaza before the Cathedral of Seville, in the centre of which stands an equestrian Statue of marble to the memory of Don Pedro, the Commandant : on the pedestal of this Statue the following inscription is carved :

     "I HERE AWAIT THE VENGEANCE DECREED BY HEAVEN UNTO THE WRETCH WHO SLEW ME."
It is about two in the morning.

SCENA XIV.—Don Giovanni, *salendo il muro; vedi* Leporello.

Gio. Ah! ah! ah! questa è buona!
        Or lasciala cercar.   Che bella notte!
        E piu chiara del giorno; sembra fatta
        Per gir a zonzo, a caccia di ragazze.
        Vediam s' è tardi? Ah, no!
        Ancor non son le due di notte. Avrei
        Voglia un pò di saper com' è finito
        L' affar tra Leporello e Donna Elvira;
        S' egli ha avuto giudizio.

Lep. [*Senza alito, dietro il muro.*]
        Aifin vuole ch' io faccia un precipizio!
Gio. È desso! Oh, Leporello!
Lep. Chi mi chiama?
Gio. Non conosci il padrone!
Lep. Cosi nol conoscessi!
Gio. Come? birbo!
Lep. Ah, siete voi? Scusate!
Gio. Cos' è stato?
Lep. Per cagion vostra io fui quasi scoppato.
Gio. Ebben, non era questo
        Un onore per te?
Lep. Signor, vel dono!
Gio. Via, via, vien quà:
        Che belle cose ti deggio dir!
Lep. Ma cosa fate quì?
Gio. Vien dentro, e lo sapprai
        Diverse istorielle,
        Che accadute mi son, dacchè partisti,
        Ti dirò un' altra volta; or la più bella
        Ti vo' solo narrar.
Lep.   Donnesca, al certo.
Gio. C' è dubbio! Una fanciulla,
        Bella, giovin, galante,
        Per la strada incontrai; le vado appresso,
        La prendo pe. la man—fuggir mi vuole;
        Dico poche parole, ella mi piglia
        Sai per chi?
Lep. Non lo sò.
Gio. Per Leporello!
Lep.   Per me!
Gio.   Per te!
Lep. Va bene!
Gio.   Per la mano
        Essa allora mi prende.
Lep. Ancora meglio!
Gio.   M' accarezza, m' abbraccia—
        " Caro il mio Leporello!
        Leporello, mio caro!' Allor m' accorsi
        Ch' era qualche tua bella.
Lep. [*Aparte.*] Oh, maledetto!
Gio. Dell' inganno approfitto: non sò come
        Mi riconosce, grida, sento gente,—
        A fuggire mi metto; e pronto pronto
        Per quel muretto in questo loco io monto.
Lep. E mi dite la cosa
        Con tal indifferenza—
Gio.   Perchè no?
Lep. Ma se fosse costei stata mia moglie?

Gio. [*Ridendo molto forte.*] Meglio ancora!
                                [*Parla la Statua.*
Com Di rider finirai
        Pria dell' Aurora!
Gio. Chi ha parlato?
 *p. Ah! qualch' anima sarà dell' altro mondo,
        Che vi conosce a fondo.
Gio. Taci, sciocco! Chi va là!
Com Ribaldo, audace!
        Lascia ai morti la pace.

SCENE XIV.—Don Juan; *afterwards* Leporello.

Juan. [*As he enters hastily.*] Ha, ha, ha, ha! this is good
        fun, now let her search away: [*looking around him,*] a
        lovely night this, almost clearer than day-light; lady
        moon gives her charter, too, toward the chasing pretty
        damsels: what hour now? oh, barely turn'd of two i'
        the morning; 'twould like me to be well acquainted
        how the matter ended 'twixt Leporello and Elvira
        heaven grant he was prudent.

Lep. [*Scrambling over the wall of the terrace, and sitting on it.*]
        He'll ne'er pause, till I'm taken in and done for.
Juan. Behold him: well, Leporello?
Lep. Who has call'd me?
Juan. Know ye not your liege lord?
Lep. O, would I ne'er had known him!
Juan. How so? villain!
Lep. Ah, is that you? your pardon.—
Juan. What has happen'd?
Lep. On your account have I nearly been murdered.
Juan. On my account, so please you; 'twere an honor for
        thee.
Lep. Which I—relinquish.
Juan. Whu! whu! and list, my bird; a pretty story I have
        to tell.
Lep. What art thou doing here?
Juan. Come down, and read that riddle. [*Leporello jumps
        down from off the wall, and advances.*] Some ten or
        twelve adventures have accrued to my share since last
        we parted: I postpone them at present, keeping the
        best for thine immediate ear.
Lep. A girl's at bottom.
Juan. I think so. [*They re-exchange dresses during this narra-
        tion.*] Round by the Prado I encounter'd a dainty
        blushing young damsel; I straight approach her—]
        touch her dimpled hand; she would escape me: but a
        word in due season bids her to take me—guess, for
        whom?
Lep. I cannot.
Juan. For Leporello.
Lep. For me?
Juan. For thee.
Lep. So far,—good.
Juan. In her turn, by the hand, she too caught me—

Lep. And so far,—better.
Juan. She caresses—embraces—" darling little Leporello!"
        —" Leporello, my darling!"—and then it struck me
        she might just be your mistress.

Lep. O malediction!
Juan. I made hay while the sun shone: she soon found her
        intense mistake, and scream'd out: steps draw near
        us; I put wings to my trotters, and deftly I vault yon
        wall to light here like a feather.
Lep. You can stand here, and tell me all this with brazen
        coldness?
Juan. And why not?
Lep. But then what wouldst have done, were she my wife
        Sir?
Juan. So come o'er her.

The Statue of the Commandant.
        With laughter chang'd to woe, greet you Aurora!
Juan. Who now spoke there?
Lep. [*Trembling.*] Ah, some spirit from the other world
        who knows you, wishing more close acquaintance.
Juan. Silence, blockhead! Who spoke there?
The Statue. Stay, ribald, this violence:
        Leave to the dead their silence!

Lep. Ve l' ho detto?
Gio. Sarà qualcun di fuori, che si burla di noi.
    [Con indifferenza e sprezzo.
Ehi! del Commendatore   [zion.
Non è questa la statua? Leggi un poco quell' iscri-
Lep. Scusate: non ho imparato a leggere
A raggi della luna.
Gio. Leggi, dico!
Lep [Legge.]
"Dell' empio, che mi trasse al passo estremo.
"Qui attendo la vendetta."
    Udiste? io tremo!
Gio. O, vecchio buffonissimo!
Digli che questa sera l' attendo a cenar meco.
Lep. Che pazzia! Vi far! Oh, Dei! mirate
Che terribili occhiate
Egli ci da! Par vivo—par che senta—
E che voglia parlar.
Gio. Orsù va là,
O quì t' ammazzo? E poi ti seppelisco!
Lep. Piano, piano, signore—
Ora ubbidisco.
O, statua gentilissima
Del gran Commendatore—
Padron, mi trema il core;
Non posso terminar.
Gio. Finiscila, o nel petto
Ti metto questo acciar.
[Aparte.] Che gusto, che spassetto!
Lo voglio far tremar.
Lep. [Aparte.] Che impiccio! che capriccio!
Io sentomi gelar!
O, statua gentilissima,
Benchè di marmo siate—
Ah, padron mio! mirate
Che seguita a guardar.

Gio.   Mori, mori!
Lep.   No, attendete!   [Alla Statua.
Signore, il padron mio—
Badate ben, non io—
Vorria con voi cenar,
Ah! ah! che scena è questa!
Oh, Ciel!
Chinò la testa!

Gio. Va là che sei un buffone—
Lep. Guardate ancor, padrone.
Gio. E che deggio guardar?
Lep. Colla marmorea testa
Ei fa così così.
Gio. Parlate, se potete,
Verrete a cena?

Com.   Si!
Lep. Mover mi posso appena!
Mi manca, oh Dei, la lena!
Per carità partiamo:
  Andiamo via di quà!
Gio. Bizzarra è inver la scena—
Verrà il buon vecchio a cena:
A preparala audiamo,
Partiamo via di quà.   [Partono.

Lep. As I told you.
Juan. It must be some one o'er the wall then playing a joke there. [He approaches the Statue, and remarks it for the first time.] Eh! that Commandant's money here has raised him a statue: read you yon inscription aloud.
Lep. Excuse me, I've heard it rated very bad to try and read by moonlight.—
Juan. Read! I tell you.
Lep. "I here—a-wait—that—vengeance, decreed—by—Heav-en—
"Unto—the—wretch—who slew me."
You hear that? I tremble!
Juan. Exquisite pithy epitaph! tell him this very ev'ning I ask him home to supper.
Lep. Gracious pow'rs! are you mad? O heav'n, observe, Sir, what a terrible light his eyes assume! he liveth! he is breathing' ye gods, he wants to speak!
Juan. About the work!
Or I will slaughter, and 'neath this turf will lay thee.
Lep. Piano, piano! Señor, now I obey thee.
[Advancing and bowing to the Statue with great civility
So please your marble mightiness,
Most statuesque Commander—
Lord, Sir! my senses wander,
I cannot get it out.
Juan. Come, finish it; or this weapon
Shall somewhat clear your throat.
(He flutters like a capon,
All flounder, quake, and float.)
Lep. (To such insane caprices
My fears refuse a vote.)
    [Approaching the Statue again
Most petrified of gentlemen,
Most polish'd marble statue—
Ah, he is gazing right at you,
Gods, how he glares about!
Juan. Die, Sir.
Lep.   Not just at present.
    [Advancing again to the Statue
My lord so bold and high now
Invites you—mark! not I, now,
To join a drinking-bout.
[The Statue bows in acquiescence; Leporello falls on his knees
Ah, ah! I sink with dread, Sir,
I swear he bow'd his head, Sir.
Juan. [Laughing.] All hope of cure you past are.
Lep. Ah, look there, dear good master!
Juan. Ah, look at what, you lout?
Lep. He made his marble helmet
To nod this way! this way! [Imitating the Statue
Juan. [Advancing himself to the Statue.
If   an answer;
W   per?
The Statue.   Yea!
Lep. Movement   denied me;
That Earth   ope, and hide me!
For mercy's   , do quit, Sir,
This most unpleasant place.
Juan. Bizarre! though justly proper!
The old boy comes to supper;
Away, bestir your wit, Sir,
To spread the board apace.   [Exeunt.

The scene changes. The stage represents a vestibule in Donna Anna's Palace leading to her more private apartments, which are seen in the background.
Don Octavio enters, tenderly leading Donna Anna, whose whole demeanor still indicates that she is plunged in the deepest grief

SCENA XV.—*Camera.*—Donna Anna, Don Ottavio.
Otto. Calmatevi, idol mio, di quel ribaldo
Vedrem puniti in breve i gravi eccessi,
Vendicati sarem

SCENE XV.—Donna Anna, Don Octavio.
Oct. Calm thee, mine own existence: thou soon shalt see this arch-ribald suffer for his vile excesses 'neath a mighty revenge.

Anna. Ma il padre, oh Dio!

Otta. Convien chinar il ciglio
Al volere del Ciel. Respira, o cara,
Di tua perdita amara
Fia domani, se vuoi, dolce compenso
Questo cor, questa mano, ch' il mio tenero amor!

Anna. Oh, Dei! che dite, in si tristi momenti?

Otta. E che vorresti con indugi novelli
Accrescer le mie pene? Crudel!

Anna. Crudele! ah, no!
Mio ben, troppo mi spiace
Allontanarti un ben che lungamente
La nostr' alma desia;
Ma il mondo? oh Dio!
Non sedur la mia costanza
Del sensibil mio core;
Abbastanza per te mi parla amore.
Non mi dir, bell' idol mio,
Che son io crudel con te;
Tu ben sai quant' io t' amai,
Tu conosci la mia fè.
Calma, calma il tuo tormento!
Se di duol non vuoi ch' io mora.
Forse un giorno il Cielo ancora
Sentirà pietà di me. [Parte.

Anna. Will't give back—my father?

Oct. We bow in mute submission to Heaven's decree
look up then, beloved; why, thy bitterest anguish on
the morrow might melt, kiss'd into gladness—for this
heart—this affection—this my tenderest love—

Anna. O God! such accents in these moments of sorrow!—

Oct. And why with this prolonged unneeded delaying increase my faithful yearning? unkind!

Anna. "Unkind" love? ah no, Octavio.
Poorly it likes me thus to defer a bliss
So long, so justly, so supremely our object:
The world though—O heaven!— [bleedeth
Still to try thy constant patience this my heart truly
For Love, all in thy cause fervently pleadeth.
Never say
That cold displeasure's
Joyless measures
Can chill my breath;
Poesy's power
In Phœbus bower,
Could not picture half my faith.
Calm, ah calm thy gentler sorrow,
If you grieve, my woes are double;
Haply these brief hours of trouble
Gem with smiles our future path. [Exit.

SCENA XVI.—Don Ottavio.

SCENE XVI.—Don Octavio, solus.

Otta. Ah! si segua il suo passo;
Io vò con lei dividere i martiri:
Saran meco men gravi i suoi sospiri. [Parte.

Oct. [Looking after her.] Yes, I follow her footsteps.
Participation can dull the edge of Sorrow,
And from Friendship, e'en Woe a sunbeam may borrow. [Departs.

The scene changes. The stage represents a grand banqueting-hall in the Palace of Don Juan: towards one side of which, a magnificent table is spread with a sumptuous repast. Don Juan is discovered seated at the table. Leporello stands at the beaufet, napkin in hand, wiping silver plates, &c., and directing the various servants in attendance on Don Juan. The gallery above is filled with musicians.

SCENA XVII.—Don Giovanni, Leporello.

SCENE XVII.—Don Juan, Leporello, Ladies, Attendants, Servants, Musicians.

Gio. Già la mensa è preparata—
Voi suonate, amici cari;
Già che spendo i miei danari,
Io mi voglio divertir.
Leporello, presto in tavola.

Lep. Son prontissimo a servir.
Bravi! "Cosa Rara."

Gio. Che ti par del bel concerto?

Lep. E conforme al vostro merto.

Gio. Ah che piatto saporito!

Lep. Ah che barbaro appetito!
Che bocconi da gigante,
Mi par proprio di svenir.

Gio. Nel veder i miei bocconi
Gli par proprio di svenir.
Piatto!

Lep. Servo

Gio. Versa 1 vino. [Beve.

Juan. Richest dainties rise before me,
Play your best, to crown the pleasure;
Let expense be free from measure!
Let me boast right royal cheer!
Leporello, now the second course.

Lep. Sir, your most obedient, here.
[The Musicians strike up an air from Martini's "La Cosa Rara."] Bravi! bravi!—"Cosa Rara."

Juan. Is it not an air of spirit?

Lep. Aye,—and suited to your merit.

Juan. Why, this cream would honor "Gunter."

Lep. (He is hungry as a hunter,
And he eats just like a giant;
I may look and—long, I fear.)

Juan. (Did his mouth feed as his eyes do,
He would swallow all, I fear.)
Plates, here!

Lep. Serv'd, Sir.

Juan. Pour some sherry.

Leporello fills his master's glass; the Musicians have now changed to another air

Lep. "Fra i due Litiganti!"

Gio. Excellente marsimino!

Lep. [Aparte.] Queste pezzo di fagiano,
Piano piano vò inghiottir.

Gio. Sta mangiando quel marrano!
Fingerò di non capir.

Gio. [Udendo ancora la musica.]
Questa poi la conosco pur troppo

Lep. From "I Due Litiganti."

Juan. 'Faith, that bottle makes us merry.

Lep. [Helping himself to the maccaroni, and eating as fast as he can.] (This small dish of maccaroni
Quickly, quickly let me clear.)

Juan. (What's that scamp at? eating, only;
Not to know it I'll appear.) [The Musicians play "Non più Andrai," from "Le Nozze di Figaro."

Lep. "Non più Andrai," from "Le Nozze," by Mozart!

Gio. Leporello!
Lep.   Padron mio!
Gio. Parla schietto, mascalzone—
Lep. Non mi lascia una flussione
    Le parole proferrir.
Gio. Mentre io mangio, fischia un poco.
Lep. Non so far.
Gio. Cos' è?
Lep.   Scusate!
    Si eccellente è il vostro cuoco,
    Che lo volli anch' io provar—
Gio. Si eccellente è il cuoco mio,
    Che lo volle anch' ei provar.

SCENA XVIII.—Donna Elvira; e detti.

Elv. [A Don Giovanni.] L' ultima prova dell' amor mio
    Ancor vogl' io fare con te: [S' inginocchia.
    Più non rammento gl' inganni tuoi,
    Pietate io sento—
Gio. } [Aparte.]
Lep. } Cos' è? cos' è?
Elv. Da te non chiede quest' alma oppressa
    Fella sua fede qualche mercè.
Gio. Mi maraviglio! Cosa volete?
    Se non sorgete—non resto in piè.
Elv. Ah, non deridere gli affanni miei!
Lep. Quasi da piangere mi fa costei!
Gio. Io tederidere! Cielo! perchè?
    Che vuoi, mio bene?
Elv. Che vita cangi!
Gio.   Brava!
Elv. Cor perfido!
Gio. Lascia ch' io mangi; a se ti piace,
    Mangia con me.
Elv. Mimanti, barbaro, nel lezzo immondo,
    Esempio orribile d' iniquità.
Lep. [Aparte.] Se non si muove al suo dolore,
    Di sasso ha il core—o cor non ha.
Gio. Vivan le femmine! Viva il buon vino!
    Sostegno e gloria d' umanità.

[Donna Elvira rushes off by one of the entrances on the left; but presently returns, uttering a piercing shriek.]

Elv. [Partendo.] Ah!   [Parte.
Gio. Che grido è questo mai?
    Va a veder che cos' è stato.

SCENA XIX.—Don Giovanni, Leporello.

Lep. Ah!   [Sorte Leporello, e ritorna spaventato.
Gio. Che grido indiavolato?
    Leporello, che cos' è?
Lep. Ah, signor, per carità,
    Non andate fuor di qua!
    L' uom di sasso, l' uomo bianco—
    Ah, padrone, io gelo, io manco!
    Se vedeste che figura,—
    Se sentiste come fa—
    Ta, ta, ta, ta!
Gio. Non capisto niente affatto
    Tu sei matto in verità.

Lep. Ah sentite!
Gio.   Qualcun batte.
    Apri!
..   Io tremo!
        Apri, dice!

        Ah! ah!

Juan. Leporello!
Lep.   Your commands, Sir?
Juan. Speak more plainly, clear your throat Sir.
Lep. I can boast no plainer note, Sir,
    Sore throat makes mine accent queer.
Juan. Nay; then whistle—this a joke is.
Lep. Don't know how—
Juan. And why?
Lep.   Excuse me;
    Such a paragon your cook is,
    I can swear he hath no peer.
Juan. "Such a paragon my cook is,
    How could he resist the cheer?

SCENE XVIII.—The same; Donna Elvira

Elv. All mine affection yearns to retrieve thee,
    Love can reprieve thee ere Error slay.
    Mem'ry doth banish all thine offences,
    'Neath Mercy, they vanish—
Juan & Lep. What does she say?
Elv. I will not hurt you clam'ring for justice;
    Learn but one virtue! Mend, while you may
Juan. Dear! how surprising! what more your will, then
    If you still kneel, then, I, too, essay,
Elv. Ah, do not ridicule such deep afflictions!
Lep. ('Gad, she is stirring up my sad reflections)—
Juan. I, lady—"ridicule?" And in what way?
    Come, love, what would you?—
Elv. Teach thee repentance!
Juan. Brava!
Elv.   Base, cruel wretch!
Juan. Sharp though that sentence, I can excuse it;
    Sup with us, pray!
Elv. Monster! I leave thee, then, slave to thy passions
    Sunken in brutal lust, hated by all!
Lep. (It is a stone heart takes it thus coolly;
    Or, to speak truly, no heart at all!)
Juan. Long live the pretty girls! long live the wine-cup!
    They are the glory of Earth's merry ball!

[Donna Elvira rushes off by one of the entrances on the left; but presently returns, uttering a piercing shriek.]

Elv. [Re-entering.] Ah!   [Escapes by another door
Juan & Lep. [To each other.] And why that shriek of terror
Juan. [To Leporello.] Run and see what is the matter

SCENE XIX.—Don Juan, Leporello.

Lep. [Goes out and returns presently, dropping his light]
    Ah!
Juan. Explain this dev'lish clatter!
    Leporello, what is up?
Lep. Ah, Señor!—I—must—im-plore
    Do—not—venture—past—the—door!
    Sir,—the—Sta-tue!—that—huge white man,
    O dear master,—I'm dying—with fright, man
    If—you—could—but see—his—figure!
    Or—could—hear—his—step—a-far!
        Ta! ta! ta! ta!
Juan. I can make nor head nor tail on't;
    You're gone mad, and very far!
        [A loud knocking is heard
Lep. Listen, listen!
Juan.   Who is knocking!
        [Drawing his sword
Lep. [Falling on his knees.] I—can—not!
Juan. [Menacing Leporello with the sword.]
    Open, quickly!
Lep. Shrieking.] Ah!

no. Matto!	*Juan.* [*Snatching a candle from the table.*]
Per togliermi d' intrico	Idiot! ye tie the knot up faster,
Ad aprir io stesso andrò!	I to gain the clue, must go. [*He goes out.*]
Lep. Non vò più veder l' amico, [*Parte.*]	*Lep.* Now adieu to thee, poor master,
Pian pianin m' asconderò.	It were best be scarce, I trow.
[*Si nasconde sotto la Tavola.*]	

[*Leporello hides himself under the table; the lights go out. Don Juan re-enters, candle and drawn sword in hand, backing before the Statue of the Commandant, which enters on foot, and advances one step into the apartment, remaining rigid and firm.*

SCENA XX.—*Il Commendatore.* E detti.

SCENE XX.—Don Juan; The Statue of the Commandant; Leporello, *under the table.*

Com. Don Giovanni, a cenar teco	*Statue.* So, Don Juan, thou didst invite me
M' invitasti—è son venuto!	To thy banquet,—lo, I am present!
Gio. Non l' avrei giammai creduto;	*Juan.* Though unlook'd for, this is pleasant,
Ma farò quel che potró.	I will strive my best to do.
Leporello, un' altra cena	[*Calling to Leporello, under the table.*]
Fa che subito si porti.	Leporello, clear the table,
	And another supper run for—
Lep. Ah, padron, siam tutti morti!	*Lep.* Ah, Señor, we all are done for
Gio. Vanne, dico!	*Juan.* Run, I tell thee—
Com. Ferma un pò!	*Statue.* Hold! do *not* go
Non si pasce di cibo mortale	He may never taste food that is mortal
Chi si pasce di cibo celeste:	Who is fed on the manna of Heaven;
Altre cure più gravi di queste—	Graver cares to these moments are given,
Altra brama quaggià mi guido!	Other purpose I come here to show.
Lep. La terzana d' avere mi sembra,	*Lep.* (O, the cold of an Arctic December
E le membra fermar più non so!	Shivers through me with terrible throe.)
Gio. Parla dunque—che chiedi? che vuoi?	*Juan.* Speak out bravely: your purpose? what want you
Com. Parlo, ascolt! più tempo non ho!	*Statue.* Listen; for Time's precious seconds, fast flow.
Gio. Parla, parla! ascoltandoti sto.	*Juan.* Speak, then, speak: I am longing to know.
Com. Tu m' invitasti a cena,	*Statue.* Thou bad'st me to thy supper;
Il tuo dover or sai!	Host of mine would I turn:
Rispondimi: verrai	And wilt thou too, in thy turn
Tu a cenar meco!	Come to my banquet—
Lep. Oibò! oibò! tempo non hà—scusate.	*Lep.* [*To the Statue.*] Hallo! He is engag'd, excuse him
Gio. A torto di viltate	*Juan.* Thy guest, none can accuse him
Tacciato mai sarò.	As one whom fear could cow.
Com. Risolvi?	*Statue.* The answer?
Gio. Ho già risolto.	*Juan.* My mind is made up.
Com. Verrai?	*Statue.* Wilt come, then?
Lep. Dite di no!	*Lep.* Please tell him "no!"
Gio. Ho fermo il core in petto;	*Juan.* With firmer heart than iron.
Non hò timor: verrò!	If so you will,—be't so!
Com. Dammi la mano in pegno!	*Statue.* Pledge me thy hand as earnest.
Gio. Eccola.	*Juan.* Take it, then.

[*The moment the marble fingers of the Statue close upon his hand, a shuddering seizes Don Juan's whole frame, and a wild terror seems to possess him.*

Ohimè.	Alas!
Che gelo è quest, mai!	Mine hour of death is nigh.
Com. Pentiti, cangia vita,	*Statue.* Turn thee, repent thy vices
E l' ultimo momento!	Ere Heav'n award the sentence.
Gio. No, no—ch' io non mi pento,	*Juan.* [*Still in the Statue's grasp.*]
Vanne lontan da me!	No, no; I scorn repentance!
	Hence, dotard! end this farce!
Com. Pentiti! scelerato!	*Statue.* Turn thee, insensate rev'ller!
Gio. No, vecchio infatuato	*Juan.* Away, thou babbling driv'ller!
Com. Pentiti!	*Statue.* Yet repent!
Gio. Nò.	*Juan.* No!
Com. & Lep. Sì!	*Statue. & Lep.* Yea!
Gio. Nò!	*Juan.* No!
Com. Ah tempo più non v' è! [*Parte.*]	*Statue.* [*Letting Don Juan's hand drop.*]
	Down to thy doom then pass!

[*The Statue sinks; flames rise on all sides; and from the abyss that has engulfed the Statue, Demons rush forth and seize Don Juan.*]

SCENA XXI.—Don Giovanni, Leporello, Chorus of Demons.

Gio.	Da qual tremore insolito Sento assalir gli spiriti! Dond' escono quei vortici Di foco piea d' orror?
	Chi l' anima mi lacera,— Chi m' agita le viscere! Che strazio ohimè! che smania! Che inferno! che terror!
Lep.	Che ceffo disperato! Che gesti di dannato! Che gridi! che lamenti Come mi fa terror!
Coro.	Tutto a tue colpe è poco, Vieni, v' è un mal peggior!

SCENE XXI.—Don Juan, Leporello, Chorus of Demons.

Juan.	Hideous fears are seizing me, Hell and its horrors rise around, The Awful Summons thundereth Thro' Fire's eternal roar!
	Each Sense that slav'd me withereth, The heart they slew is slain at last, The soul they burnt shall burn still When Time itself is o'er!
Lep.	He shews the fate that waiteth The doom'd and damn'd ungodly. What shrieks! what cries of terror! I dare to look no more!
Cho. of Demons.	These pangs but ill requite thee, Down! there are worse in store!

[*The Demons overcome Don Juan, and sink with him into the abyss*

SCENA XXII E Ultima.—Donna Anna, Zerlina, Donna Elvira, Don Ottavio, Masetto, Leporello.

Tutti.	{ Ah! dov' è il perfido? { Dov' è l' indegno? Tutto, il mio sdegno sfogar io vò.
Anna.	Solo mirandolo stretto in catene Alle mie pene calma darò.
Lep.	Più non sperate di ritrovarlo, Più non certate lontano andè.
Tutti.	Cos' è? favella—
Lep.	Venne un colosso—ma se non posso—
Tutti.	Via, presto sbrigati!
Lep.	Tra fume e foco, badate un poco, L' uomo di sasso fermate il passe— Giusto la sotto diede il gran botto— Giusto là il diavolo sel trangugiò.
Tutto.	Stelle! che sento!
Lep.	Vero è l' evento.
Tutti.	Ah! certo è l'ombra che l'incontre.
Otta.	Or che tutti, o mio tesoro! Vendicati siam dal cielo, Porgi, porgi a me un ristoro Non mi fà languire ancor.
Anna.	Lascia, o caro, un anno ancora Allo sfogo del mio cor, Al desio di chi t' adora Ceder deve un fido amor.
Zer. e Mas.	Noi { Masetto { Zerlina } a casa andiamo, A cenar in compagnia.
Lep.	Ed io vado all' osteria A trovar padron miglior.
Tutti.	Resti dunque quel birbon Con Proserpina e Pluton! E noi tutti, o buona gente Ripetiam allegramente L' antichissima canzon: Questo è il fin, di chi fa mal, E dì perfidi la morte. Alla vita è sempre ugual.

SCENE XXII AND LAST.—Donna Anna, Zerlina, Donna Elvira, Don Octavio, Masetto, Leporello, Attendants, Officers of Justice.

Anna, Zer., Elv., Oct. & Mas.	Where lurks the murderer? where hides the traitor Justice, ne'er greater, poiseth her blow.
Anna.	Viewing him bound in chains henceforth to languish Would o'er mine anguish calm gently throw.
Lep.	Gentlefolk, hope not ever to find him; Search not or grope not, he's off, I trow.
The Rest.	And how befell it?
Lep.	Came a colossus—Sirs—I can't tell it—
The Rest.	Quickly! explain yourself!—
Lep.	Lightnings and thunder rent Earth asunder,— Gazing hard at you enter'd the Statue— Here, too, his foot was; here, his huge boot was Just there, the Devil did down with him go!
The Rest.	Heav'n! speak you truly?
Lep.	All is told fully
The Rest.	Aye; sure the Statue fulfill'd its vow!
Oct.	[*To Donna Anna.*] Since thy sorrows, mine angel-treasure, Are aveng'd by mightier Powers: Bid my hopes, wing'd with vision'd pleasure, Reach the home whereto they soar.
Anna.	Let these pass, love, one twelvemonth o'er her That all tears may quit the shore, Ere the faithful true adorer Reap the rich reward in store.
Zer. & Mas.	Come, my sweet, the priest tomorrow Ushers in domestic blessing.
Lep.	Let me look to be possessing Better master . . . . fore.
Zer., Mas. & Lep.	Stay, . . u cause of all our wrong, With old Pluto's crew along! Since our ev'ry heart rejoices, Let us gladly blend our voices In an old time-honor'd song.
All.	"Such his end—who doeth ill! To a like account, the wicked Ever did come—ever will!"

THE END.

THE BARBER OF SEVILLE
(Il Barbiere di Siviglia)

by

GIOACCHINO ROSSINI

THE STORY OF
"THE BARBER OF SEVILLE"

THE Count Almaviva, desperately in love with Rosina, the ward of Doctor Bartolo after serenading his mistress, encounters Figaro, the Barber and factotum of the town, a meddling busy-body; to him the Count confesses his love, and they mutually plot for the purpose of bringing about the introduction of Almaviva to the maiden.

Rosina is strictly watched by her guardian, Doctor Bartolo, who cherishes a desire of wedding his ward himself; in this design he is assisted by Basilio, a music-master. Rosina returns the affection of the Count, to whom, in spite of the watchfulness of her guardian, she contrives to convey a letter, declaring her passion, and her intention to break through her trammels, and at the same time requesting his name.

To obtain an interview with his mistress the Count disguises himself as a drunken soldier, and forces his way into Bartolo's house. Rosina has already been told by Figaro that the name of the Count is Signor Lindor. The disguise of Almaviva is discovered by the guardian, the pretended soldier is placed under arrest, and the first act concludes.

In the second act the Count again enters Bartolo's house, disguised as a music-teacher, pretending that he has been sent by Basilio to give a lesson in music, on account of the illness of the latter. To obtain the confidence of Bartolo, he produces Rosina's letter to himself, and offers to persuade Rosina that the letter has been given to him by a mistress of the Count, and thus to break off the connection between the two. He obtains the desired interview, which proceeds satisfactorily, and Figaro manages to obtain the keys of the balcony, while at the same time an escape is determined on at midnight, and a private marriage arranged. In the meantime, Basilio himself makes his appearance, the lovers are disconcerted, and the Count makes his escape.

Bartolo, who possesses the letter of Rosina written to the Count, succeeds, by producing it, in exciting the jealousy of his ward, who, while under the influence of this feeling, discloses the plan of escape which had been arranged, and agrees to marry her guardian. At the appointed time Figaro and the Count make their appearance, and after some confusion the lovers are reconciled. A notary, procured by Bartolo, celebrates the marriage of the enamored pair. Immediately afterwards the guardian enters, accompanied by the officers of justice, into whose hands he is about to consign Figaro and the Count, when mutual explanations take place, and all parties are reconciled.

This opera was first produced at the Teatro Argentina, in Rome, at the Carnival in 1816.

IL BARBIERE DI SIVIGLIA
(THE BARBER OF SEVILLE)

ACT I.

SCENE I.—A Street in Seville.—Dawn of Morning.

Fiorello, with a lantern in his hand, introducing various Musicians; the Count Almaviva, wrapped up in a mantle.

Fiorello. Piano, pianissimo, in tender sound,
Let love's light airs now float
around.

Chorus. Piano, pianissimo,
Love's music sound.

Fiorello. All wrapped in silence, no soul is
near;
No wandering footstep falls on the
ear.

Count. Fiorello—ho!
(In a low voice.)

Fiorello. Sir, I am here.

Count. Well; and our friends?

Fiorello. They are all ready.

Count. All's well;
Keep silence.

Fiorello. Softly, softly!
Utter not a word.
Oh, moment full of rapture!
Oh, bliss almost divine!
Such beauty well may capture
A heart already thine.
Ho, Fiorello!
(They tune their instruments, and the Count sings, accompanied by them.)

Fiorello. Sir?

Count. Say, have you seen her?

Fiorello. No, sir.

Count. Ah, how vain is every hope!

Fiorello. Behold, sir, the dawn advances.

Count. Ah, what am I to think—what
shall I do?
All is vain. Well, my friends?

Chorus. Sir?
(Softly.)

Count. Retire, retire;
I have no longer need
Of your songs or your music.
(He gives a purse to Fiorello, who distributes money to all.)

ATTO I.

SCENA PRIMA.—Il momento dell'azione è sul termine della Notte.—La Scena rappresenta una Strada in Siviglia.

Fiorello, con lanterna nelle mani, introducendo vari Suonatori; indi il Conte Almaviva avvolto in un mantello.

Fiorello. Piano, pianissimo, senza parlar
Tutti con me venite quà.

Coro. Piano, pianissimo, eccoci quà
Piano, venite quà.

Fiorello. Tutto è silenzio, nessun qui c'è;
Che i nostri canti possa turbar.

Conte. Fiorello—olà!
(Sotto voce.)

Fiorello. Signor, son quà.

Conte. Ebben; gl'amici?

Fiorello. Son pronti già.

Conte. Bravi, bravissimi;
Fate silenzio.

Fiorello. Piano, pianissimo!
Senza parlar.
O, istante d'amor!
Felice momento!
O, dolce contento
Ch'eguale non ha.
Ei, Fiorello!
(Accordano gl'istrumenti, e il Conte canta accompagnato da essi.)

Fiorello. Mio signore?

Conte. Dì, la vedi?

Fiorello. Signor, nò.

Conte. Ah, che è vana ogni speranza!

Fiorello. Signor Conte, il giorno avanza.

Conte. Ah, che penso—che farò?
Tutto è vano. Buona gente?

Coro. Mio signore?
(Sotto voce.)

Conte. Avanti, avanti;
Più di suoni più di canti
Io bisogno ormai non ho.
(Dà una borsa a Fiorello, il quale distribuisce devari a tutti.)

ECCO RIDENTE IL CIELO—LO! SMILING IN THE ORIENT SKY

COUNT

Ec - co ri-den-te il cie - - lo,   Spun-ta la bel-la au-
Lo! smil-ing in the   o - ri - ent sky,   Morn in her beau-ty

ro - ra,   E tu non sor-gi an-co-ra E - - -
breck - ing,   Canst thou, my love, in - ac-tive lie My

puoi dor-mir co - si? Ah!   Sòr-gi mia dol - ce spe - - me,
life, art thou not wak-ing? A - rise, my heart's own treas - ure,

Vie-ni bell' I - dol mi - o,   Ren-di men cru-do, oh Di - o! Lo
All that my soul holds dear;   Oh! turn my grief to pleas-ure! A -

stral, lo stral che mi fe - rì; lo stral che mi, fe-
wake, my love, my love, ap - pear; a - wake, my love, ap-

rì.   Oh, sor - te! gia veg - go? Quei
pear.   Oh, joy! and do I see thee? My

ca - ro sem-bi - an - te;   Quest' a - ni-ma a-
doubts all dis - ap - pear;   Those eyes are heav-en

man - te ot - ten ne pie - ta?
to me! What have I now to fear?

Fiorello. Good night to all;
I have nothing farther for you
to do.

(The Musicians surround the Count, thanking him and
kissing his hand. Annoyed by the noise they make, he
tries to drive them away. Fiorello does the same.

Chorus. Many thanks, sir, for this favor;
Better master, nor a braver,
Ever did we sing a stave for.
Pray, good sir, command our
throats!
We will ever sing and pray for
One who gives us gold for notes!

Count. Silence! silence! cease your
bawling,
Nor like cats with caterwauling
Wake the neighbors—stop your
squalling,
Rascals, or I'll dust your coats!
If this noise you still keep making,
All the neighbors you'll be waking.

Fiorello. Silence! silence! what an uproar!
For these favors—for such honor!
(Mocking them.)
Rascals, hence, away—
Scoundrels, quit the spot!
Eh, what a devilish uproar!
Are ye mad, or not?
(Exit Chorus.)

Count. The indiscreet rabble! They had
nearly,
With their importunate clamors,
Awakened the whole neighborhood.
At last they're gone! But she
appears not.
(Looking towards the balcony.)
It is in vain to hope; yet here will I
(He paces pensively up and down.)
Wait till I behold her. Every
morning
Does she come into this balcony
To breathe the fresh air at early
dawn.
Here will I wait.—Ho, Fiorello!
Do you also retire.

Fiorello. I go. Yonder
I will await your commands.
(He withdraws.)

SCENE II.—Figaro, with his Guitar round his neck, and
the preceding.

Fiorello. Buona notte a tutti quanti;
Più di voi che far non so.

(Gli Suonatori circondano il Conte, ringraziandolo, e
baciandogli la mano. Egli, indispettito per lo strepito che fanno li và cacciando. Lo stesso fa anchè
Fiorello.)

Coro. Mille grazie, mio Signore;
Del favore, dell'onore,
Ah! di tanta cortesìa.
Obbligati in verità!
O che incontro fortunato
È un signor di qualità!

Conte. Basta! basta! non parlate,
Ma non serve, non gridate,
Maledetti, andate via,
Ah, canaglia, via di quà!
Tutto quanto il vicinato
Questo chiasso sveglierà.

Fiorello. Zitti! zitti! che rumore!
Ma che onore—che favore!
(Con ironia.)
Maledetti, andate via—
Ah, canaglia, via di quà!
Veh, che chiasso indiavolato!
Ah, che rabbia che mi fa?
(Il Coro parte.)

Conte. Gente indiscreta! Ah quasi,
Con quel chiasso importuno,
Tutto quanto il quartier han ri-
svegliato.
Alfin sono partiti! E non si vede.
(Guardando verso la Ringhiera.)
È inutile sperar; eppur quì voglio
(Passeggia riflettendo.)
Aspettar di vederla. Ogni mattina
Ella su quel balcone
A prender fresco viene in sull'
Aurora.
Proviamo.—Olà, tu ancora
Ritirati, Fiorello!

Fiorello. Vado. Là in fondo
Attenderò suoi ordini.
(Si ritira.)

SCENA II.—Figaro, con Chitarra appesa al collo, e detti.

LARGO AL FACTOTUM DELLA CITTA—*ROOM FOR THE CITY'S FACTOTUM*

FIGARO

Lar - go al fac - to__ tum del - la cit - tà   lar - go, .
Room__ for the cit - y's__ fac - to - tum, here,
La, la,
La, la

la, la, la, la, la, la, la, la. Pres-to a bot - te - ga che l'al-ba è già pres-
la, la, la, la, la, la, la, la., I must be off to my shop, for the dawn is

to, la, la, la, la, la, la, la, la, la, la. Ah, che bel vi - ve-re,
near, la, la, la, la, la, la, la, la, la, la. What a mer-ry life,

che bel pià - ce - re, che bel pia - ce-re, Per un bar - bie - re, di qua-li-
what pleas-ure gay, what pleas-ure gay, A-waits a bar - ber of qua-li-

tà, di qua-li - tà. Ah, bra - vo, Fi-ga - ro; bra - vo, bra-
ty, of qua-li - ty. Ah, bra - vo, Fi-ga - ro; bra - vo, bra-

vis - si-mo bra - vo. La, la, la, la, la, la, la, la, la, la;
vis - si-mo bra - vo. La, la, la, la, la, la, la, la, la, la;

For - tu - na - tis-si-mo, per ve-ri - tà, bra - vo, la, la, la, la, la, la, la, la,
Of men, the hap-pi-est, sure, art thou, bra - vo. la, la, la, la, la, la, la, la,

là, la; for - tu - na - tis - si - mo, per ve-ri - tà, for - tu - na-tis - si - mo
la, la; Of men, the hap-pi - est, sure, art thou, Of men, the hap-pi - est,

per ve-ri - tà, la, la, la, la, la, la, la, la, la, la, la, la, la, la, la, la, la, la, la, la, la.
sure, art thou, la, la, la, la, la, la, la, la, la, la, la, la, la, la, la, la, la, la, la, la, la.

Figaro.	Figaro.
La ran la lera,	La ran la lera,
La ran la la!	La ran la la!
Ready to do everything	Pronto a far tutto
Both by night and by day—	La notte e il giorno—

Perpetually in bustle	Sempre d'intorno
And in motion.	In giro stà.
What happier lot,	Miglior cuccagna,
What nobler life	Per un barbiere
For a barber,	Vita più nobile,
Than my own!	Nò non si dà.
La ran la lera,	La ran la lera,
La ran la la!	La ran la la!
Razors and combs,	Rasori, e pettini,
Lancets and scissors—	Lancette, e forbici—
Everything is	Al mio comando
Ready at command!	Tutto quì stà!
Then there are the snug	Vi è la risorsa
Perquisites of business	Poi del mestiere
With gay damsels,	Colla donnetta,
With cavaliers.	Col cavaliere.
La ran la lera,	La ran la lera,
La ran la la!	La ran la la!
All call for me,	Tutti mi chiedono,
All want me—	Tutti mi vogliono—
Dames, maidens,	Donne, ragazze,
Old and young:	Vecchi, fanciulle:
My peruke! cries one;	Quà la parucca!
Quick, my beard! another;	Presto la barba!
Here, bleed me! a third:	Quà la sanguigna:
Figaro! Figaro!	Figaro! Figaro!
I am here, I am here.	Son quà, son quà.
Figaro up, Figaro down!	Figaro sù, Figaro giù!
Figaro here, Figaro there!	Figaro quà, Figaro la!
I am activity itself—	Pronto prontissimo—
I'm quick as lightning—	Son come un fulmine—
I'm the factotum	Sono il factotum
Of the city.	Della città.
Ah, bravo, Figaro!	Ah, bravo, Figaro!
Bravo, bravissimo!	Bravo, bravissimo!
Most fortunate of men	Fortunatissimo
In every truth.	Per verità.
La ran la lera,	La ran la lera,
La ran la la!	La ran la la!
Ah! ah! what a happy life!	Ah! ah! che bella vita!
But little fatigue, and abundant amusement;	Faticar poco, e divertirsi assai;
Always with some doubloons in my pocket,	È in tasca sempre aver qualche doblone,
The noble fruit of my reputation.	Gran frutto della mia reputazione.
So it is: without Figaro	Ecco quà: senza Figaro
There's not a girl in Seville will marry;	Non si accasa in Siviglia una ragazza;
To me the little widows	A me la vedovella
Have recourse for a husband: I, under excuse	Ricorre per marito: io, colla scusa
Of my comb by day,	Del pettine di giorno,
And under favor of my guitar by night,	Della chitarra col favor la notte,
Endeavor—though I don't do it for the sake of saying so—	A tutti onestamente—

	To please all in an honest way.
	Oh, what a life, what a life! Oh,
	what business!
	Now, away to the shop—
Count.	(It is he, or I am much deceived.)
Figaro.	(Who may this be?)
Count.	It is no less than himself.
	Figaro!
Figaro.	Good master!
	Oh, whom do I see?—your
	Excellency—
Count.	Hush! hush! be prudent;
	I am not known here,
	Nor do I wish to be—for this
	I have the best of reasons.
Figaro.	I understand, I understand—
	I'll not interrupt you.
Count.	Stop!
Figaro.	For what purpose?
Count.	No, I tell you—stop here:
	I will explain myself. On the Prado
	I beheld a flower of beauty—a
	maiden,
	The daughter of a certain silly old
	physician, who
	Within these few days has estab-
	lished himself here.
	Enamored of this damsel, I have
	left
	My country and relatives; and here
	I am come,
	Under the name of Lindor;
	And, night and day,
	I watch and wander near this
	balcony.
Figaro.	Near this balcony?—a physician?
	Zounds!
	You are very fortunate:
	And must make hay while the
	sun shines.
Count.	Explain!
Figaro.	Certainly.—In this house
	I am a barber, perruquier,
	surgeon,
	Botanist, apothecary, veterinary—
	The major-domo of the house.
Count.	Oh, how fortunate!
Figaro.	But this is not all: the girl is not
	The daughter of the physician—
	she is only his ward.
Count.	Oh, what a consolation!

	Non fo per dir—m'adatto a far
	piacere,
	Oh, che vita, che vita! oh, che
	mestiere!
	Orsù, presto a bottega—
Conte.	(È desso, o pur m'inganno.)
Figaro.	(Chi sarà mai costui?)
Conte.	Oh, è lui senz' altro.
	Figaro!
Figaro.	Mio padrone!
	Oh, chi veggo?—Eccellenza—
Conte.	Zitto! zittoù prudenza:
	Quì non son conosciuto,
	Nè vò farmi conoscere—per questo
	Ho le mie gran ragioni.
Figaro.	Intendo, intendo—
	La lascio in libertà.
Conte.	No!
Figaro.	Che serve?
Conte.	No, dico—resta quà:
	Ora mi spiego. Al Prado
	Vidi un fior di bellezza—una
	fanciulla,
	Figlia di un certo medico barbogio,
	Che quà da pochi dì s'è stabilito.
	Io di questa invaghito
	Lasciai patria e parenti; e quà
	men venni,
	Col nome di Lindoro;
	E quà, la notte e il giorno,
	Passo girando a quei balconi
	intorno.
Figaro.	A quei balconi?—un medico? Oh,
	cospetto!
	Siete ben fortunato:
	Sui maccheroni il cacio v'è
	cascato.
Conte.	Come!
Figaro.	Certo.—Là dentro
	Io son barbiere, parucchier,
	chirurgo,
	Botanico, spezial, veterinario—
	Il faccendier di casa.
Conte.	Ah, bella sorte!
Figaro.	Non basta: la ragazza
	Figlia non è del medico—e soltanto
	La sua pupilla.
Conte.	Ah, che consolazione!

Figaro.	How so? but hush!		*Figaro.*	Perciò? zitto!
Count.	What is it?		*Conte.*	Cos'è?
Figaro.	See, the balcony opens.		*Figaro.*	S'apre il balcone!

Figaro. See, the balcony opens.
They retire under the Portico.)

Figaro. S'apre il balcone!
(Si ritirano sotto il Portico.)

SCENE III.—Rosina; afterwards Bartolo, on the Balcony; and the preceding, in the Street.

SCENA III.—Rosina; e poi Bartolo, sul Balcone; e detti in Strada.

Rosina. Is he not come yet? Perhaps—

Count. Oh, my life! my angel! my treasure!
At length do I behold you—at length—

Rosina. (Oh, how provoking! I wished to give him this note.)

Bartolo. Well, daughter,
It is fine weather. Pray, what letter is that?

Rosina. Nothing, sir: only the words
Of an air in the "Useless Precaution."

Count. Well and good!—of the "Useless Precaution!"

Rosina. Unfortunate that I am! I have let drop the air.
Make haste and pick it up.

Bartolo. I go, I go.
(He goes down.)

Rosina. Hist! hist!—

Count. I understand—

Rosina. Make haste!

Count. Never fear.

Bartolo. Here I am. What is it?
(Coming into the Street.)

Rosina. Oh, the wind
Has carried it away—
Look again.

Bartolo. I can't see it:—where, young lady?
I'll search no more. (Zounds!
She may have tricked me!) In! into the house!
Come, come! Do you mind what I say?
Quick, into the house!

Rosina. Well, I am going;—what a fury!

Bartolo. I will surely have that balcony walled up.
In, I say!

Rosina. Oh, what a scolding life I lead!
(Entering.)

Rosina. Non è venuto ancora?—forse—

Conte. Oh, mia vita! mio nume! mio tesoro!
Vi veggo al fine—al fine—

Rosina. (Ah, che vergogna!
Vorrei dargli il biglietto.)

Bartolo. · Ebben, ragazza,
Il tempo è buono. Cos'è questa carta?

Rosina. Nulla, signore: sono le parole
Dell'aria dell' "Inutil Precauzione."

Conte. Ma brava!—dell' "Inutil Precauzione!"

Rosina. Ah me meschina! l'aria mi è caduta:
Raccoglietela presto.

Bartolo. Vado, vado.
(Scende.)

Rosina. Pst! pst!—

Conte. Ho inteso—

Rosina. Presto!

Conte. Non temete.

Bartolo. Son quà. Dov'è?
(Uscendo in Strada.)

Rosina. Ah, il vento
Se l'ha portato via—
Guardate.

Bartolo. Io non la veggo;—ehi, signorina?
Io non vorrei. (Cospetto!
Costei m'avesse preso!) In casa! in casa!
Animo, sù! A chi dico?
In casa, presto!

Rosina. Vado, vado;—che furia!

Bartolo. Quel balcone lo voglio far murare.
Dentro, dico!

Rosina. A che vita da crepare!
(Entrando.)

Count.	Poor unhappy maid! Her wretched situation Still more interests me in her behalf.
Figaro.	Come, come— Let us see what she has written.
Count.	Well, read.
Figaro.	"Your assiduous attentions have excited my curiosity. My guardian is shortly going out: as soon as you perceive him quit the house, devise some ingenious method of acquainting me with your name, circumstances, and intentions. I can never appear at the balcony without being haunted by the inseparable attendance of my tyrant. Be, therefore, assured, that entirely disposed to break her chains, is the unhappy—Rosina."
Count.	Yes, yes, she shall break them;— but tell me, What kind of fellow is this guardian of her's?
Figaro.	Oh, a very demon! All avarice and suspicion, a terrible blusterer, But have a care, have a care!
Count.	Oh what?
Figaro.	The door opens.
Bartolo.	So; I shall return in a few minutes. (Coming out of the door, and speaking towards the side.) Don't let any one in. If Don Basilio Should come to inquire for me, let him wait. (He shuts the door cautiously.) I wish to hurry on my marriage with her. Yes, this very day I am going to conclude the affair. (Exit.)
Count.	This very day conclude his marriage with Rosina? Oh, the foolish old dotard! But tell me, who is this Don Basilio?
Figaro.	A famous intriguing match-maker— A hypocrite, a desperate fellow, With never a farthing in his pocket. He has lately turned music-master. And teaches this girl.

Conte.	Povera disgraziata! Il suo stato infelice Sempre più m'interessa.
Figaro.	Presto, presto— Vediamo cosa scrive.
Conte.	Appunto, leggi.
Figaro.	"Le vostre assidue premure hanno eccitato la mia curiosità. Il mio tutore è per uscir di casa: appena si sarà allontanato, procurate con qualche mezzo ingegnoso di indicarmi il vostro nome, il vostro stato, e le vostre intenzioni. Io non posso giammai comparire al balcone senza l'indivisible compagnia del mio tiranno. Siate però certo che tutto à disposto a fare per rompere le sue catene, la sventurata Rosina."
Conte.	Sì, sì le romperò;—su, dimmi un poco Che razza d'uomo è questo suo tutore?
Figaro.	Un vecchio indemoniato! Avaro, sospettoso, brontolone; Ajuto, ajuto!
Conte.	Che?
Figaro.	S'apre la porta.
Bartolo.	Ehi; fra momenti io torno. (Uscendo dalla porta, e parlando verso le quinte.) Non aprite a nessun. Se Don Basilio Venisse a ricercarmi, che m'aspetti. (Chiude la porta di casa.) Le mie nozze con lei voglio affrettare. Sì, dentr'oggi finir vò quest'affare. (Parte.)
Conte.	Dentr'oggi le sue nozze con Rosina. Ah vecchio rimbambito! Ma dimmi or tu, chi è questo Don Basilio?
Figaro.	È un solenne imbroglion di matrimonj— Un collo torto, un vero disperato. Sempre senza un quattrino. Già è maestro di musica, Insegna alla ragazza.

Count.	Well and good! It is right to know all these things; And you shall be well rewarded for your trouble.	*Conte.*	Bene, bene! Tutto giova saper; di tue fatiche Largo compenso avrai.
Figaro.	Indeed!	*Figaro.*	Davver!
Count.	On my word.	*Conte.*	Parola.
Figaro.	Then, shall I touch the gold hand- somely?	*Figaro.*	Dunque oro a discrezione?
Count.	To your heart's content. Come, be active.	*Conte.*	Oro a bizzeffe. Animo, via.

Figaro.	I'm all readiness. You cannot
	    imagine
	What a prodigious effect the idea
	    of a
	Reward has produced on me; and
	    what sympathy
	I feel in the success of Signor
	    Lindor.
		Figaro.	Son pronto. Ah, non sapete
			I simpatici effetti prodigiosi;
			Che ad appagare il mio Signore
			    Lindoro
			Produce in me la dolce idea dell'
			    oro.

ALL' IDEA—*MIGHTY JOVE* (Duet)

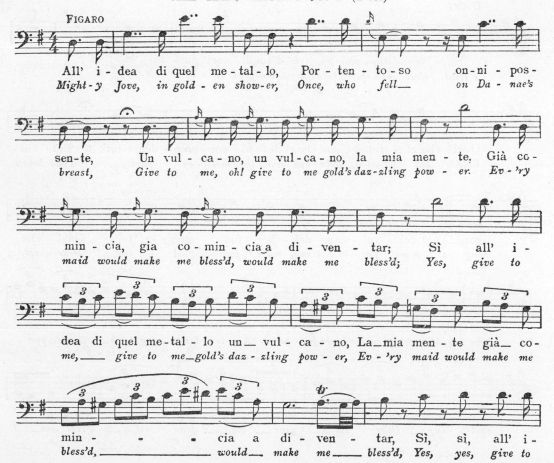

dea_ di quel_ me-tal - lo un_ vul - ca - no, La_mia men - te già co -
me,____ give_ to me_gold's daz - zling pow - er, Ev - 'ry maid would make me

min - - - cia a di - ven - tar, a di - ven - tar, a di - ven -
bless'd,_____ would make me _bless'd, would make me bless'd, would make me

tar, Un vul - ca - no in - com - in - cia a di - ven - tar.
bless'd,. Ev - 'ry_ maid_ would_ make_ me_____ bless'd.

COUNT

Su ve - dia - mo, su ve - diam di quel me - tal - lo,
Hold thy pom-pous, hold thy pom-pous sil - ly rail - ing,

Qual che ef - fet - to, qual che ef-fet - to sor - pren - den - te: Del vul -
Gold but wins,_ gold but wins the mean - er part:__ True love's

can,___ del vul - can del - la tua men - te, Qual - che
song is more pre - vail - ing, more pre - vail - ing, Dear - est,

mos-tro, qual-che mos-tro, sin - go - lar, sì, Del vul - can_ del - la_ tua
give me, dear-est, give me heart for heart; Ah, true love's song_ is_ more pre -

men - te,___ Qual - che_ mo - - - stro,_ sin - go -
vail - ing,__ Dear - est,_ give_ me,_ dear - est,_ give me_

lar, sì, sì, Del vul - can - del - la__ tua__ men - te,__ Qual - che__
heart for heart, True love's song__ is__ more pre - vail - ing__ Dear - est,__

mo - - - stro__ sin - go - lar, sì, sin - go -
give__ me,__ dear - est,__ give me__ heart for heart, oh,

lar, sì, sin - go - lar; Qual - che__ mo - stro sin - go - lar.
give me heart for heart; Dear - est,__ give__ me__ heart_for__ heart.

Figaro.	You must disguise yourself— For example, as a soldier.	*Conte.*	Da soldato?
Count.	As a soldier?	*Figaro.*	Sì, signore.
Figaro.	Even so, sir.	*Conte.*	Da soldato!—e che si fà?
Count.	As a soldier!—and for what purpose?	*Figaro.*	Oggi arriva un reggimento.
Figaro.	To-day a regiment is expected here.	*Conte.*	Sì, m'e amico il Colonello.
Count.	Yes; the Colonel is a friend of mine.	*Figaro.*	Va benon!
Figaro.	Excellent!	*Conte.*	Ma, e poi?
Count.	Why so?	*Figaro.*	Cospetto!
Figaro.	Zounds! By means of a billet, yonder door Will soon open to you. What say you to this, my good sir? The invention is not amiss.		Dell' alloggio col biglietto, Quella porta si aprirà. Che ne dite, mio signore? L'invenzione è naturale.
Count.	What an original genius. Excellent! excellent in truth!	*Conte.*	Oh, che testa universale! Bravo! bravo in verità!
Figaro.	What a capacious head is mine! Excellent! excellent in truth! Softly, softly—another thought. See the power of your gold! Drunk!—yes, my good sir, You must pretend to be drunk.	*Figaro.*	Oh, che testa universale! Bella—bella in verità! Piano, piano—un altra idea. Veda l'oro cosa fà! Ubriaco!—sì ubriaco, Mio signor, si fingerà.
Count.	Drunk?	*Conte.*	Ubriaco?
Figaro.	Even so, sir?	*Figaro.*	Sì, signore.
Count.	Drunk!—but for what purpose?	*Conte.*	Ubriaco!—ma perchè?
Figaro.	Because the guardian, believe me— The guardian would less distrust (Imitating the movements of a drunken man.) A man not quite himself But overcome with wine.	*Figaro.*	Perchè d'un che poco è in se— Che dal vino casca già (Imitando i moti di Ubriaco.) Il tutor credete a me, Il tutor si fiderà.

Both.	This is excellent, by my faith. Bravo! bravo! excellent truly!		*Assieme.*	Questa è bella per mia fè. Bravo! bravo! in verità!
Count.	Well, then?		*Conte.*	Dunque?
Figaro.	To business.		*Figaro.*	All' opra.
Count.	Let us to it.		*Conte.*	Andiam.
Figaro.	With spirit.		*Figaro.*	Da bravo.
Count.	I go.—Oh, I had forgotten the important part of the business: Tell me, where is your shop? That I may not miss finding you.		*Conte.*	Vado.—Oh, il meglio mi scordavo: Dimmi un po, la tua bottega? Per trovarti dove stà.
Figaro.	My shop?—you cannot mistake it. Look yonder, there it is: *(Pointing to the side.)* Number fifteen, on the left hand, With four steps, a white front— there, Five wigs in the window; On a placard, "Pomade Divine;" A show-glass, too, of the latest fashion, And my sign is a lantern. There, without fail, you will find me.		*Figaro.*	La bottega?—non si sbaglia. Guardi bene, eccola là. *(Additando fra le quinte.)* Numero quindici, a mano manca, bianca— Quattro gradini, facciata bianca Cinque parrucche nella vetrina; Sopra un cartello, "Pommata Fina;" Mostra in azzurro alla moderna; V'è per insegna una lanterna. Là senza fallo mi troverà.
Count.	Do you be upon the alert.		*Conte.*	Ho ben capito.
Figaro.	Leave the rest to me.		*Figaro.*	Or, vado presto.
Count.	I perfectly understand.		*Conte.*	Tu guarda bene.
Figaro.	Haste, no delay!		*Figaro.*	Io penso al resto.
Count.	I repose in you.		*Conte.*	Di te mi fido.
Figaro.	I shall wait for you yonder.		*Figaro.*	Cola l'attendo.
Count.	My dear Figaro!		*Conte.*	Mio caro Figaro!
Figaro.	I understand, I understand.		*Figaro.*	Intendo, intendo.
Count.	I will bring with me—		*Conte.*	Porterò meco—
Figaro.	A purse well filled?		*Figaro.*	La borsa piena?
Count.	Yes, to your heart's content.		*Conte.*	Sì quel che vuoi.
Figaro.	And as for the rest— Oh, doubt not of our complete success.		*Figaro.*	Ma il resto poi— Oh, non si dubiti che bene andrà.

(Figaro enters the House.—Exit the Count.)   *(Figaro entra in Casa.—Il Conte parte.)*

SCENE IV.—A Chamber in Don Bartolo's House.   SCENA IV.—Camera nella Casa di Don Bartolo.
(Rosina, with a letter in her hand.)   *(Rosina, con lettera in mano.)*

Rosina.	A little voice I heard just now: Oh, it has thrilled my very heart! I feel that I am wounded sore; And Lindor 'twas who hurled the dart. Yes, Lindor, dearest, shall be mine! I've sworn it, and we'll never part. My guardian sure will ne'er consent; But I must sharpen all my wit:		*Rosina.*	Una voce poco fà: Quì nel cor mi risuonò! Il mio cor ferito è già; E Lindor fu che il piagò. Sì, Lindoro mio sarà! Lo giurai, la vincerò. Il tutor ricuserà; Io l'ingegno aguzzerò:

AH, CHE D'AMORE—*WHEN SONG IS FLOWING* (Duet)

Content at last, he will relent,
  And we, oh, joy! be wedded yet,
Yes, Lindor I have sworn to love!
  And, loving, we'll our cares
  forget.
Yes, yes, he shall triumph. Could
  I but
Send him this letter!—but how?
There is no one here I can trust:
My guardian has a hundred eyes.
  —Well, well,
At least I will seal it.
From my window I beheld him
  conversing
For more than an hour with Figaro
  the barber;—

Alla fin s'acchetterà,
  E contenta io resterò,
Sì, Lindoro mio sarà!
  Lo giurai—la vincerò.
Sì, sì, la vincerò. Potessi almeno
Mandargli questa lettera!—ma
  come?
Di nessun quì mi fido:
Il tutor ha cent'occhi.—Basta,
  basta,
Sigilliamo intanto.
Con Figaro il barbiere dalla
  finestra
Discorrer l'ho veduto più d'un
  ora;—

IO SONO DOCILE—*WITH MILD AND DOCILE AIR*

ce - de - re, fa - rò gio - car,___ fa - rò___ gio - car, E cen-to
way - ward tricks, and sub-tle wiles,_____ I'd___ play, Ere they my

trap-po-le, Pri-ma di - ce - de - re, fa-rò gio - car,___ fa - rò___ gio -
will should guide, Ere they my will should guide, Ere they my will_____ should__

car; E - cen-to trap-po-le, Pri-ma di - ce - de - re, E cen-to
guide; A__ thou-sand, thou-sand tricks, And sub - tle__ wiles I'd play, Ere they my

trap-po- - le fa - rò, fa - rò gio - car.
will, my_____ will should_____ guide, my_____ will should_____ guide.

Figaro is an honest fellow,	Figaro è un galantuomo,
A good-hearted lad:	Un giovin di buon cuore:
Who knows but he may favor our love?	Chi sà ch'ei non protegga il nostro amore?

SCENE V.—Rosina and Figaro.	SCENA V.—Rosina e Figaro.
Figaro. Oh, good day! Signorina.	*Figaro.* Oh, buon dì! Signorina.
Rosina. Good day! Signor Figaro.	*Rosina.* Buon giorno! Signor Figaro.
Figaro. Well, what are you doing?	*Figaro.* Ebbene, che si fa?
Rosina. I am dying with ennui.	*Rosina.* Si muor di noja.
Figaro. Oh, the deuce! impossible! For one so handsome, so full of spirit.	*Figaro.* Oh, diavolo! possibile! Una ragazza bella e spiritosa.
Rosina. You make me smile, Figaro: Of what use is my spirit, What avails my beauty, If forever shut up between four walls, Which appear as dreary as a sepulchre?	*Rosina.* Ah, ah, mi fate ridere Che mi serve lo spirito,— Che giova la bellezza, Se chiusa io sempre sto fra quattro mura, Che mi par d'esser proprio in sepoltura?
Figaro. A sepulchre! good Heavens! (Taking her aside.) I wish to know—	*Figaro.* In sepoltura! oibò! (Chiamandola a parte.) Sentite, io voglio—
Rosina. See! see! my guardian!	*Rosina.* Ecco il tutor!
Figaro. Indeed!	*Figaro.* Davvero!
Rosina. Certainly, certainly! it is his voice!	*Rosina.* Certo, certo! la sua voce!

Figaro. Adieu! adieu! in a few moments
(Exit.)
I will see you again—I have some-
thing to tell you.

Rosina. And so have I, Signor Figaro.

Figaro. Adieu, fair lady!

Rosina. A civil fellow this.
(Exit.)

SCENE VI.—Bartolo and Don Basilio.

Bartolo. Don Basilio,
You come just in time. I wish
Within to-morrow, either by force
or love,
To espouse my Rosina.—Do you
understand?

Basilio. Ah! you speak wisely;
And I was just coming myself to
advise with you.
(Taking him aside.)
But be secret!—The Count
Almaviva
Is arrived.

Bartolo. What! the unknown lover
Of Rosina?

Basilio. The very same.

Bartolo. Oh, the devil
Something must be done here.

Basilio. Certainly; but, between ourselves—

Bartolo. That is to say—

Basilio. We must boldly
Begin by inventing
Some plausible story, that may
Disgrace him in the eyes of the
public.

Bartolo. And would you? But a calumny—

Basilio. Oh, then,
You don't know what a calumny
is?

Bartolo. No, indeed.

Basilio. No?—Then hear, and be silent.
Oh! calumny is like the sigh
Of gentlest zephyrs breathing by;
How softly sweet, along the
ground,
Its first shirll voice is heard
around:
So soft, that, sighing 'mid the
bowers,
It scarcely fans the drooping
flowers.
Thus will the voice of calumny,

Figaro. Salva! salva! fra poco
(Parte.)
Ci rivedremo—ho a dirvi qualche
cosa.

Rosina. E ancor io, Signor Figaro.

Figaro. Bravissima, vado!

Rosina. Quanto è garbato.
(Parte.)

SCENA VI.—Bartolo e Don Basilio.

Bartolo. Don Basilio,
Venite a tempo. Oh io voglio
Per forza, oh per amor, dentro
domani
Sposar la mia Rosina.—Avete
inteso?

Basilio. Eh, voi dite benissimo;
E appunto io quì veniva ad
avvisarvi.
(Chiamandola a parte.)
Ma segretezza!—è giunto
Il Conte d'Almaviva.

Bartolo. Chi! l'incognito amante
Della Rosina?

Basilio. Appunto quello.

Bartolo. Oh, diavolo!
Ah quì ci vuol riparo.

Basilio. Certo; ma, alla sordina—

Bartolo. Sarebbe a dir—

Basilio. Così con buona grazia
Bisogna principiare
A inventar qualche favola
Che al pubblico lo metta in mala
vista.

Bartolo. E vorreste?—Ma una calunnia—

Basilio. Ah, dunque,
La calunnia cos'è voi non sapete?

Bartolo. No, davvero.

Basilio. No?—Uditemi, e tacete.
La calunnia è un venticello
Un'auretta assai gentile;
Che insensibile, sottile,

Leggermente, dolcemente

Incomincia a susurrar

Piano piano, terra terra,

Sotto voce sibillando,

More subtle than the plaintive sigh,
In many a serpent-wreathing, find
Its secret passage to the mind,—
The heart's most inmost feelings
    gain,
Bedim the sense, and fire the brain.

Then passing on from tongue to
    tongue,
It gains new strength, it sweeps
    along
In giddier whirl from place to
    place,
And gains fresh vigor in its race;
Till, like the sounds of tempests
    deep,
That through the woods in mur-
    murs sweep
And howl amid their caverns
    drear,
It shakes the trembling soul with
    fear.
At length the fury of the storm
Assumes its wildest, fiercest form,—
In one loud crash of thunder roars,
And, like an earthquake, rocks the
    shores.

While all the frowning vault of
    heaven,
With many a fiery bolt is riven.
Thus calumny, a simple breath,
Engenders rain, wreck, and death;
And sinks the wretched man
    forlorn,
Beneath the lash of slander torn,
The victim of the public scorn.

(Exeunt.)

SCENE VII.—Figaro, coming forth with precaution; then
    Rosina.

Figaro. Bravo! all goes on well!
I have overheard everything.
So, so, good Mr. Doctor!
Your spouse!—a good joke. The
    grapes are sour.
While they remain shut up yonder,
I will endeavor to speak to the girl;
But here she is, *à propos.*

Rosina. Well, Signor Figaro?

Figaro. I have great things to tell you,
Signorina.

Rosina. Indeed!

Figaro. We shall eat weding-cake shortly.

Rosina. What do you mean?

Và scorrendo, và ronzando
Nelle orecchie della gente,—
S'introduce destramente,
E le teste ed i cervelli,
Fà stordire, e fa gonfiar.

Dalla bocca fuori uscendo,

Lo schiamazzo và crescendo;

Prende forza a poco a poco,

Scorre già di loco in loco,
Sembra il tuono, la tempesta,

Che nel sen della foresta,

Va fischiando, brontolando,

E ti fa d'orror gelar.

Alla fin trabocca, e scoppia,
Si propaga, e si raddoppia,
E produce un esplosione
Come un colpo di cannone.

Un tremoto, un temporale,

Un tremoto generale,
Che fa l'aria rimbombar.
E il meschino, calunniato,
Avvilito, calpestato,

Sotto il pubblico flagello,
Per gran sorte và a crepar.

(Partono.)

SCENA VII.—Figaro. uscendo con precauzione;
    indi Rosina.

Figaro. Ma bravi! ma benone!
Ho inteso tutto. Evviva il buon
    dottore!
Povero babbuino!
Tua sposa!—eh via. Pulisciti il
    bocchino
Or che stanno là chiusi,
Procuriam di parlare alla ragazza;
Eccola appunto.

Rosina. Ebbene, Signor Figaro?

Figaro. Gran cose Sigorina

Rosina. Sì, davver!

Figaro. Mangerem dei confetti.

Rosina. Come sarebbe a dir?

Figaro.	I mean That this fine guardian of yours has settled That to-morrow he is to be your husband.		*Figaro.*	Sarebbe a dire Che il vostro bel tutore ha stabilito Esser dentro doman vostro marito.
Rosina.	Oh, pooh!		*Rosina.*	Eh, via!
Figaro.	Yes, I swear it: Even now he is closeted With your music-master, Drawing up the contract.		*Figaro.*	Oh, ve lo giuro; A stendere il contratto Col maestro di musica, Là dentro si è serrato.
Rosina.	Indeed! In truth he is much mistaken! Poor fellow! he shall find with whom he has to do. But tell me, Mr. Figaro, Just now, below my window, You were speaking to a gentleman—		*Rosina.*	Sì! L'ha sbagliata affè! Povero sciocco! l'avrà da far con me. Ma dite, Signor Figaro, Voi poco fa sotto le mie finestre, Parlavate a un signore—
Figaro.	Oh, a cousin of mine— An excellent young man, with a good head, And the best of hearts; he is come here To finish his studies, and to try, poor fellow, To make his fortune.		*Figaro.*	Ah! un mio cugino— E' un bravo giovinotto; buona testa, Ottimo cuor! quì venne I suoi studj a compire, e il poverino, Cerca di far fortuna.
Rosina.	His fortune?—Oh, he will make it.		*Rosina.*	Fortuna?—eh, la farà.
Figaro.	Aha, I doubt it much; in confidence, I tell you he has one great failing.		*Figaro.*	Oh, ne dubito assai; in confidenza, Ha un gran difetto addosso.
Rosina.	A great failing, said you?		*Rosina.*	Un gran difetto?
Figaro.	Yes, a great one; He is dying in love.		*Figaro.*	Ah, grande; E'innamorato morto.
Rosina.	Ah, indeed? Do you know that this young man Interests me extremely.		*Rosina.*	Sì, davvero? Quel giovine, vedete M'interessa moltissimo.
Figaro.	Good Lord!		*Figaro.*	Per Bacco!
Rosina.	Don't you believe it?		*Rosina.*	Non ci credete?
Figaro.	Oh, certainly.		*Figaro.*	Oh sì.
Rosina.	But tell me, does this fair one Live far from this place?		*Rosina.*	Ma la sua bella Dite, abita lontano?
Figaro.	Oh no!—that is— But two paces from hence—		*Figaro.*	Oh nò!—cioè— Quì a due passi—
Rosina.	Is she handsome?		*Rosina.*	Ma è bella?
Figaro.	Oh, very much so—behold her portrait, Which I give you in two words: A handsome, graceful figure, Jetty locks, a rosy cheek, An eye that speaks, a hand whose touch thrills one.		*Figaro.*	Oh, bella assai—eccovi il suo ritratto, Che vi fo in due parole: Svelta, gentil, vezzosa, Capelli neri, guancia porporina, Occhio che parla, mano che innamora.

Rosina. And her name?	*Rosina.* E il nome?
Figaro. Ah, her name too?	*Figaro.* Ah, il nome ancora?
Her name?—Ah, what a sweet name!—	Il nome?—Ah, che bel nome!—
She's called—	Si chiama—
Rosina. Well, what is she called?	*Rosina.* Ebben? si chiama?
Figaro. Sweet creature!	*Figaro.* Poverina!
She's called Ro-ro-ro-si-na—Rosina.	Si chiama Ro-ro-ro-si-na—Rosina.

DUNQUE IO SON—*WHAT AM I, OR DOST THOU MOCK ME?*

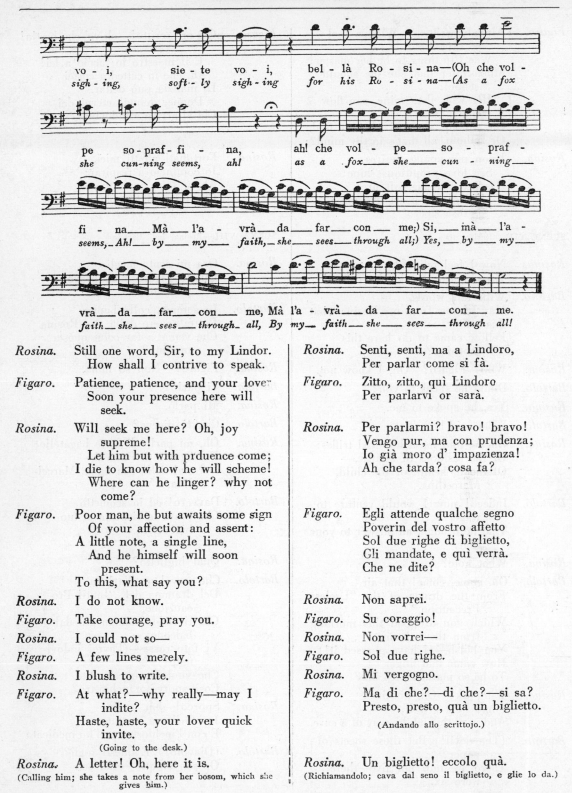

vo - i, sie - te vo - i, bel - là Ro - si - na—(Oh che vol -
sigh - ing, soft - ly sigh - ing for his Ro - si - na—(As a fox

pe so-praf-fi - na, ah! che vol - pe___ so - praf -
she cun-ning seems, ah! as a fox___ she___ cun - ning___

fi - na___Mà___l'a - vrà___da___far___con___me;) Si, ___mà___l'a -
seems,___Ah!___by___my___faith,—she___sees___through all;) Yes, ___by___my

vrà___da___far___con___me, Mà l'a - vrà___da___far___con___me.
faith___she___sees___through_ all, By my___faith___she___sees___through all!

Rosina. Still one word, Sir, to my Lindor.	*Rosina.* Senti, senti, ma a Lindoro,
How shall I contrive to speak.	Per parlar come si fà.
Figaro. Patience, patience, and your lover	*Figaro.* Zitto, zitto, quì Lindoro
Soon your presence here will seek.	Per parlarvi or sarà.
Rosina. Will seek me here? Oh, joy supreme!	*Rosina.* Per parlarmi? bravo! bravo!
Let him but with prduence come;	Vengo pur, ma con prudenza;
I die to know how he will scheme!	Io già moro d' impazienza!
Where can he linger? why not come?	Ah che tarda? cosa fa?
Figaro. Poor man, he but awaits some sign	*Figaro.* Egli attende qualche segno
Of your affection and assent:	Poverin del vostro affetto
A little note, a single line,	Sol due righe di biglietto,
And he himself will soon present.	Gli mandate, e quì verrà.
To this, what say you?	Che ne dite?
Rosina. I do not know.	*Rosina.* Non saprei.
Figaro. Take courage, pray you.	*Figaro.* Su coraggio!
Rosina. I could not so—	*Rosina.* Non vorrei—
Figaro. A few lines merely.	*Figaro.* Sol due righe.
Rosina. I blush to write.	*Rosina.* Mi vergogno.
Figaro. At what?—why really—may I indite?	*Figaro.* Ma di che?—di che?—si sa?
Haste, haste, your lover quick invite.	Presto, presto, quà un biglietto.
(Going to the desk.)	(Andando allo scrittojo.)
Rosina. A letter! Oh, here it is.	*Rosina.* Un biglietto! eccolo quà.
(Calling him; she takes a note from her bosom, which she gives him.)	(Richiamandolo; cava dal seno il biglietto, e glie lo da.)

Figaro.	Already written!—What a fool
	(Astonished.)
	Was I to thing to be her master!
	Much fitter that she me should school:
	Her wits, than mine, can flow much faster.
	Oh, woman, woman! who can find,
	Or fathom, all that's in thy mind?
Rosina.	Upon my young desires,
	See love propitious shine;
	'Tis he, with his soft fires,
	Must ease a heart like mine.
	(Exit Figaro.)

SCENE VIII.—Rosina, then Bartolo.

Rosina.	Now I feel relieved.
	This Figaro is a kind creature!
Bartolo.	With fair words,
	May I know from my Rosina what this
	Fellow came to do here this morning?
Rosina.	Who? Figaro?—Oh, I know not.
Bartolo.	Didn't he speak to you?
Rosina.	Yes, he spoke to me.
Bartolo.	What said he?
Rosina.	Oh, he told me a hundred trifles:
	Of the fashions of France,—
	Of the ill health of the child, Marcellina.
Bartolo.	Indeed! now I would venture to wager
	That he brought an answer to your note.
Rosina.	What note?
Bartolo.	Oh, come, come! that air
	From the drama of the "Useless Precaution,"
	Which you dropped this morning from the balcony.
	You blush—(I have guessed it!)
	How came that finger
	To be so marked with ink?
Rosina.	With ink!—Oh, nothing:
	I had hurt myself,
	And used this ink by way of a cure.
Bartolo.	(The devil!) But these sheets of paper?
	There are now but five—there were six.

Figaro.	Già era scritto!—oh ve' che bestia!
	(Attonito.)
	E il maestro io faccio a lei!
	Ah, che in cattedra costei
	Di malizia può dettar.
	Donne, donne! eterni dei,
	Chi vi arriva a indovinar?
Rosina.	Fortunati affetti miei,
	Io comincio a respirar;
	Ah tu solo, amor tu sei,
	Che mi devi consolar.
	(Figaro parte.)

SCENA VIII.—Rosina, indi Bartolo.

Rosina.	Ora mi sento meglio.
	Questo Figaro è un bravo giovinotto!
Bartolo.	In somma, colle buone,
	Potrei sapere dalla mia Rosina
	Che venne a far colui questa mattina?
Rosina.	Figaro?—Non so nulla.
Bartolo.	Ti parlò?
Rosina.	Mi parlò.
Bartolo.	Che ti diceva?
Rosina.	Oh, mi parlò di certe bagatelle:
	Del figurin di Francia,—
	Del mal della sua figlia, Marcellina.
Bartolo.	Davvero! ed io scometto
	Che portò la risposta al tuo biglietto.
Rosina.	Qual biglietto?
Bartolo.	Che serve! quell'arietta.
	Del dramma del' "Inutil Precauzione,"
	Che ti cadde staman giù dal balcone.
	Vi fate rossa—(l'avrei indovinato!)
	Che vuol dir questo dito
	Così sporco d'inchiostro?
Rosina.	Sporco!—Oh, nulla:
	Io me l'avea scottato,
	E con l'inchiostro or l'ho medicato.
Bartolo.	(Diavolo!) E questi fogli?
	Or son cinque—eran sei.

Rosina.	Those sheets? Oh, true:
	I made use of one of them
	To send some sweetmeats to
	    Marcellina.
		Rosina.	Quei fogli? E vero:
			D' uno mi son servito
			A mandar de' confetti a Marcel-
			    lina.

Bartolo.	Most excellent! And the pen— For what purpose has that been cut?	*Bartolo.*	Bravissima! E la penna— Perchè fu temperata?
Rosina.	(Confound him!) That pen? To design a flower on my tambour.	*Rosina.*	(Maledetto!) La penna? Per disegnare un fiore sul tamburo.
Bartolo.	A flower?	*Bartolo.*	Un fiore?
Rosina.	A flower.	*Rosina.*	Un fiore.
Bartolo.	A flower! Ah, you cunning minx!	*Bartolo.*	Un fiore! Ah, fraschetta!
Rosina.	It's true.	*Rosina.*	Davver.
Bartolo.	Silence!	*Bartolo.*	Zitto!
Rosina.	Believe me.	*Rosina.*	Credete.
Bartolo.	Enough of this.	*Bartolo.*	Basta così
Rosina.	Sir—	*Rosina.*	Signor—
Bartolo.	No more—be silent. To a doctor of my rank, These excuses, Signorina, I advise another time That you better should invent. The sweetmeats for the girl! The embroidery on the tambour! Out of my sight! begone! And is it thus my more than daughter Dares to trifle with me? Why is the paper missing? That I would wish to know. Useless, ma'am, are all your airs— Be still, nor interrupt me so. Another time, sweet Signorina, When the doctor quits his house, He will carefully provide For the keeping you inside. Useless now are your grimaces, No one heeds your affectation! A vow I make that no one now Shall come within my habitation. And poor innocent Rosina, Disappointed, then may pout: In her room shall she be locked, Till I choose to let her out. (Exeunt.)	*Bartolo.*	Non più—tacete. A un dottor della mia sorte, Queste scuse, Signorina, Vi consiglio mia carina Un pò meglio a imposturar. I confetti alla ragazza! Il ricamo sul tamburo! Vi scostate, e via! Ci vuol altra figlia mia Per potermi corbellar? Perchè manca là quel foglio? Vo' saper cotesto imbroglio. Sono inutili le smorfie— Ferma là, non mi toccate. Signorina, un altra volta Quando Bartolo andrà fuori, La consegna ai servitori A suo modo dar saprà. Ah, non servono le smorfie, Faccia pur la gatta morta! Cospetton per quella porta Nemmen l'aria entrar potrà E Rosina, innocentina, Sconsolata, disperata: In sua camera serrata, Fin ch'io voglio star dovrà. (Partono.)

SCENE IX.—Bertha, alone.

SCENA IX.—Berta, sola.

Bertha.	Methought just now
	I heard a noise within this
	    chamber,
	It perhaps was the guardian with
	    his ward;
		Berta.	Finora in questa camera
			Mi parve di sentir un mormorìo;
			Sarà stato il tutor colla pupilla;

He has never an hour's peace.
These girls
Will not hear;—some one knocks.
(A knocking is heard.)

Count.   Open the door!
(Within.)

Bertha.   Poor girl! she will be driven to
some rash act,
If she be longer confined in this
sepulchral place.
(Bertha opens the door, and exits.)

SCENE X.—The Count, disguised as a Soldier, and pretending to be drunk; then Bartolo.

Count.   Hallo! house here!—Hey! good
people!
Hallo! house here!—Faith, you'll
sleep ill.

Bartolo. Who can this be?—Ugly fellow!
Drunken rascal, thus to bellow!

Count.   Hallo! house there!—All are still
here!

Bartolo. Signor Whiskers, what's your will
here?

Count.   Hey! oh, oh!—Pray, how d'ye do,
sir?
(Seeing him, he searches in his pocket.)

Bartolo. Stupid puppy!—Who are you sir?

Count.   Are not you, sir—but steady—
order!
Doctor Balordo?

Bartolo. What, Balordo?

Count.   Ah, ah! Bertoldo—
(Reading.)

Bartolo. Pooh! pooh! Bertoldo!
No such person.—Hear me,
fool, do!
Doctor Bartolo!

Count.   Ah, bravissimo!
Doctor Barbaro; well and good;
The difference, after all, is but
trifling.
(She appears not! what impatience
I feel!
How long she delays!—where can
she be?)

Bartolo. I am already out of all patience.
Prudence is necessary here.

Count.   You, then—are a doctor?

Bartolo. I am a doctor—yes, sir.

Non ha un'ora di ben. Queste
ragazze
No la voglion capir;—battono.
(Si ode picchiare.)

Conte.   Aprite!
(Di dentro.)

Berta.   Alla fine farà qualche stortura?
O anderà dalla noja in sepoltura.

(Apre e parte.)

SCENA X.—Il Conte travestito da Soldato contrafucando
i moti d'ubriaco; indi Bartolo.

Conte.   Ehi di casa!—buona gente!
Ehi di casa!—niun mi sente!

Bartolo. Chi è costui?—Che brutta faccia!
E ubriaco, chi sarà!

Conte.   Ehi di casa!—maledetti!

Bartolo. Cosa vuol, Signor Soldato?

Conte.   Ah! sì, sì!—Ben obbligato?
(Vedendolo, cerca in tasca.)

Bartolo. Quì costui!—che mai vorrà?

Conte.   Siete voi—aspetta un poco!
Siete voi—Dottor Balordo?

Bartolo. Che Balordo?

Conte.   Ah, ah! Bertoldo—
(Leggendo.)

Bartolo. Che Bertoldo.
Eh, andate al diavolo!
Dottor Bartolo!

Conte.   Ah, bravissimo!
Dottor Barbaro; benissimo;
Già c'è poca differenza.
(Non si vede! che impazienza!
Quanto tarda!—dove stà?)

Bartolo. Io già perdo la pazienza.
Quì prudenza ci vorrà.

Conte.   Dunque voi—siete Dottore?

Bartolo. Son Dottore—sì, Signore.

Count. / Conte.	Ah, how fortunate! let me embrace— Here, fellow collegian.	Ah, benissimo! un'abbraccio— Quà collega.
Bartolo.	Stand off.	Indietro.
Count. / Conte.	Here! (Embracing him by force.) I also am a doctor of full degree, And marshal of the regiment: Here on the billet for my lodgings. (Presenting a billet.) Look, here it is.	Quà! (Lo abbraccia per forza.) Sono anch' io Dottor perfetto, Marescalco al reggimento: Dell' alloggio sul biglietto. (Presentando il biglietto.) Osservate, eccolo quà.
Bartolo.	(With rage and vexation I'm ready to burst in good earnest; Ah, let me be cautious Not to commit some rash act!) (Reads the billet.)	(Dalla rabbia—dal dispetto Io già crepo in verità; Ah ch'io fo se mi ci metto Qualche gran bestialità!) (Legge il biglietto.)
Count. / Conte.	(Ah, would my heart's dear idol come— Sole object of my love, appear; Haste, oh, haste; thy fond adorer, Full of love, awaits thee here.)	(Ah, venisse il caro oggetto— Della mia felicità; Vieni, vieni; il tuo diletto, Pien d'amor, t'attende quà.)

SCENE XI.—Rosina, and the preceding. SCENA XI.—Rosina, e detti.

Rosina.	Methought I overheard e'en now, A most unusual clamor here. A soldier!—and my guardian!— What can they be doing here? (She advances softly.)	D'ascoltar quà m'è sembrato, Un'insolito rumore. Un soldato!—ed il tutore!— Cosa mai faranno quà? (Si avanza piano piano.)
Count. / Conte.	It is Rosina!—I now am content.	E' Rosina! Or son contento.
Rosina.	He looks at me, he approaches me!	Ei mi guarda, e s'avvicina!
Count. / Conte.	I am Lindor. (Softly, to Rosina.)	Son Lindoro. (Piano, a Rosina.)
Rosina.	Heavens! what do I hear? Prudence, for mercy's sake!	Oh, ciel che sento? Ah, giudizio, per pietà!
Bartolo.	The Signorina here? Quick, quick, your exit make. (Pushing Rosina.)	Signorina che cercate? Presto, presto, andate via. (Vedendo Rosina.)
Rosina.	I am going; don't hallo so.	Vado, vado, non gridate.
Bartolo.	Quick, quick, away, I tell you.	Presto, presto, via di quà.
Count. / Conte.	Well, sweetheart, and I'll follow you.	Ehi ragazza vengo anch'io.
Bartolo.	Follow! where, sir?	Dove, dove, Signor mio?
Count. / Conte.	To my quarters: oh, this is excellent!	In caserma: oh, questa è bella!
Bartolo.	To your quarters? a pretty joke!	In caserma? bagatella!
Count. / Conte.	Dearest!	Cara!
Rosina.	Help!	Ajuto!
Bartolo.	Hold! zounds!	Olà! cospetto!
Count. / Conte.	Quick, let drop your handkerchief; Quick, for goodness' sake! (To Rosina, showing her a note by stealth.)	Via, gettate il fazzoletto; Fate presto per pietà! (A Rosina mostrandola furtivamente un biglietto.)

Rosina. Ah, he's looking!	*Rosina.* Ah, ci guarda!
(To the Count.)	(Al Conte.)
How unlucky!	Maledetto!
Ah, discretion, for goodness' sake!	Ah, giudizio, per pietà.
(Eyeing Bartolo.)	(Guardando Bartolo.)
Bartolo. A curse on this drunken fellow!	*Bartolo.* Ubriaco maledetto!
I am ready to burst with vexation	Ah costui crepar mi fa.
Count. Then I go—	*Conte.* Dunque vado—
Bartolo. Oh no; stop, sir!	*Bartolo.* O no; Signore!
(Retaining him.)	(Trattenendolo.)
You can have no lodging here.	Quì d'alloggio star non può.
Count. How say you?	*Conte.* Come, come?
Bartolo. Oh, it is in vain to remonstrate;	*Bartolo.* Eh, non v'è replica;
I am exempt from lodging troops.	Ho il brevetto d'esenzione.
Count. How are you exempt?	*Conte.* Che brevetto?
(In a rage.)	(Adirato.)
Bartolo. Oh, my good sir,	*Bartolo.* Oh mio padrone,
A moment, and I will show you.	Un momento, e il mostrerò.
(Goes to his desk.)	(Và allo scrittojo.)
Count. Ah, if I cannot here remain,	*Conte.* Ah, se qui restar non posso,
Quick, take it—	Deh, prendete—
(Making signs to her to take the note.)	(Accennandolo di prendere un biglietto.)
Rosina. He looks at me again.	*Rosina.* Ahimè! ci guarda.
Rosina and Count. Oh, this heart is filled	*Rosina e Conte.* Cento smanie io sento
with pain!	addosso!
Myself no more can I contain.	Ah, più reggere non so.
Bartolo. At present I have searched in vain,	*Bartolo.* Ah trovarlo ancor non posso,
But soon I hope to find it.	Mà sì, sì, lo troverò.
(Searching in the desk.)	(Cercando nello scrittojo.)
Oh, here it is.	Ecco quì.
(Reads.)	(Legge.)
"By these presents,	"Colla presente,
(He comes forward with a parchment.)	(Venendo avanti con una pergamena.)
The Doctor Bartolo, etc., etc.	Il Dottor Bartolo, *et cetera.*
We exempt"—	Essentiamo"—
Count. Oh, go to the devil!	*Conte.* Eh, andate al diavolo!
(With a dash of his hand he sends the parchment into the air.)	(Con un rovescio di mano manda in aria la pergamena.)
Bartolo. My dear sir, what would you?	*Bartolo.* Cosa fa, Signor mio caro?
Count. Silence, Mr. Doctor Lomaro!	*Conte.* Zitto là, Dottor Lomaro!
My lodging is fixed here,	Il mio alloggio è quì fissato,
And here will I remain.	E in alloggio quì vo star.
Bartolo. Will remain!	*Bartolo.* Vuol restar!
Count. Yes, will remain.	*Conte.* Restar, sicuro.
Bartolo. My good sir, I have something else to do:	*Bartolo.* Ah, son stufo, mio padrone:
I beg you will begone, or a cudgel	Presto fuori, o un buon bastone
Shall dislodge you.	Lo farà di quà sloggiar.
(Threatening him.)	
	(Minacciandolo.)
Count. Then you—you wish to fight with me?	*Conte.* Dunque lei—lei vuol battaglia?

Well, you shall have your way.
(Drawing back.)
A battle is a fine thing, truly!
(Laughing.)
A specimen I'll show you duly.
(Advances, pretending to fight.)
This is the trench, observe,
And you are the enemy.
(Makes a pass at him.)
Now, mark! (Drop your hand-
kerchief.)
(Aside, to Rosina.)
Our friends are stationed here—
Now mark!
(He seizes the moment when Bartolo is less attentive. and lets fall the note; Rosina drops her handkerchief upon it.)

Bartolo. Hold! hold!

Count. What is it?—ah!

Bartolo. Let me see it.

Count. Prescriptions only are for you;
But letters go where they are due.
I ask your pardon.
(He bows to Rosina, and gives her the note and the handkerchief.)

Rosina. Charming, charming, how
delightful!

Bartolo. Charming, truly!
Oh, 'tis frightful.

Count. Some little girlish love affair.
(Drawing him aside; meanwhile, Rosina changes the letter.)

Rosina. Could I but change the letter there!

Bartolo. I wish to see it.

Rosina. 'This naught to see.

Bartolo. Quick, give the paper—give it me.
(Enter Basilio on one side; Bertha on the other.)

Basilio. Look here!—what do I see?

Bertha. The barber! Eh, what stir is here!

Bartolo. Give here the paper, impertinence!
(To Rosina.)
Do you mind what I say—quick!

Rosina. The paper, sir, you wish to have,
Which slipped by chance from out
my hand,
Is but a list of linen.

Bartolo. Quick, give it here, hussy!
(He seizes it violently.)
What do I see?—I am mistaken!
This list I'd for a letter taken.
Oh, what a fool, indeed, am I!
Oh, what immense stupidity!

Ben, battaglia le vuò dar.
(Tirandosi indietro.)
Bella cosa una battaglia!
(Ridendo.)
Ve la voglio or quì mostrar.
(Avvicinandosi, amichevolmente a Bartolo.)
Osservate! questo è il fosso,
L'inimico voi sarete.
(Gli da una spinta.)
Attenzion! (Giù fazzoletto.)

(Piano, a Rosina.)
E gli amici stan di quà—
Attenzione!
(Cogli il momento in cui Bartolo l'osserva meno attenta-
mente, e lascia il biglietto, e Rosina vi fa cadere sopra il fazzoletto.)

Bartolo. Ferma! ferma!

Conte. Che cos' è?—ah!

Bartolo. Vo' vedere.

Conte. Sì, se fosse una ricetta;
Mi dovete perdonar.

(Fa una riverenza a Rosina, e le da il biglietto, e il fazzoletto.)

Rosina. Grazie, grazie!

Bartolo. Grazie, come!
Vo saper cotesto imbroglio!

Conte. Qualche intrigo di fanciulla.
(Tirandolo a parte; intanto, Rosina cambia la lettera.)

Rosina. Ah, cambiar potessi il foglio!

Bartolo. Vuò veder.

Rosina. Ma non è nulla.

Bartolo. Quì quel foglio, presto quà!
(Escono da una parte Basilio; e dall'altra, Berta.)

Basilio. Ecco quà!—oh, cosa vedo?

Berta. Il barbiere! Oh, quanta gente!

Bartolo. Quà quel foglio, impertinente!
(A Rosina.)
A chi dico?—presto quà!

Rosina. Ma quel foglio che chiedete,
Per azzardo m'è cascato,
E la lista del bucato.

Bartolo. Ah, fraschetta presto quà!
(Lo strappa con violenza a legge.)
Ah, che vedo?—ho preso sbaglio!
E la lista, son di stucco!
Ah, son proprio un mamalucco!
Ah, che gran bestialita!

Rosina and Count. Bravo! bravo! the old
       fool
     In his own snare at last is caught.

Basilio and Bertha. What it means I cannot
       tell:
     Confusion here some work has
     wrought.

Rosina. 'Tis ever thus you rate and school
       (Weeping.)
     me,
     And with rod of iron rule me;
     But I no more this life will lead—
     I'll from such tyranny be freed.

Bartolo. Ah, Rosina! poor young lady!

Count. Leave her, sir! What have you
     done?
  (Threatening him, and pushing him away by the arm.)

Bartolo. Holloa! help, there!

Rosina. Nay, be quiet.

Count. Unhand me, sir!

All. What's all this riot?

SCENE XII.—Enter Figaro, with a basin under his arm
  and the preceding.

Figaro. Holloa here!
     What has happened?--my good
       people,
     What clamor's this? Great gods!
     This tumult has together drawn
     Into the street one-half the city.
       (Softly to the Count.)
     (Prudence, sir, in pity!)

Bartolo. This is a rogue!
       (Pointing to the Count.)

Count. This is a knave!

Bartolo. Ah, the scoundrel!

Count. Ah, the rascal!
      (Threatening him with his sword.)

Figaro. Mr. Soldier, have a care,
   (Raising his basin and threatening the Count.)
     Or this basin soon shall teach you
     Of your manners to beware.

Count. You ugly savage—
      (To Bartolo.)

Bartolo. You low-born scoundrel—

All. Peace, Doctor—

Bartolo. I'll not hold my peace—

All. Hold, sir!
     (To the Count.)

Count. I am determined to kill him.

Rosina e Conte. Bravo! bravo! il mama-
       lucco
     Che nel sacco entrato e già.

Basilio e Berta. Non capisco, son di stucco:
     Qualche imbroglio qui ci stà.

Rosina. Ecco quà sempre un istoria,
       (Piangendo.)
     Sempre oppressa, e maltrattata:
     Ah, che vita disperata—
     Non la so più sopportar.

Bartolo. Ah, Rosina! poverina!

Conte. Via quà tu! Cosa l'hai fatto?
   (Minacciando, e afferrandolo per un braccio.)

Bartolo. Gente, ajuto! soccorretemi!

Rosina. Ma chetatevi.

Conte. Lasciatemi!

Tutti. Gente, ajuto per pietà!

SCENA XII.—Figaro, entrando con bacile sotto il braccio; e detti.

Figaro. Alto là! Alto là!
     Che cosa accadde?—Signori miei.
     Che chiasso è questo? Eterni Dei!
     Già sulla piazza a questo strepito
     S'e radunata mezza città.
       (Piano, al Conte.)
     (Signor, prudenza, per carità!)

Bartolo. Questo è un birbante!
      (Additando il Conte.)

Conte. Questo è un briccone!

Bartolo. Ah disgraziato!—

Conte. Ah maledetto!
      (Minacciandolo con la sciabola.)

Figaro. Signor Soldato, porti respetto,
   (Alzando il bacile, e minacciando il Conte.)
     O questo fusto, corpo del diavolo,
     Or le creanze le insegnera.

Conte. Brutto scimiotto—
      (Al Bartolo.)

Bartolo. Birbo malnato—

Tutti. Zitto, Dottore—

Bartolo. Voglio gridare—

Tutti. Fermo, signore!
      (Al Conte.)

Conte. Voglio ammazzarlo.

All.	Silence, silence! For goodness' sake! (A knocking at the street door.) Silence! Who is it knocks? Who can it be?	*Tutti.*	Fate silenzio! Per carità! (Si ode bussare con violenza alla porta di strada.) Zitti, che battono? Chi mai sarà?
Bartolo.	Who is it?	*Bartolo.*	Chi è?
Chorus.	Open, and you soon shall see. (Within.)	*Coro.*	La forza. Aprite quà! (Di dentro.)
All.	The police!—Oh, the devil!—	*Tutti.*	La forza!—Oh diavolo!
Figaro.	You have done it now! (To the Count, Rosina, and Bartolo.)	*Figaro.*	L' avete fatta! (Al Conte, Rosina, e Bartolo.)
Count.	Fear not.	*Conte.*	Niente paura.
Bartolo.	Let them come in.	*Bartolo.*	Vengan pur quà.
All.	I wonder How the deuce This adventure will terminate!	*Tutti.*	Questa avventura Ah, come diavolo Mai finirà!

SCENE THE LAST.—An Officer, with Soldiers; and the preceding.

SCENA ULTIMA.—Un Uffiziale; con Soldati; e detti.

Officer.	Hold, here! Let no one stir. Good Sirs, what is the matter? What's the cause of this disturbance? What's the reason of this clatter?	*Uffiziale.*	Fermi tutti! Niun si muova. Miei Signori che si fa? Questo chiasso donde è nato? La cagione presto quà.
Count.	The reason—	*Conte.*	La cagione—
Bartolo.	It is not true.	*Bartolo.*	Non è vero.
Count.	Yes, sir.	*Conte.*	Si, Signore.
Bartolo.	No, sir.	*Bartolo.*	Signor nò.
Count.	He is a rascal.	*Conte.*	E un birbante.
Bartolo.	He is an impostor.	*Bartolo.*	E un impostore.
Officer.	One at a time.	*Uffiziale.*	Un per volta.
Bartolo.	But I will speak! Sir, this soldier has abused me, Like a very dog has used me.	*Bartolo.*	Io parlerò! Questo soldato, M' ha maltrattato.
Rosina.	Pray, sir, pity the poor fellow, Wine has made him rather mellow.	*Rosina.*	Il poverino, Cotto è dal vino.
Bartolo.	Pity! he his sabre drew! The villain spoke of murder, too.	*Bartolo.*	Cava la sciabola! Parla d'uccidere.
Figaro.	Sir, I came to hear the clatter, But know nothing of the matter.	*Figaro.*	Io son venuto Quì per dividere.
Officer.	Silence! silence! Hark ye, fellow, (To the Count.) You're our prisoner,— Quick, away! (The Soldiers are about to surround him.)	*Uffiziale.*	Fate silenzio! Che intesi già, (Al Conte.) Siete in arresto,— Fuori di quà! (I Soldati si muovano per circondarlo.)
Count.	I your prisoner? hold awhile— Now what is't you please to say?	*Conte.*	Io in arresto?— Io, fermi, ola?

(Repulsing the Soldiers with an air of authority, he calls the Officer towards him, privately shows him the order of the Grandees of Spain, which he has under his uniform, and whispers to him his name. The Officer surprised, makes a sign to the Soldiers, who retire, and he does the same. All remain astonished.)

(Con gesto autorevole trattiene i Soldati; chiama a se l'Uffiziale, gli mostra segretamente l'ordine di Grande di Spagna, che ha sotto l'uniforme, e gli dice all' orecchio suo nome. L'Uffiziale sorpreso, fa cenna ai Soldati che si ritirino, e anch'egli fa lo stesso. Tutti restano attoniti.)

FREDDO ED IMMOBILE—*COLD AND IMMOVABLE* (Trio)

ROSINA

Fred - da ed im - mo - bi - le   Co - me u - na sta - tua, Fia - to non
Cold and im - mo - va - ble   as sculp-tured fear,   All pow'r has

e - sta - mi   Da re - spi - - rar;   Fia - to non
left   me to see or   hear;   All pow'r has

COUNT

Fred - da ed im -
Cold and im -

re - sta - mi   Da re - spi - rar,   Fia - to   non
left me to see or hear,   All pow'r has

mo - bi - le   Co - me u - na sta - tua, Fia - to non
mo - va - ble as sculp-tured fear,   All pow'r has

re - sta - mi   Da re - spi - rar;   Fia - to non
left me to see or hear;   All pow'r has

re - sta - gli   Da re - spi - - rar,   Fia - to non
left him to see or hear,   All pow'r has

BARTOLO

Fred - da ed im -
Cold and im -

Figaro.	To see the doctor's	Figaro.	Guarda Don Bartolo
	Frantic fear,		Sembra una statua,
	I'm laughing so,		Ah, che dal ridere
	I scarce can hear.		Sto per crepar.
Bartolo.	But, sir—	Bartolo.	Ma, Signore—
	(To the Officer.)		(All' Uffiziale.)
Chorus.	Silence!	Coro.	Zitto tu!
Bartolo.	For a doctor—	Bartolo.	Ma un dottore—
Chorus.	I have done!	Coro.	Oh non più.
Bartolo.	But if she—	Bartolo.	Ma se lei—
Chorus.	Hold your tongue.	Coro.	Non parlar.
Bartolo.	She wished—	Bartolo.	La vorrai—
Chorus.	How you bawl.	Coro.	Non gridar.
All Three.	But if we—	A 3.	Ma se noi—
Chorus.	Silence, all.	Coro.	Zitti voi.
All Three.	But if—	A 3.	Ma se poi—

Chorus.	We'll think of it. Let every one the house now quit. Let altercation cease.	Coro.	Pensiam noi. Vada ognun pe' fatti suoi. Si finisca d' altercar.

MI PAR D'ESSER—*WHAT CONFUSION*

BARTOLO AND CHORUS

Mi___ par__ d'es- ser__ col- la__ te- sta! In___ un___
What___ con- fu - sion! with___ the___ din - ning, Round___ {my___ {his___

or - ri - da__ fa - ci - na! Par__ mi__ d'es - ser__
gid - dy__ head___ is___ spin - ning! What___ con - fu - sion__

col - la - te - sta! In___ un__ or - ri - da___ fa -
with___ the__ din - ning! Round___ {my gid - dy__ head___ is___ {his___

ci - na! Do - ve__ cre - sce e mai___ non re - sta, e
spin - ning! No___ one__ end -- ing,_ each___ be - gin - ning,

mai___ non re - sta,_____ Dell'__ in - cu - di - ni___ so -
each___ be - gin - ning,_____ What___ con - fu - sion! with___ the__

no - ra L'im - por - tu - no__ stre - pi - tar!___
din - ning, Round___ {my__ gid - dy__ head___ is__ spin - ning!
                        {this__

Chorus.	Like hammers on the anvil ringing, Till, echoing with the horrid sound, The walls and vaulted roofs rebound. Thus does your outrage stun the brain, That seeks for quiet here in vain,	Coro.	Alternando questo e quello, Pesantissimo martello, Fà con barbara armonìa Muri e volte rimbombar. E il cervello poverello.

Where furious tongues the sense
    confound,
Till reason's in the clamor
    drowned,
And madness seems to rage
    around!

    END OF ACT I.

Già stordito, sbalordito,

Non ragiona, si confonde,

Si riduce ad impazzar!

    FINE DELL' ATTO PRIMO.

ACT II.

SCENE I.—A Room in Bartolo's Home.

Bartolo. Do but see my ill-fortune! That
        (Alone.)
    soldier,
As far as I can learn,
Is known by no one in the regi-
    ment.
I doubt—zounds!
Doubt, did I say?—I would ven-
    ture to wager
That this fellow was sent here
By the Count Almaviva,
To sound the heart of Rosina.
Not even in one's own house
Can one be secure! but I—
    (A knocking is heard.)
Who knocks?
Holloa! who's there? they knock
    again,
Don't you hear?
I am in my own house, why should
    I be afraid?
Open the door.
    (Speaking to the side.)

ATTO II.

SCENA I.—Camera in Casa di Bartolo.

Bartolo. Ma vedi il mio destino! Quel
        (Solo.)
    soldato
Per quanto abbia cercato,
Niun lo conosce in tutto il reg-
    gimento.
Io dubito—oh cospetto!
Che dubitar?—scommetto
Che dal Conte Almaviva,
E stato quà spedito quel Signore,
Ad esplorar della Rosina il core.
Nemmeno in casa propria
Sicura si può star! ma io—
    (Battone.)
Chi batte?
Ehi! chì è di la? battono,
Non sentite?
In casa io son, non ho timore?
Aprite.
    (Verso le quinte.)

SCENE II.—The Count, dressed as a Music-master, and
    the preceding.

Count. May heaven send you peace and
    joy!

Bartolo. A thousand thanks! no more, good
    sir.

Count. Joy and peace for thousands of
    years!

Bartolo. In truth I'm very much obliged.
    (That face is not unknown to me,
    I don't recollect—I can't
      remember—
    But that countenance—that dress—
    I can't devise who it can be.)

Count. (Ah, if before I was unsuccessful
    In deceiving this simpleton.
    My new metamorphosis
    May prove more propitious to me.)
    Joy and peace; peace and joy.

SCENA II.—Il Conte, travestito da Maestro di Musica;
    e detto.

Conte. Pace e gioja il ciel vi dia!

Bartolo. Mille grazie! non s'incommoda.

Conte. Gioja e pace per mille anni!

Bartolo. Obbligato in verità.
    (Questo volto non m' è ignoto;
    Non ravviso—non ricordo—
    Ma quel volto—ma quell' abito—
    Non capisco chi sara.)

Conte. (Ah, se un colpo è andato a vuoto
    A gabbar questo balordo,
    La mia nuova metamorfosi
    Più propizia a me sarà.)
    Gioja, e pace; pace e gioja.

Bartolo. Enough—(Heavens! what an annoyance!)

Count. Joy and peace from my very heart.

Bartolo. Enough, enough! for mercy's sake.
(What a wretched fate is mine:
Every knave conspires against me!
What a cruel destiny.)

Count. (The old fellow knows me not:
How fortunate for me!
A few short moments, my love,
And we shall speak wthout restraint.)

Bartolo. In a word, sir,
Who are you? may I know?

Count. Don Alonzo,
Professor of music, and pupil
Of Don Basilio.

Bartolo. Well?

Count. Don Basilio,
Poor man, is taken ill; and in his stead—

Bartolo. Taken ill, say you?—I'll run and see him.
(About to depart.)

Count. Gently, gently,
(Detaining him.)
His illness is not so serious.

Bartolo. (I do distrust this fellow.) Come, let us go.

Count. But, sir!

Bartolo. Well, what?

Count. I wished to say—
(Taking him aside, and in a whisper.)

Bartolo. Well, speak out.

Count. But—

Bartolo. Speak out, I say!

Count. Well, as you wish:
(Raising his voice.)
Then you shall know who Don Alonzo is.
I came from the Count Almaviva—
(Going.)

Bartolo. Softly, softly—
(Gently restraining him.)
Speak, speak, I can hear you.

Count. The Count—
(Raising his voice.)

Bartolo. Softly, for goodness' sake.

Bartolo. Ho capito—(oh ciel che noja!)

Conte. Gioja e pace, ben di cuore.

Bartolo. Basta, basta! per pietà.
(Ma che perfido destino:
Tutti quanti a me davanti!
Che crudel fatalità.)

Conte. (Il vecchion non mi conosce:
Oh mia sorte fortunata!
Ah! mio ben, fra pochi instanti,
Parlerem con libertà.)

Bartolo. In somma, mio Signore,
Chi è lei, si può sapere?

Conte. Don Alonzo,
Professore di Musica, ed allievo
Di Don Basilio.

Bartolo. Ebbene?

Conte. Don Basilio,
Sta male il poverino, ed in sua vece—

Bartolo. Sta mal?—Corro a vederlo.
(In atto di partire.)

Conte. Piano, piano.
(Trattenendolo.)
Non è un mal così grave.

Bartolo. (Di costui non mi fido.) Andiamo, andiamo.

Conte. Ma, Signore!

Bartolo. Che c'è?

Conte. Voleva dirvi.
(Tirandolo a parte, e sotto voce.)

Bartolo. Parlate forte.

Conte. Ma—

Bartolo. Forte, vi dico.

Conte. Ebben, come volete.
(Alzando la voce.)
Ma chi sia Don Alonzo apprenderete.
Vo dal Conte Almaviva—
(In atto di partire.)

Bartolo. Piano, piano—
(Trattenendolo con dolcezza.)
Dite, dite, v'ascolto.

Conte. Il Conte—
(A voce alta.)

Bartolo. Piano, per carità.

Count. This morning he came by chance
To the same inn! and by accident
I took up this note, which I found
Directed to him by your ward.

Bartolo. What do I see? It is indeed her writing!

Count. Don Basilio being engaged with the lawyer,
Knows nothing of this letter, and I, being sent
To give lessons to your ward, in his stead,
Wished to make a merit of the thing with you;
Because, by means of this letter I might—

Bartolo. You might what?

Count. I will tell you,
If I could but speak a few words with her,
I think, with deference be it said, that I could
Make her believe that it was given to me by a mistress of the Count's:
A tolerable good proof to Rosina,
That she is only made a fool of by the Count,
And therefore—

Bartolo. Softly, softly;—a calumny this!
Oh, I see very well that you are
A scholar worthy of Don Basilio!
I shall know how to reward
(Embraces him and puts the note in his pocket.)
So happy a suggestion;
I will go and call the girl.
And as you interest yourself so much about me,
I recommend myself to your good offices.
(He goes into Rosina's apartment.)

Count. Ne'er doubt me.
This affair of the note
Slipped from my tongue against my will.
But what was I to do? Without some strategem
I should have gone away like a simpleton
I must now acquaint her
With my plan: if she consent,
I shall be completely happy.
She comes! How my heart beats in my bosom!

Conte. Stamane,
(Calmandosi.)
Nella stesa locanda
Era meco d'alloggio, ed in mie mani
Per caso capitò questo biglietto
Dalla vostra pupilla a lui diretto.

Bartolo. Che vedo? È sua scrittura!

Conte. Don Basilio occupato col curiale,
Nulla sà di quel foglio, ed io per lui
Venendo a dar lezione alla ragazza,
Volea farmene un merito con voi;
Perchè, con quel biglietto, si potrebbe—

Bartolo. Che cosa?

Conte. Vi dirò,
S' io potessi parlare alla ragazza,

Io creder, verbigrazia le farei

Che me lo diè del Conte un' altra amante:

Prova significante,
Che il Conte di Rosina si fa gioco,

E perciò—

Bartolo. Piano un poco;—una calunnia!
Or sì vi riconosco
Bravo e degno scolar di Don Basilio!
Io saprò come merita
(La abbraccia e mette in tasca il biglietto.)
Ricompensar sì bel suggerimento;
Vò a chiamar la ragazza.
Poichè tanto per me v'interessate,
Mi raccomando a voi.
(Entra nella camera di Rosina.)

Conte. Non dubitate

L'affare del biglietto
Dalla bocca mi è uscito non volendo.
Ma come far? Senza di un tal ripiego
Mi toccava andar via come un bagiano,
Il mio disegno a lei
Ora paleserò: s'ella consente,
Io son felice appieno.
Eccola! Ah, il cor sento balzarmi in seno!

SCENE III.—Bartolo, bringing in Rosina; and the preceding then Figaro.

Bartolo.	Come, Signorina; Don Alonzo, Whom you see here, will give you your lesson.
Rosina.	Ah!
	(Starting.)
Bartolo.	What's the matter?
Rosina.	It is a cramp in my foot.
Count.	Oh, nothing at all. Seat yourself by my side, fair lady; And, if not disagreeable, I will give you A little lesson in place of Don Basilio.
Rosina.	Oh, sir! with the greatest pleasure.
Count.	What will you sing?
Rosina.	Whatever you please.
Bartolo.	Well, let us hear, then.
Rosina.	Here it is.
Count.	Now let us begin with spirit.
	(Rosina sings an Air. chosen, ad libitum, for the occasion.)
Count.	Bravissimo! a fine voice, truly!
Rosina.	A thousand thanks!
Bartolo.	Yes, truly, a fine voice; But, then, good Lord! that air is very tiresome. In my time music was another thing: Oh! when, for instance, Cafariello sung that wondrous air— "La, la, la!" List, Don Alonzo, I will give it you. With that bewitching mien, ah! Oh, come to me, Rosina! And on my arm, oh, lean, ah! There let me chant my lay; Or, if you more incline, ah! To dancing, so divine, ah! Then thus in grace we'll twine, ah! With minuetto sway.
	(To Figaro. who enters, mimicking him.)
	Bravo! Mr. Barber.
Figaro.	Oh! no harm, sir; Excuse my folly.
Bartolo.	Well, rogue, And what are you come here for?
Figaro.	Here for! Why, I am come to shave you— this is your day.

SCENA III.—Bartolo, conducendo Rosina; e detti; indi Figaro.

Bartolo.	Venite, Signorina: Don Alonzo, Che quì vedete, or vi darà lezione.
Rosina.	Ah!
Bartolo.	Cos'è stato?
Rosina.	È un granchio al piede.
Conte.	Oh, nulla. Sedete a me vicin, bella fanciulla; Se non vi spiace, un poco di lezione Di Don Basilio invece io vi darò.
Rosina.	Oh! col più gran piacer la prenderò.
Conte.	Che vuol cantare?
Rosina.	Quel che lei aggrada.
Bartolo.	Or ben, dunque sentiamo.
Rosina.	Eccola quì.
Conte.	Da brava incominciamo.
	(Rosina canta qualche Aria, scelta, ad libitum, per l' occasione.)
Conte.	Bela voce! bravissima!
Rosina.	Oh, mille grazie!
Bartolo.	Certo, bella voce; Ma quest' aria, cospetto! è assai nojosa. La musica a miei tempi era altra cosa: Oh! quando, per esempio, cantava Cafariello Quel' aria portentosa—"Là, là, là!" Sentite, Don Alonzo, eccola quà. Quando mi sei vicina, Amabile Rosina, L' aria dicèa Giannina, Ma io dico Rosina; Il cor mi balza in peïto, Mi balla il minuetto.
	(A Figaro, che entra contra fiecondolo.)
	Bravo! Signore Barbiere!
Figaro.	Eh niente affatto. Scusi sue debolezze.
Bartolo.	Ebben, gridone, Che vieni a far?
Figaro.	O bella! Vengo a farvi la barba—oggi vi tocca.

Bartolo. Oh, not to-day—I don't wish it.

Figaro. Not to-day? but
To-morrow I can't come.

Bartolo. And why not?

Figaro. Because I am otherwise engaged.
And then—and then—what matters
it?
I cannot come to-morrow.

Bartolo. Come, less chattering;
I'll not be shaved to-day.

Figaro. What? Do you treat me
As you would some country
barber?
E'en find some other person;—I
am off.

Bartolo. Well, what signifies it?—this is his
way—
What a whimsical dog!
Quick! into my room, and bring
the cloth.
No; I'll go myself.

Figaro. (Oh, if he would but hand me
That bunch of keys, all would be
right.)
Tell me, is not the key
(To Rosina.)
Which opens that lattice among
them?

Rosina. Yes; and it is the newest.

Bartolo. (Oh, I'm mighty wise
To leave that devil of a barber
here!)
Here, go yourself:
(Giving the keys to Figaro.)
Pass yonder corridor, and on the
shelf
You will find everything.
Have a care, but touch nothing.

Figaro. Eh, I am no fool.
O be joyful! I'll be back in an
instant.
(The trick is done!)
(He goes in.)

Bartolo. That's the rascal, sir, who brought
(To the Count.)
The Count's letter to Rosina.

Count. He seems a very adept in intrigue.

Bartolo. Ah, he'll not trick me—
(A noise within, as of some earthen vessels breaking.)
Oh, I'm undone.

Rosina. What noise was that?

Bartolo. Oggi non voglio.

Figaro. Oggi non vuol? domani
Non potrò io.

Bartolo Perchè?

Figaro. Perchè ho da fare.
E poi—e poi—che serve?
Doman non posso.

Bartolo. Orsù, meno parole:
Oggi non vo' far barba.

Figaro. Ma? che mi avete preso
Per un qualche barbier da contadino?
Chiamate pur un altro;—io me
ne vado.

Bartolo. Che serve?—a modo suo—
(Vedi che fantasía!)
Và in camera a pigliar la bian-
cheria.
No; vado io stesso.

Figaro. (Ah, se mi dava in mano
Il mazzo delle chiavi, ero a
cavallo.)
Dite, non è fra quelle
(A Rosina.)
La chiave, che apre quella gelosía?

Rosina. Sì certo; è la più nuova.

Bartolo. (Ah son per buono
A lasciar quì quel diavolo di
barbiere!)
Animo, va tu stesso:
(Dando le chiavi a Figaro.)
Passato il corridor, sopra l'
armario
Il tutto troverai.
Bada non toccar nulla.

Figaro. Ah, non son matto.
(Allegri!) Vado e torno.
(Il colpo è fatto!)
(Entra.)

Bartolo. E quel briccon, che al Conte
(Al Conte.)
Ha portato il biglietto di Rosina.

Conte. Mi sembra un imbroglion di prima
sfera.

Bartolo. Eh, a me non me la ficca—
(Si sente di dentro rumore come di vasellonne che si
spezza.)
Ah, disgraziato me.

Rosina. Ah, che rumore?

Bartolo.　Oh, the rascal! I felt my heart mis-
　　　　give me.
　　　　　(Goes in.)
　　　　He has broken everything,
　　　　Six plates, eight basins, one tureen.

Figaro.　A might matter, truly! had I not hit
　　　　Upon the key by good fortune,
　　　　(Showing the Count the key of the veranda.)
　　　　In that same cursed
　　　　Corridor, I should have broken
　　　　My head against the wall.
　　　　He keeps every room so dark; and
　　　　then—

Bartolo.　No more of this!

Figaro.　Come, then. (Be prudent.)
　　　　　(To the Count and Rosina.)

Bartolo.　Proceed to business.
(He seats himself to be shaved; at this moment enter
　　　　　Basilio.)

SCENE IV.—Don Basilio, and the preceding.

Rosina.　(Don Basilio!)

Count.　(What do I see?)

Figaro.　(What an unfortunate encounter!)

Bartolo.　How is this?

Basilio.　Good day to you all.

Bartolo.　(What an unexpected visit!)

Figaro and Count.　(Some courage here is
　　　　necessary.)

Rosina.　(Alas! what will become of us!)

Bartolo.　Basilio, how do you find yourself?

Basilio.　Find myself!

Figaro.　Who is to wait here?
　　　　　(Interrupting him.)
　　　　That blessed beard of yours!
　　　　Shall I operate on it or no?

Bartolo.　I'l be with you directly.
　　　　　(To Figaro.)
　　　　And the lawyer—
　　　　　(To Basilio.)

Basilio.　The lawyer!—

Count.　I have already told him
　　　　That everything is arranged;
　　　　Is it not true?

Bartolo.　Yes; I know it all

Basilio.　But, Don Bartolo, explain to me—

Count.　Doctor, a word with you—
　　　　　(Interrupting him.)

Bartolo.　Ah, che briccon! me lo diceva il
　　　　core.
　　　　　(Entra.)
　　　　Tutto mi ha rotto, tutto;
　　　　Sei piatti, otto bicchieri, una
　　　　terrina.

Figaro.　Vedete che gran cosa! ad una
　　　　chiave
　　　　Se mai non m'attaccava per
　　　　fortuna.
　　　　(Mostrando al Conte la chiave della golosia.)
　　　　Per qual maledettissimo
　　　　Corridor, così oscúro,
　　　　Spezzato mi sarei la testa al muro.
　　　　Tiene ogni stanza al bujo; e poi—
　　　　e poi—

Bartolo.　Oh, non più.

Figaro.　Dunque, andiam. (Giudizio.)
　　　　　(Al Conte, e Rosina.)

Bartolo.　A noi.
　　　　(Si siede a farsi radere.—Entra Basilio.)

SCENA IV.—Don Basilio, e detti.

Rosina.　(Don Basilio!)

Conte.　(Cosa veggo?)

Figaro.　(Quale intoppo!)

Bartolo.　Come quà?

Basilio.　Servitor di tutti quanti.

Bartolo.　(Che vuol dir tal novità!)

Figaro e Conte.　(Quì franchezza ci vorrà.)

Rosina.　(Ah, di noi che mai sarà!)

Bartolo.　Don Basilio, come state?

Basilio.　Come sto!

Figaro.　Or che s'aspetta?
　　　　　(Interrompendolo.)
　　　　Questa barba benedetta!
　　　　La facciamo sì, o nò?

Bartolo.　Ora vengo.
　　　　　(A Figaro.)
　　　　E là il curiale—
　　　　　(A Basilio.)

Basilio.　Il curiale!—

Conte.　Io gli ho narrato
　　　　Che già tutto è combinato;
　　　　Non è ver?

Bartolo.　Sì; tutto io sò.

Basilio.　Ma, Don Bartolo spiegatemi—

Conte.　(Ehi, dottore, una parola—)
　　　　　(Interrompendolo.)

Don Basilio, I shall be with you
immediately.
(To Bartolo.)
Listen to me a moment.
(To Figaro.)
(Try and get him off,
Else I fear he will discover us.)
(Softly, to Bartolo.)
(Of the affair, sir, of the letter,
Recollect, he knows nothing.)

Bartolo. With this fever, Don Basilio,
Who taught you to walk abroad?
(Figaro, listening with attention, prepares to second the
Count.)

Basilio. With a fever!
(Astonished.)

Figaro. Why, what think you?
You are as yellow as a corpse.

Basilio. As a corpse, say what?

Figaro. Heavens, man!
(Feeling his pulse.)
Zounds, what a galloping pulse!
It's certainly the scarlet fever.

Figaro and Count. Go home, take medicine.
(The Count secretly gives a purse to Basilio.)

Figaro. Quick, quick, home to bed—

Count. I am quite alarmed for you—

Bartolo and Rosina. He says well; go home
to bed—

All. Quick, retire, and rest yourself.

Basilio. (A purse!—Go to bed!—
They all seem of the same mind.)

All. Quick, home to bed.

Basilio. Eh, I'm not deaf;
Pray cease your entreaties.

Figaro. What a color—eh!

Count. Oh! what a rueful visage!

Bartolo. Rueful visage!

Figaro and Count. Rueful, truly.

Basilio. Well, I'm going.

All. Go, go!

Don Basilio, son da voi.
(A Bartolo.)
Ascoltate un poco quà.
(A Figaro.)
(Fate un pò ch'ie vada via,
Ch'ei ci scopra ho gran timore.)
(Piano, a Bartolo.)
(Della lettera, Signore,
Ei l'affare ancor non sa.)

Bartolo. Colla febbre, Don Basilio,
Chi v'insegna a passeggiare?
(Figaro, ascoltando con attenzione, si prepara a secondare
il Conte.)

Basilio. Colla febbre!
(Attonito.)

Figaro. E chi vi pare?
Siete giallo come un morto.

Basilio. Come un morto?

Figaro. Bagatella!
(Tastandogli il polso.)
Cospetton che tremarella!
Questa è febbre scarlatina.

Figaro e Conte. Via, prendete medicina.
(Il Conte da a Basilio una borsa di soppiatto.)

Figaro. Presto, presto andate a letto—

Conte. Voi paura in ver mi fate—

Bartolo e Rosina. Dice bene, andate a
letto—

Tutti. Presto andate a riposar.

Basilio. (Una borsa!—Andate a letto!—
Ma che tutti sian d'accordo.)

Tutti. Presto a letto.

Basilio. Eh, non son sordo,
Non mi faccio più pregar.

Figaro. Che color—eh!

Conte. Che brutta cera!

Bartolo. Brutta cera!

Figaro e Conte. Oh, brutta assai.

Basilio. Dunque vado.

Tutti. Andate, andate.

BUONA SERA—*FARE YOU WELL, THEN* (Duet)

Rosina. (Plague upon you, can't you stir, ah!)
Quick, begone, and nurse yourself.

Basilio. Oh, good night, I quite agree—
Much obliged I really am.
(Guardy's in the trap I see!)
Cease your noise, I go, good man.
(Exit.)

Bartolo. I am here.
(Bartolo seats himself, and Figaro prepares to shave him, during the operation he conceals the two lovers.)
Now, work away.

Count. Rosina, now attend to me.

Rosina. I'm all attention, sir.
(They sit down. pretending to be at their musical studies.)

Count. At midnight precisely,
(Cautiously, to Rosina.)
We'll wait for you here;
For since we've the keys
We have nothing to fear.

Figaro. Ahi! ahi!
(Calling off Bartolo's attention.)

Bartolo. What's the matter?

Figaro. Something flew in my eye,
Look, but don't touch it:
Blow, for pity's sake.

Rosina. At midnight, precisely,
My love, I'll await thee;
Oh! fleet be the moments
That to thee shall unite me.

Bartolo. Nay, let me look!

Figaro. Well, look; who hinders you?

Rosina and Count. Do, re, mi, fa, sol, la.

Count. But now I tell you,
(Bartolo rises, and draws near the lovers.)
That I showed your letter,
In order that I might disguise
Myself much better.

Bartolo. Oh, excellent, forsooth!
Excelent, in very truth!
Rascals! scoundrels!
I see you've all
Conspired this day
To haste my fall.
Avaunt!
Or I shall slay you all!
With rage I'm nearly
Like to die.

Count, Rosina and Figaro. Your friend is delirious:
His head is oppressed.
Be silent, good doctor,

Rosina. (Maledetto seccatore!)
Presto, andate via di quà.

Basilio. Buona sera—ben di cuore—
Obligato—in verità.
(An, che in sacco va il tutore!)
Non gridate, intesi già.
(Parte.)

Bartolo. Son quà.
(Bartolo siede, e Figaro disponesi a fargli la barba; durante l'operazione va coprendo i due amanti.)
Stringi bravissimo.

Conte. Rosina, deh ascoltatemi.

Rosina. V'ascolto, eccomi quà.
(Siedono fingendo studiar la musica.)

Conte. (A mezza notte in punto,
(A Rosina con cautela.)
A prendervi quì siamo;
Or che la chiave abbiamo.
Non v'e da dubitar.)

Figaro. Ahi! ahi!
(Distrando Bartolo.)

Bartolo. Che cosa è stato?

Figaro. Un non sò che nell' occhio!
Guardate, non toccate—
Soffiate per pietà.

Rosina. A mezza notte in punto,
Anima mia, t'aspetto;
Io già l'istante affretto,
Che teco m' unirà.

Bartolo. Ma lasciami vedere!

Figaro. Vedete, chi vi tiene?

Rosina e Conte. Do, re, mi, fa, sol, la.

Conte. Ora avveritirvi voglio,
(Bartolo si alza. e si avvicina agli amanti.)
Cara che il vostro foglio,
Perchè non fosse inutile
Il mio travestimento.

Bartolo. Ma bravi, ma bravissimi!
Ma bravi, in verità!
Bricconi! birbanti!
Ah, voi tutti quanti
Avete giurato
Di farmi crepar.
Uscite furfanti!
Vi voglio accoppar!
Di rabbia, di sdegno
Mi sento crepar.

Conte, Rosina e Figaro. L' amico delira;
La testa gli gira.
Dottore, tacete,

'Tis only a jest.
Peace, peace, let's away;
We've been overheard.
This clamor is useless—
He'll not hear a word.
(Exeunt.)

SCENE V.—Bertha, alone.

There is nothing but noise and
    clamor in this house;
Nothing but disputing, weeping,
    and threatening.
There's not an hour's peace
With this avaricious old wrangler.
Oh, what a house! what a house of
    confusion!
The fond old dotard seks a wife,
    The merest girls for husbands
    pine
The one a fool, the other mad—
    In jacket straight I'd all confine.
What con this love be
    That drives the folks mad?
Some all happiness seem,
    While other are sad.
'Tis something that teases,
    That plagues and inspires;
Even I am its prey,
    And am scorched by Love's fires.
But because I am old,
    I by all am passed by;—
Ah, with rage I expire!
    With vexation I die!
(Exit.)

SCENE VI.—Don Bartolo, introducing Don Basilio.

Bartolo. Then you don't know
    Don Alonzo at all?

Basilio. Not at all.

Bartolo. Ah, surely
    He was sent by the Count! Some
    great scheme
    Is, no doubt, in agitation.

Basilio. I tell you
    That this friend
    Was no other than the Count
    himself.

Bartolo. The Count himself?

Basilio. The Count!
    (This purse clearly bespeaks it.)

Bartolo. Let him be what he may—to the
    notary
    I will hasten this moment,
    And settle the marriage contract.

Vi fate burlar.
Tacete, partiamo;
    Non serve a gridar.
Intesi ci siamo—
    Non v'è a replicar.
(Partono.)

SCENA V.—Berta, sola.

Sempre gridi e tumulti in questa
    casa;
Si litiga, si piange, si minaccia.
Non v'è un'ora di pace
Con questo vecchio avaro e bron-
    tolone.
Oh, che casa! oh, che casa di
    confusione!
Il vecchietto cerca moglie,
    Vuol marito la ragazza:
    Quello freme questa è pazza—
Tutti e due son da legar.
Ma che cosa è questo amore
    Che fà tutti delirar?
    Egli è un male, universale,
Una smania, un pizzicore,
    Un solletico, un tormento;
    Poverina! anch'io lo sento,
Nè so come remediar.
Ah, vecchiaia maledetta!
Son da tutti disprezzata,
    E arrabiata—disperata,
    Mi convien così crepar!
(Parte.)

SCENA VI.—Don Bartolo. introducendo Don Basilio.

Bartolo. Dunque voi Don Alonzo
    Non conoscete affatto?

Basilio. Affatto.

Bartolo. Ah, certo
    Il Conte lo mandò. Qualche gran
    trama
    Quì si prepara.

Basilio. Io dico
    Che quel garbato amico,
    Era il Conte in persona.

Bartolo. Il Conte?

Basilio. Il Conte!
    (La borsa parla chiaro.)

Bartolo. Sia che si vuole—amico, al notaro
    Vo' in questo punto andare, in
    questa sera
    Stipular di mie nozze io vo' il
    contratto.

Basilio.	To the notary! are you mad? It rains in torrents; and, besides, This evening the notary is to be with Figaro: the barber Gives his niece in marriage.

Bartolo.	His niece?
	What niece?—The barber
	Has no nieces. Ah, there must be
	    some plot here.
	This very night the scoundrels will
	Lie in wait to betray me. Haste,
	    and call!
	The notary, instantly;
	Here is the key of the door—go,
	Make haste, for goodness' sake.
	(Gives him a key.)

Basilio.	Don't be alarmed; in two minutes I will be here again. *(Exit.)*

SCENE VII.—Bartolo, then Rosina.

Bartolo.	Either by force, or love,
	Rosina shall yield, I am deter-
	    mined!—
	I have another thought. The note,
	(Takes from his pocket the note given him by the Count.)
	Which the girl wrote to Almaviva,
	May serve—Oh, what a masterly
	    thought!
	That rascal, Don Alonzo,
	Has undesignedly put weapons into
	    my hands.
	Eh, Rosina! Rosina!
	(Rosina comes from her room without speaking.)
	Come here, come here;
	I have some news from your lover
	    to give you.
	Poor unhappy girl! in truth,
	You have placed your affections on
	    a noble object!
	Know that, in the arms of another,
	He makes a joke of your affections;
	Behold the proof.
	(He gives her a note.)

Rosina.	Oh, heaven! my note!
Bartolo.	Don Alonzo and the barber Are conspiring against you: do not trust them. They wish to give you up Into the arms of Count Almaviva—
Rosina.	(Into the arms of another! What do I hear?—Oh, Lindor!— Oh, betrayer! Ah, yes!—vengeance—I will teach the wretch,

Basilio.	Il notar! siete matto? Piove a torrenti; e poi, Questa sera il notaro È impegnato con Figaro: il barbiere Marita una nipote.

Bartolo.	Una nipote!
	Che nipote?—Il barbiere
	Non ha nipoti. Ah, qui v'è qualche
	    imbroglio,
	Questa notte i bricconi
	Me la voglion far. Presto, il
	    notaro
	Quà venga sull' istante;
	Ecco la chiave del portone—
	    andate,
	Presto, per carità.
	(Gli dà una chiave.)

Basilio.	Non temete; in due salti io torno quà. *(Parte.)*

SCENA VII.—Bartolo, indi Rosina.

Bartolo.	Per forza, o per amore,
	Rosina avrà da cedere, cospetto!—
	Mi viene un altra idea. Questo
	    biglietto,
	(Cava dalla tasca il biglietto datogli dal Conte.)
	Che scrisse la ragazza al Conte
	    Almaviva,
	Potria servir—Che colpo da
	    maestro!
	Don Alonzo, il briccone,
	Senza volerlo mi diè l' armi in
	    mano.
	Ehi, Rosina! Rosina!
	(Rosina dalla sue camere esce senza parlare.)
	Avanti, avanti;
	Del vostro amante io vi vo' dar la
	    novella.
	Povera sciagurata in verità,
	Collocaste assai bene il vostro
	    affetto!
	Del vostro amor, sappiate,
	Ch'ei si fa gioco in sen d'un altro
	    amante;
	Ecco la prova.
	(Le dà il biglietto.)

Rosina.	Oh cielo! il mio biglietto!
Bartolo.	Don Alonzo, e il barbiere Congiuran contro voi; non vi fidate. In potere del Conte d' Almaviva Vi vogliono condurre—
Rosina.	(In braccio a un'altro!— Che mai sento?—Ah Lindoro!— Ah traditore!

	Who Rosina is.)		Ah sì!—vendetta! e vegga
	Tell me, sir, do you		Quell'empio chi è Rosina.)
	Wish to marry me?		Signore, sposarmi,
Bartolo.	I do.		Voi bramavate?
Rosina.	Well, let it be done!	*Bartolo.*	E il voglio.
	I am content—let it be instantly.	*Rosina.*	Ebben, si faccia!
	Listen:		Io son contenta—ma all'istante.
	At midnight the wretch will be here,		Udite:
	With Figaro, the barber;—and it was settled,		A mezza notte quì barbier;—con lui fuggire,
	That I should fly and espouse him.		Per sposarlo io voleva.
Bartolo.	Oh, wretches!	*Bartolo.*	Ah, scellerati!
	I hasten to bar the door.		Corro a sbarrar la porta.
Rosina.	Oh, my dear sir!	*Rosina.*	Ah, mio Signore!
	They are to enter by the window: they have the key.		Entran par la finestra: hanno la chiave.
Bartolo.	I will not stir from this spot!	*Bartolo.*	Non mi muovo di quì!
	But supose they should be armed? My dear child,		Ma—e se fossero armati?—Figlia mia,
	Since you are now so awake to your situation,		Poichè ti sei si bene illuminata,
	Let us act thus. Shut yourself up in your room,		Facciam così. Ti chiudi a chiave in camera,
	While I go and see for assistance.		Io vo a chiamar la forza.
	I will declare they are two thieves, and as such,		Dirò che son due ladri, e come tali,
	By Bacchus! we shall see what the consequence will be!		Corpo di Bacco! l' avremo da vedere!
	Child, shut yourself up immediately: I go.		Figlia, chiuditi presto: io vado via.
	(Exit.)		(Parte.)
Rosina.	How cruel! how cruel is my fate!	*Rosina.*	Quanto, quanto è crudel la sorte mia!
	(Exit.)		(Parte.)

(A storm. The veranda is seen to open, and one after the other, Figaro and the Count enter, wrapped up in mantles.)

(Un temporale. Si vede aprire la gelosia, ed entrare un dopo l'altro Figaro, ed il Conte avvolti in mantelli.)

SCENE VIII.—The Count, Figaro, then Rosina.

SCENA VIII.—Il Conte, Figaro, indi Rosina.

Figaro.	At last, here we are.	*Figaro.*	Al fine eccoci quà.
Count.	Figaro, your hand. By the powers!	*Conte.*	Figaro, dammi man. Poter del mondo!
	What a tempestuous night!		Che tempo indiavolato!
Figaro.	Truly, a lover's night!	*Figaro.*	Tempo da innamorati!
	(Figaro lights the candles, and looks around.)		(Figaro accendde i lumi spiando.)
Count.	Eh, show a light.	*Conte.*	Ehi, fammi lume.
	Where can Rosina be?		Dove sarà Rosina?
Figaro.	We soon shall see—	*Figaro.*	Ora vedremo—
	There she is.		Eccola appunto.
Count.	Ah! treasure of my soul—	*Conte.*	Ah mio tesoro—
	(With transport.)		(Con trasporto.)
Rosina.	Stand off,	*Rosina.*	Indietro,
	(Repulsing him.)		(Respingendolo.)

Wretch that thou art! I am come here
To repair the fault of my
Too foolish credulity; to show thee
What I am, and what a mistress
Thou hast lost, unworthy and thoughtless man.

Count. I am petrified!

Figaro. I know not what this can mean.

Count. But, for mercy's sake!—

Rosina. Peace! You have pretended love,
In order to sacrifice me to the wishes
Of the vile Count Almaviva—

Count. To the Count?—
Ah, you are deceived. Happy that I am!
Then you return with truth
The affections of Lindor!—answer—

Rosina. Ah, yes! I loved him but too well!

Count. This, then, is the moment
At which to reveal myself. My sweetest life,
(He kneels, throwing aside his mantle.)
Behold one who so long
Has followed thy steps; who sighs for thee:
Who hopes to possess thee. See, treasure of my kind
I am Almaviva: I am not Lindor.

Rosina. What unexpected bliss,
What peace without alloy!
Oh, heavens! 'tis he indeed,
I'm almost mad with joy!

Count. My triumph is complete
No more shall doubt annoy!
This moment all repays,
I'm almost mad with joy!

Figaro. One moment all was grief!
The next they kiss and toy;
But thanks to my designs,
Their hearts are filled with joy!

Rosina. Dear sir—but you—but I.

Count. Nay, never fear, my love!
The blessed name of wife
Awaits thee from above.

Rosina. The blessed name of wife!
What joy it gives my heart.

Rosina and Count. Oh, happy bond of love,
We'll never, never part!

Anima scellerata! Io qui di mia
Stolta credulità venni soltanto
A riparar lo scorno; a dimostrarti
Qual io sono, e quale amante
Perdesti, anima indegna, e sconoscento!

Conte. Io son di sasso!

Figaro. Io non capisco niente.

Conte. Ma per pietà!—

Rosina. Taci! Fingesti amore,
Sol per sagrificarmi
A quel tuo vil Conte Almaviva—

Conte. Al Conte?—
Ah, sei delusa. Ah me felice! adunque!
Tu di verace amore.
Ami Lindor!—rispondi—

Rosina. Ah, sì! t'amai pur troppo!

Conte. Ah, non è tempo
Di più celarsi. Anima mia! ravvisa,
(S'inginocchia, gettando il mantello.)
Colui che sì gran tempo:
Seguì tue traccie; e che per te sospira:
Che suo ti vuol. Mirami, o mio tesoro!
Almaviva son io: non son Lindoro.

Rosina. Ah, qual colpo inaspettato,
Egli stesso! oh ciel! che sento!
Di sorpresa, di contento,
Son vicina a delirar!

Conte. Qual trionfo inaspettato!
Me felice! oh bel momento!
Ah, d'amore, di contento,
Son vicino a delirar!

Figaro. Son rimasti senza fiato!
Ora muojon dal contento;
Guarda, guarda il mio talento,
Che bel colpo seppe far!

Rosina. Mio Signore—ma voi—ma io—

Conte. Ah, non più, non più, ben mio!
Il bel nome di mia sposa
Idol mio! t'attende già.

Rosina. Il bel nome di tua sposa;
Ah, qual gioja al cor mi dà.

Rosina e Conte. Dolce nodo avventurato,
Che fai paghi i miei desiri!

The fates propitious proved,
  And gave us heart for heart.
	Alla fin de' miei martiri,
	  Tu sentisti Amor, pietà.

Figaro.   Quick, let us hence: have done
      with sighs,
    All difficulty's passed;
    But often, acts too long delayed,
    To nothing come at last.
	Figaro. Presto, andiamo: vi sbrigate,
	    Via, lasciate quei sospiri;
	    Se si tarda, i miei raggiri,
	    Fanno fiasco in verità.

Rosina and Count. Oh, happy bond of love!
    We'll never, never part!
    The fates propitious proved,
    And gave us heart for heart.
    (Figaro runs to the balcony.)
	Rosina e Conte. Dolce nodo avventurato!
	    Che fai paghi i miei desiri;
	    Alla fin de' miei martiri,
	    Tu sentisti, Amor, pietà.
	    (Figaro va al balcone.)

Figaro.   Ah, zounds! what do I see?
    At the door—a lantern—
    Two persons—what is to be done?
	Figaro. Ah, cospetto! che ho veduto?
	    Alla porta—una lanterna—
	    Due persone—che si fa?

ZITTI, ZITTI, PIANO, PIANO—*STEP AS SOFT AS ZEPHYRS DYING* (Trio)

dia - mo, _ via _ di _ quà!   Pia - no,   pia - no!   Per la
light-ly _ and _ a - way!   Pia - no,   pia - no!   Down the

dia - mo, _ via _ di _ quà!   Pia - no,   pia - no!   Per la
light-ly _ and _ a - way!   Pia - no,   pia - no!   Down the

dia - mo, _ via _ di _ quà!   Pia - no,   pia - no!   Per la
light-ly _ and _ a - way!   Pia - no,   pia - no!   Down the

sca - la   dal bal - co - ne, Pres-to an - dia - mo via di quà!
lad - der quick-ly fly - ing, Trip it   light-ly and a - way!

sca - la   dal bal - co - ne, Pres-to an - dia - mo via di quà!
lad - der quick-ly fly - ing, Trip it   light-ly and a - way!

sca - la   dal bal - co - ne, Pres-to an - dia - mo via di quà!
lad - der quick-ly fly - ing, Trip it   light-ly and a - way!

Count.	What has happened? (About to depart.)	Conte.	Che avvenne mai? (Vanno per partire.)
Figaro.	The ladder—	Figaro.	La scala—
Count.	Well—	Conte.	Ebben—
Figaro.	The ladder is gone.	Figaro.	La scala non v'è più.
Count.	What say you?	Conte.	Che dici?
Figaro.	Who could have taken it away?	Figaro.	Chi mai l'avrà levata?
Count.	What a cruel obstacle!	Conte.	Quale inciampo crudel!
Rosina.	Unhappy that I am!	Rosina.	Me sventurata!
Figaro.	Ah, hush! somebody is coming, and here we are. What is to be done?	Figaro.	Ah, zitti! sento gente, (ora ci siamo.) Signor mio, che si fa?
Count.	Courage, my dear Rosina. (Wraps himself in his mantle.)	Conte.	Mia Rosina, coraggio. (Si ravvoglie nel mantello.)
Figaro.	Here they are. (They retire to the side.)	Figaro.	Eccoli quà. (Si ritirano verso le quinte.)

SCENE IX.—Don Basilio with a lantern, introducing a Notary with a paper in his hand.)

Basilio. Come in, Don Bartolo.

Figaro. Don Basilio!
(Calling to the opposite side, beckoning to the Count.)

Count. And that other?

Figaro. Oh, oh, our notary. Delightful! Leave the affair to me. Mr. Notary.
(Basilio and the Notary turn round, and remain surprised. The Notary approaches Figaro.)

This evening
You were to settle in my house,
The marriage contract between
The Count Almaviva and my niece
Here are the parties! Have you indorsed
The papers? Oh, very well!
(The Notary takes out a paper.)

Basilio. But softly;
Where is Don Bartolo?

Count. Here, Don Basilio,
(Calling Basilio aside, and taking a ring from his finger, beckons him to be silent.)
This ring is for you.

Basilio. But I—

Count. You
(Taking out a pistol.)
Will have two balls in your head
If you offer any opposition.

Basilio. O Lord! I take the ring.
Who signs?

Rosina and Count. Here we are.
(They sign.)

Count. Figaro and Don Basilio
Are witnesses;—this is my wife.

Figaro and Basilio. Viva!

Count. How am I blessed!

Rosina. Oh, long-sighed-for happiness!

All. Viva!
(While the Count is kissing the hand of Rosina, and Figaro is embracing Basilio, enter Bartolo in haste.)

SCENE THE LAST.—Don Bartolo; an Alcalde, Alguazils, Soldiers; and the preceding.

Bartolo. Hold, all of you. There they are.
(Pointing out Figaro and the Count to the Alcalde, and rushing towards Figaro.)

Figaro. Softly, sir, softly.

Bartolo. Sir, they are thieves;
Arrest them, arrest them.

SCENA IX.—Don Basilio con lanterna, introducendo un Notajo con carta in mano.

Basilio. Entrate quì Don Bartolo.

Figaro. Don Basilio!
(Chiamando dalla quinta apposta, accennando al Conte.)

Conte. E quell'altro?

Figaro. Ve', ve', nostro notajo. Allegramente!
Lasciate fare a me. Signor Notajo.
(Basilio e il Notajo si rivolgono, e restano sorpresi. Il Notajo si avvicina a Figaro.)

Dovevate in mia casa
Stipular questa sera
Un contratto di nozze
Fra il Conte d' Almaviva e mia nipote
Gli sposi, eccoli quà! Avete indosso
La scrittura? Benissimo!
(Il Notajo cava una scrittura.)

Basilio. Ma, piano;
Don Bartolo dov'è?

Conte. Ehi, Don Basilio,
(Chiamande a parte Basilio e cavandosi un'anello dal dito, e gli addita di tacere.)
Quest'anello è per voi.

Basilio. Ma io—

Conte. Per voi
Vi sono ancor due palle nel cervello
(Cavando una pistola.)
Se v'opponete.

Basilio. Oibò prendo l'anello.
Chi firma?

Rosina e Conte. Eccoci quà.
(Sottescrivone.)

Conte. Son testimonj
Figaro e Don Basilio;—essa è mia sposa.

Figaro e Basilio. Evviva!

Conte. Oh mio contento!

Rosina. Oh, sospirata mia felicità!

Tutti. Evviva!
(Nell' atto che il Conte bacia la mano a Rosina, e Figaro abbraccia Basilio, entra Bartolo come appresso.)

SCENA ULTIMA.—Don Bartolo, un Alcalde, Alguazils, Soldati, e detti.

Bartolo. Fermi tutti. Eccoli quà.
(Additando Figaro e il Conte all' Alcade, e slanciandosi contro Figaro.)

Figaro. Colle buone, Signor.

Bartolo. Signor, son ladri;
Arrestate, arrestate!

Officer.	Sir, your name. (To the Count.)		*Uffiziale.*	Signore, (Al Conte.) il suo nome.
Count.	My name? It is that of a man of honor; I am husband to this lady—		*Conte.*	Il mio nome? Egli è quel d'un nom d'onore; Lo sposo io son di questa—
Bartolo.	Eh! go to the devil! Rosina is to be mine;—is it not true?		*Bartolo.*	Eh, andate al diavolo! Rosina esser dève mia sposa, non e vero?
Rosina.	How! yours! No; not even in thought.		*Rosina.*	Come debbo esser sua? Oh nemmen per pensiero.
Bartolo.	How now, hussy! Ah, I am betrayed! Arrest him, I tell you: He is a thief! (Pointing to the Count.)		*Bartolo.*	Come, come, fraschetta! ah, son tradito. Arrestate, vi dico: E un ladro!
Figaro.	I shall be the death of him.		*Figaro.*	Or, or l'accoppo.
Bartolo.	He is a rogue—a scoundrel!		*Bartolo.*	E un birbante, è un briccone.
Officer.	Sir? (To the Count.)		*Uffiziale.*	Signore? (Al Conte.)
Count.	Stand off!		*Conte.*	Indietro!
Officer.	Your name—		*Uffiziale.*	Il nome—
Count.	Stand off, I say; stand off.		*Conte.*	Indietro, dico; indietro!
Officer.	Eh, my good sir, lower that tone;— Who are you?		*Uffiziale.*	Ehi, mio Signor, abbassi quel tuono;— E chi è lei?
Count.	I am the Count Almaviva! (Discovering himself.)		*Conte.*	D' Almaviva il Conte io sono. (Scoprendosi.)
Bartolo.	The fact is, I bear all the blame.		*Bartolo.*	Insomma, io ho tutti i torti.
Figaro.	Ay, and justly, too.		*Figaro.*	Pur troppo è così.
Bartolo.	But you, you rascal— Even you to betray me, and turn witness!		*Bartolo.*	Ma tu briccone— Tu pur tradirmi, e far da testimonio!
Basilio.	Ah, Doctor, The Count has certain persuasives And certain arguments in his pocket, Which there is no withstanding.		*Basilio.*	Ah Dottore Bartolo mio, Quei Signor Conte certe ragioni Ha in tasca; certi argomenti A cui non si risponde.
Bartolo.	Ay, ay! I understand you.		*Bartolo.*	Sì, sì, ho capito tutto.
Count.	Well, Doctor?		*Conte.*	Ebben, Dottore?
Bartolo.	Well, well, what matters it? what's done is done. Go; and may Heaven bless you!		*Bartolo.*	Sì, sì, che serve? quel ch'è fatto è fatto. Andate pur; che il Ciel vi benedica!
Figaro.	Bravo, bravo, Doctor! Let me embrace you.		*Figaro.*	Bravo, bravo, un'abbraccio! Venite quà, Dottore.
Rosina.	Oh, how happy we are!		*Rosina.*	Ah, noi felici!

Count.	Oh, propitious love!	*Conte.*	Oh, fortunato amore!
Figaro.	Young Love, triumphant smiling,	*Figaro.*	Di si felice innesto,
	All harsher thoughts exiling,		Serbiam memoria eterna,
	All quarrels reconciling.		Io smorzo la lanterna,
	Now waves his torch on high!		Quì più non ho che far!
Bartolo.	Young Love, our hearts beguiling,	*Bartolo.*	Amore e fede eterna,
	Bids care and sorrow fly.		Si vegga in voi regnar.
Rosina.	May all our lot now viewing,	*Rosina.*	Costò sospiri e pene,
	Find every hour renewing		Un sì felice istante
	The joys of youth's first wooing,		Alfin quest'alma amante,
	And happy prove as I.		Comincia a respirar!
Count.	The humble Lindor wooed thee,	*Conte.*	Dell' umile Lindoro,
	And kind was thy reply;		La fiamma a te fu accetta
	A brighter fate pursued thee—		Più bel destin t'aspetta,
	No more, then, heave a sigh.		Sù, vieni a giubilar.
Chorus.	May love, our hearts beguiling,	*Coro.*	Amore e fede eterna,
	Bid care and sorrow fly!		Si vegga in voi regnar!

END OF THE OPERA.